McCAWLEY AND *TRETHOWAN*: THE CHAOS OF POLITICS AND THE INTEGRITY OF LAW

VOLUME 1: *McCAWLEY*

In this two-volume work, Ian Loveland offers a detailed exploration and analysis of two Australian entrenchment cases which have long been a source of fascination and inspiration to lawyers.

This first volume, focusing on the *McCawley* case, introduces non-Australian readers to the remarkably rich legal and political history of constitutional formation and development in New South Wales and Queensland in the nineteenth and early twentieth centuries. It culminates with a deeply contextualised analysis of the emergence of the bizarre 'Two Act entrenchment' principle which emerged in Queensland's constitutional law in 1908 and the subsequent and celebrated *McCawley* judgments of the Australian High Court and Privy Council.

The judgments are placed in both their deep and immediate historical and political contexts; from the legal formation of New South Wales in the late 1700s, through the creation of New South Wales and Queensland as distinct colonies in the 1850s and the subsequent passage of the Colonial Laws Validity Act 1865, and on to the fiercely contested reformism espoused by Labour governments in Queensland in the early part of the twentieth century.

McCawley and *Trethowan*: The Chaos of Politics and the Integrity of Law

Volume 1: *McCawley*

Ian Loveland
Professor of Public Law, City, University of London

·HART·
OXFORD · LONDON · NEW YORK · NEW DELHI · SYDNEY

HART PUBLISHING

Bloomsbury Publishing Plc

Kemp House, Chawley Park, Cumnor Hill, Oxford, OX2 9PH, UK

1385 Broadway, New York, NY 10018, USA

29 Earlsfort Terrace, Dublin 2, Ireland

HART PUBLISHING, the Hart/Stag logo, BLOOMSBURY and the Diana logo are trademarks of Bloomsbury Publishing Plc

First published in Great Britain 2021

Copyright © Ian Loveland, 2021

Ian Loveland has asserted his right under the Copyright, Designs and Patents Act 1988 to be identified as Author of this work.

All rights reserved. No part of this publication may be reproduced or transmitted in any form or by any means, electronic or mechanical, including photocopying, recording, or any information storage or retrieval system, without prior permission in writing from the publishers.

While every care has been taken to ensure the accuracy of this work, no responsibility for loss or damage occasioned to any person acting or refraining from action as a result of any statement in it can be accepted by the authors, editors or publishers.

All UK Government legislation and other public sector information used in the work is Crown Copyright ©. All House of Lords and House of Commons information used in the work is Parliamentary Copyright ©. This information is reused under the terms of the Open Government Licence v3.0 (http://www.nationalarchives.gov.uk/doc/open-government-licence/version/3) except where otherwise stated.

All Eur-lex material used in the work is © European Union, http://eur-lex.europa.eu/, 1998–2021.

A catalogue record for this book is available from the British Library.

Library of Congress Cataloging-in-Publication data

Names: Loveland, Ian, author.

Title: *McCawley* and *Trethowan* : the chaos of politics and the integrity of law / Ian Loveland, Professor of Public Law, City, University of London.

Other titles: Chaos of politics and the integrity of law

Description: Oxford, UK ; New York, NY : Hart, 2021- | Discusses the cases: McCawley v The King [1920] UKPC 22, [1920] AC 691; (1920) 28 CLR 106 (8 March 1920), Privy Council (on appeal from Australia); Attorney General for New South Wales v Trethowan [1932] AC 526, before the Privy Council | Includes bibliographical references and index. | Contents: v. 1. McCawley—v. 2 Trethowan

Identifiers: LCCN 2021011467 (print) | LCCN 2021011468 (ebook) | ISBN 9781509927111 (v. 1 ; hardback) | ISBN 9781509948260 (v. 1 ; paperback) | ISBN 9781509927135 (v. 1 ; pdf) | ISBN 9781509927128 (v. 1 ; Epub)

Subjects: LCSH: Constitutional history—Australia—20th century. | Political questions and judicial power—Australia—History—20th century | Legislative power—Australia—History—20th century | Queensland—Political and government. | New South Wales—Politics and government. | McCawley, Thomas William, 1881–1925—Trials, litigation, etc. | Trethowan, Arthur King, 1863–1937—Trials, litigation, etc.

Classification: LCC KU1760 .L68 2021 (print) | LCC KU1760 (ebook) | DDC 342.9402/9—dc23

LC record available at https://lccn.loc.gov/2021011467

LC ebook record available at https://lccn.loc.gov/2021011468

ISBN: HB: 978-1-50992-711-1
ePDF: 978-1-50992-713-5
ePub: 978-1-50992-712-8

Typeset by Compuscript Ltd, Shannon

To find out more about our authors and books visit www.hartpublishing.co.uk. Here you will find extracts, author information, details of forthcoming events and the option to sign up for our newsletters.

PREFACE

This book has been a rather long time in the making. *Trethowan v Attorney General for South Wales*[1] is one of the two seminal entrenchment cases to which most British law students are introduced during their LLB or GDL studies. The other, the South African case of *Harris v Donges (Minister for the Interior)*,[2] was one I explored in a book published by Hart some 20 years ago.[3] That book, and this one, were written because I came to the view very early on in my career as a constitutional law scholar that the UK's constitutional arrangements were grotesquely unsatisfactory, principally because of our unhappy attachment to the idea that sovereign lawmaking power lies – and should lie – with bare majorities in the two Houses of Parliament (or even just the Commons if Parliament Act legislation is in issue), and that it is therefore possible for seismic changes to constitutional arrangements to be made by legislators who may represent at best only a large minority of the population, and who cast their legislative votes on the basis of palpably ill-informed consideration (or even no consideration at all) of the issue before them.

Harris and *Trethowan* are both offered up to British law students as vehicles for exploring the supposed legal impossibility of entrenching any political or moral values in a form that would safeguard them from alteration through that normal lawmaking process. The simple lesson generally presented is that, as a matter of law, *Harris* and *Trethowan* offer no assistance to achieve that objective. The purpose of this book is not to rebut that conclusion, but rather to offer an antidote – a supplement might be an appropriate and less pejorative term – to the cursory treatment that many supposedly seminal constitutional law cases are accorded in terms of their sociological and political contexts.

The primary difficulty arising in any attempt to produce a 'contextual' study is dealing with the realisation that there is always much more to be said than there is space to say it. I am acutely aware that a great many people, incidents and ideas which I regarded when I encountered them as being of considerable interest and value have received little or no attention in the text. I therefore offer a pre-emptive apology-cum-explanation to those readers who find themselves asking themselves: "But why doesn't he mention that?"

As it is, the study has grown beyond its original conception and appears as a linked two-volume project. When I began my research, I had not appreciated how significant events in Queensland were to any attempt to gain a full understanding of *Trethowan*,

---

[1] [1930] 31 SR (NSW) 183 (New South Wales Supreme Court), [1931] CLR 394 (High Court), [1932] AC 526 (Privy Council).
[2] 1952 (2) 428 (AD).
[3] (1999) *By due process of law? Racial discrimination and the right to vote in South Africa*.

and as I dug deeper into Queensland constitutional history, I found so many interesting and illuminating seams of legal and political theory and practice – culminating in the *McCawley* litigation – that my treatment of *Trethowan* itself was pushed further and further back, to the point where it seemed sensible to explore it in a second, sequential volume.

These books have been written primarily for a British and American audience for whom Australian political and legal history is a very unfamiliar terrain, and to whom Jack Lang, Thomas Bavin, Ted Theodore, Tom Ryan, William Wentworth, Samuel Griffith and William Kidston are likely unknown names. I hope at least to introduce those (and other) characters – some of them politicians, some lawyers and many both – and their careers and ideas to my readers, on the basis that the personal is not just political, but also constitutional. Similarly, even for non-Australian readers knowledgeable about their respective country's constitutional law arrangements, such seminal Australian cases as *Cooper v Commissioner of Income Taxes*,[4] *Taylor v Attorney-General*,[5] *McCawley v The King*[6] and *Trethowan* itself may be largely unknown quantities. Those cases are likely well known to Australian readers, but I hope that even that audience will find material here that adds some detail or insight to their understanding of their country's political and constitutional history.

I have also assumed that readers have at least a rudimentary familiarity with basic principles of British constitutional law. For the benefit of those who do not, I have occasionally made reference to passages in my own constitutional law textbook to offer some background explanation of the matters being discussed.

I do not doubt that there are errors in the text, arising from the inadequacies of my own research or understanding; such errors are, of course, entirely my responsibility.

Ian Loveland
London, 2020

---

[4] [1907] ST R Qd 110 (Queensland Supreme Court), (1907) 4 CLR 1304 (High Court).
[5] [1917] St R Qd 208 (Queensland Supreme Court), (1917) 23 CLR 457 (High Court).
[6] [1917] St R Qd 62 (Queensland Supreme Court), (1918) 26 CLR 9 (High Court), [1920] AC 691 (Privy Council).

ACKNOWLEDGEMENTS

I should initially record my thanks to Kate Whetter at Hart Publishing for commissioning this project on the strength of a proposal and couple of draft chapters, and to both Kate and her colleague Rosemarie Mearns for accommodating changes to the proposal – most notably releasing it as a two-volume publication – which developed as I found myself digging deeper and deeper into Queensland's and New South Wales's political and constitutional history. I am also very grateful to Professors George Williams and Sean Brennan for hosting me as a Visiting Professor at the School of Law at the University of New South Wales in July 2019, a visit which gave me the opportunity to consult a wider range of primary and secondary sources than are available in London. Thanks are owed to the Robert Menzies Bicentennial Fund at King's College London, which graciously provided a grant towards the cost of that visit.

I have made extensive use of state and national election results in the text, and am very grateful in doing so to have been able to draw on the excellent electoral database maintained by the University of Western Australia.[1] I have also made frequent resort to the marvellous Trove newspaper archive established by the Australian government, and express my admiration for the many long-dead journalists and publishers who reported on political and legal issues in colonial Australia with such rigour and thoroughness. I must also record my gratitude to the law library staff at City, especially Conor Jackson and Robert Hodgson, who have been unfailingly helpful in responding to my requests for assistance in tracking down obscure source materials.

---

[1] http://elections.uwa.edu.au/electionsearch.lasso. For an explanation of the site, see Sharman (2002) 'A web-based database on Australian government and politics', *Australian Journal of Political Science* 347.

BRIEF CONTENTS

Preface .... *v*
Acknowledgements .... *vii*
Detailed Contents .... *xi*
Abbreviations .... *xix*
Table of Cases .... *xxi*
Table of Legislation .... *xxv*

1. Constituting New South Wales 1787–1850 1

2. 'Constituting' New South Wales – And Queensland – 1850–1861 33

3. The Colonial Laws Validity Act 1865 – I: Origins 67

4. The Colonial Laws Validity Act 1865 – II: Policy (?) and Text 101

5. Constitutional Developments in New South Wales and
   Queensland 1865–1900 123

6. Australian Confederation 157

7. Constitutional Controversy in Queensland: Kidston and *Cooper* 210

8. Constitutional Controversy in Queensland: Ryan and *Taylor* 239

9. Constitutional Controversy in Queensland: Ryan, Theodore
   and *McCawley* in the Queensland Courts 267

10. Constitutional Controversy in Queensland: Ryan, Theodore
    and *McCawley* – In the High Court 280

11. Constitutional Controversies in Queensland: Ryan, Theodore
    and *McCawley* – Before the Privy Council 305

Bibliography *339*
Index *343*

DETAILED CONTENTS

Preface .... *v*
Acknowledgements .... *vii*
Brief Contents .... *ix*
Abbreviations .... *xix*
Table of Cases .... *xxi*
Table of Legislation .... *xxv*

1. **Constituting New South Wales 1787–1850** 1
    I. An Unusual Type of Colony 1
        The Governor's Commission and *Instructions* 2
            'Exclusives', 'Emancipists' and the Emergence of Pastoralism
            as an Economic and Political Force 4
            From Prison Towards Colony … and from Prisoners Towards Colonists 5
    II. The New South Wales Act 1823 8
        The 'Legislative Council' 8
            Legislative Competence and 'Repugnancy' 9
        The Judicial and Executive Branches of the Colony's Government 11
            Darling's Commission and *Instructions* 13
        Pre-legislative Colonial Judicial Review of Colonial Legislation –
            The Newspaper Licence and Tax 'Laws' 15
    III. The Australian Courts Act 1828 16
        Increasing Regulation of Land Disposition and Occupation 17
    IV. The Australian Constitutions Act 1842 18
        The 'Constitution' of the New Legislative Council 19
        The Powers of the New Legislative Council 20
        The 1842–47 Land 'Reforms' 21
            The Australian Land Sales Act 1842 21
            The 1846 Act and the 1847 Order in Council 22
        Van Diemen's Land's Dog Act – Post-Enactment Colonial
            Judicial Review of Colonial Legislation 24
            Amoving the Judges 27
    V. The Australian Colonies Constitution Act 1850 29

2. **'Constituting' New South Wales – And Queensland – 1850–1861** 33
    I. The New South Wales Constitution Bill 1853 33
        The Composition and Powers of the New Legislature 34
            The Proposed Council 35

xii *Detailed Contents*

		The Proposed Assembly	36
		Legislative Powers	37
		The Lawmaking Process: The 'Ordinary Way' of Legislating	37
		The Lawmaking Process: The Absolute and Two-Thirds Majority Provisos	40
		An 'Independent' Judiciary	42
		The Legal Source (?) of Responsible Government	43
	II.	The New South Wales Constitution Act 1855	44
		The Purpose and Wording of s.1 [BAA] of the New South Wales Constitution Act 1855	45
		The Purpose (?) and Wording of s.4 [BAA] of the Constitution Act 1855	46
		Debate in the Imperial Parliament	47
		The Secretary of State's Despatch	48
		A Diversion from s.4 [BAA]: Mid-Nineteenth-Century Presumptions as to the 'Manner' of Lawmaking by the British Parliament …	49
		… and Back to s.4 [BAA] …	50
		Another Diversion from s.4 [BAA]: And Another Mid-Nineteenth-Century Presumption as to (Judicial Regulation of) the 'Manner' of Lawmaking by the British Parliament …	52
		… and Back (again) to s.4 [BAA]	52
		The Governor's Commission and *Instructions*	53
		Responsible Government by Implication?	53
		Matters Reserved for the Royal Assent	55
	III.	The Law and the Politics of 'Dis-Entrenchment'	56
		The New South Wales Constitution Act 1857	56
		Electoral Reform … and Swamping the Council	58
		The Electoral Act 1858	60
		Robertson's 1861 Land Reforms – And the First 'Swamping'(?) of the Council	60
	IV.	The Creation of Queensland as a Separate Colony	63
		The First Queensland Government	65
3.	**The Colonial Laws Validity Act 1865 – I: Origins**		**67**
	I.	Constitutional Controversies in Early 1860s Queensland – Lutwyche	68
		The Two-Thirds Clauses in the Queensland Constitution – A Question of when …	68
		The Initial Electoral Law – And Sir Alfred Lutwyche's View of the Constitution	70
		The Pugh Seditious Libel Case …	75
		Lutwyche's Final Fling	77
	II.	South Australia's Constitutional Crises – Boothby and Gwynne	80
		The First Dismissal Attempt	81
		The Torrens Land Act …	81
		Hutchinson v Leeworthy – April 1860 – Judicial Invalidation of 'Repugnant' Colonial Statutes	83

Detailed Contents xiii

   Payne v Dench – April 1861 – The Constitutionality of the
    'Court of Appeals' 85
   McEllister v Fenn – June 1861 – The Invalidity of 'Acts' Consented
    to by the Governor in Breach of his *Instructions* 87
   The First Addresses for Removal and Boothby's 'Evidence' to the
    Assembly 89
   McEllister v Fenn (again) – November 1861 – The Continued
    Non-Existence of the Court of Appeals 92
   The Imperial Government's Response to the Dismissal Addresses 93
   The Controversy Continues … and Deepens … and Broadens 96
   Driffield v Torrens – December 1862 – The Entrenchment Proviso
    in the South Australia Constitution 97
   Auld v Murray – October 1863 – Assessing the Effect of Validating
    Legislation 99
   The 1864 Validity Petitions 100

4. **The Colonial Laws Validity Act 1865 – II: Policy (?) and Text** 101
 I. Palmer and Collier's Report 101
 II. The Act – And its Enactment 105
   Parliamentary Consideration – Or Not – Of the Bill 105
   The Secretary of State's Despatch 106
   The Text of the Act: ss.1–5 107
    Temporal Effects 109
    'Colonial Legislatures' and 'Representative Legislatures' 110
    The Powers of Colonial and Representative Legislatures 110
    … 'Such Manner and Form' 112
   The Text: s.6 114
   The Text: s.7 114
 III. Meanwhile – And Afterwards – On the South Australia
   Supreme Court 115
   The Queen v Neville – June 1865 – Criminal Courts and Repugnancy 115
   Dawes v Quarrell – July 1865 – There are No Local Courts 116
   Walsh v Goodall (1865) – October 1865 – Gwynne and Boothby
    on the Construction of the CLVA 1865 118
   Not Dismissal, but Amoval – The End of Boothby's Judicial Career 120
 IV. Conclusion 121

5. **Constitutional Developments in New South Wales and
 Queensland 1865–1900** 123
 I. The 'Two-Thirds' Clauses in the Queensland Constitution Act 1867 123
   Putting – Or Keeping – Them in: The Queensland Constitution
    Act 1867 124
   Taking (One of) them Out – The Constitution Act Amendment Act 1871 127
    Lilley's 'Singular Omission' Analysis of the Special Majority Clauses 128
   The Amended Bill – Repealing s.10; Retaining s.9 129
   Electoral Reform … or Not 131

    II.   Queensland – Griffith … and McIlwraith 133
            Points of Division in a 'No-Party System' 134
            Political and Legal Dimensions of Assembly Council Relations 135
                Swamping or Radical Reform of Queensland's Legislative Council? 139
            To the Left … to the Right … to the Court … the Final Steps
            of Griffith's (Party) Political Career.. 141
    III. New South Wales – Parkes 144
            Assembly–Council Relations 145
            The Emergence and Consolidation of a Formal Party System 147
    IV. Towards Australian Federation? 149
            Colonial Legislatures have Plenary, Not Delegated Powers –
            The *Apollo Candle* (and *Burah*) Litigation 150
            The Immediate Origins of Federation.. 153

6. **Australian Confederation** **157**
    I.   The Terms of Federation 157
            The Commonwealth Parliament 158
                The Composition of the House of Representatives and the Senate 158
                Parliament's Powers 158
                Deadlock Provisos 159
                Disallowance and Reservation... 160
            The National Government 160
            State Autonomy 161
                'Fiscal' Autonomy 162
            The High Court 163
            The Constitutional Amendment Process 164
            The Continuing Significance of the CLVA 1865? 165
    II.   Party Political Alignments in the Commonwealth Parliament
            in Early Twentieth-century Australia.. 166
            The 1901 Election 167
                The Judiciary Act 1903 and the First High Court Judges.......................... 168
            The Rise and Fall and Rise and Fall and Rise and Fall of the Deakin
            and Labour Governments 169
    III. In the High Court and Privy Council – The Implied Immunity
            of Instrumentalities Doctrine 172
            In re the Income Tax Acts (No 4); *Wollaston's Case* 172
                An American Diversion – The Judgment in *McCulloch v Maryland* 173
                On Judges as Jurists – *McCulloch* in the Privy Council 175
                On Judges as Statesmen... 177
                Wollaston's Case in the State Supreme Court 179
                    Counsel and Submissions 179
                    The Judgment 181
            D'Emden v Pedder 182
                In the State Supreme Court.. 183
                    Counsel and Submissions 183
                    The Judgment 184

		In the High Court 185
		Counsel and Submissions 185
		Judgment 186

        Deakin v Webb 188
            In the Victoria Supreme Court 189
                Judgment 189
            In the High Court 189
        Webb v Outtrim (*Outtrim's Case*) 191
            The Privy Council Bench 191
            Counsel 192
            Judgment 193
        Railway Servants 195
            The High Court's Judgment 195
        Baxter v Commissioners of Taxation 196
        An Uneasy Settlement? 199
        The *Harvester* Judgment and the Constitutionality of 'New Protection' 200
        The Constitutionality of the Excise Tariff Act 1906 201
    IV. Conclusion 201
        The New South Wales Constitution Act 1902 202
            The Reduction of Members Referendum Act 1903 206
            The Reduction of Members Referendum Bill 206
        The Australian States Constitution Act 1907 208

7. **Constitutional Controversy in Queensland: Kidston and *Cooper*** **210**
    I.   William Kidston and the Politics of Progressive Coalition 211
    II. Income Tax and the Judges – The *Cooper* Litigation 214
        In the Lower Queensland Courts 219
        In the Queensland Supreme Court 221
        In the High Court 222
            Counsel and Submissions 222
            Judgment 222
    III. The Constitution Act Amendment Act 1908 and the Parliamentary
        Bills Referendum Act 1908 228
        The Constitution Act Amendment Act 1908 229
            In the Assembly 230
            In the Council 232
        The Parliamentary Bills Referendum Act 1908 233
            In the Assembly 233
            In the Council 236
    IV. Conclusion 238

8. **Constitutional Controversy in Queensland: Ryan and *Taylor*** **239**
    I.   Abolishing the Queensland Legislative Council? 240
        Ryan, Hughes and Conscription – Round 1 241
        The Legislative Council Abolition Bill 242

xvi *Detailed Contents*

		The First Conscription Referendum and Hughes's Desertion of the Labour Party	243
		The Legislative Council Abolition Referendum	245
		Duncan v Theodore – At Trial before Pope Cooper	246
		The Background to *Duncan v Theodore*	247
		Cooper's Judgment	248
	II.	*Taylor* in the Queensland Courts	250
		Counsel and Submissions	250
		Judgment	253
		The State Supreme Court's Judgment in *Duncan v Theodore*	255
		The High Court's Judgment in *Duncan v Theodore*	256
		The Judges	256
		The Judgments	257
	III.	*Taylor* in the High Court	259
		Counsel and Submissions	259
		The Judgments in *Taylor*	262
		Ryan, Hughes and Conscription – Round 2	264

9. **Constitutional Controversy in Queensland: Ryan, Theodore and *McCawley* in the Queensland Courts** 267
    I. In the Queensland Courts 269
       'Counsel' and 'Submissions' 269
       The Judges 272
       The 'Judgment' 272
    II. Regularising the Proceedings 276
       The 1918 Assembly Election 277
    III. *Taylor* before the Privy Council 278

10. **Constitutional Controversy in Queensland: Ryan, Theodore and *McCawley* – In the High Court** 280
    I. The Hearing 280
    II. The Majority Judgments 282
       Griffith 283
       Barton 285
       Gavan Duffy 287
       Powers 287
    III. The Dissenting Judgments 288
       Isaacs and Rich 288
         On the CLVA 1865 s.5 289
         On the 1855 Act, the 1859 Order and the 1867 Act 293
         On Empirical Inconveniences and Logical Inconsistencies 294
         On *Cooper* 296
         On the Validity of the Commission and the Meaning of 'Five Years' Standing' 296
       Higgins 297
       Conclusion 298

IV.	Abolition of the Legislative Council and the 1919 National Election 298
	Abolishing Queensland's Legislative Council? 299
	The 1919 National Election 302

11. Constitutional Controversies in Queensland: Ryan, Theodore and *McCawley* – Before the Privy Council 305

    I.   The Hearing 305
            The Judges – A Court of Statesmen, Not Jurists? 305
            Counsel and Submissions 306
    II.   The Judgment 308
            Answered Questions 308
            An Unanswered Question? 313
            The Meaning (and Vires) of the Commission 314
            Reaction(s) in Queensland 314
    III. The Eventual Abolition of the Queensland Legislative Council 315
            The Judges' Retirement Act 1921 319
                In the Assembly 319
                In the Council 323
            The Labour Party's (1921) 'Socialisation Objective' 324
            The Legislative Council Abolition Legislation 325
                In the Assembly 325
                In the Council 327
            The 'New' Supreme Court 329
    IV. National Developments 330
            A Judicial Rebalancing of Commonwealth–State Constitutional
            Relations? The *Engineers* Case and the Implied Immunity
            of Instrumentalities Doctrine 330
            Deposing Hughes 333
            A Political Rebalancing of Commonwealth–State Financial Relations?
            Control of the Note Issue and the Creation of the Loan Council 334
    V.   An Opportunity Not Taken – Or Not Realised? 336
            McCawley – An Unanswered (and Unasked) Question 337

Bibliography *339*
Index *343*

ABBREVIATIONS

BC	*The (Brisbane) Courier* (newspaper)
CAG	Commonwealth of Australia Gazette
HCD	House of Commons Debates
HLD	House of Lords Debates
HRA	Historical Records of Australia
HRD	House of Representatives Debates
JRAHS	*Journal of the Royal Australian Historical Society*
JRHSQ	*Journal of the Royal Historical Society of Queensland*
LD	*Labour Daily* (newspaper)
NSWLAD	New South Wales Legislative Assembly Debates
NSWLCD	New South Wales Legislative Council Debates
ODNB	Oxford Dictionary of National Biography
QGG	Queensland Government Gazette
QLAD	Queensland Legislative Assembly Debates
QLCD	Queensland Legislative Council Debates
SAA	*South Australia Advertiser* (newspaper)
SAR	*South Australian Register* (newspaper)
SMH	*Sydney Morning Herald* (newspaper)
SD	Senate Debates
VPLA (NSW)	Votes and Proceedings of the Legislative Assembly (of New South Wales)
VPLC (NSW)	Votes and Proceedings of the Legislative Council (of New South Wales)

TABLE OF CASES

Many of the early Australian colonial cases discussed in this book were not formally reported. Where what seems to me to be an adequate newspaper report of such cases is available, I have provided the relevant newspaper citation and a link to the newspaper report.

New South Wales

Powell v Apollo Candle (1883) 4 NSW LR 167 150

Queensland

Australian Alliance Insurance Co v A-G (Qld) [1916] ST R Qld 135 270
'*Cooper*' – formally *Commissioner of Income Tax v Cooper* (Small Debts Court) unreported 219
'*Cooper*' – formally *Commissioner of Income Tax v Cooper* (District Court) – *The Telegraph (Brisbane)* 9 February 1907 p13, http://trove.nla.gov.au/newspaper/article/175277634 219
'*Cooper*' – formally *In re the Income Tax (Consolidated Acts, 1902–1904, and the Income Tax Declaratory Act of 1905* (Supreme Court) [1907] ST R Qd 110 220
Duncan v Theodore [1917] St R Qd 250 .... 246–47, 249, 255–59, 270
Gibson v Lennon [1918] St R Qd 1 .... 278, 301
In re McCawley [1917] St R Qd 62 269–77
R v Pugh – BC 24 August 1861 p5, http://nla.gov.au/nla.news-article4600656; *The Empire* 2 September 1861 p2, https://trove.nla.gov.au/newspaper/article/60484143 76
R v Ryan The Queensland Times 6 December 1917; https://trove.nla.gov.au/newspaper/article/121979458/10314361; *The Daily Standard* 6 December 1917 p7, http://trove.nla.gov.au/newspaper/article/179432907 .... 265, 270
Taylor v Attorney General [1917] St R Qd 208 250–55

South Australia

Auld v Murray – SAR 17 December 1863 p3, https://trove.nla.gov.au/newspaper/article/50165392 99–100

xxii Table of Cases

Dawes v Quarrell – *SAA* 28 July 1865 p4, https://trove.nla.gov.au/newspaper/
article/31852008 116
Driffield v Torrens – *Adelaide Observer* 29 November 1962 p3,
https://trove.nla.gov.au/newspaper/article/158190041; *Adelaide Observer*
20 December 1862 p3, http://nla.gov.au/nla.news-article158190406 97–98
Hutchinson v Leeworthy – *SAR* 26 April 1860 p3, https://trove.nla.gov.au/
newspaper/article/49891143; *SAR* 29 May 1860 p3, http://nla.gov.au/
nla.news-article49892802 83–85
McEllister v Fenn – *SAR* 27 June 1861 p3, https://trove.nla.gov.au/newspaper/
article/50018147 87–88
McEllister v Fenn – *SAR* 9 November 1861 p3, https://trove.nla.gov.au/
newspaper/article/50080889 92–93
Payne v Dench – *SAA* 7 November 1860 p3, https://trove.nla.gov.au/
newspaper/article/826197 85
Payne v Dench – *SAA* 26 December 1860 p2, http://nla.gov.au/nla.
news-article828278 85
Payne v Dench – *SAR* 19 March 1861 p3, http//nla.gov.au/nla.news-
article50019491 85
Payne v Dench – *SAA* 18 April p3, https://trove.nla.gov.au/newspaper/
article/50017763 85
R v Neville – *SAR* 26 June 1865 p3, http://nla.gov.au/nla.news-article39123875 116
Ridpath v Murray – *SAR* 5 March 1866 p3, https://trove.nla.gov.au/newspaper/
article/41029961 119
Walsh v Goodall – *Adelaide Observer* 28 October 1865, p3, http://nla.gov.au/
nla.news-article159498701 118–19

Tasmania (and Van Diemen's Land)

D'Emden v Pedder [1903] TLR 146 183–88
Symons v Morgan (Hobart Magistrates Court) – *Hobart Courier* 18 September
1847 p3, https://trove.nla.gov.au/newspaper/article/2970922 .... 1, 25
Symons v Morgan (Hobart Quarter Sessions) – *Hobart Guardian* 3 November
1847 p2, https://trove.nla.gov.au/newspaper/article/163501445 25
Symons v Morgan (Supreme Court) – *Hobart Courier* 2 February 1848,
https://trove.nla.gov.au/newspaper/article/2969922 .... 24–25, 27

Victoria

Deakin v Webb (1904) 29 VLR 748 188–91
Webb v Outtrim – *The Argus* 11 February 1905 pp 14–15, https://trove.nla.
gov.au/newspaper/article/192234507, https://trove.nla.gov.au/newspaper/
article/9891194 191
Webb v Outtrim (permission to appeal to Privy Council) [1905] VLR 463 191
Wollaston's Case (1902) VLR 357 .... 172–73, 179–82

Table of Cases xxiii

Australia

Amalgamated Society of Engineers v Adelaide Steamship Co Ltd (1920)
   28 CLR 129... 331–33
Attorney-General for the Commonwealth v Colonial Sugar Refining Co
   (1918) 26 CLR 9..284
Baxter v Ah Way (1909) 8 CLR 626 225
Baxter v Commissioners of Taxation (1907) 4 CLR 1087....................... 196–200
Cooper v Commissioner of Income Tax (1907) 4 CLR 1304..................... 222–26, 250–52,
                                                                                                              259–64, 281–96
D'Emden v Pedder [1904] 1 CLR 91 ....182–88, 223, 333
Deakin v Webb (1904) 1 CLR 585.. 188–91, 223
Duncan v Queensland [1916] HCA 67, (1916) 22 CLR 556....................................247
Duncan v Theodore [1917] HCA 38, (1917) 23 CLR 510 .... 246–48, 255–59, 270
'Engineers' – see Amalgamated Society of Engineers v Adelaide
   Steamship Co Ltd (1920) 28 CLR 129 above ....
Ex parte HV McKay ('Harvester') (1907) 2 Car 1 200
Federated Sawmill Employees of Australia v Jones Moore and
   Sons Pty Ltd (1909) 8 CLR 465... 331
Gibson v Lennon (1918) 24 CLR 140...301
'Harvester' (Ex parte HV McKay) (1907) 2 Car 1 200–01
Federated Amalgamated Government Railway and Tramway Service
   Association v New South Wales Traffic Employees Association
   ('Railway Servants') (1906) 4 CLR 488 ....195–96, 331, 333
McCawley v The King (1918) 26 CLR 9............................... 280, 283–87, 290, 294–95, 297
Municipal Council of Sydney v The Commonwealth (1904) 1 CLR 208 188
R v Barger; R v Mackay (1908) 6 CLR 4...201
'Railway Servants'- formally Federated Amalgamated Government
   Railway and Tramway Service Association v New South Wales
   Traffic Employees Association (1906) 4 CLR 488 ....195–96, 331, 333
Taylor v Attorney General [1917] [1917] HCA 45; (1917) 23 CLR 457 ..... 259–64, 274–75,
                                                                                                              280, 287, 313–14

United Kingdom

Attorney-General v De Keyser's Royal Hotel [1917 D 582], [1919] 2 Ch 197,
   [1920] AC 508..278
Attorney-General for New South Wales v Rennie (1896) AC 376....................261
Australian Alliance Insurance Co v A-G (Qld) [1917] AC 537........................270
Bank of Toronto v Lambe [1887] AC 575..175, 177, 181, 188, 190
Bullock v Dodds (1819) 2 B and Ald 358; 106 ER 361 6–8
Calvin's Case (1606) 7 Co Rep 1...2
Campbell v Hall (1774) 1 Cowp 204...2
Churchwardens and Overseers of West Ham v Fourth City Mutual Building
   Society and Another [1892] 1 QB 654 216

Citizens Insurance Co v Parsons (1881) 7 App Cas 96 177
Conservators of the River Thames v Hall (1868) Law Rep 3 C P 415 216
Dean and Chapter of Ely v Bliss (1842) 5 Beavan 574; 49 ER 700 49
Dean of Ely v Bliss (1852) 2 De Gex Macnaghten & Gordon 459; 42 ER 950 49
Dimes v Grand Junction Canal (1852) 3 HL Cas 759; 10 ER 301 .... 90, 190
Edinburgh and Dalkeith Railway v Wauchope (1842) 8 Cl & 710; 8 ER 279 52
Eastman Photographic Materials Co v Comptroller- General of Patents
  [1898] AC 571 197
Fitzgerald v Champneys (1861) 70 ER 958 86
Fort Frances Pulp v Man Free Press [1923] AC 695 305
Garnett v Bradley (1878) 3 App Cas 944 216
Heydon's Case (1584) 76 ER 637 197
Hodge v R (1883) 9 App Cas 117 151
Imperial Hydropathic Hotel Co, Blackpool v Hampson (1882) 23 Ch D 1 282
In re Patent Invert Sugar (1885) 31 Cd D 166 282
In re Williams (1887) 36 Ch D 573 216
Liquidators of the Maritime Bank of Canada v The Receiver-General of
  New Brunswick [1892] AC 437 178
Lennon v Gibson [1919] AC 709 .... 301, 307, 319
McCawley v The King [1920] AC 691 305–14
Ontario (AG) v Canada (AG) (Local Prohibition Reference) [1896] AC 348 178
Powell v Apollo Candle (1885) 10 App Cas 282 150
R v Burah (1878) 3 App Cas 889 .... 151, 153, 282, 312
Reference re Board of Commerce Act [1922] 1 AC 191 305
Re Petition of Right [1915] 3 KB 649 278
Taff Vale Railway Company v Amalgamated Society of Railway Servants
  [1901] AC 426 192
Taylor v Attorney-General [1918] St R Qd 194 (PC permission to appeal) 278–80, 305
Theodore v Duncan [1919] AC 696 .... 301, 307–08
Toronto Electric Commissioners v Snider [1925] AC 396 305
Webb v Outtrim [1907] AC 81 .... 191, 193–94, 221
Winthrop v Lechmere (1727–1728); unreported Pricy Council 'judgment' 10

United States

Central Pacific Railroad v California (1896) 162 US 91 182
Cohens v Virginia (1821) 19 US 264 157
Collector v Day (1870) 78 US 113 .... 180, 196
Dobbins v Commissioners of Erie County (1842) 41 US 435 .... 180, 182, 191
Fletcher v Peck (1810) 109 US 87 157
Marbury v Madison (1803) 1 Cranch 137 .... 157, 174
Martin v Hunters Lessee (1816) 14 US 304 .... 157, 197
McCulloch v Maryland (1819) 4 Wheaton 316 .... 159, 173–78, 180–81,
                                                                            183–88, 191, 193, 197, 199
Railroad Company v Peniston (1873) 85 US 18 .... 182, 184–86

TABLE OF LEGISLATION

New South Wales

Constitution Act 1855[1]	33, 44, 73, 105, 272
s.1	45, 48, 64–65, 125, 135, 151
s.2	45, 47, 125, 135
s.3	45, 47, 70, 74
s.8	47, 49, 52
s.10	47, 49, 52, 123
s.11	36
s.12	36
s.13	36
s.14	36
s.15	42, 48–49, 51–52, 64, 69, 123, 126, 231
s.21	36
s.23	47, 49, 52
s.36	42, 48, 52, 64, 69, 123, 126, 231
s.37	42
s.38	45
s.39	42
s.40	42
s.41	35
s.43	37
s.45	37
s.49	37
s.51	35, 43
s.54	38
Constitution Act 1857	
s.1	56
s.2	56
Constitution Act Amendment Act 1884	206
Constitution Act Amendment Act 1890	206, 223
Constitution Act 1902	202–08
s.2	205–06
s.3	204

[1] *Sensu stricto*, the New South Wales Constitution Act 1855 is a schedule of the Imperial New South Wales Constitution Act 1855. I have listed it here (as well as listing it as schedule 1 to the Imperial Act) as it is often regarded in common usage as a New South Wales statute.

s.5 ....204, 207
s.7 204
s.10 205
s.16 205
s.32 205
s.33 205
s.34 205
s.47 205
Schedule 1 205–06
Crown Land Protection Act 1833 – formally 'An Act for Protecting the Crown
 Lands of this Colony from Encroachment, Intrusion and Trespass 1833' 17
Crown Lands Unauthorised Occupation Act 1836 – formally 'An Act to
 Restrain the Unauthorized Occupation of Crown Lands 1836' 17
Customs Regulation Act 1879
 s.133 150
Electoral Act 1858 .... 71, 204, 217
s.2 60
s.9 60
s.13 60
s.41 60
s.42 60
s.43 60
Electorates Redistribution Act 1904 208
Industrial Arbitration Act 1901 203
Parliamentary Representatives Allowance Act 1889 148
Reduction of Members Referendum Act 1903 206
Women's Franchise Act 1906 1902
 s.4 203

Queensland

Constitution Act 1867 ..... 124, 127, 218–20, 223–25, 233, 261, 275, 285–86, 291–92, 295
s.1 125
s.2 125
s.9 ....123, 126, 217, 228, 234
s.10 217
s.14 273
s.15 ....126, 271–73, 297
s.16 ....271–73, 297
s.17 ....126, 215, 226, 272
s.26 ....126, 130
s.54 295
s.55 295
s.56 295

Constitution Act Amendment Act 1871 .... 127–30, 217
Constitution Act Amendment Act 1908 228–38
The Constitution Act Amendment Act 1922 325–329
Electoral Act 1872
   s.3 132
Electoral Districts Act 1887 .... 133, 139
Industrial Arbitration Act 1916 267
   s.6 268
   s.6(6) 268
   s.6(7) 272
   s.7 268
Judges Retirement Act 1918
   s.3 322
Legislative Assembly Act 1867
   s.13 126
Meat Supply for Imperial Uses Act 1914 .... 248–49, 256, 258
   s.6 247
   s.7 247
Members Expenses Act 1886 138
Parliamentary Bills Referendum Act 1908 .... 228–38, 243, 251–52, 260, 262–63, 274, 279, 287–88, 307
   s.3 245
   s.4 .... 233, 235
   s.10 255
Public Curator Act 1915 270
Sugar Acquisition Act 1915 .... 247, 249, 258
   s.7 .... 248, 256, 301
   s.10 .... 248, 256
Supreme Court Act 1867 218
Supreme Court Act 1889 218
Supreme Court Act 1892 218
Tax Declaratory Act 1905
   s.2 218

South Australia

Appointment Act 1862 – formally 'An Act to Remove Doubts as to the Appointments to and Dismissal from Office of Certain Persons 1862' 96
Cooper's Pension Act 1861 92
Court of Appeals Act 1861 .... 87, 91
   s.3 87
   s.4 87
Electoral Act 1856 95
Electoral Act 1861 97

Local Courts Act 1861
  s.8 115
  s.13 115
  s.115 115
  s.116 116
Real Property Act 1858 .... 83–84, 88
  s.77 82
Real Property Act 1860 88
  s.118 82
Real Property Act 1861
  s.41 99
Registration of Deeds Act 1841 .... 97, 118, 122
Registration of Deeds Act 1862 .... 97, 118, 122
South Australia Constitution Act 1856 .... 68, 83, 85–86
  s.1 87
  s.6 97
  s.30 89
  s.31 89
  s.33 96
  s.34 .... 96, 104
  s.36 81
Supreme Court Act 1837
  s.16 85
Supreme Court Consolidation Act 1856
  s.18 85

Tasmania/Van Diemen's Land

Dog Act – formally 'An Act to Restrain the Increase of Dogs 1846' 24, 26–27, 29,
                                                                                                            42, 280–81, 309
  s.2 25
  s.6 25
Stamp Duties Amendment Act 1902
  s.5 182

Victoria

Constitution Act 1855 35

Australia

Australian Notes Act 1911 335
Commonwealth Bank Act 1911
  s.12 335

Commonwealth Bank Act 1920
  s.6...335
Commonwealth Bank Act 1924
  s.7...335
Commonwealth Conciliation and Arbitration Act 1904 ....170, 331
  s.4...195
Commonwealth of Australia Constitution Act 1900[2] 157, 172, 175, 180,
                                                                187–88, 195, 197–98, 224
BAI[3]
  s.5... 161, 193–94

  s.1... 157–58
  s.7...158
  s.9...167
  s.22...158
  s.23...158, 165
  s.30...158, 167
  s.39...158
  s.40...158, 165
  s.51.. 162–63
  s.51(ii)..170
  s.51(xii)..159
  s.51(xxxix)...163
  s.51(xxxv)...169, 332
  s.52...162, 165
  s.53...204
  s.57...235, 243
  s.59...160
  s.63...160
  s.65...160
  s.71...163, 194
  s.72...163
  s.73...163, 194
  s.74... 163–64, 227
  s.75...163
  s.76...163
  s.87.. 162–63
  s.90...162
  s.106 ....161, 193
  s.107 .... 161–62, 193
  s.109 ....161–62, 193–94
  s.111 162
  s.114 .... 162, 184, 194

---

[2] This *sensu stricto* is a UK statute, but entries are duplicated here to acknowledge the political reality of the Act being Australia's Constitution.
[3] For an explanation of the [BAI] prefix, see p 157 above n 1.

s.115 162
s.128 .... 164–65, 235
Commonwealth Franchise Act 1902
    s.4 168
Commonwealth Salaries Act 1907 199–200
Conciliation and Arbitration Act 1904 .... 170, 331
    s.4 195
    s.25 170
Excise Tariff Act 1906
    s.2 .... 170, 200–01
Immigration Restriction Act 1901 167
Invalid and Old Age Pensions Act 1908 .... 170, 321
Judiciary Act 1903 168
Judiciary Act 1908 199
Military Conscription Referendum Act 1916 245
Pacific Islands Labourers Act 1901 167
War Precautions Act 1914 .... 244, 265

United Kingdom

Act of Settlement 1701 .... 11, 295
Australian Colonies Act 1861
    s.3 .... 77, 126
Australian Constitutions Act 1842 – formally 'An Act for the Government
    of New South Wales and Van Diemen's Land' 18
    s.2 20
    s.4 20–21
    s.5 19
    s.12 19
    s.24 21
    s.27 21
    s.29 20–21
    s.31 20–21
    s.32 21
    s.33 88–89
    s.40 88
Australian Constitutions Act 1850 115–16
    s.8 117
    s.12 88
    s.14 .... 84, 95, 117
    s.25 28
    s.29 117
    s.32 .... 30–31, 68, 81, 83, 90, 94, 98, 206
Australian Constitutions Act 1862 – formally 'An Act to explain an Act,
    intituled An Act for the Better Government of Her Majesty's Australian
    Colonies 1862' 94

Table of Legislation xxxi

Australian Courts Act 1828
    s.16 17
    s.21 16
    s.22 17
    s.25 24
Australian Land Sales Act 1842 21
    s.2 22
    s.4 22
    s.6 22
    s.15 22
    s.19 22
Australian States Constitution Act 1907 6.51 .... 326, 328
    s.1 .... 208–09, 234, 237
    s.2 .... 209, 252
British North America Act 1867 176–78
    s.90 .... 162, 181
    s.91 175
    s.92 175
Burke's Act – see Colonial Leave of Absence Act 1782
Colonial Act Confirmation Act 1863 98
    s.2 .... 99, 112, 119
    s.3 102–03
Colonial Laws Validity Act 1865 .... 67–121, 151, 193, 221, 236–37, 251, 288
    s.1 .... 113, 122, 152, 165, 253, 260–61
    s.2 .... 126, 209, 225, 284, 286, 290, 336
    s.3 204
    s.4 168
    s.5 .... 108–09, 112–15, 118–19, 121–22, 126,
                                          128, 141, 164–65, 204, 207–09, 217, 232,
                                          250, 252–53, 260–62, 274, 279, 284, 289–94,
                                          296–97, 311, 313, 336
    s.6 114–15
    s.7 .... 68, 114–15, 118–19, 122, 293
Colonial Leave of Absence Act 1782 (Burke's Act) 43, 120
    s.2 27
Commission and Salaries of Judges Act 1760 215
Commonwealth of Australia Constitution Act 1900 .... 157, 172, 175, 180, 187–88,
                                          195, 197–98, 224
BAI[4]
    s.5 .... 161, 193–94
———
    s.1 157–58
    s.7 158
    s.9 167

---

[4] For an explanation of the [BAI] prefix, see p157 above n 1.

xxxii Table of Legislation

    s.22 158
    s.23 .... 158, 165
    s.30 .... 158, 167
    s.39 158
    s.40 .... 158, 165
    s.51 162–63
    s.51(ii) 170
    s.51(xii) 159
    s.51(xxxix) 163
    s.51(xxxv) 169, 332
    s.52 .... 162, 165
    s.53 204
    s.57 .... 235, 243
    s.59 160
    s.63 160
    s.65 160
    s.71 .... 163, 194
    s.72 163
    s.73 .... 163, 194
    s.74 .... 163–64, 227
    s.75 163
    s.76 163
    s.87 162–63
    s.90 162
    s.106 .... 161, 193
    s.107 .... 161–62, 193
    s.109 .... 161–62, 193–94
    s.111 162
    s.114 .... 162, 184, 194
    s.115 162
    s.128 .... 164–65, 235
Duties in New South Wales Act 1819 5
Federal Council of Australasia Act 1885
    s.13 149
    s.15 149
    s.20 149
    s.22 .... 149, 193
Judicial Committee Act – An Act for the Better Administration of
    Justice in His Majesty's Privy Council 1833 279
New South Wales Act 1823 .... 10, 13–14, 16
    s.2 11
    s.19 .... 12, 17
    s.20 .... 12, 17
    s.24 .... 8–9, 12, 15
    s.29 .... 15, 20
    s.30 11

s.32 .... 9, 19
s.44 11
New South Wales Constitution Act 1842 – see Australian Colonies Constitution
    Act 1842 88
New South Wales Constitution Act 1855
[BAA][5]
    s.1 45–46
    s.3 .... 53, 55, 204
    s.4 .... 46–53, 57–58, 64–65, 69, 104, 106, 113,
                                                           128–29, 152, 206–07, 216, 224, 313
    s.7 .... 63, 65, 68, 70–72, 74, 78, 126, 223, 231, 286
    s.9 .... 46, 53, 204
    Schedule 1 .... 34, 45, 49, 60, 64, 98, 203–06
    s.1 .... 64–65, 135, 151, 206, 313
    s.2 206
    s.3 .... 70, 74
    s.8 206
    s.10 47
    s.11 .... 36, 204
    s.12 .... 36, 204
    s.13 .... 36, 204,
    s.14 204
    s.15 .... 40–42, 47–49, 57–59, 69–70, 126, 231
    s.21 36
    s.23 .... 36, 37, 49, 52
    s.36 .... 40–42, 47, 48–49, 57–59, 69–70, 126, 231
    s.37 .... 42, 204
    s.38 45
    s.39 .... 42, 43, 45
    s.40 45
    s.41 34
    s.43 37
    s.45 37
    s.49 37
    s.51 43
    s.54 38
New South Wales Courts Act 1787 1
Parliament Act 1911 .... 192, 243, 209
South Australia Act 1834 – formally 'An Act to Empower His Majesty
    to Erect South Australia into a British Province or Provinces and to
    Provide for the Colonisation and Government thereof' 19, 83
    s.2 116
South Australia Act 1842 – formally 'An Act to Provide for the Better
    Government of South Australia' 117

---

[5] For an explanation of the [BAA] label, see ch 2 n 46.

Trade Disputes Act 1906 192
Union Act 1840 – formally 'British North America Act 1840' 35
    s.3 41
Waste Land Occupation Act 1846 22
    s.3 23
    s.4 23
    s.5 23
    s.6 23
    s.12 23

United Kingdom Orders in Council

Order in Council 1859 creating Queensland – formally 'Order
    in Council empowering the Governor of Queensland to make laws,
    and to provide for the Administration of Justice in the said Colony' 70, 72, 79,
                                                                           121, 226–27, 231, 293, 310
    cl. 1 .... 68, 125
    cl.2 .... 64, 125
    cl.3 .... 64, 319
    cl. 4 .... 70, 74, 235, 319
    cl. 6 .... 64, 70–71
    cl.8 .... 64–65, 69–71, 74, 126, 230
    cl. 16 215
    cl.22 .... 64–65, 69, 74, 125, 128, 141, 217, 222–25,
                                                                   230, 243, 250–54, 260–61, 263, 272, 274,
                                                                   284, 286, 294, 297–98, 313, 336–37

United States

Constitution of the United States 158, 162–64, 168, 176, 178,
                                                                        180, 185, 187, 190, 196–98, 290
    Art I s.8 159
    Art VI 161, 173

1
Constituting New South Wales 1787–1850

> This, said the learned gentleman (holding up the Act) is a piece of waste paper – a nullity – but such a piece as it is, it is at an end, and thank God for it!
> The learned gentleman concluded his address amidst the applause of the crowd who filled the office.
>
> Mr Alfred Montagu, of counsel, addressing the court on behalf of the defendant in *Symons v Morgan* before the Hobart Police Magistrate's Court, as reported in *The Courier (Hobart)* 18 September 1847 p3.

It is perhaps difficult for contemporary observers to imagine the extraordinary emptiness – from a European perspective[1] – of the Australian continent in the early to mid-nineteenth century. The cultural and political flavour of the period (from that viewpoint) is perhaps best caught in Kate Grenville's celebrated novels *The Secret River* and *The Lieutenant*. By 1855, Britain laid claim to a continental patchwork of Australian colonies whose land mass dwarfed what we now recognise as western Europe, a land mass to which British governments had been sending colonists of various sorts for some 80 years.

I. An Unusual Type of Colony

New South Wales, occupying the continent's eastern half, was invaded by the British in 1788 for use as a penal colony,[2] centred on a settlement named Sydney after the then Secretary of State for the Colonies, where the Governor, a crown appointee, exercised complete legislative and executive authority.[3] The governmental system differed

---

[1] The land had, of course, been populated by indigenous peoples for many centuries. The genocide wrought on those peoples by the British is a well-known element of Australian history, and is not studied here. Readers unfamiliar with that history might usefully consult, inter alia, Ward (1992) *Concise history of Australia* chs 1–3; Evans (2007) *A history of Queensland* chs 1–2; Hughes (1987) *The fatal shore* pp 272–81, 414–24.

[2] There is a lively and much-joined debate as to Imperial motives in founding the colony, which motives are portrayed variously as simply creating a distant prison, as establishing a strategically significant Imperial way station or as a kaleidoscopic melange of aspects of both perspectives. The literature is accessibly reviewed in Atkinson (1990) 'The first plans for governing New South Wales 1786–87' *Australian Historical Studies* 24.

[3] The New South Wales Courts Act 1787 ('An Act to enable His Majesty to establish a Court of Criminal Judicature on the Eastern Coast of New South Wales, and the Parts adjacent 27 Geo III c 2'), http://foundingdocs.gov.au/item-did-36.html. See especially Melbourne and Joyce (1963) *Early constitutional development in Australia* pp 1–37. I draw heavily on this work in this and subsequent chapters. I am also indebted to Clark (1994) *A history of Australia* (a remarkably florid book in style, which ought to be read sceptically on issues of substance). Readers seeking a similarly dramatic account of early colonisation might refer to Keneally (2007) *The Commonwealth of thieves*; Hughes op cit chs 1–3.

markedly from those established in Britain's North America and Caribbean colonies. Governance in (most of) those colonies proceeded on the assumption that the colonies' respective inhabitants (or at least the more affluent – white – male inhabitants) should enjoy appreciable political autonomy over domestic issues and that their political preferences should be expressed through some form of representative assembly.[4]

Granting such autonomy could manifestly be a perilous enterprise. The American revolution was a very recent experience for British politicians as colonisation of Australia began. But such assumptions as to the propriety of representative government were not seen as applicable to a colony whose population consisted primarily of convicts. Nor, more pertinently, were they considered by successive British governments in the late eighteenth and early nineteenth centuries appropriate for a colony where many residents were 'emancipists' – ie former prisoners – and their immediate descendants.[5]

Convicts (and their guards) were not the only immigrants. A trickle of free British and Irish (before and after the Act of Union between Britain and Ireland in 1800) settlers – known in then and later popular parlance as 'exclusives' – settled before 1820, drawn primarily by the prospects of acquiring large tracts of land at minimal cost and/or lucrative placements in government service.[6] Even as late as 1820, however, over 60% of the colony's inhabitants were current or former prisoners.[7]

To that point, colonial governance had lain almost entirely in the hands of a Governor appointed by the Secretary of State for the Colonies. The early era Governors were military officers, the dominant rationale for their appointment being that the colony was in (very) large part a prison, more in need of firm disciplinary control than subtle skills of political governance.

The Governor's Commission and *Instructions*

Governors' discretion was in formal terms constrained both by their respective Commissions and *Instructions*. Both measures were issued by the Crown under prerogative powers, the Commission being in effect the Governor's initial terms of appointment and the *Instructions* – which might be updated periodically during the Governor's tenure – a more detailed series of commands which responded (as best could be done given the year which might well elapse in a communication being sent from New South Wales to London, considered, replied to and received by the Governor) to changing policy circumstances.

---

[4] Bailyn's 1967 study *The ideological origins of the American revolution* provides an illuminating guide to the contested ideas informing this area of British imperial history. The classic legal statements of the presumption are respectively *Calvin's Case* (1606) 7 Co Rep 1 and *Campbell v Hall* (1774) 1 Cowp 204. *Campbell* confirmed that in using the royal prerogative to grant a colony an Assembly, the Crown had 'irrecoverably' (ibid 1050) deprived itself of the capacity to revoke or alter such a grant. Any such alternation or revocation would have to be made by statute.

[5] See especially Atkinson op cit.

[6] The categories of settlers are nicely described in Karskens (2013) 'The early colonial presence, 1788–1822' in Bashford and MacIntyre (eds) *The Cambridge history of Australia*.

[7] Melbourne and Joyce op cit p102.

The Commission given to the first Governor, Arthur Phillip,[8] who sailed to the colony in a convoy of ships containing some 780 prisoners and 200 marines to guard them, was brief in scope and loosely framed in substance. Phillip was told he should collect cattle, sheep and pigs en route and not allow them to be eaten until they had bred sufficiently to form a viable population.[9] Quite what the livestock and settlers would eat in the short term was a matter for speculation. Phillip was ordered to: "proceed to the cultivation of the land" – having acquired grains and seeds along with the sheep and cows – and the Imperial government seemed to think (obviously on no good evidential basis) that the task would be any easy one: "as the settlement will be amply supplied with vegetable production and most likely with Fish, Fresh Provisions, excepting for the sick and Convalescents, may in a great degree be dispensed with …".

Convicts were put to work at cultivation. That per se made their sentences very different from those they would have served in Britain, but Phillip's Commission also offered a second, more significant distinction. The Governor was authorised to pardon any convicts "who shall from their good conduct and a disposition to Industry, be deserving of favour", and to grant them ten-year licences of land (30 acres for a single man, plus 20 acres for a wife and 10 for each child) at no cost conditional upon the grantee residing on and cultivating the land. Such former convicts became known as 'emancipists'. The longer-term presumption was that emancipists who fulfilled those occupancy conditions would subsequently be granted a freehold estate in their land. Phillip was soon afterwards (in 1789)[10] authorised to make land grants to 'the exclusives' – military officers and government officials in the colony and to people who might come as free settlers. Grants of land were accompanied by assignment of convict labour to assist with cultivation. New South Wales was an unusual colony in being primarily a prison; but it was also an unusual prison in being without walls and also being reliant for its sustainability on the very cheap and immobile source of labour which the prisoners provided.

Such formal land grants coexisted with a wholly informal system in which settlers of all types simply occupied patches of land, marking boundaries, building dwellings or beginning cultivation, both in Sydney's immediate environs and further into the colony's interior. Such 'naked possession', as it came to be known, existed with no formal legal underpinnings whatsoever, yet quickly became so firmly established as an element

---

[8] http://adb.anu.edu.au/biography/phillip-arthur-2549. Phillip was a career naval officer, who had served with distinction in both the British and Portuguese navies. He had some professional connection with Sydney, having led a successful military engagement against the Spanish some years earlier, but was not especially well connected politically. His appointment as the first Governor seems to have been given to him on the – for the time by no means usual – basis that he was technically and temperamentally suited to the task of establishing a British presence in a certainly distant and probably unwelcoming environment.

[9] In a tacit acknowledgement of the gender imbalance (overwhelmingly male) of the initial immigrant population, Phillip was told that the convict ships should: "at any of the Islands in the seas … take on board any of the women who may be disposed to accompany them".

[10] Secretary of State for the Colonies to Phillip 22 August 1789 *HRA* Series 1 vol 1 p124. There is a substantial literature on early land allocation policies in New South Wales. I have found particularly helpful Campbell (1966) 'Conditional land grants by the Crown' *Sydney LR* 267; Weaver (1996) 'Beyond the fatal shore: pastoral squatting and the occupation of Australia' *The American Historical Review* 98; La Croix (1992) 'Sheep, squatters and the evolution of land rights in Australia' *3rd Annual Conference of the International Association for the Study of Common Property*; Karskens (2013) op cit; Karskens (2012) 'Naked possession: building and the politics of legitimate occupancy in early New South Wales Australia' in Shammas (ed) *Investing in the early modern built environments*.

of the initial colonial order that a thriving secondary market in the 'sale' and 'letting' of such plots of land emerged.[11]

The notion that the land which Phillip bestowed on the colonists – or which they occupied themselves – might be 'owned' by the indigenous population was not one that then appeared to occur to, still less to trouble, either British or colonial politicians. British colonisation proceeded on the basis of (for the British) the convenient fiction that New South was *terra nullius*, with the consequence – according to prevailing western European legal norms – that the Crown could assert ownership of the land without either conquest of the native population nor cession of lands by treaty or other formal legal mechanism.[12] Assertion of *terra nullius* also spared the British government any costs that a treaty or cession might incur. As Phillip's *Instructions* took pains to confirm: "we are desirous to diminish as much as possible the Expences which the intended Establishment occasions".

Little was spent on the machinery of government in any recognisably civilian sense. The 'executive' branch was essentially the Governor and the military forces. The colony initially contained but two courts, one for criminal and one for civil matters. Both were notionally headed by a Deputy-Judge-Advocate appointed by the British government. It was not until 1809 that the Deputy-Judge-Advocate was a qualified lawyer. The additional 'judges' on the criminal court were military personnel not required to have legal training and appointed by the Governor. The civil court consisted of the Deputy-Judge-Advocate and two other persons – not necessarily lawyers – chosen by the Governor.[13]

The extreme privations endured by the early colonists have been widely documented.[14] But within 20 years – the prosaic problem of avoiding starvation resolved – more complex difficulties emerged.

'Exclusives', 'Emancipists' and the Emergence of Pastoralism as an Economic and Political Force

Phillip had remained as Governor until 1792. The most well known of his early successors was perhaps Sir William Bligh, whose name has passed into history primarily because of his role as the captain of *The Bounty*. Bligh had the singular misfortune of having endured mutinies not only by the sailors on *The Bounty*, but also by the colony's soldiery when Governor of New South Wales. Much modern recounting of Bligh's tenure has cast him very firmly as the villain of the piece – Manning Clark's account is especially scathing[15] – portraying Bligh as a brutal autocrat.[16] A distinctly contrasting view

---

[11] Karskens (2012) op cit, (2013) op cit.

[12] For an account of how the original colonists interpreted and presented the indigenous population's presence in a fashion which closely fitted the juridical notion of terra nullius see Frost (1981) 'New South Wales as terra nullius the British denial of aboriginal land rights' *Australian Historical Studies* 513. For a more sceptical view see Fitzmaurice (2007) 'The genealogy of terra nullius' *Australian Historical Studies* 1.

[13] On the early judicial system see Neal (1991) *The rule of law in a penal colony*, especially chs 3 and 7.

[14] See eg Hughes op cit ch 4 and Clarke op cit ch 2, the chapters being respectively entitled 'The starvation years' and 'Hunger'.

[15] (1994) *History of Australia* pp 39–44. For a more benign view see http://adb.anu.edu.au/biography/bligh-william-1797.

[16] A more recent revisionist analysis roots opposition to Bligh largely in his decision to override the accepted practice of 'naked possession' and bring all aspects of land grant and usage firmly under governmental control; see Karskens (2012) op cit, (2013) op cit.

is offered by Herbert Evatt,[17] who casts Bligh as a principled opponent of a thuggishly corrupt military establishment which extorted vast sums from the non-military population by the creation of a complete monopoly over alcohol imports (which for good measure contributed to the physical and moral degradation of the civilian colonists).

Bligh's principal antagonist was a former soldier, and by 1808 an extremely wealthy man (by virtue of his alcohol ventures and his occupancy of vast areas of land on which he grazed similarly vast numbers of sheep, kept primarily for their wool rather than their meat), named John Macarthur.[18] Macarthur and his family proved pre-eminent representatives of the so-called 'pastoral'[19] interest in early New South Wales society, both within the colony itself and via his many and carefully cultivated connections with persons of influence in British political circles.

From Prison Towards Colony ... and from Prisoners Towards Colonists

By 1810, any presumption that New South Wales should exist only – or even predominantly – as a prison was being undermined by a gradual influx of voluntary immigrants and a rapidly growing population of released prisoners and their spouses and offspring. (The indigenous aboriginal population was of course regarded by colonial authorities and white residents as largely irrelevant to any political questions.) It had also become increasingly apparent to successive British governments that the Governor appointed in 1809 – a Colonel Lachlan Macquarie – frequently and substantially exceeded the limits of his legal powers.[20]

This was a quality which became both more visible and more politically problematic as the character of the colony (and its overall white population) became decreasingly penal in nature. Dissatisfaction with the legitimacy of the court system had led to a modest reform in 1814, which included – under the exercise of the royal prerogative rather than statute – the creation of a Supreme Court staffed by a judge and two magistrates.[21] The new Court was accompanied by a 'Charter of Justice' outlining the Court's jurisdiction. The British government resisted Macquarie's suggestion that the time was ripe to introduce trial by jury either in criminal or civil cases, evidently for fear

---

[17] Evatt (1947) *Rum rebellion*. (Evatt appears in this book in several guises; as politician, as counsel, as academic analyst and as judge.) See also the relatively pro-Bligh account in Ward (1992) *Concise history of Australia* pp 63–66.

[18] http://adb.anu.edu.au/biography/macarthur-john-2390; Clark op cit chs 3–5; Ward (1992) op cit pp 63–69. For more detail see Kerr (1961) 'The Macarthur family and the pastoral industry' *JRAHS* 131. Kerr (atypically) notes that Macarthur's success was largely due to Macarthur's wife Elizabeth, who often managed the business alone while her husband was in England. I use the term 'occupancy' as Macarthur ran his enterprise both on granted land and land held under 'naked possession'.

[19] Much of the land was not well suited to intensive or even subsistence agricultural production, but could support sheep. And even many of those areas sufficiently fertile for crop production were used for pastoral purposes.

[20] Melbourne and Joyce note that by 1818 the British government was sufficiently concerned that Macquarie was levying taxes without legal power to do so that it promoted legislation, enacted in 1819 (Duties in New South Wales Act 1819; 59 Geo III c 114), retrospectively authorising the taxes being levied; op cit pp 34–35. See also Clark op cit ch 8.

[21] Melbourne and Joyce op cit pp 44–46. The Letters Patent are at *HRA* Series 4 vol 1 p77.

that emancipists or their children could not be trusted with such responsibility and that there were too few exclusives to make a jury system practical.[22] Macquarie was, however, firmly wedded to a rehabilitationist policy towards emancipists, and was happy to mix with them socially, to appoint them to governmental positions and – crucially – to make them substantial grants of land.[23]

The leading player in the emancipist camp was William Wentworth.[24] Wentworth was likely conceived in 1790 on board a convict ship. His mother was a convict and his father – D'Arcy Wentworth – the ship's surgeon. Wentworth's parents never married, and his mother died in 1800. His father also laboured under some social stigma; he had reputedly accepted his commission as surgeon to escape prosecution for robbery. Wentworth's father nonetheless proved a favourite of Governor Macquarie, and was appointed to several government offices. By his death in 1827, D'Arcy Wentworth had become one of the colony's wealthiest men.[25] The family was sufficiently well connected for William to receive some education in England. On returning to Sydney in 1810, William also fell within Macquarie's benevolent orbit: the Governor appointed him to a minor office and granted him 1750 acres of land, with a further 1000 acres following as a later reward for leading an exploration of hitherto unknown (to whites) parts of the colony's interior.

Wentworth's early political beliefs and career were substantially shaped by his perception that even though his father was – strictly speaking – never a convict and so an exclusive rather than an emancipist – he and his family were the object of sleight and disdain from the exclusivist interests, a perception that public office and 2750 acres did not dispel. That personal concern was married with a broad knowledge of and sincere attachment to the political theory of colonial autonomy. Returning to England in the early 1820s to read for the Bar and (briefly) study at Cambridge, Wentworth fashioned himself as an advocate for mass free settler emigration to New South Wales and as a champion of emancipist interests. Wentworth also articulated a comprehensive programme for constitutional reform, aimed at replicating a British system of parliamentary government in the colony, in support of which he tirelessly lobbied British politicians and newspapers. Wentworth's activities were consistently countered by Macarthur and the squatting interest, which maintained a permanent lobbying presence (frequently one of Macarthur's sons) in London.

Wentworth's arrival in England coincided with a Court of King's Bench judgment which had seriously unfavourable consequences for emancipists. The claimant in *Bullock v Dodds*[26] was a former convict, who returned to England having been pardoned by Macquarie. The then general presumption in English law was that a convicted felon was in many senses legally incapacitated, most pertinently here in the sense of being unable to bring legal proceedings in defence of her/his property. Various statutes had provided that transported prisoners were regarded as pardoned – and so no longer legally

---

[22] ibid 44–45: Neal op cit pp 171–75.
[23] See Melbourne and Joyce op cit pp 20–22: Hughes op cit pp 293–301.
[24] Melbourne and Joyce op cit pp 65–70, http://adb.anu.edu.au/biography/wentworth-william-charles-2782. See also the colourful account in Hughes op cit pp 361–66.
[25] Keneally op cit pp 450–52.
[26] (1819) 2 B and Ald 358, 106 ER 361. For discussion of *Bullock* in the wider context of the so-called 'infamy law' see Woods (2002) *A history of criminal law in New South Wales* pp 99–100.

incapacitated – once their sentence had expired. The same result could be achieved by a royal pardon issued under the Great Seal. But a pardon granted by the Governor did not per se have that effect; and would not do so until the person's name had been promulgated under the Great Seal. Because of administrative shortcomings in the Governor's administration of the colony's affairs, many pardons granted were not forwarded to London, were not included in periodic royal pardons under the Great Seal and so – per *Bullock* – the persons concerned were still legally incapacitated. The upshot of this in New South Wales was that many emancipists who 'owned' land or other property could not initiate or defend proceedings in relation to it; a consequence which was obviously very problematic both for the individuals concerned and more broadly for the colony's economy. The judgment thus provided Wentworth with a focus for his lobbying, which much enhanced his colonial status as a champion of emancipist interests.

The cleavage between 'emancipists' and 'exclusives' is a helpful if simplistic label with which to describe early political divisions in the colony. In part, the dichotomy speaks to issues of social and cultural status. Emancipists were regarded by exclusives as morally tainted; a taint which attached to emancipists' children as well. Yet it was not uncommon for male exclusive settlers to have children with or marry convict or emancipist women. The dichotomy also had an economic dimension. In crude terms, exclusives were much the wealthier of the two groups. But not all free settlers were from affluent backgrounds; not all prospered economically in New South Wales; and many emancipists very quickly became wealthy as result of land grants or involvement in trade.[27] Questions of status and money might also pull in different political directions. Continued convict immigration on any large scale undermined New South Wales's claim to be treated as a 'normal colony' with its own civilian government, but it provided landowners and occupiers with a steady supply of very cheap labour for pastoral and (to a lesser extent) cultivation purposes. Those two generally distinct types of land use also fostered a political division which could cut across emancipist and exclusivist lines.

Furthermore, even by 1820 there was an emerging fragmentation within what one might loosely call 'the landed classes' between individuals whose land was wholly or substantially held on a regularised legal basis consequent upon grants by the Governor or lease or purchase of previously granted lands in the secondary market, and those who were wholly or primarily referred to as 'squatters',[28] that is, people who occupied land without having either a legal estate in it (whether freehold or leasehold) or permission in the form of a licence to do so; in essence. asserting 'naked possession' over very large rather than small areas of land.

Continued internal political pressure from exclusivists with pastoral interests opposing Macquarie's 'idiosyncratic'[29] personal rule and seeking a more orthodox form of colonial government – one in which exclusivists themselves played a more meaningful part – led to various petitions being sent by the colony's pastoralists to the House of

---

[27] The only 'industries' of significance were whaling and sealing, predominantly Sydney based, and timber production. Emancipists played a major role in these activities, and in the economic superstructure (banking, shipping, insurance, accounting) which grew out of them; see Ward (1992) op cit pp 77–80: Karskens (2013) op cit.

[28] Although some people had feet firmly in both camps.

[29] His inclination to grant lands to emancipists offended some exclusives for both cultural and economic reasons.

Commons between 1810 and 1820, and thence to a governmental Commission headed by John Bigge[30] established in 1819 to inquire into conditions in New South Wales and to consider the colony's future governance. Bigge and the then Secretary of State for the Colonies Henry Bathurst[31] (in Lord Liverpool's Tory administration) seemingly approached the inquiry with the firm belief that Macquarie's (enlightened for the time) approach to penal policy was wholly misconceived, Bathurst expressing the view that prospective criminals should view transportation to New South Wales as "an object of real terror".

Bigge's personal relations with Macquarie were difficult during the inquiry, in which Bigge accorded significant weight to the views of the Macarthur faction both in gathering his evidence and formulating his recommendations. Bigge subsequently produced several reports for the Commons in 1822 and 1823, which reports prompted enactment of the New South Wales Act 1823 and some initially tentative attempts to exercise greater governmental control over the occupancy and use of the colony's lands.[32]

II. The New South Wales Act 1823

The 1823 Act retrospectively reversed *Bullock*, providing that all pardons made by the Governor in New South Wales should be treated as made under the Great Seal.[33] In institutional terms, the Act was notable for creating a Legislative Council and modifying the judicial system.

The 'Legislative Council'

Wentworth's vigorous lobbying for New South Wales to be treated like the North American colonies bore little fruit in the 1823 legislation. However, the Act made tentative steps towards diffusing governmental power. The 'Legislative Council' created by 's.24'[34] began life as a tiny body (5–7 members) appointed (by the Monarch/Governor). The Act's preamble explained the initiative:

> And whereas it may be necessary to make laws and ordinances for the welfare and good government of the said colony of New South Wales and the dependencies thereof the occasions of which cannot be foreseen nor without much delay and inconvenience be provided for without entrusting that authority for a certain time and under proper restrictions to persons resident there and whereas it is not at present expedient to call a legislative assembly in the

---

[30] Bigge was born into a politically well-connected family, and entered the Bar after studying at Oxford. After a few years in practice he was appointed as Chief Justice of the British colony of Trinidad in 1813, a post he held until he began his New South Wales inquiries, http://adb.anu.edu.au/biography/bigge-john-thomas-1779.

[31] Bathurst was then the (second) Earl of Bathurst. A biographer describes him as a moderate Tory, albeit that Bathurst's 'moderation' in that era accommodated opposition to the abolition of slavery and to electoral reform, http://adb.anu.edu.au/biography/bathurst-henry-1751.

[32] Melbourne and Joyce op cit ch s 8 and 9; Ward (1992) op cit pp 71–73; Clark op cit pp 96–97.

[33] See further Melbourne and Joyce op cit ch XI; Twomey (2004) *The constitution of New South Wales* pp 2–3. The Act is at http://foundingdocs.gov.au/item-sdid-73.html#history.

[34] The numbering is a post hoc addition. Legislation enacted in that era was not numbered in the modern fashion. The text is at http://foundingdocs.gov.au/item-sdid-73.html.

said colony Be it therefore enacted that it shall and may be lawful for his Majesty his heirs and successors by warrant under his or their sign manual to constitute and appoint a council ...

That it was not yet 'expedient' to create an elective Assembly was attributable to a British government presumption that emancipists were not to be trusted with any powers of self-government, but that it would be impolitic given the number of emancipists – and the wealth of some of them – to create a representative Assembly composed of and chosen by only free settlers. Indeed, it seems that creating the Council was largely a means to reduce the likelihood of a future Governor following in Macquarie's overly indulgent (towards convicts and emancipists) footsteps.[35] The British government's assumption was that many, if not most, of the Council's original members would be government officials, including inter alia the Chief Justice and the Colonial Secretary.[36]

S.24 also provided that only the Governor could propose laws. Ordinarily, a proposed law required support from a bare majority of Council members to be enacted, but s.24 allowed that in circumstances where the Governor considered a law was needed to prevent 'extreme injury' the support of just one member was sufficient. S.24 further provided that in cases of insurrection or rebellion (a lively fear given the number of convicts and emancipists) the Governor could make law without the approval of any Council members.

The Council's appointive nature obviously compromised its 'representative' character in any electoral sense. That quality was further undermined by the Act's curious provision – inserted into the councillor's oath by s.32 – which forbade Council members from discussing Council business with anyone who was not a member.

Legislative Competence and 'Repugnancy'

The Governor and Legislative Council were given a general grant of lawmaking authority in s.24, subject to a 'repugnancy clause' (in italics below):

... [T]he governor or acting governor for the time being of the said colony with the advice of the council to be appointed as aforesaid or the major part of them shall have power and authority to make laws and ordinances for the peace welfare and good government of the said colony such laws and ordinances *not being repugnant to this act or to any charter or letters patent or order in council which may be issued in pursuance hereof or to the laws of England but consistent with such laws so far as the circumstances of the said colony will admit* ...

Whether 'the laws of England' referred only to statute or also embraced the common law[37] was not made clear. The 'circumstances' proviso was presumably intended to allow some – and possibly substantial – variation from 'English laws'.[38]

The notion of 'repugnancy' as a substantive limit derived from common law on the lawmaking powers of colonial legislatures was by then an accepted if ill-defined element

---

[35] Melbourne and Joyce op cit chs 10–11.
[36] An executive office established under the prerogative in 1821, whose holder would assume very substantial administrative responsibilities over the governmental system; Melbourne and Joyce op cit pp 104–05.
[37] I use the term loosely to embrace all judge-made law.
[38] Four obviously relevant circumstances being the tiny and wholly non-urbanised population, the large percentage of prisoners, the millions of acres of 'unowned' (except by the Crown) land and the presence of a potentially hostile indigenous population.

of British constitutional law. Its first judicial articulation seems to have been the Privy Council's 1727 decision in *Winthrop v Lechmere*,[39] in which a Connecticut statute dealing with intestacy was held invalid because of inter alia its inconsistency with a distinct rule of English common law. There is no reasoning of any sort in the 'judgment', just a bald statement of the legal position. It is oversimplistic to view *Winthrop* as a 'judgment' in the orthodox sense; the Privy Council was still over 100 years away from being formally designated by statute as a judicial court of appeal from the colonies.[40] Nor could *Winthrop* be seen unequivocally as asserting that common law had an autonomous restraining effect on the competence of colonial legislatures, since there was an express element in Connecticut's founding charter (itself a common law instrument) that its legislation not be inconsistent with common law principles.

Winthrop prompted the issue of an opinion on the matter from the then Law Officers of the Crown (Attorney General Phillip Yorke and Solicitor General Charles Talbot) in 1729. Both Yorke and Talbot subsequently became eminent judges.[41] The very brief opinion, distinctly lacking in any kind of reasoning, lends itself to interpretation either as being limited specifically to Connecticut or as having a general application. Its most notable passage suggested that:

> [I]t is a necessary qualification of all such laws, that they be reasonable in themselves and not contrary to the laws of England; and if any laws have been there made, repugnant to the laws of England, they are absolutely null and void.[42]

Yorke's views on the issue qua Attorney-General were prima facie a marvel of inconsistency. In 1729 he had offered the opinion that British statutes which were not stated in terms that would apply to a colony presumptively did not do so and could gain local effect only if a local Act so provided; although that presumption *might* be rebutted through long usage, which usage *might* be seen as demonstrating a tacit consent to the law.[43] Quite why such a statute was not a 'law of England' in the repugnancy sense while the common law was Yorke did not explain. There is again no reasoning in the opinion.

---

[39] Graber and Gilman (2015) *The complete American constitutionalism vol 1: introduction and the colonial era* pp 154–55 has lengthy excepts from *Winthrop*.

[40] Act for the Better Administration of Justice in His Majesty's Privy Council 1833 (3 & 4 Wil IV c 41).

[41] Yorke, the son of an attorney of no great repute, began his career as an articled clerk and did not attend university. He nonetheless had an extremely successful early career at the Bar, and having become something of a favourite of the then Duke of Newcastle was returned to the Commons for one of Newcastle's rotten borough seats in 1713. He served as both Solicitor-General and Attorney-General in various Walpole-led administrations, and was appointed Lord Chief Justice in 1733 and Lord Chancellor, as the first Earl of Hardwicke in 1737; see Thomas (2007) 'Yorke, Philip, first earl of Hardwicke' *ODNB*. Talbot was a bishop's son. After attending Oxford and being briefly a fellow of All Souls, Talbot pursued a dual career at the Bar and in politics, being returned as a Walpole-ite for a Cornwall rotten borough in 1720. Walpole appointed him Solicitor-General in 1726 and then Lord Chancellor in 1733. He died in office just four years later aged 52; Macnair (2008) 'Talbot, Charles, first Baron Talbot of Hensol' *ODNB*. The York and Talbot ensemble as givers of legal opinions are best – and most unfavourably – known for their 1729 statement, once again bereft of any reasoning, denying that slaves who were brought to England or were baptised as Christians thereby became free; see Glasson (2010) '"Baptism doth not bestow freedom": missionary anglicanism, slavery, and the Yorke-Talbot opinion, 1701–30' *The William and Mary Quarterly* 279. The 'opinion' is reproduced in full in Glasson op cit p279.

[42] The opinion is in Chalmers (1814) *Opinions of eminent lawyers on various points of English jurisprudence* p208.

[43] ibid.

Campbell's survey and analysis of the repugnancy doctrine in eighteenth- and early nineteenth-century colonial constitutional law[44] indicates that the doctrine was both very uncertain in scope and very rarely invoked in practice. Her suggestion is that the doctrine's main utility was as a background principle which might dissuade colonial politicians from promoting markedly radical legislative initiatives.

Should such laws be enacted, they could be revoked under the British government's retained power (then in s.30 of the 1823 Act) to 'disallow' colonial legislation. That power could be exercised by the Crown simply on policy grounds, without any need for 'repugnancy' in a legal sense (whatever that sense might actually be) to be established. Disallowance was, however, generally a time-limited power.[45] The repugnancy doctrine was not time-limited, and was presumptively a mechanism to empower courts – either colonial or (qua the Privy Council) Imperial – to invalidate a colonial statute. It is, however, perfectly credible to conclude that there was no certainty in New South Wales (nor in the Colonial Office in London or within the English courts) in 1823 as to what the repugnancy clause in s.24 actually meant.

The Judicial and Executive Branches of the Colony's Government

The 1823 Act also substantially reformed the colony's judicial system by empowering the Crown to create a new Supreme Court (for both New South Wales and Van Diemen's Land),[46] staffed by a Chief Justice (and up to two additional judges) appointed by the Crown. Per s.2, the Supreme Court(s) would have all the powers of the English courts of King's Bench, Common Pleas and Exchequer.[47] Criminal matters would be tried by a judge and a 'jury' of seven serving or retired military officers. The default tribunal in civil matters would be a judge and two Justices of the Peace,[48] although the parties could agree to have a 12-person jury if they wished. Jury eligibility was set at a level which excluded most emancipists: either freehold ownership of 50 acres of cleared land or a dwelling valued at £300 or more.[49]

The Supreme Court judges would not have security of tenure in the British sense, which, since the passage of the Act of Settlement 1701, permitted judges to be dismissed only on an address of the Commons and Lords consequent on some form of judicial misbehaviour. Such misbehaviour was not defined in the Act, but was widely presumed *not* to include giving judgments which the Crown found politically unpalatable.

---

[44] Campbell (1965) 'Colonial legislation and the laws of England' *University of Tasmania LR* 148. See also McGoveny (1944) 'The British origin of judicial review of legislation' *University of Pennsylvania LR* 1.

[45] The s.30 variant had a three-year time limit.

[46] Now Tasmania, but then governed as an adjunct of New South Wales with its administration headed by a Lieutenant Governor. The legislation (s.44) also empowered the Crown to separate Van Diemen's Land from New South Wales and establish it as an autonomous colony. The separation was effected by Order in Council in 1825, www.foundingdocs.gov.au/item-did-73.html.

[47] What we would now regard as the High Court in England and Wales. S.15 created a (misnamed) Court of Appeals for the colony, which was apparently to comprise the Governor sitting alone for New South Wales cases and with the New South Wales Chief Justice for Van Diemen's Land cases.

[48] Council members were automatically appointed as Justices. Other Justices were appointed by the Governor.

[49] The Act empowered the Crown to extend or modify these provisions.

The supposed purpose of the Act was to safeguard the 'independence of the judiciary' against political pressure from the Crown. Judges in New South Wales and Van Diemen's Land had no such security against the Crown: the 1823 Act provided that "it shall and may be lawful for his Majesty ... from time to time as occasion may require to remove and displace any such judge ... and in his place and stead to appoint another fit and proper person". No misbehaviour on the judge's part was legally required.

Ss.19–20 respectively empowered the Governor and the Legislative Council to create Courts of Quarter Sessions to deal with criminal matters and 'Courts of Requests' to hear minor civil litigation. The Governor was empowered to appoint a Justice of the Peace to sit in the Quarter session and 'commissioners' to conduct matters in the Court of Requests.[50]

Although the Act did not per se remodel the executive branch of the colony's government, its introduction coincided with moves towards a more formal executive structure. The post of 'Colonial Secretary' created under the prerogative in 1821 was followed by that of 'Colonial Treasurer' in 1823.

The Governor charged with overseeing the initial implementation of these reforms was Sir Thomas Brisbane, who replaced Macquarie in 1821. Brisbane has acquired considerable notoriety as the proponent of brutal penal regimes, a policy linked to establishing convict outposts much further north in the colony.[51] Brisbane was also less accommodating to emancipist sentiment than his predecessor. He was, however, also notably more willing to make land grants than Macquarie (albeit more readily to exclusives than emancipists), especially to enable expansion of the amount of land available for the pasturing of sheep and cattle.

Brisbane's successor from 1825, General Ralph Darling, shared Brisbane's preference for stringent penal policy and disdain for emancipists. Melbourne, a commentator not given to hyperbole, described him as:

[P]robably the most unpopular of all the early Governors ... His military experience had rendered him unfit to occupy any important civil administrative post ... [H]e resented the imposition of limitations on his authority. He quarrelled with the Chief Justice and nearly every other official, he ignored that part of his instructions which enjoined him to consult, on all things, with his Executive Council.[52]

These changes were given a more systematic character in 1825, when prerogative powers were used to create the aforesaid 'Executive Council', comprising senior officials appointed by the Imperial government rather than the Governor, whose presumed remit was to advise the Governor and rein in any inclination he might have towards unacceptably idiosyncratic policies.[53]

---

[50] The latter had a statutory basis in s.20. The Act made no provision for appointment of Justices of the Peace (save that, per s.24, members of the Legislative Council were automatically Justices of the Peace), presumably on the basis that such a power was given to the Governor in his Commission.

[51] See eg Evans (2007) *A history of Queensland* pp 26–30; Hughes op cit pp 366–68.

[52] Melbourne and Joyce op cit p109. This is not an isolated view; see also Clark op cit 107–18; Evans op cit pp 38–41; http://adb.anu.edu.au/biography/darling-sir-ralph-1956.

[53] Melbourne and Joyce op cit pp 104–09. The Executive Council's creation was announced in the Commission granted to Governor Darling, discussed further below. Its original members were all senior government officials (including the Chief Justice and Colonial Secretary) appointed by the Crown rather than the Governor.

Darling's Commission and Instructions

Darling's Commission nonetheless granted him very extensive personal powers. He was authorized, for example, inter alia:

> [T]o suspend any of the Members of our said [Executive] Council from siting voting or assisting therein if you shall find cause for so doing ...

> [T]o constitute and appoint Justices of the Peace Coroners Constables and other necessary officers and ministers ... for the better administration of justice and putting the laws in execution ...

> [T]o pardon all offenders ... treason and wilful murders only excepted ...

In respect of the Governor's powers over land allocation, Darling's Commission contained two important provisions. One, which came towards the end of the document, was explicit:

> We hereby give and grant unto you full power and authority with the advice of our Executive Council ... to agree for such Lands Tenements And Hereditaments as shall be in our power to dispose of to grant to any person or persons upon such terms ... according to such instructions as shall be given to you ...

The second, earlier in the document, was more opaque. Darling was given:

> Full power and authority with the advice and consent of our said Executive Council to issue a proclamation dividing our said territory of New South Wales and its dependencies into District Counties Hundreds Towns Townships and Parishes and appointing the limits thereof respectively ...

The proclamation identifying the so-called 'limits of location' appeared as Government Notice No 35 on 5 September 1826.[54] The area identified was subject to survey during the next three years, the results of which were promulgated in a notification[55] in October 1829. The 19 counties of surveyed land comprised a tiny – almost inconsequentially so – percentage of the continental territory.[56]

The 1826 proclamation introduced three distinct forms of land disposition. Grants would be made of up to four 640-acre parcels to persons who could show capital resources of £500[57] per parcel. Grantees would have to reside on the land – or employ a free person[58] who did so – and enhance its value within seven years under threat of forfeiture. Land could also be purchased, in totals of no more than 9600 acres, under a system of sealed bids. Purchased lands could immediately be sold on. Grantees could not alienate any part of their grant until several years had elapsed. The third method was

---

[54] The full text is in *The Sydney Gazette and New South Wales Advertiser* 13 September 1826 p1, https://trove.nla.gov.au/newspaper/article/2186529.

[55] 'Notification' rather than proclamation as Darling expressly disclaimed that the announcement was a proclamation in accordance with his Commission and *Instructions* as the boundaries of the counties etc had not yet been fixed with sufficient precision to be given legal force. The notification is printed in full in *The Sydney Gazette and New South Wales Advertiser* 17 October 1829 p1, https://trove.nla.gov.au/newspaper/article/2193642.

[56] See the map at mass www.records.nsw.gov.au/archives/magazine/onthisday/14-october-1829.

[57] Which could be livestock, agricultural tools or government pensions.

[58] Which person would obviously be a shepherd.

for the Governor to give permission for people to occupy unspecified amounts of land on payment of an annual 'rent' of £1 per 100 acres.[59]

For most emancipists and the more impecunious free settlers, neither grant nor purchase direct from the Governor were feasible routes to land ownership. Their prospects of acquiring freehold or long leasehold possession was dependent entirely on small parcels of land being made available in the secondary market. Nor were such colonists well placed to participate in what had by 1829 become a more significant route to land occupation.

The limits of location initiative spoke to an Imperial government preference to curb the colony's geographical spread, primarily out of concern to avoid the expense of having to administer a large territory. But that was a policy couched more in terms of hope than expectation. Darling must surely have issued his 1826 proclamation knowing – as did the colonists who might be disposed to flout it – that his government had no credible capacity to enforce the (miniscule in relative terms) limits he had identified. From the mid-1820s onwards a steady stream of land-hungry pastoralists took themselves – and many thousands of their sheep – far beyond the 19 counties, laying claims in a practical (if not legal) sense to the occupation (if not 'possession') of what, if placed in a British context, would have seemed unimaginably large tracts of land.

This was occurring to a limited extent within the 19 counties, much of which remained in the Crown's possession because grants or sales or leases could not be made until the relevant land had been surveyed, and the colonial government's capacity to conduct such surveys was very limited. But a much greater amount of land was affected beyond the limits of location.

Such 'squatters'[60] were primarily, but not solely, drawn from the exclusive faction of the population. Some emancipists (and by 1829 their free- and Australian-born children) had also 'established'[61] themselves as wealthy squatters, a development which – having collapsed the economic basis of differentiation between some exclusives and emancipists – began also to lead to greater commonality of political interests among the more affluent members of each group.

The political tensions created by the wish of successive British governments to keep the New South Wales colonists within the limits of location in the face of many colonists' wish to exploit more far-flung areas for pastoral purposes were a constant theme of Darling's governorship. But he also faced more obviously 'constitutional' difficulties. For present purposes, one example arising from a confluence of personal and legal matters must suffice as an illustration.

---

[59] The term 'rent' might suggest that the interest created was a lease rather than a mere licence, but its use might simply be the result of careless drafting.

[60] The term is a dissonant one from a British perspective, as a 'squatter' in modern British parlance generally denotes a very impoverished class of persons. By 1830, New South Wales 'squatters' were in contrast often men occupying huge tracts of land, and whose wealth and political influence led to the coining of the label 'squattocracy' to describe their (elevated) class position.

[61] As in the early 'naked possession' era in the original settlement, squatting beyond the limits was considered so legitimate by its practitioners that vigorous secondary markets for the lease and sale of squatted lands emerged even though there were no formal means of asserting or defending 'ownership'; see especially Weaver op cit; La Croix op cit.

Pre-legislative Colonial Judicial Review of Colonial Legislation – The Newspaper Licence and Tax 'Laws'

S.29 of the 1823 Act granted the Chief Justice a potentially significant legislative role in prohibiting the Governor from proposing any law to the Legislative Council unless the Chief Justice had certified that "such proposed law is not repugnant to the laws of England but is consistent with such law so far as the circumstances of the colony will admit". S.29 was a further precaution against Macquarie-esque 'misfeasance' in the lawmaking process.[62] For no obviously good reason, the s.29 repugnancy clause is framed differently from the one in s.24. S.29 refers only to "the laws of England". Standing alone, that notion would presumably include the 'this Act and letters patent etc' elements of s.24; though, since s.24 also refers to 'the laws of England', one might credibly assume that the 'this Act and letters patent etc' part of s.24 is not embraced by the 'laws of England' in s.29. It may be that sloppy drafting rather than subtle and deliberate design is the reason for the different wording.

Wentworth became a prominent political force from the mid-1820s onwards on returning to New South Wales,[63] partly from his activities at the Bar, but also from his astute decision to become a newspaper journalist and publisher. He used his paper, provocatively titled *The Australian*,[64] zealously and often intemperately to press his political agenda; an agenda which coincided not at all with Darling's instinctive unwillingness – reinforced by MacArthur and the squatter interest's constant lobbying – to support emancipist demands.

A particular cause célèbre arose in November 1826, when a former soldier convicted of theft, one Joseph Sudds, died in the chains imposed – at Darling's intervention – as part of his sentence.[65] Wentworth called for Darling's prosecution for his involvement in the death,[66] and imaginatively linked the metal yoke around Sudds's neck with the political yoke under which emancipists in the colony felt themselves imprisoned. Darling's response was to propose laws requiring that newspapers would have to apply and pay for a licence from the Governor to operate, which licence could be withdrawn if the paper published seditious material.

This essentially political battle then acquired a legal dimension. As noted above, s.29 empowered the Chief Justice to block presentation of bills which he considered 'repugnant to the law of England'. The then Chief Justice, Francis Forbes,[67] appointed in 1823, had previously served as Chief Justice of Newfoundland, where he had built a reputation as a judge ready to compel autocratically inclined Governors to respect legal limits on their powers. Forbes developed friendly relations with Brisbane, less so with

---

[62] Melbourne and Joyce op cit pp 103–04.
[63] See generally the florid but fascinating account in Clark op cit chs 3–4.
[64] The first edition (14 October 1824) is at https://trove.nla.gov.au/newspaper/article/37074013.
[65] *The Australian* 29 November 1826 p2, https://trove.nla.gov.au/newspaper/article/37073689.
[66] *The Australian* 20 December 1826 p2, https://trove.nla.gov.au/newspaper/article/37071618.
[67] http://adb.anu.edu.au/biography/forbes-sir-francis-2052. For a fuller account see Bennet (2003a) *Sir Frances Forbes* chs 1–2.

Darling, and reputedly favoured political developments in the colony consistent with Wentworth's aspirations.

Forbes refused to certify provisions in the bills which empowered the Governor to license (and delicense) the colony's newspapers. They were, in Forbes's view, 'repugnant to the law of England' per s.29; not because they contravened any statute or common law rule, but because 'the laws of England' controlled freedom of the press only by the imposition of post-publication sanctions (be they criminal measures such as sedition or blasphemy or civil law suits in defamation) and not by pre-publication censorship. In essence, Forbes asserted that the Legislative Council's lawmaking powers were constrained by quite abstract notions of constitutional morality rather than by 'law' in any formal statutory or judicially made sense.[68]

The episode triggered a sharp deterioration in Forbes's relationship with Darling, and prompted recurrent, unsuccessful attempts by Darling to undermine Forbes's position in the colony and in British government circles. Forbes nonetheless remained in office until 1837, and played a significant role, as an adviser to the Colonial Office, in formulating the next two stages in the colony's constitutional development.

III. The Australian Courts Act 1828

Wentworth had orchestrated a petition to the Commons in mid-1828 which, highlighting an emerging shift in political forces, had been signed by wealthy representatives of both exclusive and emancipist interests, calling for an extension of trial by jury and an elective Assembly. Wentworth's efforts were consistently countered by the MacArthur faction, and the next stage in the colony's constitutional development made little advance towards Wentworth's position.[69]

The 1828 Act *expressly* repealed the entire 1823 statute. The 1828 Act did not re-enact the Governor's personal legislative powers under the 1823 Act, and the Council was increased in size to a maximum of 15 (appointed) members. The Council would not be quorate unless at least two-thirds of members were present, although if that quorum was met the Council could decide any matter by a simple majority vote.

In respect of the Council's legislative powers, the 1828 Act modified (in s.21) the 'repugnancy clause' by omitting the above-quoted italicised words in the 1823 Act's provision (... *but consistent with such laws so far as the circumstances of the said colony will admit*). The obvious legal inference to draw from the omission – an inference surprising in political terms if one takes the 1828 Act's objective to have been to increase the colony's capacity to manage its internal affairs – is that the reformed Legislative Council could not, unlike its 1823 predecessor, invoke the colony's 'circumstances' to justify making laws inconsistent with British statute or the common law. The omission was likely the result of governmental carelessness in drafting the bill, rather than considered policy.

---

[68] For a broader analysis of Forbes's jurisprudence see Castles (1975) 'The judiciary and political questions: the first Australian experience 1824–25' *Adelaide LR* 294. For a detailed account of the newspaper case see Bennett (2003a) op cit ch 7.

[69] The reasoning of the then British government (the Duke of Wellington's Tory administration) is outlined at the Commons first reading debate for the 1828 bill at *HCD* 1 April 1828 c 1431.

The 1828 Act did not alter the tenure of the Supreme Court judges, who remained dismissible at the Queen's pleasure. It did, however, modify the judges' role in certifying that proposed laws were not 'repugnant'. Under s.22, a law would come into effect unless one or more of the judges informed the Governor that he/they considered the law repugnant. In such circumstances, the Council could nonetheless enact the measure, but was obliged to refer it to the Imperial government along with the judges' explanation for their repugnancy conclusion. The Governor and Council's power to create Courts of Quarter Sessions and a Court of Requests in ss.19–20 of the 1823 Act was repeated in s.16 of the 1828 Act.

The Act came into force in the context of rapidly changing social circumstances in New South Wales. Darling's drawing of the limits of location and the disdain showed for them by the squatters has already been remarked upon. The number of free settlers of no or modest financial means was rising, as was the number of time-served prisoners. Internal political pressure to end transportation of convicts was also growing. That pressure had in part an enlightened moral base, but it was also rooted in economic tension. Many pastoralists (whether squatters or in possession of land within the limits) favoured continued transportation as both a direct source of cheap labour and an indirect way to depress the wages of free settler or emancipist workers. Those workers' interest obviously favoured ending transportation.

Increasing Regulation of Land Disposition and Occupation

Darling's tenure as Governor ended in 1831. His departure coincided with a significant change in land disposition policy within the 19 counties. In future, no more grants were to be given; disposition could be only by sale through public auction with a minimum reserve price.[70] The shift in policy was effected through the prerogative rather than enactment of an Imperial statute. Colonial legislation was passed shortly afterwards, creating the posts of Commissioners of Crown Lands to police squatting within the limits.[71]

Shortly afterwards, the Imperial government and Governor conceded the practical futility of preventing squatting beyond the limits, and in 1836 introduced a licensing system (again through prerogative powers) for such occupancy beyond the limits and legislation criminalising occupancy without a licence.[72] The designation of the entitlement to occupy as a licence rather than a lease was intended to convey that squatters' occupancy was a matter of Crown sufferance rather than one of legal rights. But for the squatters themselves a licence was regarded as a first 'official' step towards leasehold or freehold, especially as Crown Commissioners were increasingly drawn into settling

---

[70] Goderich to Darling 9 January 1831 *HRA* series 1 vol 16 pp 19–21. The then Secretary of State was Lord Goderich, serving in the Whig/Liberal administration led by (the second) Earl Grey, which was soon to embroiled in the Great Reform Act crisis; see Loveland (2018) op cit pp 171–75. However, the 1831 initiative was substantially the work of Goderich's junior minister, Henry Grey, the Prime Minister's son, http://adb.anu.edu.au/biography/grey-henry-george-2126.

[71] An Act for Protecting the Crown Lands of this Colony from Encroachment, Intrusion and Trespass 1833 (4 Wil IV No 10).

[72] An Act to Restrain the Unauthorized Occupation of Crown Lands 1836 (7 Wil IV No 4).

disputes between squatters concerning the boundaries of licensed land, a development which both lent further 'official' status to occupancy and provided a (crude) survey of the lands concerned which would facilitate the future grant or sale of more formal legal interests.[73]

These land innovations had occurred under the stewardship of Darling's successor, Sir Richard Bourke, yet another senior military officer.[74] Responsibility for their longer-term implementation, and the colony's adjustment to being no longer a destination for convict transportation, fell to Bourke's successor, Sir George Gipps, appointed in 1838. A career soldier – though an administrator rather than warrior – Gipps had made his reputation through his work on the issue of the governance of Canada in the 1820s and 1830s. He had only attained the rank of major on his appointment in 1838, but in a sign perhaps of the predominance of the political rather than military nature of his career thus far he had also been knighted.[75]

Gipps's arrival in the colony was followed shortly afterwards by the Imperial government's[76] announcement of the cessation of convict transportation to New South Wales (but not to Van Diemen's Land or Western Australia) in an Order in Council issued in May 1840.[77] Viscount Melbourne's administration adopted the new policy in large part in response to continued pressure from a group called the Australian Patriotic Association, which had emerged in 1835 to represent the interests of the more affluent faction of the emancipist population and in which Wentworth played a major part. The decision had significantly adverse economic implications for many pastoralists, in that it deprived them of a continuing supply of cheap labour.[78] Under Gipps's governorship (he served until 1846), the next formal development in the legal treatment of the land issue occurred simultaneously with significant changes in the colony's constitutional ordering.

IV. The Australian Constitutions Act 1842

While the 1828 Act expressly repealed the 1823 legislation, the 1842 Act made no reference to the 1828 statute. If read strictly, the 1842 Act did not 'alter' the composition of the New South Wales Legislative Council. Rather, it created a new Legislative Council.[79] The new Council would be a hybrid chamber: 12 members were to be appointed by the

---

[73] See Weaver op cit pp 98–100.

[74] http://adb.anu.edu.au/biography/bourke-sir-richard-1806.

[75] http://adb.anu.edu.au/biography/gipps-sir-george-2098.

[76] Viscount Melbourne's Whig administration, which won comfortable majorities in the post-Reform Act elections of 1835 and 1837.

[77] On the reasons underlying the shift in policy see Clark op cit pp 203–05; Melbourne and Joyce op cit chs VI and IX. The Order is reproduced at https://dictionaryofsydney.org/entry/order-in-council_ending_transportation_to_new_south_wales_22_may_1840.

[78] The policy's political complexities are illustrated by the fact that as a pastoralist Wentworth's short-term economic interests were harmed by ending transportation. But at this juncture of his political career he attached more importance to the long-term political implications of the change: namely, that it would much strengthen the case for New South Wales to be granted a 'normal' form of colonial government (within which no doubt he expected to play a prominent part).

[79] The governmental and legislative assumption presumably being that in creating a new Council the Act impliedly abolished the former Council and so express abolition was unnecessary.

Governor and 24 would be 'elected'.[80] That the British government would now accept an at least partially elected (and so to a limited extent) representative legislature in the colony was primarily a consequence of discontinuing transportation in 1840: as time passed, New South Wales would have a decreasing proportion of convicts and ex-convicts in its population, and so it would become increasingly inconsistent with traditional colonial policy to deny its inhabitants some kind of elected representation.[81]

The 'Constitution' of the New Legislative Council

The Council would sit for five-year terms (subject to earlier dissolution by the Governor), at the end of which both elected and appointed members would vacate their seats. The choice of appointed members was for the Governor to make, subject to various statutory constraints. Per s.12, no more than half the appointed members could hold office under the Crown (although any such office holders could contest an elected seat so that many more than six such persons might sit on the Council). There was no formal barrier to emancipists being appointed; nor did appointed members have to satisfy any property-owning requirements.

In contrast, all elected members had to own freehold land valued at £2000 in toto or with an annual value of £100, be over 21 and be British subjects. Emancipists were not barred from election. Nor were emancipists barred from the electorate. S.5 required electors either to own freehold land in the relevant electoral district valued at £200 or to occupy a dwelling valued at £20 or more annually.[82] The Act used the term 'person' rather than 'man' or 'male person' in referring both to electors and Council members, but there is no suggestion in the events either in New South Wales or Britain before the Act's passage that 'persons' might include women. As in Britain, voters were not restricted to qualifying in just one district; a 'person' owning sufficient property in several districts could vote in each (although time and geography placed practical limits on that possibility).

---

[80] Preamble. The Act had no section numbers in its original form. The numbering here follows the numbering inserted in the version of the Act retrievable through Westlaw.

[81] By this time, South Australia had also been established as a distinct colony. An initial Act was passed in 1834 (An Act to Empower His Majesty to Erect South Australia into a British Province or Provinces and to Provide for the Colonisation and Government thereof); 4 & 5 William IV c 95, www.foundingdocs.gov.au/resources/transcripts/sa1_doc_1834.pdf) authorised the King to establish such a colony, a step taken in an Order in Council issued in February 1836 (www.foundingdocs.gov.au/resources/transcripts/sa4_doc_1836.pdf). Unlike New South Wales, South Australia was to be settled only by free persons. The colony's governmental system was also reformed by statute in 1842 (An Act to Provide for the Better Government of South Australia, 5 & 6 Vict c 61). The 1842 Act made provision for the Queen to create a Legislative Council comprising "the Governor and seven other persons ... to make laws for the peace order and good government of the said colony". But the 1842 Act also empowered the Queen to summon a general assembly elected by freeholders, and thereafter to refashion the Legislative Council into a mixed elective and appointive legislature or to create a bicameral legislature comprising both the Assembly and the Council. That the British government was willing to countenance an elected Assembly in South Australia was an understandable consequence of the colony's free settler policy, but the prospect was an obvious source of potential discontent in New South Wales.

[82] These limits were more restrictive than in Britain. The Representation of the People Act 1832 (s.26) set the sum at £10 in the boroughs. In the counties, freeholders *and* long leaseholders owning property with an annual value of £10 (£50 for short leaseholders) were also enfranchised (s.19). The 1832 Act also retained (s.32) the melange of other routes to eligibility, some of which enfranchised men unable to meet the property threshold; see generally Loveland (2018) op cit pp 172–77.

The Act also empowered (in s.2) the colonial legislature constituted under it to draw electoral district boundaries for the new Council, subject only to a requirement that Sydney should return two members and Melbourne one, while the Port Phillip area should have at least five. There was no requirement – there was none under then extant British electoral legislation – that electoral districts contain even approximately equal numbers of voters. Nor did the Act require that each district return only one member. S.2's obvious and intended consequence was that boundaries were drawn in a fashion which advantaged rural over urban areas.[83] The Act's underlying rationale was that elected members would represent 'interests' rather than people – and the interests of small farmers and the people who lived and worked in 'urban' areas paled besides those of the large landowners and squatters.

The Powers of the New Legislative Council

S.29 apparently granted a very expansive legislative power to the Governor and Legislative Council:

S.29 Governor and Legislative Council authorized to make Laws

… [T]he Governor of the said Colony of New South Wales, with the Advice and Consent of the said Legislative Council, shall have Authority to make Laws for the Peace, Welfare, and good Government of the said Colony:

> Provided always, that no such Law shall be repugnant to the Law of England, or interfere in any Manner with the Sale or other Appropriation of the Lands belonging to the Crown within the said Colony, or with the Revenue thence arising.

This is yet another formulation of 'repugnancy'. The 'circumstances' clause of the 1823 Act has not been reintroduced. The 'this Act and letters patent …' provisos of both the 1823 and 1828 Acts were removed, and the sole yardstick was now 'the Laws of England', which concept might or not include common law (and Forbes's much more abstract moral principles) as well as statute. There is no immediately apparent explanation of why this new form of words was adopted.

S.29's general grant of legislative power – saving the hugely important excepted matter of disposition of Crown lands – was not exhaustive. The Act also made specific provision for making laws relating to particular issues. The obvious inference to draw from the presence of such specific provisions would be that laws on such matters did not lie within the general s.29 power.

The most significant example was s.4, which empowered the new Council to alter the initial electoral district boundaries and (while maintaining the two-thirds elected to one-third appointed ratio) to increase the number of members. There was nothing in s.4 itself to suggest that laws dealing with such issues be made in a manner which differed in any respect from those made under s.29. However, s.31 of the Act did identify 's.4 laws' as one of several matters reserved for the Monarch's personal assent.[84]

---

[83] I use the terms 'rural' and 'urban' guardedly, and not in their modern sense; but even in 1842 there was a discernible split of that sort within the Australian population; see especially Ward (1992) op cit pp 119–21.

[84] The others being laws altering the salaries of the Governor or the judges or changing customs duties.

S.4 did not extend on its face to such matters as the qualifications of either members of the Council or the electorate. There is nothing in the history of the bill's enactment to suggest that the British government assumed that such matters fell outwith both s.4 and s.29: the assumption rather seems to have been that these were issues to be addressed by the Council periodically under s.29.

S.31 provided that the Governor might assent to the bill, withhold assent or reserve the bill 'for Her Majesty's pleasure' (ie send the bill for consideration to the British government). The Governor enjoyed a presumptive discretion on that question, subject to any constraints imposed either by the Act itself or by the *Instructions* sent to him by the British government. Indeed, s.31 explicitly provided that the Governor could not assent to a bill if to do so would contradict his *Instructions*. Per s.32, any bill to which the Governor had assented could be disallowed by the British government within two years of it having been received in Britain.

S.27 authorised the Council – subject to the Governor's approval – to adopt standing orders to regulate its business. In respect of the passage of bills, the subsequently adopted orders followed the model used in the House of Commons: a first reading; second reading; committee stage; report stage; and third reading. The s.27 power was constrained by other provisions in the Act. Most notably, per s.24, the Council would only be quorate if at least one-third of its members were present. That number attending, members could determine 'any question' by a (bare) majority.

A bare majority of those present would therefore suffice for a law made under the s.29 'general power' or the issue-specific grants of lawmaking power such as that arising under s.4. The only distinction the Act drew as to the manner in which laws addressing different subjects had to be made was s.31's aforementioned proviso that in respect of some matters the relevant bill had to be reserved for the royal assent.

The 1842–47 Land 'Reforms'

The express exclusion of land disposition from s.29 underlined the political significance of that issue to the British government, both because of the land's intrinsic economic value and because of the intense political disagreement which the question generated in New South Wales. For the 1842 Act to have bestowed such power on a Legislative Council likely dominated by representatives of the pastoral squatter interest would likely lead to enactment of measures which would both enable squatters to gain formal legal title to their occupied lands and skew the grant or sale of as yet unsquatted Crown lands in directions very favourable to squatter interests. That prospect was distinctly unpalatable to the increasingly voluble liberal sentiment developing in the colony, which could not hope to exercise much influence on laws passed by the Legislative Council as constituted by the 1842 Act.

The Australian Land Sales Act 1842

Nonetheless, the Australian Land Sales Act 1842[85] took some significant steps – at least in form – further to regularise the basis of land occupation in the colonies.

[85] 5 & 6 Vict c 36.

The Act gave statutory effect to the policy pursued under the prerogative since 1831 which ended the Governor's power to grant *freehold or leasehold interests* in Crown land. S.2 provided that all future conveyances would have to be by sale in accordance with regulations promulgated under the Act.[86] S.4 precluded any such conveyance until the land concerned had been formally surveyed (by government surveyors), and presumptively limited the size of conveyed lots to no more than one square mile. S.6 required that all such lands be offered for sale at public auction with a minimum price of £1 per acre (higher prices being in the Governor's discretion). Per s.12, an immediate 10% deposit was required for land bought at auction, with the balance payable within one month.[87]

However, s.15 also empowered the Governor to grant *licences* of any Crown lands for periods of up to 12 months. No minimum price was set for licence payments; nor was any prohibition made on repeated renewals. S.15 also provided that land could not be conveyed either freehold or leasehold while a licence was extant. Per s.19, half of all proceeds raised by sales or licences was to be used to subsidise migration to the colonies from Britain and Ireland.

Gipps was replaced as Governor in 1845 by Sir Charles Fitzroy, a grandson of both the Duke of Grafton and the Marquis of Londonderry. Originally pursuing a career as a soldier, Fitzroy held a Commons seat (a rotten borough seat controlled by the Grafton family) in 1831–32, and subsequently relied on his family connections to secure appointments as Lieutenant Governor first of Prince Edward Island and then of the Leeward Islands.[88] His tenure as Governor was especially notable for two matters pressed on the colony while Henry Grey[89] was Secretary of State for the Colonies in Lord John Russell's Whig/Liberal government.[90] The second, to which we return below, related to convict transportation; the first related to land regulation.

The 1846 Act and the 1847 Order in Council

The Waste Land Occupation Act 1846[91] and an 1847 Order in Council[92] went some substantial distance towards further regularising squatters' occupancy of land beyond the limits of location. The 1846 and 1847 initiatives appeared as British politics were

---

[86] S.3 made exceptions for disposition made for various public purposes (roads, cemeteries, defence, etc) and grants to serving military personnel.

[87] The deposit and land were forfeit if payment was not made.

[88] http://adb.anu.edu.au/biography/fitzroy-sir-charles-augustus-2049.

[89] See n 70 above. Grey had succeeded to the earldom on his father's death in 1845. To avoid confusion, he is referred to as Henry Grey hereafter.

[90] Born in 1792, Russell was the third son of the Duke of Bedford. After attending Edinburgh University, and steeping himself in elite Whig culture and ideology, Russell was 'elected' to the Commons for a (family-controlled) rotten borough seat in 1812. Prominent as an advocate of electoral reform in the 1820s, Russell played a large part in drafting the 1832 Reform Act and served as a junior minister in Earl Grey's government. Russell was subsequently appointed as Home Secretary in Lord Melbourne's mid-1830s administration, and was Prime Minister of a mildly reformist Whig administration between 1846 and 1852. While Prime Minister, much of Russell's political energy was directed to contesting for eminence within the Whig party with Lord Palmerston – a contest he lost in 1852. The brief summary here is taken from Prest (2004) 'Russell, John [*formerly* Lord John Russell], first Earl Russell' *ODNB*.

[91] 9 & 10 Vict c 104.

[92] 9 March 1847; reproduced in Bell and Morrell op cit p241 et seq.

being convulsed by the dispute over repeal of the Corn Laws. Melbourne's Whig government had fallen at the August 1841 election, to be replaced by a Tory administration led by Sir Robert Peel. Peel's eventual decision to lead a minority of his party to vote with the Whigs to repeal the Corn Laws in May and June 1846 triggered the defeat of his ministry and brought a minority Whig government led by Lord John Russell into power, a situation which continued after the 1847 general election.[93]

The 1846 Act was formally a Russell government measure, but it differed little in terms either of principle or detail from a bill promoted earlier that year during Peel's ministry.[94] Most significantly, s.1 permitted the granting of leases rather than licences for occupancy of squatted lands. The duration of leases was limited to a maximum of 14 years. Ss.3–5 made provision for the prompt removal of any persons unlawfully occupying Crown lands and also made such occupation a criminal offence (although no explicit provision was made for financial or administrative resources to ensure that ss.3–5 were effectively enforced). More significantly, s.6 Act empowered the Queen to make regulations under an Order in Council: "to … establish all such rules and regulations as to Her Majesty shall seem meet" to implement the provisions of the 1842 and 1846 Acts.[95]

The Order in Council appeared in 1847. Within what were termed 'the unsettled districts', the Governor could grant leases of up to 14 years' duration. The size and rent payable for each leased area (a 'run') would be calculated according to the number of sheep (with a minimum set at 4000) each run could sustain. The minimum rent for a 400-sheep run was set at £10 per year, with an additional £2 10s for each extra 1000 sheep. Crucially from the perspective of the occupants of squatted lands, a lease brought with it a pre-emptive right of freehold purchase to the lessee (and precluded freehold sale to anyone else). The minimum size of any sold land was to be 160 acres, with a minimum purchase price fixed at £1 per acre. Selling of larger lots – or fixing higher prices – was left to the Governor's discretion.

The 1846/1847 reforms did not, however, satisfy many of the colony's most prominent pastoralists, among whom the Macarthurs still played a leading role. While the new rights of pre-emption offered squatters the eventual prospect of long leasehold or freehold possession, they regarded both the rents and the purchase price as too high. Their primary concern was not simply to alter the Imperial law which controlled land disposition, but to have the matter in its entirety brought within the control of the colony's own legislature – within which the squatting interests expected to exercise a dominant influence. Wentworth's personal politics had begun to shift significantly by the mid-1840s. His earlier political radicalism ebbed as his economic interests as a pastoralist deepened, to the point where he was essentially making common cause with the Macarthur faction. The fruits of that alliance began to emerge towards the end of the decade, but in the interim a controversy in Van Diemen's Land presented the colonists and the Imperial government with questions which went more to constitutional principle than political expediency.

---

[93] The Whigs did not win a Commons majority, but the split between Peelite and protectionist Tories was sufficiently rancorous to preclude a Tory administration being formed.
[94] See Henry Grey's speech introducing the bill's second reading at *HLD* 14 August 1846 c 700 et seq.
[95] S.12 expressly repealed the 1842 Act to the extent of any inconsistency within it with the 1846 Act.

Van Diemen's Land's Dog Act – Post-Enactment Colonial Judicial Review of Colonial Legislation

The 1842 Act did not retain the Chief Justice's power under s.22 of the 1828 Act to certify proposed laws as 'repugnant' in New South Wales. Nevertheless, s.22 remained in force in Van Diemen's Land. S.25 of the 1828 Act had imposed various substantive and procedural restrictions on the Council/Governor's taxing powers, including that:

> ... the purposes for which every such tax or duty may be so imposed and to or towards which the amount thereof is to be appropriated and applied shall be distinctly and particularly stated in the body of every law or ordinance imposing every such tax or duty.

John Pedder, a Charterhouse- and Cambridge-educated English barrister, was appointed Chief Justice of Van Diemen's Land in 1824, aged 31, after just two years in practice. Initially regarded in the colony as very much the Lieutenant Governor's man – Pedder sat in both the Executive and Legislative Councils and approved a newspaper licensing bill identical to the one rejected by Forbes[96] – Pedder gradually developed an increasing independence.[97] His judgment in *Symons v Morgan*[98] was an early application of the principle that (some) colonial courts had jurisdiction to invalidate 'Acts' passed by colonial legislatures.

In 1847, the then Lieutenant-Governor was William Denison,[99] a career soldier appointed in 1846 by William Gladstone qua Secretary of State for the Colonies and War in Peel's Conservative government. Denison took with him firmly established views (also held by Brisbane and Darling) that the purpose of imprisonment was punishment rather than rehabilitation, and steered the colony's penal policy firmly in that direction. He also inherited a governmental and fiscal crisis on his arrival: six of the Legislative Council's members had resigned in protest at the British government's refusal fully to meet the costs of the colony's jails and police force. Amidst much political controversy and doubts over the lawfulness of his actions, Denison subsequently reappointed them. The episode cast an immediate shadow over his administration's legitimacy; a shadow darkened by the antics of a Mr John Morgan.

Morgan was an English émigré, a former soldier, who established several Hobart-based newspapers after a string of ill-fated commercial ventures.[100] As a journalist he pressed a liberal, pro-self-government agenda, of which embarrassing Denison formed a substantial part. Morgan opposed Denison's policy of having the Council pass taxation legislation used to finance continued transportation. Morgan appeared to think that one such measure was a so-called 'Dog Act' passed in 1846,[101] which imposed a modest tax on dog ownership. The preamble to the Act recorded a different motivation:

> WHEREAS Dogs have increased in this Island to such an extent as to be injurious to Sheep-owners and a nuisance to the Public and there is no sufficient check by law to this evil

---

[96] Bennet (2003a) pp 86–87, (2003b) *Sir John Pedder*.
[97] http://adb.anu.edu.au/biography/pedder-sir-john-lewes-2542; Swinfen op cit pp 47–49; Castles op cit.
[98] The case predated thorough official law reports. The judgment, handed down on 29 November 1847, is published in *The Courier (Hobart)* 2 February 1848, https://trove.nla.gov.au/newspaper/article/2969922.
[99] http://adb.anu.edu.au/biography/denison-sir-william-thomas-3394.
[100] http://adb.anu.edu.au/biography/morgan-john-2479.
[101] 'An Act to Restrain the Increase of Dogs'; 10 Vict No 5, www.austlii.edu.au/cgi-bin/viewdb/au/legis/tas/num_act/aatrtiod10vn5377/.

and it is advisable in order to restrain the increase of Dogs and to make their destruction lawful in certain cases that a remedy be provided ...

Nonetheless, Morgan, who owned several dogs, refused to buy a licence,[102] and was prosecuted under s.1, which imposed a penalty of £2 (per dog) on any person 'keeping' an unlicensed dog.[103] His primary defence was that the Act was per se invalid because it did not satisfy s.25's 'distinctly and particularly stated ...' proviso.

The Courier (Hobart)[104] recorded that the public benches were packed for the trial before a Police Magistrate. Morgan's barrister, a Mr Alfred Montagu,[105] playing more to the gallery than the bench, ended his submissions with a flourish:

> This, said the learned gentleman, (holding up the Act,) is a piece of waste paper – a nullity – but such a piece as it is, it is at an end, and thank God for it!
>
> The learned gentleman concluded his address amidst the applause of the crowd who filled the office.[106]

The Police Magistrate, a Mr Wilmott, showed no inclination to engage with Montagu's submissions, and offered an immediate judgment without reasons: "I convict the defendant of the offence laid in the information, and sentence him to pay a fine of £1 and costs."[107] Morgan refused to pay.

Morgan subsequently appealed to the Court of Quarter Sessions in Hobart, which – sitting with six lay members – accepted that the Act's validity was properly a question it could address. The bench, however, divided 3–3 on that issue, which left Morgan's conviction in place.[108] Commenting on the judgment, the *Hobart Guardian* sympathised with Morgan's end, but not with his means:

> We are perfectly aware, and we quite agree with the general feeling, that the Dog Act is very unjust, but at the same time it would be a most dangerous precedent to try the legality of the Act of Legislative Council before a Bench of Magistrates. All these gentlemen, or the Police Magistrate have to do, is to carry out the intentions of the Acts as they find them, not to alter or amend them.[109]

Morgan then pressed the case to the Supreme Court. Pedder sat as one of a two-man bench.[110] His position was ostensibly complicated by the fact that he had been a member of the Legislative Council when the Dog Act was passed and had not exercised

---

[102] 5s for a male dog and 10s for a female (s.2).
[103] S.6 imposed a reverse burden of proof. Anyone occupying land on which an unlicensed dog was found was presumed to be the dog's keeper unless he/she proved to the contrary.
[104] 18 September 1847 p3, https://trove.nla.gov.au/newspaper/article/2970922.
[105] Alfred Montagu emigrated from England to Hobart in 1843 to practise at the Bar on the recommendation of his brother Algernon. The Montagus were grandsons of the fourth Earl of Sandwich. Algernon Montagu did not attend university, and was called to the Bar in London in 1826 when 24 years old. After only two years in practice, Montagu managed to have himself appointed as Van Diemen's Land's Attorney-General. He was appointed to the Supreme Court in 1833: http://adb.anu.edu.au/biography/montagu-algernon-sidney-2470; Bennet (2003b) op cit pp 80–83.
[106] *The Courier (Hobart)* 18 September 1847 p3, https://trove.nla.gov.au/newspaper/article/2970922.
[107] ibid.
[108] *Hobart Guardian* 3 November 1847 p2, https://trove.nla.gov.au/newspaper/article/163501445.
[109] ibid.
[110] *The Courier (Hobart)* 2 February 1848 p3, https://trove.nla.gov.au/newspaper/article/2969922. His colleague, who concurred with Pedder's reasoning and result, was Algernon Montagu, the elder brother of Mr Morgan's counsel.

the s.22 power. Having heard the arguments Morgan adduced, Pedder accepted that the terms of the Dog Act breached s.25. The large question was whether, that being so, the Supreme Court could invalidate the legislation.

The government's (Denison's) position was that the Supreme Courts of New South Wales and Van Diemen's Land stood vis-à-vis the Legislative Councils in just the same position as the higher British courts stood vis-à-vis the British Parliament, ie that they had no power to invalidate colonial legislation.[111] Any such power would have to be expressly granted in Imperial legislation. It could not be implied, for three suggested reasons.[112] Firstly, the Supreme Court had been given an express power under s.22 of the 1828 Act to prevent the enactment of bills, which power should be taken to preclude the implication of any post-enactment jurisdiction to invalidate a colonial statute. Secondly, a more appropriate remedy for an 'unlawful' Act was available through the Queen's power of disallowance, since such a solution would not entail – as would post-enactment invalidation – any suggestion that colonial courts were in some sense more powerful than colonial legislatures. Thirdly, invalidation of this Act would undermine legal certainty – create 'confusion and anarchy', as Attorney-General Horne more melo-dramatically put it – as no one could be sure that other revenue-raising Acts would not also be invalidated in future.

Pedder was not persuaded by these arguments. He concluded that drawing an analogy between the normative relationship of Parliament and the British courts and that of the Council and the colonial courts was misconceived. While British courts were required to apply British legislation, irrespective of its content:

> [T]his case was widely different. I then read the 21st, and 25th clauses of the [1828] Act ... and observed that the Legislative Council of this Colony was an inferior Legislature, having no existence by the Common Law, but created by the Act of Parliament for a temporary purpose, and having the power of making laws under certain limitations and restrictions the principal of which was, that the laws to be made by it were not to be repugnant to the laws of England or to that Statute. That this is a condition inseparably annexed to the power or making laws, and must therefore be strictly complied with ...
>
> And I concluded therefore that if, in any case before the Court, the question arose whether a given Act of Council was one which the Council had not the power to enact, or whether it

---

[111] The then obvious point of reference – invoked by Denison's counsel – being the following passage in *Blackstone's Commentaries on the laws of England*, first published in 1765, which stated the orthodox understanding of the normative relationship between Parliament and the courts which was presumed to have been created (some might prefer the term confirmed) after the 1688 revolution: "I know it is generally laid down more largely, that acts of parliament contrary to reason are void. But if the parliament will positively enact a thing to be done which is unreasonable, I know of no power in the ordinary forms of the constitution that is vested with authority to control it: and the examples usually alleged in support of this sense of the rule do none of them prove, that, where the main object of a statute is unreasonable, the judges are at liberty to reject it; for that were to set the judicial power above that of the legislature, which would be subversive of all government"; vol 1 p90. On the consolidation of the doctrine see generally Loveland (2018) op cit ch 2.

[112] Denison's counsel was the then Attorney-General Thomas Horne. Horne was an Oxford-educated English émigré, called to the Bar in London, who arrived in Hobart in 1830. Despite his comfortable family origins and a reasonably successful practice, Horne accumulated (repeatedly) substantial debts and was consequently widely regarded in liberally inclined quarters as very much disinclined to question Denison's preferences for fear that would lead to his dismissal and financial ruin, http://adb.anu.edu.au/biography/horne-thomas-3798.

was repugnant to the Act of Parliament, and therefore void, it was not only competent to the Court, but it was our duty to decide upon it, unless the Court was prevented from so doing by something contained in the Act of Parliament.[113]

Pedder concluded that the Dog Act was indeed a taxation measure within s.25, rather than – as Horne had urged, citing the preamble – an Act to deal with nuisance caused by dogs in which the licence fee was an incidental regulatory measure. While it might be a credible inference that the licence fees would be used to finance administration of the licensing system, the Act did not contain any explicit provision to that effect. Consequently, Pedder and Montagu concluded that the 'Act' did not satisfy s.25's 'distinctly and particularly stated' proviso. As such, it was necessarily invalid.

The judgment was a considerable embarrassment and irritation to Denison. But its implications went beyond the Dog Act itself. If that Act was invalid because of non-compliance with s.25, the strong presumption arose that other tax-raising statutes might also breach s.25. Denison was much concerned by the threat that this posed to the colony's fiscal viability. However, he also appeared to regard the judgment as a personal affront; and, giving rein to a soldier's perception of the judiciary as his subordinates rather than as a more seasoned politician might have done as a coordinate branch of government, sought to have the judges dismissed from their posts.

Amoving the Judges

Both Pedder and Montagu held office under the terms of the 1828 Act, and so were dismissible at pleasure by the Queen. Rather than seek the Imperial government's assistance to dismiss the judges, Denison proceeded against Montagu through the Colonial Leave of Absence Act 1782[114] (often referred to as Burke's Act). The Act, applicable to all British colonies, provided in s.2 – entitled 'Governor and Council may amove Officers for Neglect of Duty' – that if any appointee to public office "shall neglect the duty of such office, or otherwise misbehave therein, it shall be lawful for the Governor and Council to remove such person from the office in question". The Act's long preamble indicated that the 'neglect or misbehaviour' in issue was the practice of people accepting colonial offices in the Americas (and the often large associated salaries) and then remaining in Britain while appointing a deputy to undertake the necessary official tasks on their behalf (for a presumably small share of the official salary). S.2 was, however, cast in unqualifiedly general terms. Nor did the Act specify how any 'amoval' proceedings should be conducted; although s.2 did permit an amoved person to appeal the decision to the Privy Council.

Montagu was vulnerable to such proceedings because he had consistently behaved boorishly and intemperately on the bench, and enjoyed little affection or respect among the legal profession. He was also reputed to have severe financial difficulties, and rumours circulated that he may have exploited his office unethically to ease these problems. Denison and the Executive Council seized on these issues as sufficient reason

---

[113] *The Courier (Hobart)* 2 February 1848, https://trove.nla.gov.au/newspaper/article/2969922.
[114] The Act is most readily found through the JustisOne website.

to amove Montagu in December 1847. His subsequent appeal to the Privy Council was dismissed without reasons being given.[115] He was replaced on the bench in January 1848 by the Attorney-General Thomas Horne, a man widely regarded as a Denison loyalist.[116]

Denison trod more circumspectly with Pedder, whose personal integrity was unquestioned. Denison's initial 'suggestion' was that Pedder take a prolonged leave of absence pending referral of the matter to the Colonial Office. When Pedder refused to do so, Denison initiated amoval proceedings.[117]

Pedder was refused an oral hearing. He subsequently pleaded his own case in writing, his argument being that for a judge to change his mind on a legal question having heard arguments in court could not remotely be thought to amount to misbehaviour in the s.2 sense. To Denison's chagrin, the majority in the Executive Council accepted Pedder's contention and the amoval initiative failed. Denison had rashly taken all these steps without seeking the Colonial Office's approval. He subsequently explained his conduct in a despatch[118] to the Secretary of State (then still Henry Grey), seemingly expecting approval for his actions. He received instead a lengthy condemnation, which accused him of undermining public confidence in the colony's governmental system by his attack on the independence of the judiciary.[119] Denison's behaviour also received fierce criticism in the Commons on 12 July 1849;[120] criticism that was subsequently reproduced verbatim in the local press.[121]

Grey's admonition had been sent in a confidential despatch, which did not find its way into the New South Wales newspapers, and the British government appeared keen to draw a veil over the episode and leave Denison in post. The fiscal difficulties which had so concerned Denison were eventually removed by s.25 of the Australian Constitutions Acts 1850,[122] in which the Imperial Parliament both repealed s.25 of the 1828 Act and provided that no tax law made at any time by the Governor and Council would be invalid because of non-compliance with s.25.

Fortunately perhaps for Denison's longer-term career prospects, his particular difficulties were overshadowed by a British initiative towards all of the Australian colonies.

---

[115] (1849) 13 ER 773. The process was peremptory at best, and provoked considerable press and public hostility to Denison, primarily on the basis that he was abrogating the principle of the independence of the judiciary. See the *Colonial Times* 14 January 1848 p2, https://trove.nla.gov.au/newspaper/article/8762091; The *Courier (Hobart)* 8 January 1848 p2, https://trove.nla.gov.au/newspaper/article/2970097. The dominant public mood is best caught by a leader in the *Launceston Examiner* 19 January 1848 p3, https://trove.nla.gov.au/newspaper/article/36253871: "There was a rash recklessness in the 'amoval' of Mr. Montagu, which was peculiarly refreshing; and when the real grounds of his dismissal were known, the character of the ruler stood revealed. His will was to be law: the opinion of an irresponsible executive council respecting legal enactments was to be enforced; and the judges who decided differently were to do so at the peril of removal, pecuniary loss, and disgrace." A lengthy article defending Denison appeared in the *Hobart Guardian* 15 January 1848 p3, https://trove.nla.gov.au/newspaper/article/163501752.

[116] See the *Colonial Times* 7 January 1848 p3, https://trove.nla.gov.au/newspaper/article/8762061; *The Courier (Hobart)* 15 January 1848 p2, https://trove.nla.gov.au/newspaper/article/2970050.

[117] Summarised in Bennett (2003b) op cit pp 98–101.

[118] Denison's despatch is reproduced in full in the *Launceston Examiner* 13 December 1848 p5, https://trove.nla.gov.au/newspaper/article/36256257/3641603.

[119] See Bennet (2003b) op cit pp 101–02.

[120] *HCD* 12 July 1849 c 252 et seq.

[121] *Colonial Times* 23 November 1849 p4, https://trove.nla.gov.au/newspaper/article/8766082.

[122] 13 & 14 Vict c 59. S.25 was appropriately entitled 'Removing Doubts as to certain Taxes imposed by Governor and Council of Van Diemen's Land'.

The Imperial Act, which retrospectively validated the Dog Act and all the other Van Diemen's Land tax statutes which breached s.25 (and which inferentially conceded the correctness of the Dog Act judgment), dealt primarily with rather larger issues.

V. The Australian Colonies Constitution Act 1850

The Dog Act controversy coincided with a more acute but not so overtly 'constitutional' political crisis in New South Wales. In part in response to pressure from Wentworth and some of the squatter faction (which was disproportionately well represented in the Legislative Council) and in part for reasons of domestic penal policy, the Imperial government decided to reinstate convict transportation to New South Wales in the late 1840s. Grey had erroneously assumed that the support for renewed transportation offered by Wentworth and the squatter faction on the Legislative Council – who had obvious economic interests qua 'employers' in a renewed supply of cheap labour – reflected wider political sentiments in the colony. He was rapidly disabused of that presumption.

The shift in policy excited widespread opposition in the colony, and when the convict ship *Hashemy* arrived in Sydney in June 1849 it met a large and noisy demonstration.[123] The *Hashemy* promptly sailed several hundred miles further north to the colony's Moreton Bay region, where the pre-eminence (both economic and political) of squatting pastoralists keen to acquire indentured labourers ensured the convicts a warmer welcome. The vehement opposition which had greeted the *Hashemy* was channelled into a fierce and quickly successful campaign within the colony to bring a final end to transportation.

The British government's acquiescence to press and popular sentiment in New South Wales on the transportation issue was a particularistic manifestation of a more pervasive shift emerging in Imperial policy. In May 1849, shortly before Denison's conduct towards Pedder had been vigorously criticised in the Commons and just weeks before the *Hashemy* reached Sydney, the Colonial Office had issued a circular to the Governors of the Australian Colonies[124] which indicated significant changes would be made to the colonies' governmental systems. The circular contained a Privy Council report – instigated by Henry Grey – that considered the colonies' future development.

The report began by noting that the established seventeenth- and eighteenth-century practice towards British colonies was that the Monarch, through prerogative powers, would "establish a local legislature consisting of three estates – that is of a Governor appointed by the sovereign, of a Council nominated by the Sovereign, and of an Assembly elected by the people". That policy had not been followed in more recently

---

[123] Ward (1992) op cit pp 135–38; Clark op cit pp 216–17; Hughes op cit pp 552–62. *The People's Advocate and New South Wales Vindicator* had issued a rousing call to (metaphorical) arms on 9 June (p2, https://trove.nla.gov.au/newspaper/article/251540221): "The crisis has at length arrived. The first convict ship is now at anchor in our cove. Now is the time for the citizens to make themselves heard ... Citizens, be not backward – assemble in thousands to raise your voices against this most iniquitous act." For coverage of the protest see the *SMH* 12 June 1849 p2, https://trove.nla.gov.au/newspaper/article/12907428.

[124] Reproduced in *The Courier (Hobart)* 3 September 1849, https://trove.nla.gov.au/newspaper/article/2965074.

acquired colonies, including those in Australia. The report was coy about the reason for this. No mention was made of the use of New South Wales as a prison. The justification offered for not thus far having followed this model in Australia was instead that the colonies had not been sufficiently populous and wealthy to finance such a governmental arrangement from their own resources. Western Australia, which the British initially settled in 1826, had yet to reach that position. But the Privy Council considered that New South Wales, South Australia and Van Diemen's Land were now competent to do so.

Although the Privy Council suggested that it would be in principle desirable for Parliament to create the traditional three-part legislature in those colonies, it was persuaded that the more practical short-term course was to give each colony a hybrid Legislative Council on the New South Wales model and then to empower those Councils if their respective colonies so wished to amend their own compositions, subject, however, to any colonial legislation introducing such reforms to be reserved for the Queen's assent.

The second major issue addressed in the report concerned the partitioning of New South Wales. Throughout the 1840s, the southern region of New South Wales surrounding Melbourne (what was known as the Port Phillip district) played host to increasing political pressure for separation into a new colony.[125] The 1849 Circular accepted such pressure as legitimate,[126] and indicated that such a colony – Victoria – would be created, and would initially be governed by a hybrid Council as in New South Wales.

The report was enthusiastically received in all of the colonies, and its policy objectives were promptly enacted in the Australian Colonies Constitution Act 1850. For present purposes, the Act's key provision was s.32:

> 32. [N]otwithstanding anything herein-before contained, it shall be lawful for the Governor and Legislative Council of the Colony of New South Wales, after the Separation therefrom of the Colony of Victoria, and for the Governors and Legislative Councils of the said Colonies of Victoria, Van Diemen's's Land, South Australia, and Western Australia respectively, after the Establishment of Legislative Councils therein under this Act, from Time to Time, by an Act or Acts to alter the Provisions or Laws for the time being in force under this Act, or otherwise, concerning the Election of the elective Members of such Legislative Councils respectively, the Qualification of Electors and elective Members, or to establish in the said Colonies respectively, instead of the Legislative Council, a Council and a House of Representatives, or other separate Legislative Houses, to consist respectively of such Members to be appointed or elected respectively by such Persons and in such Manner as by such Act or Acts shall be determined, and to vest in such Council and House of Representatives or other separate Legislative Houses the Powers and Functions of the Legislative Council for which the same may be substituted: Provided always, that every Bill which shall be passed by the Council in any of the said Colonies for any of such Purposes shall be reserved for the Signification of Her Majesty' s Pleasure thereon; and a Copy of such Bill shall be laid before both Houses of Parliament for the Space of Thirty Days at the least before Her Majesty's Pleasure thereon shall be signified.

---

[125] Melbourne and Joyce op cit pp 331–46.
[126] Primarily on the basis that Sydney was too remote to afford residents of the Port Phillip area a sufficiently responsive seat of government.

The then prevalent style of legislative drafting generally eschewed sub-sections or short sentences. S.32 is a 263-word single sentence, which conflates several separate issues. The effect of s.32 would apparently be to empower the colonies' existing Legislative Councils to pass colonial legislation – subject to reservation to the Queen and laying before the Commons and Lords – which could radically redefine the composition of each colony's legislature. S.32 indicated that the Legislative Councils might create unicameral, bicameral or even multi-cameral legislatures, with members either appointed or elected on such basis as each Council thought fit. The likely expectation was that each colony would model its proposals broadly on the British example; on its face, however, s.32 was notably non-directive on questions of detail. What s.32 did not do – and nor did any other provision in the 1850 Act – was grant those newly fashioned legislatures, whatever form(s) they might take, any greater power than already possessed by the Legislative Councils.

In terms of the Australian legislatures' future institutional structures, however, s.32 passed the reform process firmly back into colonial hands. The details of the conduct and outcome of that process in South Australia and Victoria is beyond the scope of this book. The focus of chapter two is on how the 1850 Act led to constitutional change in New South Wales. And on that question, it was William Charles Wentworth who took centre stage. He did so in the context of two other significant changes in the colony's fortunes.

The potentially important developments heralded by s.32 took shape contemporaneously with the discovery of large gold deposits in New South Wales and Victoria. The gold rush triggered a big influx of (entirely non-convict) immigrants from Britain and Ireland, but also from China. It also, at least in the short term, led to substantial increases in the colony's wealth and, by extension, to its capacity to be fiscally self-supporting.[127]

As Secretary of State between 1846 and 1852, Henry Grey was firm in insisting that the colonists who regarded Crown lands as entirely a resource for the colony's benefit (or, more accurately, for the benefit of a particular political faction within the colony) were acting under a misapprehension. In Grey's view, such lands were held on trust by the Crown for the benefit of the Empire as a whole.[128] Since land leases and sales were much the most important source of potential revenue, Grey's position was essentially incompatible with any meaningful form of colonial self-governance.

Wentworth was the primary influence behind a *Petition on the general grievances of the colony*, adopted by the New South Wales Legislative Council on 5 December 1851.[129] Amidst warnings that the British Parliament's failure to redress the grievances might trigger an Australian revolution akin to that in the North American colonies in the 1770s, the petition offered to resolve the difficulties by – crudely stated – proposing that the colonists would meet all costs of the government system in return for the grant of much more substantial internal political autonomy.

---

[127] See generally Goodman (2013) 'The gold rushes of the 1850s' in Bashford and McIntyre op cit; Ward (1992) op cit pp 139–44; Clark (1993) op cit 243–66.
[128] Despatch from Henry Grey to Fitzroy 23 January 1852, *Parliamentary Papers* 1852 No 34; reproduced in Bell and Morrell op cit pp 262–65.
[129] *VPLC (NSW)* No 31, 5 December 1851, www.parliament.nsw.gov.au/lc/papers/Documents/1851/5-december-1851-minutes/Minutes%20No%2031%20-%205%20Dec%201851.pdf (reproduced in Bell and Morrell op cit p137).

The proposal did not much commend itself to Henry Grey, whose perception of colonial lands as being held on trust for the Empire – and so subject to close and constant Imperial control – had been reiterated in February 1852. But 10 months later, a despatch from the Colonial Office to Fitzroy announced a radical reconsideration:

> Her Majesty's Government are ready to accede to the wishes of the Council and of the Colony in a spirit of entire confidence ... They have arrived, after full consideration, at the conclusion that, under the new and rapidly changing circumstances of New South Wales, the time is come at which it is their duty to advise her majesty that the administration of these lands should be transferred to the Colonial Legislature.[130]

The author of the despatch was Sir John Pakington.[131] Pakington had succeeded Grey as Secretary of State for the Colonies when Russell's government fell in February 1852, to be replaced by a Tory administration led by Lord Derby. Derby retained power at the election of November 1852, but his ministry remained in office barely a month, before collapsing as Peelite and free trade factions within the Tory party moved into coalition with the Whigs/Liberals in a government led by the Earl of Aberdeen in December 1852. Pakington's despatch to Fitzroy on 15 December 1852 had been virtually his last action in office. However, the new government – and the new Secretary of State, the Duke of Newcastle[132] – saw no need to depart from the policy Pakington had announced. The scene was therefore firmly set for New South Wales' politicians to write the next stage of the colony's constitutional development.

---

[130] Despatch from Sir John Pakington to Fitzroy 15 December 1852, *Parliamentary Papers* 1852 No 63; reproduced in Bell and Morrell op cit p265.

[131] Pakington, the son of minor gentry, initially began his career as a clergyman. He was (in the main) a Peelite Conservative, appointed apparently to his own surprise (and that of many of his colleagues) as Secretary of State for War and the Colonies in Lord Derby's 1852 administration; Chilcott (2004) 'Pakington [*formerly* Russell], John Somerset, first Baron Hampton' *ODNB*.

[132] Henry Clinton, the fifth Duke, was a man of relatively liberal political inclinations, being a close friend both of William Gladstone and Robert Peel. He sat in the Commons as a Whig/Liberal before inheriting the dukedom in 1851. He was Colonial Secretary under Palmerston from 1855 to 1858 and again from 1859 until shortly before his death in 1864: Munsell (2009) 'Clinton, Henry Pelham Fiennes Pelham, fifth duke of Newcastle under Lyme' *ODNB*.

2

'Constituting' New South Wales – And Queensland – 1850–1861

> With respect to the quoted opinions of certain English statesmen in opposition to the principle of a nominated Upper House, he would remind the Council that those gentlemen had no stake in this colony, and were safe in theorising and indulging in constitutional speculations which would not injure themselves. They coolly put forth untried theories, much upon the same principle that young surgeons acted when they tried reckless experiments with patients in the hospital ... He was certain that if it were proposed to the Duke of Newcastle or to Mr Gladstone that an elective House should be substituted in England for the present House of Lords that they would theorise very differently ...
>
> Charles Wentworth, speech at third reading in the Legislative Council of New South Wales during passage of the Constitution Bill 1853, 21 December 1853.

The power given to Legislative Councils by s.32 was not sufficient to placate political discontent in New South Wales. S.32 related to the future institutional structure of the colony's legislature, but not to its future powers. For Wentworth and his supporters, the minimum requirements were that the Legislature should control not just its own structure, but also – additional to its existing authority – that it should acquire unfettered control over the disposition of Crown lands and other locally generated revenues, that it should determine the appointment and salaries of government officials, and that the Governor's power to reserve bills should be confined to measures affecting Imperial interests.[1]

I. The New South Wales Constitution Bill 1853

That settlement eventually took legal form as a statute enacted by the British Parliament, (hereafter referred to as) the New South Wales Constitution Act 1855.[2] Wentworth, by then a proponent of ensuring that enhanced colonial autonomy would support

---

[1] I have drawn here on Irving (1964) 'The idea of responsible government in New South Wales before 1856' *Historical Studies: Australia and New Zealand* 192; Main (1957) 'Making constitutions in New South Wales and Victoria, 1853–1854' *Historical Studies: Australia and New Zealand* 369; Twomey (2004) *The constitution of New South Wales* ch 1; Melbourne and Joyce op cit part V. The description offered here is at best very truncated.

[2] 18 & 19 Vict c 54.

conservative, even reactionary, political ideology – and consequentially having drifted into effective rapprochement with the Macarthur faction[3] – was the dominant force in designing the legislation and steering it through the Legislative Council. Since the Council was seeking both to redefine the Legislature's composition and extend its competence, its objectives could not all be achieved through s.32. British legislation was also required. The Council chose to combine its preferences as to the new Legislature's composition with those relating to its powers in a single bill which, once approved by the Council, would have to be re-enacted in some fashion by the British Parliament.

The political heart of the 1855 Act was the 'recognition' that New South Wales should be granted both 'representative' and 'responsible' government. The term 'recognition' is used cautiously, as the 1855 Act – following prevalent British constitutional traditions – left important political matters unsaid.

The Composition and Powers of the New Legislature

Although the Legislative Council had no power, whether under s.32 or in any other source, to extend the colonial legislature's lawmaking competence, it nonetheless framed its proposed constitutional settlement as if it were a bill in the usual sense, eventually producing in late 1853 a document[4] styled as 'An Act to confer a constitution on New South Wales and to grant a Civil List to Her Majesty'.[5] According to the measure's preamble, it was indeed rooted in s.32, and so was reserved by the Governor for the royal assent. The Council was evidently alert to its lack of capacity to extend its powers, as the Bill included a section (s.66) providing that even if the Bill received the royal assent, it would have 'no force or effect' until the British Parliament had repealed existing Imperial legislation which would prevent the new Legislature from exercising its desired new powers. The Bill fell broadly into two parts. The first, achievable through s.32, related to the new Legislature's composition; the second, beyond s.32, to the Legislature's powers.

S.32 empowered the mixed Councils either to alter their own composition or to establish a new Legislature *instead of* their 1850 Act selves. The Bill's preamble indicated that the second option was being followed in New South Wales: "a Legislative Council and a Legislative Assembly, as *constituted* by this Act, should be *substituted* for the present Legislative Council".[6] The 1853 Bill thus began by providing in s.1[7] [s.1] that it would when enacted create a Legislative Council and a Legislative Assembly which would exist *in place of* the mixed Council.[8]

---

[3] Clark op cit pp 142–14: Ward (1992) op cit pp 162–64.

[4] Hereafter referred to as 'the Bill' – the capital B being used to acknowledge the measure's historical significance.

[5] 17 Vict c 41.

[6] Emphases added.

[7] I have inserted in the following pages in [ ] the section number of the provisions in sch.1 of the 1855 Imperial statute (18 & 19 Vict c 54) (which reproduces most of the provisions of the 1853 New South Wales Bill) immediately after the section number in the 1853 New South Wales Bill when the provision is identical (or close thereto) in each measure. The original text of the Imperial Act uses Roman numerals, but I have replaced those with Arabic numerals.

[8] S.48 [s.41] underlines this point by providing that all laws and ordinances in force in the colony when the Bill was enacted would retain their pre-existing effect. It is not immediately apparent why legislators

The Proposed Council

Per s.4 [s.2], the Legislative Council would consist of at least 21 'persons' appointed by the Governor for (s.5 [s.3]) an initial five-year term, although any person appointed thereafter would be a member for life. Save that members had to be at least 21 years old and British subjects (and save the unspoken assumption that only men could be 'persons'), the Bill placed no qualifications restricting eligibility for Council membership.

Wentworth initially proposed that the Council be a hereditary body, with its version of 'peers of the first creation' appointed by the Governor from the ranks of wealthy landowners and government officials. He found little support for that idea in New South Wales,[9] and reverted promptly to advocating a nominated (by the Governor) second chamber. There was a broad consensus in New South Wales, the other Australian colonies and British political circles as to the role that second chambers should perform in colonial government systems:

> It is on all hands admitted that there should be a second branch of the legislature, less easily swayed by the popular feeling of the moment than the representative Assembly, and capable of acting as check and counterpoise to that body, in order to guard against hasty legislation, without requiring the too frequent interference of the Governor or the Crown.[10]

There was less consensus over how best to compose the Council to achieve that objective. Wentworth rooted his eventual preference for a nominated chamber in Canadian precedent. Since the passage of Union Act 1840,[11] Canada's second chamber had been appointive and the offer the Council made to the British government in December 1851 was premised on the colony being granted a constitution similar to Canada's. Pakington, as Secretary of State for the Colonies, had also indicated that he favoured a nominated upper house. Some eminent British politicians, however, most notably Newcastle and William Gladstone, influenced, it seems, by very effective lobbying from anti-Wentworth forces – and especially by Robert Lowe MP

---

in New South Wales considered such a saving clause necessary, but there was presumably concern that it might be thought that the statutory abolition of a Legislature (the 1842 Act mixed Council) impliedly brought with it the abolition of the laws that Legislature had enacted. A similar provision (s.51) is found in the 1842 (Imperial) Act, in relation to laws in force in the colony prior to the 1842 Act hybrid Council being created. Victoria's 1855 Constitution Act had an identical clause to s.41. The notion that existing laws had to be 'saved' by express enactment when a new Legislature was created was therefore not a novel (nor solely colonial) idea. S.49 [s.42] – unnecessarily, one might think, given the scope of s.48 [s.41] – expressly preserved the continued existence of all courts previously created in the colony. S.48 [s.41] also perhaps explains what might otherwise be an ostensibly strange omission from the Bill: namely, that it did not contain any express repugnancy clause qualifying the Legislature's general or specific grants of lawmaking power. It is plausible, if by no means obvious, that the repugnancy clause in s.29 of the 1842 Act was by virtue of s.48 [s.41] implicitly incorporated into the Bill. An alternative possibility is that Wentworth and his colleagues assumed that the common law repugnancy doctrine (p 9 above) would be reasserted. It seems unlikely that the colony's legislators considered that the new Legislature would not be subject to the doctrine in some form.

[9] Ward (1992) op cit p164. Wentworth's proposal is the source of the derisive term 'bunyip aristocracy'; ibid.

[10] The quotation comes from a Privy Council report relating to the governance of the Cape Colony in South Africa; cited in Melbourne and Joyce op cit p404.

[11] Which Act merged the formerly separate colonies of Upper Canada and Lower Canada into a single entity; see Morton (2006 6th edn) *A short history of Canada* ch 5: Bothwell (2006) *Penguin history of Canada* pp 183–86.

(of whom more is said below) – had publicly favoured an elected second chamber. Wentworth found such interventions intolerable:

> With respect to the quoted opinions of certain English statesmen in opposition to the principle of a nominated Upper House, he would remind the Council that those gentlemen had no stake in this colony, and were safe in theorising and indulging in constitutional speculations which would not injure themselves. They coolly put forth untried theories, much upon the same principle that young surgeons acted when they tried reckless experiments with patients in the hospital ... He was certain that if it were proposed to the Duke of Newcastle or to Mr Gladstone or that an elective House should be substituted in England for the present House of Lords that they would theorise very differently ...

Wentworth's argument was obviously undermined by the fact that both Victoria and South Australia were contemporaneously adopting elective second chambers – on a very restrictive property franchise – within their new s.32-derived Legislatures.[12] But, as discussed further below, it should not be assumed that proponents of elected second chambers uniformly regarded them as likely to be more liberal – still less radical – in political outlook than an appointive house. Insofar as New South Wales's new constitution would have an obviously 'democratic' – in a limited sense – element, that element would be found in the Legislative Assembly

The Proposed Assembly

S.12 [s.10] provided that the Assembly would consist of 54 members. The electorate was identified in ss.13–14 [ss.11–12] and would comprise men[13] who satisfied various property criteria (rather more expansive than those then in force in Britain for the Commons electorate), which would enfranchise dramatically varying proportions of the adult male population depending upon the demographics of the particular electoral districts.[14] Eligibility for election to the Assembly was based on the same criteria. The Assembly would sit (s23 [s.21]) for a maximum period of five years, but could be dissolved by the Governor at any point.[15]

At first glance, so broad a franchise seems hard to reconcile with Wentworth's avowedly anti-democratic intentions. On close examination, the generous franchise appeared – at least in the short and medium term – as something of a mendacious sop to 'democratic' sentiment. S.15 [s.13] defined the constituencies which Assembly members would represent. Although it is not apparent from s.15's text, constituency apportionment was initially designed to give a substantial weighting advantage to rural areas; a skewing intended, very much at Wentworth's instigation, to favour conservative

---

[12] See especially Main op cit pp 381–83.

[13] S.13's text used the term 'man' rather than 'person' throughout.

[14] The qualifications inter alia being: a freehold estate worth £100 or more; owning a leasehold estate of £10 or more annual value or occupying a property of such value; having a salary of £100 or more per year; paying board and lodging of £40 or more per year; or holding a squatting licence. One analyst has credibly suggested that the criteria enfranchised as many as 70% of adult men in urban areas, around 50% in agricultural areas and only 23% in the pastoral districts; Loveday (1965) 'The Legislative Council in New South Wales 1856–1870' *Australian Historical Studies* 481, 483. There was no bar on multiple voting; an individual meeting the property threshold in several constituencies could vote in all of them.

[15] The Act did not place any express limits on the Governor's power of dissolution.

political sentiment; to represent, as was the case with the elected members of the then Council, 'interests', not people. The Bill contained no requirement for even approximate parity of constituency electorates. Many men would be entitled to vote for members of the Assembly; but many of those with liberal political inclinations, especially in Sydney and its suburbs, would cast their votes in more populous constituencies than those lived in by more conservatively inclined voters. A Sydney vote was worth much less than a vote in a pastoral constituency.[16]

Legislative Powers

The Bill repeated the grant of general lawmaking power given to the 1842 Act mixed Council.[17] In its new formulation in s.1 [s.1], that general power was expressed as enabling the Assembly, the Council and the Queen: "to make laws for the peace welfare and good government of the said Colony in all cases whatsoever". Despite the 'in all cases whatsoever' proviso in s.1 [s.1], the general power was accompanied by several *specific grants* of legislative authority. For Wentworth and his faction, the most important was in s.50 [s.43]: "Subject to the Provisions herein contained, it shall be lawful for the Legislature of this Colony to make Laws for regulating the Sale, Letting, Disposal, and Occupation of the Waste Lands of the Crown within the said Colony."

A related provision in s.57 [s.49] guaranteed an annual payment to the Crown of up to £64,300 to meet a scheduled list of governmental expenses, related primarily to the salaries and pensions of various government officials (the civil list payment). The quid pro quo for this commitment was identified in s.58 [s.50]:

> The said several Sums mentioned in Schedules A. B. and C. shall be accepted and taken by Her Majesty, Her Heirs and Successors, by way of Civil List, instead of all territorial, casual, and other Revenues of the Crown (including all Royalties) from whatever Source arising within the said Colony, and to the Disposal of which the Crown may be entitled either absolutely or conditionally, or otherwise howsoever.

S.52 [s.45] anticipated enhancement of the Legislature's powers over customs duties, expressly allowing the Legislature to impose: "such Duties of Custom as to them may seem fit" and also expressly providing that any Imperial legislation restricting the scope of that power were no longer applicable to the colony. There was, however, a clumsily worded caveat to the effect that any import duties on particular types of goods could not differentiate according to the goods' place of origin.

The Lawmaking Process: The 'Ordinary Way' of Legislating

The new Legislature's s.1 [s.1] capacity to 'make laws' was conditioned by several provisions relating to issues of quora and decision-making majorities in the Council and Assembly. S.25 [s.23] required that at least 20 members (of the 54) be present in the

---

[16] Although as under the similarly skewed scheme created for elected members of the 1842 Act Council, the huge distance between Sydney and the rural constituencies made it difficult for members from those areas to attend regularly.
[17] In s.29 thereof; p 20 above.

Assembly to conduct any business; that quorum being reached: "all questions (*except as herein excepted*) which shall arise in the said Assembly shall be decided by a majority of votes of such Members as shall be present ...".[18] In the Council (per s.10 [s.8]), the quorum would be at least a third of the members – maybe just seven – and all questions arising (without the exception applied to the Assembly)[19] would be decided by "a majority of the Members present", ie by as few as four.[20] There seems no scope to doubt that for the purposes of making laws per s.1 the 'majority' referred to in s.25 [s.23] and s.10 [s.8] was a bare majority of the members present in each quorate chamber, as in the Commons and Lords.[21]

Following the controversy fought out in Britain over the passage of the 1832 Great Reform Act, a previously tentative constitutional assumption began to harden in Britain that the Lords was the inferior partner within the British Parliament's bicameral structure, and that, even though in legal terms it was the equal of the Commons, it should refrain from exercising that power when it was clear that the Commons' majority sentiment coincided with the wishes of the electorate.[22] The New South Wales Bill did not adopt that premise as a matter of law in respect of the relationship between the Assembly and the Council. With the exception of a clause in s.1 [s.1] which required that: "all Bills for appropriating any part of the Public Revenue or for imposing any new rate tax or impost ... shall originate in the Legislative Assembly", the Bill envisaged that the Assembly and Council would exist in a relationship of perfect equality within the lawmaking process.

The Bill certainly made no explicit provision fully to enact a non-legal principle which was by then a long-established feature of the relationship between the Commons and the Lords: namely, that the Upper House should not seek to amend – although it might simply refuse to pass – any money bills passed in the Commons. That principle had pre-1688 revolutionary roots, spelled out in a 1678 House of Commons resolution:

> All Bills for granting such Aids and Supplies ought to begin with the Commons: And that it is the undoubted and sole right of the Commons to direct limit and appoint in such Bills the Ends, Purposes, Considerations, Limitations and Qualifications of such Grants: which ought not to be changed or altered by the House of Lords.[23]

Nor did the Bill explicitly provide a mechanism to resolve difficulties that might arise if Assembly and Council majorities held different views on the desirability of passing a bill and voted accordingly. However, the Bill – and this is a point which Wentworth

---

[18] Emphasis added. On the 'exceptions' see pp 40–42 below.

[19] The omission of the 'exception' proviso vis-à-vis the Council in the New South Wales Bill is repeated in the Imperial Act. I have not found any explanation for the differential drafting, and assume it is attributable to carelessness by both legislators and parliamentary draughtsmen. There are other textual errors which also point to such carelessness. S.1 of the 1853 Bill referred the reader to s.62. Following the Bill's renumbering when it became the schedule to the Act, s.62 became s.54 (and there was no s.62), but s.1 of the schedule still refers to s.62.

[20] S.10 [s.8] is drafted in terms of 'members present' rather than 'members voting', so presumably would not be satisfied if, with seven members present – six of whom abstained – just one member voted in favour. Similarly, in the Assembly 'the majority' would require at least 11 positive votes.

[21] Although neither the Commons nor Lords then had (or has ever had) a *statutory* quorum.

[22] See generally the discussion in Loveland (2018) op cit pp 138–41, 171–76.

[23] S.1 [s.1] enacted the first clause of the resolution, but not the second.

evidently considered insignificant – arguably did so implicitly if the Bill were indeed to institute a system of 'responsible government' in New South Wales.

If the Governor were to act on the advice of his ministers, and his ministers were his ministers because they enjoyed majority support in the Assembly,[24] what was to prevent ministers faced with a bill that had been passed by the Assembly but was obstructed in the Council from advising the Governor to appoint sufficient new members of the Council to create a pro-ministerial majority which would pass the bill? The 1853 Bill proposed a minimum number (21) of members of the Council, but did not set a maximum. Nor did the Bill propose any criteria constraining the Governor's discretion as to who might be appointed.[25]

Proponents of elective second chambers in the Australian colonies were alert to the possibility – of which British history furnished two examples (one recent) – that a government controlling a majority in the Commons but in a minority in the Lords could create an upper house majority by (in form) 'advising' but (in practice) 'instructing' the Queen to pack or swamp the Lords with new members who were government supporters. This had occurred in 1713, when Queen Anne had acceded to her government's advice to create 12 new government party peers to produce a Lords majority supportive of the various measures that would be needed to enable the government to sign the treaty of Utrecht, which ended the War of the Spanish Succession.[26]

The passage of the 1832 Great Reform Act was the more relevant and recent example. No new peers had actually been created in 1832 to secure enactment of the Whig government's electoral reform bill. Rather, after much prevarication and initial refusal, William IV had intimated that if Tory peers continued to obstruct the bill he would appoint many new members of the Lords to provide the government with a majority.[27] The threat was sufficient for the Tory peers to allow the bill to pass.

That difficulty could (perhaps) be countered in the New South Wales Legislature by fixing the maximum number of members for an appointive Council, and either not granting the Legislature the power to alter that number or providing that the power could only be exercised if specific restrictive conditions are met. That idea seemed to have little currency in New South Wales, in part perhaps because Wentworth and his supporters considered that other aspects of the new Legislature's composition would preclude such circumstances arising.

The politically skewed nature of constituency apportionment militated against radically inclined majorities controlling the Assembly. And in the unlikely event such a majority did emerge, the Council's appointive character made it similarly (perhaps even more) unlikely that a similar majority would appear there. Wentworth did not, however, equate the unlikely with the impossible, and successfully proposed provisions

---

[24] These two principles being at the heart of the notion of 'responsible government' as that term was understood in mid-19th-century Britain.

[25] Albeit that the persons referred to in s.4 [s.2] had to be British subjects aged at least 21 and (almost certainly) men.

[26] Littleton (2013) 'The Peace of Utrecht, 1713', https://thehistoryofparliament.wordpress.com/2013/04/30/the-peace-of-utrecht-april-1713/; Hill (1973) 'Oxford, Bolingbroke and the Peace of Utrecht' *The Historical Journal* 241; Turbeville (1927) *The House of Lords in the eighteenth century* pp 111–18.

[27] Although neither William IV nor the then Prime Minister, Earl Grey, could be sure that such members would actually vote for the bill after they were appointed; see Loveland (2018) op cit pp 171–75.

designed to limit the impact that such a two-house majority might have. The 'except as herein excepted' proviso in s.25 [s23] seemed applicable to two sections in the Bill: s.17 [s.15] and s.42 [s.36].

The Lawmaking Process: The Absolute and Two-Thirds Majority Provisos

S.17 [s.15] empowered 'the Legislature' to alter the number of Assembly members and/or to change constituency apportionment, but coupled that power with a proviso:

> [1] Provided always that it shall not be lawful to present to the Governor of the Colony for Her Majesty's Assent any Bill by which the number or apportionment of Representatives in the Legislative Assembly may be altered unless the second and third readings of such Bill in the Legislative Council and the Legislative Assembly respectively shall have been passed with the concurrence of *a majority of the Members for the time being of the said Legislative Council* and of <u>two-thirds of the Members for the time being of the said Legislative Assembly</u>.[28]

S.17 [s.15] evidently modified s.10 [s.8] slightly, in that it required – and on two separate occasions – a majority of 'members for the time being' (ie, assuming there to be 21 members of the Council, at least 11 members) rather than those 'present', which could be as few as four (ie a bare majority of the quorum of seven).[29] The modification to s.25 [s.23] is more significant. The 'two-thirds of members for the time being' (not 'members present', as in s.25 [s.23]) proviso suggests that at least 36 members of the Assembly would have to attend for the Assembly to be quorate for s.17 [s.15] purposes, and that, irrespective of whether attendance was 36, 37 or any number up to 54, that at least 36 voted – again on two separate occasions – for the proposed alterations: a 35–0 vote would not suffice.

S.42 [s.36] modified s.10 [s.8] and s.25 [s.23] more radically:

> [1] Notwithstanding anything herein-before contained, the Legislature of the said Colony, as constituted by this Act, shall have full Power and Authority, from Time to Time, by any Act or Acts, to alter the Provisions or Laws for the Time being in force under this Act or otherwise, concerning the Legislative Council, and to provide for the Nomination or Election of another Legislative Council, to consist respectively of such Members to be appointed or elected respectively by such Person or Persons, and in such Manner, as by such Act or Acts shall be determined:
>
> [2] Provided always, that it shall not be lawful to present to the Governor of the said Colony, for Her Majesty's Assent, any Bill by which any such Alteration in the Constitution of the said Colony may be made, unless the Second and Third Readings of such Bill shall have been passed with the Concurrence of Two-thirds of the Members for the Time being of the said Legislative Council and of the said Legislative Assembly respectively:
>
> [3] Provided also, that every Bill which shall be so passed for any of such Purposes shall be reserved for the Signification of Her Majesty's Pleasure thereon, and a Copy of such Bill shall be the laid before both Houses of the Imperial Parliament for the Period of Thirty Days at least before Her Majesty's Pleasure thereon shall be signified.[30]

---

[28] [1] is my addendum; emphases added.

[29] Although the point is not spelled out, s.17 [s.15] effectively increases the Council's necessary quorum from one-third to just over one-half of the Council's members.

[30] The [1] etc are my addenda.

As per s.17 [s.15], s.42 [s.36] required a *two-thirds majority of 'members for the time being' of the Assembly* to vote in favour of any such Bill at second and third reading. Unlike s.17 [s.15], s.42 [s.36] also required a *two-thirds majority of members for the time being to do so in the Council*. Additionally, s.42 [s.36] demanded that any such bill be reserved for the Monarch's assent rather than being assented to by the Governor; and that the bill be placed before both the Commons and the Lords for 30 days prior to assent being given.

The two-thirds majority provisos were unusual conditions in the context of the British parliamentary tradition, where it was assumed that any bill could be passed by a simple majority of members voting at any stage of the bill's passage. Wentworth was entirely candid as to his purpose in proposing special majorities. Their intended effect was to render it even more unlikely that either house (and almost impossible that both houses) would support changes to their respective compositions that would lend the lawmaking process a 'democratic' character; which character might, in turn, lead to enactment of laws unpalatable to Wentworth's faction.

The two-thirds majority proviso was not without colonial precedent. The Union Act 1840, which had combined the separate colonies of Upper and Lower Canada into a single entity, provided that 'Canada' would (per s.3) have a legislature composed of an elected Legislative and an appointed (members being appointed by the Governor, for life) Legislative Council, which would legislate in most cases by simple majority in both houses. However, s.26 provided that the number of Assembly members (and by implication the boundaries of Assembly constituencies) could not be altered unless the relevant Act had been approved by two-thirds majorities (of the total membership) in both chambers at second and third reading.

The Council's petition had asked for New South Wales to be given a constitution like Canada's.[31] Wentworth had likely pressed that point primarily to legitimise by invocation of precedent the creation of an appointive second chamber and the use of a two-thirds clause in New South Wales. The analogy is manifestly bogus. Canada's two-thirds clause was an obvious response to the concerns of French Canadians that their distinctive interests could be placed at the mercy of a bare Anglophile majority created by gerrymandering legislation supported by the more numerous (but not to the extent of two-thirds more numerous) English majority.[32] A two-thirds majority requirement precluded that possibility.

The reference to 'second and third readings of such bills' in s.17 [s.15] and s.42 [s.36] is itself a curiosity from a strictly legalistic perspective. The 1853 Bill did not specify the procedures that either house should follow in their lawmaking processes. As previously noted, the Council had been empowered by s.27 of the 1842 Act to adopt standing orders regulating its internal procedures, and had modelled them on those followed by the Commons.[33] Within the 1853 Bill, s.37 [s.35] echoed the former s.27 in empowering the Assembly and Council to promulgate standing orders regulating their proceedings. The standing orders would become 'binding' when approved by the Governor. As in the 1842 statute, what 'binding' meant, and who or what would be 'bound' was not explained.

---

[31] 'Canada' at this time being per the Union Act 1840 only what are now (broadly) the provinces of Ontario and Quebec.
[32] cf Bothwell op cit n 11 above.
[33] Pp 21 above.

Since s.37 [s.35] expressly stated that the power could be used from 'time to time', the inference is that each chamber would be 'bound' by its respective standing orders until such time either as the Governor approved new standing orders or the Legislature (or Imperial Parliament) amended s.37 [s.35]. The assumption of legislators in New South Wales seems to have been that it was so obvious that the new Assembly and Council would adopt the Commons-derived model followed by the Council since 1842 that there was no need to legislate expressly for them to do so.[34]

The 'second and third reading' clause in both s.17 [s.15] and s.42 [s.36] is also a peculiarity in a more limited sense. Presumably it meant that if a measure did not attract the requisite majority in either chamber at second reading it would be precluded from going to third reading. The requirement for enhanced majorities at both stages might be thought a mechanism designed to give legislators the opportunity to reflect upon their second reading votes, and for press and public opinion to be expressed. However, it was not unusual for bills before the pre-1855 Council to pass second and third readings on consecutive days, and not unheard of for both to occur on the same day. Since the Act did not specify a minimum period between readings, there was no guarantee that any opportunity for reflection or expression of public opinion would arise.

A matter perhaps of more significance is the Act's silence as to how s.17 [s.15] and s.42 [s.36] might be enforced. What was to happen if the relevant officer of the chamber (who would presumably be identified in standing orders made under s.37 [s.35]) where the Bill ended its passage tried to present the Governor with a bill which had not received the necessary majority (or if a bill which did not receive the special majority at second reading was sent for third reading)? Could presentment be injuncted? If so, by whom and before which court? Relatedly, if the Governor (purportedly) assented to such a bill, would a court have the power to invalidate the measure because it was not an 'Act' as one or more of the s.17 [s.15] or s.42 [s.36] requirements had not been met? Or, if compliance with those requirements was disputed, how and by whom was such a dispute to be resolved? The Bill did not even hint as to how those questions should be answered.[35]

An 'Independent' Judiciary

The Bill's provisions concerning the Supreme Court were limited to judicial tenure, salaries and pensions. S.44 [s.39] provided that Supreme Court judges would hold office during good behaviour, although per s.46 [s.40]: "It shall be lawful, nevertheless, for Her majesty, Her Heirs or Successors, to remove any such judge or Judges upon the Address of both House of the Legislature of this Colony." S.46 [s.40] then provided that the judges' salaries would be payable throughout their tenure.

---

[34] Clune and Griffith op cit pp 35–36.

[35] I do not wholly exclude the possibility that New South Wales politicians assumed, without discussion – perhaps with the Dog Act controversy in mind – that a judicially enforceable remedy for legislators' non-compliance with specified procedural requirements was already available. But, as possibilities go, it strikes me as remote.

The New South Wales Legislative Council was not competent to disapply Burke's Act[36] to the colony, and there is no indication that the Imperial government gave any consideration to the matter. Burke's Act provided an 'easier' route to remove (amove) a judge than s.39 [s.46], since it did not require the colonial government to seek the approval of the British government. Denison's attempts to amove Pedder and Montagu[37] must have been fresh (and prominent) in the minds of New South Wales politicians, which suggests that the failure to address Burke's Act's application to Supreme Court judges was deliberate rather than accidental.

The Legal Source (?) of Responsible Government

The Bill was concerned primarily but not exclusively with the composition and powers of the reformed Legislature. What the Bill did not do was spell out in any meaningful fashion the nature of the relationships that would arise between that Legislature and the colony's government, and between the government and the Governor. S.65 [s.58] was an interpretation provision which (impliedly) confirmed that the Governor remained legally in charge of the colony's executive government: "In the construction of this Act the term 'Governor' shall mean the person for the time being lawfully administering the Government of the Colony ..."

The 'clearest' – really the only – textual hint in the Bill that New South Wales might have 'responsible government' in the British sense – that the government would be drawn from the political grouping with majority Assembly support and that the Queen (Governor) would exercise her legal powers on the advice of that government – was in s.44 [s.37]:

> The Appointment to all Public Offices under the Government of the Colony hereafter to become vacant or to be created whether such Offices be salaried or not, shall be vested in the Governor, with the Advice of the Executive Council, with the Exception of the Appointments of the Officers liable to retire from Office on political Grounds as herein-after mentioned, which Appointments shall be vested in the Governor alone ...[38]

S.59 [s.51] then provided that pensions would be payable inter alia to: "certain Officers liable to Removal from Office on Political Grounds". The officers identified were all members of the Executive Council: the Colonial Secretary, Colonial Treasurer, Attorney-General, Solicitor-General and Auditor-General. The entitlement was for the 'present incumbents' only. The unwritten assumption seems to have been that the occupants of these offices would be replaced after the first Assembly elections by others who were chosen on 'political grounds', and that those 'political grounds' would be that they represented the political grouping commanding majority support in the Assembly, and the offices identified (other than the Auditor-General) would comprise the inner core of a government cabinet.

---

[36] P 27 above.
[37] Pp 27–28 above.
[38] The 'Executive Council' having been established under the prerogative in 1825; p 12 above. S.32 did not empower the mixed Legislative Council to alter or abolish the Executive Council.

II. The New South Wales Constitution Act 1855

Wentworth's political standing in the hybrid Council in 1853 was such that there was little opposition there to his proposed constitution. The official records[39] of the proceedings of the Legislative Council at the Bill's third reading on 21 December 1853[40] concluded succinctly:

> 6. Constitution Bill: – Mr Wentworth moved, That this Bill be now read a third time.
>
> Debate ensued.
>
> Question put.
>
> Council Divided.
>
> Ayes 27 Noes 6.

In a rumbustious speech during the third reading debate, Wentworth – his radical past now far behind him – took evident delight in emphasising that voices in the colony that sought a more egalitarian constitutional settlement had been roundly defeated:

> They soon found that the spirit of democracy had no chance in New South Wales – that loyal and constitutional sentiments and principles were the characteristics of this community, and if they wished to live under those republican institutions they so loudly belauded they had better take themselves to that republican state which was situated within six weeks sail of this country …[41]

Whether the vote in the hybrid Council accurately reflected the sentiments of the colony's population at large was a more uncertain question. The Bill's passage had been attended by innumerable public meetings and protests, at many of which the consistent and fiercely expressed critique of the Bill was that it pandered unacceptably to pastoral and squatting interests.[42] Press sentiment was also divided. While the colony's leading newspaper, the *Sydney Morning Herald*, firmly supported the Bill, there were clearly divergent voices. The strongest was perhaps a newly founded paper called *Empire*, edited by a young man with obvious and obviously liberal political ambitions, Henry Parkes.[43]

---

[39] The 'official records' of the pre-1855 Council are at www.parliament.nsw.gov.au/hansard/pages/first-council.aspx.

[40] www.parliament.nsw.gov.au/fcdocs/FCDocuments/1853/Minutes%20No%2086%20-%2021%20Dec%201853.pdf.

[41] *SMH* 22 December 1853 p4, http://nla.gov.au/nla.news-article12955456. See also Main's comment on the draft Bill: "as a social document the constitution faithfully reflected the wealth and status of the pastoralists … it was a monument to the political dominance which they had striven for in earlier years …"; op cit p379.

[42] By 1853 those interests did not always coincide. While squatters were almost invariably pastoralists, some pastoralists held their lands on a fully regularised freehold or leasehold basis and regarded squatters as an economic enemy rather than ally; see Baker (1958) 'The origins of Robertson's land acts' *Australian Historical Studies* 166.

[43] Parkes was an English émigré from a very impoverished background. With no formal education to speak of, but having had substantial exposure to radical political ideas and activities in Birmingham, he had emigrated to Sydney in 1839. Despite his lack of education, Parkes rapidly established himself as a poet, journalist and political commentator. He worked closely with Robert Lowe (see p 47 below), vocally protested against the resumption of transportation when the *Hashmeny* docked in Sydney and was likely the author of the call to arms noted at p 29 above. He created the soon-to-be influential *Empire* in 1850, and was sufficiently well established politically and personally to win a Council seat in 1854; http://adb.anu.edu.au/biography/parkes-sir-henry-4366.

Having completed its parliamentary passage, the Bill was reserved for the royal assent. It was accompanied on its journey to Britain by Wentworth, who had been deputed by the Council, along with the then Colonial Secretary Edward Deas Thomson,[44] to lobby British politicians to secure its unaltered adoption. In that task, Wentworth and Deas Thomson achieved mixed results.

The Colonial Secretary at that time was Lord John Russell, serving in Palmerston's Whig/Liberal administration. From the British government's perspective, the most significant alterations to the Bill were the excision of s.2 and s.3. S.2 had sought to limit the Governor's power to reserve bills and the Queen's power to disallow bills to measures addressing six subject matters, regarded by Wentworth and his colleagues as dealing with 'Imperial' rather than 'local' questions. S.3 then provided that the Privy Council should have the jurisdiction to determine if a bill fell within those particular categories.[45] Russell would not accept that the New South Wales Legislature should have any role in this issue. On that point, Wentworth's best efforts as a lobbyist were to no avail.

With the exception of those alterations, however, sch.1 of the 1855 Act 'reproduced' (the term is used guardedly for reasons explored below) the text of the 1853 New South Wales Bill more or less verbatim. However, from Wentworth's perspective, that ostensibly very successful outcome was compromised – and perhaps very significantly – not just by the aforementioned excision of s.2 and s.3 from the Bill, but also by Parliament's enactment of several new provisions proposed by the British government.

The Purpose and Wording of s.1 [BAA] of the New South Wales Constitution Act 1855

The New South Wales Constitution Act 1855 was a brief nine section measure[46] followed by two schedules, the first reproducing in amended form the 1853 Bill sent for the Queen's assent. Sch. 1 was therefore not a text passed by the Legislative Council under s.32. It was thus not a 'Bill' in the s.32 sense, and so there was nothing – per s.32 – for the Queen to assent to.

This point was not lost on the British government, which persuaded Parliament to address this issue in s.1 [BAA] of the 1855 Act, which provided that:

Power to Her Majesty to assent to the reserved Bill in schedule 1

1. It shall be lawful for Her Majesty in Council to assent to the said reserved Bill, as amended as aforesaid, and contained in schedule 1, anything in the said specified Acts of Parliament, or any other Act, law, statute, or usage, to the contrary in anywise notwithstanding.

---

[44] http://adb.anu.edu.au/biography/thomson-sir-edward-deas-2732. Thomson, the son of a senior naval officer, was a career civil servant deployed to New South Wales in 1829. He maintained good personal relationships with successive Governors and was widely regarded as an able administrator. He was appointed as Colonial Secretary (and, as such, was a member of the Legislative Council) in 1837.
[45] Ss. 38–41, which dealt with the detailed issues relating to the Governor's assent and reservation powers, were consequential upon acceptance of the s.2 distinction, and were removed, along with s.2, from the Bill presented to Parliament by the British government.
[46] Whenever I refer to one of those nine sections I style it as s.1 [BAA] or s.2 [BAA], the [BAA] denoting British Act Addendum. As already noted, a reference styled s.1 is to the New South Wales Bill; a reference styled [s.1] is to the sections in sch.1 of the Act.

46 'Constituting' New South Wales – And Queensland – 1850–1861

This unusual way of proceeding raises an obvious – and obviously important – question. Was 'schedule 1' to be regarded as an Act of the New South Wales Legislature or as part of an Act of the British Parliament? The latter conclusion seems the more obvious; although the import of s.1 [BAA]'s convoluted language may be that s.32 Act was being retrospectively amended so that the amended Bill (ie sch.1) – which the Council had not actually passed – was to be a s.32 measure (ie a New South Wales bill) and so the Queen could assent to it. The reason why (one might have thought) this was an important question is that if sch.1 was a 'British statute' it would prima facie not be amendable (whether in whole or in part(s)) by a subsequent *New South Wales* statute unless the Imperial Parliament granted the New South Wales Legislature such an amending power.

The Purpose (?) and Wording of s.4 [BAA] of the Constitution Act 1855

At third reading before the Council, Wentworth asserted that such a power was provided for in s.1 [s.1]: "... if there were subsidiary and minor grievances, and he admitted there might be, there was a clause in the Bill giving the future legislature of the colony plenary powers of legislation for their redress ...".[47] Whether Wentworth's apparent confidence at third reading as to s.1 [s.1]'s effect was sincere is an open question. The confidence was evidently not shared by the British government. Within the nine sections in the main body of the 1855 Act, the provision of most interest – which caused Wentworth such concern – (such concern being the reason one might doubt his sincerity as to s.1's [s.1] effect) was s.4 [BAA]:

> It shall be lawful for the Legislature of New South Wales to make laws altering or repealing all or any of the provisions of the said reserved Bill in the same manner as any other laws for the good government of the said Colony subject however to the conditions imposed by the said reserved Bill on the alteration of the provisions thereof in certain particulars until and unless the said conditions shall be repealed or altered by the authority of the said legislature.[48]

Russell evidently proposed the s.4 [BAA] amendment on the basis that the 'all cases whatsoever' clause in s.1 of the New South Wales Bill (enacted as [s.1] in sch.1 of the 1855 Act) did not mean what it might be thought plainly to have said. Rather, it meant 'all cases whatsoever *except for those matters contained in the said reserved Bill reproduced in sch.1 of this Act*'.[49] Quite what – as a matter of legal analysis – led Russell to that conclusion is a puzzle. Neither s.1 [s.1] nor any other part of the schedule expressly states that reform of the schedule is not a 'peace welfare and good government' matter. Russell's position seems, however, to have been that a legally significant distinction existed between the matters addressed in the schedule and all other colonial laws; that the former were more important in normative legal terms than the latter, and as such alterable only by explicit grants of lawmaking authority. That presumption seems to

---

[47] *SMH* 22 December 1853 p4, http://nla.gov.au/nla.news-article129555456.
[48] S.9 [BAA] filled a gap left by the original Bill, in explicitly specifying the elements of which the (original) 'Legislature' would be composed: "... the word 'Legislature' shall include as well the Legislature to be constituted under the said reserved Bill and this Act, as any future Legislature which may be established in the said Colony under the powers in the said reserved Bill and this Act contained".
[49] Like the 1853 Bill, the [BAA] sections of the 1855 Act did not contain an express repugnancy clause constraining the s.1 [s.1] or s.4 [BAA] powers.

be expressed in s.4 [BAA] of the 1855 Act, which explicitly distinguishes between 'the provisions of the said reserved bill' and 'any other laws'.

S.4 [BAA] thus raises several important questions about how the New South Wales Legislature could – to invoke a designedly generic term – 'make law'. The 'same manner' referred to in s.4 [BAA] would seem to be – arising inferentially from the combined effects of s.10 [s.8] and s.25 [s.23], and the more amorphous assumption shared by politicians in New South Wales and Britain that the new Legislature was modelled on the British Parliament – by bare majorities in the (quorate) Assembly and Council plus the royal assent given by the Governor.

But s.4 [BAA] also indicates that the 'same manner' of lawmaking would not apply to 'certain particulars' of the reserved Bill which had 'conditions' attached to them. Those 'certain particulars' would be (primarily) s.17 [s.15] and s.42 [s.36], which both contained precise 'conditions' as to majorities and (for s.42 [s.36]) reservation and laying before the Lords and Commons. 'The conditions' might be characterised in various ways. They might be seen as providing for a special type of lawmaking procedure to be followed for the specified s.17 [s.15] and s.42 [s.36] objectives to be achieved. Alternatively, they might be portrayed as altering the composition or identity of 'the' Legislature when such objectives were in issue.

S.4 [BAA] also provided that the 'conditions' could be: "repealed or altered by the authority of the said legislature". What s.4 does not expressly state is whether 'the said legislature' which could alter or repeal s.17 [s.15] and/or s.42 [s.36] could do so through the 'same manner' (bare majorities plus royal assent; hereafter referred to as 'the ordinary way' of legislating) or would have to conform to the 'conditions' (enhanced majorities/reservation/laying before) specified in each respective provision.

Debate in the Imperial Parliament

There was little Commons discussion of the Bill and the British government's amendments. *Hansard* records two brief substantive debates, on 14 June 1855 (second reading) and 25 June 1855 (committee), respectively.[50] The excisions of s.2 and s.3 and the addition of s.4 – the issues most concerning the British government – were made before the Bill reached the Commons.

Much of the (brief) second reading debate was taken up with a fierce attack on Wentworth and his supporters by Robert Lowe,[51] then a backbench MP and nominally a Liberal. After Oxford and a brief career at the English Bar, Lowe had emigrated to New South Wales, where he had practised law and journalism, and had also been appointed to the Council by Governor Gipps in 1843. Lowe, having fallen out of favour with Gipps, who considered Lowe far too liberal on governmental matters, won a Council seat for Sydney in 1848, running second to Wentworth.[52] Although Lowe shared

---

[50] *HCD* 14 June 1855 c 1989: *HCD* 25 June 1855 c 100.
[51] http://adb.anu.edu.au/biography/lowe-robert-2376.
[52] Lowe's career in New South Wales is detailed in Knight (1966) *Illiberal liberal; Robert Lowe in New South Wales 1842–1850*. He had made a particular dramatic and widely reported speech (from the top of an omnibus parked at the dockside) as the *Hashemy* pulled into Sydney harbour; *SMH* 12 June 1849 p2, https://trove.nla.gov.au/newspaper/article/12907428).

Wentworth's desire to enhance New South Wales' control over its own affairs, he vehemently opposed what he regarded as Wentworth's primary political concerns, namely to acquire and safeguard squatter control over the colony's (as yet unallocated) 'waste' lands and reinstate transportation to provide cheap labour.[53]

In committee, Lowe unsuccessfully moved an amendment to remove the two-thirds clause from s.17 [s.15] and to omit s.42 [s.36] entirely.[54] Russell resisted the amendment, on the basis that s.4 [BAA] would empower the New South Wales Legislature to achieve that result through bare majority legislation, and it was politically more desirable that any such decision be made there rather than in London:

> In proposing the present measure the Colonial Office was only acting in accordance with the express decision of the Legislative Assembly [sic[55]], and with a view to the best interests of the colony. All that it was now proposed to do was that which the colonists themselves had decided upon, as likely to prove beneficial to the colony.[56]

The Secretary of State's Despatch

Despite the difficulties Denison suffered as Lieutenant Governor of Van Diemen's Land, his stock with successive British governments remained sufficiently high for him to be appointed Governor of New South Wales in late 1854.[57] Russell had not elaborated his views on the need for and effect of s.4 [BAA] during the Bill's passage, but did so subsequently in a despatch to Denison:

> 13. The effect of this provision, as now introduced, will, it is conceived, be as follows: – In the first place, the new Legislature will have full power to alter all the provisions of the bill not specified in clauses 17 and 42 aforesaid. In the next place it will have power to alter the portions specified in those clauses, subject to the conditions imposed by these clauses. And finally, it will have power to repeal those conditions themselves, if it shall think proper, by enactment passed by simple majorities ... By this provision her Majesty's Government conceive[s] that the purpose of the Council will be most effectually answered because, if the bill had been passed under their ordinary powers, it is clear that, although they might have imposed these conditions, any subsequent Legislature might have repealed the clauses imposing them by simple majorities. But, in any case of a bill being offered for your assent, repealing these conditions, you will reserve such bill for her Majesty's pleasure.[58]

---

[53] Wentworth's concern was in part simply to acquire more lands (Gipps had also vetoed an extraordinary proposal from Wentworth that Wentworth buy most of the south island of New Zealand for a pittance). However, Wentworth also recognised that allowing the Governor to sell or lease the waste lands provided him with a substantial source of revenue free of Legislative Council control, which weakened the influence of colonial politicians on all matters. Lowe returned to Britain in 1850 and was elected to the Commons in 1852. He subsequently served as Home Secretary and Chancellor of the Exchequer in the 1870s.

[54] HCD 25 June 1855 c 101. Lowe did not object to s.15 [s.13].

[55] There are repeated references by several MPs to the 'Assembly' rather than the 'Council'. Since there was no 'Assembly', the erroneous nomenclature is surprising.

[56] HCD 25 June 1855 c 104.

[57] He was also appointed as Governor-General of all the Australian colonies, which placed him on some matters in an intermediary role between the other colonies' Governors and the British government.

[58] It is on this point that the sincerity of Wentworth's aforementioned third reading assertion as to s.1 [s.1] rather founders. Wentworth and Deas Thomson fiercely opposed the suggested s.4 [BAA] – and pressed the point vigorously to British MPs and ministers – because they assumed it would empower the Legislature to repeal or alter s.17 [s.15] and/or s.42 [s.36] through the simple majority express or implied repeal process. Russell's closing comment that bills altering any of the conditions should be reserved is inconsistent with the Bill, which specified reservation only for s.42 [s.36] measures.

Russell's analysis seems prima facie rather odd. He suggests that a mere *alteration* to s.17 [s.15] and/or s.42 [s.36] would require the identified special majorities, but their complete *repeal* would demand only bare majorities. So the more substantively radical option was to be less difficult to achieve in terms of the political support required in the Assembly and Council than a more modest alteration. The oddity becomes more pronounced when one sets this analysis alongside the wording of s.4 [BAA], which at first glance appears to treat 'altering' or 'repealing' the entrenched clauses without distinction. Either objective might be achieved by the New South Wales Legislature to alter or repeal any or all provisions of sch.1 of the 1855 Act in just the same 'manner'; that manner being the process used in the Imperial Parliament.

A Diversion from s.4 [BAA]: Mid-Nineteenth-Century Presumptions as to the 'Manner' of Lawmaking by the British Parliament …

Although Russell did not spell the points out in his despatch, and nor were they discussed in the Commons or Lords during the 1855 Act's passage, that 'manner' was in the mid-nineteenth century accepted to have had four important elements.

The first was that bills would pass their various stages in the Commons and Lords by simple majority at each point before being given the royal assent. There was no 'law' to this effect, but rather an unquestioned reality of centuries – predating the 1688 English revolution – of unbroken political practice. That practice was given legal expression in the 1855 Act by s.10 [s.8] and s.25 [s.23], which identified bare bicameral majoritarianism as the usual (although not the only) manner in which the New South Wales Legislature would enact statutes.

The second element – which had a legal basis in the formal sense of being endorsed by the courts – was that if the provisions of any two Acts contradicted each other, then the earlier Act's provisions were repealed and replaced by those in the later Act even if that later Act made no reference to the earlier one. That orthodoxy – now known as the 'doctrine of implied repeal' – had been firmly stated by the Court of Chancery in 1842, in *The Dean and Chapter of Ely v Bliss*:[59]

> [I]f two inconsistent Acts be passed at different times, the last is to be obeyed, and if obedience cannot be observed without derogating from the first, it is the first which must give way. Every Act of Parliament must be considered with reference to the state of the law subsisting when it came into operation, and when it is to be applied; it cannot otherwise be rationally construed. Every Act is made, either for the purpose of making a change in the law, or for the purpose of better declaring the law, and its operation is not to be impeded by the mere fact that it is inconsistent with some previous enactment.

On appeal[60] – decided as the New South Wales Legislative Council was considering how to exercise its s.32 powers – the then Lord Chancellor (Lord St Leonards) approved that analysis, even if the proposition might seem peculiar or objectionable as a matter of politics or morality:

> Without reference to the language of the Acts, it would certainly require a very strong and clear case to enable the Court to say that a statute, passed so recently after a former one

---

[59] (1842) 5 Beavan 574; 49 ER 700, 704 (Lord Langdale MR). The case concerned payment of tithes.
[60] *The Dean of Ely v Bliss* (1852) 2 De Gex Macnaghten & Gordon 459; 42 ER 950.

(upon the occasion of which it is impossible to suppose that there was not some knowledge of the former statute, creating, as it did at the time, a great sensation with respect to the rights of the Church), and which does not profess to repeal a leading enactment in that former statute, should by implication have that effect. Under such circumstances, it would be natural to expect to find upon the face of the later Act a reference to what had been done the year before – an intention to diminish the time limited by the previous Act, and to make a new enactment upon the subject. Still, however, if by the later Act the Legislature has really done what is represented, I must give effect to it, though the operation would be to abrogate a portion of the former Act of Parliament.

The third element – again a matter of evidently unshakeable political understanding rather than law – was that (with one exception)[61] the substantive moral nature of the matter addressed by the statute was not relevant to operation of the first two principles. A legislative provision altering, for example, the number of members in the Commons or the property threshold determining the right to vote would be produced by Parliament and treated by the courts in just the same way as a statutory term changing the cost of a dog licence.[62]

The fourth, and perhaps the most important, element was that the Imperial Parliament apparently did not have the power to alter its manner of lawmaking. Legislative provisions which might specify that future Acts on particular subjects be entirely prohibited, be passed by enhanced majorities at any point in either house, be subject to some other unusual procedural requirement or could not have implied effect would be perfectly valid as laws when enacted, but could at any point be overridden by an Act passed in that ordinary manner.[63] No political or moral values could be granted an 'entrenched' legal status which safeguarded them to any degree against subsequent legislation passed in the 'ordinary way'.

... and Back to s.4 [BAA] ...

S.4 [BAA]'s wording seems to accept the doctrine of implied repeal principle, given that it says 'repealed or altered' (ie 'alteration' need not be preceded by 'repeal') and it does not say 'expressly' repealed or altered. So, even if one were to accept that the matters dealt with in sch.1 were in some sense more morally significant than other New South Wales laws (a dichotomy perhaps between 'constitutional law' and 'ordinary law'), that distinction would have no relevance in terms of how such laws might be affected by subsequent legislation.

---

[61] That exception being a presumption, which must arise at common law, that the Crown is not bound by legislation except to the extent that the relevant Act expressly has such an effect; see the pre-1855 cases cited in Maxwell (1875) *On the interpretation of statutes* pp 112–19.

[62] There were also by then some qualifications – if not quite stark exceptions – to the general rule. For present purposes, the most important was the (strong) presumption that a statutory provision dealing with a specific issue would not be impliedly repealed or altered by a later provision having a (much) wider scope within which the specific matter addressed in the earlier provision might be thought to fall; see especially Maxwell's 1875 survey (the style of the treatise is too descriptive to merit portrayal as an analysis) of *the generalia specialibus non derogant* pricinciple, ibid pp 157–65.

[63] Hereafter I use the terms 'entrenched' and 'entrenchment' to signify departures from the 'ordinary way' of legislating (ie bicameral bare majoritarianism plus royal assent by the Queen – or the Governor in a colony – expressly or impliedly) which made enacting a statute politically more difficult than under that ordinary process.

S.4 [BAA] – read in the context of accepted notions of 'the manner' of the British Parliament's lawmaking power relating to bare majoritariansim and implied alteration and repeal – would suggest that the New South Wales Legislature could, by bare majority at each stage in the Assembly and Council, pass a bill entitled, for example, The Legislative Assembly (Additional Members for Sydney) Bill 1858, which said simply:

1. With effect from the next election for members of the Legislative Assembly, which election shall be held on 1 March 1859, the Legislative Assembly shall have six additional members.
2. The six aforesaid members shall all be elected, in accordance with the scheme detailed in schedule 1 herein, to represent voters in the City of Sydney.

So long as that bill then received the royal assent from the Governor, it would become a valid Act, even though it made no reference at all to altering or repealing s.17 [s.15]. A fortiori, there could be no need for the legislature to enact a preliminary statute expressly repealing s.17 [s.15] prior to enacting a second statute altering the number of members for Sydney.

On the basis of Russell's despatch, however, that hypothetical Act – qua a measure effecting an *alteration* to rather than a *repeal* of s.15 [s.17] – could not have been passed unless the special majorities were achieved.[64] If the hypothetical Act is, however, taken to have *repealed* s.17 [s.15] (insofar as it relates to the members for Sydney), Russell's despatch suggests that the 'ordinary manner' would suffice.

It is perhaps fanciful to assume that Russell in his despatch was *sub silentio* drawing a legally significant distinction between 'alter' and 'repeal'. It would presumably be for a court with the requisite jurisdiction to determine if Russell's reading of s.4 [BAA] was correct should the matter ever be put to a legal test. It may well be that the alter/repeal dichotomy to which Russell alluded was a slip of the pen, and that he assumed that any legislative 'alteration' to, for example, the number of members of the Assembly necessarily 'repealed' the previous statutory provision dealing with that issue.

But Russell did not directly address in his despatch a second point that would arise in this hypothetical scenario: namely, that it would prima facie seem that until such time as s.17 [s.15] was repealed, it would be unlawful for the relevant official in either the Assembly or Council to present the hypothetical 'Additional Members Bill' to the Governor for the royal assent unless the requisite special majorities had been achieved at second and third reading. In other words, there would in such circumstances be no 'bill' for the Governor to assent to. Or, to frame the point in yet another fashion, s.17 [s.15] and s.42 [s.36] did not place limits on the Legislature's powers (because 'the Legislature' is the Council, Assembly and royal assent ensemble), but on the powers of the Assembly and Council and Governor *as individual elements of* that ensemble.[65]

---

[64] Unlike s.42 [s.36], s.17 [s.15] did not additionally have 'conditions' relating to reservation and laying before; p 40 above.

[65] On Russell's analysis of s.4 [BAA], that difficulty could presumably be met by the Legislature enacting a bill ('The Royal Assent Bill') which authorised the relevant officer to present any bill for the royal assent so long as the bill had achieved a bare majority in the Assembly and Council, even if 'The Royal Assent Bill' made no reference to s.17 [s.15] or s.42 [s.36]. Since 'The Royal Assent Bill' would not be addressing matters identified in s.17 [s.14] or s.42 [s.36], it would not be unlawful to present it to the Governor without the enhanced majorities having been achieved. (Although this would, of course, raise a question about the applicability of the doctrine of implied repeal inasmuch as the latter statute would be of general application while s.17 [s.15] and s.42 [s.36] had a very particularistic scope; p 50 above.)

Another Diversion from s.4 [BAA]: And Another Mid-Nineteenth-Century Presumption as to (Judicial Regulation of) the 'Manner' of Lawmaking by the British Parliament ...

This point perhaps simply did not occur to Russell or his advisers; or, if thought about, was dismissed as inapplicable. Shortly before the 1855 Act was passed, the House of Lords had decided in *Wauchope v Edinburgh and Dalkeith Railway*[66] that a court could not inquire into whether an Act had completed its parliamentary passage in accordance with the Commons' and/or Lords' standing orders, regarding this as a matter of parliamentary privilege relating to each house which was inextricably linked to Parliament's sovereign lawmaking power.[67] If the *Wauchope* principle applied to the New South Wales Legislature, then s.17 [s.15] and s.42 [s.36] would simply be unenforceable at law: they were merely moral impediments to the legitimacy of bare majority legislation.

Wauchope might be thought of limited relevance to the New South Wales scenario outlined above, since the procedure that was allegedly not complied with in *Wauchope* did not derive from a statutory source, as would be the case for a two-thirds bill – and, indeed, for the Assembly and Council's standing orders themselves – in New South Wales. But there was manifestly no explicit provision anywhere in the 1855 Act to confirm that the *Wauchope* principle was not applicable to the New South Wales Assembly or Council. This was another particularistic manifestation of a general trend; the Act omitted entirely to address both the legal consequences of a failure by the Assembly, Council or Governor to comply with the Act's 'requirements' concerning their respective roles in the lawmaking process and the mechanisms through which any such alleged non-compliance might be investigated and (if established) remedied.

... and Back (again) to s.4 [BAA]

Nor did the Act itself or Russell's despatch consider another potentially significant issue. If, as seemed to be Russell's expectation, the two-thirds clauses were repealed, did s.4 [BAA] empower the Legislature at some future date to reinstate them (or to create some other 'manner' of lawmaking other than by bare majority in each house)? Relatedly, did s.4 [BAA] permit similar 'conditions' being created de novo in respect of other parts of sch.1? And if so, was it also to be possible for s.4 [BAA] to be used to attach legally enforceable 'conditions' (or 'manners' of legislating) to the repeal or amendment of those reinstated or de novo conditions? In other words, was s.4 [BAA] to be not simply a 'disentrenching' device (ie permitting such matters in future to be addressed by legislation passed in the 'ordinary way'), but also a 're-entrenching' provision (ie permitting legislation to be passed in the 'ordinary way' which in future required 'the Legislature' to comply with additional conditions)?[68]

---

[66] (1842) 8 Cl & 710; 8 ER 279.

[67] A 'better' way – in the sense of adhering to then orthodox notions of constitutional propriety – to reach the same result might be to suggest that any such investigation was precluded by statute: namely, Art 9 of the Bill of Rights 1689, which provided inter alia that: "proceedings in parliament ought not to be impeached or questioned in any court or place out of Parliament"; see generally Loveland (2018) op cit pp 200–15.

[68] Most obviously by altering the presumptive bare majority requirements in s.10 [s.8] and/or s.25 [s.23] to require enhanced majorities for Acts seeking, for example, to impose requirements as to a person's religion

Had the Bill received more extensive attention in the Commons or Lords, there might be some evidence as to legislators' intention on the question. As it is, we are left only with the Act's text. The phrasing of s.4 [BAA] can credibly be read as pointing to s.4 [BAA] being a grant of general power in the *dual* 'disentrenching *plus* re-entrenching' senses. That proposition gains particular strength from the clause in s.9 [BAA] which not only defined the Legislature in terms of its original composition, but also referred to: "*any future Legislature which may be established* in the said Colony under the powers in the said reserved Bill and this Act contained" (emphasis added).

Attempting to discern s.4 [BAA]'s meaning on this issue by placing it in its political context is problematic, as several quite distinct contexts are identifiable. The first and most obvious is that Russell and (by extension, if only as a matter of form) the Imperial Parliament regarded s.4 [BAA] solely as a device irrevocably to align the New South Wales Legislature's lawmaking process with the British model as soon as political circumstances in the colonial society had matured sufficiently for the safeguard of enhanced majorities to no longer be necessary. On that reading of context, that New South Wales's constitution was to mirror the British constitution, s.4 [BAA] would be simply a disentrenching device. A second contextual perspective, premised on the presumption that the Imperial Parliament was content to allow the colonists to design their own constitutional system, would be that s.4 [BAA] might be used to attach all sorts of – in a British sense – unusual (and legally impossible) 'conditions', 'restrictions' or 'manners' to how various sorts of colonial law might be made.

Any effort to identify a dominant context on this issue is further complicated by s.3 [BAA], which expressly preserved the measures enacted in the 1842 and 1850 statutes in respect of the types of colonial bills to be reserved for the Queen's assent, and the Queen's powers of disallowance of colonial Acts and issuing *Instructions* to the Governor.[69]

The Governor's Commission and *Instructions*

Russell's despatch as to the Legislature's powers reached the colony alongside Denison's revised Commission and *Instructions*.[70] Through a process of deduction, one can infer from those *Instructions* that New South Wales was intended by the Imperial government to have a governmental system modelled on that existing in Britain. But neither the Commission nor the *Instructions* remedied the 1855 Act's lack of reference to such politically (if not legally) recognisable aspects of the British constitutional order as the notion of responsible government, the office of Prime Minister and the institution of the Cabinet.

Responsible Government by Implication?

While responsible government in New South Wales could readily, as a matter of principle, entail that the colony's government command majority Assembly support, the

---

in respect of holding public office or prohibiting use execution as a punishment; or by altering the default 'manner' of passing such laws by adding conditions such as reservation to the Monarch and/or laying before the Common and Lords.

[69] Pp 20 and 30 above.
[70] *VPLC (NSW)* 1855 v 1 p635 et seq.

associated (in Britain) notion that the government should in effect control the Monarch's legal powers was much more problematic. The Governor occupied an obviously dual position, embroiled in a political relationship with both the colony's government and the Imperial government.

The 1855 Act said little in express terms about 'responsible government' in New South Wales. Denison's Commission (taking the legal form of Letters Patent issued under the prerogative) and *Instructions* were slightly less opaque on the point. Russell's despatch to Denison had included this observation at para 21:

> The only remaining instructions which I have to convey relate to the introduction of responsible government: but it is so evident from the provisions of the Colonial Bill before me, that your advisers and the Legislature have had fully in view the exigencies of that system, that I am not aware that any special directions are required from myself.

That the text of the Bill – or the subsequent Imperial Act – put the meaning of responsible government in New South Wales 'fully in view' is perhaps less a preposterous inaccuracy than a complacent assumption that many of the most important principles regulating a 'British' governmental system need not and should not be given legal expression. Denison's *Instructions* from Russell brought the issue, if not fully, then closer into view.

Rather than referring to a 'Cabinet', the Commission announced that it would be "expedient" for the Governor to be "advised and assisted" by an 'Executive Council',[71] the members of which the Governor could: "from time to time nominate and appoint". Neither the Commission nor the *Instructions* gave any indication as to who those persons might be, nor on what basis they should be appointed. Certainly, no express suggestion was made that the Governor should appoint a 'government' drawn from whichever political grouping had majority support in the Assembly. Per para 10 of the Commission, appointees would hold office at pleasure: no guidance was given as to the circumstances in which the Governor might dismiss members of the Executive Council.[72]

The *Instructions* were similarly reticent in an express legal sense. Para 12 seemed to accord the Executive Council considerable importance, in that it commanded the Governor that:

> ... you do in all things consult and advise with Our said Executive Council, and that you do not exercise the powers and authorities aforesaid, or any of them, except by and with the concurrence and advice of our said Council.[73]

Para 12 continued however by identifying exceptions to that command; notably matters which were respectively urgent, or trivial, or regarding which such consultation and advice might in the Governor's judgment cause 'material prejudice' to the Crown.

---

[71] This presumably being in legal terms the Executive Council created under the prerogative in 1825; p 12 above.

[72] Although the final paragraph of the Commission informed Denison that the Governor could suspend *any* office holder: "upon sufficient cause to you appearing ...". 'Sufficient' was not further defined.

[73] This general instruction as to acting on advice coexisted with more specific manifestations of the general power; see eg para 3 regarding appointments to the Legislative Council.

Para 13 then gave the Governor a power which seemed substantially to undermine the command made in para 12: "We do authorise you in your discretion ... to act ... in opposition to the advice which may in any such case be given to you by the Members of Our said Executive Council."

Other than requiring the Governor promptly to inform the British government when he exercised the para 13 power – and to offer reasons for having done so – the *Instructions* placed no textually explicit restrictions at all on its use.

No mention was made of a Prime Minister or Premier, though para 10 – which indicated that the Governor would preside over Executive Council meetings – did allow the Governor to appoint a member of the Council who would preside when the Governor was absent.

'Responsible government' – like the office of Prime Minister or the Cabinet – had no express legal basis in the British constitution, and so it is perhaps unsurprising to see it dealt with in so opaque a fashion in the colonial context. Dickey's characterisation is entirely apt: "The Letters Patent and the *Instructions* sent to Denison simply reveal the lawyers capacity to conceal the real seat of power."[74] Para 12 and para 13 are a clear illustration of the dichotomous political position occupied by the Governor; a dichotomy underlined by the *Instructions*' provisions about the giving of the royal assent to bills passed by the Assembly and Council.

Matters Reserved for the Royal Assent

While the giving of royal assent by the Queen to a British bill passed by the Commons and Lords was regarded as a mere formality in Britain, Denison's *Instructions* contained several significant departures from that principle, all of which clearly envisaged that the Governor was expected by the British government to give careful consideration to granting assent. He was told, for example, that he should: "Take especial care in passing such laws ... that the provisions contained in Acts of Parliament ... and also in Instructions given to you are strictly complied with".

Para 5 seemed to order the Governor to ensure that the doctrine of implied repeal should *not* operate in the colony in telling him that:

> No Act whatever be suspended, allowed, continued revived or repealed by general words, but that the title and date of such Act so suspended, allowed, continued revived or repealed be particularly mentioned and expressed in the enacting part ...

As noted above, s.42 [s.36] had expressly required that a bill altering the composition of the Legislative Council be reserved for the Queen's assent. S.3 [BAA] had also retained the reservation requirements laid out in the 1842 and 1850 Acts.[75] Para 6 of the *Instructions* identified 12 additional types of bill to be reserved. This comprised an eclectic list, including inter alia bills allowing divorce, granting land or money to a Governor, creating paper currency, establishing a lottery, containing terms inconsistent with a treaty entered into by the Imperial government, interfering with the armed

---

[74] Dickey (1969) *Politics in New South Wales 1856–1900* p106.
[75] P 53 above.

forces and intended to be in force for less than a year.[76] Like the Act itself, Denison's *Instructions* were silent about the legal consequences ensuing if a Governor deliberately or erroneously assented to a bill supposed to have been reserved for assent.

It is unsurprising, given their origins in British political traditions, that New South Wales's new constitutional arrangements should leave so much legally unsaid about the nature and content of the governmental system. And is it similarly unsurprising that those arrangements were also immediately put to the test.

III. The Law and the Politics of 'Dis-Entrenchment'

Despite Wentworth's best efforts to secure a conservatively inclined Assembly alongside a still more conservative Council, the first Assembly elections in March/April 1856 produced a house with many liberally inclined members. There were no 'parties' in the modern sense, albeit that most members could credibly be identified as having liberal or conservative dispositions, and Assembly majorities shifted so quickly on the basis of personal loyalties and issue-specific policy disagreements that four different governments held office before a second election was called in January 1858.[77]

The New South Wales Constitution Act 1857

The most notable 'constitutional achievement' during the first Legislature was removal of the enhanced majority provisions of s.15 [s.17] and s.36 [s.42]. In 1857, the new bicameral Legislature enacted Act 20 Vict No 10 (hereafter referred to as the Constitution Act (NSW) 1857).[78] The Act was short in terms and clear in purpose:

> An Act to repeal so much of the Constitution Act as requires the concurrence of unusual majorities of Members in the Legislative Council and Legislative Assembly respectively in the passing of Bills to alter the constitution conferred by the said Act or the number and apportionment of Representatives in the said Legislative Assembly.

The Act contained only two sections. S.1 repealed entirely s.17 [s.15]. S.2 repealed the two-thirds majority requirements of s.42 [s.36], although it did not alter the provision's reservation and laying before elements.

The Act's preamble offered little indication as to why the provisions should be repealed, stating only:

> … And whereas it is deemed fitting to repeal the hereinbefore recited provisoes to the said fifteenth and thirty-sixth sections of the said Constitution Act to the end that it may become competent to the Legislature of the Colony at any time after this Act shall have received the Royal Assent to amend the provisions of the said Constitution Act in the particulars in the

---

[76] Which last category, given the time that would be required for a bill to travel to and back from London, virtually negated the possibility of such short-term Acts being passed.
[77] See generally the detailed analysis by Clune and Griffith (2006) *Decision and deliberation: the Parliament of New South Wales 1856–2003* pp 17–19.
[78] www.austlii.edu.au/au/legis/nsw/num_act/caaa1857n6316.pdf.

said provisoes mentioned in the same manner and by the same majorities of Members as any of the other provisions of the said Act or any other law for the good government of the Colony...

The Act initially appeared as a bill promoted by Stuart Donaldson in the Assembly on 7 August 1856. Donaldson was an ideological conservative, and was briefly Premier in 1856.[79] The two-thirds clauses had been in issue during the election campaign, although land reform was the dominant controversy. That Donaldson had initially promoted the measure indicated that the two-thirds clauses attracted little electoral support, even within the restricted electorate the 1855 Act had created.

The bill eventually resurfaced for second reading in the Assembly on 30 October 1856,[80] at the behest of the then Premier Sir Henry Parker. Parker was a career New South Wales civil servant, previously an appointed member of the hybrid Council. Denison had invited Parker to form a government earlier that month, evidently hoping that Parker could fashion a ministry which would attract support from both liberal members and Wentworth's faction.[81] Parker's ministry survived barely a year, though it succeeded in garnering virtually unanimous Assembly support for the two-thirds repeal bill.

Parker introduced the bill with a firm statement that only a simple majority was required to enact it. Curiously, however, he also indicated that this measure would have to be passed before any change could be introduced – by a subsequent and separate Act – to alter the law regulating the Legislature's composition.[82] Parker was either not alert to the relevance of the doctrine of implied repeal or considered it (for reasons he did not explain) inapplicable to these provisions. Of the other 12 members who spoke at second reading, none voiced any doubt that a simple majority would suffice. All, however, also accepted that an Act explicitly repealing the two-thirds clause would have to be passed *before* any other Act addressing the s.17 [s.15] and s.42 [s.36] issues could be enacted. The prevailing assumption was that two separate Acts were required to 'alter' these substantive elements of New South Wales's constitution: the first to empower the Legislature to make the change; the second actually to make the change.

Much of the debate was taken up with criticism from liberally inclined members of the fact that members of Parker's ministry had been vocal proponents of the two-thirds clause, and had now become in barely a year vocal proponents of its repeal. No one spoke to oppose repeal of the clause, which was variously described as: "the obnoxious, Un-English two third clause" and as a "blot". S.4 [BAA], in contrast, along with Russell's despatch, was identified by several members as a 'boon' to the colony. The bill passed second reading and committee without division. Report and third reading were undertaken on 7 November 1856, and were again both passed without division.[83]

Deas Thomson, so supportive of the two-thirds clauses in 1855, used the Council's second reading debate on 19 November 1856 to explain why he and other members of the government had so promptly changed their minds.[84] Deas Thomson maintained

---

[79] http://adb.anu.edu.au/biography/donaldson-sir-stuart-alexander-3425.
[80] *SMH* 31 October 1856 p4, http://nla.gov.au/nla.news-article12988530.
[81] http://adb.anu.edu.au/biography/parker-sir-henry-watson-4364.
[82] *SMH* 31 October 1856 p4, https://trove.nla.gov.au/newspaper/article/12988530.
[83] *SMH* 7 November 1856 p8, https://trove.nla.gov.au/newspaper/page/1498883.
[84] *SMH* 20 November 1856 p4, https://trove.nla.gov.au/newspaper/article/12989178.

that he still considered the two-thirds majority desirable, and referred approvingly to the various constitutional entrenchment devices used in the United States which he saw as a counterweight to: "the large amount of freedom which prevailed [there]".[85] Nonetheless, he felt it inappropriate to oppose the new bill, given: "The universal opinion which had been expressed throughout the land that as the legislature of the colony was at present constituted, the two House of Parliament ought to have unreserved power to deal with the Constitution".[86] In any event, Deas Thomson was confident that if the Assembly should ever pass an improper bill, the Council would prevent such a measure becoming law.

As in the Assembly, all Council members who spoke at second reading accepted both that the two-thirds clauses could be repealed by a simple majority and that an Act to that effect should be passed before any subsequent changes were made to the Assembly's electoral system or the Council's composition.

Debate ended with Deas Thomson's explanation of what he saw as the Council's proper constitutional role:

> It was true that the House was independent alike of the Government, the Assembly, and the popular voice; but when they saw independent popular opinion brought to bear upon a particular question, he felt that they were bound to give weight to the public voice. If they believed that the popular feeling had been led away, so that a demand was made which would prove injurious to the people themselves, he thought they would be bound to stand firm, and resist the demand but that could not be the case here.

The bill passed second reading and all subsequent stages without division, and was reserved for royal assent by Denison on 20 January 1857. Royal assent was subsequently proclaimed in New South Wales in October 1857.[87]

There is no indication in the debates that any member thought s.4 [BAA] might permit reinstatement of s.17 [s.15] or s.42 [s.36], or the creation of some similar departure from bicameral bare majoritarianism. S.4[BAA] seems to have been regarded entirely as a device to impose bare bicameral majoritarianism not just as the *default* 'manner' of lawmaking on all matters, and not just as the *only* 'manner' of lawmaking on all matters *for the time being*, but as the *only* 'manner' of lawmaking on *all matters* for the time being *and for the future*.

Electoral Reform ... and Swamping the Council

Having removed the two-thirds clauses, liberally inclined Assembly members, gathered under the leadership of Charles Cowper[88] and John Robertson, proceeded with plans to reform the house's electoral system. Cowper, the son of an English clergyman, had emigrated to New South Wales when a young child. He had pursued a career in the colony's nascent civil service, and by the mid-1830s had variously bought and been

---

[85] ibid.
[86] ibid.
[87] *SMH* 23 October 1857 p3, https://trove.nla.gov.au/newspaper/article/13001976.
[88] http://adb.anu.edu.au/biography/cowper-sir-charles-3275.

granted substantial land holdings with the colony. He was not, however, a squatter, used his lands primarily for agricultural rather than pastoral purposes and had no particular sympathy with squatters' interests. Describing himself somewhat ambiguously as a political moderate, Cowper had won election to the mixed Council in 1843, defeating one of the Macarthur family in doing so. Cowper's political views, in marked contrast to Wentworth's, shifted in a liberal direction over the next decade and by the time the 1855 Act came into force he was among the most prominent figures in an emerging liberal faction within the Legislature,[89] and won a Sydney seat in the March 1856 Assembly election.

Cowper was closely aligned personally and politically with Robertson, who was also a substantial landholder and agriculturalist, but not a squatter. His family had emigrated to Sydney from London in 1822 at the suggestion of Governor Brisbane, who was a personal friend. Robertson was educated in Sydney at a school run by the (very) radical political activist and clergyman John Dunmore Lang, and seemingly imbibed elements of Lang's political philosophy. Although a vocal and visible opponent of the 1853 Bill, Robertson had not to that point sought elected office. He was returned to the first Assembly in 1856, on a distinctly radical platform, advocating manhood suffrage and sweeping land reforms, which was distinctly antagonistic to the squatter interest.[90]

The undisciplined nature of political alignments in the first Assembly meant that governments formed and fell with remarkable rapidity. Donaldson and Parker both headed short-lived conservative ministries in that period, and Cowper was Premier twice: for just a month in August/September 1856 and again between September 1857 and January 1858. The instability was such that the Assembly did not last its scheduled three years, but was dissolved during Cowper's second administration. Despite the skewed nature of the electoral system, Cowper's liberal faction secured an initial majority in the Assembly, where its primary concern was enactment of legislation to amend the colony's electoral law.

Cowper's electoral bill had faced significant opposition (led by Deas Thomson) in the Legislative Council. Cowper put the question of to what extent the Governor would act on the advice of the 'Executive Council' by requesting Denison to appoint 15 new members (nominated by Cowper in the expectation that they would support his ministry's bill) to the Legislative Council.[91] Denison, seemingly construing para 13 of his *Instructions* as overriding para 12, initially refused the request, though by the end of the year some 13 Cowper nominees had been appointed, mostly replacing original appointees who had died or stepped down.

Cowper and Robertson remained well short of commanding a majority in the Council, however, and faced a well-disciplined 'opposition' faction in the Council unofficially led by Deas Thomson, which persistently obstructed the government's appropriation, taxation and electoral reform bills. Those tensions were resolved by Denison dissuading Deas Thomson's bloc from continuing its intransigence by

---

[89] He had made a long and forceful speech criticising various aspects of Wentworth's Bill at second reading; *SMH* 31 August 1853 p4, http://nla.gov.au/nla.news-article28644777.
[90] http://adb.anu.edu.au/biography/robertson-sir-john-4490.
[91] Clune and Griffith op cit pp 106–07.

threatening to allow the Council to be 'swamped' with government supporters if it did not give way,[92] and Cowper and Robertson's electoral reform bill eventually received assent on 24 November 1858.[93]

The Electoral Act 1858

S.2 of the Electoral Act 1858[94] *expressly* repealed many provisions in sch.1 of the 1855 Act that regulated the Assembly's composition and the qualifications of members and voters. The Act increased the Assembly's size from 54 to 80 members and reapportioned electoral districts in a fashion which reduced the original pro-rural bias. Perhaps most notably, s.8 introduced near-universal male adult suffrage, conditional only on six months' residency in a particular electoral district.[95] Non-residents could qualify for the franchise by meeting the pre-existing property criteria (per s.9),[96] and a new route to eligibility was also granted to anyone in possession of a miner's licence for at least six months prior to any election (per s.13). The quantitative effect was substantial: there were 44,451 registered voters in the 1856 election, and 78,231 in 1859.[97] The Act also introduced a secret ballot (per ss.41–43).

The first election fought on the reformed franchise was held in June 1859. Although Cowper managed to form a new administration, it was unstable, and the Assembly was again dissolved late in 1860. At the December 1860 election, Cowper passed the mantle of liberal leadership to Robertson. The initial balance of forces in the Assembly after the election enabled Robertson to form a new ministry, although he promptly stood aside in favour of Cowper to concentrate on securing enactment of his land reform legislation.

Robertson's 1861 Land Reforms – And the First 'Swamping' (?) of the Council

Robertson's land reform bills had several significant elements.[98] The 1847 initiative to regularise occupation of waste lands under short-term leases[99] had been notably

---

[92] Loveday (1965) op cit pp 488–89; Clune and Griffith op cit pp 110–11.

[93] Inter-house disputes over whether the Council was entitled to *amend* – rather than simply pass or reject – taxation and appropriations measures were not so readily resolved. The position consistently taken by the Council was that because sch.1 of the Constitution Act 1855 did not expressly provide that the Council could not amend such bills, it had the power to do so. The view taken by Cowper and Robertson was that the strict letter of the law had to be read against a contextual presumption that on this question the Assembly and Council stood vis-à-vis each other as the Lords stood vis-à-vis the Commons: namely, that as a matter of convention the upper house could not exercise such power; see generally Clune and Griffith op cit pp 75–78. In this period, Cowper and Robertson also made several somewhat faint-hearted attempts to recast the composition of the Council on an elective basis, none of which were successful; Twomey (2004) op cit pp 362–64; Clune and Griffith op cit pp 145–47.

[94] 22 Vict No 20, www.austlii.edu.au/cgi-bin/viewdb//au/legis/nsw/num_act/teao1858n23179/.

[95] A decade was still to pass before enactment of Disraeli's electoral reform legislation in Britain, which, while it significantly lowered the property threshold, fell far short of a universal male adult franchise; Loveland (2108) op cit pp 175–77.

[96] So multiple voting remained possible for voters who met the threshold in several constituencies.

[97] (1856) http://elections.uwa.edu.au/elecdetail.lasso?keyvalue=1306; (1859) http://elections.uwa.edu.au/elecdetail.lasso?keyvalue=1308.

[98] For detailed analysis see Baker op cit.

[99] P 23 above.

ineffective. This was primarily because leases could be issued only after land had been surveyed by government surveyors, and the Survey Department was notoriously inefficient and corrupt. Areas surveyed were let at very low rents, but the vast majority of unsurveyed pastoral land was held on yearly licences, for which low fees were payable and which also granted squatters pre-emptive purchase rights when surveys were eventually completed.

The central element of Robertson's reform was popularly known as 'free selection before survey'. The policy would entitle any person to select plots of 40–320 acres which could be bought on a freehold basis before surveys were carried out on land which was unoccupied or held under a squatting licence. The purchase price would be £1 per acre, with a 5/- per acre down payment and the balance payable after three years, conditional upon the purchaser residing on the site and improving its value (by erecting buildings and/or cultivating it for agricultural use) by £1 per acre.

It may be a mischaracterisation to regard the dominant purpose and likely effect of Robertson's proposed reform as being to trigger a proliferation of small freehold farmers, although it seems credible that a romanticised vision of that sort accounted for much of the electoral support that Cowper and Robertson received from less affluent voters in both 1859 and 1860. Robertson's own motives were perhaps directed more at undermining squatting-based pastoralism as a political force.[100] But it was likely that, if rigorously implemented, the reforms would be significantly detrimental to squatter's economic interests and, by extension, to their political influence. Consequently, the bills were consistently rejected in the Council.

Denison's term as Governor ended early in 1861.[101] His replacement was Sir John Young, a man whose career marked him out as a very different character to Denison. Young, born into a minor aristocratic family, had attended Oxford and pursued a dual career as a barrister and Conservative MP (with liberal leanings), holding several low-level ministerial positions before accepting a diplomatic post as High Commissioner for the Ionian Islands in 1855.[102] Young's 1861 *Instructions* were essentially a verbatim repetition of those given to Denison in 1855. They made no reference to the 1858 franchise legislation or to its implications for the nature of the relationship between the government and the Governor, and retained the internally contradictory provisos in paras 12 and 13.[103]

Young's arrival in March 1861 coincided with the acute political controversy raised by the Legislative Council's refusal to pass the land reform bills. The broader basis of dispute was the general issue of the propriety of the Legislative Council's power – not as a matter of law, but as a matter of political morality – to block government bills which had majority Assembly support; a power already discernibly being used much

---

[100] Baker's (op cit) analysis of the policy in this way is eminently credible.
[101] He was appointed Governor of Madras, where he served until his retirement in 1866. Denison then returned to England, where he died in 1871.
[102] http://adb.anu.edu.au/biography/young-sir-john-4905.
[103] Young's *Instructions* did reduce the categories of bill to be reserved for the royal assent from 12 to 11. The removed category was an Act intended to be in force for less than a year. As in the 1855 *Instructions*, there was no indication as to the legal consequences of the Governor assenting to a bill he had been told to reserve.

more frequently in respect of bills promoted by liberal rather than conservative administrations.[104]

Cowper's solution to the impasse was precisely the scenario which had prompted politicians in South Australia and Victoria to opt for a fixed-size, elective second chamber. Cowper proposed that Young appoint 21 new Council members – enough to secure Cowper and Robertson a reliable Council majority. With evident reluctance, Young accepted Cowper's advice and issued the necessary writs to appoint the persons concerned. Cowper's efforts to acquire a Council majority were, however, frustrated by a combination of unfortunate timing and astute (or cynical) manoeuvring by the government's Council opponents.[105] The Legislative Council's original five-year term was approaching its end – the 21 new appointees would serve only for a few days[106] before the original councillors would be replaced by members who would hold office for life. Cowper and Robertson's intention was that the expanded Council would spend those last few days passing blocked government bills.

The initiative was, however, stymied by the prosaic device of the existing Council majority resigning their seats, walking out of the chamber and rendering the Council inquorate prior to the new members taking office. Under the Council's standing orders, the Council was therefore adjourned till the next sitting day; which day fell after the end of the five-year period.

Henry Clinton, the fifth Duke of Newcastle, had again become Colonial Secretary in June 1859.[107] In a despatch which suggested that the then British government (this being still a Palmerston-led Liberal administration) held a very restrictive view of what responsible government meant in New South Wales, Newcastle indicated that both Cowper's and Young's behaviour had been politically indefensible:

> I regret that your Ministers should have offered you such advice and that you, even under the circumstances you described, should have accepted it. A measure so violent, and in its nature, so unconstitutional, could only be justified by circumstances of the gravest danger and the greatest urgency.[108]

Young nonetheless managed to appoint a successor Council (of lifetime appointees) which seemed in terms of composition to satisfy all shades of political opinion in the colony and at the Colonial Office, and which promptly passed Robertson's land bills. Wentworth agreed to serve as its President, in the context of various 'understandings' – none of which were given any legal status – arrived at by Young, Cowper and other

---

[104] See the table in Clune and Griffith op cit p107. It should not be assumed that the Council's position was always what would now be regarded as illiberal; see especially Clune and Griffith's analysis of Deas Thomson's opposition to a bill proposing to curb Chinese immigration (much of which was triggered by the gold rush): op cit pp 104–05.

[105] For an extensive treatment of the episode, see Currey (1943) 'The Legislative Council of New South Wales 1843-1943: constitutional changes attempted and achieved' *JRAHS* 337, 361-67; Currey (1929) 'The first proposed swamping of the Legislative Council of New South Wales' *JRAHS* 282.

[106] Young approved the appointments on a Friday; the five-year term ended on the following Tuesday.

[107] Russell had left office in July 1855. Two Whig/Liberal politicians succeeded him during the remainder of Palmerston's administration, and two Tories held the post during Lord Derby's short-lived 1858–59 government. Neither the change of personnel nor the change of ministry heralded any noticeable shift in colonial policy towards New South Wales.

[108] Newcastle to Young, 14 December 1861, cited in Griffith (2009) 'Young, Sir John' in Clune and Turner (eds) *The Governors of New South Wales 1728-2010* pp 257–58.

senior political figures as to the proper role of the Council in blocking legislation and of the Governor in acceding to government requests to swamp the Council:

> [T]he Council is not to be swamped on any future occasion, until after the rejection by it of some vital question upon which the opinion of the country had previously been taken, after a dissolution of the Assembly for that express purpose.[109]

The 'understanding' had obvious parallels with the emergent presumption in Britain as to the proper role of the House of Lords in obstructing measures which had passed the Commons,[110] and offered the prospect of a relatively harmonious relationship between the two houses for the foreseeable future.[111]

IV. The Creation of Queensland as a Separate Colony

Pressure had been building in New South Wales throughout the 1840s for the colony to be divided to give separate colonial status to its northern areas as well as the south-western region, which became Victoria in 1855. The pressure was in part a principled ideological objection by residents of settlements on the northern coast to being governed from a place (Sydney) so far away in miles and time.[112] Its primary source seems, however, to have been pastoralists – both emancipists and exclusives – who occupied even larger tracts of land than in the colony's south and who opposed ending transportation as that had deprived them of cheap labour.[113] Their hope was that they would be able to dominate the governmental process in a new colony – and thereby gain control over land disposition – in a fashion by then beyond them in New South Wales.[114]

By 1855, the British government had bowed to that pressure. S.7 [BAA] of the 1855 Act empowered the Queen, through Letters Patent, to create one or more separate colonies in northern New South Wales, and to establish a Government and Legislature for any such colony(ies) which would:

> in manner as nearly resembling the Form of Government and Legislature which shall be at such time established in New South Wales as the Circumstances of such Colony will allow; and full power shall be given and by such Letters Patent or Order in Council to the Legislature of the said colony to make further provision in that Behalf.

The new colony of Queensland was separated from New South Wales in May 1859; the Order in Council establishing its Government and Legislature was promulgated on 6 June 1859.[115]

---

[109] Wentworth to Young 14 June 1861, cited in Loveday 1965 op cit p495. See further Griffith (2009) op cit pp 257–62.
[110] Loveland (2018) op cit pp 139–41.
[111] That relationship was to continue without Wentworth, who returned to England permanently in 1862. Wentworth eventually died in 1872, and was buried with a state funeral in New South Wales the next year.
[112] This having been accepted by the Privy Council as the primary justification for creating Victoria as a separate colony in the south of New South Wales; p 30 above.
[113] Evans op cit ch 3; Melbourne and Joyce op cit pp 443–47.
[114] The complexities of the political pressures at play both in New South Wales and London are explored in Knox (1976) '"Care is more important than haste": Imperial policy and the creation of Queensland, 1856-9' *Historical Studies* 64.
[115] www.foundingdocs.gov.au/item-sdid-48.html.

The Order created a Legislative Council and Legislative Assembly and provided in cl.2 (reproducing s.1 [s.1] of the 1855 Act):

> [W]ithin the said Colony of Queensland, Her Majesty shall have power by and with the advice and consent of the said Council and Assembly to make laws for the peace welfare and good government of the said Colony in all cases whatsoever ...

Cl.3 provided that the Governor of New South Wales would summon at least five persons[116] to form an initial Legislative Council. Cl.6 empowered the Governor to draw boundaries for Assembly electoral districts, with qualifications of members and electors fixed "As nearly as may be" to the relevant law in force in New South Wales. Cl.8 followed that method by providing that all provisions in sch.1 of the 1855 Act relating to, inter alia: "the constitution, functions and mode of proceedings of the Legislative Council and of the Legislative Assembly respectively" would be in force in Queensland: "unless and until altered in the manner hereafter specified".

At first sight, cl.8's wording produced the apparently (in political terms) peculiar consequence that the two-thirds clauses in s.17 [s.15] and s.42 [s.36] of the 1855 Act, repealed in New South Wales in 1857, would resurface two years later in Queensland. Given that other references in the Order to laws subsisting in New South Wales were to those applicable when the Order came into force (ie in 1859), the cl.8 reference was presumably the result (yet again) of carelessness in drafting, rather than a deliberate British government decision to give Queensland provisions so widely – and recently – condemned in New South Wales

If oversight it was, cl.8 was apparently to be – as had been s.17 [s.15] and s.42 [s.36] in New South Wales – readily amendable. The ostensible equivalent of s.4 [BAA] of the 1855 Act appeared in cl.22 of the Order, which appears to combine in a single source s.4 [BAA] and s.1 of sch.1 of the 1855 Act:

> *xxii.* The Legislature of the Colony of Queensland shall have full power and authority from time to time to make laws altering or repealing *all or any of the provisions of this Order in Council* in the same manner as any other laws for the good government of the Colony except so much of the same as incorporates the enactment of the fourteenth year of Her Majesty chapter fifty-nine and of the sixth year of Her Majesty chapter seventy-six relating to the giving and withholding of Her Majesty's assent to bills and the reservation of bills for the signification of Her Majesty's pleasure and the instructions to be conveyed to Governors for their guidance in relation to the matters aforesaid and the disallowance of bills by Her Majesty Provided that every bill by which any alteration shall be made in the Constitution of the Legislative Council so as to render the whole or any portion thereof elective shall be reserved for the signification of Her Majesty's pleasure thereon and a copy of such bill shall be laid before both Houses of the Imperial Parliament for the period of thirty days at least before Her Majesty's pleasure thereon shall be signified.[117]

The reason that cl.22 might be seen as only the ostensible equivalent of s.4 [BAA] is this. S.4 [BAA] was a British statutory provision which gave the New South Wales Legislature powers to alter any of the provisions in sch.1. S.4 [BAA] did not in terms empower the New South Wales Legislature to alter any of the [BAA] parts – including s.4 [BAA]

---

[116] With the same qualifications as under the 1855 Act.
[117] Emphases added.

itself – of the 1855 Act. So, unless s.1 of sch.1 was to be taken as empowering the Legislature to do so, and Russell and by extension the British Parliament seemed decidedly of the view that it did not, s.4 [BAA] was not amendable other than (whether expressly or impliedly) by subsequent British legislation.

Cl.22, in contrast, is itself part of the Order, not of a distinct British Act, and is said to give a power in relation to 'all or any' of the provisions of the Order – which 'all or any' must presumably include (subject to its reservation and laying before provisos) cl.22 itself. For s.4 [BAA] and cl.22 to be true equivalents, s.4 [BAA] would have had to have been drafted in these (added text in italics) terms:

> It shall be lawful for the Legislature of New South Wales to make laws altering or repealing all or any of the provisions of the said reserved Bill *and all or any of the provisions of this Act* in the same manner ...

To approach the point from a different perspective, had the Order been a British statute, then by s.22 Parliament would have given the Queensland Legislature a power it had not given to the Legislature of New South Wales.[118]

There is no obvious evidence to explain why New South Wales and Queensland were treated differently in this respect. It may have been assumed by ministers or civil servants at the Colonial Office – perhaps because this Order was issued under statutory powers in s.7 [BAA] of the 1855 Act rather than being a free-standing exercise of the royal prerogative – that cl.22 mirrored s.4 [BAA] in a normative sense. If so, the assumption was ill-founded. It would in principle be possible for Parliament to specify explicitly that an Order in Council be treated as a statute, but that was not done in s.7 [BAA] (nor by any other legislative provision, whether in the 1855 Act or elsewhere). There is no basis for thinking that an Order could acquire that status implicitly. Perhaps the most likely explanation for the difference is (once again) British government carelessness in drafting the Order.

The First Queensland Government

The first Governor of Queensland per se was Sir George Bowen, who took office in December 1859.[119] Bowen, the son of an Irish clergyman, was educated at Charterhouse and Oxford. He pursued an academic career in Corfu and then at Oxford. Bowen moved in Gladstone's political circles, and owed his Queensland appointment to Gladstone's patronage. Bowen was accompanied to Queensland by Robert Herbert, scion of a well-connected aristocratic family, who after education at Eton and Oxford became a fellow of All Souls.[120] Bowen, likely at Gladstone's prompting, chose Herbert as his

---

[118] The 'manner' referred to in cl.22 must be – via cl.8 – the 'manner' created for the New South Wales Legislature by s.1 of sch.1 of the 1855 Act. And that manner was presumptively the manner followed by the British Parliament, ie a simple majority in both houses plus royal assent by either explicit or implied repeal/amendment.

[119] http://adb.anu.edu.au/biography/bowen-sir-george-ferguson-3032. See further Joyce (1978) 'George Ferguson Bowen and Robert George Wyndham Herbert: the imported openers' in Murphy and Joyce (eds) *Queensland political portraits 1859–1952*.

[120] http://adb.anu.edu.au/biography/herbert-sir-robert-george-wyndham-3757; Joyce op cit.

(interim) Colonial Secretary, on the understanding (rooted in the legally unarticulated presumption that Queensland, like New South Wales, would have a system of responsible government) that to continue in that role Herbert would have to secure election to Queensland's Assembly. Bowen also appointed several resident Queenslanders to office, most notably Ratcliffe Pring[121] as the government's Attorney-General.

Bowen's government began promptly to prepare for Queensland's first Assembly elections. But even before the election was held, the new colony was gripped by acute constitutional controversy, the understanding of which requires rigorous examination both of the Order's statutory source and of its terms. In New South Wales, that initial controversy had initially been fought out over the issue of the relationship between the Assembly and the Council; in Queensland, the battle was between the two legislative houses together and the colony's senior judiciary.

---

[121] Pring, an English born and educated émigré, achieved some distinction as a barrister and legal academic, and some notoriety as a foul-tempered drunk: http://adb.anu.edu.au/biography/pring-ratcliffe-4416. For a racier sketch, casting Pring in equal measure as a gambler and womaniser, see Bernays op cit pp 11–12.

3
The Colonial Laws Validity Act 1865 – I: Origins

Unless some Imperial Act should be raised legalising the acts of this legislature in the meantime, the Judicial Committee of the Privy Council will, some fine day, set Queensland aghast. I believe that the Acts of this legislature will not be worth the paper they may be printed upon unless the Imperial Parliament intervenes ... And as the mere hint of such a doctrine would be sure to produce infinite confusion, I shall take steps to keep it to myself ...

Albert Luytwyche, judge of the Supreme Court of Queensland, to Governor Bowen on 20 July 1863.

... Relieve us from suffering under this enormous evil unknown to England's law, to wit, the power claimed by our Judges to declare laws passed by the Parliament of this Province illegal.

Petition from the House of Assembly of South Australia to the Secretary of State for the Colonies June 1864.

Enactment of the Colonial Laws Validity Act 1865 (hereafter CLVA 1865) was prompted by a Report[1] by the British Government's then Law Officers,[2] Sir Roundell Palmer (Attorney-General)[3] and Sir Robert Collier (Solicitor-General).[4] Their Report was triggered in part by a South Australia dispute about the validity of certain measures 'enacted' by that colony's Legislature through processes inconsistent with the

---

[1] Cited here as Palmer and Collier (1864) *The Law Officers to Mr Cardwell: colonial laws validity report*. (I have capitalised the R in this Report when citing it hereafter to denote its significance.) Edward Cardwell was then Secretary of State for the Colonies. He entered the Commons as a Tory in 1842, but switched allegiance to the Liberals in 1853. He served in Palmerston's governments as Secretary of State for Ireland and Chancellor of the Duchy of Lancaster 1859–64, and as Secretary of State for the Colonies 1864–66, in which role his primary achievement was facilitating Canadian federation; Bond (2004) 'Cardwell, Edward, first Viscount Cardwell' *ODNB*.
[2] The then government being Palmerston's Liberal administration.
[3] Palmer, elected a Conservative MP in 1857, crossed to the Liberals in 1859. He served both as Solicitor-General and Attorney-General, and was appointed (as Lord and subsequently Earl Selborne) Lord Chancellor in 1872 in Gladstone's administration; see generally Steele (2004) 'Palmer, Roundell, first Earl of Selborne' *ODNB*. Palmer's view – as Lord Chancellor – of the Act's effect is returned to below. Palmer attended school at Winchester, where he befriended Robert Lowe. Palmer's rise in status as a politician and lawyer mirrored Lowe's. When Palmer became Lord Chancellor in 1872, Lowe was Chancellor of the Exchequer.
[4] Collier achieved fame as a criminal defence counsel before becoming a Liberal MP in 1851. He was Solicitor-General and Attorney-General in various Liberal administrations, and was appointed to the bench in 1871; Pugsley (2004) 'Collier, Robert Porrett, first Baron Monkswell' *ODNB*.

colony's 'constitution'.[5] That is made clear by s.7 – the final section – which, unusually, had its own preamble:

> And whereas doubts are entertained respecting the validity of certain Acts enacted or reputed to be enacted by the legislature of South Australia: Be it further enacted as follows:
>
> **7. Certain Acts enacted by Legislature of South Australia to be valid.**
>
> All Laws or reputed Laws enacted or purporting to have been enacted by the said Legislature, or by Persons or Bodies of Persons for the Time being acting as such Legislature, which have received the Assent of Her Majesty in Council, or which have received the Assent of the Governor of the said Colony in the Name and on behalf of Her Majesty, shall be and be deemed to have been valid and effectual from the Date of such Assent for all Purposes whatever; provided that nothing herein contained shall be deemed to give Effect to any Law or reputed Law which has been disallowed by Her Majesty, or has expired, or has been lawfully repealed, or to prevent the lawful Disallowance or Repeal of any Law.

The South Australian controversy, considered in section II below, was not the sole reason for the CLVA's enactment. The statute also addressed more pervasive colonial 'constitutional' difficulties in which Queensland played a prominent role.

I. Constitutional Controversies in Early 1860s Queensland – Lutwyche

Cl.1 of the 1859 Queensland Order repeated the proviso in s.7 [BAA] of the 1855 Act that any Order creating such a colony would:

> Make provision for the Government of any such colony and for the establishment of a Legislature therein, in manner as nearly resembling the ... Legislature which shall be at such time established in New South Wales as the circumstances of such colony will allow; and full power shall be given by such ... Order in Council to the Legislature of the said colony to make further provision in that behalf.

Cl.1 immediately prompted two political disputes; each arose because in the brief period between 1855 and Queensland's creation the New South Wales Legislature enacted two significant political reforms: the 1857 repeal of the two-thirds clauses; and the 1858 franchise extension. The disputes raised the same question: was Queensland's constitutional law controlled by New South Wales law as it was in 1855 or in 1859?

The Two-Thirds Clauses in the Queensland Constitution – A Question of when ...

The obvious inference arising from cl.1's text – "... Legislature which *shall be at such time*[6] established in New South Wales" – was that the Order, whenever promulgated,

---

[5] Introduced through the 1850 Act s.32 process as the South Australia Constitution Act 1856.
[6] Emphasis added.

would give Queensland a Legislature identical to that of New South Wales *at the date that the Order was issued*. Had the Order been promulgated in 1856, that Legislature would have been subject to the two-thirds clauses. By 1859, those clauses had gone. This would suggest that Queensland's Legislature would come into being without such special majority clauses.

However, if one reads on into the Order, one finds cl.8, which points firmly in the opposite direction. Cl.8 states that all provisions contained *in the 1855 Act*:

> ... which relate to the constitution, functions and mode of proceeding of the Legislative Council and the Assembly respectively, and to the qualification and disqualification of electors and members of the Assembly, shall be of force within the said colony of Queensland, unless and until altered in the manner hereinafter specified; and shall be deemed to be incorporated in this present Order in Council.

The two-thirds provisions were certainly in the 1855 Act. The 'hereinafter specified' proviso can only be a reference to cl.22, which, as noted in chapter two, essentially reproduced the text of s.4 [BAA] of the 1855 Act, namely that Queensland's Legislature would have "full power" to alter any of the provisions of the Order in Council "in the same manner as any other laws for the good government of the colony ...".[7]

Linguistic carelessness in drafting colonial statutes was a recurrent feature of nineteenth-century British legislation; the 1859 Order perhaps shares that weakness. A superficial delineation of that controversy might focus solely on matters of chronology. Cl.8 strongly suggests that Queensland's Legislature would have the characteristics defined in the 1855 Act *as originally enacted*. Cl.1 implies – strongly – that Queensland's Legislature would have the characteristics defined in the 1855 Act *as subsequently amended*. Accepting that an express provision should override a mere implication, cl.8 indicates that the two-thirds provisos would apply. But this ignores the point that the relevant substantive provisions of cl.1 and cl.8 and of s.15 [s.17] and s.36 [s.42] are framed in quite different ways.

S.36 [s.42] was cast in very general terms, ie any law *'concerning'* the Legislative Council. Cl.8 seems to achieve a similar effect with a rather longer form of words, ie *'the constitution, functions and mode of proceeding of the Legislative Council'*. Cl.8's chronological reach would therefore be relevant, which would indicate that the special majority provisions would apply in Queensland to any mooted reform of the Council.

In contrast, s.15 [s.17] imposed the special majority proviso *only* on Assembly constituency apportionment laws and/or the number of members. The proviso did not extend to the qualifications of members or electors, or to any other aspect of the Assembly. However, cl.8 applies not only to the qualifications of members and electors, but also (as per the Council) to *'the constitution, functions and mode of proceeding of the ... Assembly'*. Cl.8 does not *expressly* include apportionment or number questions,[8] but it is credible to assume that such questions would be encompassed by the notion of the Assembly's 'constitution'. If so, cl.8's express chronological reach (ie the *1855 Act as originally enacted*) is also relevant to apportionment questions.

---

[7] Subject to the same reservation, disallowance and laying before provisos in s.4 [BAA].
[8] cf the assertion – not very fully reasoned – of Melbourne and Joyce (op cit p450) that the Order: "provided that the whole of the New South Wales Constitution Act should be applied to Queensland ... (fn. Sec 8)".

The wide drafting of cl.1 – *in manner as nearly resembling* – also credibly includes inter alia apportionment and number issues. Consequently, cl.1's implied chronological reach (ie the *1855 Act as subsequently amended*) would be relevant to such matters. But that implied reach would again be overridden by cl.8's express terms, so the special majority provisions of the 1855 Act would also apply in Queensland to apportionment and number questions.

However, this analysis overlooks a normatively higher level of abstraction. The 1859 Order was not a free-standing exercise of the prerogative, but was issued under s.7 [BAA],[9] which provided that the Order was to (emphasis added):

> ... make provision for the Government of any such colony, and for the Establishment of a Legislature therein, in manner as nearly resembling the Form of Government and Legislature *which shall be at such Time established in New South Wales* as the circumstances of the colony will allow ...

S.7 points expressly to New South Wales law *at the date any such Order is made*, and not the date the 1855 Act itself came into force, as the relevant date. This is the date impliedly provided for in cl.1. Cl.1, then, is chronologically consistent with s.7 [BAA]. Cl.8, which expressly points to the 1855 Act coming into force as the relevant date, is prima facie incompatible with s.7 [BAA], and so is presumptively ultra vires. The larger and more problematic consequence of that conclusion would be that any provisions made in pursuance of the chronology of cl.8 rather than cl.1 might themselves be invalid: crudely stated, the Legislature itself might be ultra vires the 1855 Act.

Any such incompatibility might be argued away by invoking the 'as the circumstances of the colony will allow' clause, ie that the Order chose through cl.8 to make the unamended 1855 New South Wales law applicable to Queensland because of the then (1859) circumstances of the colony. There is no evidence to suggest that such a choice was considered and made in the Colonial Office. The more likely explanation of the apparently poor fit between s.7 [BAA] and cl.8 is lazy thinking and slipshod drafting in the Colonial Office in 1859, akin to the drafting errors in the 1855 Act itself.[10] But while the point may have escaped the attention of Colonial Office officials and draftsmen, it caused acute political controversy immediately Queensland came into being over the pressing issue of identifying the electorate for the 1860 election.

The Initial Electoral Law – And Sir Alfred Lutwyche's View of the Constitution

The electoral districts were defined in a proclamation issued by Denison (qua interim Governor under the powers contained in cl.6 of the Order) on 31 December 1859 in the

---

[9] This was because the Order carved out portions of New South Wales territory, which territory as a matter of law existed through statute. Free-standing exercise of the prerogative could not have achieved that effect.

[10] A glaring example is cl.4, the last word of which identifies the Order as an 'Act', the (poor) reason being presumably that cl.4 verbatim repeats s.3 of sch.1 of the 1855 Act, in which the word 'Act' is apposite. In theory, s.7 [BAA] could have given the Order issued under it the status of an 'Act', but it did not do so expressly and there is no credible basis to assume that it was intended by Russell or British legislators that it did so impliedly. In its other clauses, the Order self-references correctly.

Queensland Government Gazette.[11] Denison's choice on that issue appeared more akin to Wentworth's political philosophy than to the 'democratic' sentiment then prevailing in New South Wales. The Queensland districts – which returned 26 members – were skewed distinctly to favour pastoral interests.

The more contentious issue was who within those districts could vote. The 1855 Act applied a relatively restrictive property threshold for the franchise in New South Wales. But that threshold was significantly loosened by the Electoral Act 1858.[12] Per (the implicit effect of) cl.1, the 1858 Act should determine the franchise for the first Queensland election; per (the express words of) cl.8, the 1855 rules would apply. But if cl.8 was in turn ultra vires s.7 [BAA], then cl.1 would be determinative. The answer would likely significantly affect the election's outcome: the 1855 criteria would be more favourable to the squatter interest than those of 1858.

Denison's proclamation assumed cl.8 to control the issue. He came to that view having asked the Chief Justice of New South Wales, Sir Alfred Stephen, for an advisory opinion.[13] Stephen's father John had been an early appointee to the New South Wales bench, where he developed a reputation for delivering robust, often intemperate opinions.[14] Alfred followed in his father's official footsteps and, using various family connections, managed to have himself appointed – with no significant legal experience – as Solicitor General in Van Diemen's Land in 1825. Although – as tradition then permitted – Stephen maintained an extensive private practice while Solicitor-General, he assiduously discharged his official responsibilities, and became Attorney-General in 1833. He subsequently took judicial office in New South Wales, and became Chief Justice in 1845. He intervened a little in subsequent debate about the structure of the post-1850 Legislature, advocating a mixed appointive/elective Council. He accepted Denison's invitation to become Council President in 1856, apparently seeing no conflict between his judicial and legislative roles until 1858, when he resigned the presidency.

Stephen's opinion on the chronology was clear:

> The answer to this question, I conceive ... is found in Clause 8 of the Order in Council. And I am of opinion, that, by the plain and unequivocal terms of that clause, the Qualifications both of electors and members in Queensland is established and is declared and ordered to be that which was created, or fixed by the Constitution Act of [1855].[15]

Assuming the Order was intra vires s.7 [BAA], Stephen was correct. However, he entirely overlooked s.7 [BAA].[16]

This was not just an abstract controversy. The June 1859 election in New South Wales involved voters who by December 1859 lived in Queensland. One-third of the electors who voted in that 1859 election had done so because of the 1858 extension of

---

[11] P16 et seq, www.textqueensland.com.au/item/journal/76f8c7c165766f9cc52232c780933004.
[12] P 60 above.
[13] Stephen's opinion is at *QGG* 31 December 1859 pp 20–21, www.textqueensland.com.au/item/journal/76f8c7c165766f9cc52232c780933004.
[14] http://adb.anu.edu.au/biography/stephen-john-1292.
[15] *QGG* 31 December 1859 p20.
[16] *QGG* 31 December 1859 pp 20–21. On first reading, cl.6 of the Order might also point towards an 'as amended' reading of the Act on this issue, but when cl.6 is carefully read it applies only to the machinery for running the election, including compiling voter lists, but not to voter qualifications.

the franchise; those voters were positively *disenfranchised* under Queensland electoral law by Denison's acceptance of Stephen's opinion.

Intriguingly, when Stephen produced this opinion he was embroiled in a bitter personal conflict with a liberal faction in the Assembly on the issue of whether he could be granted paid leave to spend a year in England, a conflict not resolved until April 1860 – and then not on terms Stephen wished. Whether this predisposed Stephen towards favouring a pre-1858 electorate in answering Denison's query is a matter for speculation. His overlooking of s.7 [BAA] is, however, peculiar. The peculiarity becomes more pronounced because in his opinion Stephen said that, before coming to a decision, he had conferred with his judicial colleagues, one of whom, since February 1859, had been Sir Alfred Lutwyche.

Lutwyche, a Charterhouse- and Cambridge-educated barrister and journalist, reached New South Wales – surviving shipwreck en route – in 1853. After establishing himself at the Bar, Lutwyche declined a seat on the Legislative Council in 1856, but subsequently accepted a seat and the office of Solicitor-General in Cowper's 1856 and 1857 ministries. He cultivated a reputation as a democratic reformer, positioning himself as an early champion of male adult suffrage, before accepting a Supreme Court seat in 1859. Lutwyche's seat was based at Moreton Bay, which became part of Queensland under the 1859 Order.

Lutwyche had difficulty accepting that being on the bench precluded political activity. He volubly criticised Denison's franchise decision – by extension acquiesced in by Bowen – and lobbied for new Imperial legislation to impose the New South Wales law in Queensland.[17] Bowen considered the matter should be dealt with by Queensland legislation; a solution Lutwyche doubted would lead to reformist legislation given that an election fought on the 1855 franchise would surely return a squatter-dominated Assembly.

While Lutwyche's motivations were to a degree 'party political' – in the limited sense of being antagonistic to the squatter interest – they were also 'constitutional'. It is difficult to accept that Stephen's December 1859 opinion had involved any meaningful conferral with Lutwyche. On 9 January 1860, Lutwyche had written to Governor Bowen suggesting he had not been consulted, and that he disagreed with Stephen's view:

> I should probably have come to the same conclusion if I had reasoned from their premises. But it seems to me that the root of the real question lies much deeper than the construction of the Order in Council. The question is does the 8th section of the Order in Council pursue the authority given by [s.7 [BAA] of the 1855 Act]?[18]

Lutwyche reasoned that s.7 [BAA] required Queensland law to follow 1859 New South Wales law. He saw no basis for assuming that the 'circumstances' clause would justify adopting the 1855 law and therefore: "the 8th section of the Order and Council is null and void".[19] He continued:

> Happily the error cannot be visited on the government of Queensland; but it is not difficult to foresee that it will occasion much discontent … it is not likely that the people of Queensland

---

[17] Evans (2007) *A history of Queensland* pp 80–81.
[18] The letter is reproduced in *BC* 29 August 1861 p2, http://nla.gov.au/nla.news-article4600736.
[19] ibid.

will be satisfied with a smaller measure of political privileges than are enjoyed by their fellow-colonists in New South Wales, Victoria and South Australia.

The proper solution, he suggested, was for the Imperial Parliament to pass an amending Act.

It would be erroneous to dismiss Lutwyche's concern with legal rigour as a product of partisan political obstructionism. Bowen's Commission appointing him Governor in 1859 had contained the following admonition immediately after a passage which referred to the various circumstances (some statutory, some identified in the Order) in which the Legislature was not permitted to make law by the ordinary bare bicameral majority plus Governor's assent process:

> ... [W]e ... hereby require and command that you do take *especial care* in making and passing such laws with the advice and consent of the said Legislative Council and Legislative Assembly the provisions regulations restrictions and directions contained in the said Acts of Parliament and in our said Order ... be *strictly* complied with ... (emphasis added)

Lutwyche's view – that the proposed election was to be fought on an unlawful basis – was rooted in such strict compliance. And his opinion was – if not rooted with quite such legal rigour – widely shared in Queensland.[20] The 1860 election was conducted with only 4790 voters on the electoral roll. Only 2176 votes were cast in the 26 seats.[21] There were no organised political parties; all 26 elected members were nominally 'independents'. Herbert (formally Colonial Secretary) became Premier and Pring remained as Attorney-General; both were elected unopposed. But as Lutwyche expected, there was little indication that the elected Assembly would favour populist electoral reform.[22] Indeed, Herbert promoted bills in 1862 and 1864 which would have added education and extended residence requirements which, if enacted, would likely have reduced the electorate.[23]

Herbert and Assembly and Council majorities took serious offence at Lutwyche's analysis, for immediately after the 1860 election a bitter dispute arose over the judge's salary. The Order had fixed the salary of a Queensland Supreme Court judge at £1200 pa. Under the 1855 Act, New South Wales Supreme Court judges received £2000. This seems to have been another error, rather than considered policy on the Colonial Office's part. Herbert's government promoted a new Supreme Court Bill which confirmed judicial salaries at £1200. Governor Bowen reserved the bill for the royal assent.

---

[20] See Shaw (1980) '"Filched from us"; the loss of universal manhood suffrage in Queensland 1859–1863' *Australian Journal of Politics and History* 372.

[21] http://elections.uwa.edu.au/electionsearch.lasso. Of those votes cast, a significant number were likely plural votes cast by the same person who had the requisite property in two or more constituencies. On the personalities returned, see Bernays op cit pp 7–10.

[22] cf Herbert's comment at the 1861 opening of the parliamentary session that he would: "introduce a bill for reforming the franchise, when the circumstances of the colony should appear to demand it. The present state of the law, in his opinion, gave the privilege of voting to every man who chose to obtain it, and he did not see that greater freedom could be accorded"; QLAD 30 April 1861p6, www.parliament.qld.gov.au/documents/hansard/1861/1861_04_30_A.pdf.

[23] Joyce (1978) 'George Ferguson Bowen and Robert George Wyndham Herbert: the imported openers' in Murphy and Joyce (eds) *Queensland political portraits*; Bernays op cit pp 209–10; Lauchs (2010) 'The return of manhood suffrage to Queensland, 1863–1872' *Journal of Australian Colonial History* 119.

Lutwyche then wrote to Bowen, on what he said was a confidential basis, on 20 July 1860.[24] Lutwyche said that he would refuse to accept a post on £1200 per year, on the twin bases that the £1200 figure in the Order was ultra vires the 1855 Act and that the Legislature had the power per cl.22 to restore the £2000 figure. Should Bowen respond to that refusal by suspending or removing Lutwyche from office, Lutwyche informed the Governor that he would bring legal proceedings in the Privy Council for loss of office and would petition the Queen to refuse assent to the Supreme Court bill. Lutwyche then added further fuel to the constitutional fire: repeating his view on cl.8 being ultra vires s.7 [BAA], he informed (threatened might be a more apposite characterisation) Bowen that:

> [u]nless some Imperial Act should be raised legalising the acts of this legislature in the meantime, the Judicial Committee of the Privy Council will, some fine day, set Queensland aghast. I believe that the Acts of this legislature will not be worth the paper they may be printed upon unless the Imperial Parliament intervenes ... And as the mere hint of such a doctrine would be sure to produce infinite confusion, I shall take steps to keep it to myself ...

Bowen passed the letter to Herbert, but it was not immediately given wider circulation.[25] Lutwyche's petition to the Queen repeated the assertion that the 1860 Assembly had been unlawfully elected, but then added a further reason for assuming that: "it is doubtful whether the legislature of Queensland, as at present constituted, possess [sic] any legislative power or authority".[26] This related to the Legislative Council. In 1859, per s.3 of sch.1 of the 1855 Act, legislative councillors would initially hold office for five years, after which they could be appointed for life. Cl.4 of the Order, however, empowered the Governor of Queensland to appoint councillors for life before that five-year period had elapsed; a power which Bowen had exercised. But, Lutwyche suggested, in that respect, cl.4 was ultra vires s.7 [BAA] and Bowen's appointments would have been unlawful.

Lutwyche's petition to the Queen to refuse the assent to the Supreme Court was successful, and the then Secretary of State (the Duke of Newcastle)[27] indicated that a £2000 salary was appropriate, whereupon in July 1861 the Legislature passed an amended bill. This was done with evident ill grace in both houses. On 26 July the Council passed a resolution fiercely attacking Lutwyche professionally and personally, concluding:

> (6) That this House ... feels constrained to place on record its condemnation the conduct of Mr Justice Lutwyche in practically evincing a political partisanship, calculated seriously to impair confidence in the administration of justice in this colony: also, in formally impugning the legality of the Constitution and Acts of Parliament of Queensland ...[28]

Some Council members seemed particularly perturbed[29] by Lutwyche's response to a letter sent to him by the Mayor of Brisbane, John Petrie, following a public meeting on 9 May 1861, which congratulated Newcastle on his decision to withhold assent to

---

[24] The letter is reproduced in *BC* 29 August 1861 p2, http://nla.gov.au/nla.news-article4600736.

[25] See the *QLAD* 1 August 1861 pp 11–12, www.parliament.qld.gov.au/documents/hansard/1861/1861_08_01_A.pdf.

[26] The petition, not dated, but presumably sent in July or August 1860, is in *BC* 29 August 1861 p2, http://nla.gov.au/nla.news-article4600736.

[27] P 32 above.

[28] *QLCD* 26 July 1861 pp 1–3.

[29] cf the comment of a Mr MacDougall *QLCD* 26 July 1861 p3.

the Supreme Court bill and hoped that Lutwyche would: "be long spared to exercise his functions for the benefit of the colony". In reply, Lutwyche expressed thanks and commented that: "it will be my constant endeavour ... not to swerve for one instant from the broad and plain path of duty, but to stand between the people and the crown, and to do justice to both".[30]

The Council's resolution, and its endorsement by the Assembly, then prompted a similarly fierce response in a leading article in *The (Brisbane) Courier* on 30 July 1861 that the Council's criticism of Lutwyche was ill-founded. The article was certainly vituperative. It lamented that the resolution:

> ... proved that men who are destitute of gentlemanly feelings, who lack common christian charity, who have an utter disregard for truth, who have not the slightest acquaintance with the first principles of justice, and who betray the most "crass ignorance" (as Lord BROUGHAM would say) on all matters connected with the history and constitution of their country, may yet figure among our senators ...

The 'crass ignorance' theme was returned to further on:

> ... [W]e find the President of the Legislative Council, and three or four other equally sapient members, resting on the declaration made by the Judge, in his letter to the Mayor of Brisbane, that he would "stand between the Crown and the people," as sufficient proof of partisanship. Can the force of stupidity go further? Where ought a Judge to stand, if not between the Crown and the people? The Judges are made independent of the crown and of the legislature, in order that they may not be tempted to side with the crown, as they were formerly too apt to do ... For our own part, we are very thankful that the people have such shield against oppression as the present Judge of the Supreme Court ...

The article concluded by accusing the Council majority of deliberately lying on several points in the resolution.

The Pugh Seditious Libel Case ...

Rather than letting the matter rest, the Council intensified the controversy by passing a resolution instructing the Attorney-General,[31] still Ratcliff Pring, to begin seditious libel proceedings against *The (Brisbane) Courier*'s publisher, Theophilus Pugh. Pugh, British educated, had emigrated to Brisbane in 1855 and worked initially for the *Moreton Bay Free Press*, a very pro-squatter journal. On joining *The (Brisbane) Courier* as editor in 1859 he championed a distinctly anti-squatter perspective, more in accord with his own political preferences.[32] Pugh may have authored the article, but there was widespread suspicion that Lutwyche had either contributed some of its pithier elements or provided helpful raw material. The indictment motion passed in the Council by nine votes to four on 1 August, and was approved in the Assembly that night by 11 votes to eight.[33]

---

[30] The letters are reproduced in *BC* 29 August 1861 p2, http://nla.gov.au/nla.news-article4600736.
[31] *QLCD* 1 August 1861 pp 1–3. Pring's response – "I have the honor to inform the council, that I shall consider it to be my duty to give effect to the request therein contained" – is at *QLCD* 9 August 1861 p5. Pring spoke in support of the Council's resolution against Lutwyche in the Assembly; *QLAD* 1 August 1861 p16.
[32] http://adb.anu.edu.au/biography/pugh-theophilus-parsons-4417.
[33] *QLAD* 1 August 1861 p18.

A leader in the *Rockhampton Bulletin and Central Queensland Advertiser* on 17 August 1861[34] castigated the majorities in both houses, suggested that Herbert was behind the initiative, and predicted that the Council was embarking on an ill-advised adventure:

> [T]he Legislative Council will appear to great disadvantage, absurdly so, in fact. If the prosecution takes place, the verdict rests with a jury of twelve, and such juries are not in the habit of lending their aid to the hampering of the press ... It is evidently the wish of the Minister, and the clique they have at control, to hound the Judge from the bench, but they will find the old gentleman a doughty antagonist yet. The fact is the Judge has the people at his back, while the Government crew have comparatively few sympathisers.

The warning proved prescient, although it was not really the jury that bloodied the Council's nose.

The indictment was grandiloquently framed, asserting inter alia that: "Pugh, being a wicked, malicious, seditious and ill-disposed person, and having no regard for the law of this colony", had "most wickedly and audaciously" sought to "make it to be believed that the said Legislative Council in Parliament assembled, were a most wicked base and corrupt set of persons".[35]

The judge presiding was, of course, Lutwyche. The hearing on 21 August lasted five and a half hours, beginning with the surreally ironic objection from Pugh's counsel, a Mr Jones, that if the Queensland Legislature had always been unlawfully constituted, then Lutwyche, who now held office under a Queensland statute,[36] was not actually a judge and so could not preside. After some bickering between Pring (leading the prosecution) and Jones, Lutwyche, one suspects with relish, concluded that while Jones's objection had force, he held judicial office under a New South Wales statute which granted him the requisite jurisdiction. Pring made submissions throughout the morning. After lunch, Jones, in submissions amounting to a hilarious tour de force even more critical of various Council members and more approbatory of Lutwyche than Pugh's article, sought to persuade the jury that nothing written therein was seditious because it was a perfectly fair comment on a matter of pressing political importance.

Jones was surely pitching his submissions to the presumably friendly political inclinations of the jury. It may be that he would have persuaded them. But the matter was largely taken out of their hands by Lutwyche's subsequent instruction as to the law.

Lutwyche's charge to the jury is an arresting blend of recourse to English judicial authority, liberal political theory and scarcely veiled personal sleights. He began by saying that he found himself qua judge in an invidious position, given that *The (Brisbane) Courier*'s article was largely directed to defending his own reputation; he would nonetheless do his judicial duty. That 'duty' apparently entailed him casting the Council majority as a motley body of slanderers sheltering behind parliamentary privilege.[37]

---

[34] P2, https://trove.nla.gov.au/newspaper/article/51554503.
[35] The indictment is reproduced, with a full record of the hearing, in *BC* 24 August 1861 p5, http://nla.gov.au/nla.news-article4600656. Lutwyche's charge to the jury is not included there, but is in *The Empire* 2 September 1861 p2, https://trove.nla.gov.au/newspaper/article/60484143.
[36] His acceptance was confirmed in the Assembly on 6 August 1861; *QLAD* 7 August 1861 p1.
[37] *BC* 24 August 1861 p5: "Unfortunately, experience tells us that men, who neither nature nor education have fitted for the position, occasionally find their way into Colonial Legislatures. Men of this stamp, sometimes from mere thoughtlessness, sometimes from the workings of an ill-regulated mind, indulge themselves by scurrilous attacks upon public and private character ..."

That privilege did not, however, protect councillors from public criticism of their political behaviour. With – presumably – some sarcasm, Lutwyche explained that such criticism should bear only upon a councillor's political conduct, not his private character. A critical citizen:

> could not be justified for example in saying, for instance, of one member that he was a murderer … or of another that he was an adulterer, a gambler and a drunkard; or of a third that he was a griping landlord and a tyrannical master to his servants.[38]

The general thrust of Lutwyche's charge to the jury was that *The (Brisbane) Courier*'s article was entirely justifiable. The coup de grace came, however, towards its end, when Lutwyche instructed the jury that seditious libel required an attack on *the government*: the Legislative Council was not, however, part of the government, but of the Legislature: "Theoretically as well as practically, the Legislature and the Executive are separate bodies, with distinct functions, and any attempt to amalgamate them would only result in confusion and disorder."[39] Pugh might properly have been prosecuted for the distinct offence of a *scandalous* libel vis-à-vis the Council, but that offence was not before the court.

The (Brisbane) Courier's report of the hearing suggested Lutwyche was pushing at a wide-open door:

> The jury having retired for a very brief period, returned with a verdict of "not guilty." Loud cheers, which his Honor at once suppressed, broke forth when the verdict was announced. During the whole of the trial the court was densely crowded.[40]

Lutwyche's Final Fling

Shortly afterwards, Lutwyche could also derive some satisfaction from the Imperial government's recognition that his analysis of the constitutional position concerning the franchise arrangements and the position of life appointee legislative councillors was correct.[41] The Australian Colonies Act 1861 was – inter alia – "An Act to remove Doubts respecting the Authority of the Legislature of Queensland" with both prospective and retrospective effect.[42] S.3 provided:

> … All the provisions made in the afore-mentioned Letters Patent and Order in Council of the said sixth day of June one thousand eight hundred and fifty-nine, for establishing the colony of Queensland, and for the government of the said colony, and for the establishment of a Legislature therein, shall be and be deemed to have been valid and effectual for all purposes

---

[38] The second descriptor was likely targeted at Pring; see Bernays op cit pp 11–12. I have not been able to establish the identities of Lutwyche's other targets.

[39] *BC* 24 August 1861 p5.

[40] *BC* 22 August 1861 p2, https://trove.nla.gov.au/newspaper/article/4600634. For Pugh's immediate reactions, see *BC* 26 August p2, https://trove.nla.gov.au/newspaper/article/4600634.

[41] See Newcastle's (very brief) second reading speech at *HLD* 21 March 1861 c 153. There was no discussion of the bill at Lords second reading, and although Hansard records (ibid) that the bill was committed for consideration to a committee of the whole, there is no record of any such debate. The bill was passed without amendment to the Commons. There was no substantive debate in the Commons on the issue Lutwyche raised either respecting Queensland per se or as a matter of relevance to all colonies; *HCD* 9 July 1861 c 632.

[42] 24 & 25 Vict c 44. The bill is indexed in Hansard as the 'Queensland Government Bill'.

whatever; and all acts and proceedings of the said government and Legislature shall be and be deemed to have been from the date of the said Order in Council of the same force and effect as if the last mentioned Order in Council had been in all respects valid and free from doubt.

Assent was given on 22 July 1861, and vindicated Lutwyche's analysis of the constitutional position. Given that it then took at least two months for communications between London and Brisbane, its enactment, although anticipated by the Governor and Herbert,[43] was not known about in Queensland when the Council passed its denunciatory resolution nor when Pugh's trial was held.[44]

The 1861 Act did not, however, end Lutwyche's 'constitutional objections'. A year later he raised the larger argument that because – in his view – two members of the Assembly elected in 1860 had not taken their seats in a lawful manner, all the measures enacted in the ensuing session were invalid.[45] Lutwyche's scarcely veiled threat that he might so decide in judicial proceedings prompted Governor Bowen to seek advice from Newcastle. Newcastle referred the matter to the British Government's Law Officers, who reported to him on 10 November 1862.[46] Roundell Palmer[47] was then Solicitor-General. The Attorney General was Sir William Atherton, a notably progressive Liberal politician, who had achieved distinction both at the Bar and as an academic author before being appointed a QC in 1851 and elected as a Liberal member for Durham in 1852. His served as Solicitor-General between 1859 and 1861, before becoming Attorney-General. His tenure in that post was brief, ill-health causing him to retire in 1863.[48]

Neither Atherton nor Palmer accepted Lutwyche's views as to the invalidity of Queensland Acts passed when some Assembly members may have taken their seats unlawfully:

> It appears to us, on principle, that the validity or invalidity of Acts of Parliament cannot be made to depend upon the legal sufficiency or insufficiency of the title to sit and vote of particular members of the Assembly, such members being, for the time, accepted and received by the Parliament itself as members thereof. It would be dangerous in the last degree if the validity and force of Acts of Parliament could be made to depend upon the due constitution, in whole or in any part or proportion, of the Parliament by whom [sic] they were enacted.[49]

---

[43] See Herbert's explanation of the measure at *QLAD* 22 May 1861 p2: "After the close of last session, the Judge [Lutwyche] petitioned her Majesty to disallow the Supreme Court Bill; and as the same petition expressed a doubt whether the Acts of the Queensland Parliament were not invalid, this petition was transmitted by the Governor at the Judge's request on the 4th October, 1860, and in transmitting it the Governor remarked, that as much confusion might arise from the possible refusal of the Judge to carry out the Acts of the Queensland Parliament, it would probably be safe to pass an Imperial Act removing his Honor's doubts."

[44] Bowen had, however, sent a message to the Assembly on 7 August (two weeks after the Council's resolution) both confirming Lutwyche's acceptance of the Queensland judgeship and saying that: "As to the alleged illegality of the present legislature, it was anticipated that an act had already passed the Imperial Parliament, and would arrive by the next mail, rectifying this defect"; *QLAD* 7 August 1861 p2, www.parliament.qld.gov.au/documents/hansard/1861/1861_08_07_A.pdf.

[45] The premise here being that the Legislature did not meet the requirements of the Order, rather than that the Order was ultra vires s.7 [BAA].

[46] The full report is most easily found in *Rockhampton Bulletin and Central Queensland Advertiser* 9 May 1863 p1, https://trove.nla.gov.au/newspaper/article/51558030.

[47] n 3 above.

[48] Spencer (2004) 'Atherton, Sir William' *ODNB*.

[49] n 46 above.

The Law Officers agreed that a judge of the Queensland Supreme Court did have the authority in certain circumstances to hold that Acts of the Legislature were invalid. This, however, was not such a circumstance:

> ... [I]f with the view of forming such an opinion he should embark upon an inquiry into the legal vacancy of certain seats for which members were permitted to sit and vote, and did sit and vote, we think he would take a very erroneous view of his duties and functions, and would justly expose himself to severe animadversion on the part of Her Majesty's government.

Although the Law Officers did not cite the case in their opinion, their view reflected the conclusion reached by the House of Lords in 1842 in *Wauchope*.[50] As noted in chapter two, applying the so-called 'enrolled bill rule' to a colonial legislature was problematic since the component parts of such legislatures (and the standing orders they adopted) would, unlike the Commons and Lords, have a statutory source. They could therefore, at least as a matter of theory, act ultra vires that statutory authority. The obvious inference from Atherton and Palmer's opinion does, however, seem to be that some internal proceedings of the houses of colonial legislatures did not raise a justiciable issue. As in Britain, the only solution for such a failing – if failing indeed there was – would be new legislation.

Newcastle's despatch enclosing and approving the report did not reach Queensland until early May 1863.[51] But while Lutwyche accepted the Law Officers' opinion, his more general antagonism towards many of the colony's politicians did not abate. The tension culminated in an extraordinary intervention by Lutwyche in the June 1863 Assembly election[52] in an address to the East Moreton electorate, published more widely in *The (Brisbane) Courier* on 28 May 1863.[53] Lutwyche began with a broad attack on the Legislature: "FELLOW ELECTORS, The first Parliament of Queensland has been dissolved. Let us hope that we may never look upon its like again." His critique caustically attacked the Herbert administrations for their fiscal profligacy in general and projected railway expenditure in particular, reiterated his populist position on the current franchise law – "We are certainly entitled to ask for a restoration of the franchise which was filched from us by the Order in Council of 1859 ..." – and ended with a personal denunciation:

> Perhaps it is unnecessary for me to add that I should not vote, under any circumstance, for Mr. Herbert, Mr Macalister, or Mr. Moffatt ... I have no confidence in them, collectively or individually. I look upon them as the agents of a despotism cloaked in the guise of responsible government.[54]

---

[50] (1842) 8 Cl & Fin 710; 8 ER 279; p 52 above.
[51] The despatch is also reproduced verbatim at https://trove.nla.gov.au/newspaper/article/51558028.
[52] In which Theophilus Pugh was returned as a member for Brisbane.
[53] https://trove.nla.gov.au/newspaper/article/3163541.
[54] Macalister, of whom more is said in ch 5, was a Scot who emigrated to Sydney in 1839. He had established himself as a solicitor by 1850, and won an Assembly seat in 1859. Originally a professed opponent of Herbert, he became Secretary for Lands in a Herbert administration in 1862; http://adb.anu.edu.au/biography/macalister-arthur-4055. Thomas De Lacy Moffat was a squatter with substantial landholdings. He had become Colonial Treasurer in 1862, but died in 1864 aged just 38; http://adb.anu.edu.au/biography/moffatt-thomas-de-lacy-4216. Both voted in the Assembly for the resolution criticising Lutwyche; *QLAD* 1 August 1861 p8.

Matters reached the point where Bowen had asked the British government if he might lawfully dismiss Lutwyche from office. The situation was, however, effectively defused by the arrival in the colony of a newly appointed Chief Justice, James Cockle.[55]

Cockle was born in Essex in 1819. After schooling at Charterhouse, he studied mathematics at Cambridge before being called to the Bar. As well as building a successful legal practice, Cockle developed a considerable reputation as an academic mathematician, an interest he maintained throughout his life. He was appointed directly to the Chief Justiceship in 1862, largely because it was assumed he would be unaffected by any political considerations in discharging the role. Cockle acquired a reputation as a careful and thoughtful judge, who indeed remained aloof from partisan politics, and served as Chief Justice until retiring in 1879.[56] One of Cockle's early successes, likely the result of his non-partisan reputation and courteously emollient personality, was to persuade Lutwyche to end his wrangling with the government and the Legislature and to concentrate on his judicial duties.

Tension between the judiciary and the government and legislature was not an exclusively Queensland phenomenon, however. In South Australia, similar forces were in play.

II. South Australia's Constitutional Crises – Boothby and Gwynne

The immediate cause of the difficulties in South Australia was the evident antagonism of one of the colony's (three) Supreme Court judges, Benjamin Boothby, to many of the political initiatives that the Legislature wished to undertake.[57] Boothby,[58] born in Nottingham in 1803, spent his early career working in his family's iron ore business. After dabbling on the fringes of radical electoral politics as a Chartist[59] and developing an interest in constitutional issues, Boothby was called to the Bar in 1841 at the

---

[55] See generally Bennet (2003) *Sir James Cockle; First Chief Justice of Queensland*. Chs 2–3 provide a more extensive account of Lutwyche's disputes.

[56] http://adb.anu.edu.au/biography/cockle-sir-james-3240; www.sclqld.org.au/judicial-papers/judicial-profiles/profiles/jcockle.

[57] cf McWhinney (1953) '"Sovereignty" in the United Kingdom and the Commonwealth countries at the present day' *Political Science Quarterly* 511, 5 –: "[The Act was] rendered necessary by the curious perversity of a colonial judge, one Mr Justice Boothby of South Australia, who persisted in holding statute after statute passed by the legislature of that colony invalid on the score of a supposed conflict with the English Common Law …" As suggested below, McWhinney rather misrepresents the reality. Boothby's views were not entirely 'perverse'; nor was he the only South Australian judge to hold (some – even most – of) them. More significantly, many of his opinions rested on the incompatibility of colonial statutes with Imperial legislation, not with 'English common law'.

[58] http://adb.anu.edu.au/biography/boothby-benjamin-3025; Williams (2007) 'Justice Boothby: a disaster that happened' in Winterton (ed) *State constitutional landmarks*; Swinfen (1970) op cit ch 11. Boothby's life and career have prompted a quite substantial body of academic literature. In addition to the Williams and Swinfen articles, I draw here on Taylor (2013) 'The early life of Mr Justice Boothby' *Adelaide LR* 167; Pike (1960–62) 'Introduction of the Real Property Act in Australia' *Adelaide LR* 169, 185. The most comprehensive source is an unpublished (but much cited) monograph: Hague (1992) *The judicial career of Benjamin Boothby*. The account I give here is necessarily rather selective.

[59] Taylor op cit pp 169–71.

advanced age of 38. He practised and published in the field of criminal law, and was appointed Recorder of Pontefract in 1849. Newcastle was a family friend, and promoted Boothby's appointment to the South Australian Supreme Court in 1853.

The First Dismissal Attempt

On arrival in Adelaide in August 1853, Boothby complained volubly about the inadequacy of his salary. Rebuffed by the colonial government on that issue, he immediately involved himself in criticism of aspects of the colony's proposals for its constitution under s.32 of the 1850 Act. He was especially vexed by the proposal (subsequently enacted as s.36 of the Constitution Act 1856) that judges could not sit in either the Assembly or the Council; he seemingly regarded himself as an ideal candidate for such office.[60]

Boothby's constitutional views were perhaps sincerely held,[61] but his increasingly acrimonious relationship with both houses of the Legislature and the colony's legal profession owed much to his bumptiously abrasive personality and a continuing conviction that his post was substantially underpaid.[62] Unlike Lutwyche in Queensland, Boothby did not have a substantial body of (party) political public support behind him[63] as he collided repeatedly with the colony's ministers and legislators.[64] Nor was Boothby on good personal or political terms with the then Governor, Richard MacDonnell, appointed in 1855. The son of a prominent Anglo-Irish family, MacDonnell practised as a barrister and subsequently served both as Chief Justice and Governor of the Gambia. MacDonnell's personal politics veered between the Conservative and reactionary. He also considered that the Governor should play an interventionist role in the colony's politics, and his personal relationships with many of the colony's politicians were consequently very uneasy.[65]

The Torrens Land Act ...

Boothby had engendered adverse press comment by his bombastic conduct of various criminal trials. But the initial cause of acute conflict between Boothby and the government

---

[60] There was no such ban in New South Wales, where the Chief Justice, Sir Alfred Stephen, was not just a member of the Legislative Council but also its President (pp 70–71 above), a position that Boothby likely craved in South Australia.

[61] Pike notes of Boothby: "he sincerely regarded himself as the champion of English judicial standards and never mitigated his abhorrence of colonial crudities and the impertinent suggestion of those who had never eaten dinners in the Inns of Court that rules formulated by centuries of tradition should be set aside for antipodean convenience': op cit 185.

[62] Williams op cit. Boothby had 15 children, which placed great strain on his personal finances. He had also run into substantial financial difficulties in England. Suggestions that Boothby acted corruptly on the bench to secure financial benefits are made in Moore (2013) 'The corruption of Benjamin Boothby' *ANZLH E-journal*.

[63] Lutwyche was very obviously a champion of 'liberal' political values contra a conservative/reactionary ministry in Queensland. Boothby never acquired such a distinctive cachet.

[64] As in New South Wales and Queensland, there were then no clearly organised political parties in South Australia.

[65] http://adb.anu.edu.au/biography/macdonnell-sir-richard-graves-4084.

and legislature was several judgments relating to the Real Property Act 1858.[66] The Act, which introduced the Torrens system of land registration, was opposed by many large landowners and some members of the legal profession who saw its simplification of land conveyancing as threatening their livelihoods.[67] Those livelihoods had been much enhanced by the chaotic nature of land transactions in South Australia since the 1830s, which – through several periods of manic speculation and frequent subdivision and resale of plots initially sold by the Crown – had attained extraordinary evidential uncertainty. The problem is nicely captured in Pike's study of the Act's origins:

> The early titles were little more than receipts issued by the Commissioner of Public Lands and the Colonial Treasurer who "in consideration of the *sum* of Lx sterling" granted "all that section of land numbered x and delineated in the Plan of the margin hereof, – together with all timber, minerals and appurtenances, to hold unto the said (purchaser), his heirs and assigns for ever". Neither the size nor the position of the section was specified and the marginal drawing was merely a rectangle around a number … so the district maps were often inaccurate in detail. To make matters worse, they were completely destroyed by fire in 1839, together with the surveyors' field books. New maps, however, carefully constructed, multiplied the errors, for survey marks had been obliterated and fences were erected "within a chain or so of the boundaries".[68]

The crux of the Torrens system was a system of government-administered land registration which would produce titles which could not be challenged in legal proceedings,[69] an innovation which Boothby found objectionable because it inter alia reduced the role of the judge in such proceedings, did away with the need for a jury, deprived the legal profession – especially the junior Bar – of much lucrative work and, perhaps most importantly for Boothby, deprived litigants in land disputes of the entitlement to have their argument resolved by a court.

By 1859, Boothby was one of three judges on the Supreme Court. The then Chief Justice was Sir Charles Cooper. Born in 1795, Cooper had practised at the English Bar from 1827 to 1838, when he was appointed to the judgeship of the South Australian Supreme Court, where he remained the sole judge until 1850.[70] Cooper, a man of conservative views and habits, gradually developed a reputation as a conscientious and able, if slow and hesitant, judge.[71]

The third judge, appointed in 1859, was Edward Gwynne.[72] Gwynne had qualified as a solicitor in England before emigrating to South Australia in 1837. He subsequently

---

[66] No 15 of 21 Vict 1857–58. See especially Pike op cit for discussion of these cases from a land policy perspective. The Act is at www.foundingdocs.gov.au/item-sdid-43.html.

[67] See generally Taylor (2008) *Law of the land: the advent of the Torrens System in Canada* chs 1 and 2. Torrens, the son of a prominent colonial official, emigrated to South Australia from Ireland. He had a short and controversy-ridden career as a civil servant before being appointed to the mixed Legislative Council in 1851 and subsequently being elected to the Assembly. He served briefly both as Colonial Treasurer and Premier, before returning to England in 1862; http://adb.anu.edu.au/biography/torrens-sir-robert-richard-4739.

[68] (1960–62) op cit p173.

[69] A certificate produced in accordance with the Act was to be conclusive evidence (save for certain specified exceptions) of title for the purposes of a defence against an action for ejectment: s.77 of the 1858 Act; re-enacted as s.118 of the Real Property Act (No 11 of 23 & 24 Vict 1860).

[70] Supreme Court Act (No 12 of 12 & 13 Vict 1849) provided for a second judge.

[71] http://adb.anu.edu.au/biography/cooper-sir-charles-1918.

[72] The Supreme Court Act (No 31 of 19 Vict 1855–56) seemingly – and imprecisely – permitted the appointment of additional judges.

read for the Bar and established a successful practice in various fields. As counsel, Gwynne clashed frequently with Boothby on criminal law matters, although he shared Boothby's distaste for the Real Property Act. He served briefly as a member of the (elected) Legislative Council and even more briefly (just 10 days) as Attorney-General before accepting the Court's third seat in 1859.[73] Shortly thereafter, the Supreme Court delivered several judgments interpreting the Real Property Act 1858[74] (and successive amendments thereto) in ways which substantially compromised the statute's apparent objectives.

Hutchinson v Leeworthy – *April 1860 – Judicial Invalidation of 'Repugnant' Colonial Statutes*

During submissions in *Hutchinson v Leeworthy* in April 1860,[75] Boothby indicated that some aspects of the Act – notably its conclusive certificate provisions in s.77 – might be inconsistent with English common law principle, and as such invalid on the basis of repugnancy to Imperial law. As noted in chapter one,[76] the statutory definition of repugnancy in New South Wales had varied – for no readily discernible reason – during the early nineteenth century. The history of repugnancy provisions relating to South Australia was similarly chaotic. The 1834 Act, in its provisions empowering the Monarch to appoint persons to make laws for South Australia, limited repugnancy regarding such laws only to the requirements: "of this Act". The 1836 Order simply repeated that provision. The 1842 Act repealed the 1834 Act and did not contain any repugnancy clause at all relating to laws enacted by new Legislative Council; s.1 stated only that the Council's power would be: "to make laws for the peace order and good government of the said colony". The 1850 Act, applicable to all the Australian colonies, provided in s.14 that the lawmaking powers of *the Legislative Councils created under that Act* were subject to a repugnancy clause framed in these terms: "that no such Law shall be repugnant to the Law of England" (s.14 did not further define the 'Law of England'). By 1855–56, those Legislative Councils were superseded by the Legislatures created pursuant to s.32. S.32 did not contain a repugnancy clause, nor did it refer to s.14. And since, in referring to bicameral legislatures, s.32 provided that such legislatures would be created 'instead of' (and not as an amended version of) the 1850 Act Legislative Councils, it is credible to assert that there was no *Imperial* statutory repugnancy clause in force vis-à-vis the s.32 legislatures. Whether a common law repugnancy principle applied to them, and, if so, with what scope, was equally uncertain.

South Australia's Constitution Act 1856 – arguably – enacted a colonial repugnancy clause. There is no such express clause in the Act. But s.1 provided that the bicameral Legislature: "shall have and exercise all the powers and functions of the existing Legislative Council", a form of words which might be construed as implicitly incorporating the s.14 repugnancy clause into *colonial* law.

---

[73] http://adb.anu.edu.au/biography/gwynne-edward-castres-3684.
[74] (No 16 of 22 Vict 1858).
[75] Reported at *SAR* 26 April 1860 p3, https://trove.nla.gov.au/newspaper/article/49891143.
[76] Pp 9–11, 15–16 and 20 above.

Assuming that construction to be correct, the 'law of England' formulation is manifestly imprecise. It is not textually limited to statute, but could obviously be thought to include statute, Orders in Council and the various forms of judge-made law, both in the narrow sense of specific cases and in the broader notion of underlying principle.[77] Nor is it on its face limited to such 'law' as was explicitly applicable to a colony.

In his subsequent judgment in *Hutchinson*,[78] Boothby was quite clear as to the Court's jurisdiction regarding colonial statutes:

> That the validity of any legislation in excess of the powers granted to the Parliament of this Province by the Imperial Parliament may be enquired into by this Court I have no doubt. The Parliament of this Province exists only by statutory creation, and legislates under restrictions imposed by [Imperial] statute.[79]

Boothby also suggested that 'repugnancy' – he identified the source of the concept as s.14 of the 1850 Act – vis-à-vis the 1858 Act would arise if that Act had removed a person's entitlement to have his claimed ownership of land determined in a court. Boothby did not cite either a statutory source or a specific judicial authority for that assertion, and it seems he was invoking a general notion of common law principle. In such circumstances, it would be the Court's duty to hold the Act invalid. However, since the Act allowed an applicant to have land registered to challenge in court *a refusal* to accept the registration, it necessarily followed as a matter of implication that a third party adversely affected by *an acceptance* of the applicant's application could do so as well. Repugnancy therefore did not arise on that issue.

Given that the Act did not address that matter at all, Boothby was engaging in some imaginative interpretation to reach that conclusion. But his comments as to the Court's jurisdiction to invalidate such 'Acts' were quite orthodox and, insofar as the repugnancy test was 'the law of England', his observations that repugnancy embraced common law principle were not implausible.[80]

Boothby was not a lone voice on either issue. During argument in April, Cooper had indicated that he saw nothing contentious about the notion that the court might invalidate colonial legislation. That power, he suggested, would arise in respect both of an inconsistency with an Imperial statute and with the common law. He seemed to construe that latter notion broadly, to embrace general principles and specific judicial authority, noting that if the effect of the colonial Act's certification clause was that: 'no enquiry can be made afterwards, and that a man can have no remedy and the land is taken from him, then it would be repugnant'. Cooper resolved the matter at the May hearing however by finding that the Act did not have such an effect. Gwynne did not offer judgment.

The 'constitutional' dimension of the Supreme Court's position became clearer when another Real Property Act case – *Payne v Dench*[81] – was pressed to an appeal against the

---

[77] This era predated the formal fusion of equity and common law in English law under the Judicature Acts 1873 and 1875. I refer here for convenience to all judge-made law as 'common law'.
[78] *SAR* 29 May 1860 p3, http://nla.gov.au/nla.news-article49892802.
[79] ibid.
[80] See pp 15–16 above.
[81] There are no official law reports for this era, although thorough accounts both of judgments and submissions appear in contemporary newspapers. Reports of many cases involving Boothby were subsequently

Supreme Court's judgment. The plaintiff was seeking the Supreme Court's permission to appeal. That was opposed by the defendant on, inter alia, the constitutional basis that the intended appellate court simply did not exist.

Payne v Dench – *April 1861 – The Constitutionality of the 'Court of Appeals'*

In the pre-1855 era, South Australia's then Legislature created a 'Court of Appeals' per the Supreme Court Act 1837 s.16.[82] The Court of Appeal was not an orthodox judicial body; its members were the Governor and the Executive Council (none were required by s.16 to be lawyers). The provision of such a 'Court' was not an unusual phenomenon in the early years of the Australian colonies' existence;[83] what was unusual about South Australia's Court of Appeals was that the Legislature apparently wished to retain it after the 1856 constitutional reforms were enacted. South Australia's Supreme Court Consolidation Act 1856 s.18[84] simply verbatim reproduced s.16 of the 1837 Act. This was done even though the Executive Council's composition was radically altered by the Constitution Act.[85] Prior to 1856, its members were Crown appointees holding office at pleasure. S.32 of the Constitution Act 1856 – in another example of the oblique way in which the s.32 reforms in all the Australian colonies created systems of representative and responsible government – required executive councillors also to be members of the Legislature, which, since both houses were elected in South Australia, lent their occupancy of office both a transient and politically partisan character.

The Court of Appeals' composition was listed in s.18 of the Supreme Court Consolidation Act 1856 simply as: "the Governor for the time being and the Executive Council", and it was afforded an extensive jurisdiction over the Supreme Court's judgments. No politician or official in either Britain of South Australia had thought it necessary – or, perhaps more likely, had thought about the point at all – to replace this 'Court' in 1856 with a more obviously judicial forum or simply to abolish it.

After some procedural wrangling, judgment in *Payne* was given by the Full Court on 16 April 1861. Gwynne had no difficulty in concluding that the Court of Appeals no longer existed. His primary reason was that the Constitution Act had not just altered the nature of the Executive Council, but had replaced the previous Council with a new one. Whereas the Council had previously been a Crown-appointed body, whose

---

collated in various parliamentary papers; these seem to be copies of press reports and are not available online. On *Payne v Dench* see especially *South Australian Advertiser* 7 November 1860 p3 (initial proceedings before Boothby), https://trove.nla.gov.au/newspaper/article/826197; 26 December 1860 p2 (submissions and judgment before Boothby), http://nla.gov.au/nla.news-article828278; *SAR* 19 March 1861 p3 (submissions before the Full Court), http//nla.gov.au/nla.news-article50019491; 18 April p3 (judgment of the Full Court), https://trove.nla.gov.au/newspaper/article/50017763.

[82] (No 5 of Wm IV 1837), www.austlii.edu.au/cgi-bin/viewdb/au/legis/sa/num_act/sca5o7wi1837292/.
[83] P 11, n 47 above.
[84] (No 31 of 19 Vict 1855–56), www.austlii.edu.au/au/legis/sa/num_act/sca31o19v18556260.pdf.
[85] This came into force after the Supreme Court Consolidation Act 1856, and so on orthodox principle would presumptively alter the effect of that Act to the extent of any inconsistency between them.

members served at the Crown's pleasure and who had no obvious 'political' affiliations, the Constitution Act requirement that members of the Executive Council be elected members of either the Assembly or Legislative Council meant that for them to serve as judges as well would be: "contrary to the general principles of the British Constitution".[86] Additionally, Gwynne held that since s.36 of the Constitution Act forbade judges from sitting in the Legislature, it must follow that members of the Legislature could not sit as judges.

Boothby concurred, approving both of Gwynne's reasons. Boothby's objection to the continued existence of the 'Court of Appeals' likely contained an element of personal objection to there being a 'Court' (other than the Privy Council) superior to the Supreme Court within the colony. But he and Gwynne were also motivated by what we would now recognise as separation of powers considerations, namely that in legal actions where the government was a party (either actual or interested) it was unacceptable for the colony's final Court of Appeals to be composed of government ministers. That general concern was underlined by the obvious particularistic consideration that a 'court' composed largely of ministers who promoted the Real Property Act reforms would likely reverse any Supreme Court judgment that compromised the Act's efficacy.[87] Only the plainest words in Imperial legislation would persuade Boothby that such a 'court' could exist.

Neither Boothby nor Gwynne was dissuaded from their conclusion view by the obvious fact that the 'Court of Appeals' had not been *expressly* abolished by the Constitution Act 1856 Act or Imperial legislation. As noted above, the implied repeal or amendment of statutory provisions by subsequently enacted legislation was an accepted tenet of British constitutional theory and practice in 1860. Whether that tenet was applicable to these two Acts rests on a straining of orthodox principle. Had Boothby and Gwynne looked carefully at English authority they would have found clear support for the proposition that courts should be most reluctant to assume that a very specifically focused statutory provision (as s.18 was) could be impliedly overridden by a subsequent provision having a much broader application (as did the alteration to the composition of the Executive Council).[88] The more credible analysis from an orthodox (conservative) legal perspective was that such implied inconsistency would not even be assumed, and even it were it could be overcome by reading s.18 as "the Governor and the Executive Council for the time being". That such a court might be as Gwynne had put it: "contrary to the general principles of the British Constitution" did not per se point to its legal invalidity (unless one adopted a very expansive notion of 'repugnancy').

---

[86] This was, although Gwynne did not acknowledge the point, an application of repugnancy doctrine.

[87] Boothby also asserted – without offering authority – that the Legislature could not permit the appointment as judges of: "any person not educated by the practice and administration of the law". Much of Boothby's reasoning is obviously rooted in notions of 'repugnancy' which embraced quite abstract British constitutional principle.

[88] See eg *Fitzgerald v Champneys* (1861) 70 ER 958, where Wood VC (at 968) explained the rationale for the principle, expressed in the Latin maxim *generalia specialibus non derogant*: "In passing the Special Act, the Legislature had their attention directed to the special case which the Act was meant to meet, and considered and provided for all the circumstances of that special case; and, having so done, they are not to be considered by a general enactment passed subsequently, and making no mention of any such intention to have intended to derogate from that which, by their own Special Act, they had thus carefully supervised and regulated." Maxwell's (1875) *Interpretation of statutes* devotes pp 157–65 to the principle, illustrating it almost entirely with pre-1860 judgments.

Cooper agreed with his colleagues' reasoning as to the present non-existence of a Court of Appeals in that form, although he also held that the legislature's general lawmaking power under s.1 of the Constitution Act would enable it to create a new Court of Appeals if it so wished.

That conclusion was promptly acted upon, although Cooper might have been surprised that the Court of Appeals Act 1861[89] retrospectively overrode *Payne* and provided simply that the Court of Appeals – composed of the Governor and the Executive Council for the time being – had always been and would continue to be a court to which appeals from the Supreme Court could be taken.

McEllister v Fenn – *June 1861 – The Invalidity of 'Acts' Consented to by the Governor in Breach of his* Instructions

On 26 June 1861, Boothby handed down judgment in *McEllister v Fenn*.[90] This was a slander action in which the slander complained of was that the defendant– a well-known barrister – had committed an offence under the Real Property Act. One line of the defence was that the Act was invalid; consequently there could be no such offence and so nothing defamatory had been said.

In a lengthy judgment, Boothby accepted that argument. He began – uncontentiously – by restating a basic constitutional principle:

> On this question of the jurisdiction of this Court to decide on the validity of the legislation of the Parliament of this province I have already given my opinion in the case of Hutchinson v. Leeworthy; the judgment in which case was given now thirteen months ago …

The narrow ground of Boothby's conclusion that the Act was invalid was that the Governor had acted in breach of his *Instructions* in not reserving the bill for the Queen's personal assent. Boothby's reasoning proceeded through several stages, each of which was decided on a credible, if not compelling, basis:

> Such a Bill, therefore, the Governor-in-Chief was erroneously advised to give his assent to; and having given it, contrary to the royal instructions, such assent is invalid, and cannot give the force of an Act of Parliament to such a Bill.

The Governor's *Instructions* in place when the bill was passed included the familiar proviso as to the types of bill to be reserved for the Queen's assent.[91] One such proviso in the 1856 *Instructions* was:

> [A]ny Bill of an extraordinary nature and importance, whereby our prerogative, or the rights and property of our subjects not residing in the colony, or the trade and shipping of the United Kingdom and its dependencies, *may be prejudiced*…[92]

---

[89] (No 5 of 24 and 25 Vict 1861) assented to on 31 August 1861. In anticipation of obstruction from Gwynne and Boothby, the Act imposed (in ss.3–4) obligations on Supreme Court judges to furnish the Court of Appeal with all necessary papers for the relevant appeal to be conducted; www.austlii.edu.au/cgi-bin/viewdb/au/legis/sa/num_act/coaa5o24a25v1861268/.

[90] *SAR* 27 June 1861 p3, https://trove.nla.gov.au/newspaper/article/50018147. References to the judgment in this section are to this source, which in the original is on one page, so I have not footnoted those references.

[91] Pp 21 and 55–56 above.

[92] The emphasis here and in the quotation below is in Boothby's quotation of the proviso.

When the 1858 Act was amended and consolidated by the 1860 Real Property Act, new *Instructions* were in force which expressed that proviso in a slightly different form:

> Every Bill which you shall consider to be of an extraordinary or unusual nature, or requiring our special consideration thereupon, *particularly such as may affect the property*, credit or dealings of such of our subjects as are not usually resident with ... South Australia.

Boothby did not think any discussion was needed as to whether the Real Property Acts fell within those categories, nor that the Governor had breached his *Instructions* by failing to reserve the bills.[93] The next question was what legal consequence flowed from that failure. Boothby's reasoning here began with s.12 of the 1850 Act, which made applicable to all Australian colonies the provisions in the Australian Colonies Constitution Act 1842[94] concerning inter alia reservations of bills and the Governor's *Instructions* on that matter. Two sections of the 1842 Act were relevant here. S.40 empowered the Crown to issue *Instructions* to the Governor concerning assent and reservation, and provided that: "It shall be the duty of the Governor to act in obedience to such instructions." S.31 stated that the Governor's discretion as to assent or reservation was "subject ... to the provisions contained in this Act and to such instructions as may from time to time be given in that behalf by Her Majesty".[95]

Boothby was certainly correct therefore in asserting that the requirement that the Governor follow his *Instructions* had: "a statutory force, and to be considered in reference to the validity of any assent given to the legislation of the Parliament of the province by the Governor, in Her Majesty's name". He was on less secure ground in the conclusion that a breach of the *Instructions* necessarily rendered any affected Act invalid. As previously noted, neither the 1850 Act nor the 1842 Act, or the 1828 Act, had identified expressly the legal consequences of such a breach. But Boothby's proposition was certainly plausible.[96] He also noted that he was drawing attention to a very important – and thus far overlooked – issue:

> The question as to the operation, with the force of law, of Acts of the Parliament of this province, is of so serious importance that I am surprised that the provisions of 5 and 6 Vict c.76 [the 1842 Act] have not, in the time I have had a seat on this Bench, been brought before the Court for judicial decision. In closely examining this Statute I am of opinion that it has been dangerously disregarded, and so risked the security of past legislation, probably to an extent that will require an Imperial Act to remove all doubts as to the validity of legislation since the coming into operation of 13 & 14 Vict c.5 [the 1850 Act].

Boothby also alluded to another possible consequence of s.12 of the 1850 Act. S.33 of the 1842 Act contained a provision relating to the coming into effect of bills reserved for the Queen's assent. Such bills would not have 'any force or authority in the colony' until the Governor had informed the colony's Legislative Council that the Queen

---

[93] Boothby overlooked or deliberately ignored the point that the later *Instructions* contained the "which you shall consider" phrase, the obvious implication of which is that the *Instructions* did not order the Governor to reserve a bill if he did not consider if to have the specified effects.
[94] Pp 19–21 above.
[95] Emphasis added.
[96] More so if limited to specific parts of the 'Act'. But Boothby also less plausibly suggested that invalidity would afflict the entire Act, not just specific repugnant provisions.

had given her assent, the Governor's message was recorded in the Council's official journal and a copy of the message was recorded by the Registrar of the Supreme Court. In Boothby's view, non-compliance with any such requirement would invalidate a colonial Act assented to by the Queen.

Again, there was no indication in the 1842 Act itself as to the consequence of such non-compliance. But the main – and obvious – objection to Boothby's analysis is that the 'Legislative Council' referred to in s.33 no longer existed, and so the requirements listed in s.33 had disappeared – albeit without express repeal – along with the Council itself.

The First Addresses for Removal and Boothby's 'Evidence' to the Assembly

Boothby's conduct and judgments, and the views he expressed from the bench, had antagonised many members of both the Assembly and the Council by mid-1861, to the point that both houses established committees to inquire into the correctness of Boothby's constitutional opinions. The not very veiled threat that accompanied these initiatives was that both the Assembly and the Council were taking the first steps needed to activate the power bestowed on the Queen by s.31 of the Constitution Act 1856 to remove a judge from office. S.30 – as in the other colonies – provided that Supreme Court judges were to hold office during good behaviour. But, per s.31: "It shall be lawful, nevertheless, for Her Majesty, Her Heirs and Successors, to remove any such Judge or Judges upon the address of both Houses of the said Parliament."

Given that Gwynne was evidently as willing as Boothby to identify constitutional objections to the validity of legislation, it seems likely that Boothby's eventual singling out by legislators and MacDonnell as a problem that needed to be removed owed as much to Boothby's abrasive character as to his constitutional theories. On 17 August 1861, MacDonnell sent a long despatch to Newcastle[97] deprecating both Boothby's legal ideas and his personality. That deprecation – widely (but certainly not universally) shared within the Legislature and in the colony's press – stemmed in large part from the style as well as the substance of the views Boothby expressed.

Boothby declined to assist the Council's inquiry, but cooperated after a fashion with the Assembly. He gave evidence over several days in mid-August 1861, 'answering' a list of 180 questions.[98] Although Boothby declined to discuss specific cases, he offered clear opinions on various legal issues. The cumulative impact of those opinions was also clear: that much of the colony's legislation was invalid, occasionally because of its incompatibility with (a broad notion of) the common law, but more often because it had not been 'enacted' in accordance with the requirements of Imperial statutes.

---

[97] A full copy is most readily found in the *SAA* 23 June 1862 p4, https://trove.nla.gov.au/newspaper/article/31811910.

[98] 'Answering' because it seems that Boothby substantially altered his oral evidence when he submitted his written version of that evidence for publication; *SAR* 12 September p2, https://trove.nla.gov.au/newspaper/article/877484. There are verbatim reports of the written evidence at *SAR* 11 September 1861 p2, http://nla/gov.au.nla.news-article50084957; 12 September 1861 p3, https://trove.nla.gov.au/newspaper/article/50084522; 16 September p3, https://nla.gov.au/nla.news-article50085470. In the following pages numbers in [] denote the number of the question and answer in the proceedings.

Some of these ideas had already appeared in Boothby's judgments or his musings from the bench during submissions;[99] others seem to have come to him more latterly.

The potentially most important issue derived from s.32 of the 1850 Act:[100]

> [136] It is quite clear that everything done under this clause must be reserved and must also be laid for thirty days before both House of Parliament before Her Majesty the Queen can declare her pleasure thereon.

That assertion is perfectly sound. Boothby was on similarly firm legal ground in suggesting that electoral apportionment laws fell within s.32:

> [138] What I want to point out to the Committee is the danger of pursuing a course which leaves anything open to doubt. The two Houses should exercise the utmost care in preventing any Bill from being left open to doubt, because the powers of the Houses are restricted by statute; and *if these are passed or transgressed the validity of everything is in danger* ... The only safe way of dealing with Electoral Bills is to reserve them for assent by Her Majesty ...

The significance of the '*everything is in danger*' point lay in the fact that the Electoral Act of 1856,[101] which drew the Assembly's constituency boundaries (the Legislative Council was given a single state-wide constituency) and prescribed the method of election of Assembly and Council members, had not been reserved. According to Boothby, if that Act was invalid – and he was sure that it was – then South Australia's current Legislature had no lawful basis and *all* of the 'legislation' it had 'enacted' would also be invalid.

Boothby was also pressed on the issue of judicial precedent, and more precisely on the question of whether a single judge sitting at first instance was bound to follow a judgment of the Full Court which he considered incorrect. Boothby's responses on this point were lengthy and repetitive, but would likely have left observers with the distinct impression that were many circumstances in which a judge sitting alone would not be bound by a Full Court decision. The line of questioning was presumably intended to ascertain if Boothby's views could be rendered irrelevant by a majority on the Full Court without any need arising to have Boothby removed, although, since Gwynne agreed with him on some of these issues, it was not evident that such a majority would soon appear.

Boothby was not, however, setting himself up as the ultimate arbiter of the validity of colonial legislation. He readily accepted that he would follow any Privy Council

---

[99] "68 [As to the Real Property Act] ... I expressed in my judgment in the case of McEllister v. Fenn the opinion that it removes trial by Jury in matters relating to the ownership of land, as provided by Magna Charta and the Bill of Rights, and so saps the fundamental principles of the constitution of the British Empire as to the security of every man's estate ... And because a Bill having such provisions *was not reserved for Her Majesty's consideration in obedience to her instructions*, the Privy Council would hold for such reason that it was invalid, as being repugnant to the law of England" (emphases added). Boothby similarly endorsed the correctness of his (and Gwynne and Cooper's) conclusion in *Payne v Dench*, but on broad moral grounds rather than narrow legal ones: "[148] ... The validity of an Act cannot be determined by the supposed Court of Appeal here ... [149] It would be against natural justice. The Judges of that supposed Court would be sitting in judgment on the lawfulness of their own proceedings as legislators. A case decided by the Lord Chancellor has been set aside, because he was deciding on a matter relating to some railway in which he was a small shareholder ... The first principles of justice require that the Judges who may form any court shall not decide a question in which they may be interested." (The case alluded to is *Dimes v Grand Junction Canal* (1852) 3 HL Cas 759; 10 ER 301.)

[100] Pp 29–30 above.

[101] No 10 of 19 Vict 1855–56.

judgment that held his view incorrect, and also repeated insistently that it would be a prudent course for the South Australian government to request the Imperial Parliament to enact legislation removing the doubts that he had raised.

Boothby's case before the Assembly had been championed – on the basis of principle rather than personality – by Richard Hanson, then perhaps the most eminent politician and lawyer in the colony. Hanson was born into a middle-class Methodist family in Cambridge. He grew up with radically – and very visibly – non-conformist religious views. He had a wide-ranging career, both geographically and professionally, working variously in London, Canada and New Zealand as an attorney, civil servant and as a journalist. He subsequently emigrated to South Australia in 1846, qualified for the Bar and immersed himself in the colony's politics. He was elected to the mixed Legislative Council in 1851 and the Assembly in 1857, serving at various points as Attorney-General and then as Premier from September 1857 to May 1860.[102]

Hanson had no reason to feel either professional or personal fondness towards Boothby. As counsel, he had frequently been the target of Boothby's criticisms from the bench, and was also the promoter (as Attorney-General and Premier) of legislation which Boothby regarded as invalid. Hanson nonetheless was firmly insistent that the judges had jurisdiction to assess the validity of legislation, and asserted that if Boothby was wrong on matters of law the proper forum to correct him was the Privy Council.

Hanson's view initially prevailed in the Assembly, where the proposal that the Queen be petitioned to remove Boothby from office was defeated. The Legislative Council – where deliberations had not been informed by such judicious reasoning – reached the opposite conclusion. However, despite the obvious orthodoxy of Hanson's arguments, the clamour in much of the colony's press against the Assembly's original decision was sufficiently powerful to persuade some Assembly members to change their minds. The political tension was so acute that the then government resigned from office so that a new ministry might be formed for the sole purpose of carrying a vote to seek Boothby's dismissal.[103]

Boothby nonetheless apparently saw no good reason to alter his views. In another hearing of *McEllister v Fenn* on 6 October 1861, both Gwynne and Boothby intimated during submissions that the Court of Appeals Act 1861 was invalid.[104] On 9 October 1861, a motion to send an address to the Crown seeking Boothby's dismissal was carried by 21 votes to 14.[105] Two weeks later, Governor MacDonnell sent the addresses requesting Boothby's dismissal to Britain.

---

[102] http://adb.anu.edu.au/biography/hanson-sir-richard-davies-3710. As in New South Wales and Queensland at this time, governments did not have an obviously party political identity.

[103] For a much more detailed account, see Williams op cit pp 31–35; Hague op cit pp 81–91.

[104] *South Australian Weekly Chronicle* 12 October 1861 p6, https://trove.nla.gov.au/newspaper/article/90031785.

[105] *SAR* 10 October 1861 p2, https://trove.nla.gov.au/newspaper/article/50079385. The text of the motion was unequivocal: "I. That an humble address be presented to our Sovereign Lady the Queen, setting forth that, in consequence of the position assumed by His Honor Mr. Justice Boothby, public confidence in the administration of the laws is destroyed, the validity of titles thrown into doubt, ruinous litigation threatened and the whole system of legislation in the Province involved in confusion, contradiction, and contempt: and praying that Her Majesty will be most graciously pleased to remove Mr. Justice Boothby from his office as Judge of the Supreme Court of this province."

McEllister v Fenn (again) – November 1861 – The Continued Non-Existence of the Court of Appeals

Boothby did not take that as a cue to adopt a less confrontational position. Judgment in *McEllister* was delivered on 8 November 1861.[106] Gwynne's brief judgment was blunt as to the effect of the 1861 Act: "I have already expressed my opinion in the case of *Payne v Dench* that the old Court of Appeal has died out, and that no competent authority has established a new one. I still adhere to that opinion."[107]

Boothby was similarly terse:

> … The argument for the plaintiff, resting on the effect of the Act of the present session, as giving legal validity to a Court of Appeal within the province, cannot prevail: for if the Legislature, as the judgment of this Court has pronounced, had no authority without an enabling Act of the Imperial Parliament to establish such a Court, that state of the law is not altered by the Parliament of this Province declaring to the contrary.

Cooper delivered an extempore judgment, in which he said he had changed his opinion in *Payne*. He did not offer a clear explanation for so doing. This was his last contribution to the colony's constitutional jurisprudence. In poor health and evidently wearying of the tension between the colony's judges and politicians, Cooper sought early retirement; legislation passed in late 1861 granted him a generous pension.[108]

Boothby – in a sign of his apparently growing detachment from political reality – had expected to be Cooper's successor. MacDonnell unsurprisingly regarded that expectation as preposterous, as did most members of the Legislature. Gwynne was also not regarded as a credible candidate. The position was given instead to Hanson.

Writing before news of *McEllister* reached London, Newcastle had informed MacDonnell that the British government would not disallow the Court of Appeals 1861 Act, but did so in obviously disapprobatory terms:

> But I think it necessary to record my regret that the Legislature of South Australia should have found it necessary to sanction and perpetuate a Court which, in its present shape, exists only by accident, and of which the composition is such as to be wholly indefensible on any Constitutional principle.[109]

Newcastle would likely not have anticipated that by the time his despatch reached Adelaide the Supreme Court would have held the Act invalid. His 'regret' was rooted in the objections that Boothby had identified: the obvious lack of legal competence of the 'court's' members and their similarly obvious vulnerability to being presumed to act on the basis of partisan political considerations. From the perspective of political morality, if not strict legality, the then British government was evidently in some

---

[106] *SAR* 9 November 1861 p3, https://trove.nla.gov.au/newspaper/article/50080889.
[107] ibid.
[108] Cooper's Pension Act 1861 (No 11 of 24 & 25 Vict). The pension of £1000 per year (two-thirds of Cooper's salary) was expressly stated (s.2) to be free of all taxes and charges. Cooper was then 66. He lived to 91.
[109] Newcastle to MacDonnell, Despatch No 3 of 1862, 20 January 1862, reported verbatim in *South Australian Weekly Chronicle* 17 May 1862 p7, https://trove.nla.gov.au/newspaper/article/90258800.

sympathy with Gwynne and Boothby's reasoning and conclusions in *Payne* and *McEllister*.

Colonial legislators also seemed to concede that Boothby's evidence to the Assembly in August as to the need for electoral reform bills to be reserved per s.32 was correct. On 29 November 1861, a new electoral bill[110] was reserved for the royal assent.

The Imperial Government's Response to the Dismissal Addresses

By the time Newcastle's reply to the dismissal addresses was received in Adelaide (11 June 1862), MacDonnell's term as Governor had ended (he was appointed as Lieutenant Governor of Nova Scotia in March 1862). MacDonnell was succeeded by Sir Dominick Daly. Daly came from an eminent Irish catholic family. He pursued a career in the colonial civil service and, after spending many years in Canada, served successively as Lieutenant Governor of Tobago and Prince Edward Island. Daly was much more moderate in his political views than MacDonnell, and more inclined to follow rather than seek to guide the colony's elected politicians.[111]

The reply made unhappy reading for the legislators who had sought Boothby's dismissal. Newcastle had referred the addresses to Atherton and Palmer, with a series of questions relating firstly to the correctness of Boothby's legal analyses and secondly to the propriety of the Queen removing Boothby from office. Newcastle had done so, he explained to Daly, with an essential constitutional principle in mind:

> It is of vital importance, not only to the colonies, but to all those who have dealings with them, of whatever kind, and to the Imperial Government itself, that these [colonial] Courts should exercise their functions in entire independence, not only of the Local Executive, but of the popular feelings which are from time to time reflected in the Legislature. Or of any political party which may happen to be in the ascendant ...[112]

While Newcastle's despatch offered a ringing endorsement of theoretical constitutional principles, the accompanying Law Officers' report (of 12 April 1862) was a document largely devoid either of authority or legal reasoning. It moved from repeating the questions asked to offering answers to them without troubling to engage with the intervening stages of argument and evaluation. Much the largest question had been answered in an opinion included in Newcastle's despatch of the previous day: namely, whether the Governor's failure to reserve the Electoral Act bill for the royal assent as expressly required by s.32 rendered that Act invalid.

Atherton and Palmer accepted that Boothby's view on this matter was correct: both as to the invalidity of the Electoral Act itself *and consequentially of all subsequent South Australian legislation*. The Law Officers' view on that final point had led to the

---

[110] 'Enacted' as No 20 of 24 & 25 Vict 1861. The reason for the ' ...' is addressed below. See www.austlii.edu.au/cgi-bin/viewdb/au/legis/sa/num_act/ea20o24a25v1861196/.
[111] http://adb.anu.edu.au/biography/daly-sir-dominick-3359.
[112] The reply and appended Law Officers' opinion is most easily found at *SAR* 12 June 1862 p3, https://trove.nla.gov.au/newspaper/article/50171332.

immediate enactment of retrospective validating legislation, formally titled 'An Act to explain an Act, intituled An Act for the Better Government of Her Majesty's Australian Colonies 1862'.[113] As Newcastle put it in his despatch to Daly:

> I have not lost a moment in applying to Parliament to relieve the colony of South Australia from the embarrassments into which it would have been plunged by the public adoption of this opinion, based as it appears to be on conclusive grounds.

Perusal of Hansard[114] suggests that Newcastle's allusion to 'applying to Parliament' should not be taken as an indication that the measure was either carefully explained to or considered by members of the Commons or Lords:

> **THE CHANCELLOR OF THE EXCHEQUER** said, it would be a great convenience for the public business if this Bill, which stood as the seventh order of the day for its third reading, were passed at once, that it might go up to the House of Lords that night, and be ready for the Commission which was to give the Royal assent to certain Bills to-morrow. He had, therefore, to move that the six previous orders of the day be postponed, to allow the measure to be proceeded with first.
>
> **SIR HENRY WILLOUGHBY** said, he believed that the Bill was harmless, but it had been read the second time before printed copies of it were delivered to hon. Members; and he must protest against the practice of hurrying through measures before the House had the opportunity of making itself conversant with their provisions ...
>
> *Ordered*,
>
> That the first six Orders of the Day be postponed till after the Order of the Day for the Third Reading of the Australian Colonies Government Act Amendment Bill.
>
> Bill read 3°, and *passed*.[115]

The Act's effect – exhibiting perhaps an abundance of caution on the Imperial government's part – was not limited to South Australia. Its preamble referred to (s.32 of) the 1850 Act and to subsequent Imperial and colonial legislation passed to implement s.32:

> 1. ... Every Act passed for the purposes mentioned in the said first-recited Act, or any of them, by the legislative council of any of the said colonies, and assented to in Her Majesty's name by the Governor of such colony, shall be deemed to be and to have been from the date of such assent as valid and effectual for all purposes whatever as if the same Act had been reserved for the signification of Her Majesty's pleasure, and as if the same had been duly laid before both Houses of Parliament, and as if Her Majesty's assent had been duly given ...
>
> 3. ... Every Act passed by any colonial legislature established under any such Acts or Act as aforesaid, for altering the constitution or mode of election or appointment of any or either of the legislative bodies composing such legislature, which may have been at any time heretofore assented to in Her Majesty's name by the Governor of the colony ... shall be deemed to be and to have been from the date of such assent as valid and effectual for all purposes whatever as if the same Act had been reserved for the signification of Her Majesty's pleasure thereon, and as if Her Majesty's assent had been duly given ...[116]

---

[113] (25 & 26 Vict c 11). The Act is often referred to as the Australian Constitutions Act 1862.
[114] *HCD* 10 April 1862 c 768.
[115] There is no indication in Hansard that the bill was discussed in the Lords. It received royal assent the next day.
[116] The Act had only three sections.

The Law Officers' more wide-ranging report of 12 April 1862 began by endorsing the view stated by Boothby, Gwynne and Cooper that a colonial Supreme Court was: "in our opinion bound (and certainly at liberty) to satisfy itself of the legal validity of any Act of the Colonial Legislature, the provisions of which it is called on to administer".

However, Atherton and Palmer disagreed with Boothby's analysis of the legal consequences of a Governor failing to reserve a bill in breach of his *Instructions*. Their view was that such a breach raised only a matter between the Governor and the Monarch; it had no bearing on the validity of a colonial Act so passed. This was again an entirely unreasoned assertion. The obvious objection to it is that if a Governor's failure to follow his *Instructions* was a purely internal matter vis-à-vis the Crown, there would be no need to enact a statutory requirement.

The Law Officers also rejected Boothby's apparently broad notion of repugnancy (although they agreed with his view that s.14 of the 1850 Act was the current statutory source of the repugnancy doctrine). They accepted that incompatibility with an Imperial statutory provision applicable to the colony amounted to repugnancy. Inconsistency with what was styled a 'fundamental principle of British law' would also have that effect. Repugnancy would not, however, arise if a colonial law differed from a British law which did not embody fundamental values. Unhelpfully perhaps – but unsurprisingly – Atherton and Palmer could not offer any means of distinguishing 'fundamental' and 'non-fundamental' values.[117] They did suggest, however, that it was almost unthinkable that a statute incompatible with a fundamental value would ever be passed; if it were, the Queen would surely disallow it.[118]

The Law Officers offered an equivocal view about Boothby's removal from office, couching their opinion in terms which could be construed as a warning to Boothby and/or an encouragement to his opponents. Noting that although they considered Boothby mistaken on some legal questions, he had been right on others – especially the invalidity of the Electoral Act 1856[119] – and that given Boothby was right on that point, then the Assembly and Council were both 'unlawful' bodies when they sent their addresses, Atherton and Palmer saw no present basis for Boothby's dismissal:

> But we entertain no doubt that the Crown might properly remove a Judge on the address of both Houses if satisfied that, owing to his perversity or habitual disregard of judicial propriety, the administration of justice might be practically obstructed by his continuance in office

Newcastle endorsed that equivocation, adding that it was proper for the Imperial government to accord 'great deference' to the views of colonial legislators on such matters and noting that 'perversity' might be proven if Boothby persisted in giving effect to legal opinions which the Law Officers, his fellow judges and legislators in the colony considered mistaken.

---

[117] They offered some examples. Abolishing Christianity, allowing slavery or authorising "the uncontrolled destruction of aborigines etc" (the 'etc' was not further defined) were fundamental. Allowing magistrates to try offences which required a jury in Britain, altering laws of evidence or introducing new rules of succession were not.

[118] Atherton and Palmer also concluded that Boothby was incorrect in asserting that repugnancy of particular statutory provisions mean that the entire statute was invalid.

[119] "The fault has been with the Governor in not reserving Acts for the royal assent which were expressly required by statute to be so reserved."

The Controversy Continues ... and Deepens ... and Broadens

Boothby and Gwynne were not the only office holders investigating the lawfulness of the colony's legislative and executive activity. James Fisher, President of the Legislative Council, prompted appreciable disquiet by drawing attention to s.33 of the Constitution Act 1856:

> 33. No officer of the Government shall be bound to obey any order of the Governor involving any expenditure of public money; nor shall any warrant for the payment of money, or any appointment to or dismissal from office, be valid, except as herein provided, unless such order, warrant, appointment, or dismissal shall be signed by the Governor, and countersigned by the Chief Secretary.

Successive Governors were evidently unaware of or indifferent to this limit on their power – as presumably were the various members of successive ministries. In the intervening years, many appointments and dismissals had been made without the requisite countersigning. All of these were arguably invalid. The uncertainty created was such that South Australia's legislature felt it necessary to pass a retrospective validating statute in September 1862.[120] But such curative laws were not always within that legislature's ordinary lawmaking competence.

In November 1862, Fisher wrote to Governor Daly raising a potentially more significant problem.[121] As noted above, the 1861 electoral reform bill had been reserved (per s.32) for the royal assent. Fisher suggested, however, that the 'Act' was nonetheless invalid. His point was a very simple one – which remarkably seemed to have escaped everyone's attention (even Boothby and Gwynne's thus far) – resting on s.34 of the Constitution Act 1856:

> 34. The said Parliament shall have full power and authority, from time to time by any Act, to repeal, alter, or vary all or any of the provisions of this Act, and to substitute others in lieu thereof: Provided that it shall not be lawful to present to the Governor for her Majesty's assent, any bill by which an alteration in the Constitution of the said Legislative Council or House of Assembly may be made, unless the second and third reading of such Bill shall have been passed with the concurrence of an absolute majority of the whole number of the members of the said Legislative Council and House of Assembly respectively: Provided also, that every Bill which shall be so passed shall be reserved for the signification of her Majesty's pleasure thereon.

Fisher (surely correctly) considered it obvious that the Electoral Act fell within s.34. But the bill had not been passed by an absolute majority of members on the four identified occasions. What, he asked, was the legal consequence of this failure:

> It seems clear that it must be invalid and void, as, under the section referred to, it was not lawful to present the Act to Sir Richard MacDonnell for Her Majesty's assent; and therefore he had no authority to receive it for reservation, much less to reserve it – in fact, there was nothing to reserve; and, consequently, there would be no Act which could be properly submitted for Her Majesty's assent – or to which Her Majesty could assent ...

---

[120] An Act to Remove Doubts as to the Appointments to and Dismissal from Office of Certain Persons 1862 (No 2 of 25 & 26 Vict).

[121] Reprinted in the *Adelaide Observer* 7 March 1863 p2, https://trove.nla.gov.au/newspaper/article/159516597.

This matter is one of vast importance, as, of course, if the Electoral Act is invalid, all the elections which have recently taken place, and those in progress under it, will be equally so … it would, I imagine, be necessary to apply for an Act of the Imperial Parliament to supply a remedy …

MacDonnell and the members of the Assembly and Council had little time to digest this matter before Boothby and Gwynne presented it to them in a starker form.

Driffield v Torrens – *December 1862 – The Entrenchment Proviso in the South Australia Constitution*

The *Adelaide Observer* of 29 November 1862[122] devoted almost 6000 words to an account of submissions in *Driffield v Torrens*. The formal issue was prosaic. Mr Driffield wished to register himself under the terms of the Registration of Deeds Act 1841[123] as the leaseholder of a particular plot of land. Torrens, then holding office as the colony's Registrar General of Deeds, refused the application on the basis that the 1841 registration system and registration office had been abolished with prospective effect by the Registration of Deeds Act 1862.[124] Driffield's primary argument drew on the point raised by Fisher earlier that month: namely, that the 1862 Act was invalid because it had not been passed in the manner required by s.34. Fisher's analysis had been targeted at the Electoral Act 1861, which clearly fell within the purview of s.34. Driffield's argument was more indirect.

Per s.6 of the Constitution Act 1856, the right to vote for members of the Council was granted inter alia to 'subjects of Her Majesty resident in the colony' who had registered with the General Registry Office their ownership of a lease worth in excess of £20 per annum. Driffield argued that the 1862 Act was invalid because in abolishing the registration office it had preventing him from registering his lease and so deprived him of his s.6 right to vote and had not been passed in accordance with the specified s.34 manner. He thus sought an order of mandamus requiring Torrens to register his lease.

The trial before the full court proceeded on the basis that the 'Act' had been passed only by simple majorities and had been assented to by the Governor. Randolph Stow, the then Attorney-General, led for Torrens. A Mr Belt was counsel for Driffield. Stow submitted in essence that s.34 was an irrelevance. The Legislature simply had no power to constrain either the substantive scope of its legislative competence or the procedures through which that competence was exercised. Belt's straightforward submission was that s.34 matters could only be addressed by legislation complying with s.34 procedures:

> Hanson: You contend that they [the Legislature] have no power except such as is given by the 34th clause.
>
> Belt: That is my argument. We have a written Constitution which we must abide by, or if we wish to change it we can only do so by complying with a prescribed form of legislation.

---

[122] P3, https://trove.nla.gov.au/newspaper/article/158190041.
[123] (No 8 of 5 Vict 1841).
[124] (No 27 of 25 & 26 Vict 1862).

Judgment was given in late December 1862.[125] Gwynne held that s.32 of the 1850 Act had empowered the mixed Council, which passed the 1856 Act to authorise South Australia's new Legislature, to deal with s.32 matters[126] either through legislation passed in the ordinary way or 'subject to restrictions', of which the absolute majority and reservation conditions were examples. An Act affecting a s.34 matter could therefore only be passed if the specified 'restrictions' had been complied with. Boothby concurred in the result. His reasoning was that s.34 had altered the quora required in the Assembly and Council for particular purposes, and that such an alteration imposed a judicially enforceable condition on the validity of any 'Act' not complying with its terms.[127]

Neither Boothby nor Gwynne, or either counsel, made any reference to the two-thirds clauses of sch.1 of the New South Wales Constitution Act 1855, or to their repeal in 1857 and the accompanying dispute as to whether their repeal could have been achieved by simple majority legislation. No submission was made nor was any judicial view expressed as to whether the Legislature could have repealed s.34 entirely by an Act passed in the ordinary way.

Governor Daly once again requested Imperial legislation to negate the Supreme Court's judgment – a request Newcastle granted with obvious irritation:

> It is not at all proper or desirable that the statute book of this country should be encumbered with enactments which are only required to extricate colonial government and legislatures from the consequences of their own irregularity or inadvertence, especially when the irregularity consists in an omission on the part of the legislature to conform to rules *of their own making.*[128]

The particular encumbrance to which Newcastle referred was the Colonial Act Confirmation Act 1863,[129] a statute which on its face was – like its 1862 predecessor – not confined in scope to South Australian constitutional failings:

> **2. Confirmation of certain Acts of Colonial Legislatures.**
>
> All Laws heretofore passed or purporting to have been passed by any Colonial Legislature with the Object of declaring or altering the Constitution of such Legislature, or of any Branch thereof, or the Mode of appointing or electing the Members of the same, shall have and be deemed to have had, from the Date at which the same shall have received the Assent of Her Majesty or of the Governor of the Colony on behalf of Her Majesty, the same Force and Effect for all Purposes whatever as if the said Legislature had possessed **full Powers** of enacting Laws

---

[125] There is a full report in the *Adelaide Observer* 20 December 1862 p3, http://nla.gov.au/nla.news-article158190406.

[126] Gwynne suggested that this was not a power that could be exercised with respect to other matters.

[127] Hanson produced a curious dissent. Echoing the views he had expressed in the Assembly during the first dismissal attempt, Hanson began by emphasising that it was perfectly proper for the Court to consider the validity of colonial legislation: "I cannot refrain from stating my conviction that the present question is one which it is the right and the duty of this Court to entertain and to decide." However, his solution to the question was that the 1862 Act was not invalid as the Constitution Act itself created a free-standing entitlement for voters to have their leases registered. Quite where in the Constitution Act this right was to be found, and how it was to be exercised in practice, were not matters which Hanson addressed.

[128] Newcastle to Daly 25 July 1863; emphasis added. (I should note that I originally encountered this quotation in Williams op cit p40.)

[129] (26 & 27 Vict c 84).

for the Objects aforesaid**, and** as if **all Formalities and Conditions** by Act of Parliament or otherwise prescribed in respect of the passing of such Laws had been duly **observed**.[130]

The Act obviously rests on Parliament's acceptance[131] (again) that it was proper – indeed, necessary – for colonial judges to deny that 'Acts' which had not been passed in accordance with statutory formalities and conditions had any legal effect. S.2 also indicates – echoing Newcastle's observation – in using the phrase "otherwise prescribed", that those formalities and conditions could emanate not just from Imperial Acts, but also – as in Queensland – from Orders in Council and – as in South Australia – *colonial legislatures themselves.*

Auld v Murray – *October 1863 – Assessing the Effect of Validating Legislation*

The 1863 Act's effect was addressed three months later by the Full Court in *Auld v Murray*.[132] On this occasion, s.41 of the Real Property Act 1861 was in issue. S.41 forbade registration of any estate or interest in land other than under the scheme outlined in the Act, thus prima facie excluding registration under the 1841 Act and so indirectly depriving some property owners of their voting rights.

While one might have thought that the 1863 Act had retrospectively validated any such provision, Gwynne took a different view. Gwynne noted that s.2 of the 1863 Act contained the phrase: "*with the Object of* declaring or altering the Constitution of such Legislature" (emphasis added). These (emphasised) words were not without meaning. And what they meant was that s.2 was drawing a distinction: "between what was done knowingly and designedly, and what was done unwittingly and unintentionally". Gwynne could see nothing in the text of s.41 (or any other part) of the Real Property Act 1861 which suggested such design; therefore, if s.41 did affect voting rights under s.6 – as he considered it did – any constitutional invalidity it had created would not be cured by the Colonial Act Confirmation Act 1863. More narrowly, however, he held that s.41 did not preclude registration of a lease for voting purposes, so no invalidity actually arose.

Boothby reached a different conclusion. His view – which is extremely difficult to support – was that s.41 was invalid prior to the passage of the 1863 Act and remained so afterwards. On Boothby's reading, the 1863 Act only validated measures which the colonial legislature had no power to pass. Since s.41 could have been passed by the Legislature if the Legislature had complied with s.34, s.41 did not fall within the purview of the 1863 Act. That conclusion might be thought a clear example of the 'perversity'

---

[130] The emphases are added to highlight the point that – on a strictly literal reading – s.2 treats 'full Powers' distinctly from observing 'all formalities and conditions'; the two concepts are conjoined with both a ',' and an 'and'. The separation suggests that 'full Powers' refers to a legislature's substantive competence, while 'formalities and conditions' refers to any procedural requirements that departed from the 'ordinary way' of passing a bill in respect of measures dealing with specific elements of that overall substantive competence.

[131] 'Parliament's acceptance' is used formalistically. Like the 1862 validating Act, the measure was not carefully considered in either house.

[132] *SAR* 17 December 1863 p3, https://trove.nla.gov.au/newspaper/article/50165392.

to which Atherton and Collier and Newcastle alluded in 1862. But Boothby then went further, stating he still regarded his decision in *McEllister* to be correct and would do so: "until better taught by a judgment of the Judicial Committee of Her Majesty's Privy Council, or by the provisions of Imperial legislation".[133]

The 1864 Validity Petitions

In June 1864, majorities formed in both the Assembly and the Council to deal with what was perceived to be Boothby's determined obstructionism by petitioning the Imperial government:

> [T]o take such steps as may be necessary to confirm, by Imperial legislation, the right of the Parliament of this province to pass all laws necessary for the peace, order, and good government of the province, without any exception whatever; and to enact that it shall not be competent for any Court of the province of South Australia to call in question any Act which may have been or shall be passed by the Parliament of South Australia ...[134]

The petition subsequently sent recited Boothby's supposed transgressions in considerable detail, but refrained from asking for his dismissal. The petition's focus remained on validating Imperial legislation, and concluded with an apparently heartfelt plea: "Relieve us from suffering under this enormous evil unknown to England's law, to wit, the power claimed by our Judges to declare laws passed by the Parliament of this Province illegal."

It is unclear if the Assembly's address was underpinned by ignorance or mendacity. That colonial judges might declare colonial legislation invalid was certainly not a principle 'unknown to England's [sic] law' by 1864; the power was a firmly established feature of colonial constitutional law. Nor – given the repeated enactment by the Imperial Parliament of retrospectively validating statutes which rested on the propriety of such judicial action – could it credibly be regarded as an 'evil' (save in the limited sense alluded to by Newcastle of imposing unnecessary burdens on the Imperial Parliament and the Colonial Office). But, legally ill-founded though the Assembly's plea may have been, it did prompt a 'considered' Imperial response.

---

[133] Hanson was again the lone dissentient.
[134] *South Australian Advertiser* 17 June 1864 p2, https://trove.nla.gov.au/newspaper/article/31837913. For a summary of proceedings, see Hague op cit pp 132–33. For detailed coverage, see inter alia *Adelaide Observer* 4 June 1864 p8, https://trove.nla.gov.au/newspaper/article/159524624; *South Australian Advertiser* 17 June 1864 p2, https://trove.nla.gov.au/newspaper/article/31837913; *Adelaide Observer* 22 October 1864 p7, https://trove.nla.gov.au/newspaper/article/159526941. The text of the final petition is reproduced at *SAR* 26 October 1864 p3, https://trove.nla.gov.au/newspaper/article/39134937.

4

The Colonial Laws Validity Act 1865 – II: Policy (?) and Text

… It is intended as far as possible to obviate doubt and litigation on this most important subject, by declaring that no colonial law shall be void for repugnancy to the law of England, unless it is inconsistent with an Imperial Act intended by Parliament to extend to the colony in which such law is passed, nor because it is at variance with the Governor's instructions. It also establishes the power of Colonial Legislatures to regulate the administration of justice, on which doubts had been thrown, and the power of every Representative Legislature to alter its own Constitution.

Secretary of State for the Colonies, Edward Cardwell, in a despatch to Colonial Governors explaining his understanding of the presumed purposes and effects of the Colonial Laws Validity Act 1865.

Palmer and Collier produced their 1864 Report[1] in the context of a steady stream of Imperial statutes, enacted (on an almost annual basis since 1860) to give retrospective effect to 'invalid' colonial legislation. Such statutes not only gave legal force to the disputed 'Acts', but also underlined the legal points that colonial legislatures which ignored or overlooked 'conditions' attached *either by Imperial or colonial legislation* to the way they might make law on certain subjects were acting unlawfully, that any such 'Acts' would been invalid and that it was the duty of colonial courts to pronounce upon claimed invalidities.

The Law Officers' Report was therefore directed only partly at the immediate South Australian situation; it also addressed a longer running and more territorially diverse constitutional controversy. Nonetheless, Gwynne and Boothby's decisions provided the main foci for Palmer and Collier's attention. And while the Law Officers regarded some of those judgments and opinions as 'absurd',[2] on other points Palmer and Collier were distinctly equivocal.[3]

I. Palmer and Collier's Report

Like Atherton and Palmer's 1862 opinion,[4] the 1864 Report has two parts. The first contains questions; the second, consequential answers.[5] The answers section began

---

[1] P 67 above.
[2] Palmer and Collier op cit para 7-A.
[3] ibid para 5-A.
[4] P 93 above.
[5] Cited here as para 1-Q etc; para 1-A etc.

by recommending a general change to the law of 'repugnancy' in the British colonies. The change was to adopt an explicit statutory definition taken from s.3 of the Act of Union (Canada) 1840,[6] which empowered Canada's Assembly, Council and Governor to:

> make Laws for the Peace, Welfare, and good Government of the Province of Canada, such laws not being repugnant to this Act ... or to any Act of Parliament made or to be made, and not hereby repealed, which does or shall, by express Enactment or by necessary Intendment, extend to the Provinces of Upper and Lower Canada, or to either of them, or to the Province of Canada.

Much as Wentworth glossed over the unusual political circumstances prevailing in 'Canada' in 1840 when borrowing the 1840 Act's two-thirds clauses for the Council's 1853 Bill,[7] Palmer and Collier ignored the obvious point that s.3's repugnancy provisions were narrowly drawn because Lower Canada (Quebec) had been – and was to remain – a civil law jurisdiction resting atop French cultural tradition. The common law – whether narrowly construed as case law or broadly as denoting particular moral principles – was not expected to become the legal norm there, so colonial legislation repugnant to the common law would not be politically problematic.

The Law Officers were: "... strongly inclined to think that the balance of reason and practical convenience is in favour of extending such provisions to all Her Majesty's colonial possessions".[8] They did not, however, explain what the 'reason and practical convenience' were. As noted in chapter one, successive Acts relating to New South Wales had adopted – for no obviously discernible reason – different definitions of 'repugnancy'.[9] Given that Boothby's judicial adventurism in defence of supposed common law principle was one cause of the Report being made, one might surmise that the primary 'reason and practical convenience' was to signal to colonial judges that their legal competence was normatively inferior to that of the colonial legislature except in circumstances where a British statutory provision was in issue. That is to say that Palmer and Collier's concern was more with the allocation of governmental power within the colony itself than with the normative relationship between the colony and Parliament.

However, what also seems evident from the string of curative statutes passed in the 1860s in respect of 'invalid' Acts passed in South Australia and Queensland is that 'colonial legislatures' could attach what the Colonial Act Confirmation Act 1863 had called 'formalities and conditions' to the exercise of legislative power, and that such formalities and conditions were enforceable by colonial courts. Palmer and Collier did not question the propriety of that principle, and accepted that colonial courts could properly invalidate colonial 'legislation' that did not respect those 'formalities and conditions', in essence because – although they do not expressly use the terminology – such measures would not be 'legislation' at all.

---

[6] (3 & 4 Vict c 35).
[7] Pp 41–42 above.
[8] Palmer and Collier op cit para 1-A.
[9] See pp 9, 16 and 20 above.

S.3 of the Act of Union (Canada) 1840 had also precluded argument as to the legal consequences of a Governor assenting personally to a measure that prima facie had to be reserved:

> and that all such Laws being passed by the said Legislative Council and Assembly, and assented to by Her Majesty, or assented to in Her Majesty's Name by the Governor of the Province of Canada, shall be valid and binding to all Intents and Purposes within the Province of Canada.

This issue was a major source of the problems experienced in South Australia. Palmer and Collier did not, however, recommend simple adoption of this aspect of s.3 for the Australian colonies.[10] Rather, they suggested that legislation be enacted which distinguished between circumstances where reservation was required by a British or colonial statute and those where it was required only by a Governor's *Instructions*. In the latter case, non-compliance should be retrospectively validated. In the former, it should not. As in Atherton and Palmer's 1862 Report,[11] the Law Officers offered no explanation for this distinction, beyond suggesting it was 'advisable'. (They also glossed over the intermediate position where a Governor was required by statute to follow his *Instructions* and those *Instructions* included a 'requirement' to reserve.) The unarticulated rationale perhaps again lay in considerations of normative hierarchy. Since a statutory provision was a superior form of law to a mere instruction (which derived from the Monarch's prerogative powers), it is, at least in the abstract realm of constitutional theory, more difficult to justify an indulgence or an excusing of a breach of a statutory requirement. The interesting implication of the distinction, not developed in the Report, was that in normative terms a colonial statute should be equated with a British statute and regarded as superior to a Governor's *Instructions* issued under the prerogative.

That implication also arose in paras 3-A and 4-A, which again considered the legal status of colonial 'Acts' enacted through processes which breached pre-existing legal requirements (what Palmer and Collier referred to as: "the proper forms"):

> 3. If an Act which, under some Act of Parliament or a local statute, ought to have been reserved for the signification of her Majesty's pleasure has not been reserved, or if an Act, containing provision which could only be passed by certain majorities has not been passed by such majorities, we think it is void in toto ...

> 4. When the power of legislation with regard to a particular subject is given, not to a simple majority, but to certain specified majorities in one or both branches of the Legislature, it is evident that such majorities are a *conditio sine qua non* to its exercise; and consequently that the Judges are not at liberty to treat any law on that subject as valid if it appears, either on the face of the law itself or by other proper evidence, that it was not, in fact, passed by the required majorities.

The Law Officers certainly accepted that it was proper – legally and politically – that special majority procedures should be legally enforceable by colonial courts on

---

[10] ibid para 2-A.
[11] Pp 93–94 above.

'particular subjects'. Notably, they also accepted that such majorities could be created by *either the British Parliament or colonial legislatures.* There is no allusion in the Report to s.4 [BAA] or to Russell's accompanying despatch, and so no basis to support the proposition that Palmer and Collier regarded bare majority law making as the *only* appropriate fashion in which colonial legislatures might enact statutes. Nor is it clear from this part of the Report if Palmer and Collier considered that colonial legislatures already had the power to create such special majorities (for example, in New South Wales per s.4 [BAA]) or if new Imperial legislation would be required to achieve that effect. The South Australia saga suggests that the former view had considerable currency in British governmental circles.[12]

Accepting the 'special majority' premise would, however, presumably require a departure from the *Wauchope* principle in relation to colonial legislatures. A court hearing a challenge to a colonial statute on the basis that the requisite 'special majority' had not been achieved would surely have to: "inquire into the mode in which [the bill] was introduced... or what passed... during its progress in its various stages through Parliament".[13] Palmer and Collier briefly canvassed this issue; and the potentially more difficult one of how a court should respond to a colonial law which provided, for example, that a certification from a designated person that the special majority had been achieved was conclusive of the point, if such certification was challenged as being factually erroneous:

> [We] incline to think (although this point may perhaps admit of some doubt) that the Judges ought to presume, until the contrary is proved, that every Act which has passed the Legislature, and which is authenticated as an Act of the Legislature in the ordinary way, was passed by such a majority as would be necessary, according to law, to give it effect.

Para 5-A bluntly rejected the notion that the doctrine of implied repeal should be assumed inapplicable to colonial laws purporting to alter existing colonial constitutional laws. Palmer and Collier firmly disapproved the proposition that the 'object' of any Act had to be expressly stated for the Act to be valid:[14]

> It must be presumed that a legislative body intends that which is the necessary effect of its enactments; the *object*, the *purpose* and the *intention*, of the enactment is the same; it need not be expressed in any recital or preamble; and it is not (as we conceive) competent for any Court, judicially, to ascribe any part of the legal operation of a statute to inadvertence.

The obviously interesting question arising from the interaction of paras 4-A and 5-A is whether Palmer and Collier gave any thought to whether requiring an 'express recital' in an Act for any given 'particular purpose' was equivalent to 'special majority' provisions in the sense of having to be complied with for the resultant colonial statute to be valid. The point is not pursued in the Report. However, given that a

---

[12] See especially Newcastle's comment concerning s.34 of the South Australia Constitution Act 1856 at p 98 above.
[13] (1842) 8 ER 279 at 285. See p 52 above.
[14] Original emphasis.

'special majority' provision would depart more substantially than a mere 'express repeal' provision from orthodox British presumptions about the nature of legislative lawmaking, it seems unlikely that the Law Officers – if pressed – would have rejected the assumption.

The matter discussed in paras 4-A and 5-A seem to lead fluently into the conclusory recommendation in para 6-A:

> We think it will be very expedient to pass an Imperial Act for the purpose of empowering the Legislature of that colony [South Australia] (and of any other colonies or colony that may be in like circumstances) to alter its own Constitution …

The passage suggests that any such Act would represent a new departure point in colonial legislatures' powers to control their respective constitutions; ie that they did not already have such powers (the 'its' in para 6-A clearly refers to the constitution of the legislature, not of the colony). That suggestion is perhaps difficult to square with Palmer and Collier's aforementioned conclusion that colonial legislatures could enact legally enforceable 'proper forms' to structure their lawmaking process in fashions other than the 'ordinary way'. But what did Palmer and Collier consider was included within the notion of a legislature's 'constitution'?

It seems plausible, in answering that question, to read back to paras 3-A, 4-A and 5-A. Para 3-A refers to 'proper forms' of lawmaking, including 'special conditions' relating to 'reservation' and 'certain majorities'. Para 4-A focuses solely on the 'specified majorities' point. Para 5-A is directed at matters of electoral law. This collection of issues rather suggests that Palmer and Collier had in mind the notion that the 'constitution' of legislature referred to its compositional identity in respect of 'its' power to make laws on particular subjects. There is no indication that Palmer and Collier conceived of the issue in terms of a colony having several distinct 'legislatures', the identity of each (even if composed substantially of the same people speaking and voting in the same buildings) being dependent upon the subject matter of the law enacted.

II. The Act – And its Enactment

Such were the Law Officers' reasons and recommendations. And in large part, those reasons and recommendations found their way into the Act's text.

Parliamentary Consideration – Or Not – Of the Bill

The Colonial Laws Validity Bill was promoted in the spring of 1865. As previously noted, neither the Commons nor the Lords devoted much attention to the details of colonial governance bills. Even so significant a measure as the New South Wales Act 1855 completed its parliamentary passage with only rudimentary attention in the Commons, and that driven mostly by Robert Lowe. But that cursory consideration compared favourably with the consideration given to the 1865 Bill, despite it being a measure applicable not just to the Australian colonies, but also to much of the Empire. Hansard for the Commons on 29 May 1865 records:

> HC Deb 29 May 1865 vol 179 c1042
>
> § On Motion of Mr. CHICHESTER FORTESCUE, Bill to remove doubts as to the Validity of Colonial Laws, ordered to be brought in by Mr. CHICHESTER FORTESCUE and Mr. SECRETARY CARDWELL.
>
> § Bill presented, and read 1°. [Bill 184.][15]

As to what followed in the two houses of Parliament, one might usefully refer to reports in the South Australian press:

> AN IMPERIAL ACT to validate the laws of the colonies has passed both Houses of the British Parliament; the measure having been first introduced in the Commons, and the third reading having passed in the Lords on June 22. It appears that the measure passed through Parliament not only without opposition, but without discussion.[16]

The Advertiser found that absence of discussion both puzzling and undesirable. That view was repeated in other South Australian newspapers. Describing it as a: "singular circumstance that the Parliamentary reports in the English papers contain scarcely any reference to the passage of the bill through its various stages",[17] *The Daily Telegraph* applauded the Bill's enactment, while conceding that Boothby had raised valid concerns about the lawfulness of previous 'legislation'.

The Secretary of State's Despatch

As noted in chapter two, Russell's despatch explaining the supposed effect of s.4 [BAA] was greeted in New South Wales as being as or even more significant politically than s.4 [BAA] itself. During the passage of the 1857 Act repealing the two-thirds clauses, not a single voice was raised to suggest that the result could not be achieved – as Russell's despatch had suggested – by bare majority legislation, even though many legislators had seemed to accept that two separate Acts would be required to repeal the two-thirds clauses and then reapportion the Assembly constituencies or member and voter qualification laws.[18]

The Colonial Laws Validity Act 1865 (hereafter CLVA 1865) was sent to Colonial Governors with a despatch from Secretary of State Edward Cardwell. His despatch was more modest in length and scope than Russell's. The entirety of the text relating to the CLVA 1865 is reproduced below:

> … It is intended as far as possible to obviate doubt and litigation on this most important subject, by declaring that no colonial law shall be void for repugnancy to the law of England,

---

[15] Fortescue was then Under-Secretary for the Colonies.
[16] *SAA* 12 August 1865 p2, http://nla.gov.au/nla.news-article31852506. Swinfen's careful (1970) study *Imperial control of colonial legislation 1813–1865* devotes a chapter to 'The making of the Colonial Laws Validity Act', within which (understandably) not a single word is deployed to consider parliamentary debate.
[17] *Daily Telegraph* (South Australia) 12 August 1865 p4, http://nla.gov.au/nla.news-article5786279.
[18] Pp 56–57 above.

unless it is inconsistent with an Imperial Act intended by Parliament to extend to the colony in which such law is passed, nor because it is at variance with the Governor's instructions. It also establishes the power of Colonial Legislatures to regulate the administration of justice, on which doubts had been thrown, and the power of every Representative Legislature to alter its own Constitution.[19]

Cardwell's suggestion that the Act would obviate 'doubt and litigation' was echoed in the (South Australia) *Daily Telegraph*,[20] which had welcomed: "the ample legislative powers which have at length been conferred upon [the colony], and which, it is to hoped, are now established beyond dispute". Such may have been the hope. One might wonder, on carefully reading the Act, if a future absence of dispute as to the extent of such power could credibly be regarded as going beyond the realm of hope and into that of expectation.

The absence of any (still less any *rigorous*) parliamentary debate as to the Act's various provisions and its underlying purposes leaves us with Palmer and Collier's Report as the only significant textual source concerning those points emanating from the British government or legislature. In broad terms, the Act seems to follow Palmer and Collier's analysis, but there are also points of divergence and many questions raised to which the Report offers no obvious answer.

The Text of the Act: ss.1–5

S.1 was a straightforward definition clause, which gave an expanded meaning to many of the Act's terms. As such, it was not per se problematic. Whether the definitions offered would so prove is a very different question.

1. Definitions "Colony"

The term *"colony"* shall in this Act include all of Her Majesty's possessions abroad in which there shall exist a legislature, as hereinafter defined …

The terms *"legislature"* and *"colonial legislature"* shall severally signify the authority, other than the Imperial Parliament or Her Majesty in Council, competent to make laws for any colony:

The term *"representative legislature"* shall signify any colonial legislature which shall comprise a legislative body of which one half are elected by inhabitants of the colony:

The term *"colonial law"* shall include laws made for any colony either by such legislature as aforesaid or by Her Majesty in Council …

S.2 enacted a 'repugnancy' provision which indicated the inferior status of colonial legislation to an Imperial statute:

2. Colonial law when void for repugnancy

Any colonial law which is or shall be in any respect repugnant to the provisions of any Act of Parliament extending to the colony to which such law may relate, or repugnant to any order or regulation made under authority of such Act of Parliament, or having in the colony the

---

[19] The most accessible source for the despatch is the *Adelaide Express* 19 September 1865 p3, http://nla.gov.au/nla.news-article207604078.

[20] n 17 above.

force and effect of such Act, shall be read subject to such Act, order, or regulation, and shall, to the extent of such repugnancy, but not otherwise, be and remain absolutely void and inoperative.

S.2 is drafted in the same terms as the original Bill. Its text is not an exact copy of the provision in the Act of Union (Canada) 1840 s.3 to which Palmer and Collier had referred. That text read: "… which does or shall, by express Enactment or by necessary Intendment, extend …". Whether the changed form of words was meant to embrace both the 'express' and 'intendment' elements of s.3 or just the former is unclear. By implication, since s.2 made no reference to the common law, colonial legislatures could pass Acts which modified English common law rules or principles. That implication is strengthened by s.3:

3. Colonial law when not void for repugnancy

No colonial law shall be or be deemed to have been void or inoperative on the ground of repugnancy to the law of England, unless the same shall be repugnant to the provisions of some such Act of Parliament, order, or regulation as aforesaid.

Ss.2–3 can certainly be seen as very targeted responses to the difficulties that Boothby had identified and as flowing – in policy terms – directly from the Law Officers' Report. S.4 can be viewed in the same way:

4. Colonial law not void for inconsistency with instructions

No colonial law passed with the occurrence of or assented to by the governor of any colony, or to be hereafter so passed or assented to, shall be or be deemed to have been void or inoperative by reason only of any instructions with reference to such law or the subject thereof which may have been given to such governor by or on behalf of Her Majesty, by any instrument other than the letters patent or instrument authorizing such governor to concur in passing or to assent to laws for the peace, order, and good government of such colony, even though such instructions may be referred to in such letters patent or last-mentioned instrument.

S.5 is a more complicated provision:[21]

5. Colonial legislatures may establish, &c. courts of law. Representative legislature may alter constitution

[1] Every colonial legislature shall have, and be deemed at all times to have had, full power within its jurisdiction to establish courts of judicature, and to abolish and reconstitute the same, and to alter the constitution thereof, and to make provision for the administration of justice therein; [2] and every representative legislature shall, in respect to the colony under its jurisdiction, have, and be deemed at all times to have had, full power to make laws respecting the constitution, powers, and procedure of such legislature; [3] provided that such laws shall have been passed in such manner and form as may from time to time be required by any Act of Parliament, letters patent, Order in Council, or colonial law for the time being in force in the said colony.

S.5 is drafted in ungainly terms: its 128 words collapse together several discrete ideas and myriad sub-divisions of those ideas into a single sentence.[22] If subject to literal

---

[21] The [1], [2] and [3] in the text are my addenda.
[22] This was – unhappily – the dominant drafting style of the time.

construction, s.5 appears to contain some important distinctions and ambiguities which become evident if the text is presented in a more physically segmented way. Thus:

> [1] Every colonial legislature shall have, and be deemed at all times to have had, full power within its jurisdiction to
> (a) establish courts of judicature, and
> (b) to abolish and reconstitute the same, and
> (c) to alter the constitution thereof, and
> (d) to make provision for the administration of justice therein;
>
> [2] and every representative legislature shall, in respect to the colony under its jurisdiction, have and be deemed at all times to have had, full power to make laws respecting the
> (a) constitution,
> (b) powers, and
> (c) procedure
>
> of such legislature;
>
> [3] provided that such laws shall have been passed in such manner and form as may from time to time be required by any
> (a) Act of Parliament,
> (b) letters patent,
> (c) Order in Council, or
> (d) colonial law
>
> for the time being in force in the said colony.

S.5 is an excellent vehicle through which to explore the art or science of statutory drafting, since it lends itself to analysis as either replete with subtle complexities and distinctions or as a spectacularly undisciplined shambles. As suggested below, that duality emerges whether we approach the provisions of the Act in an atomistically literalist fashion or deploy the golden rule or the mischief rule.[23] Similarly, while Palmer and Collier's Report certainly offers some assistance in ascertaining the meaning of ambiguous textual provisions if we accept that it is legitimate to apply the mischief rule to the construction of the Act, that Report is itself not a model of unrelenting clarity.

Temporal Effects

[1] and [2] share two common features. Their chronological impact is both prospective and retrospective – "shall have, and be deemed at all times to have had …". Their territorial impact is constrained to the colony whose legislature produces the law in issue, although on this point 'Parliament'[24] has managed for no apparent reason to use a different form of words in [1] than in [2].[25] A series of quite different words then appear in [1] and [2].

---

[23] I am assuming here that readers are familiar with these concepts. For those who are not, an introductory explanation can be found in Loveland (2018) op cit pp 55–61.
[24] I use the term archly because neither the Commons nor the Lords gave any substantive consideration to any part of the bill which became the Act.
[25] [1] being: "within its jurisdiction" and [2] being: "in respect to the colony under its jurisdiction". Indeed, [1] might even be taken to refer just to the issue of competence rather than territory.

'Colonial Legislatures' and 'Representative Legislatures'

[1] applies to: "every colonial legislature". That concept is defined in s.1 as: "the authority, other than the Imperial Parliament or Her Majesty in Council, competent to make laws for any colony ...". The definition is broad both institutionally (any '*authority other than ...*' rather than 'the legislature') and functionally ('competent to *make law*' rather than 'competent to enact legislation'). One might credibly assert that a colonial judge is an 'authority' who 'makes' law, although that assertion might be rebutted by the assumption that the mid-nineteenth-century British Parliament embraced a declaratory theory of the common law in which the common law – while certainly 'law' – was 'found' rather than 'made'.

S.1 identifies the notion of 'representative legislature' more narrowly, to include only: "any colonial legislature which shall comprise a legislative body of which one half are elected by inhabitants of the colony".[26] These few words are riven with imprecision. Is 'a' legislative body to include bicameral as well as unicameral institutions? If so, is that legislature 'representative' if one chamber is elective and one is not (ie 'half')? If that is Parliament's objective, why does the definition use 'are' instead of 'is'? The 'are' (as opposed to 'is') presumably refers to the members of the chamber(s), rather than the chamber(s) itself (themselves). If so, a bicameral body in which more than half of the members sat in an appointive or hereditary chamber would not be 'representative'. Further, if the number of members in each chamber varied, then the body could presumably drift in and out of 'representative' status.

One would further assume that the Monarch, in giving (through the relevant Governor or in reserved matters through the relevant British minister), was not part of the 'legislative body'. If she were to be so regarded, then a legislature with an elected chamber, an appointive chamber and the Monarch would in a narrow institutional sense be but one-third elected by inhabitants of the colony.

But, leaving that complication aside, there is an even more unhappy flaw in s.1's drafting. Taking s.1's definition at face value, a colony with a unicameral or bicameral legislature within which fewer than 50% or more than 50% of members were elected would not be 'representative'. Indeed, on a strict reading of s.1, neither South Australia nor Victoria had a representative legislature in 1865, as in both colonies both houses and all members (ie not 'half') were elective. We might readily assume that 'half' was meant to mean 'at least half of all members' and/or 'at least one house', but that simply is not what the text says.

The Powers of Colonial and Representative Legislatures

[1] then states that colonial legislatures shall 'have full power' to achieve a short list of objectives. In [2], in contrast, a representative legislature is granted 'full power to *make law*' to achieve a different list of objectives. One assumes that Parliament did not envisage that 'colonial legislatures' could achieve the objectives in [1] other than by 'making

---

[26] There is clearly no scope to include a judge in this definition.

law', but again the drafting is so sloppy that a literal construction of [1] raises that possibility. The listed objectives in [1] are confined to courts. Those in [2] are applicable only to 'representative legislatures'.

The competence evidently granted in [1] is – variously – to *establish* courts, to *abolish* courts, to *alter the constitution* of such courts and to *make provision for the administration of justice* in those courts. This was obviously one of the problems that Boothby and Gwynne's judgments had generated, although it is not actually addressed expressly in Palmer and Collier's Report.[27]

The notion of 'establish' presumably encompasses the power to define the jurisdiction of the courts established. Quite how the power to establish or abolish a court might fit with existing or future colonial law concerning the appointment and dismissal of judges is left entirely unaddressed. To take a trite example, if colonial law requires that judges be appointed during good behaviour, is it to be assumed that the abolition of a court per [1] cannot carry with it the termination of the office of judges who sit in that court? The 'constitution' of a court presumably encompasses the number and/or seniority of its judges, but is it also supposed to embrace their security of tenure? These are obvious points.

[2] does not describe the competence of representative legislatures in terms of 'establish', 'abolish' or 'alter'. The terminology used is to 'make laws respecting', and the 'respecting' (which one assumes must mean 'respecting' in the sense of 'in relation to' rather than 'according respect to') is then directed towards three phenomena, namely [2](a) the 'constitution', [2](b) the 'powers' and [2](c) the 'procedure' of 'such' legislatures. None of these concepts are defined in s.1.

One might sensibly assume that the [2](a) 'constitution' extends to the institutional structure of the legislature, the number of its members and the ways those members are chosen. It is not obvious whether 'making a law respecting its constitution' empowers the legislature to abolish itself entirely, abolish one or more of its original component parts (which might thereby deprive it of its representative character per s.1), establish additional or alternative component parts, or specify that in order to pass bills dealing with particular matters those various component parts might have to comply with provisions specifying – inter alia – enhanced majorities, particular timescales or reservation of bills to the Monarch. If the notion of the [2](a) 'constitution' does not stretch so far – ie if the legislature does not initially have the 'power' to achieve those ends – might it nonetheless be correct that the [2](b) notion 'powers' and/or the [2](c) notion 'procedures' enable the legislature to grant itself (by making a law) that capacity?

It is not fanciful to wonder if the textual sequencing of these three concepts denotes a descending normative hierarchy, ie – to invert the hierarchy – that alteration to 'procedures' could not be used to change 'powers', and that alterations to 'powers' could not be used to change the 'constitution'. It is perhaps no less fanciful to consider that parliamentary draughtsmen had just flung together three ill-defined ideas to endow the legislatures with the capacity to do whatever at all they liked, subject only to the repugnancy provisions of ss. 2–3. The obvious difficulty that attends the first contention

---

[27] The general conclusion on para 6-A refers to an Imperial Act relating to the constitution of legislatures, not courts.

is that the Act offers not the slightest clue as to how one might draw a line between the three concepts.

Palmer and Collier did not use the terms in such a distinct way. As suggested above, they seemed to use the notion of 'constitution' to embrace the legislature's composition rather than its capacity (or, to use a different dichotomy, 'identity' rather than 'competence'). The dichotomy is not a precise one, and is used here in the following sense. A proviso which, for example, required a two-thirds majority at third reading in each house in order for valid legislation to be enacted for the purposes of increasing the number of members of either house has both an 'identity' and a 'competence' dimension. A proviso requiring such a majority to raise income tax above five shillings in the pound has only the latter, 'competence', quality. The context of the CLVA 1865's enactment would point firmly to the government assuming only 'identity' matters fell within s.5, but the insertion of 'powers' into the text creates obvious uncertainty.

A further, and perhaps more important, ambiguity lies in the phrase 'full power' itself, which appears in both [1] and [2]. One plausible reading of 'full power' may be to equate it with the default position of the Imperial legislature's lawmaking process, ie that statutes on any [1] or [2] matter could be enacted by bicameral bare majorities with express or implied repeal (this default position is hereafter referred to as the 'ordinary way' of legislating). If so, any previously existing departures from the 'ordinary way' imposed on a colonial legislature by colonial or Imperial legislation (or an Order in Council) might be argued to have been impliedly repealed. S.5's underlying policy could then be seen as sweeping away all judicially enforceable restraints (other than s.2 repugnancy) on a representative legislature's capacity to make laws on [1] and [2] issues in the 'ordinary way'.[28]

But we then arrive at s.5[3], which appears at first glance to tell us that [1] and [2] measures *already passed* or *to be passed* in the future (because [1] and [2] are both prospective and retrospective) will not be valid unless they '*shall have been passed*' in compliance with the 'manner and form' 'as may from time to time be required'. [3] uses the future perfect tense ('shall have been passed') and the present tense ('as may from time to time be required'), while [1] and [2] use both the perfect and the future. There is thus no chronological symmetry between the text of [1]–[2] and that of [3]. That would require [3] to read as '*were passed* or shall have been passed' and 'as may from time to time *have been required* or be required). Such carelessness in language presented obvious scope for confusion as to s.5's effect.

... 'Such Manner and Form' ...

Palmer and Collier did not use the couplet 'manner and form' in their Report. The term 'proper forms' appeared in para 3-A in reference to special majority provisions, and it is certainly clear that Palmer and Collier saw such provisions as entirely legitimate, to the point that a purported law which was required to but did not meet such provisions

---

[28] A quite different reading, rooted in the distinction made in the Colonial Act Confirmation Act 1863 s.2 (p 98 above), is that s.5[1] is simply confirming that representative legislatures did not have to await further Imperial legislation on s.5[2] and s.5[3] issues but could enact it themselves.

would be void. It is therefore difficult to resist the conclusion that the 'manner and form' formula was designed to allow representative legislatures to give effect to all sorts of mechanisms which departed from the presumption that statutes were to be enacted through bare majoritarian bicameralism with either express or implied repeal (ie the 'ordinary way' or the 'manner' – per Russell's despatch – we find in s.4 [BAA] of the 1855 Act).[29]

Other questions which s.5[3] raises have no obvious answer. For example, New South Wales, Queensland and South Australia had (construing s.1 benevolently) representative legislatures in 1865. But each of those 'legislatures' was subject to some restrictions or conditions (manner and form requirements in the s.5[3] language) which precluded certain laws from being made in the ordinary way.

In a colony with a bicameral legislature (with one or both houses elective), a colonial Act which required that any law altering the composition of either house be passed by a three-fifths or two-thirds majority in either or both of the houses would not affect the (per s.1) 'representative' character of the legislature. Similarly, a 'manner and form' which provided, for example, that any law altering the composition of either house had to be passed by a simple majority in both houses on two separate occasions a specified time apart before the Governor could grant the royal assent would not stop the legislature from being representative. Equally clearly, a 'manner and form' which placed the relevant power in the hands only of one (elective) house would also satisfy s.1.[30]

However, in colonies with an elective and appointive house, a 'manner and form' which added further elements to the legislature would be distinctly problematic if those elements were not (per s.1) 'elected by the inhabitants of the colony'. A 'manner and form' introduced by colonial legislation which precluded alteration to the composition of either house unless the relevant bill achieved required majorities in the Assembly and the Council, the grant of the royal assent and the approval of a (let us say) statutorily created 'Constitutional Reform Committee' comprising members appointed by the Governor or the British Government would presumably not be being exercised by a 'representative legislature'. A tricameral body of that sort might be a 'colonial legislature', but a colonial legislature is not granted power to alter the 'constitution, powers or procedure' of a representative legislature.

In short, the issue raised here is whether a representative legislature can use s.5 to pass its authority to control its 'constitution, power and procedures' to a body that is not a representative legislature per s.1. The notion might seem rather peculiar in political terms. In a more narrow legal sense, one might fasten on Parliament's use of the word 'such' in the final line of [2]. Should this word be taken to indicate that a 'representative legislature' cannot deprive itself of its representative character; or is the word merely used (superfluously) to underline the s.1 definitional distinction between 'colonial legislatures' and 'representative legislatures'?

A further complication arises when one notes that plausible arguments can be made for and against the proposition that [3] applies only to [2] and not to both [1] and [2].

---

[29] Pp 48–49 above.
[30] Conversely, giving such power to the Council (if that body was appointive rather than elected) would presumably deprive the Legislature of its representative nature. This assumes that 'half' in s.1 means 'half or more than half'.

As noted above, s.5 is just one sentence: we cannot find disjunction between its various component provisions by looking for numbers or paragraphs, or even full stops.

The first word in [2] is 'and'. This could be seen as linking [1] and [2], which then as a couple are both subject to [3]. However, [3] refers to 'such laws'. The term 'laws' is used in [2] but not in [1]; and [2] and [1] refer to different categories of legislature.[31] That prompts the assumption that [3] applies only to [2] and not to [1]. Palmer and Collier's Report does not assist much here, since it drew no precise distinction between colonial legislatures which were and were not 'representative'. The proposal of a new Act made in para 6-A is suggested as desirable not just for South Australia, but also for other colonies which "may be in like circumstances": but that phrase lends itself as readily to being an allusion to colonies where Acts might be invalid whether or not the legislature is 'representative' as to colonies with 'representative' legislatures.

A close reading also reveals that – for no obviously good reason – [3] uses the term 'pass' a law, while [2] uses the term 'make' a law; and [1] does not refer to 'law' at all, whether 'passed' or 'made'. Does 'pass' mean something other than 'make'? If so, what is the distinction? If not, why are different words used? Palmer and Collier's Report sheds no light on the issue.

The Text: s.6

S.6 – a provision of general application – also appears clearer in effect. It enacted a rule that certification by the clerk or proper officer (posts not defined by the Act) of *any* legislative body in *any* colony in relation to *any* colonial Act or bill was to be prima facie evidence: "that such law has been duly and properly passed and assented to, or that such Bill has been duly and properly passed and presented to the governor". S.6 also seems to apply both to bills already passed (unlike s.5, s.6 uses only the word 'passed' and not also 'made') and those passed in future.

The purpose of s.6 was presumably to provide evidence that some types of manner and form requirement had been complied with (although s.6 is not limited by subject matter, whether to s.5[1] or s.5[2] issues or anything else; nor by the type of colonial legislature which passed the law in issue). That such certification is to be only prima facie and not conclusive obviously implies that the certification could be challenged. But what s.6 notably omits is any provision detailing how that prima facie evidence might be rebutted.

The Text: s.7

The previously quoted s.7[32] also seems straightforward in its effect, albeit that effect was limited only to South Australia. The reference to 'purported Acts' and 'Persons or Bodies of Persons for the Time being acting as' the Legislature indicates that s.7 was to be a catch-all, retrospective validation provision, unlimited either chronologically or

---

[31] [1] includes [2], but not vice versa.
[32] P 68 above.

by subject matter. The breadth of its language suggests that Palmer and Collier (and Newcastle and Cardwell) anticipated that other hitherto undiscovered 'unlawful Acts' might be uncovered by Boothby and/or Gwynne. S.7 would presumably preclude such discoveries being given legal force.

That s.7 had such precise territorial scope, and that it was preceded by its own preamble, implies that the government perceived it as essentially a separate measure to the generalist provisions enacted in ss.1–6. That s.7 was lumped in with the rest of the Act in this way, rather than being passed as a discrete statute, is perhaps a further illustration of the slapdash way in which the Act was drafted.[33]

III. Meanwhile – And Afterwards – On the South Australia Supreme Court

As the bill received the royal assent in London – it would take some months for an authoritative copy to reach the Australian colonies – Gwynne and Boothby produced majority judgments in two cases which had significant – and, from the colonial government's perspective, significantly deleterious – political consequences.

The Queen v Neville – June 1865 – Criminal Courts and Repugnancy

Neville had been convicted in the Willunga Local Court of stealing a rug. This court was one of many such courts purportedly created under the terms of the Local Courts Act 1861,[34] which amended a statute passed in 1850. The Act addressed both civil and criminal matters. The provisions in issue in *Neville* were those which gave an extensive criminal law jurisdiction to courts in which the judges might be Justices of the Peace – who need not be legally qualified and could sit without a jury, and who were appointed by and held office at the pleasure of the Governor.[35]

Neville's counsel, Randolph Stow,[36] had raised as his client's first line of defence the proposition hinted at by Boothby (four years earlier) in *Payne v Dench* and in his evidence to the Assembly[37] that the Legislature had no power at all to create courts. The secondary proposition was that – assuming the Legislature had such a power – it could not create courts which in their nature or jurisdiction were repugnant to the law of

---

[33] For no discernible reason, s.7 uses the word 'enacted', not 'passed'; s.6 uses 'passed', not 'enacted'; and s.5 uses both 'make' and 'passed'.
[34] (No 15 of 24 & 25 Vict), www.austlii.edu.au/cgi-bin/viewdb/au/legis/sa/num_act/lca15o24a25v1861242/.
[35] Ss. 115–16, s.8 and s.13. Neville was also convicted at much the same time – in a Supreme Court hearing presided over by Gwynne with a jury – of stealing a horse; *SAR* 11 May 1865 p3, https://trove.nla.gov.au/newspaper/article/39132192.
[36] Stow was then among the most eminent practitioners at South Australia's Bar. He took silk in 1865, had been a member of the Assembly since 1861 and had served as Attorney-General. He was subsequently appointed to the Supreme Court in 1874; http://adb.anu.edu.au/biography/stow-randolph-isham-4649.
[37] Pp 85 and 89–92 above. Stow's initial submissions are at *SAR* 11 May 1865 p3, https://trove.nla.gov.au/newspaper/article/39132192.

England; and to permit a court presided over by non-lawyers and acting without a jury to try felonies was repugnant in that sense.

Gwynne delivered the first – brief – judgment.[38] He dealt only with the second ground of defence, which ground he accepted with evident enthusiasm. Gwynne did not identify the source of the repugnancy principle he applied, but cast the notion in broad terms: "By repugnancy to the law of England I understand not a repugnancy to individual English Statutes, but a repugnancy to the Constitutional law of England." He continued:

> [Is] such part of the Local Courts Act as assumes to confer on three Justices of the Peace, appointed by the Governor and removable at his pleasure, the power to try felony and misdemeanours, and to sentence to imprisonment and hard labour for six months, and that without the intervention of a jury, repugnant to the Constitutional law of England? In my opinion it is.

Boothby concurred in an even shorter judgment. He also added that he considered his view in *Payne v Dench* to be correct, and that the only authority that could persuade him from that view would be the Privy Council.

Hanson recorded his disagreement with Boothby on that broader question: "I shall content myself with saying that in my opinion the words: 'peace order and good government' … comprise … every possible subject". Hanson also dissented on the repugnancy point. Noting that: "I have never met with a definition of repugnancy which seemed to me to throw any light on the subject", Hanson eventually settled on defining the concept as an Act which: "contradicts the substance and principle of the law of England". Hanson accepted that a statute which made provision for the infliction of the death penalty or forfeiture of all one's property on conviction of an offence tried without a jury would fall into that category. A law which did so for offences carrying a maximum sentence of six months' imprisonment could not defensibly be characterised in that way.

Dawes v Quarrell – July 1865 – There are No Local Courts

A month later, in *Dawes v Quarrell*,[39] Gwynne and Boothby addressed the larger issue avoided in *Neville*. Boothby and Gwynne concurred in holding that *all* of the colony's inferior courts created under the Local Courts Act 1861 were unlawful bodies, on the basis that the Legislature had had no power to bring them into being. The rationale for the conclusion lay in a presumption as to the consequences of a legislative omission in the 1850 Act.

The 1834 Act s.2 empowered the King to grant by Order power to persons resident in South Australia:

> [T]o make ordain and establish all such laws institutions or ordinances *and to constitute such courts*, and appoint such officers and also such Chaplains and Clergymen of the Established Church of England or Scotland and to impose and levy such rates duties, and taxes as may be necessary for the peace order and good government of His Majesty's subjects and others within the said province.[40]

---

[38] *SAR* 26 June 1865 p3, http://nla.gov.au/nla.news-article39123875.
[39] *SAA* 28 July 1865 p4, https://trove.nla.gov.au/newspaper/article/31852008.
[40] Emphasis added.

The 1836 Order then provided that:

> [T]he Governor for the time being of His Majesty's said Province of South Australia, or the Officer administering the Government thereof, the Judge, or Chief Justice, the Colonial Sec. the Advocate General, and the resident Commissioners thereof for the time being, so long as they shall be respectively resident in the said province, or any three of them, of whom the acting Governor to be one, shall have authority & power to make ordain & establish all such laws, institutions or ordinances & to *constitute such Courts* & appoint such offices, & also such Chaplains or Clergymen of the Established Church of England & also such Chaplains & Clergymen of the Established Church of Scotland & to impose & levy such rates duties and taxes as may be necessary or expedient for the peace order & good Government of His Majesty's subjects & others within the said Province ...[41]

The 1842 Act – which repealed the 1834 statute and did not expressly preserve the various legislative powers provided for in the 1836 Order – contained only the general power of legislation, and made no mention of specific legislative powers to create courts or legislate in relation to the administration of justice. If such a power existed, it would have to be found as an element of the general power.

S.8 of the Australian Constitutions Act 1850 expressly repealed South Australia's 1842 Act in its entirety. S.14 had made a general grant of power to the Governors and Legislative Councils *established under that Act* of all the colonies: "to make Laws for the Peace, Welfare, and good Government of the said Colonies". What the 1850 Act had not done was *explicitly* grant the new Legislatures of *all the colonies* a power to create courts and otherwise regulate the administration of justice. Such power might again be presumed implicit in general power. But s.29 *explicitly* gave that power to the New South Wales, Victoria and Van Diemen's Land legislatures.

This sequence of legislative provisions led Boothby and Gwynne to conclude that the presence of s.29 negated any inference that the s.14 power embraced an implicit power for the legislatures of *all the colonies* to create courts and regulate the administration of justice; and that South Australia's omission from s.29 (whether by parliamentary error or design, the judges evidently neither knew nor cared) indicated that the Imperial Parliament did not intend the colony's Legislature to have such authority. The omission of a grant of power to establish new courts should be read as a deliberate denial of such power; a denial too specific in its nature to be overcome by a construction of s.14's general words which brought such an authority within the scope of 'peace order and good government'.

Boothby and Gwynne's analysis can readily be both defended and attacked, primarily because the 1850 Act continued the by then well-established trend of shambolic incoherence in the textual narrative of the Imperial Parliament's colonial legislation. The judges' reasoning and conclusion can be buttressed by noting that other parts of the 1850 Act (in addition to s.29 and notwithstanding s.14) gave explicitly subject-specific powers to the new legislatures,[42] which raised the obvious presumption that the general power did not include the specific(s). A perhaps more forceful point *against* appears when one puts the specific power to create courts in the 1834 Act and the 1836 Order in their relevant textual contexts: that power was one of a cluster of specific powers contributing to the

---

[41] Emphasis added.
[42] These being s.24 (various taxing powers) and s.27 (levying customs duties).

general notion of 'peace order and good government'. The presumption that the 1850 Act subsumed that authority within the general grant was eminently plausible. This was the view that Hanson adopted in a long and carefully reasoned dissent.

The doctrinally elaborate reasoning which Gwynne and Boothby adopted was widely perceived in the colony's press and by its politicians as a deliberate judicial attempt to obstruct the orderly conduct of government. Since Boothby and Gwynne had been faced with two plausible answers to the question before them, and had chosen the one which created political chaos rather than political calm, that accusation has obvious merit. Whatever Gwynne and Boothby's motivation, *Dawes* threatened serious disruption to the administration of both the criminal and civil law. Some lower courts respected the judgment while others ignored it, and in reliance on the judgment, some losing parties in lower court litigation (in civil and criminal proceedings) began to initiate proceedings[43] for false imprisonment or to recover damages and costs awards made against them. Colonial politicians who hoped – like Cardwell – that the arrival of an authoritative copy of the CLVA 1865 would eventually settle this broad controversy were promptly disappointed.

Walsh v Goodall (1865) – October 1865 – Gwynne and Boothby on the Construction of the CLVA 1865

Walsh, a trespass action, turned on whether the Registration of Deeds Act 1862[44] had acquired validity consequent on enactment of the CLVA 1865.[45] What might have been thought the straightforward task of asserting for the plaintiff that the answer was 'Yes' fell on Randolph Stow as Attorney-General. Had Stow formed that impression, he was soon disabused. By a two to one majority (Gwynne plus Boothby contra Hanson), the Supreme Court held that the 1862 Act remained invalid.

Stow submitted simply that CLVA 1865 s.7 controlled the issue. Accepting that the 1862 Act was invalid prior to the CLVA 1865's passage, Stow argued s.7 obviously cured that invalidity. No other provision in the CLVA 1865 was relevant to this dispute: "s.7 had the effect of a separate and distinct Act".

However, Gwynne's judgment – with which Boothby briefly concurred – held that s.7 had to be read in conjunction with s.5, and specifically with s.5[3]. Gwynne and Boothby seemingly reasoned that an alteration to electors' qualifications was a 'constitution' matter within s.5[2],[46] and so, per s.5[3], had to have been passed in accordance with whatever 'manner and form' was required by – inter alia – 'colonial law' in 1862. In their view, all that s.7 did was to validate 'Acts' which could have been enacted in the 'ordinary way', but which had been invalid because when they were passed South Australia's Legislature was itself an 'unlawful' body. On this construction of s.5, the

---

[43] In the Supreme Court obviously; see Hague op cit pp 146–49.
[44] See the discussion of *Driffield v Torrens* at pp 97–99 above.
[45] The judgment is reported at *Adelaide Observer* 28 October 1865 p3, http://nla.gov.au/nla.news-article159498701. There is an extensive account of submissions in the *South Australian Advertiser* 13 October 1865 p3, http://nla.gov.au/nla.news-article31854418.
[46] There is no record of argument on the point, and neither Gwynne nor Boothby states it expressly.

'full power' referred to in s.5[1] and s.5[2] was conditional upon the Legislature legislating (or having legislated) in accordance with the relevant manner and form proviso.

Gwynne and Boothby's reading of s.5[3] seems wholly defensible on the basis of its text and of Palmer and Collier's preceding analysis. Whether voter qualifications were indeed a 'constitution' matter per s.5[2] is much less certain: most obviously – although evidently not to Gwynne or Boothby – s.2 of the Colonial Act Confirmation Act 1863[47] clearly identified the 'constitution' of a legislature as a separate matter from 'the mode of appointing or electing' its members. The subordination of s.7 to s.5 is still more problematic – fanciful might be a better descriptor – given that s.7 can readily be seen as a very specific provision while s.5 was of very general application.

The difficulty would obviously have been avoided had Parliament enacted s.7 as a one-section statute subsequent to[48] the CLVA 1865. Had the bill received even cursory consideration in the Commons or Lords prior to its enactment, that simple mechanical division might well have been made. In their 1864 Report, Palmer and Collier had recommended enactment of new Imperial legislation in part to counteract Boothby and Gwynne's evident predisposition to raise 'technical' objections to the validity of colonial legislation. To characterise colonial politicians' repeated breach of explicit statutory requirements as merely 'technical' failures is perhaps disingenuous. But Palmer and Collier's evident failure to anticipate that conflation of two distinct legislative objectives into a single statute might create new opportunities for such 'technical' objections to be raised can at best be described as carelessness on the part of the British government and its Law Officers.

Hanson, in contrast to his brethren, curtly accepted Stow's submission. He saw no basis for reading s.7 as anything other than a stand-alone provision. For Gwynne and Boothby to import the s.5[3] proviso into s.7 was: "making rather than interpreting the law".

Walsh's impact was promptly negated by circuitous means. In *Ridpath v Murray*, Gwynne and Hanson – in a very brief judgment – accepted that the CLVA 1865 confirmed the existence of the colony's Court of Appeals.[49] That 'court', moribund for some years, was promptly resuscitated and on 4 March 1866 it overturned – albeit without giving any reasons – the Supreme Court judgment in *Walsh*.[50]

---

[47] Pp 98–99 above.

[48] Had such an Act *preceded* enactment of the CLVA 1865, it is likely that Boothby (and plausibly Gwynne) would have held that s.7 was impliedly amended by the CLVA 1865. Stow had made the argument that s.7 – as a later provision in the CLVA 1865 than s.5 – impliedly overrides s.5 to the extent of any inconsistency between them. Neither Gwynne nor Boothby accepted that premise.

[49] Boothby provided a lengthy dissent. Both are reported at *SAR* 5 March 1866 p3, https://trove.nla.gov.au/newspaper/article/41029961.

[50] *SAR* 5 March 1866 p2, https://trove.nla.gov.au/newspaper/article/41029973. The absence of reasons might suggest that the 'court' could find no legal fault with Boothby and Gwynne's analysis. The peculiarity of the process was heightened by the 'court' hearing the appeal on a Saturday. This was the Saturday following the Friday on which judgment was given in *Ridpath* – a sequence of events which points to obvious collusion between the government, the Governor and Gwynne and Hanson. *The South Australian Advertiser*, while welcoming the outcome, commented on the: "very incongruous nature of the Court of Appeal, consisting, as it does, of gentlemen who have not had the advantage of a legal education, sitting in judgment and adjudicating upon a question of law rather than one of fact"; 6 March 1866 p2, https://trove.nla.gov.au/newspaper/article/2878554.

Not Dismissal, but Amoval – The End of Boothby's Judicial Career

Even though Boothby had been joined by Gwynne in *Walsh*, Boothby subsequently struck a lone furrow in which his constitutional objections to the validity of aspects of the colony's governmental system seem to have been subsumed beneath growing indignation about his presumed ill-treatment, indignation expressed in a succession of intemperate attacks on his judicial colleagues and the colonial Law Officers. Most particularly, Boothby now adhered to the view that his fellow judges had been unlawfully appointed to office as they had not been called to the Bar in Britain, with the result that only he (Boothby) was entitled to discharge judicial functions in the colony.

Boothby's actions resulted in considerable obstruction to the administration of court business and frequent personal abuse to Hanson and Gwynne in open court. His actions eventually provoked both Hanson and Gwynne into a public denunciation of his behaviour.[51] Boothby also managed to alienate the few supporters he might still have had among the Bar by threatening to remove from the Supreme Court rolls any counsel who questioned the correctness of Boothby's conclusions as to the existence of local courts and the Court of Appeals.[52]

He thus had no defenders from within the legal profession when the Assembly and Council again petitioned the Imperial government in 1867 to remove Boothby from office. Cardwell displayed no enthusiasm to do so, but proposed instead to refer the matter to the Privy Council. He did so ostensibly because he felt accusations as to Boothby's alleged obstructionism were closely tied to the question of whether his legal views were correct (which, Cardwell noted, they had previously been found to be: "on a former very important occasion"), because the 'charges' against Boothby lacked precision and because Boothby had not been given any opportunity to meet the case against him prior to the petitions being sent.

Although that reasoning suggests that the British government was much concerned both to respect broad constitutional principles and to ensure that Boothby was fairly treated, Cardwell was perhaps more concerned to insulate himself from criticism which might emanate from the Commons if he removed Boothby from the Court, since his despatch offered the South Australia government an alternative way forward:

> If Mr Boothby's conduct justified and the interests of the colony required, his prompt removal, it would have been far better to have adopted the responsibility for removing him under the authority of [Burke's Act] ... than to have transmitted an ex parte case to be dealt with by her Majesty's Government at the other side of the world ... I am inclined to think that even now your Government would act most wisely by commencing proceedings under that Act ...[53]

That Act seems no more relevant to Boothby's situation than it was to Montagu and Pedder's positions 20 years earlier,[54] but such was the weight of political opinion and

---

[51] Hague op cit pp 200–20.
[52] Hague op cit pp 154–55. It is difficult to avoid the conclusion that Boothby was mentally ill – and severely so – by this point.
[53] Quoted in Hague op cit pp 198–99.
[54] Pp 57–59 above.

press opinion against Boothby that the Burke's Act proceedings were initiated in June 1867.

Boothby was afforded rather more procedural entitlements than Denison had extended to Montagu and Pedder. He was offered the opportunity to present his case orally and in writing, although he declined to do so in any systematic way. After eight days of hearing evidence, the Governor and Executive Council determined that the requirement of the 1782 Act were met.[55] Amoval was effected on 29 July 1867. Boothby indicated that he would pursue the matter before the Privy Council. There is little reason to think he would have been any more successful than Montagu 20 years earlier.[56] The issue was never tested; Boothby died the next year before any 'appeal' was lodged.[57]

IV. Conclusion

Boothby's peculiarities of personality – it seems quite plausible that by twenty-first-century standards he would have been diagnosed as mentally ill – can obscure the point that he was on some issues espousing constitutional positions that were eminently credible from an orthodox perspective. That non-compliance with what CLVA 1865 s.5 termed 'manner and form' requirements in respect of colonial legislatures' lawmaking processes could invalidate the resultant colonial 'legislation' was not a contentious proposition – whether as a matter of legal theory or practical politics – by 1865. Australian colonial development had produced a constant series of such legislative failings, each responded to by the Imperial Parliament (or, if the matter was within colonial competence, by the colonial legislature) with what was presumed to be (retrospectively) validating legislation. The theoretical legal underpinnings of such practical politics were clear. Unlike the British Parliament, colonial legislatures were creations of a normatively superior lawmaker – the British Parliament itself[58] – and could thus be subjected – unlike the British Parliament – to legally enforceable rules about the way (or 'manner and form') in which their laws might be made. The CLVA 1865 was yet a further step on this well-worn constitutional path.

Given the myriad shortcomings afflicting the drafting of the CLVA 1865, Newcastle's above-quoted irritation with the carelessness of colonial legislators might bring to mind notions of stones and glass houses. Imperial legislation and Orders in Council creating colonial law were frequently marked by sloppy governmental thinking and drafting, which were left uncorrected by repeated patent and egregious failures by the Commons and the Lords to engage in any seriously critical evaluation of government proposals when passing bills.

---

[55] Hague op cit ch VII discusses the proceedings in detail.
[56] Pp 57–59 above.
[57] For a fierce (and near contemporaneous) criticism of the way that Boothby was treated see Todd (1894 2nd edn) *Parliamentary government in the British colonies* pp 846–55.
[58] In the Australian context, governmental bodies created by Order in Council were *sensu stricto* statutory in source as the Order in Council (as in Queensland's 1859 Order) was made under statutory authority rather than being (as had been the case for some British colonies in North America) a free-standing exercise of the prerogative.

Cardwell's assertion that the CLVA 1865 would resolve for all colonies the difficulties thrown up in Queensland and South Australia in the early 1860s was similarly ill-founded. And this was not because colonial judges might defy orthodox constitutional norms. Gwynne and Boothby's analysis of CLVA s.5 in *Walsh* – ie that s.5 did not retrospectively validate previously enacted colonial statutory provisions dealing with s.5[1] and s.5[2] matters if those provisions had not been passed in compliance with then extant manner and form requirements, whether Imperial (statute or Order in Council) or colonial (statute) in origin, and that it would not prospectively validate provisions having such qualities enacted in future – is not just persuasive but is compelling, given both s.5's text and the colonial legal history leading to its enactment.

Boothby and Gwynne's particular decision in *Walsh* is obviously flawed, given the presence of CLVA 1865 s.7. But the flaw is specific to South Australia.[59] The decision is also likely flawed on the basis that the impugned provisions of the Registration of Deeds Act 1862 did not fall within CLVA 1865 s.5[2] in any event. In respect of all other colonies with representative legislatures (per CLVA 1865 s.1), the credibility of the reasoning underpinning the majority view in *Walsh* as to the effect of s.5[3] on s.5[1] and/or s.5[2] matters presented obvious scope for considerable future difficulties. The Australian colonies' constitutions contained or had contained a panoply of 'manner and form' provisos, introduced primarily but not solely by Imperial statutes, all of which offered validity traps to careless or misinformed legislators.[60] More significantly perhaps, s.5[3] reinforced the obvious scope that Australia's colonial legislatures already seemed to possess to introduce *new* manner and form provisos of their own devising. The use of the future perfect and future tenses in s.5[3] – "shall have been passed in such manner and form as may from time to time be required" – 'constituted' an obvious Imperial approval of any initiatives colonial legislatures might take to alter how they might make law on s.5[1] and s.5[2] matters. That latter task was one to which from 1865 onwards Queensland's Legislature was turning its attention.

---

[59] And even within South Australia to *previously enacted* ("All Laws or reputed Laws enacted or purporting to have been enacted by the said Legislature") and *not to yet to be enacted* provisions.

[60] Inter alia: (i) a simple majority in both houses and Governor assent; (ii) a simple majority in both houses but assent reserved to the Queen; (iii) a simple majority in both houses but lay before the Commons and Lords and assent reserved to the Queen; (iv) an enhanced majority in one house, a simple majority in the other house and Governor assent; (v) an enhanced majority in one house, a simple majority in the other house, but assent reserved to the Queen; (vi) an enhanced majority in one house, a simple majority in the other house, but lay before the Commons and Lords and assent reserved to the Queen; (vii) an enhanced majority in both houses and Governor assent; or (viii) an enhanced majority in both houses but lay before the Commons and Lords and assent reserved to the Queen.

5

Constitutional Developments in New South Wales and Queensland 1865–1900

[I]t seemed ... absurd to argue that a clause having been inserted in the Constitution Act, which provided that that Act could not be altered except by a two-thirds majority, that clause could be repealed by a simple majority.

Colonial Treasurer Robert Ramsay during the passage of the (Queensland) Constitution Act Reform Act 1871 *QLAD* 1 December 1870 p168.

Questions of 'timing' regarding the franchise for Queensland's first Assembly election caused acute political and constitutional controversy in the early 1860s. The same issue arose – less immediately – over the two-thirds majority provisions. By 1859, these had been removed in New South Wales, but the prevailing assumption in Queensland was that, notwithstanding events in New South Wales, the two-thirds clauses were and should remain part of the colony's constitution. In 1862, an Assembly member for Ipswich, Arthur Macalister – the man shortly afterwards so excoriated by Lutwyche in his June 1863 article in *The (Brisbane) Courier*[1] – promoted a Constitution Bill which proposed, inter alia, turning the Council into an elected chamber and removing the two-thirds clauses, but the measure foundered in the Assembly.[2] Eight years after the colony was created, Queensland's Constitution Act 1867 s.9 reproduced verbatim s.36 [s.42] of the New South Wales Constitution Act 1855 concerning the Legislative Council; s.10 reproduced s.15 [s.17] of the 1855 Act.

I. The 'Two-Thirds' Clauses in the Queensland Constitution Act 1867

This ostensibly surprising innovation has a peculiar history. In 1866, the Queensland government established a Royal Commission to review all the colony's statute laws. The Commission had three members: Cockle and Lutwyche, then working in politically uncontentious judicial tandem, and the then Attorney-General, Charles Lilley.

---

[1] P 79 above.
[2] Bernays op cit pp 208–09.

Lilley was the Commission's instigator, and while he later credited Cockle with most of its work,[3] Lilley likely played a significant role.

The Commission emerged towards the end of a tumultuous first decade of responsible government in Queensland. As in New South Wales, with no clear political parties in existence, questions of personality and dispute over specific policy issues (notably land allocation and funding for public works, especially railways) led to frequent changes in the ministry. Macalister, for example, had entered the Assembly as an opponent of Herbert, but joined his government in 1862 and succeeded him as Premier in 1866. Macalister then resigned from office later that year when Bowen refused to assent to a government bill providing for unsecured government borrowing. Bowen subsequently invited Herbert to try to form a new ministry, but when that proved unstable asked Macalister to resume office in 1867.[4]

Lilley, appointed as Attorney-General in that 1867 ministry, had, even by the exacting standards of many colonial contemporaries, a remarkable life story.[5] Born in Newcastle (in England) in 1827 to a middle-class family but orphaned and raised by his grandparents, Lilley began articles with a solicitors' firm before joining the army, which subsequently jailed him for offering support to striking workers. After emigrating to Sydney in 1856 and initially working as a teacher, Lilley moved on to Brisbane, where he read for the Bar, edited the *Moreton Bay Courier* and threw himself into liberal political causes. In 1860, he was elected (by three votes) for a Brisbane Assembly seat as a radical liberal. In 1861, he was junior defence counsel in Pugh's seditious libel prosecution, having previously voted in the Assembly against proceedings being brought, and expressed support for Lutwyche's view that, as Lilley put it: "the constitution was illegal".[6] Lilley's personal politics were not straightforward. Despite his professed liberalism, he promoted a compulsory military service bill in 1862, which he withdrew when it provoked fury among his liberal constituents. In an era when politics was still not based on coherent party ideology, Lilley's liberalism did not preclude him from being appointed Attorney-General in Macalister's government.

Putting – Or Keeping – Them in: The Queensland Constitution Act 1867

The Commission reported early in August 1867, recommending enactment of 30 (mostly consolidating) bills.[7] The project was essentially non-partisan. Macalister's government fell at the June 1867 Assembly election, to be replaced by an administration led by Robert Mackenzie.[8] Lilley, although no longer in office, moved the Assembly

---

[3] As does Cockle's biographer; Bennet op cit pp 101–02.
[4] http://adb.anu.edu.au/biography/macalister-arthur-4055.
[5] http://adb.anu.edu.au/biography/lilley-sir-charles-4020; Gibbney (1978) 'Charles Lilley: an uncertain democrat' in Murphy and Joyce op cit; Morrison (1959–60) 'Charles Lilley' *JRAHS* 45 provides a thorough account of Lilley's life and career.
[6] *QLAD* 1 August 1861 p18.
[7] Bennet suggests that Cockle proposed very little to alteration to any existing laws; op cit pp 101–02.
[8] The son of a minor Scottish aristocrat, Mackenzie had emigrated to New South Wales in 1832. He acquired large holdings of freehold and squatter lands, which he managed so incompetently that he was bankrupted in 1844. On separation in 1859, Mackenzie had no particular track record of political activity, but Bowen

second reading of *all 30* measures on 22 October 1867. He suggested little parliamentary work was left to do:[9]

> The consolidation is mainly a consolidation; no very important alterations have been made in the law ... In consolidating the law, sir, the first work was upon the political Acts; and, with regard to these, four Bills have been produced, embodying all political matters – the Constitution Bill, the Legislative Assembly Bill, the Electoral Districts Bill, and the Elections Bill ... I think the House may be now disposed to take my assurance that no alteration has been made or attempted in the law of these subjects. Therefore, the House need not be alarmed at passing it in its entirety with very little or no question.

Although there was considerable agitation in the Queensland press to reform the Assembly franchise laws along the lines of those in New South Wales, Macalister's government resisted such pressure, with little parliamentary dissent.[10] Mackenzie's administration had the same view. Lilley and Cockle had made no suggestion that such reform was a desirable part of the 1867 consolidation process.

There is no indication that the Constitution Bill 1867 received any searching evaluation in either the Assembly or the Council. A Council select committee report published on 19 December 1867 recommended that the compendious list of matters relating to parliamentary privilege[11] (copied from the 1859 Order) be replaced by a simple clause equating the privileges of the Assembly and Council with those of the Commons and Lords, but that proposal was rejected.

The Constitution Act 1867 is a sloppy mishmash of substantive content and drafting. Bits of it reproduce verbatim (or nearly so) clauses of the 1859 Order; other bits reproduce verbatim (or nearly so) sections of the 1855 Act. Other parts of the Order and 1855 Act are omitted entirely. The Constitution Act 1867 has a long preamble, which roots the Legislature's power to enact it in cl.22 of the Order, but which does not expressly state that any parts of the Order are being amended or repealed. Nor does the preamble, or any other part of the Act, expressly replicate cl.22, which permitted the amendment of (most parts of) the Order.

S.1 (Act) reproduces cl.1 (Order) and s.2 (Act) verbatim reproduces cl.2 of the Order. So it is conceivable that the "all cases whatsoever" provision in s.2/cl.2 was supposed to embrace the cl.22 power (which in the Order was quite distinct from the cl.2 power) as well as the cl.2 power, but that is not made explicit in the Act and there is no parliamentary record to support or refute that assumption. It may be that Cockle and Lilley and the Queensland parliamentarians considered that in future all aspects of Queensland's law and governmental system were presumptively amendable in the 'ordinary way'

---

catapulted him into high office as Treasurer in Herbert's first government. By 1867 Mackenzie had once again established himself as a pastoralist, with large holdings of both leased and squatted land. Initially a bitter rival (for personal rather than ideological reasons) of Macalister, Mackenzie nonetheless entered Macalister's Cabinet in 1866, from where he promptly (and successfully) plotted to replace Macalister as Premier. His primary achievement as Premier was to promote legislation allowing Queensland squatters to regularise their landholdings on very favourable terms – a very different policy to that pursued in New South Wales under Robertson's land acts (pp 60–62 above); http://adb.anu.edu.au/biography/mackenzie-sir-robert-ramsay-4109.

[9] *QLAD* 22 October 1867 p543.
[10] See *BC* 18 September 1867 p2, https://trove.nla.gov.au/newspaper/article/1287382; 30 September 1867 p2, https://trove.nla.gov.au/newspaper/article/1287627.
[11] Ss.41–56 of a 57-section statute.

(subject to Colonial Laws Validity Act 1865 (hereafter CLVA 1865) s.2's general prohibition and other explicit exceptions), but that it is at best a presumption.

At the colony's inception, the chronological inconsistency between cl.1 and c.8 of the 1859 Order – and cl.8's obvious (but overlooked, other than by Lutwyche) incompatibility with s.7 [BAA][12] – raised a question regarding the existence in Queensland law of Wentworth's special majority provisions in s.17 [s.15] and s.42 [s.36] of the 1855 Act. Those doubts had been removed by the retrospective validating Imperial legislation – the Australian Colonies Act 1861 s.3[13] – which lent cl.8 an unquestionably legal basis. One consequence of that validation was that the special majority provisions, repealed in New South Wales,[14] were part of Queensland law when Cockle and Lilley began their consolidation project.

The provisions reappeared verbatim in the Constitution Act 1867. S.9 reproduced s.42 [s.36]; s.10 reproduced s.17 [s.15]. There is nothing in the parliamentary record to indicate that Cockle or Lilley or any member of either house considered that s.9 and s.10 were an exercise of the CLVA 1865 s.5[3] power. But, seen from that perspective, s.9 arguably has six 'manner and form' departures from the 'ordinary way' of legislating: (i) and (ii) a two-thirds majority at second and third readings in the Assembly; (iii) and (iv) a two-thirds majority at second and third readings in the Council; (v) reservation for the royal assent; and (vi) laying before the Commons and Lords for 30 days before assent is given. S.10 has five such departures: (i) and (ii) a two-thirds majority at second and third readings in the Assembly; (iii) and (iv) a majority of all members (rather those present) at second and third readings in the Council; and (v) an address from the Assembly to the Governor prior to assent that (i)–(iv) have been complied with.

The way that s.9 and s.10 fit with other parts of (and omissions from) the Act is distinctly uncomfortable. The rather obvious difficulties which present themselves suggest that neither Lilley nor Cockle, nor any of their parliamentary colleagues, gave any careful thought to the details of the New South Wales measures. S.26 makes provision for a quorum in the Council, this being at least one-third of the 'members' (presumably all members). S.26 also provides that *all* questions arising in the Council be decided by a bare majority of *members present*. S.26 makes no reference to s.9 or s.10. Neither s.9 nor s.10 make any reference to s.26. S.9 has a 'Notwithstanding anything hereinbefore contained' clause (ie ss.1–8), but no 'hereinafter contained' clause (ie s.26). S.10 has neither a 'hereinbefore' nor 'hereinafter' clause. If s.9 and s.10 are not included in the *all questions* of s.26, it can only be because of a presumption that a specific provision overrides a general one.

The Act says nothing regarding quorums or presumptive majorities in the Assembly. That issue was dealt with in an entirely separate Act (another of the 30), the Legislative Assembly Act 1867 at s.13, which required a quorum of 16. Notably, per s.13, the determination of questions in the Assembly is framed differently from s.26: "all questions (excepted as by law is excepted)" are to be decided by a bare majority of members present. The 'excepted' proviso presumably applies to s.9 and s.10 of the Constitution Act, but neither section is expressly identified in s.13. There is no suggestion in the text

---

[12] Pp 67–70 above.
[13] P 77 above.
[14] Pp 56–58 above.

of either Act, nor in the relevant legislative debates, that Queensland's legislators were even alert to, still less adopting, the 'Two Act' approach to amendment or repeal of the two-thirds clauses which had been considered necessary (whether legally or just politically necessary is unclear) by New South Wales legislators in 1857.[15]

Lilley's role in the consolidation initiative perhaps enhanced his reputation as a politician with broad parliamentary appeal. Mackenzie's 1867 government lasted barely a year. Following the election of September 1868, called after the Assembly's dissolution, Lilley, with Macalister's support, emerged as Premier. He held the post for just two years, during which he presided over several factious and unstable cabinets and achieved little legislative reform.

Taking (One of) them Out – The Constitution Act Amendment Act 1871

It is ostensibly surprising that s.10's repeal occurred while the Queensland government was led by Arthur Palmer, a squatter of a distinctly conservative ideological hue.[16] However, the repeal bill did not originate as a government measure. Lilley took the initiative, moving a private members bill for second reading on 1 December 1870. The bill was drafted to repeal both s.9 and s.10[17]

Lilley began by explaining why he was now moving to abolish constitutional provisions he had previously supported. His support had been based on a fear – "undefined and perhaps unjustifiable"[18] – that allowing reapportionment on a bare majority basis might enable one Assembly faction to impose unjust laws on the entire colony. But now, just three years later, Lilley considered that: "[P]opular opinion is sufficiently strong and the press watchful enough to guard the interests of all classes in the community".[19] A more cynical observer might attribute Lilley's change of heart to the fact that he was Premier between November 1868 and May 1870, and benefiting from the existing apportionment laws, but was in opposition in December 1870 and saw apportionment reform as his route back to power.[20]

---

[15] Pp 56–58 above.
[16] Palmer emigrated to New South Wales from Ireland as a 20-year-old in 1838. By 1863 he was variously leasing and squatting some 900 square miles of Queensland pastoral land. He was first elected to the Assembly in 1866 and became Premier when Lilley's government collapsed in 1870. His administration lasted for some four years, and was the first to have a credible claim to be a party-based ministry in any coherent sense; Berys op cit pp 58–59, http://adb.anu.edu.au/biography/palmer-sir-arthur-hunter-794.
[17] QLAD 1 December 1870 p155 et seq. The bill was squeezed into a busy afternoon, which began with a heated exchange about 'Outrages by the blacks' (pp 155–57), then second reading of the Gold Duty Repeal Bill (pp 157–65); after Lilley's repeal bill was debated (pp 165–72), it closed with second reading on another Lilley-sponsored measure to allow Queensland residents to sit London University exams in the colony (pp 172–75).
[18] ibid p165. One might credibly assume that in 1867 Lilley had not thought about the matter at all, but simply copied New South Wales law into the 1867 Act.
[19] ibid.
[20] See the comments of the then Secretary for Public Lands, William Walsh; ibid p171. Walsh, a squatter, is the subject of a remarkably unflattering biography in the *Australian Dictionary*, which describes him as, inter alia: "gauche, nasty, devious, highly egocentric and prone to strident appeals to English tradition … [H]e was probably one of the most hated men of his time"; http://adb.anu.edu.au/biography/walsh-william-henry-4795.

Lilley's 'Singular Omission' Analysis of the Special Majority Clauses

Such cynicism was not a point Lilley conceded. He did, however, accept that his primary motive for presenting the bill was his assumption that apportionment reform would not attract two-thirds majority Assembly support[21] in the foreseeable future and that such reform was immediately desirable. He then turned to a matter of obvious importance which he and Cockle had not addressed in 1867:

> ... [S]ome question may be raised as to whether it is competent to the House to repeal the proviso itself, without the consent of two-thirds of the whole number of members. Now, sir, I have no doubt upon that matter myself; and, whatever weight my opinion may have in this House, I am not able to say, but I think it can hardly admit of a doubt that it is competent for the House to repeal this proviso, as well as to repeal the whole Constitution Act. It would not be contended for a moment that it would be essential to have two-thirds of the entire Assembly to vote the repeal of the entire Constitution Act; and, if the entire Act may be repealed by a simple majority, there is nothing in the Act to justify the opinion that the proviso itself may not be. *It is a singular omission on the part of those who enacted the constitution itself that they did not carry out by two or three words that it shall not be lawful to prevent, with Bills for certain purposes mentioned in the proviso itself, "any Bill for the repeal of this constitution," unless two-thirds of the members of this House shall assent.* It is an omission; and that omission enables this House to repeal this proviso by a simple majority.[22]

Lilley buttressed his opinion by telling the Assembly that simple majority repeal: "is the opinion of all the lawyers in New South Wales – I never hear one express a contrary opinion on this matter".[23] That view presumably rested on the credible premise that cl.22 had the same effect in Queensland as s.4 [BAA] had in New South Wales – that effect being the one identified in Russell's despatch – although Lilley did not make the point explicitly. Lilley could not invoke repeal of the two-thirds clauses in New South Wales as a precedent, as those clauses were repealed in 1857 without division.[24]

Lilley clearly accepted that the Legislature could have protected the two-thirds clauses by making the clauses' own repeal or amendment conditional upon the garnering of two-thirds majorities; it just had not done so. Lilley made no mention of the CLVA 1865 (which of course pre-dates the 1867 Act) in his speech. Nor did he allude to the 'special majorities' suggestion in Palmer and Collier's 1864 Report,[25] a document with which he must have been familiar. One cannot therefore confidently conclude whether he had the CLVA 1865 s.5, cl.22 or some other legal source in mind as the mechanism through which that 'omission' could have been remedied.

Indeed, none of the six members[26] who spoke in the debate referred to the CLVA 1865 or cl.22. Two ministers spoke against the bill: the then Colonial Treasurer,

---

[21] Oddly, Lilley made no mention of the less likely prospect that such a Council majority could be achieved.
[22] *QLAD* 1 December 1870 p166; emphasis added.
[23] ibid.
[24] P 58 above. Nor did Lilley refer to the speeches offered by New South Wales legislators during the passage of the Act repealing the two-thirds clauses (p 57 above) that a 'Two Act' process of amendment or repeal was required.
[25] Pp 103–104 above.
[26] The Assembly then had only 32 members.

Robert Ramsay, and the Secretary for Public Lands, John Malbon Thompson, a Sydney-born solicitor.[27] Both opposed the measure per se, and contested Lilley's assertion that it could be enacted by simple majority. Neither minister offered any legal authority for that view. Ramsay, after drawing the Assembly's attention to the use of special majority measures in the United States Constitution and alluding to Wentworth qua framer of Queensland's constitution as: "one of the ablest men Australia had ever produced", could conclude only that:

> [I]t seemed to him absurd to argue that a clause having been inserted in the Constitution Act, which provided that that Act could not be altered except by a two-thirds majority, that clause could be repealed by a simple majority.[28]

Lilley's bare majority position was supported by the former Attorney-General, Ratcliffe Pring, and also by the then Speaker, the former (and future) Premier, Arthur Macalister,[29] who allowed the vote to proceed on the bare majority basis. The bill passed second reading by 15–12, albeit that the record of proceedings ended with a note that:

> The SECRETARY FOR PUBLIC LANDS objected to the decision the House had come to inasmuch as he considered that it was contrary to the provisions of the Constitution Act, which required that there should be a two-thirds majority for the passing of such a measure.

Council second reading was on 22 December 1870. The bill received a hostile reception: in part because it was thought too important to be presented so late in the session; in part because it originated in a private member's bill rather than a government bill; and in part because – and on this point several members reverentially invoked Wentworth and his concerns about 'democracy' – a two-thirds requirement was thought a valuable bulwark against unduly hasty legislation. Several members did, however, indicate that if the bill were amended to address only s.10 it would receive their support. After a short debate, the Council resolved, without division, to adjourn second reading for six months.[30]

The Amended Bill – Repealing s.10; Retaining s.9

Consideration resumed in May 1871, when Lilley – seeking a meaningful compromise with the Council majority – moved an amended version that removed the reference to s.9.[31] The terms of the debate echoed those discussed in 1870, and concluded with a spirited exchange between Pring and Malbon Thompson on whether a two-thirds majority was required to repeal s.10. Pring expressly invoked Russell's despatch as the

---

[27] Ramsay was a pastoralist whose primary political concern, shared with Mackenzie, Palmer and Macalister, was preventing redistributive land reform; http://adb.anu.edu.au/biography/ramsay-robert-4447. Both Ramsay and Thompson held rural seats with small electorates, and so were beneficiaries of numerical inequality in constituency electorate sizes; http://adb.anu.edu.au/biography/thompson-john-malbon-4712.
[28] *QLAD* 1 December 1870 p168. Ramsay presumably saw the 1859 Order as echoing the 1855 Act; that, in turn, was an echo of the 1853 Bill, which was primarily Wentworth's work. Ramsay and Thompson made no reference to s.4 [BAA] or to Russell's despatch.
[29] http://adb.anu.edu.au/biography/macalister-arthur-4055.
[30] *QLCD* 22 December 1870 p289.
[31] *QLAD* 4 May 1871 p153.

source of the Legislature's power to repeal s.10 by simple majorities in each house, a view with which Speaker Macalister, formally ruling on the matter, concurred. The final vote was 15–14 (the 14 including Palmer and all his ministers) for second reading.[32]

The bill came before the Council on 14 June. True to their comments in December, several Council members who opposed the original bill indicated that they would support the amended version. The debate was, however, most notable because of a fierce disagreement over whether a bill to repeal (rather than amend) s.10 required an absolute or simple majority in the Council. The Council vote was nine in favour and six against. While that was a majority (and, indeed, a two-thirds majority) of members voting, s.10 required a simple majority of all members. Since the Council then had 21 members, a s.10 majority would require 11 votes in favour. The then Chairman of Committees[33] who presided over the debate formally ruled, ignoring references from the bill's supporters to s.26 and Russell's despatch, that the s.10 majority applied to repeal of s.10 and so the second reading was not carried. A motion to overturn that ruling was then carried by a majority of members present and, amid scenes of confusion,[34] the bill was passed. The controversy was not reignited at third reading on 16 June. The bill passed with little debate and without division.[35] The Act came into force on 19 June.[36]

Table 5.1 The Queensland Legislative Assembly electorate, 1860–93[a]

Election	Registered voters	Seats
1860	4790	26
1863	8307	26
1867	15331	32
1868	15605	32
1870	16591	32
1871	18793	32
1873	23864	42
1878	49331	55
1883	56998	55
1888	70565	72
1893	86983	72

[a] Figures are taken from the University of Western Australia's *Politics and elections database*, http://elections.uwa.edu.au/elecdetail.lasso.

---

[32] ibid pp 157–59.
[33] This being Daniel Roberts, a Brisbane solicitor (and not a squatter), beaten by Lilley for the Fortitude Valley Assembly seat in 1860 by three votes; http://oa.anu.edu.au/obituary/roberts-daniel-foley-14622. Bowen immediately appointed Roberts to the Council. One can only speculate on the purity of Roberts's motives.
[34] *The Queenslander* described events as: "a regular muddle ... principally through the indecision of the Chairman", and expressed much surprise that anyone could have thought that s.10's special majority provisions applied to its own repeal; 17 June 1871 p10, https://trove.nla.gov.au/newspaper/article/27266418.
[35] *QLCD* 16 June 1871 pp 455–56.
[36] The Constitution Act Amendment Act 1871.

A leader in the *BC* that day welcomed repeal of: "this obnoxious clause [which] has hitherto proved an insurmountable obstacle in the way of all effective reform of Parliament". The *BC* considered repeal but a first step to reform. Three further measures were also essential: a franchise qualification (for men) based on residence coupled with a significant reapportionment of Assembly seats; and an Act introducing payment of salaries to Assembly members:

> And – there is little doubt that both measures, revolutionary as they may look, will prove in the best sense of the most conservative tendency, and will be adapted to promote the assured and permanent welfare of the country. They are both based on just principles. They possess every theoretic and historic recommendation. The sooner they are adopted by us, the better will it be for our every interest.[37]

Electoral Reform … or Not

In 1861, Lilley introduced a motion in the Assembly on the opening of the 1861 session calling for legislation to match the franchise in Queensland to the 1858 New South Wales electoral rules and accusing Herbert of reneging upon a promise to promote such a bill.[38] The motion attracted the support of only two other members,[39] but was vigorously approved in a leader in the *BC* (likely written by Pugh).[40] Lilley's own evangelism in that cause then waned; as noted above, he had not pressed the issue in 1867. In 1864, Pugh had informed the Assembly that he: "was of the opinion that every man of the age of twenty-one, in full possession of his senses, had a right to vote".[41] In the same debate, Macalister (then Secretary of Lands in a Herbert administration) felt no compunction in saying that he: "had never considered that every man should have a vote, nor had he heard any reasons to induce him to alter his opinions on the subject".[42]

Lilley's 1868–70 ministry did not press the issue. So, some 12 years after New South Wales had adopted a near-universal male adult franchise,[43] Queensland retained its restrictive property-based qualification. It is perhaps a powerful illustration of the essential incoherence of political ideology within the Assembly in this era that Queensland's eventual step in the avowedly more liberal direction of the franchise laws of New South Wales should occur during the tenure of an avowedly non-liberal government.

Despite Lilley's best efforts, Palmer emerged from the July–September 1871 election with an (initial) Assembly majority[44] of six. His new ministry included Ramsay and Thompson, who had so forcefully defended the two-thirds clauses in December 1870.

---

[37] https://trove.nla.gov.au/newspaper/article/1326544.
[38] *QLAD* 30 April 1861 p 6.
[39] ibid p 8.
[40] *BC* 14 May 1861 p6, https://trove.nla.gov.au/newspaper/article/4598880.
[41] *QLAD* 31 May 1864 p148.
[42] ibid 145. My thanks to Lauchs (2010) 'The return of manhood suffrage to Queensland, 1863–1872' *Journal of Australian Colonial History* 119, 133–34 for alerting me to these comments.
[43] Britain's 1867 Reform Act, sponsored by Disraeli, had substantially increased the size of the Commons electorate but fell far short of a universal male franchise; Loveland (2018) op cit pp 175–77.
[44] The term is again used guardedly as there was still no explicit clear party political organisation in Queensland, although there was a discernible and intensifying cleavage between squatter and 'urban' interests; see Morrison (1962) 'The town "liberal" and the squatter' *RHSQJ* 599.

The Legislature came back into session on 7 November 1871. By the end of the first parliamentary session in 1872 a new electoral law – the Electoral Act 1872 – had been enacted.

Lauchs's careful analysis of the Act's parliamentary history[45] suggests the measure was not – as one might have expected – the result of a keenly fought ideological battle between identifiably liberal and reactionary factions in the Assembly and Council. While there was certainly coherent pressure from the former direction, it was acquiesced in rather than opposed by many more conservatively inclined legislators on the basis that widespread corruption and administrative incompetence in applying the existing law had so undermined the integrity of the 1867 arrangements that little would be lost by enacting a statute which would be more straightforward to administer.

The Electoral Act 1872[46] echoed the 1858 New South Wales legislation. S.3 presumptively extended the franchise to any man over 21 years old who was a British subject and had been resident in a particular electoral district for at least six months prior to the election. Such people could also vote in any other electoral district where they held freehold property worth over £100 or were householders or leaseholders (of any land) worth over £10 per year. However, men of Chinese, South Sea Islands or indigenous Australian ethnicity could qualify only through the property criteria.[47]

The franchise legislation was rapidly followed by a reapportionment statute. The Assembly's size was increased from 32 to 42 seats in a fashion which certainly ameliorated, but equally certainly did not eradicate, the pro-rural (and hence pro-pastoralist) skewing of the previous law.

The electorate at the first post-reform Assembly election of November 1873 numbered almost 24,000, compared to 18,000 at the July 1871 poll.[48] The turnout – 55% of eligible voters – rather suggests that press enthusiasm for reform ran in advance of wider public opinion. The alterations in electoral law did not prompt any immediate hardening of party political identities. One might at most suggest that voters were presented with Palmer as the likely leader of a conservatively inclined faction, and Lilley and Macalister at the head of a more liberal grouping. In the event, Macalister emerged as Premier of yet another loosely constructed minority administration. Although the pervasive fragility of governments in that era presented Lilley with an obvious prospect of once again becoming Premier, he left the legislative arena in 1874 to accept a seat on the State Supreme Court.[49] His departure opened the door for the arrival of another ambitious young barrister on the political stage, one Samuel Griffith.

---

[45] Op cit.
[46] 35 Vict No 5.
[47] The New South Wales exclusions (persons of unsound mind, those receiving charitable sustenance, serving military officers, felons still serving their sentences) also applied per s.6. S.5 envisaged a seat for a university as and when one was established in Queensland.
[48] Some of that increase was attributable to population growth rather than franchise reform; http://elections.uwa.edu.au/elecdetail.lasso?keyvalue=1708; http://elections.uwa.edu.au/elecdetail.lasso?keyvalue=1709.
[49] Lilley's commission is at http://archive.sclqld.org.au/_digitisation/JudgesCommissions/0002_18740704_LilleyC.pdf.

II. Queensland – Griffith … and McIlwraith

Griffith was the son of an émigré English clergyman.[50] After an outstanding educational career in Australia, Griffith combined qualification as a solicitor with forays into school teaching and political journalism. He entered the Queensland Bar in 1867, and had taken silk within 10 years. He was elected as a 'liberal' member of the Assembly in 1872, espousing distinctly anti-squatter political views, and served as Attorney-General between 1874 and 1878 under Macalister's premiership and those of Macalister's short-lived successors, George Thorn and John Douglas. Despite the rapid turnover of leaders, there was some coherence in these ministries' efforts to push the colony's longer-term development in a liberal direction. Most notably, the 1878 Electoral Districts Act increased the size of the Assembly from 42 to 55 members, the additional 13 being allocated in a way that further ameliorated the pro-pastoralist apportionment bias.

Griffith has been described as a power behind the throne of these administrations,[51] but it was not until 1880 that Griffith became the obvious leader of the Assembly's liberal grouping, from which point it is perhaps credible to suggest that a liberal party had become a feature – albeit more blurred than distinct – of the political landscape.[52]

Griffith's emergence in that capacity coincided with the rise to pre-eminence in more conservative circles of Thomas McIlwraith. Perversely perhaps, given the presumed purpose of the 1878 Act as being to strengthen liberal representation in the Assembly, McIlwraith's supporters won a majority in the ensuing 1878 election. McIlwraith was a Scots émigré, who initially worked as a surveyor and engineer in Victoria, but by the mid-1860s had established himself as a pastoralist in Queensland. He was elected to the Assembly in 1871, and was appointed to Macalister's cabinet in 1874. His presence in that cabinet – alongside Griffith – points both to the emergent rather than established party character of Queensland politics in that era and also to McIlwraith's own complicated personal politics. Although a pastoralist, McIlwraith had significant financial interests in various banking, steamship and railway enterprises. As a politician, he favoured extensive public works investment, especially in railways, financed by borrowing and land grants rather than taxation. He also favoured steering a notable portion of such public investment towards companies in which he held a personal financial interest.

McIlwraith also appointed Charles Lilley Chief Justice in 1879 following Cockle's retirement.[53] That McIlwraith had offered Lilley the post, given their obvious differences on many political questions, is a testament perhaps to a shared presumption

---

[50] Joyce (1978) 'Samuel Walker Griffith: a liberal lawyer' in Murphy and Joyce op cit; Bernys op cit pp 72–73; http://adb.anu.edu.au/biography/griffith-sir-samuel-walker-445; Joyce (1974) 'SW Griffith: towards the biography of a lawyer' *Historical Studies* 235.
[51] http://adb.anu.edu.au/biography/thorn-george-4942; Joyce op cit.
[52] I use the term 'party' in a very guarded sense in the next few pages.
[53] Lutwyche had not lobbied for the post because of ill-health, and died in office in 1880. Cockle retired to England, where he pursued his interest in mathematics and astronomy with some considerable distinction prior to his death in 1895. Lilley's appointment was widely approved in the popular press; see *The Telegraph* 26 June 1879 p2, https://trove.nla.gov.au/newspaper/article/169502850; *BC* 12 July 1879 p5, https://trove.nla.gov.au/newspaper/article/886293.

among the Queensland political class as to the non-partisan nature of the judiciary; or, perhaps more cynically, as to the relative unimportance of the Court within the colony's political structure.

After the liberal grouping's election defeat in 1878, Griffith became 'party' leader and led his supporters to two election victories in the 1880s. For present purposes, the most notable events arising during his premierships was a dispute between the Assembly and the Council over, in narrow terms, the payment of a salary to Assembly members and, more broadly, the two houses' respective powers over appropriation bills.

Points of Division in a 'No-Party System'

Griffith and McIlwraith's respective rises to political eminence occurred in the context of substantial population growth in Queensland. Many recent émigrés were British and Irish, often from impoverished backgrounds, lured both by the offer of assisted passage and an unrealistically romanticised image of the economic prospects that awaited them. They arrived to find that Queensland did not offer them any immediate improvement in their living conditions.

Two other distinct groups contributed to Queensland's rapid population rise. Significant numbers of Chinese men had come to the Queensland area of New South Wales during the gold rush years of the 1850s; many others arrived following discovery of rich gold reserves in the Palmer River region in 1873.[54] The second group – colloquially referred to as 'Kanakas' – were men from the Melanesian islands,[55] brought to work on the sugar plantations that were becoming an increasingly important element of Queensland's economy. The sugar industry was in a narrow sense 'agricultural' rather than 'pastoral' in terms of its product, but its organisation built on a plantation system – with obvious parallels to the post-slavery form of indentured labour prevailing in the south of the United States – in which Kanaka men were 'employed' for limited periods on very low wages and in very poor working conditions, serving, in effect, as a replacement for the convict labour which had sustained the early growth of pastoralism.[56]

Immigration policy with respect to Chinese and Kanaka peoples provided a sharp point of division between the McIlwraith and Griffith factions in the 1880s. McIlwraith's support for substantial continued immigration was rooted primarily in support for the sugar plantation interest. Griffith's opposition was founded (much) less on a concern with protecting non-white labourers from exploitation than with his preference for seeing land development favour small agricultural producers, a policy he pursued by successfully promoting a bill which would end the importation of Kanaka labourers in 1890.

The nascent parties were similarly divided on the issue of recognising trade unions as lawful organisations, a measure which Griffith favoured and McIlwraith opposed.

---

[54] Ward (1992) op cit pp 143–44.

[55] These being among the 'South Sea islands' identified in s.3 of the 1872 Electoral Act. There was no realistic prospect of Kanaka labourers ever satisfying the Act's qualification criteria.

[56] See generally Ward (1992) op cit pp 144–45; Bernys op cit pp 64–72, who (writing in 1919) provides a remarkable insight into the presumed legitimacy among white Queenslanders of the exploitation of Kanaka labourers; Megarrity L (2006) '"White Queensland": the Queensland government's ideological position on the use of Pacific Island labourers in the sugar sector 1880–1901' *Australian Journal of Politics and History* 1.

The factions also disagreed on railways policy; Griffith was generally unsympathetic to the policy favoured by McIlwraith of financing railway expansion by giving railway companies substantial grants of Crown lands.

The ideological divisions between Griffith and McIlwraith were accompanied by quite intense personal antagonism. This reached its zenith over allegations that McIlwraith's governments had improperly awarded lucrative government contracts to companies in which McIlwraith had a substantial financial interest. The matter had been resolved on party lines in Assembly in McIlwraith's favour, but the intensity of the scandal was sufficient for a royal commission to be established subsequently in London to investigate the allegation in 1881. Griffith appeared, in effect, as prosecuting counsel. McIlwraith was eventually cleared of any wrongdoing, but Griffith nonetheless returned to Brisbane to find himself acclaimed even more loudly than before as the chief proponent of political liberalism in the colony.

In the constitutional context, however, the most significant episode during the years of Griffith–McIlwraith pre-eminence in the 1880s arose – in narrow terms – over Griffith's efforts to have legislation enacted to provide for the payment of a salary and expenses to Assembly members and – in a broader sense – concerning the two houses' respective powers over the contents of appropriation and money bills.

Political and Legal Dimensions of Assembly Council Relations

Griffith's administrations faced varying degrees of obstruction in the Legislative Council over several policy issues. There was no formal party organisation in the Council, but the effective balance of forces was such that 'liberal' measures passed in the Assembly invariably faced an ideologically hostile Council majority. The major cause of tension between Griffith's administrations and the Council was more generic. The Council consistently claimed that it was entitled to amend government appropriations bills. As a matter of strict law, the Council's position was correct. The Constitution Act 1867 drew no distinction between the two houses in terms of their respective legislative powers save for the proviso in s.2 (copied verbatim from s.1 of sch.1 of the 1855 Act), which required that appropriation bills begin their parliamentary passage in the Assembly.

The specific flashpoint for this pervasive difficulty was the Council's rejections in 1884 and 1885[57] of Griffith's bill to introduce payment of expenses to Assembly members. Griffith's proposal was a modest one, entailing the reimbursement of travel costs and a £2 daily subsistence allowance. The measure's quantitative financial impact would be negligible, although £150–200 per year would service a modestly comfortable standard of living for an individual in 1880s Brisbane.[58]

---

[57] The 1885 bill had passed Assembly second reading with little debate by 35 votes to 22; *QLAD* 14 July pp 72–75. There was no debate or division at third reading, and it passed without division; *QLAD* 16 July 1885 p114. At Council second reading the bill was adjourned for six months without division; *QLCD* 29 July 1885 p30.

[58] An eight-room house (with an attached shop) in the West End neighbourhood of Brisbane could then be bought freehold for £250; *BC* 5 June 1884 p1, https://trove.nla.gov.au/newspaper/article/3430775. The Assembly sat for 74 days in 1886, which would have yielded an inveterate attendee £148 in 'expenses'; www.parliament.qld.gov.au/work-of-assembly/sitting-dates/dates/1886/1886-12-02.

Griffith's government responded to the second defeat by tacking a sum equivalent to that earmarked to meet the costs which would have been incurred under the rejected bill (some £7000) onto a general appropriations bill under the heading 'The Legislative Assembly's Establishment'. The Council responded by amending the bill to remove the £7000.[59]

Griffith was concerned to settle the broader constitutional question and made his position clear in an Assembly speech on 12 November 1885.[60] In Griffith's view, the Council's role within the legislative process was the same as that played by the House of Lords in Britain. He maintained – speaking perhaps more as a politician than a lawyer – that the text of the Constitution Act 1867, which did not expressly deny the Council such a power, had to be read in that broader constitutional context. Griffith referred back to the Commons 1678 resolution,[61] and observed that this was not a matter over which the British houses had subsequently clashed. The rationale for the principle, rather stronger in 1885 than in 1678, was rooted in notions of representative legitimacy: a characteristic that could be claimed by the Assembly but not by the Council. Griffith also invoked and quoted extensively from Todd's treatise *Parliamentary government in the colonies* to support the assertion that no other colonial upper house had exercised the power which the Council was claiming.[62]

Assembly debate on 12 November 1885 culminated in an exchange of messages between the houses in which the Assembly demanded that the Council accept its subordination to the Assembly on this matter and the Council – standing on the text of the Constitution Act – bluntly refusing to do so.[63] The Assembly and Council subsequently agreed that a request be sent to the Privy Council asking it to determine the issue. The message of 17 November 1885 asked:

(1) Whether the Constitution Act 1867 confers on the Legislative Council powers coordinate with those of the Legislative Assembly in the amendment of all Bills, including money Bills?
(2) Whether the claims of the Legislative Assembly, as set forth in their message of the 12th November, are well-founded?[64]

Several months would pass before any reply would be received. Rather than leave the colony with no appropriations measure in place, the Council withdrew its amendments and the bill passed with the tack in place.[65]

Griffith then, it seems, engaged in some ethical sharp practice in (covertly) casting the questions put to the Privy Council as matters of politics rather than law. In a letter

---

[59] QLCD 11 November 1885 p255.
[60] QLAD 12 November 1885 p1564.
[61] P 38 above.
[62] McIlwraith expressed sympathy with Griffith's overall objective, but deplored the tack and suggested the proper way to proceed was to promote a bill to amend the Constitution Act expressly to confirm that the Council had no power to amend appropriation bills; QLAD 12 November 1885 pp 1566–68. McIlwraith had also made clear, however, that he felt the Council's 'unprecedented' action was a justifiable response to the similarly unprecedented action by the government to negate defeat on the expenses bill by tacking the £7000 onto the appropriations measure; QLAD 11 November 1885 pp 1562–63.
[63] ibid p1570.
[64] QLAD 17 November 1885 p1575.
[65] QLCD 17 November 1885 p274.

to Queensland's then Governor Sir Anthony Musgrave[66] on 26 November 1885, Griffith wrote:

> [T]he questions submitted (and in particular the second question) are rather questions as to the constitutional rights and powers of the two Houses of the Legislature than technical questions as to the construction of the statute law. So far, at least, as the Legislative Assembly are concerned, *I think I am right in saying that the literal interpretation of the words of the Constitution Act is regarded as a matter of small importance* as compared with the larger question, Whether, on a true construction of the written and unwritten Constitution of the colony, the two Houses of the Legislature should be regarded as holding and discharging, relatively to one another, positions and functions analogous to those of the House of Lords and House of Commons.[67]

Griffith enjoyed Musgrave's sympathy and support, and Musgrave, forwarded a lengthy letter to the then Lord President of the Privy Council Frederick Stanley MP,[68] hoping for an amicable long-term solution to what he regarded as an unpleasant blot on the Australian colonies' respective constitutional maps:

> Almost all collisions and complications of any importance, in the administration of this group of colonies at least, have arisen from conflicting views of the rights and privileges of the two Legislative Houses. It will tend greatly to the avoidance of future mischief, not only in this colony but in others, if it should be found possible to provide an umpire in a body whose decision will be respected as entirely free from local or official bias, and to establish a precedent for reference of doubtful or disputed points to such an arbitrator in a friendly manner.[69]

Musgrave also enclosed – undoubtedly with Griffith's approval, but without making the fact public knowledge – Griffith's own letter, which added a distinctly 'political' rider to the narrow legal question which the houses had agreed to refer.

Any hope that Musgrave might have had that the Privy Council could effectively perform that 'umpire' role was promptly disappointed. The Privy Council's 'judgment' merits extensive quotation to illustrate not simply the lamentable inadequacy of its reasoning, but the absence of any reasoning at all:

The Council Office to the Colonial Office.

Sir,
Whitehall,
Registrar, P.C.
3rd April, 1886 …

---

[66] Musgrave, a career civil servant, was born, educated and began his career in the West Indies. In the 1860s and 1870 he served successively as Governor of Newfoundland and British Columbia. He was Governor of South Australia between 1873 and 1877 and then Governor of Jamaica, before being appointed to Queensland in 1883.

[67] Emphasis added.

[68] Stanley was the second son of the 14th Earl of Derby, who had been Prime Minister in three administrations in the mid-19th century. Stanley himself held various ministerial positions under Disraeli, and served in 1885 and early 1886 as Secretary of State for the Colonies in the Marquess of Salisbury's Tory government, before moving to the Lords and becoming Lord President of the Council; Matthew (2006) 'Stanley, Frederick Arthur, sixteenth Earl of Derby' *ODNB*.

[69] 26 November 1885. Musgrave seemed unaware that the Privy Council had an obvious statutory jurisdiction to address the issue per s.4 of the Act for the Better Administration of Justice in His Majesty's Privy Council 1833 (3 & 4 Wil IV c 41) s.4: "It shall be lawful for His Majesty to refer to the said Judicial

The Lords of the Committee present on this occasion were the Lord President, the Lord High Chancellor,[70] His Grace the Duke of Richmond and Gordon, Lord Aberdare, Lord Blackburn, Lord Hobhouse, and Sir Richard Couch; and their Lordships, having considered the petition and the two questions therein raised, namely

1. Whether the Constitution Act of 1867 confers on the Legislative Council powers co-ordinate with those of the Legislative Assembly in the amendment of all Bills, including money Bills;
2. Whether the claims of the Legislative Assembly, as set forth in their message of the 12th November, are well founded

agreed humbly to report to Her Majesty that the first of these questions should be answered in the negative, and the second question in the affirmative …

The report of the Judicial Committee has been approved by Her Majesty in Council to-day …

I have, &c.,
Henry Reeve

Any sense of 'victory' which Griffith might have derived from the Privy Council's decision was in practical terms illusory. No suggestion was raised that the Imperial Parliament might legislate to confirm the Assembly's pre-eminence on this matter. Furthermore, since the Privy Council had not offered any reasoning to support its conclusion – a conclusion which on the first question had no textual basis at all in the Constitution Act – there was little prospect that any significant number of members of Queensland's Legislative Council would be persuaded on the basis either of political logic or constitutional morality to alter their previous understanding of their powers. Instead, the majority in the Legislative Council simply ignored the Privy Council's decision when it suited them to do so.[71]

That stance did not equate to complete intransigence. The Council eventually passed the payment of members bill in 1886. The Members Expenses Act 1886[72] was a brief (two-page) measure. The potential payments provided – styled as 'expenses' and not as a salary – were modest. A short schedule identified the eligible expenses as 1s 6d per mile for any land-based journey to and from the member's district to Brisbane (para 1); the actual cost of any sea journey (para 2); and £2 2s for each day when the member attended the Legislature (para 3).

There was little serious opposition to the bill at Assembly second reading, where it passed by 28–12.[73] The bill's opponents did not press the matter further, and it passed

---

Committee for hearing or consideration *any such other matters whatsoever* as His Majesty shall think fit; and such Committee shall thereupon hear or consider the same, and shall advise His Majesty thereon in manner aforesaid" (emphasis added).

[70] The Lord President in 1886 was Gathorne Gathorne-Hardy (later the Earl of Cranbrook), a long-serving Tory MP and minister, who had been at the Bar in his younger days. He did not have any judicial experience. The then Lord (High) Chancellor (in a Gladstone-led Liberal administration) was Farrer Herschell, a barrister elected to the Commons as a Liberal in 1874, appointed by Gladstone as Solicitor-General in 1880 and then – also with no judicial experience – Lord Chancellor in 1885.

[71] See eg the spat over a Council attempt to amend a financial provision of the 1886 Local Government Amendment Bill, which culminated in the Assembly sending the Council a Griffith-authored message which characterised the Council's behaviour as: "a manifest infringement of [the Assembly's] privileges, as they have always been claimed by this House, and have lately been declared by the Privy Council …"; QLAD 2 November 1886 pp 1504–06.

[72] 50 Vict No 9.

[73] QLAD 20 July 1886 p87 et seq. The vote is at p92. The most forceful critique came from Albert Norton, a close ally of McIlwraith (who did not attend the debate), who was then acting as leader of the opposition.

third reading without division.[74] Council second reading was on 1 September.[75] Debate there was much more heated, primarily because the public (and members of the Legislature) had just learned that Griffith had attached his additional letter to the documents sent to the Privy Council. The matter was not strictly in point for second reading purposes.[76] After several hours of rancorous exchanges on the broader constitutional issue, an opposition amendment was defeated 14–5 and second reading then passed without division.[77] At third reading on 8 September the bill passed without debate or division.

The following year, Griffith secured the passage of a new Electoral Districts Act. The Act increased the Assembly's size to 72 members and seemed designed at least in part further to reduce the pro-rural bias in the colony's constituency apportionment. Had Griffith assumed this would enhance his electoral prospects, he was promptly disappointed. After the April 1888 Assembly elections – still fought without any organised party political basis[78] – the factional balance within the Assembly tilted in McIlwraith's favour and he replaced Griffith as Premier.[79]

Swamping or Radical Reform of Queensland's Legislative Council?

Griffith did not seem to have countenanced large-scale swamping of the Council to resolve the appropriations impasses.[80] Six new appointees were made in 1885–86: Thomas Macdonald-Paterson in April 1885; Frederick Holburton in July 1885;[81] and John Mcansh, Henry Wood, William Taylor and Frederick Brentnall in April 1886. The limited press coverage of the 1886 appointments raised no suggestion of partisanship.[82]

---

[74] *QLAD* 22 July 1886 p138.
[75] *QLCD* 1 September 1886 p49.
[76] See the speech of Francis Gregory ibid p58 et seq and p65. Gregory was a surveyor and career civil servant who was very firmly identified with pastoral interests. McIlwraith had nominated him to the Council in 1882. A biographer commenting on Gregory's career in the Council suggests: "he opposed all radical legislation and social reform and allied himself with the most reactionary squatting group in the House"; http://adb.anu.edu.au/biography/gregory-francis-thomas-frank-3899.
[77] *QLCD* 1 September 1886 p65.
[78] 'Independents' won all 72 seats; https://elections.uwa.edu.au/elecdetail.lasso?keyvalue=1705&summary=false.
[79] McIlwraith took several forceful positions favouring colonial autonomy from British control during this administration. Musgrave had been politically and personally close to Griffith. His relationship with McIlwraith was difficult, however, and tension between the two men led to Musgrave's early recall in 1888; http://adb.anu.edu.au/biography/musgrave-sir-anthony-4283. Musgrave was replaced by Sir Henry Wylie Norman in May 1889. Norman was a career soldier, having spent much of that career in India. A General by 1882, Norman succeeded Musgrave as Governor of Jamaica in 1883; http://adb.anu.edu.au/biography/norman-sir-henry-wylie-7858. Norman's appointment was made after McIlwraith refused to accept the British government's initial choice, Sir Henry Blake, primarily because of his reputation as a brutal exponent – as a senior police officer and magistrate – of oppressive British policies in Ireland; see the scathing account of the nomination and its reception in Queensland in *The Freeman's Journal* 24 November 1888 p9, https://trove.nla.gov.au/newspaper/article/115460090.
[80] Musgrave's 'umpire letter' suggested he assumed the Legislative Council would continue to exist in its current form.
[81] www.parliament.qld.gov.au/members/former/bio?id=1008520861.
[82] See eg the *Moreton Mail* 24 April 1886 p3, https://trove.nla.gov.au/newspaper/article/234904913: "**NEW LEGISLATIVE COUNCILLORS.** – His Excellency the Governor has summoned to the Legislative Council, Messrs Brentnall, M'Cansh, Taylor, and H. C. Wood of Durundur. In the last named the Council will receive the assistance of a ripe Scholar and a liberal minded gentleman, who, will be an acquisition to their deliberations. Clearheaded and generous, with a broad and comprehensive view, of the Colony, its

The Council had 39 members in July 1886, so the six Griffith appointees could hardly be characterised as swampers.[83] Nonetheless, all six appointees had voted with the government at second reading of the expenses bill.[84] Brentnall spoke in the debate,[85] denying any broad sympathy with government but supporting the principle of the bill, and Mcansh made a similar contribution:

> I certainly am in accord with the present Ministry on their general policy, but whenever questions are brought forward by the Ministry or by anyone else with which I do not agree, I shall certainly vote against them. In regard to the question before the House I think the principle of payment of members is a very good one … and I am convinced that it will be for the benefit of the country if members are paid.[86]

Nor did Griffith give any serious attention to the prospect of radically reforming the Council's composition. The early swamping disputes in New South Wales had had a knock-on effect in Queensland. Just weeks after the 1861 episode, a Mr WH Yaldwyn, a squatter member of Queensland's Legislative Council, moved a motion that the Imperial Parliament be invited to pass an Act to replace the present Council with one modelled on Victoria's elective chamber.[87] Yaldwyn was not seized by 'democratic' sentiment, however, but by a fear of radicalism. Adopting the position favoured in South Australia and Victoria in their s.32 constitutions, Yaldwyn urged the creation of an elective Council on a restrictive franchise on the basis that such a body could not be swamped at the behest of a liberally inclined government with an Assembly majority.

The prospects of such a government being returned in 1861 were obviously remote, but were distinctly more credible in the mid-1880s. There was no obvious legal

---

politics, and necessities, we consider the district of Moreton has a high compliment paid it in the choice of Mr. H. C. Wood, who has been identified with it for many years past. Of Messrs M'Cansh and Taylor we know nothing, except that the former is the owner of Canning Downs Station, near Warwick, and the latter is a medical man in Brisbane. Mr. Brentnall is an ex-clergyman and though gentleman of high education and attainments, we cannot but object to his promotion, for that very reason. Once a priest always a priest is a dictum which ought never to be over-ridden. He, who in so high a calling having put his hand to the plough turns back, is deserving of neither credit nor consideration." Mcansh, a Scots émigré, was a pastoralist with substantial land holdings (although he had never been a squatter) but of visibly liberal political inclinations; http://adb.anu.edu.au/biography/macansh-john-donald-1144; www.parliament.qld.gov.au/members/former/bio?id=4038293882. William Taylor was a medical doctor raised and educated in Canada who had practised as a surgeon in England before emigrating to Brisbane in 1870. He was an active figure in medical and public health matters, but had no obvious partisan political affiliations; *BC* 30 June 1927 p12, https://trove.nla.gov.au/newspaper/article/21853540 has a lengthy and very approbatory obituary. *The (Brisbane) Courier* greeted his appointment with the comment that Taylor: "had not been before the public and [his] qualifications for the position of legislator are unknown"; 17 April 1886 p6, https://trove.nla.gov.au/newspaper/article/4494961. Macdonald-Paterson, a Scots émigré, had worked as a butcher and a solicitor in Rockhampton. He did have a 'party political' background, having been elected as a self-described 'working man's candidate' to the Assembly in 1878; *Morning Bulletin (Rockhampton)* 26 November 1878 p2, https://trove.nla.gov.au/newspaper/article/51977644.

[83] That such modest augmentation was not seen as swamping is perhaps underlined by the point that shortly after the 1888 election McIlwraith nominated four new members (three in August and one in November), two of whom had formerly been his supporters in the Assembly. The appointments were as unremarked as the six made by Griffith; *The Queenslander* 25 August 1889 p309, https://trove.nla.gov.au/newspaper/article/19934949.

[84] *QLCD* 1 September 1886 p65.
[85] ibid p61.
[86] ibid p60.
[87] *QLCD* 22 May 1861 p2; see also Bernays op cit pp 208–09.

impediment to legislation being enacted to effect such reform. The Constitution Act (Queensland) 1867 s.9 – left intact by Lilley's 1871 reform to s.10[88] – required two-thirds majorities in both houses at second and third reading, reservation and laying before for any such Act. But s.9's repeal in 1871 by a bare majority suggested that the two-thirds elements of that entrenchment provision were essentially illusory – although, of course, no legal challenge was made to that presumption at the time. Nor had the Legislature subsequently acted upon Charles Lilley's 1871 'singular omission' analysis[89] to attempt to enact a provision which (prima facie) would prevent repeal of s.9 by a simple majority.[90]

The obvious political impediment to any reform to the Council's composition and powers was the need to secure an upper house majority for any bill, which would remain an improbable prospect unless the Council was swamped. But the likelihood of continued conflict between the two houses substantially reduced by a very unexpected political development in the late 1880s.

To the Left ... to the Right ... to the Court ... the Final Steps of Griffith's (Party) Political Career

McIlwraith's premiership after the November 1888 election was short-lived: he resigned because of ill health a few months later, to be succeeded by Boyd Morehead, a pastoralist and banker with extensive landholdings. Morehead was first elected to the Assembly in 1871 and served in McIlwraith's cabinet between 1880 and 1883.[91]

In opposition, Griffith seemingly took several steps to the political left. In December 1888 he published a lengthy article entitled 'Wealth and want' in the left-leaning periodical *Boomerang*[92] advocating an essentially socialist political agenda on labour relations issues. He repeated and elaborated that analysis the following year in a piece called 'The distribution of wealth' in the Sydney *Centennial Magazine*.[93] Griffith also acted as something of a benevolent mentor to the first 'Labour Party' Assembly member, Thomas Glassey, elected in 1888.[94]

In July 1890, Griffith introduced a bizarrely idealistic bill to reform Queensland's land laws. The bill had its first reading on 22 July[95] and was set for second reading on

---

[88] Pp 128–129 above.

[89] P 128 above.

[90] Although – again – Lilley's analysis was itself necessarily speculative, being dependent on the colony's Supreme Court (and beyond that the Privy Council) accepting that cl.22 of the 1859 Order, CLVA 1865 s.5 or s.2 of the 1867 Act enabled the Legislature, by bare majority legislation, to enact such legally effective protective devices.

[91] http://adb.anu.edu.au/biography/morehead-boyd-dunlop-4240; Bernys op cit pp 73–74.

[92] Joyce (1978) op cit pp 171–72. *Boomerang* is not available online, but the article is reprinted in *The Logan Witness* 29 December 1888 p2, https://trove.nla.gov.au/newspaper/article/163892686.

[93] Also not available online, but reprinted in the *Mackay Mercury* 29 July 1889 p2, https://trove.nla.gov.au/newspaper/article/168434846.

[94] Glassey was a miner in Scotland and England, before emigrating to Queensland in 1884, where his career as a postman ended when he was sacked for union activism; see Rayner (1970) 'Thomas Glassey – first Labour member' in Murphy, Joyce and Hughes op cit; Fowler (1970) 'The 1890s – turning point in Queensland history' in Murphy, Joyce and Hughes op cit.

[95] *QLAD* 22 July 1890 p306.

7 August. But as Hansard on 7 August reveals, Griffith's foray into radical land reform was overtaken by events:[96]

> The PREMIER (Hon B D Morehead) said: Mr. Speaker, After the division that took place last night, the Ministry considered it was their duty to hand in their resignations to His Excellency the Governor and their resignations have been accepted. I also advised His Excellency to send for the leader of the Opposition, who, I believe, has accepted the responsibility of forming a Government ...
>
> The Hon. SIR S. W. GRIFFITH said: Mr. Speaker, I had the honour to-day to receive a communication from His Excellency the Governor requesting me to wait upon him. I did so, and His Excellency was pleased to ask if I would undertake the responsibility of forming a Government. I undertook that responsibility, and shall try to do so.

The division on 6 August 1890 was a government defeat on a motion criticising its economic policies,[97] which Morehead regarded as a no-confidence vote. The unlikely outcome of that 'responsibility' was that Griffith seemed suddenly to jettison not just his newly found leftist beliefs, but also his previous attachment to liberal ideas, by entering a formal alliance with McIlwraith and reappearing as Premier in what came to be known as the 'Griffilwraith' coalition.

Griffith remained as Premier for three years. His tenure coincided with a severe economic depression which afflicted all of the Australian colonies, and which may in part explain his sudden policy reversals on several major issues. The forthcoming ban on the import of Kanaka labourers was rescinded, ostensibly as a means to safeguard the continued existence of the sugar industry. The government's response to the shearers' strike of 1891 was also sufficiently aggressive – involving the use of military force and the prosecution and jailing of some strikers – to sustain the conclusion that Griffith now saw his political alliances lying more obviously with the pastoralists rather than the emerging Labour movement.

In 1893, Griffith was still a relatively young man – only 48 years old. He was, however, increasingly wearied by political life, and stood down as Premier to become Chief Justice of the State Supreme Court on Charles Lilley's retirement. There was little opposition to Griffith's appointment on the grounds of his ability or experience: he was perhaps even more distinguished as a lawyer and politician than his predecessor. There was, however, considerable criticism of one aspect of the appointment. Shortly before Griffith's appointment, the nominal 'leader of the opposition' – Hugh Muir Nelson[98] – had promoted a bill which would increase the Chief Justice's annual salary from £2500 to £3500. Griffith was evidently in some personal financial difficulty, and regarded £3500 per year as the minimum salary required to equate to his lost ministerial and Bar earnings. That Nelson rather than Griffith promoted the bill was widely seen as a futile attempt to disguise the fact that the additional £1000 per year was in essence a bribe – its cost borne by the taxpayer – offered by McIlwraith to Griffith to persuade

---

[96] *QLAD* 7 August 1890 pp 525–26.
[97] McIlwraith voted with Griffith against the government; *QLAD* 6 August 1890 p 525.
[98] Nelson, a Scots émigré, had acquired substantial pastoral landholdings (as a freeholder rather than squatter). He was first elected to the Assembly in 1883. He was (initially) closely aligned with McIlwraith, and held a cabinet office as Secretary for Railways in Morehead's government.

Griffith to resign the premiership in McIlwraith's favour, with the additional condition of preferment for Nelson thrown in. There was little surprise when McIlwraith immediately appointed Nelson as his government's Treasurer,[99] nor – when McIlwraith again resigned the premiership some months later because of ill-health – that Nelson was his successor.

Nelson's administrations remained in power in Queensland until the late 1890s, being variously referred as the 'Ministerialists' or 'Continuous' government. The newly emergent leading figures in the party were TJ Byrnes[100] and Robert Philp.[101] Byrnes has acquired a somewhat mythical status in Queensland folklore, primarily because he died when only 37, five months after becoming Premier in 1898. Byrnes provided a classic rags-to-riches story: born in Queensland in 1860, the son of illiterate and impecunious Irish immigrants, Byrnes's scholastic abilities propelled him through several school scholarships to the University of Melbourne before he was called to the Victoria Bar. On returning to Queensland, Byrnes became a protégé of Griffith, who arranged for Byrnes's appointment to the Council and as State Solicitor-General in 1891 in the coalition administration. Byrnes's personal politics were relatively conservative; for example, as Solicitor-General, he had extensively used criminal prosecutions against trade unions activists[102] during the 1891 shearers' strike.[103] Byrnes progressed quickly through the Ministerialist ranks to become party leader and Premier in April 1898 – when Nelson resigned as Premier to become President of the Legislative Council – only to die of pneumonia later that year.

Robert Philp, a Scot by birth, was State Treasurer during Byrnes's premiership. Philp came from a more moneyed background: his father owned a cotton mill before emigrating to Queensland in 1862 when Philp was 11. Philp entered working life as a clerk in a shipping company, proving sufficiently skilled to become a partner in a major firm with interests in shipping, banking and insurance. Philp began his political career serving on the Townsville municipal council, as a firm supporter of McIlwraith's administrations,[104] and was elected to the Assembly in 1886. He entered McIlwraith's Ministerialist cabinet in 1893 as Minister for Mines, and was appointed Treasurer by Byrnes in 1898. On Byrnes's death, Philp was the obvious replacement after a brief interregnum under the leadership of James Dickson, an English émigré who had made his fortune in Queensland as an auctioneer and estate agent rather than as a pastoralist.[105]

Despite the Ministerialists' firm hold on power in the early to mid-1890s, the long-term prospects of Ministerialist hegemony were threatened by the emergence of a

---

[99] See eg *The Week* 6 January 1893 p6, https://trove.nla.gov.au/newspaper/article/183110320; *BC* 24 January 1893 p4, https://trove.nla.gov.au/newspaper/article/3554665; *BC* 27 January 1893 p4, https://trove.nla.gov.au/newspaper/article/355486.1.

[100] Byrnes's career is traced – unflatteringly – in Gill (1978) 'Thomas Joseph Byrnes: the man and the legend' in Murphy and Joyce op cit. Gill's entry on Byrnes in the *Australian Dictionary of Biography* is equally sceptical about Byrnes's legendary status; http://adb.anu.edu.au/biography/byrnes-thomas-joseph-5458.

[101] Bolton (1978) 'Robert Philp: capitalist as politician' in Murphy and Joyce op cit.

[102] Several received lengthy jail sentences for their activities; see Kenway (1970) 'The pastoral strikes of 1891 and 1894' in Murphy, Joyce and Hughes (eds) *Prelude to power: the rise of the Labour Party in Queensland 1885-1915*.

[103] ibid.

[104] Pp 133-134, 141 above.

[105] http://adb.anu.edu.au/biography/dickson-sir-james-robert-5979.

political party from the rapidly growing trade union movement, itself rooted in the increasingly industrialised base of the economy and a wave of industrial disputes in the early 1890s – and especially the shearers' strike – prompted in part by the severe economic downturn.[106] Thomas Glassey – the first Labour member – was joined by three others in 1892. In the 1893 election, Labour's representation leapt to 16 of the Assembly's 72 seats; and then to 20 in 1896.

By this point, despite the personal cloud that had briefly hung over him because of the salary manoeuvrings, Griffith also had his eye on rather grander 'constitutional' issues than those that might be presented to the State Supreme Court. On that matter, Griffith occupied common ground with Henry Parkes, who by 1890 had moved on from his impoverished British origins and early colonial radicalism to become the foremost of politicians in New South Wales.

III. New South Wales – Parkes

The rapid turnover of short-lived governments in New South Wales immediately after the 1855 Act came into force continued throughout the 1860s. Cowper had chosen James Martin as Attorney-General in the 1857 administration and 1858 administrations. Martin's parents were Irish catholic domestic servants, who had emigrated in 1821. After elementary and some secondary schooling, Martin established himself as a journalist on *The Australian*, and worked closely with Wentworth (by then casting off his radical political roots) in arguing for representative and responsible government. Martin retained a prominent role as a journalist while qualifying as a solicitor. He was elected to the mixed Legislative Council in 1848 and played a major role assisting Wentworth in drafting the 1853 Bill. He was returned to the Assembly at the 1856 election.[107] Cowper chose him as Attorney-General in the 1857 administration and 1858 administrations. Martin, however, had limited sympathy with Cowper and Robertson's view on electoral and land reform, was on poor personal terms with both men and emerged as Premier heading a distinctly more conservative ministry after Cowper's government fell in 1863. Martin's administration also enjoyed more cordial relations with the Council than its predecessors, aided by the fact that Martin had pressed successfully for nine new appointees – increasing the Council's size to 32 – which secured the government a working majority.[108] Nonetheless, that ministry lasted only 18 months. Cowper again took office after the November 1864 election.

In 'opposition', Martin found common ground with Henry Parkes,[109] whose ascent through the colony's political hierarchy had been steady and relentless. Supported by Parkes' faction, Martin formed a government (he served as both Premier and Attorney-General) which lasted for over two years – something of an achievement in New South Wales in that era. The Martin/Parkes ministry, decried as: "scarcely more

---

[106] P 142 above.
[107] http://adb.anu.edu.au/biography/martin-sir-james-4161.
[108] Griffith and Clune op cit pp 112–13.
[109] P 44 n 43 above. For a brief guise to Parkes's career and personality, see Bolton (2006) 'Henry (later Sir Henry) Parkes' in Clune and Turner (eds) *The Premiers of New South Wales 1856–2005*.

than a marriage of convenience"[110] by one of Parkes's biographers, fell on Parkes's resignation, to be replaced by yet another Cowper/Robertson administration in 1868 which managed to retain office following the 1869 elections. Cowper's retirement from politics in 1870 then produced the unlikely spectacle of a Robertson/Martin ministry, which left Parkes as a de facto leader of the opposition until he, in turn, pieced together a government after the 1872 election.[111]

Assembly–Council Relations

Parkes's first administration was immediately thrown into a sharp dispute with the Council over passage of the government's Border Duties Convention Bill.[112] The bill – which provided for reciprocal easing of import and export duties on various goods between New South Wales, Victoria and South Australia – had passed third reading in the Assembly by 29–12.[113] Parkes could credibly claim that the policy underlying the bill had been in issue in the February Assembly election. The Council nonetheless rejected the measure by nine votes to eight[114] shortly before the legislature was prorogued.

Parkes responded by immediately announcing that in the next legislative session the government's priority would be to promote a bill to reform the Council's composition. The proposal was that the Council be reconstituted on a mixed appointive and elective basis. Current members would retain their seats, but all new members – to a maximum of 48 – would be elected on the basis of an expansive franchise so that the house would eventually acquire a fully elective character.

The bill was subsequently introduced in the Assembly and began second reading on 13 February 1873.[115] Debate spread over several days, the bill eventually passing second reading by 33–12 on 27 February.[116] Third reading subsequently passed by 26–14 on 27 March.[117]

Less than a week later, on 2 April 1873, the Council rejected the bill at first reading (by 21 votes to one) on the basis that, as a matter of parliamentary privilege, any bill affecting the Council's composition or powers should begin its passage in that house.[118] Parkes was content to accommodate that assertion, and reintroduced the bill into the

---

[110] http://adb.anu.edu.au/biography/parkes-sir-henry-4366.
[111] Parkes's political status had been compromised – albeit not fatally – by his bankruptcy in 1870, which led him to resign from the Assembly. He secured re-election in 1872. Many voters, it seems, had no qualms about entrusting the colony's finances to a man who could not successfully manage his own.
[112] The bill is most readily found in *The Australian Town and Country Journal* 15 June 1872 p5, https://trove.nla.gov.au/newspaper/article/70495159.
[113] Both Martin and Roberson had voted against third reading: *NSWLAD* 11 July 1872 in *SMH* 12 July 1872 p3, www.parliament.nsw.gov.au/dtdocs/DTDocuments/1872/07121872.pdf.
[114] *NSWLCD* 24 July 1872 in *SMH* 25 July 1872 p2, www.parliament.nsw.gov.au/dtdocs/DTDocuments/1872/07251872.pdf.
[115] *NSWLAD* 13 February 1873 in *SMH* 14 February 1873 p2, www.parliament.nsw.gov.au/dtdocs/DTDocuments/1873/02141873.pdf.
[116] www.parliament.nsw.gov.au/hansard/Documents/HHP/Pre1991/Votes/Votes/Votes%20-%20%20 7th%20Parliament%201872-73.pdf p196. Robertson was among the 12. Martin did not vote.
[117] ibid pp 256–58. Both Robertson and Martin voted against.
[118] *NSWLCD* 2 April 1873 in *SMH* 3 April 1873 p2, www.parliament.nsw.gov.au/dtdocs/DTDocuments/1873/04031873.pdf.

Council – with an added proviso that the reformed Council could not amend appropriation and money bills – in September.[119] The bill was, however, defeated at second reading by an overwhelming (16–4) majority on 8 October 1873.[120]

The government had no appetite to pursue the matter further. Nor did Parkes press for any significant number of his supporters to be appointed to the Council to resolve the dispute.[121] Only one new appointee had been made in 1872 and again in 1873;[122] two more members were added in 1874. Parkes did, however, remove Martin as a political rival in the Assembly by having him appointed Supreme Court Chief Justice in November 1873.[123]

The Parkes ministry subsequently fell after an Assembly vote of censure in November over its role in the Governor's grant of mercy to a convicted criminal, and in the ensuing election Robertson yet again garnered enough Assembly support to form a government. That ministry lasted until early 1877, when defeat on a confidence motion opened the door to a second Parkes administration which survived for barely four months. After the 1877 election, a precarious administration emerged under the leadership of James Farnell, but that, in turn, collapsed in December 1878, to be replaced by the improbable combination of a third Parkes administration sustained with Robertson's support. Parkes subsequently held office until 1883.

The question of Council reform remained a recurrent issue during Parkes's third government. In a letter to the Governor in September 1879, Parkes had intimated that radical change would soon be required:

> [T]he whole question must be considered at no distant day with a view to an organic change in the constitution of the Council, either by the substitution of nomination for a term of years for life-nomination, or by the introduction of the elective principle.

Parkes also used that letter to indicate that he considered that the Governor should not – either of his own volition or by referring back to London – obstruct any nominations that the government might make to the Council. Having obviously raised the threat of seeking to swamp the Council, Parkes concluded in an emollient fashion by noting that his government had no immediate intention to pursue that course.

---

[119] *NSWLCD* 10 September 1873 in *SMH* 11 September 1873 p2, www.parliament.nsw.gov.au/dtdocs/DTDocuments/1873/09111873.pdf.

[120] *NSWLCD* 8 October 1873 in *SMH* 9 October 1873 p2, www.parliament.nsw.gov.au/dtdocs/DTDocuments/1873/10091873.pdf.

[121] The then Governor was Sir Hercules Robinson, a career soldier and civil servant who had previously been Governor of Ceylon. He took office in New South Wales in 1872 and rapidly developed a reputation for being an interventionist Governor resistant to the notion that he should act on the advice of his ministers even on internal matters; http://adb.anu.edu.au/biography/robinson-sir-hercules-george-4493. It seems unlikely that Robinson would have acceded to a swamping request.

[122] The 1872 appointee was Saul Samuel, a long-time Assembly member who served as Parke's Postmaster-General; http://adb.anu.edu.au/biography/samuel-sir-saul-4534. The 1873 candidate was Joseph Long Innes, a barrister and Parkes-supporting member of the Assembly, who coupled his appointment to the Council with taking office as Parkes's Attorney-General; http://adb.anu.edu.au/biography/innes-sir-joseph-george-long-3836.

[123] *Empire* 12 November 1873 p2, https://trove.nla.gov.au/newspaper/article/63237038; *SMH* 12 November 1873 p5, https://trove.nla.gov.au/newspaper/article/13326445.

As during his first ministry, Parkes did not press the issue. However, he did in this period pursue a policy – slowly and steadily – of having substantial numbers of supporters appointed to the Council. In January 1879, the Council had 39 members. By the end of Parkes ministry in January 1883, that number had swelled to 53. Parkes remained in opposition between 1883 and 1887, but adopted the same policy towards the Council when he returned as Premier between 1887 and 1899. At the opening of the 13th Parliament, there were 61 members in the Council.[124] During Parke's third administration, 22 new members were appointed, increasing the Council's size (taking account of deaths and resignations) to 70.[125] The strategy fell some way short of 'swamping' in the sense of creating a drastic and instantaneous shift in the ideological disposition of the Council majority, but went some distance to legitimising the notion that governments could properly send significant numbers of their supporters to the Council.

The Emergence and Consolidation of a Formal Party System

The presumptive acceptability of that was soon to be challenged, however, by broader political developments. By this point, the multi-factional nature of New South Wales electoral politics was beginning to be replaced by a hardening of party identities around the question of free trade and protectionism.[126] Parkes emerged as the leader of a distinct 'free trade' grouping during his fourth ministry, facing a similarly distinct 'protectionist' opposition led by George Dibbs.[127] In that context, bulk appointments to the Council acquired an overt 'party political' character which they had previously lacked.

The party character of New South Wales electoral politics was then much intensified in 1891 when the newly formed Labour Party suddenly appeared as a major force, taking 36 of the Assembly's (then) 141 seats and leaving both the Free Trade and Protectionist parties reliant on Labour support to form a ministry. Parkes managed briefly to sustain an administration (his fifth) on such terms, but the ministry soon foundered when it was unwilling to accept Labour Party demands for legislative reform to the mining industry. Dibbs subsequently formed a government which survived with intermittent Labour support for almost three years.

---

[124] www.parliament.nsw.gov.au/hansard/Documents/13thParliamentindexes/1887.pdf.
[125] www.parliament.nsw.gov.au/hansard/Documents/1889%20a.pdf.
[126] See generally Clune and Griffith op cit pp 22–26.
[127] Dibbs was born into modest family circumstances in Sydney. Following a chequered commercial career (being bankrupted several times), he was elected to the Assembly in 1874 as an advocate of free trade. He shortly afterwards found himself jailed for a year after being convicted of criminal libel. The episode did no harm to his political career; he was re-elected in 1882 and shortly afterwards was serving as Colonial Treasurer. By 1887 he had recanted his free trade beliefs and become leader of the Protectionist Party then coalescing in the Assembly and the broader community; see Campbell (2006) 'George (later Sir George) Richard Dibbs' in Clune and Turner op cit, http://adb.anu.edu.au/biography/dibbs-sir-george-richard-3408.

Table 5.2 New South Wales Legislative Assembly elections, 1889 (1 February 1889) and 1891 (17 June 1891)

Party	% vote	Seats	Change[a]
1889			
Free Trade	49.1	71	n/a
Protectionist	50.9	66	n/a
1891			
Free Trade	40.7	47	−24
Protectionist	33.0	51	−15
Labour	21.9	36	+36
Independents	4.0	7	+7

[a] I have left the change column blank for the 1889 election as the previous election was not fought on an obvious party basis. The + and − figures are not the same as the Assembly increased in size from 137 members (1889) to 141 in 1891.

In a prosaic sense, the return of Labour members to the Assembly had been facilitated by the passage in 1889 of legislation providing for payments to members. The Parliamentary Representatives Allowance Act[128] came into force in September 1889, and set an annual allowance of £300 for Assembly members. Parkes was not – as Griffith had been in Queensland – a proponent of the reform, and had initially voted against it in the Assembly. His support had eventually been secured in reaction to the Council's refusal to pass the bill without amendments, a stance which the Assembly majority – Parkes among them – regarded as unacceptable interference with the lower house's privileges. The matter was eventually settled by a government-promoted compromise rather than the confrontational solution sought – somewhat pointlessly, as it turned out – by Griffith over the payments issue in Queensland.

Free Trade and Protectionist reliance on Labour support was complicated by the fact that the Labour Party managed to create a schism within its own ranks almost immediately. This fracture lay in part in differences of opinion among its members – both strategic and substantive – over the relative merits of accommodation with the Free Trade and Protectionist parties. A larger factor was the unwillingness of some Assembly members to accept a party requirement that all members should invariably vote en bloc. The initial consequence of this was that two Labour Parties fielded candidates at the 1894 Assembly election, winning 14 and 13 seats respectively, and proving unable to operate as a cohesive force on a regular basis.

By 1891, Parkes's political career in New South Wales had largely run its course. However, from the mid-1880s onwards, Parkes's political ambitions – like those of Griffith in Queensland – had also taken on a more 'national' character.

---

[128] www.legislation.nsw.gov.au/view/pdf/asmade/act-1889-23a.

IV. Towards Australian Federation?

Various tentative initiatives had been made from the 1860s to lay the ground for fashioning some kind of federal structure among the Australasian colonies.[129] Proponents of such reform could point to the obvious example offered by the British North American colonies from 1867 onwards, which, with the exception of Newfoundland, had come together in a single federally structured Dominion. Within New South Wales, Henry Parkes was a major player in these efforts. In Queensland, Griffith stood to the fore.

The first formal legal steps towards some kind of legal federation in the Australian colonies were enacted in the Federal Council of Australasia Act 1885.[130] The Act – largely Griffith's creation – announced in its preamble that:

> ... [I]t is expedient to expedient to constitute a Federal Council of Australasia, for the purpose of dealing with such matters of common Australasian interest, in respect to which united action is desirable, as can be dealt with without unduly interfering with the management of the internal affairs of the several colonies by their respective legislatures ...

The 'Federal Council' was to be a legislative body comprising the six Australian colonies, New Zealand and Fiji, each of which would select two representatives to sit on the Council. Griffith chaired the Council's proceedings on several occasions and was the prime mover in drafting the few laws that were enacted, a dual role which significantly increased his political profile among both parliamentarians from other colonies and the wider public.

S.15 granted the Council enumerated powers in subsections (a)–(g). S.15(h) empowered the colonies to add further competences both from a list of identified matters and a catch-all proviso embracing any other issues within a colony's competence. S.16 was (potentially) a similarly expansive provision, which empowered the Council to legislate to resolve any matter referred to it by two or more colonies. Per s.13, a bare majority vote in Federal Council would suffice to enact its bills, with assent to be given by the Governor of the colony where the Council was then sitting, subject to various provisions requiring reservation of some bills (s.17) and a general power of disallowance (s.18) vested in the Queen.

S.20 provided that the Federal Council's Acts would have the 'force of law' in all colonies. That concept was elaborated in s.22:

> **22. Acts of Council to supersede Colonial enactments.**
>
> If in any case the provisions of any Act of the Council shall be repugnant to, or inconsistent with, the law of any colony affected thereby, the former shall prevail, and the latter shall, so far as such repugnance or inconsistency extends, have no operation.[131]

The Act – repeating the omissions of much existing colonial constitutional law – did not define what was meant by 'repugnancy', and made no provision as to how the

---

[129] For various perspectives, see the discussions in Ward (1992) op cit pp 214–21.
[130] 48 & 49 Vict c 60.
[131] The 'affected thereby' phrase underlined the proviso in s.15 that Federal Council Acts would only apply to those colonies which had – in some undefined way – 'adopted' them.

'superseding' effect of Federal Council law would be enforced as and when any such 'repugnancy' had arisen.

The omissions did not prove problematic, as the Federal Council was not a busy legislator. The Act did not explicitly require any colony to participate in the Council, and was not seen as having that effect implicitly. The Council's political and legal significance was substantially compromised from the outset by the non-participation of successive governments in New South Wales and New Zealand. The Council passed very little legislation, and that mainly on narrowly technical subjects relating to civil and criminal legal procedures. By a perhaps curious coincidence, it had emerged at the same time as a Privy Council decision confirmed that – within their own colony's borders – the various Australian legislatures could not properly be regarded simply as delegates of the Imperial Parliament.

Colonial Legislatures have Plenary, Not Delegated Powers – The *Apollo Candle* (and *Burah*) Litigation

The Privy Council's 1885 judgment in *Powell v Apollo Candle*[132] provided a judicial confirmation (of sorts) of the gradual political trend towards enhancing the lawmaking autonomy of colonial legislatures. The dispute was in some senses prosaic, concerned with an import duty levied in New South Wales on a substance called stearine. The Apollo Candle Company, marrying entrepeneurial flair with technological innovation, decided to use stearine rather than beeswax and paraffin to make its candles, primarily because beeswax and paraffin were subject to New South Wales import duties and stearine (which Apollo imported from its own works in Victoria) was not.[133]

That innovation was then apparently trumped by the New South Wales government exercising the power granted by the Customs Regulation Act 1879 s.133, which empowered the Governor to impose an import duty on any non-taxed good which customs officials considered a substitute for an already taxed material.[134] Such a duty was imposed (Powell being the colony's Collector of Customs) on Apollo's imported stearine. The company sought a declaration that the charge was unlawful on various grounds; the one of interest here is that s.133 was ultra vires the Legislature's power.

In the State Supreme Court, that ground was upheld.[135] The leading (albeit rather cursory) judgment for a unanimous court was given by the then Chief Justice, and several times former Premier, Sir James Martin. Martin reasoned that because the New South Wales Legislature had been created by and was subordinate to the Imperial Parliament, it was also subject to an implied rule of public law that applied to all other governmental bodies created by that Parliament: namely, that a body exercising delegated authority could not itself delegate its powers to another body unless an Imperial statute expressly

---

[132] (1885) 10 App Cas 282.

[133] On the background, see *SMH* 24 August 1883 p6, https://trove.nla.gov.au/newspaper/article/13542810; *BC* 26 February 1885 p6, https://trove.nla.gov.au/newspaper/article/3439512.

[134] The de jure reference to the Governor meaning in effect the government through the device of issuing an Order in Council.

[135] (1883) 4 NSW LR 167.

authorised it do so ('delegatus non potest delegare'). Martin read s.133 as amounting to such a delegation; since no such authority had been bestowed on the Legislature by an Imperial Act, s.133 was ultra vires.

The Supreme Court's judgment was reversed in the Privy Council. The Court was not an especially strong one,[136] but was notable for including Sir Robert Collier, Solicitor-General when the CLVA 1865 was enacted. Collier's appointment to the bench in 1871 by Gladstone's Liberal government had provoked considerable political controversy,[137] but by 1885 Collier's judicial status was firmly established.

Collier delivered the Court's judgment. The decision straightforwardly followed two earlier Privy Council authorities, relating respectively to colonial legislatures in India and Ontario: *R v Burah* and *Hodge v The Queen*.[138] The decision in *Burah* (in which Collier had also sat) had been authored by Collier's sometime Attorney-General colleague Roundell Palmer, who by then was (as Baron and then later the Earl of Selborne) six years into his judicial career.[139] Collier also sat in *Hodge*, the judgment there being delivered by Lord Fitzgerald.

The crux of the *Burah* and *Hodge* decisions was that colonial legislatures should not be equated with other statutory bodies (most obviously local councils in Britain) for the purposes of the non-delegation rule. While those legislatures were created by the Imperial Parliament, their "true character and position" was that they were: "in no sense delegates or acting under any mandate from the Imperial Parliament".[140] As understood by the Privy Council in *Apollo Candle*:

> These two cases have put an end to a doctrine which appears at one time to have had some currency, that a Colonial Legislature is a delegate of the Imperial Legislature. It is a Legislature restricted in the area of its powers, but within that area unrestricted, and not acting as an agent or a delegate ...[141]

That a legislature might create an inferior body to carry out such functions – even such politically important ones as deciding what goods might be taxed and at what rate – was not in any sense an abdication or surrender of its own powers: "The Legislature has not parted with its perfect control over the Governor, and has the power, of course, at any moment, of withdrawing or altering the power which they have entrusted to him."[142]

Collier did indicate that a colonial legislature would act ultra vires if it failed to comply with procedural constraints on its lawmaking powers rooted in colonial or Imperial legislation – the germane proviso here, which had been complied with, being s.1 of sch.1 of the 1855 Act, that all appropriation or taxation bills had to begin their passage in the Assembly. However, it was not appropriate to infer from the existence of such procedural constraints implied limits on the legislature's substantive powers.

---

[136] Only one judge, Lord Blackburn, was a Law Lord.
[137] Detailed in Pugsley op cit.
[138] (1878) 3 App Cas 889 and (1883) 9 App Cas 117, respectively.
[139] Having been appointed directly as Lord Chancellor by Gladstone in 1872, serving until 1874 and then again from 1880 to 1885.
[140] *Hodge* (1883) 9 App Cas 117, 132.
[141] (1885) 10 App Case 282, 290.
[142] ibid 291. The idea that the Legislature had 'perfect control' over the Governor was a peculiar one, given the Governor's dual identity as both a colonial and Imperial official, and was presumably intended to be read as relating only to the scheme of the Act in issue.

That conclusion was reached without any reference (as in the New South Wales Supreme Court) in either the judgment or submissions to the CLVA 1865. (Nor was any such reference made in *Hodge* and *Burah*, the legislatures there in question being respectively colonial (India) and representative (Ontario) per CLVA 1865 s.1.) Collier did, however, refer in passing in *Apollo Candle* to s.4 [BAA] of the 1855 Act, describing it as: "a somewhat wide power".[143]

Observers sceptical as to the legal rigour of Privy Council judgments in this era might note that Collier made the extraordinary observation[144] that *Burah* was decided too late to have been considered by the New South Wales Supreme Court. *Burah* was handed down on 5 June *1878*; judgment in *Apollo Candle* in New South Wales was given on 22 August *1883*. Given that the New South Wales reports record that *Burah* was cited in that Court by counsel for Apollo and for Powell as a case which (pun presumably intended by Apollo's counsel) 'may throw some light'[145] on the issue, Collier's comment is inexplicable other than as carelessness on the Privy Council's part or as a patently mendacious basis to justify overturning the Supreme Court's judgment without having to criticise the competence of its judges. (None of the counsel who argued the case in Sydney appeared before the Privy Council.[146])

Nonetheless, while strictly construed, the ratio of *Apollo Candle* (and *Burah* and *Hodge*) is only that colonial legislatures are not subject to the non-delegation rule. But the reference in each case to the 'plenary powers' of such legislatures could readily be taken as an indication that, as an exercise in judicial lawmaking, *Apollo Candle* seems entirely consistent with mid- to late-nineteenth-century legislative trends towards enhancing the political autonomy of the Australian colonies, and the powers of their respective legislatures within them. More specifically, although no mention was made in *Apollo Candle*, *Burah* and *Hodge* of the CLVA 1865, both the reasoning in and outcome of those cases – unsurprisingly perhaps, given Collier's presence in all of them and alongside Palmer/Selborne in *Burah* – seems wholly consistent with the Act's rebalancing of intra-colonial lawmaking power away from courts and towards legislatures.

Apollo Candle says nothing – the point was not in issue – about the balancing of power *within* those respective legislatures. On that question, however, a passage from Selborne's judgment in *Burah* (which, at risk of repetition, did not invoke the CLVA 1865) – seems of obvious significance:

> The Indian Legislature has powers expressly limited by the Act of the Imperial Parliament which created it, and it can, of course, do nothing beyond the limits which circumscribe these powers. But, when acting, within those limits, it is not in any sense an agent or delegate of the Imperial Parliament, but has, and was intended to have, *plenary powers of legislation, as large, and of the same nature, as those of Parliament itself.* The established Courts of Justice, when a question arises whether the prescribed limits have been exceeded, must of necessity determine that question; and the only way in which' they can properly do so, is by *looking to the terms of the instrument by which, affirmatively, the legislative powers were created, and by which, negatively, they are restricted.* If what has been done is legislation, within the general

---

[143] (1885) 10 App Cas 282, 287.
[144] ibid 288–89.
[145] (1883) 4 NSW LR 160, 163 (*Apollo*) and 165–66 (*Powell*).
[146] Collier's judgment also errs in its citation of the Supreme Court judgment, although that may be a typesetter's rather than judicial error. *Hodge* was decided in the Privy Council on 15 December 1883.

scope of the affirmative words which give the power, and if it violates *no express condition or restriction* by which that power is limited (in which category would, of course, be included any Act of the Imperial Parliament at variance with it), it is *not for any Court of Justice* to inquire further, or *to enlarge constructively those conditions and restrictions*.[147]

Selborne's use of 'plenary' in *Burah* seemingly has two dimensions: one ('large') going to the question of substantive competence; the second ('same nature') going to the question of how that competence can be exercised. On that latter point, Selborne clearly indicates that 'express' conditions or restrictions are matters which courts can properly enforce. But the judicial role is limited to applying those *express* restrictions; it does not embrace searching for – still less finding – *implicit* constraints. Selborne's 'included' reference to Imperial Acts suggests such express conditions could also be created by the colonial legislature itself if such a power could be traced back to an Imperial Act[148] by which the Legislature was created or by which its original powers were modified. This is in essence the point made by Lilley in 1871, and is also consistent with Palmer/Selborne's views when Attorney-General in 1864 about (one of) the effects that the proposed CLVA 1865 should have.[149]

The Immediate Origins of Federation

The contextual irony of the *Apollo Candle* judgment was that the Privy Council's confirmation of the individual Australian colonial legislatures' expansive powers coincided with increasing internal pressure for many of those powers to be surrendered to a new 'national' governmental system. Parkes – having disdainfully kept New South Wales outside the Federal Council on the basis that it was a palpably inadequate arrangement rather than a useful first step towards a more thoroughgoing integration of the colonies – played a prominent role from 1889 onwards, during his fifth term as Premier, in promoting a much more extensive idea of federation. His enthusiasm was not uniformly shared in the other colonies, which prompted Parkes to plough something of a lone furrow. His case was assisted by a British government review of the colonies' defence capabilities in 1899, which concluded that some form of federation between the colonies would greatly enhance their military capacity. A speech Parkes made on the New South Wales/Queensland border in Tenterfield on 24 October 1889 has subsequently been credited with providing a springboard[150] for the federation movement, which took shape at successive Premiers' conferences in February 1890 and March 1891.[151]

---

[147] *R v Burah* (1878) AC 889, 914; emphases added.
[148] Of course, in some colonies – Queensland being the apposite example here – the relevant 'Act' was an Order in Council.
[149] Pp 101–105 and 128 respectively.
[150] Williams (1998) 'The Tenterfield oration of Henry Parkes' *New Federalist* 71. The text is accessible at https://web.archive.org/web/20140517152905/ and http://henryparkestenterfield.com/sir-henry-parkes/henry-parkes-tenterfield-oration-1889. There are contemporaneous reports at *Daily Telegraph* 26 October 1889 p5, https://trove.nla.gov.au/newspaper/article/235806621; *SMH* 25 October 1889 p8, https://trove.nla.gov.au/newspaper/article/13746899.
[151] The varied and many analyses of the political and/or economic and/or cultural motivations for federation are helpfully surveyed in Irving op cit.

The 1891 conference produced broad agreement for a constitutional structure that borrowed from both British and US principle and practice. The Queen, acting through a Governor-General, would be the legal heart of a new national government. In practice, the government would be drawn from whichever political grouping could command majority support in the lower of the two houses of a bicameral Parliament. In those respects, Australia's governmental system would follow a British lead. However, the national legislature would be a body – like the US Congress – of limited legal capacity. Its lawmaking powers would be enumerated in a constitutional text, and the former colonies – to be renamed states – would retain competence over all matters not granted to the national Parliament. A court would also be required to adjudicate upon the respective limits of national and state governmental power when disputes arose.

Those broad principles were adumbrated in a detailed Constitution Bill. Griffith – then Premier of Queensland – had a prominent part in its drafting, as did the Tasmanian lawyer and politician Andrew Inglis Clark.[152] Both Griffith and Clark were well versed in and admiring of US constitutional law, and saw much there in terms both of principle and detail which they thought should be borrowed in designing a constitution for an Australian nation.[153]

Despite so much detailed legalistic work being done, political impetus for federation sagged. This was partly because of ideological hostility towards the idea of federation per se among free trade politicians in New South Wales, who feared any national legislature would be dominated by protectionist sentiment, but also because all the colonies were severely affected by an economic downturn in the early 1890s. Sceptics among the free traders rallied round George Reid,[154] an increasingly eminent barrister who had vigorously championed the free trade cause and who had sat in the Assembly since 1880 predominantly as a backbench member, regularly refusing overtures from all sides to take ministerial office.[155] Reid's opposition contributed to the fall of Parkes's final ministry in October 1891. Reid promptly succeeded Parkes as the leader of the free trade grouping, opposing a Protectionist government headed by George Dibbs, whose protectionist instincts had not converted him to the federation cause.

Parkes's loss of office – and consequently influence – deprived the federation movement of one its most forceful advocates, but other prominent colonial politicians stepped into the gap. From New South Wales and Victoria respectively, Edmund Barton and Alfred Deakin proved particularly significant players both in securing the Act's passage and its early implementation.

---

[152] Clark, born in Hobart in 1848, was the son of an affluent businessman. Originally pursuing a career as an engineer, Clark was elected to the Tasmanian Assembly in 1878 – a year after beginning practice at the Bar – on a platform which expressed great enthusiasm for American republican principles. By 1890, Clark was the colony's Attorney-General and established a reputation as a vigorously progressive politician, enjoying support from both liberal voters and the emerging trade union movement. Clark led the Tasmania federation lobby in the 1890s, albeit spending most of that decade in political opposition rather than in government, before taking a seat on the Supreme Court in 1898; http://adb.anu.edu.au/biography/clark-andrew-inglis-3211.

[153] See especially Reynolds (1958) 'A. I. Clark's American sympathies and his influence on Australian Federation' *Australian Law Journal* 62: Williams (1996) 'Race, citizenship and the formation of the Australian Constitution: Andrew Inglis Clark and the Fourteenth Amendment' *Australian Journal of Politics and History* 10.

[154] On Reid and his career, see Hogan (2006) 'George (later Sir George) Houston Reid' in Clune and Turner op cit.

[155] db.anu.edu.au/biography/reid-sir-george-houstoun-8173.

Barton was born in Sydney in 1849. His parents, respectively an accountant and a school teacher, had emigrated from England 20 years earlier.[156] After attending Sydney Grammar School, Barton took a law degree at the University of Sydney. Barton began a career at the Bar in the 1870s, before being elected to the New South Wales Assembly in 1882, notionally as an independent free trader. He subsequently served several terms as Speaker. Barton was close personally and politically to Parkes. He accepted nomination from Parkes to the Legislative Council in 1887 and subsequently played a minor role in settling the text of the draft constitution bill. Barton's free trade sentiments were hardly a badge of faith, however, and – being no friend to Reid – he stood against Reid in the 1891 Assembly election on a platform which took support for federation as its main principle. He thereafter agreed to serve as Attorney-General in Dibbs's Protectionist government between 1891 and 1893. He subsequently lost his Assembly seat in 1894, and devoted his political energies to advocating the federation cause.

Alfred Deakin was born in Victoria in 1856 to lower-middle-class English and Welsh émigré parents. After a school career of no great distinction, Deakin took a law degree at Melbourne University and qualified for the Bar. He had no obvious enthusiasm for or success in legal practice, preferring instead to direct his energies towards journalism and poetry. Deakin became a protégé of David Syme, then editor of the leading newspaper *The Melbourne Age*, and flourished as a journalist. Deakin's interest in liberal politics led to his election to an Assembly seat in 1879. Deakin held various ministerial offices in Victoria in the 1880s, and was associated with the promotion of much reformist legislation. He was an opposition backbencher throughout the 1890s, when he combined his parliamentary career with a renewed practice at the Bar, continued his journalism activities and became a vigorously enthusiastic proponent of federation.[157] Like both Griffith and Clark, Deakin was familiar with and much influenced by US constitutional principle and history in formulating his preferences for Australia's proposed constitution.

Both Barton and Deakin made substantial efforts to keep the federation project alive during the mid-1890s. The movement was in part reinvigorated by proposals made by John Quick and Robert Garran,[158] both prominent in the 1891 convention, that each colony should elect delegates to a further convention which would put forward amended federation proposals that would subsequently be voted on in individual colony referendums and, if approved, sent to Britain for enactment. Reid's evident change of heart on the issue after he led the free trade party to a victory of sorts in the July 1894 election[159]

---

[156] http://adb.anu.edu.au/biography/barton-sir-edmund-toby-71. Barton is the subject of a most peculiar biography – Reynolds (1948) *Edmund Barton* – which is trite in content and cringingly hagiographic in tone. A more balanced and informative perspective is provided by Bolton (2000) *Edmund Barton*.

[157] http://adb.anu.edu.au/biography/deakin-alfred-5927.

[158] Quick had emigrated to Victoria as a child, where he grew up in straitened circumstances and left school at 10. He nonetheless secured an LLB from Melbourne University, developed a broad practice at the Bar and was elected to the Assembly in the 1880s; http://adb.anu.edu.au/biography/quick-sir-john-8140. Robert Garran was a New South Wales barrister who did not hold elected office but was politically close to both Barton and Reid.

[159] Albeit with only 50 of the Assembly's 125 seats, Reid's policy preferences on the perennially problematic land question and other social policy matters were broadly progressive, and his ministry suffered frequent obstruction in the Legislative Council. Reid called an early election in July 1895, in which he made reform to the Council's powers and composition a leading issue. Reid's Free Traders took 61 seats, against the 41 of Dibbs's Protectionists. With the informal support of the 18 Labour members, Reid formed an effective

lent further momentum to the cause, and a new Convention met several times in the year from March 1897. Queensland had not returned delegates, which prevented Griffith from having any formal role in the deliberations, although the proposals eventually offered to the colonial electorates were similar in matters both of principle and detail to the 1891 draft constitution.[160]

The draft bill was approved in four colonies in the June 1898 referenda,[161] but turnout was insufficient in New South Wales to meet the requirements of that colony's referendum legislation. Reid's at best lukewarm support (with a cautious eye on the July 1898 Assembly election) was a likely contributor to that result, but, having again led his party to electoral success,[162] he then played a major part in persuading delegates to modify the bill to meet some New South Wales concerns. The amended bill was subsequently approved in all colonies,[163] including Queensland, in 1899.

---

minority administration. The prompt appointment of nine new government supporters to the Council secured passage of land and income tax reform bills, and the prospect of more appointments muted opposition to government measures.

[160] For a brief but detailed view of the process from various perspectives, see Irving (2013) 'Making the federal Commonwealth 1890–1901' in Bashford and MacIntyre (eds) *The Cambridge history of Australia*; Williams (2003) 'The emergence of the Commonwealth Constitution' in Winterton (ed) *Australian constitutional landmarks*; Mc Minn op cit ch 5. La Nauze's (1972) *The making of the Australian Constitution* provides the most insightful analysis of the framing of the Constitution's text.

[161] Queensland did not participate.

[162] Reid's Free Traders won fewer seats (45 to 50) and votes than the pro-federation Protectionist group then led by Barton, but hung onto power as a minority administration with informal Labour (19 seats) support. Reid's ministry lasted barely a year, falling after a censure motion in the Assembly engineered by William Lyne, who had succeeded Barton as leader of the Protectionists. Lyne's manoeuvrings had depended on Labour support, which was won and maintained by his government's successful promotion of a wide range of progressive social and economic policy legislation.

[163] Reid had needed to secure 12 new appointments – including for the first time members of the Labour Party – to the Legislative Council to secure a majority there for the necessary enabling legislation; *SMH* 10 April 1899 p7, https://trove.nla.gov.au/newspaper/article/14208846.

6

Australian Confederation

> ... [W]hat you have here is nothing akin to the Constitution of the United States except in its most superficial features ...
>
> Richard Haldane QC, MP in the House of Commons during debate on the Commonwealth of Australia Constitution Bill; *HCD* 14 May 1900 c 98.

Barton and Deakin's final roles in the federation process were to lead the Australian delegation to Britain to explain and push for enactment of the proposed constitution, which subsequently took form as the Commonwealth of Australia Constitution Act 1900. Much feted in Britain, Barton subsequently 'emerged' as the preferred candidate to be Australia's first Prime Minister, initially on an interim basis pending elections to the newly created Parliament.

I. The Terms of Federation

There are distinct similarities in terms of principle, institutional structure and text between the Commonwealth of Australia Constitution Act 1900[1] and the 1787 United States Constitution. Some politicians involved in framing the Act were very familiar with and approving of the principles underlying the United States' second constitutional settlement. However, the deep familiarity displayed by Clark, Deakin and Griffith was not widely shared among the delegates. Williams records,[2] for example, a surprising exchange between Clark and Barton, in which Barton professed ignorance of the US Supreme Court's judgment in *Marbury v Madison*,[3] the landmark case which established the doctrine empowering the courts to invalidate Congressional legislation. The inference obviously arises that many politicians involved in drafting Australia's constitution had a limited understanding of the legal implications of the text they were approving.

---

[1] The Act has a stylistic quirk. Its first 'Part' contains nine sections, numbered 1–9. S.9 contains the Constitution in 'Chapters', within which sections are numbered 1 onwards. There are thus two sections 1–9. For clarity, any reference here to the first set of sections 1–9 are referred to as s.1 [BAI] (denoting British Act Introduction). Unlike the 1855 New South Wales Act, which contains distinct Imperial and indigenous elements (the BAA sections and the schedule; p 45 n 46 above), the 1900 Act makes no normative distinction between the [BAI] and 'Chapter' provisions.

[2] (2003) op cit pp 23–24.

[3] (1803) 1 Cranch 137. The doctrine was promptly extended to the actions of all state governmental bodies; see *Fletcher v Peck* (1810) 109 US 87; *Martin v Hunters Lessee* (1816) 14 US 304; *Cohens v Virginia* (1821) 19 US 264.

The Commonwealth Parliament

The American influence was clearly visible in the names chosen for the chambers of the Commonwealth Parliament. Per s.1: "The legislative power of the Commonwealth shall be vested in a Federal Parliament, which shall consist of the Queen, a Senate, and a House of Representatives ...". The Australian/American similarity went beyond matters of nomenclature, however, to also embrace the way members of the Senate and House would be chosen.

The Composition of the House of Representatives and the Senate

The House would have 75 members, distributed among the six states approximately according to their respective populations, with the minimum state representation fixed at five.[4] The House would sit for three-year terms, subject to earlier dissolution. Per ss.30–31, the qualifications for members, voters and laws regulating the electoral process would initially be those in force for each state's Assembly, but the Commonwealth Parliament was empowered to enact its own laws on those matters.

S.39 set the House quorum at one-third of the total membership. The Parliament was expressly empowered to amend that provision, although it was not authorised to alter s.40, which stated that all questions arising in the House were to be decided by a bare majority of members voting.

The Senate would have 36 members, apportioned on a state equality rather than population basis; this choice endorsed the reasoning accepted by the Americans in designing the Congress to afford small-population states a disproportionately large influence within the legislature.[5] More precisely perhaps, given the increasing consolidation of coherently organised parties on the political landscape, it gave a mildly disproportionate influence to those parties popular in the smaller states.

The Senate quorum was fixed by s.22 at one-third of total membership. Per s.23, all questions would be decided by a bare majority of members voting. That first proviso could be altered by the Parliament; the second could not. Senators would sit for six-year terms, with the franchise initially based on each state's Assembly provisions.

Parliament's Powers

Parkes's original proposals in 1889 envisaged a national Parliament exercising extensive but enumerated legislative powers, the associated assumption being that the colonies qua States would retain all lawmaking competence not granted to the national body. In that broad sense Parkes endorsed the scheme articulated in the US Constitution. That presumption was given legal expression in the Act, which identified the main body of the Commonwealth Parliament's legislative authority in a single section (the United States'

---

[4] New South Wales 23; Victoria 20, Queensland 8; South Australia 6; Western Australia 5; Tasmania 5. S.127 expressly excluded 'aboriginal natives' from the count.

[5] S.7 permitted the Parliament to enlarge or reduce the Senate, subject to maintaining equality of numbers (and a six-person minimum) between the original states.

provision being Art 1 s.8 of the Constitution, which lists 17 discrete powers and an eighteenth clause which entitles the Congress to make all laws 'necessary and proper' for giving effect to its enumerated powers). S.51 listed 38 (in Roman numerals) explicit powers that the Parliament would possess. Some such powers replicated those exercised by Congress,[6] although others concerned matters which would be a state responsibility in America.[7] At first sight, Australia's new Parliament appeared to have much more substantial legislative authority vis-à-vis the Australian states than that granted to the Congress vis-à-vis the American states. S.51 (xxxix) also empowered the Parliament to legislate in:

> Matters incidental to the execution of any power vested by this Constitution in the Parliament or in either House thereof, or in the Government of the Commonwealth, or in the Federal Judicature, or in any department or officer of the Commonwealth.

S.51(xxxix) is linguistically quite different ('incidental to') from the 'necessary and proper' clause of Art 1 s.8(18) of the US Constitution. But that clause had been lent a very wide interpretation by the US Supreme Court in the important 1819 judgment in *M'Culloch v Maryland*.[8] The first issue before the Court in *McCulloch* was whether Congress has the power to establish a national bank. No explicit mention was made in Art 1 s.8 of a national bank – an omission which raises the obvious presumption, given that the Congress was designed as a body which should exercise only those powers granted by the Constitution, that Congress could not create a national bank. The Court concluded, however, that one could not properly expect every single detail of the governmental system provided for by the Constitution to be expressly identified in its text. The 'necessary and proper' clause provided a textual basis to legitimise the assumption that the powers listed in Art 1 s.8 were neither exhaustive nor to be narrowly construed. In an imaginative use of language, Marshall CJ concluded that the term 'necessary' could be construed as meaning no more than expedient or desirable, and that consequently the Constitution's explicit grant to Congress of various substantial powers of economic management impliedly brought with it the power to create institutions – such as a national bank – which would facilitate the exercise of those express powers. If 'incidental to' in s.51(xxxix) bore the same (or a wider) meaning as Marshall's Court accorded to the 'necessary and proper' clause,[9] the long list of the Commonwealth Parliament's powers in s.51 would be far from exhaustive.[10]

Deadlock Provisos

For all but one issue, the House and Senate stood on an equal footing. S.53 required all appropriation or taxation bills to originate in the House, and while the Senate could

---

[6] For example: (i) trade and commerce with other countries, and among the states; (ii) taxation; (iii) bounties on the production or export of goods; (iv) borrowing money on the public credit of the Commonwealth; (xii) currency, coinage and legal tender; and (xxvii) immigration and emigration.
[7] Notably (xxi) marriage and (xxii) divorce.
[8] (1819) 4 Wheaton 316.
[9] The *McCulloch* point discussed here would not have arisen in Australia, as s.51(xii) expressly authorised the Commonwealth Parliament to – inter alia – incorporate banks.
[10] Marshall's methodology is considered further at pp 173–175 below.

reject such bills, it was not permitted to amend them.[11] S.57 made elaborate arrangements to address any 'deadlock' that might arise between the two chambers. Should the House pass a bill which: "the Senate rejects ... or fails to pass ... or passes ... with amendments to which the House ... will not agree" on two separate occasions at least three months apart, the Governor-General could order dissolution of both chambers. If the House again passes the bill after the double election and the Senate again rejects it, the chambers will sit in a joint session which may pass the bill by an absolute majority and then send it for the royal assent.[12]

Disallowance and Reservation

The Parliament's formal legal subordinacy to the British Crown was iterated in s.59, which provided that: "The Queen may disallow any law within one year from the Governor-General's assent ...". The disallowance power had been a ubiquitous feature in colonial constitutions, but there seemed little expectation either in Australia or before the Imperial Parliament that s.59 would be used with any frequency. Its projected role was likely limited to legislation which might interfere with the Imperial government's foreign policy concerns, particularly in relation to China, whose citizens qua Australian immigrants had been a perpetual source of political unease in the pre-federation colonies, and to other European powers maintaining a colonial presence in the Australasian region.

The National Government

Chapter II of the Act created Australia's executive government. In a strictly legal sense, governmental power was vested in the Queen and exercised on her behalf by a Governor-General. Per s.63, the Governor-General was, however, to exercise (most of) his powers qua 'Governor-General in Council' with the advice of a 'Federal Executive Council'. No explicit mention was made either of a Prime Minister or a Cabinet, or that the 'Federal Executive Council' should be composed of persons whose political party or grouping commanded a House majority. The legally unarticulated but universally shared assumption was that the Commonwealth would have responsible government in the orthodox British sense, that the Federal Executive Council would be the Cabinet and that the leader of the political grouping commanding a House majority would serve as Prime Minister. S.65 made provision for up to seven ministers of state,[13] who in formal terms held office at the Governor-General's pleasure.

The Governor-General would obviously occupy – as had Governors in the colonies in late nineteenth century – a dual political position; in one aspect exercising his powers on the advice of his ministers, but in a second aspect doing so at the command of the British government. The Act's text provided no indication as to how any tensions caused

---

[11] So providing a clear legal answer to the political controversy which had been prominent in Queensland and New South Wales in the late 19th century; pp 137–39 and 145–46 above.
[12] This was a concession extracted by Reid in 1898; before then the requisite joint session majority was 60%.
[13] S.65 empowered Parliament to increase that number.

by that duality should be resolved. Neither the Letters Patent[14] establishing the office of Governor-General nor the *Instructions* issued to the first incumbent[15] addressed that issue; the *Instructions*' five pages are composed primarily of details concerning oaths of office and the power to grant pardons. The prevailing assumption in Australian political circles was certainly that on all internal matters the Governor-General would act on the advice of his Australian ministers.[16]

State Autonomy

Much like Article VI of the US Constitution,[17] the 1900 Act expressly laid out a normative hierarchy of laws within the new constitutional order in s.5 [BAI] and s.109:

> 5. [BAI] This Act, and all laws made by the Parliament of the Commonwealth under the Constitution, shall be binding on the courts, judges, and people of every state and of every part of the Commonwealth, notwithstanding anything in the laws of any state …
>
> 109. When a law of a state is inconsistent with a law of the Commonwealth, the latter shall prevail, and the former shall, to the extent of the inconsistency, be invalid.

While ostensibly clear in their own terms, s.5 [BAI] and s.109 raise two questions which must be answered before those sections can be applied: namely, is the Commonwealth measure in issue actually a 'law' – ie does the Commonwealth Parliament have the power to enact it; and is the state measure in issue actually a 'law' – ie does the state legislature have the power to enact it?

S.106 and s.107 expressed broad statements of principle concerning the scope of state power under Australia's new constitutional arrangements:

> 106. The Constitution of each state of the Commonwealth shall, subject to this Constitution, continue as at the establishment of the Commonwealth, or as at the admission or establishment of the state, as the case may be, until altered in accordance with the Constitution of the state.
>
> 107. Every power of the Parliament of a Colony which has become or becomes a state, shall, unless it is by this Constitution exclusively vested in the Parliament of the Commonwealth or withdrawn from the Parliament of the state, continue as at the establishment of the Commonwealth, or as at the admission or establishment of the state, as the case may be.

---

[14] www.foundingdocs.gov.au/item-did-13.html.
[15] www.foundingdocs.gov.au/item-sdid-85.html. The first Governor-General was Lord Hopetoun, a senior aristocrat (the seventh Earl) and Tory politician who had been Governor of Victoria and a keen advocate of federation in the early 1890s, before serving briefly in the British Cabinet. Hopetoun resigned as Governor-General after two years on the basis that his £10,000 annual salary was inadequate (per s.48, members of the House and Senate received £400 per year). Hopetoun's tenure is best remembered for his so-called 'blunder' of initially inviting Sir William Lyne, then the (anti-federation) Premier of New South Wales, to be Australia's first Prime Minister, a decision he reversed when it became clear that neither Barton nor Deakin would serve under Lyne; http://adb.anu.edu.au/biography/hopetoun-seventh-earl-of-6730.
[16] S.58 granted the Governor-General the discretion to decide whether to approve or reject a bill passed by the House and Senate or to reserve it for the royal assent. The prerogative powers to summon, prorogue and dissolve Parliament were given a statutory basis in s.5.
[17] Although s.5 [BAI] omitted the provision in Art VI that the Constitution was the 'supreme law of the land'.

S.107 prima facie follows the lead of the US Constitution in eschewing any attempt to enumerate state powers, leaving states instead with an undefined residuum of legislative authority. That approach is quite distinct from the method adopted for Canada in the British North America Act 1867, which contains extensive provisions concerning the powers of both the national and provincial legislatures. But despite the extensive attention paid by Australian politicians and lawyers – Griffith perhaps foremost among them – to the Act's text, this cluster of provisions has obvious textual infelicities. S.107 refers to powers *exclusively* vested in the Parliament. But the only powers so described in the Act are in s.52, s.90 and s.111.[18] None of the Parliament's s.51 powers are described there (or anywhere else in the Act) as 'exclusive'. That obviously raises the inference that s.51 powers are not *exclusive*, but exist *concurrently* with state power. S.109 seemingly presumes concurrency – as it imposes a normative hierarchy on 'laws' made by each sphere of governance. If a state had no power to make law on a particular matter (because per s.109 the matter was 'exclusive' to the Commonwealth or 'withdrawn' from the state), there would be no 'inconsistency' to be overridden by a Commonwealth measure.

The obvious presumption as to s.109's impact would therefore be that state laws affecting (most) matters within s.51 would continue to be effective until such time as the Commonwealth legislated in respect of them, whereupon the state law would become ineffective to the extent of any inconsistency with the Commonwealth legislation.[19]

S.107's scope is more opaque. The Act does not provide any list of 'withdrawn' state powers. S.114 and s.115 seem to have that impact,[20] although they do not use the term 'withdrawn'. 'Withdrawal' in s.107 was presumably to be read in conjunction with the 'by this Constitution' proviso, ie 'withdrawal' was not something that the Commonwealth Parliament could effect. Consequently, if s.107 was to restrict states' legislative competence beyond the matters expressly addressed in s.52, s.90, s.114 and s.115, one would have to assume that the Act created *implied* exclusivity and/or *implied* withdrawal.[21]

'Fiscal' Autonomy

State revenues prior to federation derived substantially from customs duties and (decreasingly) sale and lease of waste lands. The transfer of exclusive powers over customs duties to the Commonwealth per s.90 presented a substantial threat to the states' fiscal positions. The (medium-term) compromise on that issue was s.87, which provided that for a 10-year period at least 75% of the Commonwealth's net revenues

---

[18] S.52 relates to laws establishing the Commonwealth's seat of government and the management of those parts of the Commonwealth civil service transferred from the states. S.90 provided that, once uniform customs duties had been imposed (which per s.88 had to be done within two years of the Act coming into force), the Parliament's power over such duties would become exclusive. S.111 concerned the governance of lands surrendered by a state to the Commonwealth.

[19] The 'most' caveat is applied because some s.51 matters (notably xxxvi–xxxix) simply could not have existed prior to the Act coming into force.

[20] S.114 forbids states from raising military forces without the Commonwealth Parliament's consent, or taxing Commonwealth property. S.115 forbids states from coining money.

[21] 'Withdrawal' in s.107 is presumably to be read in conjunction with the 'by this Constitution' proviso, ie 'withdrawal' is not something that the Commonwealth Parliament could effect.

from customs duties had to be returned to the states. S.87 had been championed by Edward Braddon, Premier of Tasmania between 1894 and 1899, and soon became popularly and pejoratively referred to as the 'Braddon blot'.

Braddon's presumption was that much of the Commonwealth government's revenue would be raised through customs duties, which would entail significant – if the 25% ceiling was imposed – revenue for the states. The presumption was eminently plausible, given the protectionist sentiments of so many advocates of federation. In its original form, s.87 had not been time limited; the 10- year period was a modification which Reid had successfully sought after the first New South Wales referendum.[22]

That Act also – in s.96 rather than in s.51 – authorised the Parliament for a 10-year period to: "grant financial assistance to any state on such terms and conditions as the Parliament thinks fit".

The High Court

The Act was underpinned by the presumption that the Commonwealth Parliament and government and the state legislatures and governments would all be bodies of limited legal competence, a necessary consequence of which was – again following the American model – that judicial institutions would have to be created and empowered to assess the constitutionality in a legal sense of the actions of the legislative and executive branches. US history had made it abundantly clear to colonial politicians that any attempt to establish a federal system of governance would inevitably generate constant legal dispute as to the proper limits of governmental institutions' respective powers.

The Act's relatively brief provisions in relation to 'The Judicature' are in Chapter III (ss.71–77). Adapting language from the US Constitution,[23] s.71 provided that: "The judicial power of the Commonwealth shall be vested in a federal Supreme Court, to be called the High Court of Australia, and in such other federal courts as the Parliament creates …". S.71 required that the High Court have a Chief Justice and at least two other judges. Per s.72, federal judges would be appointed by the Governor-General in Council, and would be dismissible only on an address from the House and Senate on the basis of "proved misbehaviour or incapacity". Judicial salaries were to be fixed by Parliament, and not reduced while the judge remained in office.

Chapter III did not expressly limit the number of High Court or other federal judgeships which the Parliament might create. No fixed retirement age was identified, nor was any provision made for judicial pensions. There was no obvious proviso in Chapter III authorising the Parliament to address either of those issues, although both matters might be subsumed within the Parliament's s.51(xxxix) powers to legislate on "matters incidental to" inter alia the national judiciary. The Act also followed the American model in both language and substance in listing specific circumstances in which the High Court would exercise original (ss.75–76) and appellate (s.73) jurisdiction respectively, though it also granted the Commonwealth Parliament expansive competence to extend those jurisdictions.

---

[22] See pp 155–156 above.
[23] In Art 3 s.1.

The Privy Council's judicial role had provoked tension between colonial politicians and the then Secretary of State for the Colonies Joseph Chamberlain. Chamberlain had trenchantly resisted the original colonial proposal that the High Court be Australia's final Court of Appeal. The compromise position eventually adopted in s.74 was that no appeal would lie to the Privy Council without the High Court's permission – given on the basis of 'any special reason' – on a matter concerning the limits of the powers of the Commonwealth or a state; so-called '*inter se*' matters. S.74 also empowered the Parliament – subject to any such bill being reserved for the royal assent – to require that the High Court grant such permission in other matters as well, subject to any such bill being reserved for royal assent. The Parliament was not, however, expressly empowered to prevent litigants appealing directly from State Supreme Courts to the Privy Council, an omission which raised the possibility of bypassing the High Court's control via s.74 on *inter se* matters.

The Constitutional Amendment Process

The enthusiasm displayed by Griffith, Clark and other framers for the American constitutional model also appeared in the Constitution's provisions for its own amendment. In strict (Imperial) legal terms, the Constitution could be altered in any fashion by an Act of the British Parliament. Whether, as a matter of practical politics, the British Parliament could do so without the approval of 'Australia' remained to be seen. But as a matter of indigenous law, the amendment process indicated that the Constitution's provisions were subject to a modest degree of legal entrenchment.

S.128 was the only provision in Chapter VIII, which was titled 'Alteration of the Constitution'. S.128 (echoing in part the formula used in s.5 of the Colonial Laws Validity Act 1865)[24] began by providing that: "This Constitution shall not be altered except in the following *manner* ..." (emphasis added). The entrenchment mechanism s.128 created was a complex one that recognised both a state and a national dimension to the question of defining Australia's national 'sovereign'. An amendment would require an absolute majority in the House and Senate (or two such majorities in one chamber if the other rejected or failed to pass a proposed amendment) and then be approved in referendums by a majority of the total voting electorate and by an electoral majority in a majority of the states. Since there were six states, four would have to approve the amendment. The majority required in the referendums was of voters who participated, not of those eligible to vote.

The entrenchment was manifestly not as deep as provided for by the US Constitution, which requires both a two-thirds majority in Congress and approval by at least three-quarters of the states. But the amendment process was significantly more onerous – in terms both of the nature of the majorities required and the time the process would take – than provided for by the bare majoritarian two-institution[25]

---

[24] See pp 108–09 above.
[25] The Commons and Lords. I am assuming there was no likelihood that the third institution, the Queen, would ever refuse the royal assent.

mechanism available to the British Parliament. S.128 identifies nine distinct actors on the amendment stage (the House, the Senate, the national electorate and the six state electorates), at least six of whom (and within which six there would have to be the national electorate and either the House or Senate) would have to provide majority support to alter the Act.

The Continuing Significance of the CLVA 1865?

There is no explicit reference in the Act to the CLVA 1865. The Commonwealth Parliament would presumably be a representative legislature per CLVA 1865 s.1[26] and, like all colonial legislatures, subject to the substantive limitations imposed by the CLVA 1865 s.2.[27] Whether CLVA 1865 s.5 was applicable to the Commonwealth Parliament is not so obvious. The presence of s.128 might be taken to indicate that the Parliament had no power to alter its (per s.5) 'constitution, powers or procedures' through its 'ordinary' lawmaking processes, ie that any such reform should be seen as an amendment to the Act requiring use of s.128. However, as noted above, the 1900 Act contained several provisions which expressly permitted the Parliament to alter the size of the House and Senate, the qualifications of their members and their respective quora, matters which could credibly be seen as falling within CLVA 1865 s.5 and so presumptively subject through legislation passed in the 'ordinary way' to 'manner and form' constraints which prevented that legislation from being amended or repealed in the ordinary way.

Notably, s.23 and s.40 simply fixed requisite majorities for all questions arising in each chamber to a bare majority and do not authorise the Parliament to alter that requirement. Similarly, the s.57 deadlock procedure is not identified as alterable through ordinary legislation. These would seem to be matters that could be changed only through s.128. There is no obvious objection to the proposition that s.128 could be invoked to amend s.23 and/or s.40 to require enhanced majorities in the House and/or the Senate for bills dealing with any (or many) particular s.52 matters.

Whether the s.128 process itself amounted to a 'representative legislature' for CLVA 1865 s.5 purposes was a question that did not seem to engage the minds of either colonial or British politicians. Nor was any great attention given to the related question of whether s.128 could be used to alter the provisions of s.128 itself.[28] Such abstract questions perhaps rather paled into contemporary political insignificance in the face of the more immediate matter of determining which political party would initially control the new Parliament and government's legal powers.

---

[26] Since all its members were elected, it did not satisfy a strict reading of s.1; pp 110–11 above.
[27] The view taken by the British government – evidently with the agreement of colonial politicians – was that the CLVA 1865 would apply to measures 'enacted' by the Commonwealth Parliament; see Joseph Chamberlain's second reading speech; *HCD* 21 May 1900 c 758.
[28] Whether by strengthening the level of entrenchment of particular matters, for example by requiring 55%, 60% or other special majorities in either the national and/or state votes, or by weakening it, for example by removing the 'and in a majority of states' requirement.

II. Party Political Alignments in the Commonwealth Parliament in Early Twentieth-century Australia

The Act came into force on 1 January 1901. Barton, the new nation's first Prime Minister, was joined in its Cabinet by Deakin and the then Premiers of several of the states. The first national election was scheduled for late March 1901. Voters faced a choice between a moderately protectionist party led by Barton and Deakin, a free trade grouping led by Reid and the newly emergent Labour Party.

The political process which led to the creation of the Federal Council had begun before the Labour Party started to take formal shape as a political force linked to the trade unions. But the federation machinations of the late 1880s onwards occurred in a decade which also saw the consolidation of the labour movement as a party political force in the Legislative Assemblies (but not, of course, the Councils) of all the states except Tasmania. That 'movement' was a very eclectic phenomenon. As in Britain, it encompassed working-class members driven towards pursuit of parliamentary representation by their experience of trade union activism and middle-class activists prompted by more abstract ideological concerns;[29] but the movement acquired added complexity in Australia because of the relative heterogeneity of economic and cultural development in the six colonies. Nonetheless, by 1900, 'Labour' had emerged as a potent electoral force.

Table 6.1 'Labour' party representation in State Legislative Assemblies, c 1900

State	Year	Labour members	Total seats
New South Wales	1901	28	(125)
	1904	25	(90)
Victoria	1900	9	(95)
	1902	12	(95)
Queensland	1899	21	(72)
	1902	25	(72)
South Australia	1899	11	(54)
	1902	5	(42)
Tasmania	1900	–	(38)
	1903	3	(35)
Western Australia	1901	6	(50)
	1904	22	(50)

---

[29] I use the term 'class' guardedly, recognising that it is oversimplistic to root the emergence of Labour parties in a straightforward binary class dynamic. For a nuanced Australian picture, see Markey (1987) 'Populism and the formation of a labor party in New South Wales, 1890–1900' *Journal of Australian Studies* 39; O'Farrell (1958) 'The Australian Socialist League and the labor movement 1887–1891' *Historical Studies* 152. The early careers of subsequently prominent Labour politicians also provide helpful insight; see especially Lang (1956) *I remember* chs 1–2; Robertson (1974) *J H Scullin: a political biography* ch 1; Fitzgerald (1994) *"Red Ted": the life of E G Theodore* ch 1; Murphy (1975) *T J Ryan* chs 1–3.

The 1901 Election

The Labour Party's significance in the first national election led it to winning 14 seats in the House and eight in the Senate.[30] Barton steered the Protectionists to electoral 'victory' in the sense of winning more seats in the House than Reid's Free Traders and thereby gaining the distinction of becoming Australia's first 'elected' Prime Minister. But Barton's party fell far short of an overall House majority, and in the Senate the Free Traders were the largest (albeit not a majority) party.

Table 6.2 The 1901 Commonwealth election (29 March 1901)

House of Representatives	% vote	Seats
Protectionist (Barton)	36.7	31
Free Trade (Reid)	30.0	28
Labour	15.7	14
Independent	1.6	2
Senate		
Protectionist	44.8	11
Free Trade	39.4	17
Labour	13.5	8
Independent	2.2	0

Single-party governance was therefore not a possibility. The Labour Party stood ideologically closer in many respects to the Protectionists than to the Free Traders, although the two more established parties perhaps stood closer to each other than to Labour. Barton subsequently led a Protectionist government – with Deakin very obviously both his second in command and likely successor – enjoying informal Labour support.[31] His administration's most notable achievement was perhaps to lay the legal foundations of what came to be known as the 'White Australia' policy in the Immigration Restriction Act 1901 and the Pacific Islands Labourers Act 1901, both being measures which the Labour Party had enthusiastically supported.[32] Barton's government also promoted a Customs Tariff Act in 1902 which introduced uniform tariffs at rates more akin to those which had prevailed in protectionist Victoria than free trade New South Wales.

The 1901 election was fought on the basis of state franchise legislation. The Commonwealth Parliament promptly exercised the power given by s.9 and s.30 of

---

[30] The then party leader was John Watson. The son of a merchant navy officer, Watson was initially raised in New Zealand. At 19, he emigrated to Sydney, working in the newspaper industry and becoming prominent in trade union circles. Watson was elected to the Legislative Assembly in 1894. Watson became an eminent figure in the colony's Labour Party, although – despite having personally opposed federation – he left state politics to contest a House seat in 1901 and was immediately selected as the national party leader; http://adb.anu.edu.au/biography/watson-john-christian-chris-9003.
[31] The strategy suited Watson's personal politics, which were moderately progressive in substance and cautiously incremental in style.
[32] Ward (1992) op cit pp 225–26. The measure was not popular in Queensland, where pastoral interests still favoured large-scale Kanaka immigration as a source of cheap labour.

the Constitution to specify the qualifications for voting in national elections. The Commonwealth Franchise Act 1902 took the then radically progressive step of extending voting rights in national elections to women on the same basis as men, removed any property qualification and prohibited plural voting. The Act's progressive character was, however, compromised by s.4, which expressly excluded aboriginal natives of Australia, Asia, Africa or the Islands of the Pacific from voting rights.[33]

The Judiciary Act 1903 and the First High Court Judges

Barton's government also promoted legislation to establish a High Court. Parliament's Chapter III powers were initially exercised in the Judiciary Act 1903. That Act was concerned primarily with jurisdictional issues, but also specified the number of High Court judges – three – and the qualifications required for office,[34] and fixed the judges' initial salaries at £3500 per year.[35] Barton, having no particular appetite for or skill in managing the political factions within the House, had stepped down as Prime Minister in September. He was replaced by Alfred Deakin – in evident and well-founded anticipation that one of the seats on the Court would be his.

The High Court was initially constituted (on 5 October 1903) with three judges, all appointed by – in effect – Prime Minister Deakin. The first Chief Justice was Sir Samuel Griffith.[36] He was joined by Barton and Richard O'Connor. Like his colleagues, O'Connor had pursued a dual career at the Bar and in electoral politics.[37] The son of affluent Irish émigré parents, O'Connor was educated in Sydney, entered the New South Wales Bar in 1876 and spent much of his early career as a Crown Prosecutor. He was appointed to the Legislative Council in 1887, and served briefly as Minister of Justice and Solicitor-General. He was a close friend and political ally of Barton during the confederation process, served in Barton's pre- and post-election Cabinets and was elected to the first Senate, where he led the government members. O'Connor was a prime mover of the bill creating the High Court, his eye presumably firmly fixed on occupying one of its seats. He developed a reputation as a conscientious and moderately liberal judge, and gave more than a passing nod to his Irish Catholic roots by twice declining a knighthood.

Neither Barton nor O'Connor could credibly claim to be lawyers of great distinction, and neither had any significant judicial experience. By 1900, Griffith had both qualities in abundance. And as a leading (perhaps *the* leading) drafter of the original constitution in 1891 and a prominent voice in its subsequent refinement, Griffith likely considered himself to have a unique insight into the meanings that the Act's various provisions were intended to bear.

---

[33] The Constitution's original draft had included – at Clark's instigation – a clause modelled on the US Constitution's Fourteenth Amendment. This was removed in the 1898 sessions at the behest of politicians who wished – at both state and national level – to discriminate in economic, social and political matters against non-white peoples; see especially Williams (1996) op cit.

[34] Appointees had to be either a State Supreme Court judge or a barrister or solicitor of at least five years' standing in any state (s.5). Per s.49, rights of audience were governed by the requirements of state law.

[35] S.47. This was almost *nine times* as much as the allowance paid to members of the House and Senate (s.48).

[36] http://adb.anu.edu.au/biography/griffith-sir-samuel-walker-445.

[37] http://adb.anu.edu.au/biography/oconnor-richard-edward-dick-1102.

The Rise and Fall and Rise and Fall and Rise and Fall of the Deakin and Labour Governments

Barton's departure from the House to the Court left Deakin as leader of the Protectionists and as Prime Minister. Deakin took his party to a 'victory' of sorts in the 1903 election. The Protectionists were the largest party in the House, but the 75 seats were shared almost equally between the Protectionists, Reid's Free Traders and an increasingly prominent Labour Party. Creating and maintaining a stable government would require either formal or informal coalition. For a brief period, Deakin remained in office with tacit Labour support. In terms of domestic economic and social policy, the Labour Party's primary concern was to secure enactment of an expansive Commonwealth Conciliation and Arbitration Bill creating a 'court' exercising a broad jurisdiction (both pre-emptive and reactive to industrial disputes) to impose wage and working condition standards on a wide range of employment relationships.[38]

Table 6.3 The 1903 Commonwealth election (16 December 1903)

House of Representatives	% vote	Seats	Change
Protectionist (Deakin)	29.7	26	–5
Free Trade (Reid)	34.3	24	–4
Labour	30.1	22	+8
Independent	5.0	3	+1
Senate – 19 seats contested			
Protectionist (Deakin)	17.5	8	–3
Free Trade (Reid)	34.3	12	–5
Labour	29.7	14	+6
Independent	13.5	2	+2

Deakin's ministry survived only until April 1904, when it was defeated in the House over a Labour amendment (opportunistically supported by Free Traders) to its proposed Conciliation and Arbitration Bill.[39] Deakin regarded the issue as one of confidence and resigned office. The resignation opened the door for the formation of Australia's first Labour government. Watson's ministry survived barely three months, itself falling (ironically) after being defeated on a proposed amendment to its version of Deakin's Conciliation and Arbitration Bill. On this occasion, the impasse was resolved by Reid cobbling together a Free Trade administration supported by a faction (not including Deakin) of the Protectionists. Reid's government did succeed in having a version of the Conciliation and Arbitration Bill enacted in 1904,[40] but that administration, in turn, was

---

[38] The bill was presumptively rooted in s.51(xxxv) of the Constitution, which empowered the Commonwealth Parliament to make laws in relation to: "Conciliation and arbitration for the prevention and settlement of industrial disputes extending beyond the limits of any one State".
[39] The amendment extended the reach of the bill to state employees, an initiative which Deakin regarded as unconstitutional in both a political and legal sense as it interfered unacceptably with state autonomy.
[40] The bill eventually received royal assent on 15 December 1904. Notwithstanding the fact that the measure was ultimately promoted by Reid's government, the Act went some substantial way towards meeting the

defeated on a confidence issue in June 1905 when Reid's former Protectionist supporters returned to Deakin's fold, enabling Deakin – once more with informal Labour support – to form his second (and the country's fourth) government in the two years since the 1903 election.[41]

The 1906 election left Deakin's Protectionist Party as only the third largest party in the House. However, supported by Watson's electorally more successful Labour Party, Deakin remained Premier as the head of a precariously informal 'coalition'. In policy terms, Deakin's fourth administration was dominated by a programme colloquially referred to as 'New Protection', which rested in large part on using the Commonwealth Parliament's taxing power in s.51(ii)[42] to 'encourage' private-sector employers to provide their employees with enhanced wages and working conditions.[43] The Excise Tariff Act 1906[44] was an obvious example of such legislation. The Act presumptively imposed a significant excise duty on a wide range of domestically produced agricultural machinery, but provided in s.2 that the duty would be waived if the producer paid 'fair and reasonable' wages – a concept which the statute did not further define – to its employees.[45]

Watson resigned as Labour leader in 1907, to be replaced by Andrew Fisher, a Scots émigré who had worked as a miner both in Scotland and in Queensland. Fisher had sat briefly in the Queensland Assembly in the 1890s, but had left state politics to contest (successfully) a House seat in 1901.[46] Despite the New Protection initiatives, Fisher

---

Labour Party's objectives, including in s.4 the extension of the Act to include state employees which had, at Labour's instigation, triggered the fall of Deakin's government. The Act created a Commonwealth Court of Arbitration and Conciliation (hereafter CCAC) staffed by a 'President' (who per s.12 would be a High Court judge sitting for a renewable seven-year term and subject to dismissal on grounds of misbehaviour at the instigation of the House and Senate) with extensive jurisdiction. Per s.16: "16. The President shall be charged with the duty of endeavouring at all times by all lawful ways and means to reconcile the parties to industrial disputes, and to prevent and settle industrial disputes, whether or not the Court has cognizance of them, in all cases in which it appears to him that his mediation is desirable in the public interest." The Act empowered the President to make binding awards concerning all aspects of the employment relationship. The President was authorised to act on his own initiative, but provision was also made (per s.19) for employers' and employees' representative organisations to make applications to the Court. O'Connor was the first holder of the office, which he held alongside his seat on the High Court. The Act was distinctly non-directive on matters of detail both as to the substance of awards that the President might make and the procedure he should follow in doing so; for example, per s.25: "25. In the hearing and determination of every industrial dispute the Court shall act according to equity, good conscience, and the substantial merits of the case, without regard to technicalities or legal forms, and shall not be bound by any rules of evidence, but may inform its mind on any matter in such manner as it thinks just."

[41] For more detailed discussion, see Sawer (1956) op cit pp 37–40.

[42] "51. The Parliament shall, subject to this Constitution have power to make laws ... with respect to:- ... (ii) Taxation; but so as not to discriminate between States or parts of States ...".

[43] Deakin successfully promoted an Invalid and Old Age Pensions Act in 1908, which provided impecunious men and women (of 65 or 60 years or more, respectively) the modest sum of 10s per week. Persons not of good character, men who had deserted their wives and children and (per s.16(1)) "Asiatics (except those born in Australia), or aboriginal natives of Australia, Africa, the Islands of the Pacific, or New Zealand" were ineligible.

[44] There are several Excise Tariff Acts 1906. The one here in issue is 1906 No 16.

[45] Which criterion could be met (per s.2) either by a House and Senate resolution, an award under the CCAA 1904 or on application by the producer to the CCCA. No 16 was a small part of a wider policy strategy; for example, the Excise Tariff Act 1906 empowered the government to impose additional duties on alcoholic drinks whose producers did not pay 'fair and reasonable wages'.

[46] Marginson (1970) 'Andrew Fisher – the views of the practical reformer' in Murphy, Joyce and Hughes (eds) *Prelude to power*.

was less willing than Watson to sustain Deakin in power rather than form a Labour administration, and pressed a successful no confidence vote against Deakin's ministry in late 1908. Fisher's subsequently appointed minority government also proved a short-lived enterprise.

Table 6.4 The 1906 Commonwealth election (12 April 1906)

House of Representatives	% vote	Seats	Change
Protectionist	16.4	16	−10
Anti-Socialist (Reid)[a]	38.1	26	+2
Labour	36.6	26	+3
Independent Protectionist	4.8	5	+5
Independent	1.5	1	−1
Western Australian	2.3	1	+1
Senate – 18 seats contested			
Protectionist	12.4	6	−2
Anti-Socialist	46.5	15	+3
Labour	38.7	13	−1
Independent	1.0	2	–

[a] The rebranded Free Trade party.

Shorn of Labour support, Deakin engineered a 'fusion' of the Protectionist and Free Trade parties. With 39 House members, the Fusion grouping – soon renamed the Liberal Party – passed a no-confidence motion against Fisher's government in May 1909 and Deakin again returned to office. That government's most notable achievement was to broker an agreement with the states – at least in the medium term – on financial matters. The 'Braddon blot' was to lose its constitutionally protected status in 1910 and Deakin had no wish to extend it. Under the terms of the Financial Agreement of 1909,[47] the Commonwealth would pay the states a flat rate of 25 s per head of population rather than a 75% proportion of its customs revenues.

Nestled among the Free Traders, Deakin's reformist instincts on social and economic policy seemed rather to wane. The electorate was consequently presented with a distinct two-party choice at the 1910 election. That voters entrusted the Labour Party with comfortable House and Senate majorities indicates that the moderate progressivism on economic and social issues that Labour embraced[48] had become a thoroughly respectable rather than dangerously radical political philosophy in early twentieth-century Australia.

---

[47] Enacted as the Surplus Revenue Act 1910 (No 8 of 1910). An attempt through s.128 to entrench the Act as part of the Constitution was unsuccessful.
[48] Deakin retained his own House seat in 1910, but did not hold government office again. He was apparently afflicted by a form of dementia shortly after the 1910 election, and died in 1919 after a reclusive retirement.

172   Australian Confederation

Table 6.5 The 1910 Commonwealth election (13 April 1910)

House of Representatives	% vote	Seats	Change
Liberal[a]	49.9	31	−11
Labour	45.1	43	+17
Independent	4.9	1	−6
Senate – 18 seats contested			
Liberal	45.5	14	−7
Labour	50.3	22	+7

[a] In the change column I have equated the Liberal Party with the Protectionists and Free Trade (Anti-socialist) parties in the 1906 election.

III. In the High Court and Privy Council – The Implied Immunity of Instrumentalities Doctrine

The High Court's early years were marked by a fierce dispute between the Court and the Privy Council as to which body was Australia's highest court of appeal. The controversy initially arose over questions of taxation; specifically, whether states could tax incomes paid by the Commonwealth government to Commonwealth officials and officers. More broadly, the cases concerned whether the national Constitution contained *implied* restrictions upon state powers, a question turning on the different views taken by the Privy Council and by Griffith, Barton and O'Connor of the relevance of US constitutional law to Australian constitutional doctrine.[49] Shortly after the 1900 Act came into force, Quick and Garran[50] had published a compendious annotated guide to the Constitution,[51] which suggested that many of the Constitution's provisions directly borrowed from the United States should be given the same meaning in Australia as by judgments of the US Supreme Court.[52] Their view was seemingly shared by many – though not all – senior Australian judges.

In re the Income Tax Acts (No 4); Wollaston's Case

The question before the Victoria Supreme Court in *Wollaston's Case*[53] in 1902 was whether Dr Wollaston, a senior Commonwealth government official, was liable to pay Victoria income tax on his government salary. The litigation was a test case pressed

---

[49] For more extensive analysis, see Sackville (1969) 'The doctrine of immunity of instrumentalities in the United States and Australia: a comparative analysis' *Melbourne ULR* 15; Goldsworthy (2006) 'Australia: devotion to legalism' in Goldsworthy (ed) *Interpreting constitutions: a comparative study*.
[50] P 155 above.
[51] (1901) *The annotated Constitution of the Australian Commonwealth*.
[52] See the discussion of the commentary's early influence in Gageler and Bateman (2018) 'Comparative constitutional law' in Saunders and Stone (eds) *The Oxford handbook to the Australian Constitution*.
[53] (1902) 28 VLR 357. Argued in June 1902 and judgment given in September 1902.

by Barton's government to establish whether the Commonwealth Constitution placed *implicit* limits on the powers (especially the taxation powers) of the states.

S.114 contained a peculiar combination of issues:

> 114. A state shall not, without the consent of the Parliament of the Commonwealth, raise or maintain any naval or military force, or impose any tax on property of any kind belonging to the Commonwealth, nor shall the Commonwealth impose any tax on property of any kind belonging to a state.

On tax matters, s.114 seemingly granted the states and the Commonwealth limited reciprocal protection. The meaning of 'property' obviously raised a question for judicial determination. But it might credibly be thought that the Act's *explicit* treatment of intergovernmental tax immunity was also *exhaustive*. Dr Wollaston, qua figurehead for Barton's administration,[54] offered an alternative thesis.

An American Diversion – The Judgment in McCulloch v Maryland

Dr Wollaston's submissions drew an analogy between the American and Australian constitutions, and more particularly borrowed from the US Supreme Court's judgment in *McCulloch*.[55] As noted above, *McCulloch*'s primary concern was whether Congress could establish a national bank. However, a secondary question – seized upon by Dr Wollaston – was whether a state could levy taxes on such a bank's activities.[56] The Constitution's text did not expressly answer that question.[57] *McCulloch* resolved that matter in the federal government's favour, expounding a principle known as the doctrine of intergovernmental immunities.

Marshall CJ – for a unanimous Court – rooted his conclusion in the Constitution's supremacy clause,[58] which in a normative sense ranked the powers of Congress above any state law. Marshall's reasoning was that this superiority necessarily – albeit implicitly – precluded state interference with federal government actions lawfully mandated by Congress: "[It] is of the very essence of supremacy to remove all obstacles to its action within its own sphere, and so to modify every power vested in subordinate governments, as to exempt its own operations from their own influence."[59] That the Constitution's text did not expressly forbid states from laying such a tax on a federal body could not be taken to indicate that they were empowered to do so.

On this issue, as on whether the 'necessary and proper' clause enabled Congress to create a bank, Marshall held that the Court could properly approach the question of

---

[54] Deakin was acting Prime Minister in 1902 while Barton attended Edward VII's coronation. Dr Wollaston's relationship with his political masters soon soured. The day before submissions in 'his' case ended (23 June 1902), he resigned his office (Controller-General of Customs), protesting what he considered overzealous enforcement of customs laws; *The Age (Melbourne)* 23 June 1902 p5, https://trove.nla.gov.au/newspaper/article/199394114.

[55] (1819) 17 US 316.

[56] The tax was imposed on a flat rate or percentage basis on the bank's issue of currency.

[57] There being no equivalent of s.114 in the US Constitution.

[58] "Article VI. This Constitution, and the Laws of the United States which shall be made in Pursuance thereof; and all Treaties made, or which shall be made, under the Authority of the United States, shall be the supreme Law of the Land; and the Judges in every State shall be bound thereby, any Thing in the Constitution or Laws of any State to the Contrary notwithstanding."

[59] (1819) 17 US 316, 427.

construing the Constitution in ways which would not be appropriate to interpreting an ordinary statute. Judges could not expect always to find clear answers to constitutional questions in the constitution's text:

> A Constitution, to contain an accurate detail of all the subdivisions of which its great powers will admit, and of all the means by which they may be carried into execution, would partake of the prolixity of a legal code, and could scarcely be embraced by the human mind ... Its nature, therefore, requires that only its great outlines should be marked, its important objects designated, and the minor ingredients which compose those objects be deduced from the nature of the objects themselves ... In considering this question, then, we must never forget that it is a *Constitution* we are expounding.[60]

To 'deduce from those objects', it is obviously necessary that a court has decided what the objects were. Before becoming Chief Justice, Marshall was a prominent politician, serving as Secretary of State in John Adams's 1797–1801 administration. Marshall had been controversially nominated as Chief Justice by Adams – and confirmed by the Federalist majority Senate along with many other appointments of Adams's political allies to posts in the federal government or judiciary[61] – in the lame duck period between the election of 1800 and Jefferson's inauguration as President in 1801. Adams's Federalists and Jefferson's Republicans held distinctly differing views as to the way the Constitution distributed powers between the federal and state spheres of governance, Adams – and Marshall – taking a much more expansive view of federal power than that adopted by Jefferson and his supporters.[62] It is plausible that Marshall had entirely eschewed his former party political beliefs when taking office on the Court, and that his subsequent judgments rested on a bona fide non-partisan reading of the Constitution's requirements. It is equally plausible that – whether consciously or unconsciously – Marshall's judicial reasoning was shaped by a firmly held presumption that those 'objects' favoured an interpretive approach enhancing rather than restricting congressional (and presidential) authority vis-à-vis the states.

Marshall's judgment lends itself both to narrow and broad interpretations. At the end of his opinion Marshall seemingly held that some state taxes impacting on federal activities were not constitutionally problematic:

> This opinion ... does not extend to a tax paid by the real property of the bank, in common with the other real property within the state, not to a tax imposed on the interest which the citizens of Maryland may hold in this institution, in common with property of the same description throughout the state. This is a tax on the *operations* of the bank, and is, consequently, a tax on the *operation* of an instrument employed by the government of the Union to carry its powers into execution. Such a tax must be unconstitutional.[63]

But that plausibly narrow construction of the judgment is overshadowed by the more expansive notion of 'exemption' offered elsewhere in the opinion. Marshall evidently did not regard this 'exemption' as a matter of degree, arising only if the state tax did *in fact* adversely affect the workings of the national bank. State power to tax the federal

---

[60] ibid 407; original emphasis.
[61] Including Mr William Marbury, the claimant in *Marbury v Madison*.
[62] It is notable in *McCulloch* that any reference to the federal government ('Congress'; 'the Union') has an upper case letter while the 'state' always begins with a lower case s.
[63] (1819) 17 US 316, 436; emphasis added.

bank *might* be exercised in so extensive a fashion as to severely impede or even 'destroy' the bank's efficacy.[64] Rejecting Maryland's assertion that the Court should simply have 'confidence' that states would not abuse the power, Marshall reasoned that any question about such abuse was irrelevant as the power simply could not exist:

> We are not driven to the perplexing inquiry, so unfit for the judicial department, what degree of taxation is the legitimate use and what degree may amount to the abuse of the power. The attempt to use it on the means employed by the Government of the Union, in pursuance of the Constitution, is itself an abuse because it is the usurpation of a power which the people of a single state cannot give.[65]

Furthermore, if a state could not tax a national bank, presumably nor could it tax any federal government activity. And if could not interfere with federal government activity through taxation, presumably nor could it do so in any other fashion.[66]

The conclusion that Marshall reached and, perhaps more importantly, the reasoning that underlay it, had obvious – and from a state's perspective, obviously unwelcome – consequences for the effective allocation of lawmaking power within the USA's constitutional system.

On Judges as Jurists – *McCulloch* in the Privy Council

Wollaston's Case brought into issue to what extent *McCulloch's* conclusion on the notion of implied intergovernmental immunity – and its invocation of a very expansive approach to constitutional interpretation – applied to the 1900 Act. In contrast, Palmer/Selborne's judgment in *Burah*[67] envisaged a juridically conservative role for the Privy Council and for colonial courts in the context of the colonies' constitutional law. The 'constructive enlargement' which Selborne deprecated in *Burah* might be thought an apt metaphor for the result and reasoning deployed in *McCulloch*.

The Privy Council expressed similar sentiments in 1887 in *Bank of Toronto v Lambe*.[68] The issue in *Lambe* was whether a Canadian province could enact legislation imposing a direct tax on a bank established under the authority of dominion legislation. S.92(2) of the British North America Act 1867 granted provinces the power to impose direct taxation within the province to raise revenue for provincial purposes. S.91(3) gave a general taxing power to the dominion Parliament, s.91(2) gave it power over trade and commerce, and s.91(15) gave it power over banking and the incorporation of banks. The British North America Act 1867 had no explicit equivalent of the US supremacy clause in respect of the normative relationship between dominion and provincial law, although the final lines of s.91 provided that a matter which fell within an enumerated dominion Parliament power in s.91 could not also fall with an enumerated provincial power in s.92.

---

[64] ibid 426 and 427.
[65] ibid 430.
[66] ibid 432–33.
[67] Pp 150–53 above.
[68] [1887] AC 575.

The Privy Council rejected the Bank of Toronto's argument that *McCulloch*'s reasoning and result should influence the construction of the British North America Act 1867. That Act might well be a 'constitution' for Canada, and the matter before the Court was:

> undoubtedly a case of great constitutional importance ... But questions of this class have been left for the decision of the ordinary Courts of law, which must treat the provisions of the Act in question by the same methods of construction and exposition which they apply to other statutes.[69]

Lord Hobhouse spoke approvingly of *McCulloch*, and indicated that he would readily apply its reasoning in a 'parallel case'. The 1867 Act did not, however, present a 'parallel case', so it was "impossible to argue from the one case to the other"[70] because, while states' powers were not exhaustively and expressly defined in the US Constitution, an omission which necessitated judicial implication, the British North America Act rested on a different basis:

> Their Lordships have to construe the express words of an Act of Parliament which makes an elaborate distribution of the whole field of legislative authority between two legislative bodies, and at the same time provides for the federated provinces a carefully balanced constitution, under which no one of the parts can pass laws for itself except under the control of the whole acting through the Governor-General.[71]

Hobhouse's insistence that a court would find answers to constitutional questions in the 'express words' of the relevant 'constitutional' Act obviously precludes adoption of Marshall's more expansive interpretive techniques, and so also precludes recognising implied limits on provincial powers. The Privy Council did not elaborate on the significance of the second clause in the above-quoted sentence. The clause is presumably a reference to s.90 of the Act, under which Canada's Governor-General in Council (in effect, the national government) could disallow any provincial statute within a year of its enactment. Hobhouse's unspoken rationale was perhaps that s.90 could negate any 'abuse' of a provincial power, although s.90 would obviously be of no assistance once a year had passed, nor if the political sentiments of the respective province and the then national government coincided on the measure in issue.

A fortiori, the Privy Council did not accept that possible 'abuse' of provincial power justified a conclusion that the power did not exist:

> Then it is suggested that the legislature may lay on taxes so heavy as to crush a bank out of existence, and so to nullify the power of parliament to erect banks. But their Lordships cannot conceive that when the Imperial Parliament conferred wide powers of local self-government on great countries such as Quebec, it intended to limit them on the speculation that they would be used in an injurious manner ... [T]o place a limit on it because the power may be used unwisely, as all powers may, would be an error, and would lead to insuperable difficulties, in the construction of the Federation Act.[72]

---

[69] ibid 579.
[70] ibid 587.
[71] ibid.
[72] ibid 586. The bizarre reference to Quebec as a 'country' might be taken as a slip of the pen which reveals a judicial presentiment to find in the province's favour.

Lambe's orthodox characterisation of the judicial role – and of the British North America Act as a 'statute like any other' – repeated the Privy Council's view in another Canadian case decided six years earlier – *Citizens Insurance Co v Parsons* – where the Court held that:

> In performing this difficult duty [of interpreting the British North America Act 1867], it will be a wise course for those on whom it is thrown, to decide each case which arises as best they can, without entering more largely upon an interpretation of the statute than is necessary for the decision of the particular question in hand.[73]

On Judges as Statesmen

But that was not the only perception of the proper nature of the Privy Council's judicial power. Among the most influential of the Privy Council's judges in that era was a Scots lawyer, William Watson. An eminent (Tory) member of the Scots Bar in the 1870s, Watson was appointed Solicitor-General for Scotland by Disraeli in 1875, and subsequently won a Commons seat for a Scots university constituency in 1876. His party political career was short-lived; he was appointed a Law Lord in 1880, and soon became widely regarded as among the most able judges of that era.[74]

Watson's understanding of the Privy Council as a colonial constitutional court – and of his position within it – is perhaps best caught in an obituary written by Richard Haldane[75] in 1899:

> The function of such a judge, sitting in the supreme tribunal of the Empire, is to do more than decide what abstract and familiar legal conceptions should be applied to particular cases. *His function is to be a statesman as well as a jurist,* to fill in the gaps which Parliament has deliberately left in the skeleton constitutions and laws that it has provided for the British Colonies. The Imperial legislature has taken the view that these constitutions and laws must, if they are to be acceptable, be in a large measure unwritten, elastic, and capable of being silently developed and even altered as the Colony develops and alters.
>
> … In a series of masterly judgments he [Watson] expounded and established the real constitution of Canada.
>
> … In all these cases he seemed to get easily into the spirit of the law which he had not merely to interpret, *but as often in reality to make.*[76]

---

[73] (1881) 7 App Cas 96, 109. Adopting orthodox methods of statutory construction, the Privy Council had concluded that the Dominion Parliament's power to enact legislation dealing with 'trade and commerce' (s.91(2)) could not be construed as preventing a province from enacting consumer protection legislation addressing insurance contracts under its power to make laws dealing with 'property and civil rights in the Province' (s.92(13)).

[74] Rigg (2004) 'Watson, William, Baron Watson' *ODNB*.

[75] A Scot and graduate of Edinburgh University, Haldane entered the English Bar in 1879. He rapidly developed a high profile in colonial constitutional matters, appearing frequently before the Privy Council. A close friend of Asquith, Haldane was active in Liberal politics, and was elected for a Scottish Commons seat in 1885. In addition to his practice – he took silk in 1891 – and burgeoning political career, Haldane maintained a strong interest in moral and legal philosophy, and published several works in the field. Among the most progressive of the turn-of-the-century Liberals, Haldane developed close ties with Beatrice and Sydney Webb and the Fabian movement, and vocally supported women's enfranchisement, trade union rights and expanded university provision.

[76] Haldane (1899) 'Lord Watson' *Juridical Review* 278, 279, 280 and 281 respectively; emphases added.

Haldane approved such creative judicial activity. In doing so, he was not seeking to justify a prima facie improper judicial invasion of the legislative sphere. His point rather was that Parliament had (sometimes) deliberately designed colonial constitutions which left important political questions to be answered by the Privy Council in its capacity as a colony's final court of appeal on the basis of considerations which could not properly inform how British courts might interpret British legislative texts. The 'constructive enlargement' which Selborne decried in *Burah* and Lord Hobhouse rejected in *Lambe* could, in Haldane's view of Watson's jurisprudence, be applauded as a judicial articulation of legislators' intentions.[77] Senior appellate judges might properly, it seems: "never forget it is a constitution they are expounding"'.

Haldane either did not see or did not acknowledge that this characterisation of Watson's colonial constitutional jurisprudence resembled Marshall's methodology in *McCulloch*,[78] and his characterisation of the textual content of (some) colonial constitutions as deliberately leaving great scope for judicial implication was very similar to Marshall's view of the US Constitution. Shortly afterwards – as a politician rather than counsel – Haldane stepped – more in form perhaps than substance – into Australia's constitutional arena.

British politicians paid more attention to the 1900 bill than they had traditionally devoted to Australian constitutional legislation.[79] Whether that attention triggered understanding of the significance of American constitutional ideas to the meaning of the Act's provisions is more questionable. A year after penning his eulogy to Watson, Haldane contributed prominently to debate on the bill. He seemed (blithely?) confident that US constitutional doctrine would be irrelevant to Australia's constitutional law:

> The difference between the Constitution which this bill proposes to set up and the Constitution of the United States is enormous and fundamental. This bill is permeated through and through with the spirit of the greatest institution which exists in the Empire, and which pertains to every Constitution established within the Empire – I mean the institution of responsible government, a government under which the Executive is directly responsible to – nay, is almost the creature of – the Legislature. This is not so in America, but it is so with all the Constitutions we have granted to our self-governing colonies. On this occasion we establish a Constitution modelled on our own model, pregnant with the same spirit, and permeated with the principle of responsible government. Therefore, what you have here is nothing akin to the Constitution of the United States except in its most superficial features.[80]

Griffith, Barton and O'Connor soon proved that assumption misplaced.

---

[77] Haldane did not acknowledge the possibility that the reality of legislative lawmaking in the colonial context was less a deliberate, carefully considered and consistently applied Imperial government strategy and more a consequence of slipshod drafting of bills and slapdash parliamentary scrutiny of their contents.

[78] If Watson was aware of the similarity, he did not acknowledge it in his Canadian jurisprudence. In that context, Watson's readiness to take a 'statesmanlike' approach to construing the British North America Act 1867 frequently led him to conclusions that enhanced provincial power vis-à-vis the Dominion rather than vice versa; see especially *The Liquidators of the Maritime Bank of Canada v The Receiver-General of New Brunswick* [1892] AC 437; *Ontario (AG) v Canada (AG) (Local Prohibition Reference)* [1896] AC 348.

[79] First reading is at *HCD* 14 May 1900 c 46. Second readings in the Commons (*HCD* 21 May 1900 c 757) and Lords (*HLD* 29 June 1900 c 9) were – compared to those relating to the 1855 Act (pp 47–48 above) – extensive and contributed to by high-profile politicians.

[80] *HCD* 14 May 1900 c 98.

Wollaston's Case *in the State Supreme Court*

Wollaston's Case came before a three-judge bench of Victoria's Supreme Court in June 1902. The Chief Justice, Sir John Madden, an Irish émigré, built a successful career at the Victorian Bar in conjunction with holding political office; he had been Minister of Justice in the 1870s and 1880s. His politics were of a largely reactionary Conservative kind, especially on matters of electoral and employment law. His appointment directly from the Bar to the Chief Justiceship in 1892 occasioned considerable controversy in legal circles.[81]

Madden was joined by Hartley Williams and Thomas à Beckett. à Beckett had been born in London, schooled in Melbourne and returned to England to qualify at the Bar. He came back to Melbourne – where his father was an eminent solicitor and legislative councillor – shortly after qualifying. His practice flourished, and he also developed a profile as a journalist and academic lawyer. He was appointed to the Court in 1886, having never pursued a political career.[82] Williams was born in New South Wales but schooled in England and called to the Bar after graduating from Oxford. Williams's father had been both a politician and Supreme Court judge in New South Wales and Victoria. On returning to Melbourne, Williams quickly established a thriving practice, and after several unsuccessful Assembly runs was appointed to the Supreme Court in 1881 when only 38 years old. Williams was a prominent supporter of federation, and held broadly progressive views on social and political matters.[83]

Counsel and Submissions

Isaac Isaacs led for Victoria. Born in 1855 in Poland of Jewish parents, Isaacs had come to Victoria in 1859. Isaacs initially worked as a teacher, before taking his law degree at Melbourne University. He was called to the Bar in 1882 and was subsequently elected to the Assembly in 1892, beginning a political career in which he pursued a broadly liberal, protectionist political philosophy in various party political guises. Isaacs strongly supported federation and had been much involved in the 1891 and 1897–98 conventions. Following enactment of the Commonwealth Constitution, Isaacs served briefly as acting Premier in Victoria, but he soon left state politics and was returned to the House as a Protectionist for a Victoria constituency in 1901 (and again in 1903).

Henry Higgins argued Dr Wollaston's case. Higgins, the son of Irish Protestant parents, his father being a Wesleyan churchman,[84] was born and educated in Dublin, emigrating to Melbourne in 1870. Higgins worked as a teacher while attending Melbourne University. He established a successful career at the Equity Bar and dabbled in politics – prominently supporting Irish home rule – in the mid-1880s. Higgins was elected to Victoria's Assembly in 1894. His politics, broadly liberal and progressive, were perhaps most clearly defined by opposition to the proposed federal constitution and to the Boer Wars, factors which led to him losing his seat in 1900. Higgins then entered

---

[81] http://adb.anu.edu.au/biography/madden-sir-john-7453.
[82] http://adb.anu.edu.au/biography/a-beckett-sir-thomas-2860.
[83] http://adb.anu.edu.au/biography/williams-sir-hartley-4856.
[84] http://adb.anu.edu.au/biography/higgins-henry-bournes-6662.

national politics, successfully standing in 1901 for a Melbourne seat as a Protectionist, albeit with overt Labour Party sympathies. He subsequently sided with the Labour Party in triggering the downfall of Deakin's administration, and accepted office as Attorney-General in the short-lived Watson Labour government.[85]

In his initial submissions, citing inter alia *Apollo Candle*,[86] Isaacs asserted that states retained 'plenary' legislative competence, subject only to *express* restrictions in the 1900 Act. Anticipating Higgins's submissions, Isaacs proposed that he demonstrate why certain American authorities were not relevant to this case: "but on an intimation from the Court that, as then advised, it did not consider them applicable to the circumstances of the Australian Federation, counsel concluded his argument".[87]

Higgins sought to dissuade the Court from that conclusion. Although he did not initially allude to Marshall's extravagant approach to constitutional interpretation,[88] Higgins noted that "whole slabs" of the US Constitution were found in the 1900 Act, argued that: "such phrases have to be construed by reference to the decisions there"[89] and asserted that *McCulloch*'s implied immunities principle was both a feature of Australia's constitutional order and applicable to Dr Wollaston's case. The law reports do not record Higgins identifying the 'phrase(s)' in either Constitution which sustained his submission. This is hardly surprising, given that – a point Higgins seemed reluctant openly to acknowledge – Marshall's reasoning in *McCulloch* rested wholly on implication. Higgins did, however, invoke several US Supreme Court judgments which had applied *McCulloch* to factual situations closely analogous to Dr Wollaston's position – most notably *Dobbins v Commissioners of Erie County*[90] and *The Collector v Day*,[91] which, extending *McCulloch*'s reach beyond governmental institutions per se to the officials who worked in them, respectively held that states could not impose income taxes on salaries of federal officials, nor could Congress do so on salaries of state officials. Higgins drew further support for applying the implied immunities principles to the 1900 Act from 'domestic' sources, notably Quick and Garran's[92] and Professor Harrison Moore's[93] respective treatises on the Australian constitution.

---

[85] Palmer (1931) *Henry Bourne Higgins* ch 17.
[86] [1884] 10 App Cas 282; p 150 above.
[87] (1902) 28 VLR 357, 361.
[88] He briefly acknowledged that point towards the end of his submissions in response to a question from Madden; ibid 368.
[89] ibid 366.
[90] (1842) 41 US 435.
[91] (1870) 78 US 113. The (unanimous) Court in *Day* explicitly rooted its judgment in Marshall's *McCulloch* analysis: "It is admitted that there is no express provision in the Constitution that prohibits the general government from taxing the means and instrumentalities of the states, nor is there any prohibiting the states from taxing the means and instrumentalities of that government. In both cases, the exemption rests upon necessary implication, and is upheld by the great law of self-preservation, as any government whose means employed in conducting its operations, if subject to the control of another and distinct government, can exist only at the mercy of that government. Of what avail are these means if another power may tax them at discretion?": ibid 127. In both *Dobbins* and *Day* the Court characterised the employee (and his salary) as 'instrumentalities' of their respective governments.
[92] P 172 above.
[93] Moore, a law professor at the University of Melbourne since 1892, was closely involved in the federation movement and was widely regarded as an expert on constitutional matters. His entry in the *Australian Dictionary of Biography* records that Moore: "was an acknowledged authority on the drafts and was 'used as a human reference library' by convention members": http://adb.anu.edu.au/biography/moore-sir-william-harrison-7645.

The Judgment

Madden's leading judgment – for a unanimous Court – upheld the Income Tax Act's applicability to Dr Wollaston's salary.[94] The bulk of Madden's opinion addressed Higgins's *McCulloch* submissions. Madden concluded that the constitutional structures of the United States and Australia were not sufficiently similar to lend *McCulloch* even persuasive authority in Australia. Madden particularly stressed the British government's power to disallow any state legislation that it regarded as interfering inappropriately with Commonwealth laws or governmental activity.[95] The relevance of the distinction to Higgins's submissions is not immediately apparent.[96] Nor is the second point of dissimilarity on which Madden relied, that being that it was politically much easier (indeed, "very easy")[97] to amend the Australian Constitution than that of the United States. His unstated rationale was presumably that if a state should intrude unacceptably into the Commonwealth sphere a prompt constitutional amendment forbidding such action in future would ensue.[98]

Madden's third basis for not accepting Higgins's submission was his view that Privy Council authority (he relied heavily on *Parsons* and *Lambe*)[99] "wholly disapprove[d]" of 'British' courts following Marshall's expansive approach to constitutional interpretation. Madden rejected Higgins's submission that these judgments had little value in the present case as they all dealt with Canadian law – and so with a constitutional structure quite distinct from Australia's – on the basis that – seemingly extrapolating from Hobhouse's brief aside in *Lambe*: "The power of disallowance by the Imperial Government ... is regarded by the Privy Council as an all-sufficient safeguard against the probability of the happening of the evils which Chief Justice Marshall desired to guard against ..."[100]

Madden also, however, suggested both that subsequent decisions had lent *McCulloch* a scope which Marshall would not have approved[101] and that, in any event, there was

---

[94] Williams simply concurred and à Beckett did so in a brief opinion.

[95] (1902) 28 VLR 357, 381. Madden and Williams both raised the point during Higgins's submissions (ibid 367–68). The report records a curious comment from Madden: "Where an Act of a State Parliament ... bore harshly on Federal offices only, then his Majesty would soon recognise it as unconstitutional and disallow it": ibid 367. Madden seems to imply that 'unconstitutional' in such circumstances was not a legally enforceable concept, but something that existed solely in the political (and Imperial) sphere. Isaacs picked up the apparent cue, submitting in his reply that: "The principle for which the United States judges had to look is found in our Constitution in [the] power of disallowance": ibid 372.

[96] If only because the disallowance power lapsed after two years. The point has (some, if not much) more force in the Canadian context, since s.90 of the British North America Act 1867 empowered the Governor-General in Council (in effect the national government) to disallow provincial legislation. That the British Parliament could at any time override any colonial law points to the same conclusion as the possibility of disallowance, but Madden did not address that matter. More fundamentally, the obviously long-accepted tenet in Australia's pre-1900 colonial constitutional law that courts could invalidate 'unconstitutional' legislation existed alongside the Crown's power of disallowance.

[97] (1902) 28 VLR 357, 383.

[98] There was obviously then no empirical evidence on how 'easy' the s.128 process was. The point does not seem to have been raised during submissions.

[99] Pp 175–77 above.

[100] (1902) 28 VLR 357, 387.

[101] Madden also intimated that *McCulloch* was not really 'law' in the sense of the British judicial tradition: "This judgment ... resembled, and possibly was meant to resemble, the Praetorian Edicts, which laid down in advance as a sort of manifesto, the principles on which the Praetor intended to adjudicate on questions which had not yet arisen": ibid 380.

US authority to the effect that: "there is nothing in Chief Justice Marshall's decision to prevent the taxation of the property of a person who is merely an agent of the Union or state".[102] Madden did not refer to the two authorities cited by Higgins – *Dobbins* and *Day* – which clearly applied the immunity principle to employees' salaries, but rather invoked two later judgments – *Railroad Company v Peniston* and *Central Pacific Railroad v California*[103] – which he asserted supported the conclusion that these cases:

> [I]nsist that, while the actual instrumentalities of Government of either the Union or a state cannot be taxed by a state or by the Union, there is nothing in Chief Justice Marshall's decision to prevent the taxation of a person who is merely an agent of Union or state.[104]

The assertion was entirely credible. The Court had concluded in *Peniston* that:

> It is therefore manifest that exemption of federal agencies from state taxation is dependent, not upon the nature of the agents, or upon the mode of their constitution, or upon the fact that they are agents, but upon the effect of the tax – that is, upon the question whether the tax does in truth deprive them of power to serve the government as they were intended to serve it, or does hinder the efficient exercise of their power. A tax upon their property has no such necessary effect.[105]

The larger doctrinal point implicit (ironically perhaps) in this part of Madden's judgment was that even if an Australian court accepted that US case law was a relevant or even persuasive source of authority as to the meaning of the Australian Constitution, a consequential problem arose. If that case law contained apparently contradictory decisions – and in over a century of case law many such contradictions had emerged – on what basis should Australian courts decide which authorities should be embraced and which discarded? That question, and many others the judgment raised, demanded more senior judicial attention. But before *Wollaston's Case* could be sent to the High Court, a second test case emerged in Tasmania.

D'Emden v Pedder

Mr D'Emden was a Commonwealth postmaster employed in Tasmania. His monthly salary, £4 9s 5d, was paid in cash by the Commonwealth, for which he was required by Commonwealth law to provide a receipt. State law imposed a 2d stamp duty on such a receipt:[106] non-payment was a criminal offence. Mr D'Emden[107] refused to pay the 2d,

---

[102] ibid 380.

[103] (1873) 85 US 18, (1896) 162 US 91.

[104] (1902) 28 VLR 357, 387.

[105] (1873) 85 US 18, 36. The Court in *Central Pacific* expressly approved *Peniston*, quoting the above passage. However, the 'instrumentality' at issue in *Peniston* was neither a federal government department nor a federal officer, but a railway company whose operations were facilitated by federal law, and the judgment can also be read as requiring evaluation of 'effect' only in such circumstances.

[106] The Stamp Duties Amendment Act 1902 (2 Edw VII No 30) s.3 and sch.1. The offence was created by s.5, and carried a maximum fine of £5; www.austlii.edu.au/au/legis/tas/num_act/tsdaa19022evn30360.pdf.

[107] Mr D'Emden was promoted to the post of Deputy Postmaster-General in late March 1903; *(Hobart) Mercury* 20 March 1903 p4, https://trove.nla.gov.au/newspaper/article/12268909. It seems likely that the promotion and the test case were linked. Mr Pedder was a Police Superintendent who charged D'Emden with the offence.

asserting that the state had no power to tax his salary. He was prosecuted in the local magistrates' court in June 1903, convicted and fined 1s,[108] but appealed immediately to the State Supreme Court.

In the State Supreme Court

The Court sat as a three-man bench: Dodds CJ and Clark and McIntyre JJ.[109] Dodds, a successful barrister and eminent politician (pursuing a mildly liberal reformist agenda), had served as both Attorney-General and Premier of Tasmania before going to the bench in 1887 and becoming Chief Justice in 1898.[110] MacIntyre was a career lawyer, qualified at the Tasmanian and English Bars, who never sought political office and was appointed to the Court in 1898.[111] The third judge was Andrew Inglis Clark, the lawyer-politician-constitutional scholar who played such a major role in drafting the Commonwealth Constitution,[112] and on whom American constitutional theory had such a profound influence.

Counsel and Submissions

Sir Herbert Nicholls, the State Attorney-General, led for Tasmania. Nicholls, a barrister of pro-federation sentiment and broadly liberal ideology, was first elected to the Tasmania Assembly in 1901 and was appointed as Attorney-General in 1903.[113] Mr D'Emden's lead counsel was Sir Elliot Lewis. Three months earlier, Lewis had been Tasmania's Premier and Attorney-General; his government was defeated – and he lost his own Assembly seat – at the April 1903 elections. Lewis was an enthusiastic proponent of federation, and while Premier had also sat briefly in Barton's Cabinet.

Lewis led with the simple point that the 'receipt' was Commonwealth property, and so protected by s.114.[114] However, his case was devoted primarily to arguing that the *McCulloch* implied immunities doctrine applied to its full extent in Australia: any state interference with a Commonwealth instrumentality – which concept included Mr D'Emden and his salary – was prohibited; a court need not concern itself with the empirical effect of such state action. Lewis invoked here another element of Marshall's reasoning in *McCulloch*: that a state power to tax a federal government body could be exercised to such an extensive degree that it might become a power to destroy.[115]

---

[108] *Tasmanian News* 4 June 1902 p3, https://trove.nla.gov.au/newspaper/article/176650414. D'Emden shared the defendant's bench that day with, inter alia: "Catherine Bradford, an old woman, charged with being an idle and disorderly person, and with being found in possession of a pair of boots for which she could not give a satisfactory account. The accused pleaded guilty, and was sent to gaol for seven days": ibid.
[109] [1903] TLR 146.
[110] http://adb.anu.edu.au/biography/dodds-sir-john-stokell-3421.
[111] *(Hobart) Mercury* 29 October 1898 p4, https://trove.nla.gov.au/newspaper/article/9433187.
[112] See pp – above. See also http://adb.anu.edu.au/biography/clark-andrew-inglis-3211.
[113] http://adb.anu.edu.au/biography/nicholls-sir-herbert-7840.
[114] There are no accounts of submissions in the Tasmania Law Reports (which – oddly and inaccurately – record argument as being on a Saturday and Sunday). There is coverage in the *(Hobart) Mercury* 18 July 1903 p2, which indicates submissions began and ended on Friday 17 July, whereupon: "The Chief Justice complimented the learned counsel on the manifest research they had made into the law bearing on the case, and the ability with which the question had been argued": https://trove.nla.gov.au/newspaper/article/12280606.
[115] There is no record of this submission in press reports; Dodds' judgment alludes to it; [1903] TLR 146, 166.

Nicholls met the s.114 point with the assertion that the receipt was Mr D'Emden's property rather than the Commonwealth's. On *McCulloch*, Nicholls took two distinct positions. Firstly, he repeated Isaacs's contention in *Wollaston's Case* that states retained plenary taxing powers subject only to express restrictions in the 1900 Act. His second proposition was that if the implied immunities principle applied in Australian law, it did so only in the limited *Peniston* sense, and these facts did not meet that test.[116] Tasmania conceded that any tax targeted specifically at a Commonwealth institution or officer would be impermissible, but maintained that bringing an officer's salary within a generally applicable taxation scheme was unobjectionable.

The Judgment

Clark had reputedly characterised Madden's judgment in *Wollaston* as: "full of false history, bad political science, bad political economy, bad logic and bad law".[117] In *D'Emden* he endorsed the arguments Higgins unsuccessfully advanced in *Wollaston's Case*, but did so in dissent. To accept Tasmania's arguments would be: "totally subversive of the unrestricted operation of the laws of the Commonwealth which the Constitution in all cases prescribes for them".[118] There is no indication in press reports of Nicholls's submissions that he relied on the disallowance point that Madden invoked in *Wollaston's Case*, but Clark rebutted that argument on the basis that – the irony of his method and conclusion apparently escaping him – the argument could only be compelling if it had an obvious textual basis in the 1900 Act.[119] Clark distinguished rather than dismissed *Peniston*, holding that its 'effect' principle applied only in circumstances where the impugned state law bore indirectly rather than, as in D'Emden's case, directly on Commonwealth action.[120]

His two colleagues held a different view. Dodds'[121] structurally rather incoherent judgment[122] offers several bases for rejecting Lewis' submissions. On s.114, Dodds considered that the receipt was the 'property' of Mr D'Emden, not of the Commonwealth, and that the tax bore on him not the Commonwealth. Dodds's analysis of *McCulloch* followed Nicholls's submission, limiting *McCulloch's* effect rather than rejecting its underlying principle: "that case and the present one are so dissimilar that it is impossible to argue from one to the other. ... [T]he difference between the two cases

---

[116] Nicholls supported this submission with a floodgates argument. If Commonwealth employees were instrumentalities, presumably so was any person or company in commercial relationship with a Commonwealth body, in which event the scope of state taxing power would substantially shrink and the complexity of administering it would substantially increase.

[117] http://adb.anu.edu.au/biography/madden-sir-john-7453.

[118] [1903] TLR 146, 152.

[119] ibid 155–56.

[120] ibid 157–58. Clark linked his indirect/direct distinction to the identity of the 'instrumentality' (D'Emden being a Commonwealth officer rather than an independent contractor) and the nature of the state interference (Tasmania's law impinging upon a specific document required by Commonwealth law rather than on Mr D'Emden's salary).

[121] McIntyre simply concurred with Dodds.

[122] The reader's task is not aided by the stylistic practice then adopted in state law reports of rendering entire judgments as a single paragraph.

is strikingly obvious".[123] Quoting the above-cited passage from *Peniston*, Dodds held that *Peniston* and other cases indicated that:

> It appears from them that the general principles laid down in *McCulloch* ... have been interpreted by the later decisions in such a way as to limit their application ... to cases where the efficiency of the instrumentality is impaired by the taxation imposed.[124]

Since Mr D'Emden: "has not even suggested that the Stamp Duties Act injuriously affects either him or his department",[125] his case would have failed in the United States.

Dodds quoted *Lambe* to rebut Lewis's 'destruction' submission, and in a more general vein invoked the Privy Council's judgment in *Parsons* to justify the court's refusal to determine the case on the basis of the effect that a state tax *might have* rather than on the basis of what effect – ie none – that the tax *had been shown to have* on Commonwealth activities.[126]

In the High Court

Wollaston's Case was not pressed to appeal,[127] which left *D'Emden* as the initial opportunity for Griffith, Barton and O'Connor to address the matter. The case – the first High Court hearing in Hobart – was argued on 24 and 25 February 1904, and judgment was delivered on 26 April 1904.

Counsel and Submissions

James Drake, the Commonwealth Attorney-General, led for D'Emden, assisted by Lewis. Drake, a Queenslander, had a chequered professional and political career which exemplifies the fluid nature of party political identity in late nineteenth- and early twentieth-century Australia. Initially a journalist, Drake was called to the Bar in 1881. He was elected to the Assembly as a Griffith supporter, flirted with the Labour Party and then held office as a Minister in a Conservative administration in the late 1890s. He was elected to the Senate as a Protectionist in 1901 and served in Barton's Cabinet, before being Deakin's Attorney-General in 1903–04. He was then a minister in Reid's short-lived government. He left national politics shortly afterwards, returning to Queensland and resuming both his journalist career and legal practice.[128] Nicholls again led for Tasmania.

Drake submitted[129] that *McCulloch* 'governed' the case before the Court,[130] and boldly asserted:

> It was open to the framers of the Constitution to expressly negative the application of the principles of *McCulloch v. Maryland*. If, with this interpretation of the *US Constitution* before

---

[123] [1903] TLR 146, 161.
[124] ibid 163.
[125] ibid.
[126] ibid 167–68. He quoted the passage from *Parsons* reproduced at p 177 above.
[127] One might wonder if this was pique on Dr Wollaston's part, following his resignation; n – above.
[128] http://adb.anu.edu.au/biography/drake-james-george-6013.
[129] [1904] 1 CLR 91, 93–103.
[130] ibid 96. Drake was not suggesting that *McCulloch* bound the court, but rather that it and related American cases were so obviously relevant to the Australian situation that their reasoning should be followed.

them, they did not do this, they may be taken to have intended that the doctrine of the supremacy of Federal law was to apply to the implied powers of the Federation, as well as to the express laws.[131]

Drake further submitted that there was no empirical question to decide as to whether state law *in fact* (ie the *Peniston/California* point) impeded the activities of the Commonwealth to any (significant) degree; if *McCulloch* 'governed' the case, then the possibility that a state tax *might* be used to 'destroy' a Commonwealth function sufficed to make the tax invalid.

Drake was inviting the High Court to construe the Constitution Act in a fashion departing radically from orthodox approaches to statutory interpretation in the British tradition. This was in part because of the prominence he gave to American cases, but also because he argued it was proper to consider and draw inferences from the 'intentions' of the 'framers' to determine what the words in the Act might mean.[132] As to who exactly 'the framers' were, and how exactly one discerned their 'intentions', Drake offered no assistance.

He raised as a secondary argument – which, if correct, would render discussion of *McCulloch* and its broad implications irrelevant – that the case could be decided by simple application of s.109. There was no doubt that Mr D'Emden's salary was paid under a 'law of the Commonwealth'. If the Tasmania law was inconsistent with that law, it was invalid to that extent. The inconsistency, Drake asserted, arose because the effect of the state tax was to diminish Mr D'Emden's salary.[133]

For Tasmania,[134] Nicholls met Drake's second argument with the assertion that making a federal officer liable to pay a generally applicable tax did not in any sense diminish his income, and so no s.109 issue arose. More broadly, Nicholls accepted the principle that the Constitution placed implied limits on state powers to prevent interference with Commonwealth activities (and also argued – though the point was not strictly in issue – that the principle had a reciprocal nature). He disputed, however, that the principle had an absolute character, and pressed the *Peniston* point that the court should measure the interference to Commonwealth activity that the state law occasioned. An obligation arising under generally applicable state income tax could not be problematic.[135]

Judgment

Griffith gave the sole judgment. He promptly announced – without any reasoning – that the stamp duty diminished D'Emden's salary and that the receipt was not 'property' within s.114.[136] His judgment was primarily concerned with identifying the extent to

---

[131] ibid 96.

[132] Drake's proposal echoed the interpretive method that Griffith qua Premier of Queensland had advocated to the Privy Council in the 1880s during the dispute over the respective powers of Queensland's Assembly and Council (p 137 above), although Drake did not draw the comparison expressly.

[133] ibid 101–02.

[134] Drake's submissions and the judges' questions to him fill 10 pages of the CLR. Nicholls's submission and questions to him cover just three.

[135] [1904] 1 CLR 91.

[136] ibid 108.

which *McCulloch* was applicable to the Australian Constitution, both in the narrow sense of the implied immunities doctrine and in the broader sense of the approach that the High Court would take to interpreting the 1900 Act.

On the narrow question, Griffith formally accorded Marshall's judgment a very persuasive – though not binding – status:

> We are not, of course, bound by the decisions of the Supreme Court of the United States. But we all think that it would need some courage for any Judge at the present day to decline to accept the interpretation placed upon the *US Constitution* by so great a Judge so long ago as 1819, and followed up to the present day by the succession of great jurists who have since adorned the Bench of the Supreme Court at Washington. So far, therefore, as the *United States* and the Constitution of the Commonwealth are similar, the construction put upon the former by the Supreme Court of the United States may well be regarded by us in construing the Constitution of the Commonwealth, not as an infallible guide, but as a most welcome aid and assistance.[137]

On the larger question, Griffith concluded that it was entirely defensible for the High Court to construe the 1900 Act in accordance with US authorities dealing with similarly phrased constitutional provisions:

> We cannot disregard the fact that the Constitution of the Commonwealth was framed by a Convention of Representatives from the several colonies. We think that, sitting here, we are entitled to assume – what, after all, is a fact of public notoriety – that some, if not all, of the framers of that Constitution were familiar, not only with the Constitution *of the United States*, but with that of the Canadian Dominion and those of the British colonies. When, therefore, under these circumstances, we find embodied in the Constitution provisions undistinguishable in substance, though varied in form, from provisions of the Constitution *of the United States* which had long since been judicially interpreted by the Supreme Court of that Republic, it is not an unreasonable inference that its framers intended that like provisions should receive like interpretation.[138]

Griffith's reference to the framers' 'intentions' remained couched at this very general level. Although there are quite extensive records of the 1891 and 1897–98 debates, Griffith was unable or unwilling to identify any specific contributions which supported his conclusion; and there is no indication in the report's summary of submissions that Drake did either. The omission is perhaps explicable on the basis that Griffith and counsel were following the principle that British courts did not then refer to parliamentary debates as an aid to statutory construction, although the analogy is not compelling, given that Griffith's methodology rested substantially on the premise that the 1900 Act was not an ordinary statute and not subject to ordinary techniques of interpretation.[139]

The above-cited passages from Griffith's judgment were followed by a three-page quotation from *McCulloch*, in turn followed by Griffith explaining that Tasmania's Supreme Court was labouring under various 'misapprehensions' about that judgment.

---

[137] ibid 112.
[138] ibid 113.
[139] Goldsworthy notes Griffith did do so in other cases; (2006) op cit pp 124–25.

The first was the erroneous conclusion that *McCulloch* had been "considerably modified by later decisions"; the second was the assumption that actual interference with federal government action by a state was necessary.[140]

Griffith did not find *Lambe* any obstacle to this conclusion. In his view, the Privy Council:

> far from depreciating the authority of that case, intimated their willingness to follow the guidance of the great American Chief Justice in a similar case, but pointed out that the principles laid down in *McCulloch v Maryland* threw no light on the question then before them ...[141]

The inevitable consequence of correcting the Tasmanian Supreme Court's 'misapprehensions' was that the Tasmanian law encroached unacceptably into the Commonwealth's legal domain. However, Griffith concluded with a skimpily reasoned passage in which he held that the Tasmanian Act was not invalid per se, but only to the extent of its application to Mr D'Emden's receipt. The 'reasoning' for this appeared twofold. Firstly, legislation should not be assumed to have 'extra-territorial' effect. Griffith evidently considered that Mr D'Emden's receipt was not 'in' Tasmania in the juridical sense of territory. Griffith also asserted that the Court could not assume that Tasmania's legislature 'intended' to make law that contravened the 1900 Act, and so the state legislation should simply be construed as not applying to Mr D'Emden's receipt. Griffith made no reference at all to the Tasmania statute's text in making this assertion.[142]

There is no record in the law reports – nor in contemporaneous press coverage – of Tasmania requesting permission to appeal to the Privy Council. It seems unlikely that any such request would have been granted.[143] *D'Emden* raised a very strong inference that the High Court would have reversed the Supreme Court's judgment in *Wollaston's Case* had that case been appealed. But another opportunity soon arose.

Deakin v Webb

Deakin had, it seemed, wearied of sending legal stalking horses to contest the issue. He himself, along with Lyne, stood as co-defendants resisting the Victoria government's efforts to subject the payments they had received as members of the House and as ministers to state income tax. Deakin was still Prime Minister when proceedings were issued, but his government had fallen and been succeeded by Watson's Labour administration when the case was heard.

---

[140] [1904] 1 CLR 91, 116 and 118 respectively.
[141] ibid 112.
[142] ibid 120.
[143] Judgment was also handed down on 26 April 1904 in *Municipal Council of Sydney v The Commonwealth* (1904) 1 CLR 208. The Court held that a municipal council could not levy property taxes on a Commonwealth building on the uncontentious basis that this was prohibited by s.114. The Court refused permission per s.74 for appeal to the Privy Council, equating the 'special reason proviso of s.74 with there having to be a credible reason for assuming the High Court's decision was wrong; ibid 242.

In the Victoria Supreme Court

Deakin v Webb emerged in Victoria as *In re the Income Tax Acts (No 4)*.[144] Madden and à Beckett remained on the Court, although Williams was replaced as its third member by Henry Hodges.[145] Isaacs and Higgins – Attorney-General in Watson's government since 27 April – reprised their *Wollaston's Case* roles as counsel. Argument was heard in May 1904 and judgment was delivered in July.

The exchanges between the bench and counsel during submissions indicated that Victoria's judges did not accept that *D'Emden* should lead them to change the reasoning or result adopted in *Wollaston's Case*.[146] *Deakin*, however, presented the added question of judicial precedent in two senses: firstly, whether the High Court's judgment in *D'Emden* applied on its facts to Deakin's case; and secondly, if so, was Victoria's Supreme Court obliged to follow it?

Judgment

Madden's sole judgment occupied many fewer pages of the law reports than the submissions, and much of it addressed the narrow question of whether the taxed payments were a 'salary' within Victoria's income tax legislation. Madden dealt with the broad constitutional questions in just two pages.[147]

In an opaque passage, Madden concluded that *Wollaston's Case* was correctly decided and was: "quite in accord with that of the High Court in *D'Emden*".[148] He did not explain how the cases – which seemingly reached very different results based on very different reasoning – were distinguishable. There was no opacity on the broader point, however. The High Court's attribution of (very) persuasive status to US judgments was dismissed both as "mere dicta"[149] and inconsistent with the Privy Council's approach in *Lambe*. Since it was not yet clear if the High Court or Privy Council was the "Court of ultimate appeal" on this issue, the Victoria Supreme Court would take its lead from the Privy Council. Should the High Court subsequently decide that *Wollaston's Case* (and *Deakin*) were wrongly decided: "we will show it all the respect we are in duty bound to show it according as it may turn out to be the ultimate Court of Appeal … on the matter".[150]

In the High Court

The appeal was promptly heard. Submissions were made in August and October 1904, and judgment delivered on 3 November.[151] Higgins – still Attorney-General in Watson's

---

[144] (1904) 29 VLR 748.
[145] Hodges had been appointed to the Court in 1890 after a prominent career at the Victoria Bar. He had no obvious party political affiliations.
[146] See especially (1904) 29 VLR 748, 755–56.
[147] ibid 763–64.
[148] ibid 763.
[149] ibid 764.
[150] ibid 764.
[151] [1904] HCA 57, (1904) 1 CLR 585.

administration as proceedings began[152] – and Isaacs remained as counsel and reiterated the submissions made in the state court. Since Deakin's claim related to the 1901 tax year, both Barton and O'Connor had an obvious personal interest in the outcome: both had received House and ministerial salaries that year. That interest would arguably have rendered any High Court judgment invalid on the grounds of bias, but the point seemed not to occur to any participant.[153]

Griffith delivered the only judgment. Consistent with his conclusion in *D'Emden*, he held that liability to income tax worked as a diminution of a salary:

> If the Federal Parliament were to attempt to impose an income tax of, say, two shillings in the pound with respect to the Governor-General's salary, the result would be that the effective salary would be reduced by ten per cent. whether the tax were deducted before payment of the salary or demanded and collected afterwards. This is the accepted view in the United States ... This would be a case in which the payment and the deduction are made by the same hands ... If, however, the levy is not made by the same Government that makes the payment, although it is not a diminution in exactly the same sense, the effect upon the recipient of the income is the same. His effective salary is diminished.[154]

He also saw no reason to doubt the correctness of the High Court's reasoning and conclusion in *D'Emden*, and no basis to distinguish the two cases. Griffith felt the need to refer to the "reasons"[155] in the Supreme Court's judgment in inverted commas before explaining why those "reasons" were poorly founded. The Supreme Court was "quite in error"[156] to assume that *D'Emden* revealed a High Court preference for American over British authority. Privy Council decisions concerning the British North America Act were no assistance to construing Australia's Constitution:

> It is a matter of common knowledge that the framers of the Australian Constitution were familiar with the two great examples of English speaking federations, and deliberately adopted, with regard to the distribution of powers, the model of the United States, in preference to that of the Canadian Dominion ... The scheme of the Canadian Constitution, which was rejected by the framers of this Constitution, is essentially different.

Griffith asserted quite credibly that this was quite consistent with *Lambe*, agreeing with Lord Hobhouse's conclusion that that it was quite "impossible to argue"[157] from the British North America Act to the US Constitution: "But it is equally impossible to argue from secs. 91 and 92 of the Dominion Constitution to the Constitution of the Australian Commonwealth."[158] The impossibility arose because the Australian Constitution, like that of the United States but unlike Canada's, did not expressly identify all the powers of the states.[159] Nor could the Imperial government's power to disallow state legislation

---

[152] Watson's government fell – and Higgins stopped being Attorney-General – on 17 August, the second day (of five) of submissions. Reid's government seemingly did not interfere with the submissions made.

[153] *Dimes v Grand Junction Canal* (1852) 3 HL Cas 759; 10 ER 310; discussed briefly in Loveland (2018) op cit pp 405–06. Given the apparently broad reach of the Court's judgment in *D'Emden*, they also had a (less obvious) financial interest in that case.

[154] (1904) 1 CLR 585, 612.
[155] ibid 603.
[156] ibid 605.
[157] P 176 above.
[158] (1904) 1 CLR 585, 610.
[159] ibid 608–09.

be equated with the Canadian government's power to disallow provincial legislation; the latter functioned to safeguard Canadian national interests, while the former was concerned only with Imperial interests.[160]

Griffith then reproduced a two-page quotation from the US Supreme Court 1842 judgment in *Dobbins v Commissioners of Erie County*[161] – the ratio of which was that state law taxing federal officials' salaries was precluded by the *McCulloch* principle – and concluded: "We are not of course bound by this case as an authority. But the reasoning of the judgment appears to us to be unanswerable."[162]

Unsurprisingly, the Court saw no 'special reason' per s.74 to allow an appeal.[163] For Victoria's Supreme Court, however, the High Court's specific conclusion on the implied immunities point and the more general issue of its position within 'Australia's' judicial hierarchy was not yet resolved.

Webb v Outtrim (*Outtrim's Case*)

Outtrim's Case reran *Deakin* in February 1905. The Victoria Supreme Court, presumably smarting at both the substance and the tone of the High Court's judgment in *Deakin*, resolved *Outtrim's Case* by simply stating it was bound to follow the High Court's judgment in *Deakin*.[164] The Supreme Court's payment of 'respect' which Madden foreshadowed in *Deakin* had a double edge, however, as the Court also granted permission for an appeal direct to the Privy Council, which was presumably a deliberate attempt to circumvent the likelihood that the High Court would – as in *Deakin* – refuse permission.[165] Eighteen months passed before the Privy Council heard argument.

The Privy Council Bench

The Privy Council in *Webb v Outtrim* sat as a four-man bench: the Earl of Halsbury, Lord MacNaghten, Sir Arthur Wilson and Sir Alfred Wills. Halsbury was the son of a former editor of the *London Evening Standard*. After attending Oxford, Halsbury

---

[160] ibid 610–11.

[161] (1842) 41 US 435.

[162] ibid 615.

[163] All three judges delivered concurring opinions on the point. Griffith recorded that he listened with "some amazement" to Isaacs's suggestion that the wishes of five state governments or of 'public opinion' to have an appeal amounted to a special reason; ibid 625. He also rejected Isaac's assertion that *D'Emden* was inconsistent with *Lambe*; ibid 626.

[164] *In re the Income Tax Acts. Outtrim's Case*. The judgment is not recorded in the official law reports. There is coverage in *The Argus* 11 February 1905 p14, https://trove.nla.gov.au/newspaper/article/192234507; ibid p15, https://trove.nla.gov.au/newspaper/article/9891194. Permission to appeal to the Privy Council was subsequently granted by Hodges on 28 March 1905; [1905] VLR 463. There was some doubt that the Supreme Court had the power to grant such permission, but the application was not opposed by Outtrim (ibid 464), who, one must assume, was the figurehead in a test case with federal government (this then being Reid's precarious coalition administration) support. Higgins did not appear for the federal government. The brief was given to William Harrison Moore; see p 180 n 93 above.

[165] The scenario was predicted and debated – but obviously not conclusively resolved – during the bill's Commons passage; see the discussion in Berriedale Keith (1908) 'Judicial appeals in the Commonwealth' *Journal of the Society of Comparative Legislation* 269, pp 270–71.

combined a very successful career at the Bar with his Tory political ambitions. He was appointed Solicitor-General in 1875 (unusually without a seat in the Commons, which he did not acquire until 1877) and became Lord Chancellor in 1885, and then again between 1895 and 1905.[166] Now perhaps best known as the first editor-in-chief of Butterworth's encyclopaedia of English law, *Halsbury's Laws of England*, as a judge Halsbury is most closely associated with the *Taff Vale* judgment,[167] in which he joined a unanimous decision – overturning the Court of Appeal – holding that trade unions could be liable in damages to employers for economic loss caused by a union's industrial action. As a politician, Halsbury was stridently reactionary, most notably in opposing the Parliament Act 1911, and virulently anti-socialist; socialism in his view aptly described Campbell-Bannerman/Asquith's 1906–16 Liberal governments.[168]

MacNaghten had also sat in *Taff Vale*, in which he wrote the leading judgment. MacNaghten, the son of an Anglo-Irish Tory MP, was called to the Bar after attending Trinity College Dublin and Cambridge University. His personal politics were conservative, and he followed his father into the Commons (in the same seat) in 1880. Having declined office in several Tory administrations, he was appointed directly to the House of Lords bench in 1887.

Sir Alfred Wills's prime claim to judicial fame is as the judge in Oscar Wilde's 1895 indecency trial.[169] Wills was a career lawyer who had not held political office. He was appointed to the High Court, where his career stalled, in 1884. He retired from the High Court in 1905. Sir Arthur Wilson had practised at the English Bar before accepting a judicial appointment in India, where he also served as Vice-Chancellor of the University of Calcutta. He returned to work as a civil servant in the India Office in 1892, and was appointed to the Privy Council in 1902.

Counsel

The case was argued in May 1906, and judgment was given on 6 December. Neither Higgins nor Isaacs journeyed to London to argue. Isaacs had been appointed Attorney-General in Deakin's government in 1905. Higgins was preoccupied in early 1906 by the prospect of being opposed by a Labour candidate in the December 1906 House elections and could not spend a lengthy period abroad.[170] Victoria's case was led by a British-based silk, Sir Robert Finlay, a barrister politician who was Attorney-General between 1900 and 1905 in the Salisbury and Balfour Conservative governments, and was to become Lord Chancellor in 1916 in Lloyd George's wartime coalition administration.

---

[166] www.lexisnexis.co.uk/HalsburysLaw/Lord_Halsbury.html.

[167] *Taff Vale Railway Company v Amalgamated Society of Railway Servants* [1901] AC 426.

[168] A view likely intensified by the 1906 Liberal government successfully promoting legislation to reverse *Taff Vale* (the Trade Disputes Act 1906).

[169] In which Wills lamented that the maximum two-year sentence was not enough. For a bizarrely contradictory assessment of Wills's 'humane' character as a criminal trial judge, see *Vanity Fair* 25 June 1896, https://scholarlycommons.law.case.edu/cgi/viewcontent.cgi?article=3712&context=caselrev.

[170] Higgins meantime authored the article 'McCulloch v Maryland in Australia' (1905) *Harvard Law Review* 559, in which he suggested that the 'man in the street' in Australia was – with good reason – 'startled' by and 'indignant about' the High Court judgment in *Deakin*. Making no mention of his own role in the litigation, Higgins expressed doubts as to the correctness of the Court's reasoning (ibid 567–69) and disapproved the substantive result (ibid 571).

The national government also briefed a British lawyer to lead its case, William Danckwerts KC.

Judgment

Halsbury gave the judgment.[171] His opinion was scornfully, witheringly dismissive of the position taken by Griffith and his colleagues in *D'Emden* and *Deakin*. The opinion is a poorly reasoned polemic, raising the inference that the Privy Council's primary concern was to put an upstart colonial court firmly back in its (to the Privy Council) subordinate place.

Halsbury began with an (imprecisely cited) reference back to what he called the Victoria Act 18 & 19 Vict c 55, misquoting (without identification) from sch.1 para 1 the provision that: "Her Majesty should have power by and with the consent of the Council and Assembly in question to make laws in and for Victoria in all cases whatsoever." Halsbury then quoted s.106 and s.107 of the Constitution Act 1900[172] and framed the issue before the Court in this way:

> That question is, whether the power given in such wide words as have been mentioned above has been curtailed and so far restricted that, if a person be an officer of the Commonwealth, though he may be resident in Victoria and may have received his salary therein, he is not taxable in respect of such salary. It is not contended that this restriction on the powers of the Victoria Constitution is enacted by any express provision of the Commonwealth Act, but it is argued that, inasmuch as the imposition of an income tax might interfere with the free exercise of the legislative or executive power of the Commonwealth, such interference must be impliedly forbidden by the Constitution of the Commonwealth.[173]

That Halsbury had quoted s.106 and s.107 but did not even allude to s.5 [BAI] and s.109[174] gave a clear indication of his likely answer to that question.

Halsbury saw no merit in the High Court's reliance on *McCulloch* as an analytical source to uncover such 'implicit' constraints on state power. Echoing Haldane's sentiments in the Commons during the Act's passage, he suggested such cross-jurisdictional borrowing was quite misconceived:

> But here the analogy fails in the very matter which is under debate. No state of the Australian Commonwealth has the power of independent legislation possessed by the States of the American Union. Every Act of the Victorian Council and Assembly requires the assent of the Crown, but when it is assented to, it becomes an Act of Parliament as much as any Imperial Act, though the elements by which it is authorized are different. If, indeed, it were repugnant to the provisions of any Act of Parliament extending to the Colony, it might be inoperative to the extent of its repugnancy (see the Colonial Laws Validity Act, 1865), but, with this exception, no authority exists by which its validity can be questioned or impeached.

---

[171] [1907] AC 81.
[172] Pp – above.
[173] [1907] AC 81, 87–88.
[174] See pp 161–162 above. Halsbury also ignored or overlooked the (to his argument) inconvenient political and legal fact that s.22 of the Federal Council of Australasia Act 1885 had expressly provided that if any Act of the Council was inconsistent with state law: "the former shall prevail, and the later shall, so far as such … inconsistency extend, have no operation".

Halsbury's reasoning here is at best inelegant, and more likely lazily ill-informed or designedly incorrect. S.5 [BAI] and s.109 obviously envisage the possibility that state law would conflict with Commonwealth law, and equally obviously s.71 and s.73 gave the High Court jurisdiction to enforce the s.5 [BAI] and s.109 principles. On a simple application of the *lex posterior* principle, the CLVA 1865 would be an entirely redundant measure in circumstances of conflict between state law and Commonwealth law.

Halsbury then engaged in an unsubtle analytical sleight of hand. Having begun his judgment by recognising that the issue was the relevance of American constitutional doctrine to determining the relative competences of the Australian states and Commonwealth Parliament, Halsbury suddenly rewrote the question as one comparing the United States and Britain.

Having observed – entirely correctly – that notions of 'unconstitutionality' with respect to British legislation were limited to the moral or political sphere and did not embrace, as in the United States, the idea that courts could declare legislation unconstitutional as a matter of law, Halsbury announced (referring back to Griffith's judgments in *D'Emden* and *Deakin*) that: "It is obvious that there is no such analogy between the two systems of jurisprudence as the learned Chief Justice suggests."[175] Given that Halsbury was so able a lawyer, the passage quoted immediately above must surely be the result of mendacity rather than misunderstanding. Griffith was not positing an analogy between the United States and Britain, but one between the United States and Australia, in both of which 'countries' the states and the 'national' legislature were bodies of constitutionally demarcated limited lawmaking competence.

Halsbury was on firmer ground in suggesting that the High Court's conclusions in *D'Emden* and *Deakin* were hard to reconcile with s.114. S.114 seemed to have dealt expressly and comprehensively with the respective competences of the states and the Commonwealth to tax each other, and had denied such competence only in respect of each other's 'property ...'. Unless a salary or receipt for a salary could be regarded as Commonwealth 'property' – a contention not pressed in *Deakin* and argued only faintly in *D'Emden* – no limits to a state's taxing power were identified in the 1900 Act.

Any such limit would have to be *express*. And Halsbury moved beyond the particular point in issue to espouse the more general principle that the Constitution did not place *any* implied limits on state power. In reaching the contrary conclusion, the High Court had erred by accepting that the political preferences of the delegates at the confederation conferences were a legitimate matter to consider when construing the Constitution Act 1900:

> It is, indeed, an expansion of the canon of interpretation in question to consider the knowledge of those who framed the Constitution and their supposed preferences for this or that model which might have been in their minds. Their Lordships are not able to acquiesce in any such principle of interpretation.[176]

Halsbury's invocation of narrow canons of interpretation – ie that the 1900 Act was a statute like any other and should be construed accordingly – is open to the accusation of

---

[175] [1907] AC 81, 89.
[176] ibid 90–91.

doctrinal inconsistency. Halsbury's position is manifestly consistent with the approach espoused by the Privy Council in cases such as *Burah* and *Lambe*,[177] but is quite inconsistent with the very different perspective which Haldane attributed to Lord Watson qua colonial constitutional judge. Unsurprisingly perhaps, Halsbury did not acknowledge that line of Privy Council authority, nor – in consequence – consider whether the High Court might properly adopt a similar approach to the 1900 Act. But just as *Webb* was being argued and decided, so Griffith and his colleagues concluded that the implied immunities doctrine was as much a protection for states against the Commonwealth as vice versa.

Railway Servants

The large constitutional issue in *Federated Amalgamated Government Railway and Tramway Service Association v New South Wales Traffic Employees Association* (TEA)[178] (hereafter *Railway Servants*) was whether the Constitution permitted the powers bestowed on the Commonwealth Court of Conciliation and Arbitration (CCCA) by the Commonwealth's Arbitration and Conciliation Act 1904 to be applied to industrial disputes and matters relating to state-owned and -managed railways. The TEA had applied to the CCCA to register under the 1904 Act. This was opposed by the state on the basis that the Act's inclusion (in s.4) of state railways was beyond the Commonwealth Parliament's powers.[179] O'Connor referred the matter to the High Court. Several other states and the Commonwealth government were given permission to intervene.

The High Court's Judgment

Railway Servants was argued for 13 days in August and September 1906. Judgment was handed down on 17 December, 11 days after the Privy Council delivered its decision in *Webb v Outtrim*. Griffith, Barton and O'Connor had presumably read *Webb v Outtrim*[180] before releasing the *Railway Servants* judgment, but they made no reference to either any of the specifics or the general tenor of Halsbury's opinion.

Isaacs, now Attorney-General in the (once again) Deakin government, led for the Commonwealth. Ironically, one might think, given that the Labour opposition's successful gambit to include state railways in the 1904 Act had led to the fall of Deakin's first ministry, Isaacs now defended the constitutionality of the Act's application to the railways. Backing Isaacs's contention that the Act could properly be applied to state railways, Higgins[181] led for the TEA.

Griffith's sole judgment in *Railway Servants* rested almost entirely – in laudatory terms – on US jurisprudence. The primary question was whether the implied

---

[177] pp [5.30] above.
[178] (1906) 4 CLR 488.
[179] Pp 169–70 and n 40 above.
[180] Transmission by telegraph would have been possible – if unwieldy – by then. See also Booker and Glass (2003) 'The Engineers case' in Lee and Winterton (eds) *State constitutional landmarks* pp 37–38.
[181] A supporter in the House of the amendment to include state railways with the CCAC's jurisdiction.

intergovernmental immunities doctrine had a reciprocal basis; and, if so, how did that doctrine condition the way the Commonwealth Parliament's powers should be interpreted?

The Court's reasoning was again structured by 'history':

> With regard to state railways it is a matter of history that before 1890 all the six Colonies had established state railways, the control of which formed a very large and important part of state administration, and that very large financial obligations, amounting to a sum far exceeding £100,000,000, had been incurred by the Colonies for their construction ...
>
> It cannot, in our opinion, be disputed that the state railways were in their inception instrumentalities of the state governments ...[182]

Relying on a lengthy quotation from the US Supreme Court's 1870 judgment in *Collector v Day*,[183] Griffith concluded that the immunities doctrine was as applicable to protecting states from Commonwealth intrusion as vice versa, which conclusion then led him to accord the various provisions of the 1900 Act which might sustain s.4 a narrow interpretation.

Noting that Parliament's 'trade and commerce' power in s.51(i) was textually virtually identical to the US Constitution's commerce clause, Griffith adopted the American authority to the effect that state action would not breach the commerce clause unless it were shown such action had a direct rather than – as on these facts – a merely incidental effect on that commerce.[184]

The High Court also used *Railway Servants* to decide that the immunities doctrine was not applicable only to taxation:

> But taxation is only an instance of interference and control. The foundation of the argument is the necessity for freedom from control, and taxation is only forbidden because it is an interference. In our opinion any authority which can lawfully say to another "Thou shalt" or "Thou shalt not" exercises control over that other in the sense in which that term is used in this argument ...[185]

Baxter v Commissioners of Taxation

The High Court handed down *Railway Servants* on 17 December 1906, 11 days after publication of *Webb v Outtrim*. The Court's response to *Outtrim* was made shortly afterwards in *Baxter v Commissioners of Taxation*.[186] By this point, Isaacs and Higgins – so frequently opposing counsel before the High Court – had been appointed by Deakin to the Court as it expanded from three members to five.[187]

Baxter, a federal employee residing in New South Wales, was found liable in a state District Court to pay state income tax on his federal salary. The trial judge applied *Webb v Outtrim* and refused to follow *Deakin v Webb*. The High Court was divided on

---

[182] (1906) 4 CLR 488, 534–35.
[183] (1870) 78 US 113; P 180 above. The quotation is at (1906) 4 CLR 488, 537–38.
[184] ibid 540–45.
[185] ibid 538.
[186] (1907) 4 CLR 1087; argued on 8–15 May 1907; judgment given on 7 June 1907.
[187] As provided for by (the Deakin government-sponsored) Judiciary Act 1906 (No 5 of 1906).

a three-to-two basis. Griffith – joined by Barton and O'Connor – authored a majority judgment which – in both substance and tone – reflected Halsbury's dismissive opinion in *Webb v Outtrim*.

The first question Griffith broached was:

> [W]hether the conventional duty of one [the High] Court, not in all respects the highest, to follow another court of higher authority, is excluded by the *implication* arising from the purpose for which this Court was established, and the place which it holds under the Constitution.[188]

In answering the question, Griffith did not consider himself limited to construing the words of the 1900 Act, which he conceded would require the High Court to follow *Webb v Outtrim*. Rather, the Court should consider the: "whole purview of the Constitution",[189] which, in turn, demanded understanding of its history.

Invoking the precedent of *Heydon's Case*[190] to justify applying the mischief rule to ascertain the Constitution's meaning on this question of judicial hierarchy, Griffith – at no point expressly alluding to his own role in drafting its text – concluded that the 'history' of the Constitution's creation indicated that: firstly, its framers had informedly adopted aspects both of the text of the US Constitution and of that Constitution's underlying principles ('objects' in Marshall's terminology) in relation to the demarcation of national and state authority; secondly, the framers had anticipated that many disputes would arise over the precise boundaries of that demarcation; thirdly, the framers had wished those disputes to be resolved in accordance with the case law of the US Supreme Court; fourthly, the framers considered that the Privy Council could not be assumed to have any familiarity with that body of judicial authority but that judges appointed to the High Court would have such expertise; and therefore, fifthly, the framers 'intended' that the High Court rather than the Privy Council should have the final say on '*inter se*' matters.

Griffith seemingly considered that the fact that the 1900 Act provided no textual basis expressing that 'intention' was no impediment to reaching that conclusion (any more than it had been presumably in his applying the implied immunities doctrine itself). Having invoked *Heydon's Case*, Griffith changed doctrinal tack and stated that the 1900 Act should be regarded as a constitution rather than an 'ordinary' statute, and as such – again citing US Supreme Court authority[191] – not subject to ordinary rules of construction.[192]

---

[188] ibid 1103; emphasis added.
[189] ibid.
[190] (1584) 76 ER 637. For a brief explanation of the case in the context of British principles of statutory interpretation, see Loveland (2018) op cit pp 57–61. Griffith also noted (at (1907) 4 CLR 1087, 1104) Halsbury's endorsement of the principle 10 years earlier in *Eastman Photographic Materials Co v Comptroller-General of Patents* [1898] AC 571. Griffith omitted to mention that *Eastman* raised a very narrow question of statutory construction of an ambiguous provision (the meaning of the phrase 'fancy word' in trademark legislation).
[191] Rather than rely on Marshall's view to that effect in *McCulloch*, Griffith cited (ibid 1105) Story J's judgment in *Martin v Hunter's Lessee* ((1816) 14 US 304), in which the Marshall Court had concluded it could invalidate state legislation that breached the Constitution.
[192] At (1907) 4 CLR 1087 at 1106–07, Griffith rehearsed – not mentioning his role in the episode – the 1885 money bill dispute between Queensland's Assembly and the Council (pp 135–138 above). Griffith applauded the Privy Council's pronouncement (it was not a reasoned judgment) as based on the 'historical' presumption that the Council stood vis-à-vis the Assembly as the Lords stood vis-à-vis the Commons on this issue.

He also devoted some time to highlighting the evident inadequacies of Halsbury's knowledge and reasoning in *Webb v Outtrim*:

> It is true that what has been called an "astral intelligence", unprejudiced by any historical knowledge, and interpreting a Constitution merely by aid of a dictionary, might arrive at a very different conclusion as to its meaning from that which a person familiar with its history might reach.[193]

Griffith additionally suggested that the Privy Council had not properly read the High Court's judgments in *D'Emden* and *Deakin* and had improperly failed to ask counsel to address obviously important issues which those cases raised.[194] That targeted criticism was coupled with a more general swipe at English lawyers and judges, invoked to underpin the 'history' which pointed towards the High Court being the final court of appeal on *inter se* matters: "The Constitution of the United States was a subject entirely unfamiliar to English lawyers, while to Australian publicists it was almost as familiar as the British Constitution."[195] Similarly, Privy Council judges would not have been regarded by the framers of Australia's Constitution as: "familiar with the history or conditions of the remoter parts of the Empire, or as having any sympathetic understanding of aspirations of the younger communities which had long enjoyed the privilege of self-government".[196] Griffith considered that all of these concerns had informed the text which the 1900 Act had adopted:

> The questions referred to in sec. 74 ... are matters of supreme importance to the working of the Australian Constitution. They are questions likely to arise from day to day, and demanding immediate and authoritative decision. In our opinion, the intention of the British legislature was to substitute for a distant Court, of uncertain composition, imperfectly acquainted with Australian conditions, unlikely to be assisted by counsel familiar with those conditions, and whose decisions would be rendered many months, perhaps years, after its judgment has been invoked, an Australian Court, immediately available, constant in its composition, well versed in Australian history and conditions, Australian in its sympathies, and whose judgments, rendered as the occasion arose, would form a working code for the guidance of the Commonwealth.[197]

Griffith's retaliatory characterisation of Halsbury as a lazy, ignorant pedant was not an especially delicate exercise in interjudiciary diplomacy; it was an example perhaps of High Court tit for Privy Council tat. The judgment nonetheless revisited *D'Emden* and *Deakin* to reconsider their correctness. Griffith saw no reason to modify either decision. He was especially concerned to discredit the argument derived from *Lambe* that the Imperial disallowance power negated any scope for the Australian Constitution to contain an implied immunities doctrine. As well as – as in *Deakin* – rooting this

---

This, Griffith had suggested, was the appropriate interpretive technique – *the literal interpretation of the words of the Constitution Act is regarded as a matter of small importance* – to follow in 'constitutional' matters: "If the Queensland Constitution had been technically construed without regard to its subject matter the result must have been different" (1107). Griffith ignored the presumably inconvenient 'history' that the Council refused to comply with the Privy Council's view and that the decision had never been legally enforced.

[193] ibid 1106.
[194] ibid 1123.
[195] ibid 1111.
[196] ibid 1112.
[197] ibid 1118.

argument in the structural differences between the Canadian and Australian constitutions, Griffith emphasised the practical absurdities of reliance on disallowance, which would require state, Commonwealth and Imperial government to establish permanent bureaux to assess the possible impact of state laws on Commonwealth activities. Furthermore, disallowance applied only to an entire Act – it could not sever objectionable provisions from otherwise valid legislation.

Baxter also indicated that divergent opinions on major constitutional matters were now embedded in the High Court itself. Isaacs concurred with the majority on both the question of judicial hierarchy and the validity in Australia of an implied immunities doctrine. His dissent was on the ground that levying state income tax on a federal employee's salary in the same way that the state taxed every other salary was not an interference with a Commonwealth body's activities. Higgins, in contrast, rejected Griffith's reasoning on judicial hierarchy.[198] He considered s.74's text perfectly clear. S.74's only effect was to empower the High Court in some circumstances to prevent its own judgment being appealed to the Privy Council. That was a qualitatively quite distinct matter from concluding that the High Court was not bound by Privy Council judgments. Given the clarity of s.74's text, there was no proper basis for the Court to resort to matters of history or presumed purpose as interpretive aids to justify lending s.74 a broader meaning. Higgins also indicated that he doubted the correctness of Marshall's reasoning and conclusion in *McCulloch*, and its application in the Australian context.[199]

An Uneasy Settlement?

Notwithstanding the judgment's three-to-two basis, the majority refused permission for appeal to the Privy Council. Barton, Griffith and O'Connor had clearly adopted a position of outright defiance towards the Privy Council, a situation which presented Deakin with obvious political difficulties both domestically and with the British government.

The Commonwealth Parliament then stepped into the controversy. Deakin's (third) administration promoted the Commonwealth Salaries Act 1907.[200] The Act expressly provided that salaries paid to ministers, to members of the House and Senate and to Commonwealth officials could be subjected to state taxes of general application. That Act was swiftly followed by a statute – the Judiciary Act 1908[201] – apparently intended entirely to remove State Supreme Courts' jurisdiction, whether original or appellate, in *inter se* matters. S.5 ordered State Supreme Courts seized of such matters to remove them immediately to the High Court. There would thus be no State Supreme Court judgment to appeal to the Privy Council.

---

[198] ibid 1161 et seq.
[199] Higgins (echoing Madden in *Wollaston's Case*) characterised the judgment as: "the utterance rather of the statesman than the lawyer": ibid 1164. Higgins did not refer to Haldane's analysis of Watson's jurisprudence, but one might surmise – given how few academic legal journals were then published – that he was familiar with the *Juridical Review* obituary; pp 177–78 above.
[200] No 7 of 1907; assent given on 8 October.
[201] No 8 of 1907; assent given on 14 October.

A month later, despite having been refused permission to appeal by the High Court in *Baxter*, New South Wales argued an application it had made directly to the Privy Council before the 1908 Judiciary Act came into force.[202] In a 'judgment' spanning barely half a page, the Privy Council did not doubt its power to grant permission, but declined to do so on the twin bases that the amount of money in issue was trivial and that enactment of the Commonwealth Salaries Act 1907 had ended the dispute. Neither reason is compelling. The sum at stake in *Webb v Outtrim* was similarly small; in both cases, the money was merely a formal peg on which to hang the substantive constitutional argument. Nor did the Privy Council address the obviously credible point that if – per the High Court – states lacked the constitutional capacity to tax federal officials' incomes, they could not be given that capacity by the Commonwealth Parliament; either an amendment per s.128 or Imperial legislation would be required.[203]

The feebleness of the reasoning and the prominence of the bench[204] suggests that the decision was an exercise more in colonial diplomacy than colonial law, and that the Privy Council was indicating that Asquith's Liberal government was content to give some legal recognition to the increasing political reality of Australia acting as an autonomous 'country' within the Empire. For the High Court's original members, the Privy's Council's decision represented a victory of sorts, but it was not the only constitutional battle between the States and the Commonwealth then being fought.

The *Harvester* Judgment and the Constitutionality of 'New Protection'

Higgins replaced O'Connor as the CCCA judge in late 1907. Four months after *Baxter* was decided, Higgins was enmeshed in litigation triggered by Deakin's New Protection programme. The applicant in *Ex parte HV McKay*[205] owned factories making agricultural machinery (hence the case's colloquial soubriquet of '*Harvester*') and sought an order under s.2 of the Excise Tariff Act 1906 that his employees' wages were 'fair and reasonable' in order to be exempted from paying the duties to which such goods were presumptively liable.

Higgins expressed obvious unease – from a traditional separation of powers perspective – with the task set him by the 1906 Act:

> [T]he Legislature has not indicated what it means by "fair and reasonable". It is to be regretted that the Legislature has not given a definition of the words. It is the function of the legislature not the judiciary, to deal with social and economic problems; it is for the judiciary to apply, and, when necessary, to interpret the enactments of the Legislature. But here, this whole controversial problem with its grave social and economic bearings, has been committed to a Judge, who is not, at least directly, responsible, and who ought not to be responsible to public

---

[202] [1908] AC 214.

[203] Although if Griffith could imply the immunities doctrine into the Constitution he could surely also have implied a Commonwealth statutory power to qualify the extent of the immunity.

[204] It was headed by Lord Chancellor Lord Loreburn (in Asquith's 1906–10 Liberal government), joined by four other Law Lords.

[205] (1907) 2 Car 1. The application was argued for 20 days in October 1907; judgment was given on 12 November.

opinion ... I do not protest against the difficulty of the problem, but: against the confusion of functions – against the failure to define, the shunting of legislative responsibility ...[206]

In accepting that responsibility – and on receiving no definitional assistance from the parties – Higgins eventually concluded that:

> I cannot think of any other standard appropriate than the normal needs of the average employee regarded as a human being living in a civilised community a wage sufficient to insure the workman food, shelter, clothing, frugal comfort, provision for evil days etc.[207]

None of the wages paid by Mr McKay satisfied that test: modest increases for all of his employees would be required.[208]

The Constitutionality of the Excise Tariff Act 1906

Notwithstanding his assertion in *Harvester* that he would pay 'fair and reasonable' wages to his employees, Mr McKay subsequently appeared as a plaintiff challenging the constitutionality of the Excise Tariff Act per se. The High Court heard argument in *R v Barger; R v McKay*[209] in March 1908, and delivered judgment on 26 June. The now five-judge Court was starkly divided between the three original appointees and its two Deakin-appointed members. Griffith delivered the majority judgment; Isaacs and Higgins issued separate – similarly reasoned – dissents. Both the majority and the dissentients relied heavily (and selectively) on US Supreme Court opinions – a method presumably intended at least in part as a uniform refusal to accept Halsbury's dismissal of the relevance of such authority to Australian constitutional law.

Griffith's judgment rested on the premise that the High Court was both entitled and obliged to look behind the form of the Excise Tariff Act 1906 and to consider both the legislative purpose that underlay it and the practical effect that it would have. Seen from those perspectives, the Act was properly classified not as a lawful exercise of the Commonwealth's taxing power, but as an unlawful interference with the states' control over their respective internal industrial relations laws. The conclusion was an obvious (and heavy) further counterweight to any suggestion that the implied immunities doctrine betokened a predisposition on the original judges' parts to resolve any constitutional ambiguities in favour of expanding Commonwealth power at the states' expense.

IV. Conclusion

The first decade of Australia's existence as a national legal entity was marked by significant instability in terms of the formation and collapse of national governments and the emergence of an obvious cleavage within the High Court between the three original judges and Deakin's two 1906 appointees as to the approach the judiciary should take to

---

[206] ibid 2–3.
[207] ibid 3–4.
[208] 'Fair and reasonable' rates for all of McKay's various types of employees were detailed in a schedule at ibid 23–25.
[209] (1908) 6 CLR 4.

construing the Constitution. As chapter seven suggests, those themes of governmental instability and judicial cleavage were similarly evident during a constitutional controversy playing out in Queensland in that era. But before attention turns to that issue, two further early twentieth-century matters merit consideration.

The New South Wales Constitution Act 1902

Australia's creation as a constitutional entity provided some incentive for New South Wales to reconsider its own constitutional arrangements. The (New South Wales) Constitution Act 1902 was a brief measure, self-described as consolidating legislation. The initiative to promote the Act was not taken on partisan party grounds. The 1901 state elections had left the Assembly with a distinctly fragmented composition, compounded by yet more realignments and name changes within the parties and factions seeking representation.

Table 6.6 New South Wales Legislative Assembly election, 1901 (3 July 1901)

Party	% vote	Seats	Change[a]
Progressive	22.0	41	−9
Liberal	33.3	37	−5
Labour	18.7	24	+9
Independent	15.5	16	+7
Independent Liberal	6.2	3	
Independent Labour	1.8	4	

[a] For the purposes of the change column relative to the previous (1898) election, I have equated the Progressives with the Protectionists; the Liberal and Independent Liberals with the Free Traders; and grouped the Labour and Independent Labour members together.

The transfer of legislative power over customs duties to the Commonwealth Parliament deprived New South Wales politicians of the primary ideological fault line which shaped colonial politics in the 1880s and 1890s. In this first post-federation election, the largest bloc in the Assembly comprised former Protectionists, who had morphed into a 'Progressive Party', aligned with Barton and Deakin's national Protectionist grouping. Many former Free Traders reinvented themselves as a newly named 'Liberal Party', which took 37 of the Assembly's 125 seats. Labour, with 28 seats, and a group of 16 nominally Independent members held the balance of power.

A minority Progressive ministry led by Sir John See was subsequently formed. See's family – his father was an agricultural labourer – had emigrated from England in the 1850s and established themselves as small farmers.[210] By 1890, See had become an extremely wealthy man, with substantial interests in agricultural production, shipping and property. He initially restricted his political activities to local matters. First elected

---

[210] http://adb.anu.edu.au/biography/see-sir-john-8380.

to the Assembly in 1880, See subsequently held various ministerial posts under George Dibbs and William Lyne. Having vigorously supported federation, he was Lyne's obvious successor as leader of the New South Wales protectionists/progressives when Lyne took a seat in Barton's national Cabinet. It was not ideologically difficult for See's Progressives to fashion policy initiatives attracting Labour support, most notably a 1901 industrial arbitration measure which foreshadowed Deakin's eventually enacted national scheme and the extension of voting rights to women in 1902.[211]

The Constitution Act 1902 (hereafter CA 1902) came into being – like Queensland's Constitution Act 1867 – as one bit of a multi-part package of consolidating bills dealing with myriad matters, none of which received any searching consideration from legislators.[212] All these bills began their passage in the Council. The second reading, committee and report stages did not long detain the legislators. Hansard records on 2 July 1902 at p836:

> LAW CONSOLIDATION BILLS. The following bills (on motion by the Ron. B. R. Wise) were read the second time, and reported from Committee without amendment.

The list contained 56 bills: the Constitution Bill was lumped in with, inter alia, the Pawnbrokers Bill, the Billiards and Bagatelle Bill, the Butchers Shops Sunday Closing Bill and the Smoke Nuisance Abatement Bill. The 56 bills then progressed through third reading without any discussion at all.[213]

In the Assembly, the bills were given first reading in the 9 July session at 2.50 am the next morning.[214] The passage of all the measures was marked by a brief but very fractious dispute between the government and opposition members as to the propriety of presenting so many bills en masse when it appeared self-evident that some (and perhaps many of them) actually amended existing legislation rather than simply repackaging it.

The Constitution Bill was one of many such measures which went through second reading and committee stage on 17 July.[215] The second reading debate occupies two pages of Hansard, most of which was bickering between See and opposition members on procedural points. The bill then moved immediately into committee, where discussion prior to the bill being passed without amendment spanned one page of Hansard. At third reading on 6 August opposition members pointed to various apparent errors in the bill and to several unexplained alterations to sch.1 of the 1855 Act. See was, however, unwilling to allow any substantive debate, and third reading passed with a government majority of 28.[216] Assent was given by the Governor – the bill was not reserved – on 18 August.

Much of the 1902 Act was indeed a verbatim or approximate repetition of the 1855 measure, albeit that the ordering and precise wording of many sections was altered.[217]

---

[211] Respectively the Industrial Arbitration Act 1901 and the Women's Franchise Act 1902. S.4 of the latter Act expressly precluded women from being elected to the Assembly.
[212] Pp 123–125 above.
[213] *NSWLCD* 9 July 1902 p995.
[214] *NSWLAD* 9 July 1902 p1072.
[215] *NSWLAD* 17 July 1902 p1278.
[216] *NSWLAD* 6 August 1902 pp 1705 (debate), 1710 (vote).
[217] To facilitate cross-referencing between the CA 1902 and the 1855 measure, I use ordinary text to identify 1902 provisions (ie s.1), put any 1855 section from sch.1 in [ ] (ie [s.1]) and render the BAA parts of

Many parts of sch.1 of the 1855 Act did not feature in the 1902 Act, having been hived off at various points in the intervening 47 years into other legislation which did not bear the 'Constitution Act' label. Most notably, these included [ss.37–40], dealing with Supreme Court judges' tenure, removal from office and pensions, and [ss.11–14], addressing the qualifications of voters and compilation of the electoral roll.[218]

S. 3 [s.9 BAA] offered a definition of the Legislature:

> 3. In this Act, unless the context or subject-matter otherwise indicates or requires, "The Legislature" means His Majesty the King, with the advice and consent of the Legislative Council and Legislative Assembly.

S.3 omitted the 'any future legislature' phrase in [s.9 BAA], but the 'unless' addendum might suggest that 'the Legislature' could take different forms (or, if one prefers, could make law in different ways) in addition to the ordinary form spelled out in s.3. There is no reference or allusion to CLVA 1865 s.5 in s.3 or anywhere else in the 1902 Act. But the 1902 Act contained one provision that could be construed as (if not explicitly described as) an 'unless' or 'manner and form' requirement under CLVA 1865 s5[3]: this being a version of the 1857 amendment removing the [s.36] two-thirds majority requirement:[219]

> 7. The Legislature may, by any Act, alter the laws in force for the time being under this Act or otherwise concerning the Legislative Council, and may provide for the nomination or election of another Legislative Council to consist of such members to be appointed or elected by such persons and in such manner as by any such Act is determined: Provided that every Bill passed for any such purpose shall be reserved for the signification of His Majesty's pleasure thereon, and a copy of such Bill shall be laid before both Houses of the Imperial Parliament thirty days at least before His Majesty's pleasure thereon is signified.

The Legislature's powers were then (broadly) identified in s.5 [s.1]:[220]

> 5. The Legislature shall, subject to the provisions of the Commonwealth of Australia Constitution Act, have power to make laws for the peace, welfare, and good government of New South Wales in all cases whatsoever: Provided that all Bills for appropriating any part of the public revenue, or for imposing any new rate, tax or impost, shall originate in the Legislative Assembly.

Ss 16–22 [ss. 2–8] retained the Legislative Council in unchanged form. Despite the various 'swamping' disputes which had attended Council–Assembly and government–Governor relations since 1855, s.16 simply repeated [s.2]:

> 16. It shall be lawful for His Majesty, by an instrument under the Sign-Manual, to authorise the Governor to summon to the Legislative Council by instrument under the Great Seal any person he thinks fit, and every person so summoned shall thereby become a Member of the Legislative Council …

---

the 1855 Act as [s.1 BAA]. The 1902 Act was a single Act rather than – as had been the case with the removal of the two-thirds clauses and electoral reform legislation in 1857–58 – the first part of a Two Act strategy; see pp 56–57 above. The notion that a 'Two Act' mechanism was required to alter the Constitution Act – evidently so firmly and widely held in 1857 – seemed to have disappeared from the New South Wales political landscape in 1902.

[218] This having been done in the Electoral Act 1858; p 60 above.

[219] Pp 56–58 above.

[220] Despite s.5's broad phraseology, CA 1902 retained (in s.8 [s.53]) the specific power to dispose of waste lands.

That the power remained with the Governor, rather than the Governor-in-Council, underlined the point that a Premier could only request and not insist upon additional Council appointments being made.

Like the 1855 Constitution, the 1902 consolidation made no explicit mention of responsible government in general terms, nor of a Premier or a Cabinet. Nor was any textual indication given that that principle was to structure the exercising of the Governor's specific powers. S.16 is an obvious example. Similarly, s.10 retained [s.9] the Governor's broad discretion in relation to summoning, proroguing and dissolving the Legislature:

> 10. The Governor may fix the time and place for holding every Session of the Legislative; Council and Assembly, and may change or vary such time or place as he may judge advisable and most consistent with general convenience and the public welfare, giving sufficient notice thereof. He may also prorogue the Legislative Council and Assembly, and dissolve the said Assembly by proclamation or otherwise whenever he deems it expedient.

The 1902 Act contains several peculiarities and errors. Had See allowed more time for debate, some of these might have been identified and remedied. A remarkable infelicity arises in s.47 [s.37], concerning the Governor's power to appoint 'cabinet ministers':

> 47. Subject to the provisions of the Public Service Act, 1902, and of all other enactments relating to the appointment of officers and being in force at the passing of this Act, *the appointment of all public offices under the Government, whether such offices are salaried or not, shall be vested in the Governor with the advice of the Executive Council, with the exception of the appointments of the officers liable to retire from office on political grounds as hereinbefore mentioned, which appointments shall be vested in the Governor alone* ...

The italicised text in s.47 is nearly a verbatim recitation of [s.37], the difference being that [s.37] refers to 'herein*after* mentioned', and there is indeed a list of 'herein*after* mentioned' offices in [s.51], these being inter alia the Colonial Secretary (Premier), Treasurer, Attorney-General and Solicitor-General. However, neither these offices nor any others are 'hereinbefore mentioned' in the 1902 Act.

A similar error arises regarding the Assembly's powers. S.32(2) stated that all questions in the Assembly were to be decided by a majority of members present, but also contained an "except as herein excepted" qualification to the bare majority presumption. However, there is not actually any matter which is 'excepted' in the CA 1902. S.32 was a verbatim repetition of [s.23], in which the 'herein excepted' initially made sense as it referred to the s.15 and s.36 two-thirds majority procedures repealed in 1857. That no member of the government or either house noted the redundancy of the phrase in 1902 is rather surprising.[221]

In a more systemic vein, CA 1902 s.2 and sch.1 expressly repealed various Acts. One such 'Act' was identified as 17 Vict No 41. This measure is the 'Bill' passed by the

---

[221] The CA 1902 also made provision in sch.3 for payment of £3000 in salary to 'Two Puisne Judges' of the Supreme Court. In 1902, there were four puisne Supreme Court judges, two of whom would presumably have to find their salaries from some other source (which source, if the CA 1902 impliedly repealed any inconsistent earlier legislation, might no longer exist). Similarly, the 1902 Act reproduced verbatim (ss.33–34) the 1855 provisions ([ss.25–26]) concerning resignation or forced vacation of Assembly seats, but omitted to reproduce [s.27], which provided for an automatic by-election in such cases.

New South Wales Legislative Council in 1853, which in amended form became sch.1 of the 1855 Act (18 and 19 Vict c 54) enacted by the British Parliament. CA 1902 s.2 and sch.1 did not identify sch.1 of the 1855 Act itself as being repealed. The inference that s.2 and sch.1 raise is that sch.1 of the 1855 Act was regarded by New South Wales legislators in 1902 as a New South Wales statute, even though – since its text was amended by the British Parliament – it had not actually been passed by the Legislative Council (under s.32 of the 1850 Act).[222] Seen from a different perspective, CA 1902 s.2 and sch.1 purported to repeal a measure that did not actually exist.

S.4 [BAA] of the 1855 Act clearly empowered the Legislature to 'alter or repeal all or any' of the provisions of sch.1 of the 1855 Act.[223] The absence of any serious debate in the Assembly or Council on the 1902 Act means that there is no indication as to whether legislators considered that they were proceeding under the s.4 [BAA] power or instead (or additionally) assumed – almost certainly incorrectly[224] – that the 'all cases whatever' power given in [s.1] provided the legal source for the 1902 Act. The CA 1902's preamble states simply: "An Act to consolidate Acts relating to the Constitution." The 1902 Act does not purport to repeal any of the BAA sections of the 1855 Act. Any attempt to do so would presumably have been legally futile, since s.4 BAA only embraced sch.1, not the BAA parts of the Act.

The Reduction of Members Referendum Act 1903

The paucity of legislative debate on the CA 1902, the drafting errors in its text and the evidently non-contentious nature of the fact that such matters as electoral qualification and the tenure of Supreme Court judges need not feature in the state's 'Constitution Act' might all be thought rather surprising, given the immense care which had recently been taken in drafting and enacting Australia's Constitution. That degree of legislative rigour had evidently not permeated the state's constitution-making processes. And the CA 1902 certainly did not foreshadow two significant constitutional innovations which occurred in 1903 and 1904.

The Reduction of Members Referendum Bill

See introduced the second reading of the Reduction of Members Referendum Bill into the Assembly on 12 November 1903.[225] The bill proposed that voters be asked in a referendum whether they wished the Assembly to continue to have 125 seats, or to be reduced to 100, 90 or 80 seats. See presented the bill as a response to public and press demands that the Assembly be reduced in size (largely consequential on the assumption

---

[222] The Legislature made a different error in the Constitution Act Amendment Act 1890, which reduced the Council's quorum to one-quarter from one-third. The 1890 Act purported to amend s.8 of 18 & 19 Vict c 54, ie s.8 in the BAA part of the 1855 Act, which was the commencement proviso. What the 1890 Act should have referred to was s.8 of sch.1 of the 1855 Act, which dealt with the Council quorum. (Unlike the 1902 Act, the 1890 Act makes no mention of 17 Vict No 41.) In contrast, the Constitution Act Amendment Act 1884 – which addressed the issue of which Crown offices precluded membership of the Assembly or Council – had correctly identified (in s.1) sch.1 of the 1855 Act as the measure amended.
[223] P 46 above.
[224] Pp 46–47 and 50–54 above.
[225] *NSWLAD* 12 November 1903 p4203.

that creation of the national government and Parliament meant there would be less for the state government and legislature to do), and characterised it as a non-partisan measure on which members should vote according to conscience and as a 'constitutional' issue.[226]

It apparently did not strike See as odd that the CA 1902 made no mention of referendums; and while he accepted that the bill did indeed raise a 'constitutional matter', he did not suggest that any explicit amendment of the CA 1902 was required. See announced that he would regard himself as bound to promote a bill to implement the referendum result,[227] but there was no such requirement in the bill itself.

See then ended the first stage of the second reading debate with the (legally) curious proposition that approval in a referendum followed by legislation enacted in the ordinary way would somehow preclude the Assembly's size being altered again in the future by legislation which was not itself also supported by another referendum:

> The question is whether the present proposal is the best means of ascertaining the voice of the people on the question of reduction of members. In my judgment it is the best way and the only way. A vote of this House would have no effect. If I carried a bill through Parliament that the number should be reduced to seventy or eighty, the next Parliament might undo it.[228]

There was, however, no provision in the bill to (try to) enact that idea, and See made no suggestion that CLVA 1865 s.5, s.4 [BAA] of the 1855 Act or CA 1902 s.5 might provide the means to do so

Debate resumed on 17 November;[229] proceedings lasted into the early hours. Many members spoke, although contributions were frequently notable more for the variety and vigour of personal insults thrown across the chamber than for searching constitutional or legal analysis. See secured a comfortable second reading majority and – at 1.30 am – pushed the bill straight into committee.[230] Just over eight hours later – hours mostly spent on vituperative bickering between government members and the Liberal opposition – the bill left committee essentially unchanged.[231] A similarly fractious report stage ensued that afternoon. The debate's character was nicely caught by a contribution from William Ferguson, the member for the mining constituency of Sturt:

> I have listened very carefully to-night to a type of melodramatic acting such as I have never before seen since I have been in the House. The two Ministers who have spoken on this question with their hysterical speeches, their extravagant braggadocia, and their drivelling imbecility, will not, I am sure, receive the indorsement of the people.[232]

Third reading debate continued in similar vein, the bill eventually passing by 50 (See's Progressives with Labour support) to 35 (Liberals).[233]

---

[226] ibid.
[227] ibid pp 4203–04.
[228] ibid p4208.
[229] *NSWLAD* 17 November 1903 p4228.
[230] ibid pp 4821–82.
[231] Although Liberal members mustered considerable indignation over the removal of the option for 80 members from the referendum question.
[232] *NSWLAD* 18 November 1903 p4329. Ferguson was elected in 1894 as a Labour member, but left the party in 1899 and was returned as an 'Independent Labour member' in 1901. In late 1903 he was just about to cross the floor to join the Liberals.
[233] *NSWLAD* 18 November 1903 p4360.

There is no indication in the debates that any Assembly member considered that the bill required any alteration to the CA 1902, nor that the use of a referendum might amount to a 'manner and form' proviso within CLVA 1865 s.5[3] and/or an 'unless' redefinition of the legislature per CA 1902 s.1. Nor were those points raised in the Legislative Council, although there was a spirited exchange of views on whether the bill, once passed, had to be reserved for assent rather than just approved by the Governor. See's administration was evidently impatient to resolve matters and procured a majority to suspend Council standing orders so that second reading, committee and third reading could all be completed in an afternoon.[234] The bill was not reserved, and came into force on 1 December.

The referendum was subsequently held on 16 December 1903. Some 73% of voters supported a 90-member Assembly. Although the 1903 Act did not require that the referendum result be given legislative effect, See's government promptly promoted a bill enacted as the Electorates Redistribution Act 1904 which reduced the Assembly to 90 seats, with all members returned from single-seat constituencies on a first-past-the-post basis.

Despite See's comments at second reading of the 1903 Act, there was no indication in the 1904 Act's text that its enactment of the referendum result lent it any kind of special legal status, nor that its future amendment or repeal was subject to any type of CLVA 1865 s.5[3] 'manner and form' proviso or a CA 1902 s.1 'unless' exception. And like the 1903 Act, there was no indication in the Act's text that it should be regarded as amending New South Wales's Constitution.

The Australian States Constitution Act 1907

Seven years after enactment of the Constitution Act, the Imperial Parliament again legislated on Australian constitutional issues. The Australian States Constitution Act 1907 was a more modest affair, concerned with state rather than national matters. Its primary focus was to resolve an uncertainty typified by the discussion in the New South Wales Legislative Council during the passage of the 1903 Act: namely, which state bills had to be reserved for royal assent. S.1 provided that, in future, that requirement would attach to any bill which:

> 1(1) ...
>
> (a) Alters the constitution of the Legislature of the state or of either House thereof; or
> (b) Affects the salary of the Governor of the state; or
> (c) Is, under any Act of the Legislature of the state passed after the passing of this Act, or under any provision contained in the Bill itself, required to be reserved;
>
> but, save as aforesaid, it shall not be necessary to so reserve any Bill passed by any such Legislature ...[235]

---

[234] *NSWLCD* 24 November 1903 p4458 et seq.

[235] S.1(4) lent s.1(1) an exhaustive character by repealing all existing statutory provisions or clauses of Orders in Council which imposed reservation requirements on state bills (on which see inter alia pp 20–21, 30–31 and 48–49), save that s.1(1) also expressly reserved the Queen's power to require reservation in her *Instructions* to Governors. S.1(1)(c) confirms the point established in 1863 (p 98 above) that colonial legislatures could

S.1 further defined 'constitution' in s.1(1)(a) in narrow terms. Alterations to the apportionment of electoral districts, the number of members in either chamber or the qualifications of members or votes would not be 'constitutional' matters for s.1(1) purposes.

S.2 had obvious echoes of the constitutional difficulties which had arisen in Queensland and South Australia in the 1860s, which had prompted successive validating Acts passed by the Imperial Parliament and culminated in the CLVA 1865. S.2 enacted a sweeping retrospective validation provision in respect of any state (including, per s.2(2), any measure passed by a colony prior to federation) legislation which had been 'passed' without compliance with any then extant reservation requirement.

Introducing the Lords second reading on 26 February 1907, the Secretary of State for the Colonies Lord Elgin (in Asquith's 1906–10 Liberal administration) informed the house that the measure was being promoted at the request of all six Australian States "to deal with a great complication of legal difficulties"[236] arising from the patchwork of statutory provisions then applicable to reservation. Second reading passed without division or substantive debate. At Commons second reading on 28 June 1907, Winston Churchill, then Under-Secretary of State for the Colonies, told the Commons that: "the measure had been agreed upon by all the Australian States, and there was nothing to discuss. He had every reason to believe that it was a non-controversial Bill."[237] There was subsequently no significant discussion at either second or third reading; on each occasion it passed without division.[238]

The passage of the 1907 Act indicated that questions as to the 'manner and form' required for state legislatures to enact valid legislation on particular matters remained contentious in early twentieth-century Australia. Just how contentious was then becoming clear in Queensland, when Griffith's successor as Chief Justice became embroiled in a constitutional controversy of his own design with the state's then Premier, a by-then former Labour politician for whom the lure of a House or Senate seat proved insufficient temptation to leave Queensland politics for a role in the national arena.

---

enact such requirements, but does not address the question of whether a colonial Act requiring reservation of certain types of bill could itself be repealed without reservation, nor if any attempt to require reservation of any repealing bill would be effective. The Act makes no reference to the CLVA 1865 s.5. S.1 also provided that reservation was not required if the Queen had previously authorised a Governor to assent to a particular bill.

[236] HLD 26 February 1907 c 1394.
[237] HCD 11 June 1907 c 1340.
[238] HCD 28 June c 242; HCD 31 July 1907 c 1129.

7

Constitutional Controversy in Queensland: Kidston and *Cooper*

> The Conservative Party have found a last hope in the Legislative Council ... We are forced to ask ourselves whether we are willing to permit the political prejudices of a few nominees to continue to override the wishes of the elected representatives of the people. This has become the most important question in Queensland politics, and on its satisfactory solution rests the hope of democratic progress in Queensland.
>
> William Kidston, Premier of Queensland, 1907.[1]

As well as dominating the Queensland Assembly in the 1890s, the Ministerialists enjoyed the benefit of a usually reliable (and substantial) Council majority. While Griffith in his liberal period secured nomination of some like-minded members, most councillors were either expressly or implicitly aligned to the conservative wing of the Ministerialist party. There was consequently little scope for systemic conflict between the Assembly and Council; such problems would only arise if the Ministerialists split once more into distinct liberal and conservative factions, or if the emerging Labour Party – which won 20 of the Assembly's 72 seats in the 1896 election – garnered sufficient electoral support to form a government.

That scenario occurred briefly in December 1899, when a Labour administration led by Anderson Dawson, formerly a miner's union official and journalist, held office for just one week.[2] Labour won only 21 of the 72 seats at the 1899 election; the Ministerialists had 42 and there were nine 'independent' members. Dawson had evidently been misled by Griffith, then Chief Justice and acting as Lieutenant Governor, into thinking that the independents and more than a handful of Ministerialists would desert the government, which had lost an Assembly vote on a railway issue. The defectors never appeared, however; Dawson's government lost its first Assembly vote and resigned immediately, opening the door for Robert Philp to lead a new Ministerialist administration.

---

[1] Quoted in Murphy (1978) 'William Kidston: a tenacious reformer' in Murphy and Joyce (eds) *Queensland political portraits* p 253.
[2] See Murphy (1970) 'Notes on four parliamentary leaders' in Murphy, Joyce and Hughes op cit; http://adb.anu.edu.au/biography/dawson-andrew-5921.

I. William Kidston and the Politics of Progressive Coalition

The prime political mover in the early stages of what proved a protracted process of Council abolition was William Kidston,³ a Scot who emigrated to Queensland aged 33. Kidston's father was an iron worker, a trade Kidston himself initially adopted while also pursuing (having left school at 13) some further education in chemistry. Kidston was active in party politics and trade union organisation in Scotland, and maintained both interests in Queensland, where he set up a bookshop in Rockhampton.

While Kidston's political sympathies were distinctly (and consistently) a mix of Fabianism on economic policy and liberalism on matters of political representation, he (with similar consistency) equivocated on the question of his party political allegiance.⁴ Having achieved prominence in labour and union circles by vigorous support of workers involved in the 1891 shearers' strike,⁵ Kidston first stood (unsuccessfully) for the Assembly as a Workers Political Association (a strand of the nascent Labour Party) candidate in 1893. He ran successfully in 1896, with Labour support, but formally as an independent 'Democrat' on a platform calling for cooperation between Liberal and Labour interests to oust the Ministerialist government. Shortly after his election, Kidston formally joined the Labour caucus. His rise in the Queensland party – he was Treasurer in Dawson's 'one week' Labour government – seems attributable primarily to his own abilities, albeit aided by the departure of some senior Labour figures to the Commonwealth Parliament in 1901.⁶

Table 7.1 Queensland Legislative Assembly elections, 1893–1902

Year	Party	% vote	Seats	Change
1893	Ministerialist	44.8	42	–
	Labour	33.3	16	+12
	Independentª	21.0	14	−12
1896	Ministerialist	47.8	41	−1
	Labour	35.0	20	+4
	Independent	15.0	10	−4
	Farmer	2.4	1	+1

(continued)

³ http://adb.anu.edu.au/biography/kidston-william-6949; for a fuller account of Kidston's career, see Murphy (1978) op cit: Wanka (1970) 'William Kidston – the dilemma of a powerful leader' in Murphy, Joyce and Hughes op cit.
⁴ He supported women's enfranchisement and had unsuccessfully promoted a Private Members' bill to that effect in 1901.
⁵ An involvement which placed Kidston squarely in opposition to pastoral interests.
⁶ Dawson ran successfully for the Senate. The most significant departee was Andrew Fisher; see pp 170–171 above.

Table 7.1 *(Continued)*

Year	Party	% vote	Seats	Change
1899	Ministerialist	49.3	43	+2
	Labour	35.5	21	+1
	Independent	15.0	8	-3
1902	Ministerialist	48.1	40	-3
	Labour	39.3	25	+4
	Morganites[b]	12.5	7	-1

[a] I have included in this group a faction sometimes referred to as 'Opposition' members, who might best be portrayed as 'Liberals', ideologically left of the Ministerialists and right of the Labour Party.
[b] A group I have equated (roughly) with the 1899 Independents.

At the 1902 election, Philp led the Ministerialists to an eight-seat overall majority. Labour won 25 (of 72) seats. Seven seats went to a breakaway group of former Ministerialists (including the Speaker, Arthur Morgan),[7] whose political sentiments were more centrist than Philp's. Although the Labour opposition was formally led by a man named Billy Browne,[8] Kidston was its dominant figure in terms of policy formation and parliamentary manoeuvrings designed to solidify the Morgan group in opposition to Philp and peel away a handful of former Philp loyalists. By late 1903 the Ministerialist majority had ebbed away and Philp resigned. Kidston's strategy was not that Labour should try to form a government alone, even though it was in numbers the official opposition, but to serve in a coalition administration headed by Morgan, with Kidston as Treasurer.[9] Kidston subsequently became leader of the Labour Party on Browne's death in April 1904. Morgan secured the appointment of three Labour nominees to the Council during his first government, but lost his effective Assembly majority when several Ministerialists who had deserted Philp resumed their former loyalties, triggering an election in August 1904.

The Morganites and Labour fought the 1904 election as informal allies. While Labour won 34 (of 72) seats and the Morganites only 21, Morgan remained as Premier, with Kidston as Treasurer. Philp had stepped down as Ministerialist party leader before the election, but took the post on again when his successor lost his seat. Philp's opposition commanded only 17 seats.[10]

---

[7] http://adb.anu.edu.au/biography/morgan-sir-arthur-7652. Morgan came from a wealthy family in rural Queensland. His father owned the *Warwick Argus* newspaper and sat briefly in the Assembly. Arthur Morgan combined his political career with editing the *Argus* – in which capacity he vocally supported Byrnes in the 1890s – until 1907. See further Morgan (2004) 'The life and career of Sir Arthur Morgan' *JRHSQ* 555.
[8] Browne (born in 1846) was a merchant seaman, miner and trade union organiser before being elected to the Assembly in 1893. He became party leader in 1900; http://adb.anu.edu.au/biography/browne-william-henry-5395.
[9] On the intricacies of the manoeuvring, see Crook (1970) 'The crucible – Labour in coalition 1903–1907' in Murphy, Joyce and Hughes op cit.
[10] Bolton op cit pp 210–13.

Table 7.2 Queensland Legislative Assembly elections, 1904

Party	% vote	Seats	Change
Morganites	30.0	21	+14
Labour	36.0	34	+9
Ministerialist[a]	29.0	15	−25
Independent	5.0	2	+2

[a] Many former Ministerialists and some former Independents stood as Morgan supporters. To avoid confusion, I have retained the Ministerialist label for the rump group led by Philp and refer to Morgan's group as 'Morganites'.

Morgan's second administration pursued a reformist legislative agenda on both political and economic matters, much of which faced obstruction in the Council, which still contained a clear Philpite majority.[11] The government did secure enactment of some significant measures, including electoral reform legislation in 1905 which enfranchised women and abolished plural voting. The election legislation was also initially obstructed in the Council, but was approved following indications from Morgan that he would, if necessary, ask the 'Governor' to swamp the Council with government nominees. Whether Morgan's request would have been granted is doubtful. There was no (in formal terms) Governor in office during most of 1905; the Governor's powers were being exercised temporarily by the Lieutenant-Governor and former Premier, Hugh Muir Nelson.[12] On passing the Premier's mantle to Byrnes, Nelson became President of the Legislative Council before acting as Lieutenant-Governor. Morgan and Nelson had been political allies prior to the Morgan/Labour coalition being formed, but Nelson's personal political sympathies were more conservative than Morgan's, and it seems unlikely that he would have granted any swamping requests.

Morgan disliked the hurly burly of governance, and stepped down from the premiership in January 1906 to accept the more congenial post – replacing Nelson – of President of the Council. Kidston became Premier, but almost immediately found himself at odds with the state Labour Party, which had adopted an explicit socialisation policy as the centre of its economic programme in 1905, along with a prohibition on future sale of Crown lands. Kidston had no ideological sympathy with that agenda and, having tried and failed to secure a reversal of the policy, left the party shortly before the (May) 1907 state election.[13] Accompanied by many former Labour and Morganite Assembly members, Kidston contested the election as leader of a new party styled – immodestly – 'the Kidston Party'. While his party won only 24 of the Assembly's 72 seats and Philp's Ministerialists won 29, Kidston's personal attributes and policy programme were such that he could run a minority government with the tacit support of remaining Labour members, 18 of whom were elected under the leadership of David Bowman.[14]

---

[11] The Council vetoed measures on inter alia land reform, establishing wages boards for factory and shop workers, and income tax reform; Murphy (1978) op cit pp 250–51.
[12] P 142 above.
[13] The formal response of the Kidston wing to the 1905 socialisation policy is reproduced in Murphy, Joyce and Hughes op cit at pp 279–80.
[14] Born in 1860 in Victoria, Bowman – a miner's son – moved to Queensland in 1888, where he worked as a bootmaker and became an active trade unionist. First returned to the Assembly in 1899, Bowman's

Table 7.3 Queensland Legislative Assembly elections, 1907

Party	% vote	Seats	Change[a]
Ministerialist	40.5	29	+14
Kidston	31.8	24	+3
Labour	26.3	18	−16
Independent	1.1	1	−1

[a] For the purposes of this column, I have treated all of the seats won by the Morganites in 1904 as Kidston seats.

Kidston's attention soon turned to what he regarded as the most pressing problem in Queensland politics: the Ministerialists' constant capacity to block government bills through their control of the Council. In a letter to Bowman urging cooperation between their two parties, Kidston wrote:

> The Conservative Party have found a last hope in the Legislative Council ... We are forced to ask ourselves whether we are willing to permit the political prejudices of a few nominees to continue to override the wishes of the elected representatives of the people. This has become the most important question in Queensland politics, and on its satisfactory solution rests the hope of democratic progress in Queensland.[15]

Before broaching that issue, however, Kidston faced another constitutional challenge.

II. Income Tax and the Judges – The *Cooper* Litigation

Kidston's break from the Labour Party and his administration's difficulties with the Legislative Council rather overshadowed in political and constitutional terms a bizarre legal controversy between the government and the Supreme Court Chief Justice, Pope Cooper, which ran its course in 1906–07. Cooper was born in 1846 to wealthy landowner parents.[16] Educated in Sydney, he qualified for the Bar in London and returned to practise in Queensland as a Crown prosecutor. He served briefly and unhappily as a member of the Assembly and Attorney-General between 1881 and 1883 before accepting a Supreme Court seat. Although Cooper did not re-enter electoral politics, his personal politics were visibly located at the reactionary end of the conservative spectrum. He was nonetheless appointed Chief Justice in 1903 to succeed Griffith by the first Morgan coalition government. As Premier, Kidston was less impressed with Cooper's personal and political qualities. In 1906, the then Governor Lord Chelmsford[17] had

---

subsequent election as party leader following the Kidston split perhaps owed more to his personal popularity than his abilities as a strategic tactician or parliamentarian, and he was dogged throughout his career by ill-health; http://adb.anu.edu.au/biography/bowman-david-5315.

[15] Quoted in Murphy (1978) op cit p253.

[16] http://adb.anu.edu.au/biography/cooper-sir-pope-alexander-5771.

[17] Chelmsford was unexpectedly appointed to the post in 1905, having previously (after education at Winchester and Oxford) been called to the English Bar and appointed a fellow of All Souls. In 1909 he became Governor of New South Wales and subsequently served as Viceroy of India, then as First Lord of the Admiralty in Ramsay Macdonald's 1926 Labour government; http://adb.anu.edu.au/biography/chelmsford-third-baron-5573.

wanted Cooper appointed as Lieutenant-Governor, but Kidston successfully insisted on the role being given to the (to Kidston) much more politically palatable Morgan.[18]

Cooper's party political conservatism took a constitutional dimension when he brought a legal challenge to the constitutionality of various income tax statutes passed in 1902–05.[19] The first such measure, enacted in 1902, was Philp's initiative, designed to fill the fiscal hole that federation had dug for Queensland by removing the state's control over import and export duties.[20] In prosaic terms, Cooper's objection was that Supreme Court judges were – like everyone else in Queensland – required to pay income tax. This, he argued, was inconsistent with the Queensland's Constitution Act 1867 s.17, which re-enacted cl.16 of the 1859 Order:

> *xvi.* Such salaries as are settled upon the Judges for the time being by law and also such salaries as shall or may be in future granted to Her Majesty Her Heirs and Successors or otherwise to any future Judge or Judges of the said Supreme Court shall in all time coming be paid and payable to every such Judge and Judges for the time being so long as the patents or commissions of them or any of them respectively shall continue and remain in force.

Cl.xvi/s.17 was an essentially verbatim restatement of British legislation, the Commission and Salaries of Judges Act 1760.[21] The UK Parliament had expressly legislated in 1842 that judges' salaries were liable to income tax deducted at source, evidently without any suggestion being raised that this contradicted the 1760 Act. That legislation might have been thought unhelpful to the narrow focus of Cooper's argument, which was that a law recouping part of the judges' salaries through taxation necessarily meant that the entire salary was no longer 'paid and payable' per s.17.

The broader constitutional argument – Cooper's main concern – was more complex, since the British Parliament's sovereign nature meant it could impliedly repeal any existing legislation. The Queensland legislature obviously was not sovereign. Cooper did not dispute that Queensland's Legislature could *ultimately* reduce judges' salaries by any amount, or indeed alter the basis of their tenure of office or reconstruct the court entirely. His contention was that s.17 – and any other provision of the Constitution Act 1867 – could only be altered by a two-stage – or, more precisely, a '*Two Act*' – legislative process. The first Act would *in express terms* have to state that it was enacted to permit (by a subsequent Act) amendment or repeal of the relevant provision of the Constitution Act. Thereafter the legislature could enact whatever policy it wished to address the issue concerned, which issue would – consequent upon the first Act's passage – have lost its 'constitutional' status. Cooper did not accept that both steps could be taken in one statute, irrespective of the clarity of the language that a single statute might use.

To put the point more abstractly, Cooper contended that the terms of the 1867 Act were 'fundamental' or – as his counsel was eventually to put it – 'organic law'; that they

---

[18] Murphy (1978) op cit p 250.
[19] Cooper presented his case as resting on a matter of constitutional principle. That it was initiated very shortly after Kidston torpedoed Cooper's ambition to become Lieutenant-Governor – over legislation in force for several years – might suggest Cooper was also motivated by personal pique. Cooper's entry in the *Australian Dictionary of Biography* suggests he was a prickly character with an exaggerated sense of self-importance; see http://adb.anu.edu.au/biography/cooper-sir-pope-alexander-5771.
[20] Bolton op cit pp 210–11.
[21] 1 Geo III c 23.

were in normative terms superior to 'ordinary' (Queensland) legislation. The superiority was of a very weak, procedural kind. It was not protected by a requirement of enhanced majorities in either house (as per s.9) or a specified timespan. All that was required was that the first Act's text be explicit in confirming that the Act was intended to permit repeal or modification of a particular 'constitutional' provision contained in the 1867 Act. A second Act, drafted in terms which expressly modified the particular provision, could then be passed.

Cooper's presumption seems to have been that governments would be less willing to promote bills that altered 'constitutional' principles – and Assembly and Council members would be less likely to pass such bills – if ministers and legislators were required candidly to acknowledge their intentions and so risk encountering hostile press and public attention. The argument might be thought to have merit in terms of political theory, but it is prima facie a curious one from a legal perspective, in several senses.

The first is its obvious inconsistency with the doctrine of implied repeal. We saw in chapter two that the doctrine was firmly established as a matter of British constitutional law by the time the New South Wales Act 1855 was enacted.[22] It also seems tolerably clear that this is what was meant by Russell when promoting what became s.4 [BAA] of that Act, in which the 'manner' of lawmaking was presumed to be bicameral bare majoritarianism by express or implied repeal.

The doctrine had not been shaken later in the nineteenth century. It had been clearly restated in English courts on several occasions when optimistic litigants had raised fanciful arguments against it;[23] and there is no reason to doubt that its restatement in *In re Williams*[24] was not authoritative in the early 1900s:

> Now, it is clear that the provisions of an earlier Act may be revoked or abrogated in particular cases by a subsequent Act, either from the express language used being addressed to that particular point, or from implication or inference from the language used.

Application of the doctrine in any given case is, of course, dependent upon the court finding an inconsistency between two statutory provisions.[25] But Cooper's argument was couched at the level of grand principle. His contention was that the laws enacted in the Constitution Act 1867 were not only immune to implied repeal, but that the express repeal needed to amend them had to be contained in an Act *passed prior to and separate from* the amendments themselves.[26] Cooper apparently considered the argument applicable to the entirety of the 1867 Act, irrespective of the political significance of the provision.

---

[22] Pp 48–52 above.

[23] cf the House of Lords' judgment in *Garnett v Bradley* (1878) 3 App Cas 944, especially 952 (Lord Hatherley): *Conservators of the River Thames v Hall* (1868) Law Rep 3 C P 415.

[24] (1887) 36 Ch D 573, 578 (North J).

[25] It was on this point, rather than the correctness of the doctrine per se, that most 'implied repeal cases were argued. See *Churchwardens and Overseers of West Ham v Fourth City Mutual Building Society and Another* [1892] 1 QB 654, 658 (Smith J): "The test of whether there has been a repeal by implication by subsequent legislation is this: Are the provisions of a later Act so inconsistent with, or repugnant to, the provisions of an earlier Act that the two cannot stand together? In which case 'Leges posteriores contrarias abrogant.'"

[26] The departure from the ordinary lawmaking process would be slightly more than just linguistic (ie just requiring express rather than implied repeal or alteration) since two separate Acts would be required. Cooper did not seem to dispute, however, that the two Acts could be passed in (very) quick succession (even perhaps on the same day).

The second curiosity is that Cooper's 'Two Act' thesis has no obvious *textual* root. In principle, a 'Two Act' requirement could be a 'manner and form' provision within CLVA 1865 s.5 (ie a variation of Palmer and Collier's 'special majority' concept).[27] But s.5 extended only to measures 'establishing, abolishing and reconstituting courts' and those affecting the 'the constitution, powers, and procedure' of a colony's legislature, rather than to all 'constitutional' matters.[28] So, even if a s.5 provision requiring a 'Two Act' process had been enacted by either the Imperial Parliament or the Queensland legislature – which it had not – it would not be relevant to the specific question in issue in Cooper's case (unless one accepted the prima facie outlandish proposition that requiring judges to pay income tax amounted to 'establishing, abolishing or reconstituting' a court).

Nor was there any textual base within the Constitution Act 1867 for Cooper's argument. S.9 (and the by then repealed s.10)[29] could credibly be seen as impliedly distinguishing between 'ordinary' and 'organic/fundamental' law, but did so through the 'two-thirds majority', 'reservation' and 'laying before' provisos, not by a 'Two Act' mechanism, and was of course applicable only to ('such') constitutional measures concerning the Council. It might be contended that s.2 of the 1867 Act and/or cl.22 of the 1859 Order – the general grants of legislative authority[30] – had an effect equivalent to CLVA 1865 s.5 in empowering the Legislature to impose 'manner and form' requirements in respect of all matters of Queensland law. But even if that argument was correct legally, it was a power that had never actually been used. The 1867 Act had been passed with virtually no legislative debate,[31] and there is no evidential basis to assume that either Cockle and Lilley qua the Act's drafters or members of either the Assembly or Council, when voting for its enactment, regarded *all* of its terms as 'different' in any legally significant sense from any other Queensland statute.

There was certainly *precedent in political practice* to support Cooper's argument. As noted in chapter two, legislators in New South Wales in 1857 had (seemingly unanimously) considered that a 'Two Act' process was required to repeal the two-thirds clauses.[32] Within Queensland, the obvious reference point is what had happened in 1871 when the Legislature passed the Constitution Act Amendment Act 1871 to remove the special majority provision in s.10 of the Constitution Act 1867 relating to electoral apportionment. That Act was very clearly part of a deliberate 'Two Act' strategy, the second part of which was the electoral reform legislation of 1872.[33] But the fact that the Legislature might have chosen, as a matter of political morality, to proceed in that way did not mean it was legally required to do so.[34]

Nor had Lilley and Cockle given any indication in 1867 when presenting the Act qua bill to the legislature that the Constitution Act was to have a normative status superior

---

[27] Pp 101–105 above.
[28] Pp 112–114 above.
[29] Pp 127–128 above.
[30] Pp 125–126 above.
[31] Pp 123–127 above.
[32] Pp 56–58 above.
[33] Pp 127–132 above.
[34] The 'Two Act' process had also been presumed to be required by New South Wales legislators when repealing the two-thirds clauses (pp 56–58 above), although the Electoral Act 1858 (p 60 above) did not expressly state that it was amending the initial allocation of Assembly constituencies in s.13 of sch.1 of the 1855 Act.

to other legislation. Lilley had explicitly grouped the Constitution Bill with three other measures, referring to them en bloc as the 'political Acts'.[35]

There were, however, political precedents supporting the assertion that an Act altering the Constitution should be entitled a 'Constitution Act Amendment Act'. In 1890, the Legislature passed such an Act fixing the maximum period between Assembly elections at three years.[36] A similarly titled Act was passed in 1896 to provide for payment of salaries to Assembly members.[37] However, neither measure was part of a 'Two Act' scheme. The desired substantive change was enacted – expressly – within the text of the relevant Constitution Act Amendment Act itself. And again, a legislative choice as a matter of political morality to use express repeal does not mean the Legislature was legally compelled to do so.

Similarly, the Constitution Act made provision for only two Supreme Court judges.[38] Yet the Supreme Court Act 1867 – which received assent on the same day as the Constitution Act – permitted the appointment of three judges.[39] That number was increased to five by the Supreme Court Act 1889. Neither increase was part of a 'Two Act' scheme, and neither Supreme Court Act gave any textual indication that it was amending the Constitution Act. Relatedly, legislation has also been passed which – without making any reference to the Constitution Act – authorised appointment of Supreme Court judges on a temporary basis.[40]

Morgan's coalition government had evidently anticipated Cooper's objection to paying income tax – if not his broader constitutional arguments – as it included a provision in the Income Tax Declaratory Act 1905 (s.2) which said:

> 2. It is hereby declared that each of the persons for the time being holding the following offices in the state of Queensland, namely, the office of Chief Justice, Judge of the Supreme Court, Judge of District Courts … is and always has been chargeable with and liable to pay income tax in respect of his official salary under and in accordance with the provisions of the laws imposing a tax on income.

On Cooper's argument, s.2 would be irrelevant, as it was not preceded by a 'constitutional' Act amending or repealing s.17.

The position of the Queensland government (Kidston's Labour administration) was – assuming the colonial legislation in issue was not repugnant to an Imperial statute – that, save in circumstances where Imperial or colonial law prescribed particular lawmaking procedures as necessary to achieve certain specified outcomes,[41] the Legislature could

---

[35] P 125 above.
[36] http://www.austlii.edu.au/au/legis/qld/hist_act/caaao189054vn3366.pdf. The period had been five years per s.29 of the 1867 Act. There is no indication in the Assembly debates that any members (including Griffith) considered two Acts necessary; second reading QLAD 17 July 1890 p274; committee QLAD 30 July 1890 p431; third reading QLAD 5 August 1890 p462.
[37] http://www.austlii.edu.au/au/legis/qld/hist_act/caaao189660vn5366.pdf. This initiative was promoted by Nelson's government.
[38] Somewhat obliquely perhaps, in that Schedule A's civil list provisions identified only two judicial salaries.
[39] The Constitution Act 1867 was No 38; the Supreme Court Act was No 31. One might take this to mean that the Supreme Court Act was the 'earlier' of the two statutes.
[40] The Supreme Court Act 1892.
[41] Cl.22, for example, specified that any bill introducing an elective element into the Council be laid before the Commons and Lords for 30 days before receiving the royal assent; see p 64 above.

enact any law through its usual simple majority in both houses procedure and any such law would override any existing inconsistent statutory provision, whether in the Constitution Act 1867 or any other legislation. There was no need for provisions of the Constitution Act to be repealed or amended before a second measure could be passed that was inconsistent with their terms, nor need any express reference be made to the Constitution Act in any such Act. The government adhered wholeheartedly to the (in the colonial context) rebuttable (but not on these facts rebutted) presumption that the doctrine of implied repeal prevailed.

In the Lower Queensland Courts

The litigation began in December 1906 as an action for debt against Cooper by the state Commissioner of Income Tax for non-payment of Cooper's 1905–06 tax bill, some £77 19s 4d. The first hearing was in the City Small Debts Court, before a police magistrate, William Yaldwyn, who found for Cooper without giving a reasoned judgment.[42] William was also both a pastoralist and a Council member between 1868 and 1877, before being appointed as a police magistrate. The *Cooper* case was among the last he heard. Yaldwyn had been served with a compulsory retirement notice effective on 31 December 1906 by Kidston's Attorney-General, William Blair,[43] in September 1906, as Yaldwyn was now 70 years old, the then statutory retirement age for magistrates. Blair's retirement letter to Yaldwyn was politely drawn,[44] and makes no suggestion of anti-Labour sentiment on Yaldwyn's part, but one might wonder if the unreasoned judgment in *Cooper* was a party political last hurrah from a magistrate who likely had little empathy with Kidston's governmental programme. Whatever the basis of Yaldwyn's judgment, the matter was appealed by the government to a single judge in the District Court, where it was heard on 8 February 1907.[45]

The judge was Granville Miller. Miller had grown up in England, attending Cambridge University and being called to the English Bar. He emigrated to Queensland in 1866 and, after practising as a Crown prosecutor, was appointed as a district judge in 1882. He seems to have had no explicit party political affiliations or sympathies, and was widely considered an able, assiduous judge. He was still in post when he died in 1910.[46]

---

[42] www.revolvy.com/main/index.php?s=William%20Henry%20Yaldwyn&uid=1575. Waldwyn senior was the man who moved the 1861 Council motion calling for the Council to be placed on an elective footing, an initiative taken for conservative rather than liberal reasons; Bernays op cit p208; p 140 above.
[43] Of whom more is said at Pp 229–30 below.
[44] Reproduced in the *Queensland Times* 15 September 1906, http://trove.nla.gov.au/newspaper/article/124378903.
[45] There is a full account of the District Court hearing in *The Telegraph (Brisbane)* 9 February 1907 p13, http://trove.nla.gov.au/newspaper/article/175277634. The summary of and quotations from the hearing are taken from this source.
[46] http://adb.anu.edu.au/biography/miller-granville-george-4436. See also the obituaries in *BC* 7 July 1910, http://trove.nla.gov.au/newspaper/article/19643976; 8 July 1910, http://trove.nla.gov.au/newspaper/article/19643727.

Queensland's case was argued by Lionel Lukin.[47] Born in Queensland in 1868, Lukin joined the Bar in 1890 after a brief career in the mining industry. Lukin developed a wide-ranging practice and had no obvious party political affiliations. He was later appointed (in 1910) to the Queensland Supreme Court by the (third) Kidston government.

Cooper's case was led by Edwyn Lilley. Lilley was formerly a controversial figure at the Queensland Bar because of suspicions that he received inappropriately favourable professional treatment whenever he appeared before his father, Charles Lilley, the former Premier who held office as Chief Justice between 1879 and 1891.[48] Charles Lilley had veered radically to the political left after retirement,[49] but his son, while occasionally dabbling in electoral politics,[50] had no such evident inclinations. Edwyn's reputation had sufficiently recovered for him to be appointed KC in 1910.[51]

In the District Court, Lilley's submissions were directed primarily to contending that subjecting judges to income tax was an indirect government attempt ('juggling', as he styled it) to subvert judicial independence by reducing judges' salaries:

> [I]ncome tax was a reduction. It was juggling with words to say that it was not. Was it not a reduction to pay a man £2500 a year with one hand and take away £100 with the other. If it were admitted that tax to the extent of 1d could be imposed, the limit of taxation knew no bounds, and the judge could be taxed up to the full amount of his salary.

Miller seemed unreceptive to this point;[52] he could not see how an income tax statute of general application could be regarded as being targeted at judges as a distinct group, nor as attacking their independence: "in the slightest degree". Lilley also invoked *Deakin*[53] and *D'Emden*[54] to bolster the proposition that judges should not be subject to income tax. Miller considered those authorities irrelevant, even if they retained any force after *Webb v Outtrim*,[55] as being concerned with the relationship between the Commonwealth and the states rather than purely internal state matters.

In grander theoretical terms, Lilley rooted the independence of the judiciary concept in the Constitution Act 1867, which he referred to as: "the charter of the people's liberties", and as such protected by the 'Two Act' entrenchment principle. Miller apparently saw no merit in Cooper's constitutional arguments. He accepted Lukin's submissions that 'ordinary' legislation would suffice for the purpose of establishing judges' liability to income tax, and concluded that the terms of the Income Tax Declaratory Act of 1905 settled the issue. Cooper was not deterred by defeat, and pursued an appeal before the State Supreme Court.

---

[47] http://adb.anu.edu.au/biography/lukin-lionel-oscar-7261.
[48] http://adb.anu.edu.au/biography/lilley-sir-charles-4020. See the discussion of one such notorious case in Gibbs (1987) 'A nineteenth century cause célèbre: Queensland Investment and Land Mortgage Company v Grimley' *Royal Historical Society of Queensland Journal* 73.
[49] Gibbney (1978) 'Charles Lilley: an uncertain democrat' in Murphy and Joyce op cit.
[50] http://trove.nla.gov.au/ndp/del/article/3670607.
[51] For a brief biography, see *BC* 19 November 1910 p5, http://trove.nla.gov.au/ndp/del/article/19665261.
[52] Miller's judgment is reproduced as fn 1 in the subsequent Supreme Court judgment; *In re the Income Tax (Consolidated Acts, 1902–1904, and the Income Tax Declaratory Act of 1905* [1907] ST R Qd 110.
[53] Pp 188–191 above.
[54] Pp 185–88 above.
[55] Pp 191–195 above. The High Court did not decide *Baxter* until 7 June 1907; pp 196–199 above.

In the Queensland Supreme Court

The Court heard argument on 12 March 1907 and delivered judgment the next day. Its brief (unanimous) opinion was written by Real J.[56] Real was appointed to the Court in 1890 by the Griffith administration. The son of Irish immigrants, Real left school at 12 and studied successfully for the Bar after periods as a carpenter and railworker. He built a flourishing practice in various fields before his appointment to the bench. Real did not have overt party political sympathies, and had never sought elected political office. He was joined in *Cooper* by Chubb and Power JJ.

Unlike Real, Chubb had pursued a political career.[57] Chubb, whose father was an English émigré solicitor, had also qualified as a solicitor before being called to the Bar. Politically, he was a protégé of McIlwraith's, who arranged a safe Assembly seat for him and appointed him Attorney-General in 1883. Chubb left the Assembly in 1890 to accept a Court seat, where he served until 1921.

Virgil Power was the Court's first native-born Queenslander.[58] Born to affluent Irish parents, Power studied at Trinity College Dublin, and was called to the English and Irish Bars before returning to practise in Queensland. After 20 years in practice, much spent as Crown prosecutor, Power was appointed to the Court in 1895 during Nelson's premiership. He did not hold political office, and remained on the Court until retiring in 1910.

Lilley was joined as counsel for Cooper by GW Power, who made many of the oral submissions. Power had come to the (Victorian) Bar in 1890 with an exceptionally distinguished scholastic record. He relocated to Brisbane that year, and joined Byrnes' chambers. He was active in Ministerialist party politics, and shortly after the Supreme Court hearing stood unsuccessfully as a Philpite in the 1907 elections. He died of pneumonia in 1910 aged only 45.[59]

Real's opinion covers barely a page of the state reports.[60] In respect of Cooper's 'Two Acts' argument, the judgment relied entirely on a passage from *Webb v Outtrim*:

> Every Act of the Victorian Council and Assembly requires the assent of the Crown, but when it is assented to, it becomes an Act of Parliament as much as any Imperial Act, though the elements by which it is authorized are different. If, indeed, it were repugnant to the provisions of any Act of Parliament extending to the Colony, it might be inoperative to the extent of its repugnancy (see the Colonial Laws Validity Act 1865), but, with this exception, no authority exists by which its validity can be questioned or impeached.[61]

Real continued:

> So far as we can see, a Queensland Act is within Queensland, of like force as a Victorian Act within Victoria, and we cannot discover anything in the Income Tax Acts ... repugnant to any Imperial Act extending to this state.[62]

---

[56] http://adb.anu.edu.au/biography/real-patrick-8169.
[57] http://adb.anu.edu.au/biography/chubb-charles-edward-3207.
[58] www.sclqld.org.au/judicial-papers/judicial-profiles/profiles/vpower.
[59] https://trove.nla.gov.au/newspaper/article/19635761#. He does not appear to be related to Virgil Power.
[60] There is no account of counsels' submission in the reports, beyond a suggestion they reproduced those made before District Judge Miller; [1907] ST R Qd 110, 111. There is a long account in *The Telegraph (Brisbane)* 12 March 1907, http://nla.gov.au/nla.news-article178243281.
[61] [1907] AC 81, 89.
[62] [1907] ST R Qd 110,t 113.

So peremptory a dismissal did not lead Cooper C to abandon his case. A month later, the matter was before the High Court of Australia.

In the High Court

Griffith, Barton, O'Connor, Isaacs and Higgins delivered judgment in *Cooper v Commissioner of Income Tax (Qld)*[63] on 28 June 1907 (shortly after Kidston's success in the May election and three weeks after judgment was given in *Baxter*), having had heard argument on 23 and 24 April.[64]

Counsel and Submissions

Neither party had changed either counsel or argument for the High Court hearing.[65] On 23 April, Griffith CJ set the tone for a discursive exchange about the origins of the legislature's power by asking:

> I should like to know by what authority the Legislature of Queensland passed that statute called the Constitution Act of 1867? I have never yet been able to find out ... It seems a singular thing that the power of the Legislature to make laws was conferred upon it by itself.[66]

No clear answer was offered ether by counsel or other members of the Court to that large question, although one might have thought cl.22 of the 1859 Order provided that source.[67] Much of the subsequent exchanges was directed at deciding whether income tax – a tax of general application – could credibly be regarded as effecting any reduction in a judge's salary. Despite Lilley's continuing attachment to his 'juggling' metaphor, all the judges rejected that proposition.

Judgment

The five judges agreed that a generally applicable income tax statute was consistent with s.17:

> The object of the section on its face is to secure the due payment of the salaries according to the terms on which they are allotted, and as long as the commissions of those entitled to them remain in force. That is what is said, and I think it is all that is meant ... I have no doubt that the judicial independence was meant to be protected by that and subsequent legislation so far that even a sovereign Parliament would not dream of reducing a Judge's salary during his tenure of office. But the ordinary taxation of the state stands on a different footing. It is imposed on all who come within the area prescribed for taxation, whatever their rank or

---

[63] [1907] HCA 27, (1907) 4 CLR 1304.

[64] *BC* 23 April 1907 p3, https://trove.nla.gov.au/newspaper/article/19502999; 24 April 1907 p3, https://trove.nla.gov.au/newspaper/article/19472088.

[65] It does not seem that Lukin at any point in any hearing referred to previous one-Act reforms of the Constitution Act to counter Cooper's argument.

[66] Griffith was called to the Queensland Bar the year the Constitution Act was passed. Given his precocity as both lawyer and political journalist, it seems unlikely that he had not closely followed the measure's enactment, although he was on a grand tour of Europe throughout 1866.

[67] Pp 64–65 above.

occupation. It is raised for revenue purposes, and one does not think of a Colonial Treasurer trying to levy a tax on the whole people, yielding many hundreds of thousands of pounds, for the mere purpose of vindictively obtaining a few pounds from one or half a dozen Judges. To reduce the salaries of officiating Judges is, or may be, an attack on their independence – a punishment for its exercise. To subject them, in common with all their fellow citizens, to a general tax, is not likely to be anything of the kind …[68]

That conclusion is ostensibly difficult to square with Griffith's conclusions (for a unanimous Court) in *D'Emden* and *Deakin*[69] that subjecting a salary to tax was a diminution. It may be that Griffith's concern to promulgate the implied immunities doctrine led him to find a 'diminution' so that he had a precise factual peg on which to hang his broader theory; but it is surprising that Griffith did not confront this issue squarely in *Cooper*. Cooper was unlikely to have been dismayed by that conclusion. His primary objective was to have the High Court explore the soundness of his constitutional reasoning; on that score he was not disappointed.

Griffith determined the point wholly in Cooper's favour. Answering the question he had raised during submissions, he reasoned that since the Constitution Act 1867 (Qld) derived directly from the 1859 Order, which, in turn, was rooted in an Imperial statute (the New South Wales Constitution Act 1855 s.7 [BAA]),[70] the 1867 Act was properly regarded as Queensland's 'fundamental' law:

> The distinction between what are called in jurisprudence "fundamental laws" and other laws is, no doubt, unfamiliar to English lawyers. Nor under the Constitution of England is there any such distinction. The Parliament of the UK is supreme, and can make any laws it thinks fit, and the question whether a law once passed is beyond the competency of the legislature or not cannot arise. If, therefore, a later is inconsistent with an earlier law, the later must prevail. But in States governed by a written Constitution this doctrine has no application.[71]

Cl.22's literal meaning[72] that the Legislature could make laws in' all cases whatsoever' had to be conditioned by this contextual consideration:

> … [T]hese words must be read with the rest of the Order in Council, and clearly did not authorize the legislature, while the provisions of the Constitution remained unaltered, to make any law inconsistent with it. They referred to the scope of authority under the Constitution. The re-enactment of the provisions of paragraph *ii.* in the Act of 1867 did not make any difference in this respect. The powers of the legislature still depended upon the Order in Council, and not upon its own restatement of those powers … I think that the mere re-enactment of the provisions of the original Constitution *totidem verbis* did not alter the fundamental character of the provisions themselves, which still took effect as substituted in, and, so to say, forming part of, the Order in Council. In my opinion, therefore, the legislature could not after the Act of 1867, any more than before, disregard the provisions of the Constitution as existing for the time being, so as to be able to pass a law inconsistent with them, without first altering the Constitution itself …[73]

---

[68] (1907) 4 CLR 1304, 1319–20 (Barton).
[69] P 186 and p 190 above.
[70] Pp 63–64 above.
[71] (1907) 4 CLR 1304, 1313–14.
[72] Quoted in full at p 64 above.
[73] (1907) 4 CLR 1304, 1314. Griffith (unsurprisingly) saw no need to recall that this apparently fundamental point had not occurred to him – or any other Assembly member – during the passage of the Constitution Act Amendment Act 1890; p 218 above.

Griffith's treatment of the point was perhaps rather cursory. He quoted cl.22 in full, but did not address the significance of the phrase (emphasis added) that:

> The Legislature of the Colony of Queensland shall have full power and authority from time to time to make laws altering or repealing all or any of the provisions of this Order in Council *in the same manner as any other laws* for the good government of the Colony …

The reference to laws amending the Order being made 'in the same manner' as any other laws might be thought an obvious obstacle to Cooper's contentions. Cl.22 draws no distinction between 'constitutional' laws and 'other laws'. Indeed, it appears in express terms to treat all laws in just the same way irrespective of their substantive content. And that conclusion is reinforced if one traces cl.22's lineage back to s.4 [BAA] of the 1855 Act and from there back to the 'intention' revealed in Russell's despatch to Denison, and to the consistency of that intention with the orthodox doctrine of implied repeal.[74]

Griffith's reasoning seems unconvincing. Even if one accepts that the 1867 Act was tantamount to an Imperial statute – and that contention is itself odd – the Act does not contain, and nor did the Order, any reference to a 'Two Act' amendment process. One might wonder if Griffith's conclusion was driven by his (here unvoiced) fondness for American-influenced constitutional analysis (so firmly criticised by the Privy Council in *Webb v Outtrim*),[75] ie that if a constitution did not provide express protection for 'fundamental law' it should be read as doing so implicitly. Griffith referred at the start of his judgment to the State Supreme Court's reliance on *Webb*, but did not return to *Webb* to explain why its reasoning was not pertinent in this case.

The Chief Justice did, however, take some care to refer throughout his judgment to 'the Constitution' rather than 'the Constitution Act 1867'. He noted that in 1867 the Legislature had set out the provisions of 'the Constitution': "in the *form* of an Act";[76] the reference to 'form' was presumably made to reinforce his conclusion that the *substance* of 'the Constitution' was in some normative sense superior to an ordinary 'Act'.

Griffith's judgments in the implied immunities cases indicated that he was not a judicial prisoner of interpretive literalism. In those cases, however, his 'constructive enlargement'[77] of the 1900 Act could with some defensibility be rooted both in the 'history' of its enactment and in particular the presumption that its meaning be informed by US jurisprudence (and with rather less defensibility in his own role in drafting the text). Neither factor was pertinent in the context of Queensland's Constitution Act 1867. The Act had no Queensland history to speak of; such history as it had was traceable to the 1855 Act and was informed only by British constitutional orthodoxies.

As noted in chapter six, Clark had dismissed Madden's judgment in *Wollaston's Case* as: "full of false history, bad political science, bad political economy, bad logic and bad law".[78] Griffith's opinion in *Cooper* perhaps merits similar characterisation. His analysis

---

[74] Respectively pp 46, 48 and 49 above.
[75] Pp 193–94 above.
[76] (1907) 4 CLR 1304–1313; emphasis added.
[77] P 152 above.
[78] P 184 above.

nonetheless seemed authoritative to Isaacs, whose two-line judgment simply concurred with the Chief Justice's opinion.[79]

O'Connor, also concurring,[80] set up the issue in concise terms:

> The whole controversy really turns on the question whether the Constitution Act 1867 does stand in the same position as any other Act of the Queensland legislature, or whether it is in reality a fundamental law which, although capable of being amended by that legislature, binds it until amended, just as a Constitution embodied in an Imperial Act would bind it.[81]

Unlike Griffith and Isaacs however, O'Connor found the answer to the substantive question before the Court question in the interactive effect of cl.22 and CLVA 1865 s.2.[82] O'Connor's reasoning seems rather confused. He accepted that cl.22 empowered the Legislature: "to repeal or amend any or all of the provisions of the Order in Council". But this ostensibly unrestrained power could not be used:

> [T]o treat the Constitution as non-existent ... [nor] to abolish the constitution altogether nor to substitute for the Constitution under the Order a body of provisions which, although embodied in a Constitution Act, gave no rights and no security whatever either in respect of forms of Government or legislative bodies or officers. It was a power to substitute for the fundamental law of the Constitution under the Order in Council another fundamental law in the form of a Constitution in whole or in part of Queensland's own making, and which, when made and while it existed, would be as binding on the Queensland Parliament as the original Constitution under the Order.[83]

O'Connor then held that because the Constitution Act 1867 was itself an exercise of the power given in cl.22, in turn derived from Imperial legislation, its terms should be regarded as having the 'force and effect' of an Act of (the Imperial) Parliament for the purposes of the CLVA 1865 s.2.[84] Any subsequent Queensland Act 'repugnant to' a term of 'the Constitution' would therefore be – per s.2 – 'void and inoperative'.

The logic of that line of argument seemed rather to be undermined by O'Connor's subsequent observation that, notwithstanding the apparently superior status of 'the Constitution' to other Queensland statutes, the Legislature could repeal or amend any of its terms if it followed Cooper's suggested 'Two Act' process:

> The position generally may be thus stated. The Queensland Parliament may repeal or alter any portion of its Constitution, and when the repeal or alteration has taken effect, that portion

---

[79] Isaacs reiterated his agreement at greater length two years later in *Baxter v Ah Way* (1909) 8 CLR 626), a case which in essence repeated in respect of the Commonwealth Parliament the inapplicability of the non-delegation principle to New South Wales' Legislature articulated by the Privy Council in *Apollo Candle* (pp – above). Isaacs's comment at (1909) 8 CLR 626, 643, which was at best obiter and arguably wholly irrelevant to the issue arising in *Ah Way* (neither Griffith, O'Connor nor Higgins made any reference to *Cooper*; Barton did not sit), was: "... the power of the legislature must depend upon the terms of the Constitution as it exists at the given moment. It is not a sound argument that, because a change might be deliberately made by Parliament in a Constitution, therefore any ordinary Act whatever may be passed, though in contravention of constitutional provisions as they stand. The case of Cooper v. Commissioner of Income Tax ... is a clear authority against such a contention." The obvious inference of the passage is that Isaacs accepted 'Two Act entrenchment' for Queensland's 'organic law' was a legally enforceable constitutional 'provision'.
[80] Albeit unlike Griffith, O'Connor referred with similar frequency both to 'the Constitution' and to 'the Constitution Act 1867'.
[81] (1907) 4 CLR 1304, 1327.
[82] Pp 150–151 above.
[83] (1907) 4 CLR 1304, 1328.
[84] Pp 107–108 above.

is as if it never had been. But so long as it exists no Act conflicting with it can be passed. In other words, before an Act can be passed taking away any right given by the Constitution, the Queensland Parliament must first repeal the portion of the Constitution which gives the right.[85]

Barton's treatment of the broad constitutional question was also truncated: the greater part of his judgment addressed the narrow issue of whether the income tax legislation breached s.17. Like Griffith, Isaacs and O'Connor, Barton was persuaded by Cooper's argument. He accepted that the Legislature could alter the terms of the Constitution Act 1867 and the 1859 Order, and could do so through the 'normal' legislative process. Until it had exercised this power, however, the legislature had no power to enact provisions inconsistent with the terms of either instrument. In essence, such an Act would deprive a particular value of its previously 'constitutional status' and so render it amenable to alteration (presumably impliedly as well as expressly) by subsequent legislation. The first Act was a 'condition precedent' to the validity of the second one:

> Legislation, which could not be undertaken at all without the antecedent authority of the fundamental law, cannot overstep the bounds set for it by that law and yet stand good. Before it can avail, the bounds must have been lawfully extended. That is a condition precedent, even if the makers of the disputed law had power to make the extension themselves. They cannot omit to make it, and at the same time proceed as if it had been made.[86]

What Barton did not, however, do at any point was explain how it was that the terms of 'the Constitution' [Act 1867] had acquired that 'fundamental law' status. He did not identify any source for that conclusion in Imperial legislation or the 1859 Order. Nor did he cite any previous judicial authority to support it. He also did not cross-refer to any of the reasoning deployed by Griffith or O'Connor.[87] He did, however – like his colleagues – consistently refer to 'the Constitution' rather than to 'the Constitution Act 1867'. The inference perhaps was that Barton et al had implicitly assumed that because the terms of the 1867 Act had been styled as 'the Constitution' they were necessarily distinct from and normatively superior to 'ordinary legislation'.

Higgins was the only judge who considered it unnecessary, given the court's holding on the narrow question of whether levying an income tax on judges breached s.17, formally to address the broader constitutional question. He nonetheless indicated that he agreed with Griffith's analysis on that point:

> I assume also that, notwithstanding the exceptionally wide and very peculiar powers contained in par. xxii. of the Order in Council, of altering the Constitution, the legislature of Queensland has no power to pass a law forbidden by the Constitution as it stands, unless and until the Constitution has been definitely so altered, with His Majesty's consent, as to give the legislature power to pass such a law.[88]

And like Griffith and Barton, Higgins consistently referred in his judgment to 'the Constitution' and not to 'the Constitution Act 1867'.

---

[85] (1907) 4 CLR 1304, 1329.
[86] ibid 1330.
[87] Although neither of those judges had offered an obvious source to sustain it.
[88] (1907) 4 CLR 1304, 1331.

The judgment fully vindicated Cooper's argument. However, the decision did not excite much interest in the Queensland press. The *BC* offered a short summary without any editorial comment.[89] Given that the government had 'won' the case, it could not appeal to the Privy Council.[90] Cooper had in strict terms lost, but did not press the matter further, perhaps because the High Court's decision on the 'organic/ordinary' law issue was not obviously reconcilable with the Privy Council's comments in *Webb v Outtrim*.[91] Given the fierce criticism *Webb* made of the High Court's implied instrumentalities doctrine, there would have been credible grounds for believing that the 'organic/ordinary' law analysis might receive similarly short shrift. For the short term, however, the doctrine was 'good' law.

There is an ostensibly surprising absentee from the *Cooper* litigation. It evidently did not occur to any party, their counsel or the judges who sat at any stage of the litigation that Pope Cooper's theory was prima facie bluntly inconsistent with the principle enunciated by Selborne in *Burah* 30 years earlier.[92] That principle seemed to be that Queensland's Legislature could enact any measure within its substantive competence in the same way as the British Parliament enacted legislation, unless one could find in the 1855 Act, the 1859 order or the 1867 Act 'an *express* restriction or condition' on its capacity to do so.[93] Such condition and restrictions had to have an explicit legislative base: "it is not for any Court of Justice ... to enlarge constructively those conditions and restrictions".[94] In accepting Cooper's argument, an argument espousing a 'restriction' which had no such explicit base, the High Court appeared to have done precisely what Selborne had identified in *Burah* as quite unacceptable. *Burah* was perhaps overlooked because it was perceived as a case solely concerned with the non-delegation point rather than as stating a principle of general application. Had Kidston been able to press the matter to the Privy Council, *Burah*'s significance might not have again been ignored.

The judgment also prompted a curious response from Arthur Berriedale Keith. The first edition of Keith's *Responsible government in the Dominions* was published in December 1908. Keith was by then regarded as an eminent commentator on colonial legal and political matters, and his status in that regard increased markedly in later years.[95] *Responsible government's* treatment of *Cooper* was puzzling. Keith cited the case as supporting the proposition that Queensland law drew a distinction between 'ordinary' and 'constitutional' (he did not say 'organic') legislation. However, he then observed that such a distinction could only arise where: "Imperial or local legislation

---

[89] http://trove.nla.gov.au/ndp/del/page/1557312.
[90] There was obviously no *inter se* issue here, so s.74 of the Constitution Act 1900 was inapplicable.
[91] Pp 193–95 above.
[92] Pp 152–153 above.
[93] [1878] AC 889, 914; emphasis added. Those measures were the 'instruments' (in the *Burah* sense) creating the legislature and its powers.
[94] ibid.
[95] Born in Edinburgh in 1879, Keith proved himself an outstanding scholar at both Edinburgh and Oxford universities. His initial field of expertise was Sanskrit and oriental studies, but he also took law degrees at Oxford and was called to the English Bar. After a brief period as a civil servant in the Colonial Office, Keith accepted an academic post at Edinburgh in 1914 as Professor of Sanskrit and subsequently maintained a prodigious output and profile on colonial constitutional law matters; see Shinn (2008) 'Keith, Arthur Berriedale' *ODNB*.

has established a special procedure in passing constitutional Acts".[96] Keith subsequently listed many such special procedures in various colonies which had an explicit statutory base.[97] It seemed, however, to escape his attention that the *Cooper* 'Two Act entrenchment' principle did not have such a textually precise legislative root.

Argument and judgment before the High Court had straddled the 1907 Assembly elections which saw Kidston returned as Premier. Chief Justice Cooper likely remained a source of irritation to Kidston's government, but after the election the Premier and the Queensland press had weightier matters to address.

III. The Constitution Act Amendment Act 1908 and the Parliamentary Bills Referendum Act 1908

Kidston's second administration pursued a reform agenda in both electoral and social policy terms which, while too centrist for Labour tastes, proved far too radical for many members of the Council, which vetoed several government bills, among them measures introducing wages boards for shop and factory workers. Chelmsford refused Kidston's requests to pack the Council with government supporters to facilitate passage of the bills, on the basis that Kidston's own party did not command an Assembly majority.[98] Even while the informal coalition with Labour remained viable, Kidston's government had no prospect of commanding even the bare Council majority needed to pass legislation, let alone the two-thirds majority apparently required by s.9 of the Constitution Act 1867 to alter the Council's composition. Kidston then resigned as Premier in November 1907. Controversially, Chelmsford refused to grant a dissolution and invited Philp to form a (short-lived) government, which, in turn, resigned in February 1908. The (February) 1908 election – fought primarily on the issue of the propriety of the Council blocking government bills – once again left Kidston as Premier of an informal coalition (with Labour) government.

Table 7.4 Queensland Legislative Assembly elections, 1908

Party	% vote	Seats	Change
Ministerialist	40.3	22	−7
Kidston	24.0	25	+1
Labour	29.8	22	+4
Independent	2.1	1	–
Country	3.6	2	+2

Kidston's route through the problem of an impasse between the Assembly and Council was a bill which proposed that if a bill was twice approved in the Assembly but twice rejected by the Council then it could be submitted to a referendum and, if approved,

---

[96] (1908) *Responsible government in the Dominions* p88.
[97] ibid pp 88–89.
[98] After the 1907 election, the Assembly's composition was Ministerialist 29; Kidston 24; Labour 18.

sent to the Governor for the royal assent without the Council's concurrence. The bill was subsequently enacted – with 'unanimous'[99] support in both houses – as the Parliamentary Bills Referendum Act 1908. That measure was, however, designed as the second stage of a two-part process of constitutional reform. The first stage, which Kidston had regarded as a vital step in securing the legality of his proposals to bypass the Council, took the form of the Constitution Act Amendment Act 1908 (hereafter CAAA 1908). This would be followed by the Parliamentary Bills Referendum Act 1908 (hereafter PBRA 1908), which would allow for overriding the Council's failure to pass a bill by a vote in a referendum.

Given the reason for Chelmsford's refusal to allow Kidston to swamp the Council in 1907, Kidston had little basis to think that any such request would be more successful in 1908 to secure the government even a simple, let alone a two-thirds, Council majority. (Kidstonites and Labour combined had just under two-thirds (47 of 72) of the seats in the Assembly, but Kidston's party had only 25 of those.) And while Kidston raised the threat of swamping as a last resort to achieve reform, his government's preferred route was rather more subtle.

The legal rationale underlying the Kidston government's legislative scheme was the presumption that while s.9 (specifically, s.9[1] and [2]) of the 1867 Act was an entrenching provision vis-à-vis the Council, s.9 itself was not expressly entrenched. Consequently, s.9 could be repealed or amended by simple majorities in the Assembly and Council, whereupon the existence or powers and/or composition of the Council could then also be altered by an Act attracting only simple majority support in each house.[100]

The strategy seems to some extent to have accepted and applied the High Court's endorsement of Cooper's 'Two Acts' thesis of constitutional reform. The first measure was explicitly styled as a Constitution Act Amendment Bill, which provided simply that:

1. This Act may be cited as the 'The Constitution Act Amendment Act of 1908' and shall be read with, and as an amendment of the 'Constitution Act of 1867', herein called the Principal Act.
2. In section nine of the Principal Act the first and second provisos shall be and the same are repealed.

The Constitution Act Amendment Act 1908

Responsibility for promoting the bill at Assembly second reading (on 18 March 1908)[101] was taken by Kidston's Attorney-General, James Blair. Blair was born in Queensland in 1870, and attended grammar school until he was 18. He was called to the Queensland Bar and in 1894 joined the chambers of the then Attorney-General, Byrnes (who Blair described as his 'hero', but whose conservative politics he did not embrace). Blair built a varied practice, before standing successfully as an Independent at the 1902 state

---

[99] The term is used guardedly for reasons fleshed out below.
[100] Which is, of course, the rationale accepted in New South Wales in the 1857 repeal of the two-thirds clauses; pp 56–58 above.
[101] QLAD 18 March 1908 p163 et seq, www.parliament.qld.gov.au/documents/hansard/1908/1908_03_18_A.pdf.

elections. His political views were broadly Fabian and reformist, and, given the dearth of lawyers in Labour ranks, he was appointed as Attorney-General in the Morgan/Browne coalition administration. Although Blair did not formally join the Labour Party, Kidston kept him in that post during the first Kidston government, and reappointed him after the 1908 election.[102]

In the Assembly

Blair candidly accepted that this bill was a precursor to a bill to provide for a referendum as a means to overcome Council obstruction of bills that passed the Assembly.[103] He was equally clear (if somewhat optimistic as to Chelmsford's likely response) that if this bill was not enacted the government would proceed with plans to pack the Council to create a pro-government two-thirds majority. Blair devoted some of his speech to justifying the bill (and the proposed subsequent referendum bill) in political terms, on the basis that since both the Labour Party and the Kidston Party had fought the 1908 election principally on the issue of removing the Council's veto powers, there was a clear majority among 'the people'[104] supporting the government's proposal. He drew on two conservative English authorities – Walter Bagehot and Professor Dicey – to make the political points that Queensland's Council, like the House of Lords in Britain, should function as a subordinate chamber to the Assembly when the Assembly majority had a clear electoral mandate; and that if the Council declined to accept that role it was entirely proper that it be swamped with government supporters.[105]

However, the greater part of Blair's speech addressed legal matters. Blair took the 1859 Order as his starting point, specifically cl.22. His immediate cue for doing so was Griffith's judgment in *Cooper*.[106] The point that Blair took pains to extract from his review of Queensland's constitutional history was that the two-thirds majority provision in s.9 of the 1867 Act was not copied from the Order in Council: it was a creation of the Queensland Parliament, not of the Imperial Parliament:

> I want hon. Members to recollect this – to be certain of this – because it is the very basis on which we rest our position in this matter. There is no restriction by the Imperial Authority, and it is not until we come to an Act passed by the Queensland Legislature that we find anything related to a two-thirds majority. I hope this will serve to dispel the idea that a two-thirds majority is a safeguard introduced by the Imperial Order in Council and preserved by the Constitution Act of 1867.[107]

---

[102] http://adb.anu.edu.au/biography/blair-sir-james-william-5266.
[103] *QLAD* 18 March 1908 p 163.
[104] ibid.
[105] ibid pp 166–67. Blair quoted from p349 of the 4th edition of Dicey's *Law of the Constitution*: "If there is a difference of opinion between the House of Lords and the House of Commons, the House of Lords ought, at some point, not definitely fixed, to give way, and should the Peers not yield, and the House of Commons continue to enjoy to confidence of the country, it becomes the duty of the Crown or of its responsible advisers, to create or to threaten to create enough new peers to override the opposition of the House of Lords, and thus restore harmony between the two branches of the Legislature."
[106] *QLAD* 18 March 1908 p165.
[107] Philp, in contrast, correctly observed that s.9's two-thirds majority provision was rooted in the Order (through cl.8) rather than in Queensland law; *QLAD* 18 March 1908 p165.

This is somewhat disingenuous. The two-thirds majority in both houses proviso in respect to matters concerning the Council had appeared in s.36 [s.42] of the New South Wales Constitution Act 1855. The provision did not appear *expressly* in the 1859 Order that brought Queensland into being, but was obviously incorporated *implicitly* by s.7 [BAA] of the 1855 Act.[108] Blair would have been correct had he asserted that the first *explicit* appearance in *Queensland* law of the two-thirds requirements was in s.9 and s.10 of the 1867 Act.

Blair also offered the Assembly several 'precedents' for the view that s.9 could be repealed by a simple rather than a two-thirds majority vote. The first of these was the New South Wales Constitution Act 1857, which repealed the two-thirds majority clauses in s.15 [s.17] and s.36 [s.42] of the New South Wales Constitution Act 1855.[109] The second was Lilley's 'singular omission' speech – invoked presumably as a constitutional authority because of his later role as State Chief Justice – in the Assembly second reading of his original 1870 bill which had been drafted to repeal both s.9 and s.10.[110] Blair noted that the then Speaker had endorsed this view. The third authority was the fact that the two-thirds majority provision in s.10 of the 1867 Act had indeed been repealed and replaced by a simple majority vote in the 1871 Act.[111] Blair did not expressly invoke *Cooper's* 'Two Act' entrenchment thesis as an additional precedent to support the government's strategy, even though the strategy seemed to adopt that thesis to some extent.

But nor did Blair suggest s.9[1] and/or [2] could be *directly* amended or repealed by simple majority legislation. An Act which sought that particular result would require a two-thirds majority. This bill, however, did not affect the Council's constitution; that it might pave the way for such measures was not in point.

Kidston limited his interventions at second reading to the bill's political defensibility as a first step to ensuring that the Council could no longer block 'the people's' wishes:

> THE PREMIER: We believe – I do not think that anyone doubts it – we believe that the people of Queensland – and when we speak of the people of Queensland we mean the majority of the people of Queensland – the effective majority of the people of Queensland – have authorised Parliament to make a certain constitutional change. Some of them want a larger change
>
> LABOUR MEMBERS: Hear hear.[112]

---

[108] Pp 63–65 above.
[109] Pp 56–58 above.
[110] Pp 128–29 above. Cited by Blair in *QLAD* 18 March 1908 p169.
[111] The rationale received contemporaneous approval in Berridale Keith's (1908) *Responsible government in the Dominions* pp 127–29, which described the Philpites' critique of the scheme as a means to bypass the two-thirds majority proviso as: "true but irrelevant"; ibid p 128 fn (z). It may be that Berriedale-Keith's analysis, or the episode itself, was noted and acted upon in British government circles. The next year, Parliament enacted the South Africa Act 1909, which created the new colony of South Africa. South Africa was to have a bicameral plus royal assent Parliament, competent to enact laws on almost any matter in the ordinary British fashion. However, the Act contained two entrenched clauses, each requiring a joint session two-thirds majority for amendment: s.137 gave both Dutch and English official language status; s.35 precluded restriction of voting rights on the basis of a person's race. Per s.152, neither of the entrenched sections could be repealed unless by the same two-thirds majority joint session. See generally Loveland (1999) *By due process of law?* pp 121–28. As far as I could ascertain, the 'double entrenchment' proviso in the South Africa Act 1909 was a wholly South African initiative, prompted by a former Premier of the Cape Colony, John Merriman. It is credible to think that Merriman may have read Berriedale Keith's book; less credible that he was aware of Lilley's singular omission speech.
[112] *QLAD* 18 March 1908 p 172.

Kidston also underlined Blair's point that while this was the 'better' way to achieve the government's desired result, he would, if necessary, press the Governor to add 40 or 50 government sympathisers to the Council.[113]

Philp, leading the opposition case, did so in a rather lacklustre and counterproductive manner, on the disingenuous bases that the Council had never rejected any government measures which enjoyed popular support and that the bill presaged abolition not just of the Council but also perhaps of the Assembly:

> HON R. PHILP: I think it is unwise to alter the two-thirds majority at all ... If this Bill is passed, what is the use of the Legislative Council at all?
>
> LABOUR MEMBERS: Hear hear! and laughter ...
>
> HON R. PHILP: ... As I was going to say, if we commence by abolishing one House it will be an easy matter to abolish the other. I hope hon members will be exceedingly careful with regard to this matter ...[114]

Despite Philp's melodramatic warnings, the bill passed second reading without division and went into committee the next day. Given the bill contained only one substantive clause, the committee stage did not take much time. The bill in its original form was approved by 44 votes to 22.[115] There was no substantive debate at third reading; the bill passed by 41 votes to 19.[116] No member of the Assembly made any mention during debate of the possible significance of the CLVA 1865 s.5 to the lawfulness of the proposed Act.

In the Council

Nor was s.5 considered in the Council's debates. With Morgan (qua President) in the chair, the bill came on for second reading in the Council on 25 March.[117] Little was said that day beyond the government rehearsing Blair's Assembly speech. Debate resumed on 31 March. The (Philpite) opposition case was championed by FI Power, a solicitor appointed to the Council in 1901 and Minister of Justice in the short-lived 1907–08 Philp administration. While debate lasted several days, and despite the opposition's notional (and substantial) majority in the Council, there was no serious indication that the bill would not pass. The bill cleared its second reading on 2 April by just 17 votes to 15.[118] The government then pushed the bill straight into committee and through to third reading, where it passed without division.[119] Chelmsford gave the royal assent the next day.[120]

---

[113] ibid 173.
[114] ibid 171.
[115] QLAD 19 March 1908 p218. Ironically a two-thirds majority, although only of members voting, so not an s.9 two-thirds majority.
[116] QLAD 20 March 1908 p231.
[117] QLCD 25 March 1908 p276.
[118] QLCD 2 April 1908 p495.
[119] ibid pp 495–96.
[120] QLAD 3 April 1908 p535.

The Parliamentary Bills Referendum Act 1908

The broad brush of the government's policy was to ensure that if a bill which twice passed the Assembly in successive sessions was not passed by the Council, the government could put the bill before the electorate in a referendum. If approved in the referendum, the bill would go directly to the Governor for the royal assent (subject to any provision requiring reservation to the Monarch).

In the Assembly

Blair again opened for the government at second reading on 6 April.[121] Curiously, the government did not follow Cooper's 'Two Act' process with this measure. Cl.1 (enacted unamended) provided that: "This Act may be cited as 'The Parliamentary Bills Referendum Act of 1908' and shall be read and construed with and as an amendment of the Constitution Act of 1867." So, while the Act expressly purported to amend the Constitution, it arguably did not fully meet the High Court's *Cooper* methodology. That would have required the PBRA 1908 to have been preceded by a separate Constitution Act Reform Act – or, indeed, a provision in the CAAA 1908 itself – which said something like:

> The Legislature may at such time of its choosing legislate to provide that any bill passed in the Assembly but not passed in the Council may be submitted to the Governor for the Royal Assent if such bill has been approved by a majority of electors in a referendum; and upon receiving the Royal Assent such bill shall become an Act of the Legislature.

Blair and Kidston's assumption may have been that CAAA 1908 sufficed for *Cooper* purposes. Whether that assumption was correct would depend on the level of precision which the courts would require in the first of the 'Two Acts'. Given the 'Two Act' process had no textual basis in any legislation (whether Imperial or Queensland) but was a purely judicial creation, one could not confidently predict how much linguistic precision might be required.[122]

The caveat arises because one reading of *Cooper* would be that the PBRA 1908 would empower the 'Legislature' (qua Assembly, referendum majority and royal assent) to legislate on matters of 'ordinary law' but not of 'organic law'. For the referendum device to be effective in respect of 'organic law', *Cooper* might be taken to require that the 'organic law' concerned be identified in the PBRA 1908 as amenable to change through the referendum mechanism or to be so identified in a subsequent Act, whereupon a second Act produced through the referendum process would be effective as a means to reform. If this caveat did occur to either Kidston or Blair, it did not lead either man to address the point in the bill or canvass the point in the parliamentary debate.

The Act's detailed scheme (as finally enacted) was straightforward. S.4 provided that if a bill 'has been twice rejected' by the Council in two successive sessions of Parliament,

---

[121] *QLAD* 20 March 1908 p566.
[122] Taken to a not illogical extreme, the 'Two Act' process could be assumed to require that Act One inserted an explicit textual amendment into the Constitution Act 1867.

the Governor could issue a proclamation announcing that the bill would be the subject of a referendum. Per s.10:

> If the referendum poll is decided in favour of the Bill, the Bill shall be presented to the Governor for His Majesty's assent, and upon receiving such assent the Bill shall become an Act of Parliament in the same manner as if it had been passed by both Houses of Parliament, and notwithstanding any law to the contrary.[123]

'Rejected' in s.4 was defined in s.3 to include rejection per se, but also a failure to pass the bill or passing it with amendments not accepted by the Assembly. S. 5 and s.7 provided that the referendum electorate would be voters qualified to vote in Assembly elections, and s.11 gave the Governor in Council a general power to put the Act into effect.

Blair apparently entertained no doubts in his second reading speech that the Act would be legally valid. He rooted the measure in (the now amended) s.9 of the Constitution Act 1867, as a measure 'otherwise concerning' the Council. He expressed some uncertainty as to whether it affected the 'constitution' of the Council per s.1 of the Australian States Constitution Act 1907 (and would have to be reserved for the Monarch's assent),[124] but indicated that the government would comply with that requirement in any event.

Blair was primarily concerned with defending the bill's moral legitimacy, doing so in terms emphasising its 'British' nature:

> After all, the whole essence of our Constitution – the whole essence of the British Constitution in so far as we have adopted it – is this: To see that the sovereignty of the people is supreme (Hear, hear!), to see that their will ultimately prevails, and this is a method which will provide that in a direct, sure speedy fashion their will shall become the law of the land.[125]

Blair was also keen to debunk the notion that a referendum undermined a long-standing British tradition of responsible government:

> There are some who believe that this legislation is an attack on the Constitution – of which every member in this House is proud and none prouder than I – who would have you believe that it as old, practically, as history itself. I say those critics never made a greater mistake in their lives. What we know as modern responsible government dates really from the 1832 reform Act … when, with the broadening of the franchise, came far greater power for the expression of the will of the people.[126]

Kidston spoke at length. He stressed that he thought that a referendum would only be triggered in the most extreme circumstances, and that the Act's most likely consequence would be to exert 'moral' pressure on the Assembly and the Council to find common ground on disputed measures.[127] Kidston happily concurred with a suggestion from an opposition member that the Act would put a 'whip' over the Council:

> I have no objection to the phrase at all. People in using such a phrase imagine that it is derogatory to the honour of the Council. Is there not a whip over this Chamber? (Hear hear!)

---

[123] 'In favour' was taken to mean a bare majority.
[124] Pp 208–209 above.
[125] *QLAD* 6 April 1908 p568.
[126] ibid pp 568–69. He did not refer to the 1903 New South Wales referendum; p 206 above.
[127] ibid p573.

And was it not cracked a few months ago? ... Why should the Council be more independent of public opinion than this Chamber.[128]

Several Philpites spoke briefly in opposition, and suggested – disingenuously – that they would support reform to give the Council an elective basis. The most substantial 'opposing' speech came from a Labour member, Joe Lesina,[129] who dismissed it as a half-hearted measure that might enhance, rather than diminish, the Council's status. Bowman, qua leader of the Labour members, expressed sympathy with that view, but pledged Labour support for the bill on the basis that it would pave the way for the Council's 'total abolition'.[130]

The bill passed second reading without division. The Assembly moved immediately into committee, during which Blair accepted several minor amendments. The first, pushed by Philp, was that the Act should have only prospective effect, ie it could not be applied to bills already rejected by the Council. The second was a minor question of grammar. S.4 had initially provided that the second rejection of a bill had to occur in the 'next succeeding' session of Parliament after the one in which the first rejection had occurred. Amid some hilarity, Blair agreed to remove 'succeeding' as it added nothing to 'next'.[131]

The government refused to accept two more substantial Philp amendments. The first proposed there be at least a three-month gap between the Council's two rejections of the relevant bill. Philp offered two linked reasons for the amendment. The first was that a three-month gap would give legislators time to reflect on the merits of the bill; the second was that a three-month gap was deployed (for substantive reasons) in the deadlock provisions of the national Constitution.[132] Blair insisted any such delay was unnecessary. The second sought a minimum absolute majority requirement (of at least 26% of registered electors voting in favour) for a referendum result to be effective. Philp presented the amendment as a device to ensure that a bill passed in a referendum enjoyed the positive support of at least a significant electoral minority (in the sense of eligible rather than actual voters), but Kidston dismissed the amendment as a means to: "fence the Bill about with restrictions".[133]

Blair also took pains to explain the broad definition of 'reject' in cl.4. The 'failure to pass' and 'unacceptable amendments' provisos – borrowed from s.57 and s.128 of the Commonwealth Constitution Act 1900 respectively[134] – were to catch situations

---

[128] ibid p572. The 'few months ago' refers to the 1908 election.
[129] Lesina sat in the Assembly from 1899 to 1912. Originally a signwriter, he built his political career on union activism and a torrential stream of journalism in Labour-friendly newspapers. He was a trenchant critic of Labour accommodation to centrist parties, and was expelled from the party in 1909: http://adb.anu.edu.au/biography/lesina-vincent-bernard-joe-7174: see also Crook op cit. On the variegated nature of the Labour-friendly press in that era, see Guyatt (1978) 'The publicists: the Labour press 1880–1915' in Murphy, Joyce and Hughes op cit.
[130] *QLAD* 6 April 1908 p575.
[131] ibid pp 593–94: "Mr LESINA supported the amendment. If I were waiting for a tram and the hon. Member ... asked me if I was going home I would not say No, I am waiting for the next succeeding tram [Laughter] That would be absurd ... Why should I say I am going to take the next succeeding tram (Laughter) ... The ATTORNEY-GENERAL: In order that hon. members might not be kept waiting longer for their train or 'their next succeeding train' I consent to the amendment."
[132] Pp 159–60 above.
[133] *QLAD* 6 April 1908 p596.
[134] Pp 159–60 and 164–65 above.

in which the Council simply adjourned consideration of a bill, while the 'unacceptable amendment' clause would forestall arguments that amendment of a bill did not amount to 'rejection'.

The bill returned to the Assembly the next day for third reading, when it again passed without division.[135] As with the CAAA 1908, Assembly debates made no reference at all to the CLVA 1865.

In the Council

Philp's rejected amendments were pressed in modified form when the bill moved to the Council the next day. Although the bill passed Council second reading without division, the opposition moved amendments again in committee on 9 April. The government immediately accepted an amendment (modifying s.3) that a bill's first 'rejection' had to occur at least one month before the end of the parliamentary session: the point being to prevent a government presenting a bill at the last minute, which would not permit the Council to give it proper consideration.[136]

Power then moved an amendment requiring at least a six-month (modifying the three months proposed by Philp) gap between the end of the parliamentary session in which the first rejection occurred and the second rejection. After a spirited exchange, Power modified his amendment to three months, and it was carried 19–12.[137] The government had made it clear that it anticipated that a 'second rejection' could occur in a special parliamentary session, called in effect for no purpose other than to reconsider the rejected bill. Power consequently moved an amendment that the rejection in the second session had to occur at least one month before the session ended. This was effectively a wrecking amendment designed to make a special session administratively impractical, as members would likely have nothing else to do for that final month. The government was willing to accept a one-week period, to which Power agreed. The government accepted an amendment moved by Power (enacted in s.4(2)) that, in giving notice of the referendum, the government would publish both a copy of the bill and a copy of any Council amendments which the Assembly rejected.

There was no agreement to Power's next amendment, however, which proposed a supermajority for certain purposes:

> Provided that where the Bill is a Bill for altering or amending the Constitution of the Legislature, or either House thereof, the referendum poll shall not be deemed to be decided in favour of the Bill unless at least two-thirds of the votes recorded at the poll are recorded in favour of the Bill.[138]

Power suggested such reforms were too important to be left to bare majorities. Given that CAAA 1908 was introduced solely to remove such an entrenching majority in the Assembly and Council, there was no credible prospect that the government would accept the amendment. Power championed amendment in comically apocalyptic terms.

---

[135] QLAD 7 April 1908 p607.
[136] QLCD 9 April 1908 p706.
[137] QLCD 9 April 1908 p708.
[138] ibid p715.

He was much concerned (echoing mid-nineteenth-century cultural tropes) that a narrow referendum majority might include substantial numbers of 'criminals', or of 'ladies' whose voting preferences would be controlled by persons who supplied 'the ladies' with 'delicious pies'. He ended his speech with a hysterical personal attack on Kidston:

> [T]he policy was to sweep away anything that stood in the way of the Constitution. The only constitution that was required was the constitution of one individual who led a certain party. When he spoke everyone else was to bow down, subject, of course, to the consent of the Trades Hall. People who did not see as he saw, and did not agree with what he suggested, were to be swept off the face of the earth, and even the King of England was not to be excluded.[139]

Despite – or perhaps because of – the virulence of his speech, Power could not muster a majority for the amendment. After the committee stage, the bill was immediately given its third reading without division and returned – as amended – to the Assembly. Again, no reference was made to the CLVA 1865.

The government indicated it would accept all of the Council's amendments other than the 'three months from the end of the session' proviso. Blair proposed a further amendment to that amendment, starting the three-month period from the date of the rejection, not the end of the session. The proposal was approved without division and the bill returned to the Council, which accepted that alteration.[140] Blair by then had indicated that he considered that the Act would fall within s.1 of the Australian States Constitution Act 1907 and so have to be reserved for the Monarch's assent.[141] The bill received the royal assent in London on 4 July.[142]

The generally muted nature of Philpite opposition to the bill in the Assembly and Council (Power's speech was an exception) merits further consideration. It may be that (some) members were motivated by the presumption that the results of the 1907 and 1908 elections provided Kidston with an irresistible mandate for change. Similarly, if one takes the speeches made during the bill's passage at face value, many opposition members professed approval of the referendum idea in principle. But it was also likely that the more astute Philpites expected that the Act would weaken the hand of a future Labour Premier who wanted to press the Governor to pack the Council to overcome its obstructionism. It would be difficult for a Premier convincingly to make the argument that the Council was frustrating the wishes of the people if the referendum mechanism existed to ascertain just what 'the people' actually thought about a given issue.[143] In contrast, the *BC*, the leading voice of conservative political sentiment, saw no such beneficial subtleties in the Act, which it denounced as a 'hasty and ill-considered measure". Echoing Power's denunciation of Kidston, the *BC* castigated "the Labour masters of the Government" for their avowed intention to "destroy the upper house or subvert its functions as a revising Chamber".[144]

---

[139] ibid p717.
[140] *QLCD* 13 April 1908 p801.
[141] Pp 208–209 above.
[142] *QLCD* 17 November 1908 p3.
[143] See *The Capricornian (Rockhampton)* 11 April 1908 p17, http://trove.nla.gov.au/ndp/del/article/69164555. See also the article – likely written by Lesina – in the *Gympie Times and Mary River Mining Gazette* 11 April 1908 p5, https://trove.nla.gov.au/newspaper/article/188296749.
[144] 10 April 1908 p4, http://nla.gov.au/nla.news-article19518258.

IV. Conclusion

The 1908 Acts' passage was followed by another major realignment in Queensland's party politics. Evidently cowed by the prospect of being overruled by a referendum, the Philpites in the Council approved bills to introduce wages boards, even in relation to agricultural workers, and to establish old age pensions. But having achieved those successes with Labour's assistance in the Assembly, Kidston – obviously not subject, as the *BC* had suggested, to 'Labour masters' – discarded Labour support and fused his party with the Philpites on the basis of a mildly reformist agenda. (Given that Kidston initially entered politics as a Deakinite, there is some symmetry between his manoeuvrings here and Deakin's own creation of 'the Fusion' on the national political stage.[145]) The move prompted several former Labour Kidstonites to rejoin Labour, depriving Kidston of a reliable majority. But at the 1909 election, the fused party won 41 (of 72) seats. Blair initially declined to join the new party, instead leading a small (four-member) 'independent opposition' grouping. Kidston, though, had wearied of party politics and retired after securing further electoral reform legislation.[146] For the next six years, an increasingly Philpite government led by Digby Denham (always ideologically, if not tactically,[147] a Philpite) was in power.

On the world stage, the outbreak of war was the most significant event of that era. In Australian national politics, the key player was to be an émigré Welshman named Billy Hughes. And in the Queensland sphere, Kidston's abandoned reformist mantle was picked up by Tom Ryan and Ted Theodore, leading an increasingly popular state Labour Party.

---

[145] Pp 169–72 above.

[146] Which inter alia allowed a maximum 20% size variation in constituency electorates.

[147] Denham deserted Philp in 1903 to take office in Morgan's ministry, served under Kidston until 1907, then returned to the Philpites as Treasurer in Philp's 1907–08 government. Denham then served under Kidston in the Fused Party, succeeding him as Premier in 1911; http://adb.anu.edu.au/biography/denham-digby-frank-5953.

8

Constitutional Controversy in Queensland: Ryan and *Taylor*

The fact that it is before the Court does not prevent us from pursuing the campaign. It is our intention to go straight ahead in order to obtain the verdict of the people. I regard the will of the people as the supreme law. If there are any legal technicalities in the way of the will of the people no doubt there will be ways found of removing them, and so shaping the law that their will shall prevail.

Tom Ryan, Premier of Queensland, 20 April 1917, during his attempt to abolish Queensland's Legislative Council.

There is some irony – given the battles Kidston fought over the Council before fusing with the Philpites – that Denham's first period as Premier was notable for an acute conflict between his government and the Council over a proposed liquor licensing law.[1] The measure provided for local referendums to consider introducing rigorous licensing or total prohibition of alcohol sales in local areas. There were significant pro-temperance lobbies in Denham's party – now renamed the Liberal Party – and the Labour Party. Although Labour's official position was to oppose the bill and introduce a state monopoly on alcohol sales, the measure attracted majority Assembly support.

However, among Liberal 'supporters' in the Council, the pro-temperance group was outnumbered by a pro-business lobby whose commercial interests were seriously threatened by prohibition. The bill twice passed in the Assembly and twice failed in the Council. Early in 1912, Denham announced that he would put the question to a PBRA 1908 referendum. This was a potent vindication of Kidston and Blair's position that the 1908 Acts were not party political measures: a position Denham had then rejected.[2]

In addition to being unable to control his party's Council members, Denham faced growing discontent from some Assembly members representing rural constituencies who, echoing Morgan's previous break with Philp,[3] considered the government insufficiently sensitive to pastoral and agricultural concerns. Denham was spared the immediate consequences of these political difficulties by the outbreak of a general strike in Brisbane later in 1912.[4] The strike was triggered by the refusal of the (American) owner of Brisbane's tramway company to recognise trade unions, and his subsequent

---

[1] The episode is reviewed in Murphy (1975) *T J Ryan* pp 58–61.
[2] Pp 228–36 above.
[3] Pp 211–12 above.
[4] Morrison (1970) 'The Brisbane general strike of 1912' in Murphy, Joyce and Hughes (eds) op cit.

decision to sack tramworkers who worked wearing a union badge. The strike reflected a broader pervasive tension between the parliamentary and militant wings of the trade union movement, with the latter faction temporarily holding the upper hand. But its primary immediate effect was to offer Denham an 'enemy' against whom he could rally public and electoral support. Denham's instincts were certainly confrontational. Fisher's Commonwealth government refused Denham's request to provide military support to break the strike. Denham found a more receptive audience in the state's new Governor.

Chelmsford had stepped down in 1909, moving southwards to become Governor of New South Wales. His successor, Sir William Macgregor, was a Scots-born and educated medical doctor and career civil servant, previously Governor both of Lagos and Newfoundland.[5] Macgregor played a notably partisan role during the strike, seemingly prepared to countenance permitting Denham's government (extraordinarily, given the European geo-political situation) to request military assistance from German troops stationed on ships visiting Queensland. In the event, the request was not made. Economic rather than military pressure eventually forced the strikers back to work and contributed to a handsome Liberal victory in the 1912 election.[6]

Table 8.1 Queensland Legislative Assembly election, 1912 (27 April 1912)

Party	% vote	Seats	Change
Liberal[a]	51.3	46	+5
Labour	46.7	25	−2
Independent	1.7	1	+1
Independent Opposition[b]	−	−	−4

[a] The rebranded Ministerialists.
[b] Absorbed into the Liberal Party during the 1912–15 parliamentary session.

Denham's Liberals enjoyed the dubious benefit of their vote being heavily concentrated in small (in terms of voter numbers) rural constituencies; their increased number of seats in the Assembly was achieved despite Labour securing an increase in its share of the vote from 37% to 46%. By the 1915 election, that upward trend in the Labour vote had continued to the point that Denham not only lost his government, but also his own Assembly seat.

I. Abolishing the Queensland Legislative Council?

The imminent prospect of abolishing the Council arose in 1915, when an initiative was taken by a majority Labour government led by Thomas Ryan.[7] Ryan, the child of

---

[5] http://adb.anu.edu.au/biography/macgregor-sir-william-4097.
[6] "The strike … had completely changed Denham's political standing. No longer was he the incompetent premier stirring opposition among his associates and supporters over the Liquor Bill. Now, by enrolling sturdy special constables and preventing unruly unionists from holding processions, he had become the protector of citizens' freedom": Murphy (1975) op cit p63.
[7] A fascinating account of Ryan's life and political career is provided in Murphy (1975) *T J Ryan*. Condensed biographies are at http://adb.anu.edu.au/biography/ryan-thomas-joseph-tom-8317; Murphy (1978) 'Thomas Joseph Ryan: big and broadminded' in Murphy and Joyce (eds) op cit.

illiterate Irish immigrants, was born in 1876 in Victoria. He worked as a schoolteacher before going to the Queensland Bar, having taken a law degree at Melbourne University. He established a substantial practice representing workers and trade unions before becoming active in politics. Ryan was initially Kidston's protégé; his first electoral contest was an unsuccessful candidature for a Queensland House seat in the 1903 national elections standing as an Independent supporting Deakin's government. Ryan subsequently decided that his political sympathies lay with Labour rather than Kidston's party, and stood successfully for Labour in the 1909 state elections.

Ryan's political career was enhanced by the fact that his Bar earnings – he acted regularly for wealthy landowners as well as trade union clients – enabled him to buy a local newspaper, the Rockhampton-based *Daily Record*.[8] His meteoric progress within Labour circles was facilitated by the departure of Kidston and his supporters from the party and by loyalist Labour members entering national politics; but Ryan possessed a considerable intellect, a vast capacity and appetite for hard work at the Bar and within his party, and an instinctive ability to make friends rather than enemies among the labour movement's many factions. Ryan became party leader in 1912, when only 36 years old. He had played a particularly skilful dual role during the general strike, acting both as counsel for unionists and – as a politician – managing both to disapprove of general strikes in principle while castigating Denham's government's aggressive behaviour towards the unions.[9] While Ryan shared many of Kidston's political ideals, he remained determined to pursue those ideals in a Labour Party that maintained a united rather than divided front among its parliamentary and trade union wings.

Ryan, Hughes and Conscription – Round 1

The May 1915 elections were a triumph for Ryan. Labour won 42 of the Assembly's 72 seats and an absolute majority of votes cast. Denham lost his own seat; his party's representation dropped to only 21 members, with seats falling both to Labour and to a newly emergent Farmers party.[10]

Table 8.2 Queensland Legislative Assembly election, 1915 (22 May 1915)

Party	% vote	Seats	Change
Liberal	42.0	21	–25
Labour	52.0	45	+20
Queensland Farmers Union	5.0	5	+5
Independent	0.9	1	–

Most of Ryan's Cabinet were new to office, including William Hamilton, whose previous experience of government accommodation was of a rather different order; he was jailed

---

[8] Murphy (1975) op cit pp 43–44.
[9] See especially Murphy (1975) op cit pp 64–69.
[10] Blair joined the Liberal Party and Denham's government in 1912. However, he stood (unsuccessfully) as an Independent in 1915, having resigned from the government, and returned to practise at the Bar.

in 1891 for his part in the shearers' strike.[11] Hamilton was subsequently Minister for Mines and government leader in the Council.

Change also occurred in the Governor's office. Macgregor was replaced in 1914 by Sir Hamilton Goold-Adams. Goold-Adams was a career soldier, reaching the rank of major and serving as Lieutenant Governor of the South African Orange River colony during the Boer Wars.[12]

The Legislative Council Abolition Bill

Although abolition featured prominently in the Labour Party's 1915 campaign programme, Ryan – who served as Attorney-General and Premier – had not prioritised the issue. The potential for Council–Assembly conflict was, however, obvious; of the Council's 36 members, only three took the Labour whip.[13] Ryan had not asked Goold-Adams for many Labour appointees, an omission which rather suggests that he was expecting Council obstruction to the government's programme, which would strengthen the political case for abolition. The expectation proved well founded. The Council majority showed little inclination to defer to Ryan's electoral mandate; by November 1915 it had rejected government bills on industrial relations, land tenure reforms for small farmers and the meat industry.[14]

Ryan consequently moved a short abolition bill, which had its Assembly second reading on 17 November:[15]

> **A Bill to Amend the Constitution of Queensland by Abolishing the Legislative Council ...**
>
> **Abolition of Legislative Council**
>
> 2 (1) The Legislative Council of Queensland is abolished.
>
> (2) The office of member of the said Legislative Council is abolished.
>
> (3) All offices constituted or created in or in connection with the said Legislative Council are abolished.
>
> (4) The Parliament of Queensland (or as sometimes called the Legislature of Queensland) shall be constituted by His Majesty the King and the Legislative Assembly of Queensland in Parliament assembled ...

Rising to Labour cheers, Ryan announced that the bill was: "the most important and, at the present juncture, the most necessary motion that I have moved since I have been in Parliament".[16] Having condemned all of Australia's Legislative Councils (whether appointive or elected) as 'relics of feudalism', Ryan then suggested (disingenuously perhaps) that the obstruction posed to his government's bills had an added urgency

---

[11] P 143 above.
[12] http://adb.anu.edu.au/biography/goold-adams-sir-hamilton-john-6425.
[13] Harding (2000) 'Ideology or expediency? The abolition of the Queensland Legislative Council 1915–1922' *Labour History* 162. Harding's analysis suggests Ryan was at best a lukewarm proponent of abolition. For a more supportive view, see Murphy (1980) 'The abolition of the Legislative Council' in Murphy, Joyce and Hughes op cit.
[14] ibid p99. A fuller account is at Murphy (1975) op cit ch 6. Ryan's summary is at *QLAD* 17 November 1915 pp 2167–68.
[15] ibid p2163 et seq.
[16] ibid.

given that those bills were designed to aid the war effort. Ryan also referred to the recent curbing of the powers of the House of Lords in the Parliament Act 1911 as an indication that a fully bicameral legislature could no longer be regarded as an essential element of the British constitutional tradition, and noted that seven of Canada's nine provinces had unicameral legislatures. Ryan invoked cl.22 of the 1859 Order rather than CLVA s.5 as providing the legal basis for the Council to be abolished by the Legislature.

While that view seems correct in a narrow sense, Ryan's speech took an ostensibly rather surprising view of *Cooper*. Ryan explicitly referred to Griffith's judgment in *Cooper* as an authoritative statement of the constitutional position, ie that two Acts would be required to effect any alteration to Queensland's Constitution. The government's proposed (one) Act, however, announced both that the Constitution was being amended and that the Council was being abolished; ie only one Act, albeit an Act perfectly explicit as to its purpose and effect, was being used. If *Cooper* was indeed correct, the 'One Act' route to abolition would not be effective. It seems implausible that Ryan did not grasp this point. It may be that he thought that the then High Court[17] (or beyond that, the Privy Council) might reverse *Cooper* if given the opportunity. The more likely explanation to be deduced from Ryan's second reading speech is that he expected the bill would twice be rejected in the Council and then be enacted through the PBRA 1908 mechanism.[18]

The bill, along with other parts of the new administration's economic programme, was blocked in the Council. The bill was promoted again in September 1916 and again failed to pass the Council. Ryan nonetheless continued to favour abolition and invoked the 1908 Act to put the matter to a referendum, scheduled for 5 May 1917.

The First Conscription Referendum and Hughes's Desertion of the Labour Party

There was little prospect that the referendum question would stand uppermost in voters' minds on 5 May, given the broader political context. The primary issue was Australia's participation in World War I – more specifically, a bitter political controversy over whether to introduce conscription for military service overseas.[19]

Labour had won a majority under Fisher's leadership in both houses in the September 1914 national election. The election was triggered by the former Liberal government's request for a double dissolution (per s.57 of the 1900 Act) in June 1914. Deakin's Fusion party was rebranded as the Liberal Party for the 1913 election. Led by Joseph Cook,[20] in his (by then distant) youth a Labour politician and subsequently a member of Reid's administrations in New South Wales, the Liberals had in the narrowest sense 'won' the 1913 election: they took 38 of the House's 75 seats. Since the Speaker

---

[17] Whose composition had changed markedly since *Cooper*; p 196 below.
[18] Murphy's (1975) op cit biography suggests Ryan expected to use the PBRA route. An unresolved question – perhaps because no one thought to ask it – was whether, if *Cooper* was 'correct', any use of the PBRA 1908 mechanism would in turn require *two* PBRA Acts, the first explicitly permitting a constitutional change and the second explicitly effecting it.
[19] Ward (1992) op cit ch 6; (1978) op cit pp 111–16.
[20] http://adb.anu.edu.au/biography/cook-sir-joseph-5763.

came from among the 38, the Liberals had no House majority. They held only nine Senate seats to Labour's 27. Cook consequently sought the double dissolution hoping to secure a bicameral majority.[21] That hope proved ill-founded: Labour won comfortable House and Senate majorities.

Table 8.3 Commonwealth elections, 1913 (31 May 1913) and 1914 (5 September 1914)

Year	House	% vote	Seats	Change
1913	Labour	48.5	37	−6
	Liberal	48.9	38	+7
	Independent	2.6	−	−1
	Senate[a]			
	Labour	48.7	29	+7
	Liberal Nationalist	49.3	7	−7
1914	House			
	Labour	50.1	42	+5
	Liberal Nationalist	47.2	32	−6
	Independent	1.8	1	+1
	Senate[b]			
	Labour	52.1	31	+2
	Liberal Nationalist	47.8	5	−2

[a] 18 seats contested.
[b] 36 seats contested.

The British government had declared Britain (and, by extension, the Empire) at war in August 1914. Fisher's government promptly persuaded the Commonwealth Parliament to enact the War Precautions Act 1914 – mirroring legislation enacted in Britain and other colonies – the purpose and effect of which were to grant the Commonwealth government the power to issue regulations giving it much more extensive powers than would be considered proper in peacetime. The Act, barely three pages long,[22] created, per s.6 and s.7, criminal offences – punishable with up to six months' imprisonment – of breaching any such regulation or aiding and abetting anyone to do so.

Military conscription was not immediately introduced in either Britain or Australia. Conscription legislation was enacted in Britain in 1916, but the issue was much more contentious in Australia. Fisher opposed conscription, but continuing ill-health led him to stand down as Prime Minister in October 1915 to take the less arduous post of Australia's High Commissioner in London.

Fisher was succeeded as Prime Minister and party leader by (William) Billy Hughes. Hughes was born in London in 1862. His parents were Welsh, his father employed as a carpenter. Hughes worked initially as a teacher in London, before emigrating in 1884.

---

[21] Ward (1978) op cit pp 87–93. The political manoeuvrings leading to the double dissolution are succinctly assessed in Sawer (1956) op cit pp 121–25.
[22] The text is at www.legislation.gov.au/Details/C1914A00010.

He had various jobs before opening a small shop in Sydney in 1890. His shop became a venue for Labour activists, and Hughes's developing enthusiasm for the cause led to his election to the Assembly in 1894, where he displayed considerable skill in using growing Labour numbers to wring legislative concessions from both Free Trade and Protectionist ministries. Hughes left state politics in 1901 to take a seat in the House and read for the Bar. He was a minister in Watson's short-lived 1904 administration, and combined his parliamentary and legal careers with trade union organisation, particularly on behalf of shearers and dockworkers. Hughes was Attorney-General in Fisher's 1910–13 government, and again after the 1914 election.[23]

As the war progressed, Hughes became increasingly supportive of conscription, but the national party was deeply split on the issue. In Queensland, Ryan led a Labour Party which endorsed an anti-conscription policy and a Labour government in which several leading members held the opposite view. While Ryan consistently supported voluntary enlistment, he was personally unsympathetic to conscription and was also concerned to reduce the likelihood that the question would trigger a schism in the state and national parties.

Hughes eventually decided the most likely route to achieve his conscription objective was to raise the matter in a national referendum. The Military Conscription Referendum Act 1916 made voting compulsory; the poll was scheduled for 29 October 1916. After a rancorous campaign, the electorate voted narrowly against conscription. Immediately after the referendum, Hughes and 24 other Labour House members quit the party to form a new 'National Labour' party, with Hughes as Prime Minister of a minority government. 'National Labour' promptly pursued merger negotiations with the Liberals, and by February 1917 Hughes led a new 'National Party', which held over 50 House seats.

The Legislative Council Abolition Referendum

Hughes's manoeuvrings had potentially adverse implications for Labour's electoral prospects in Queensland, although an election was not due until 1918. Ryan was nonetheless confident that the abolitionist view would prevail in the projected Council referendum. But before he could put the question to Queensland's voters, he had to overcome a legal challenge.

On 3 April 1917, the government issued a proclamation under the PBRA 1908 s.3 fixing the referendum vote for (Saturday) 5 May 1917,[24] the same day as the scheduled House and Senate national elections. The Governor also appointed a returning officer, and issued regulations under the Act providing for the conduct of the referendum.

Several Council members (nominally headed by William Taylor)[25] then initiated two sets of proceedings in the Queensland courts to injunct the referendum, contending

---

[23] http://adb.anu.edu.au/biography/hughes-william-morris-billy-6761.
[24] The text of the proclamation is in *Taylor v Attorney General* [1917] St R Qd 208, 210.
[25] This being the William Taylor nominated to the Council in 1886 by Griffith; pp 139–40 and n 82 above. Taylor had not voted against the 1908 Act being passed. By 1916, Taylor was a medical doctor of considerable

that the 1908 Act was invalid, either per se or – more narrowly – as a device competent to effect Council abolition.

Ryan, embracing a notion of electoral rather than parliamentary sovereignty, did not seem much concerned by the action, even if Taylor's case proved soundly based:

> The fact that it is before the Court does not prevent us from pursuing the campaign. It is our intention to go straight ahead in order to obtain the verdict of the people. I regard the will of the people as the supreme law. If there are any legal technicalities in the way of the will of the people no doubt there will be ways found of removing them, and so shaping the law that their will shall prevail.[26]

Ryan might nonetheless have had good reason not to have felt particularly sanguine about the prospects of arguing the referendum case in the State Supreme Court. Shortly before the referendum proclamation was issued, Pope Cooper had handed down judgment following a trial in which he had castigated Ryan's political behaviour from both ideological and personal perspectives.

Duncan v Theodore – At Trial before Pope Cooper

Popularly known as the *Mooraberrie* case, *Duncan v Theodore* was argued at trial before Cooper over several weeks in March 1917.[27] The lead defendant in the litigation was one Edward (Ted) Theodore, the Treasurer in Ryan's government and the deputy leader of the state Labour Party. Theodore's father was the son of an orthodox priest in Romania, and grew up in an affluent middle-class family. Leaving behind his country, faith and family, Basil Teoderescu travelled the world in the merchant navy before ending up in South Australia, where he met and married an English woman, became active in trade union circles, dabbled in party politics and made no success at all of being a small farmer. His children grew up in straitened circumstances and had little formal education. Having been sent to work aged 12, Ted Theodore left home at 16, and after several years wandering the country doing various menial jobs, settled in Queensland. With much greater success than his father, Theodore threw himself into trade union organisation in the mining and sugar industries, devoting considerable energy to trying to draw myriad smaller unions within the auspices of the multi-industry Australian Workers Unions (hereafter AWU).[28] Theodore's subsequent rise within both the labour movement and Queensland's Labour Party was as rapid as Ryan's. Elected to the Assembly in 1909, Theodore was chosen – aged 28 – by caucus as Ryan's deputy in 1912. Following

---

distinction. Save for his prominence on this issue, Taylor had managed his life and career in a fashion in which politics seemingly played second fiddle to medicine; see https://trove.nla.gov.au/newspaper/article/21853540; www.parliament.qld.gov.au/members/former/bio?id=405626570.

[26] *Hobart Mercury* 20 April 1917 p5, http://trove.nla.gov.au/ndp/del/article/1070900.

[27] Cooper's judgment is reported at [1917] St R Qd 250. For a summary of the trial, see *The Queenslander* 10 March 1917 p34, https://trove.nla.gov.au/newspaper/article/22336602; 17 March 1917 p34, https://trove.nla.gov.au/newspaper/article/22336932; 24 March 1917 p34, https://trove.nla.gov.au/newspaper/article/22337043; 31 March 1917 p34, https://trove.nla.gov.au/newspaper/article/22337369.

[28] Fitzgerald (1995) *"Red Ted": the life of E.G. Theodore* ch 1 recounts the early years in detail. See also http://adb.anu.edu.au/biography/theodore-edward-granville-8776.

Labour's election victory in 1915, Theodore served as Deputy Premier, Treasurer and Secretary of Public Works.

The Background to Duncan v Theodore

The claimant in *Duncan* was suing Theodore for trespass to her land and to her cattle; Mooraberrie was the name of Duncan's run – a run of some 120 square miles – in south western Queensland. Mrs Duncan had been suffering some financial difficulties, which she hoped to alleviate by selling 600 of her cattle at auction in Adelaide. The initial complications she faced arose from the terms of the Meat Supply for Imperial Uses Act 1914[29] (hereafter the Meat Act), promoted by Denham's government shortly after the outbreak of war. The Act's general scheme was (per s.6) to vest ownership of all livestock in the Imperial government and to transform the previous owners' rights into an entitlement to compensation, assessed by a statutory Board of Control, when the Chief Secretary (de facto the Premier) or any other nominated minister issued (per s.6(2)) an order taking possession of particular animals. Per s.7, the original owners were prohibited from selling or otherwise disposing of their livestock without permission from the Chief Secretary. In May 1916, Mrs Duncan had been refused permission to send her cattle to Adelaide. Mrs Duncan then promptly issued proceedings in the High Court claiming that the Meat Act was invalid as it breached s.92 of the Commonwealth Constitution.[30] The hearing was scheduled for September 1916.

Ryan was apparently concerned that assertion might be well founded as, on 1 June 1916, a proclamation was issued under the Sugar Acquisition Act 1915[31] (hereafter the Sugar Act) asserting the Crown's ownership of all 1700 cattle on Mooraberrie. Theodore subsequently instructed two police officers to 'seize' the cattle; which instruction and actions prompted Mrs Duncan's suit.[32]

The Sugar Act was one of the first measures promoted by Ryan's government after the May 1915 election. The Act had been foreshadowed by a proclamation, issued on 30 June 1915, de jure by (with some irony given later events) Pope Cooper, who was temporarily deputising for Goold-Adams. The proclamation in essence replicated in relation to sugar the powers given to the government in relation to meat and livestock by the Meat Act 1914. The proclamation also acknowledged it might not have a defensible legal base,[33] and indicated that an Act would be passed to validate it retrospectively. There were some notable differences between the Sugar Act and Meat Act schemes. The Sugar Act vested the ownership of sugar in the state government rather than the Imperial government; the Treasurer rather than the Colonial Secretary was made responsible for the Act's administration; and prices for sugar actually requisitioned by the government would be fixed by the Governor General in Council rather than by a statutory board.

---

[29] 5 Geo V No 2, http://www.austlii.edu.au/cgi-bin/viewdb//au/legis/qld/hist_act/msfiuao19145gvn2421/.
[30] Which provided that trade among the states be 'absolutely free'.
[31] 6 Geo 5 No 2.
[32] Judgment in Mrs Duncan's challenge to the Meat Act was subsequently given on 16 October 1916. The High Court upheld the Act; *Duncan v Queensland* [1916] HCA 67, (1916) 22 CLR 556.
[33] Which was surely correct. The legislative session was not due to begin until 12 July. The intimation that any Act would be retrospective was presumably made to 'encourage' compliance with a proclamation which at the time of issue was unlawful.

The Sugar Act in s.10 also granted the government the power to extend the Act's reach:

> 10. The operation of this Act may at any time and from time to time be extended by the Governor in Council, by Proclamation published in the *Gazette*, so as to authorise the acquisition by His Majesty of raw sugar to be manufactured in any future year, or of any foodstuffs, commodities, goods, chattels, livestock, or things whatsoever (in this Act referred to as commodities) in such Proclamation mentioned. Thereupon any such commodity may be acquired by a Proclamation containing provisions similar to those of the Proclamation set forth in the Schedule to this Act, [Sch.] with such modifications as may be deemed necessary ...[34]

The Sugar Act also contained a 'protective clause'[35] in s.7. This was cast in wide terms: actions taken or purportedly taken under the Act or a proclamation issued under the Act were not found to have any legal liability beyond payment of the value of the property requisitioned.[36]

A proclamation was subsequently issued in November 1915 which prima facie extended the Act: "so as to authorise the acquisition by his Majesty of *cattle* now or hereafter to come within Queensland".[37] Various proclamations were subsequently made authorising the acquisition of specific herds of cattle,[38] including one dated 16 June 1916 – that is, shortly after Mrs Duncan had issued her High Court claim in respect of the Meat Act's validity – which (purportedly) acquired all the (1700) cattle at Mooraberrie.

Cooper's Judgment

The trespass action came before Cooper on 1 March 1917. Ryan led for the government, but was not present throughout the trial. Much of the government's case was entrusted to John Woolcock and Hugh Macrossan.[39] Arthur Feez KC[40] led for Mrs Duncan.

---

[34] The only discussion of s.10 during the bill's passage – at *QLAD* 27 July 1915 pp 242–43 – was an explanation from Theodore that the extension power was seen as necessary as the Legislature would not be in session for large parts of the year, which would preclude enactment of additional primary legislation. The Legislature was subsequently prorogued from 25 January 1916 to August 1916.

[35] An ouster clause in English legal parlance.

[36] "7. No action, claim, or demand whatsoever shall lie, or be made or allowed by or in favour of any person whomsoever, against His Majesty or the Treasurer or any officer or person acting in the execution of the Proclamation hereby ratified and confirmed, or any other Proclamation made under this Act, or of this Act, for or in respect of any damage or loss or injury sustained or alleged to be sustained by reason of the making of the said or any such Proclamation or the passing of this Act, or of the operation thereof, or of anything done or purporting to be done thereunder, save only for or in respect of the value as ascertained under this Act of any raw sugar (or other commodity) acquired by His Majesty thereunder." Other than an amendment to insert 'Treasurer' instead of 'Chief Secretary', there was no discussion of s.7 in the Assembly during the bill's passage; *QLAD* 27 July 1915 p242.

[37] *QGG* 12 November 1915; emphasis added for reasons discussed below.

[38] *BC* 13 November 1915 p4, https://trove.nla.gov.au/newspaper/article/20091934; *Darling Downs Gazette* 16 September 1915 p4, https://trove.nla.gov.au/newspaper/article/182686184.

[39] The son of an émigré English clergyman, Woolcock studied at the University of Sydney before becoming Griffith's private secretary while Griffith was Premier and reading for the Bar in Griffith's chambers. He spent much of his career as a parliamentary counsel and draughtsman, but also maintained a small private practice; http://adb.anu.edu.au/biography/woolcock-john-laskey-9186. Macrossan married a successful career at the Bar with political activism. Originally elected to the Assembly as a Denham protégé in 1912, Macrossan drifted leftwards politically and stood unsuccessfully as an Independent in 1915. Ryan was evidently impressed with Macrossan's skills as counsel and at ease with his politics, as Macrossan was frequently instructed for the government after 1915; http://adb.anu.edu.au/biography/macrossan-hugh-denis-7445.

[40] On whom see P 251 below.

The judgment proved something of a triumph for Feez: he won not only on points that he argued, but also on some that he did not, and he also secured a favourable costs ruling which might substantially protect his client should she lose a subsequent appeal. Cooper devoted much of his judgment to reciting the background facts. On questions of law, he reached several conclusions, all adverse to the government.

Cooper's first ground of judgment was structured in this way. He observed that the Meat Act had vested property in all livestock in the Crown qua Imperial government. The Sugar Act, because it prima facie vested property in all cattle to the government of Queensland, was therefore taking property away from the (Imperial) Crown. Cooper invoked the long-established principle that the (Imperial) Crown was not bound by legislation unless the legislation in issue expressly stated it was to have that effect. Since the Sugar Act did not do so, it was ineffective as a legal device in respect of cattle.[41]

Cooper applied the same argument – superfluously, if his first conclusion was correct – to invalidate the 1 June 1916 proclamation. Since that proclamation purported to transfer property in Mrs Duncan's cattle to the state government rather than to the Imperial Crown, it was necessarily invalid as that object could only be achieved by expressly framed legislation.[42]

Cooper's third conclusion was that the November 1915 proclamation had extended the reach of the Sugar Act to 'cattle' – that is, to 'cattle' as a class (in its totality). That was consistent with s.10, which required permitted extension of the Act to other 'commodities' but not to parts of such commodities. Any subsequent proclamation authorising the taking of 'cattle' had to have the same scope, ie it had to apply to *all cattle* in the state. Since the June proclamation applied only to Mrs Duncan's cattle, it was ultra vires s.10.[43]

Such conclusions on points of law were not wholly implausible. However, other aspects of the judgment suggest Cooper's decisions on the law were driven by more partisan considerations. Firstly – and quite remarkably – Cooper's judgment made no reference *at all* to the protective clause in s.7 even though Ryan had explicitly raised the issue in his submissions.[44] Secondly, Cooper of his own volition put to the jury the question of whether Theodore had acted in good faith or for an (unspecified) ulterior motive.[45] The jury's 'Yes' answer cast no light on what this ulterior motive might be. Thirdly, Cooper at several points in his judgment indicated that he considered that Theodore (and, by extension, Ryan) had not simply acted in bad faith, but were trying to undermine the war effort.[46] Cooper concluded with a decision as to costs, stating that he considered Ryan and Woolcock's cross-examination of witnesses was so lengthy and

---

[41] Feez does not appear to have argued this point according to the reports in *The Queenslander*; n 27 above.
[42] Nor did Feez argue this point.
[43] This was the central element of Feez's submissions.
[44] *The Queenslander* 31 March 1917 p34, https://trove.nla.gov.au/newspaper/article/22337369.
[45] [1917] St R Qd 250, 254. Feez had opened his submissions with a ludicrously hyperbolic denunciation of (by inference) Ryan and Theodore, telling the jury that: "they might have an idea that we lived in a free and democratic country; but they would hear that we lived under a form of tyranny at the present time; that acts had been committed that showed one of the most tyrannical and oppressive state of things that could possibly be imagined": *The Queenslander* 10 March 1917 p34, https://trove.nla.gov.au/newspaper/article/22336602. However, Feez led no evidence as to Ryan and Theodore's motivations, nor did he broach the issue on cross-examination of government witnesses (not including Ryan or Theodore). There was simply no evidence at all on the point: Cooper's putting of the question to the jury was completely improper.
[46] ibid 254, 262 and 263 (twice).

unnecessary that even if the government had won he would have not awarded them any costs for the seven days of the hearing.[47]

The government immediately made arrangements to appeal the judgment to the full court. Argument was set down for early May. Before then, Ryan had another pressing court engagement to fulfil.

II. *Taylor* in the Queensland Courts

Taylor came on for argument before the Supreme Court – with Cooper presiding – just a few weeks after Cooper handed down judgment in *Duncan*.[48] Lionel Lukin (government counsel in *Cooper* and appointed to the bench by Kidston in 1910) also sat, alongside Real and Chubb, both of whom sat in *Cooper*. Argument ran from 25 to 28 April. Judgment was given on 1 May.[49]

Counsel and Submissions

Ryan led the government's case, assisted by Blair. His submissions (aside from several quibbling jurisdictional points, which the Court curtly rejected) were brief and straightforward, and rooted in the wording of cl.22 of the 1859 Order and – a source not invoked in his 17 November 1916 Assembly speech – the CLVA s.5.[50]

Ryan made the case that cl.22's 'full power' of 'altering or repealing' any provision of the Order included turning the Legislature into a unicameral chamber, and that was a power now exercisable by the lawmaker created by the PBRA 1908 as well as by the Legislature in its original composition. Choosing his words carefully – but, one might have thought, rather disingenuously (or hopelessly), given the wording of the bill which the Council had rejected (ie 'A Bill to Amend the Constitution of Queensland by Abolishing the Legislative Council') – Ryan asserted that the bill was directed towards securing an 'alteration' of the Legislature rather than abolition of the Council.[51]

As noted in chapter seven, the CLVA 1865 had not been invoked at all in parliamentary debates on the two 1908 Acts. Ryan seems to have been the first Queensland politician to appreciate the Act's potential legal significance as a device to create departures from the 'ordinary way' of legislating. Ryan contended that CLVA 1865 s.5 gave the Legislature wider powers than cl.22, so that if the former source did not suffice to 'alter' the Legislature by recomposing it without the Council, the latter certainly would, given that it empowered representative legislatures to alter their 'constitution, powers and procedures'. Ryan appeared to acknowledge that s.5 also empowered Legislatures to impose special lawmaking requirements in relation to laws which did alter their

---

[47] ibid 266. On that point, the reports in *The Queenslander* (n 27 above) offer some support for Cooper's conclusion.
[48] A thorough contemporaneous account of proceedings is in *The Queenslander* 5 May 1917, http://trove.nla.gov.au/newspaper/article/22338401.
[49] [1917] St R Qd 208.
[50] Cl.22 is at p 64 above. S.5 is at pp 108–09 above.
[51] [1917] St R Qld 216.

'constitution, powers and procedures'.[52] But since no such measure had been enacted in Queensland,[53] the 'same manner' proviso of cl.22 remained authoritative for such purposes, albeit that on the logic of Ryan's position there were now two 'same manners' – that used by the Legislature as initially composed and that used by the Legislature as 'altered' by the PBRA 1908.

Ryan's argument echoed – although it did not acknowledge – Sir Henry Jenkyns' view of s.5, put forward in 1902 in what was to become an influential doctrinal work on colonial constitutional law, *British rule and jurisdiction beyond the seas*:

> [S.5] appears to mean that if any Act, Imperial or colonial, requires Bills varying the constitution of a colonial legislature to be specially reserved for the Royal Assent, or to be passed by any particular majority, such requirements must still be observed; but that if no such requirements exist, a colonial legislature may alter its constitution by ordinary enactment.[54]

Answering a question from Lukin as to *Cooper*'s significance, Ryan seemingly chose his language both carefully and carelessly. Carelessly, given that in his earlier submission he acknowledged that the referendum was intended to abolish the Council. Carefully, given that *Cooper* apparently required reform of 'organic law' to be effected by two Acts. Ryan responded that if *Cooper* did indeed require two legislative *steps* to be taken to abolish the Council, then both such steps could be taken in a single statute and that the PBRA 1908 was such a statute since it did: "pro tanto, abolish the Council for it took away its powers".[55] That submission might be thought optimistic, both because the PBRA 1908 gave no indication as to the scope of measures it might be used to effect and certainly made no reference to abolishing the Council, and also because *Cooper* clearly required two *separate* Acts, each explicit as to its purpose.

Taylor's case was argued by two King's Counsel, Arthur Feez and Charles Stumm. Feez, a native-born (in 1860) and educated Australian of German descent, entered the Queensland Bar in 1881. His practice flourished and he took silk in 1909. Feez also maintained an interest in conservative party politics. His pursuit of elected office – including standing against Kidston in 1908 – was notably less successful, but he channelled much of his political energy into his practice; his entry in the Australian dictionary of biography records: "Feez was senior counsel in many of the bitter anti-socialist constitutional actions brought against the T.J. Ryan government".[56] His ambition to be appointed to the bench was not indulged either by successive Queensland or Commonwealth governments. Charles Stumm, born in Queensland in 1865 and also of German parentage,[57] initially entered Queensland's legal profession as a solicitor in 1899 after working as

---

[52] ibid.

[53] The inference in Ryan's argument was that such a measure would have to have a *textually clear statutory (or Order in Council) basis*, and as such the argument seems to suggest that *Cooper* was wrongly decided insofar as it rested (at best) on a *judicial implication* of 'Two Act' entrenchment into the general scheme of the 1859 Order.

[54] At p73. Jenkyns had been a senior parliamentary draftsman for much of the latter third of the 19th century. The book was published posthumously.

[55] ibid 217–18.

[56] http://adb.anu.edu.au/biography/feez-adolph-frederick-6150. See also White and Wessels (1998) 'The Australian Feez family: its contribution to the law' *JRHSQ* 76.

[57] www.sclqld.org.au/judicial-papers/judicial-profiles/profiles/cstumm. On Stumm's life and career, see the peculiar but intriguing article: Leiboff (2016) 'Theatricalising law in three, 1929–1939 (Brisbane)' *Law Text Culture* 93.

a teacher. He was called to the Bar in 1894 and appointed Kings Counsel in 1910. Although Stumm was active in many civic organisations, he did not cultivate an obviously party political profile.

Feez and Stumm presented the court with a list of 11 grounds.[58] Some were trivial technical points, and there was some overlap between the substantive assertions. The technical points were directed to attacking the legal validity per se of both the CAAA 1908 and the PBRA 1908 on the basis that neither measure received the royal assent in the required form (ie expressly reserved to the King and lain before the Commons and Lords). Those grounds were not vigorously pressed – they seemed inapplicable given s.2 of the Australian States Constitution Act 1907[59] – and were rejected by the Court.[60]

The heart of Taylor's argument was that those two Acts could not provide a legal basis for a referendum the purpose of which was to abolish the Council, and so the relevant proclamation and regulations were ultra vires those Acts and the court should issue an injunction against the appointed returning officer forbidding the referendum to be held.

Those grounds rested on three alternative propositions, which, in descending order of constitutional magnitude, were: firstly, the Queensland Legislature had no power in any circumstances to abolish the Council – such a reform could only be effected by the Imperial Parliament: secondly, if the Queensland Legislature had such power, then the reform was properly categorised per *Cooper* as altering organic or fundamental law, and could only be effected by *Cooper*'s 'Two Act entrenchment' method; and thirdly, relatedly, those two Acts could only be enacted by 'the Legislature' qua the Assembly, the Council and the royal assent; such power could not be 'delegated' to the Assembly, a referendum and the royal assent.

On the first ground, Feez and Stumm relied largely on cl.22's text, and specifically on the proviso relating to any alteration of the Council to give it an elected character. In Feez's submission, cl.22's explicit reference to the *alteration* of the Council precluded any implicit authorisation that the 'full power' given to the Legislature included the power to *abolish* either (or both) of its chambers. In other parts of the Order – with respect, for example, to courts – abolition was expressly provided for. Had abolition of the Council been countenanced by the Imperial Parliament, that term would also be found in cl.22.

Feez deployed the same argument in respect of CLVA 1865 s.5. S.5 explicitly provided in its first part for the 'abolition' of courts, but it did not use that term in its second part, which empowered legislatures to 'make laws respecting the[ir] constitution powers and procedure'; those terms could not properly be taken to include abolition of one chamber. What they provided for was adjustment or amendment of a legislature's original component parts, not complete removal of one of them.

---

[58] [1917] St R Qd 208, 213–15.

[59] P 208 above.

[60] A question on the point had been planted in the Commons in 1911. The reply was not helpful to Feez and Stumm's cause, but does not seem to have been referred to in the *Taylor* litigation (HC Deb 6 March 1911 c 991): "Mr. NEVILLE asked the Secretary of State for the Colonies whether the Parliamentary Bills Referendum Act of 1908 (Queensland, 8 Edw. 7, No 16) was reserved by His Majesty's Governor of Queensland for the signification of His Majesty's pleasure thereon; whether the same was laid before both Houses of the Imperial Parliament for the period of thirty days before His Majesty's pleasure thereon was signified; and, if so, on what date did such thirty days begin? Mr. HARCOURT The Bill in question was reserved by the Governor and was assented to by Order in Council. Under the Australian States Constitution Act, 1907, it was not necessary to lay the Bill before the Houses of Parliament."

Feez also contended that if Ryan's view was correct, then s.5 could be used to end the Monarch's role as part of the legislature. The soundness of that argument in legal terms rested on the proposition that the Monarch was indeed part of the legislature at all. The force of the submission seemed to lie more in the realm of politics than law: it was just unthinkable that the Monarch's role could be ended in this fashion. Feez did not make – and perhaps did not even perceive – the point that if the Monarch was indeed a part of the legislature then Queensland's Legislature might not have been 'representative' per CLVA 1865 s.1 when created, had never yet acquired that status and would only become so when the Council was abolished.[61]

Judgment

Lukin authored the Court's single judgment. After devoting several pages to rejecting each party's technical and jurisdictional arguments, Lukin presented a detailed recitation of Queensland's legislative history, quoting verbatim cl.22 and CLVA 1865 s.5.

Lukin explained that he and Cooper had concluded – accepting the first of Taylor's alternative propositions – that Queensland's Legislature simply lacked the power in any circumstances to abolish the Council. That result could only be achieved by Imperial legislation. That conclusion clearly goes far beyond Cooper's 'Two Act' thesis, and entrenched the existence of the Council as a matter substantively rather than just procedurally beyond the Legislature's normal lawmaking process.

Lukin's analysis of s.5 also accepted Feez's submission that s.5 extended only to altering the *internal* characteristics of the original legislature (for example, by altering the numbers of members or their methods of election and selection). Abolishing the Council was a quite different enterprise, one not within the compass of a representative legislature. The argument drew on s.5's text; the express grant of powers to 'colonial legislatures to 'abolish' courts was not repeated in the grant of power to representative legislatures as to their 'constitution, powers and procedures'. This argument was deployed in a subtle way to attack the validity of the 1908 Act on the basis that limiting the Council's power to veto a bill was 'abolition' on a selective rather than absolute basis.

Real and Chubb[62] considered that the Legislature did have the capacity (through cl.22) to grant itself such a power, but – following *Cooper* and accepting that abolition of the Council would be a matter of *organic* rather than *ordinary* law – the question which arose was whether, in enacting the two 1908 Acts, the Legislature had done so.

Lukin's judgment proceeded on the basis that the High Court in *Cooper* correctly stated the law.[63] After citing passages from both Griffith and Barton's opinions in *Cooper*, Lukin offered this analysis:

> Some of us think, and we all assume for the purpose of this branch of the case, that the words "shall have full power and authority ... to make laws altering or repealing all or any of the provisions of this Order-in-Council in the same manner as any other laws" authorise the

---

[61] See the discussion of the possible meanings of s.1 at pp 110–111 above.
[62] Real and Chubb did not deliver separate opinions. Their view is recorded by Lukin at 239.
[63] In a strict sense, *Cooper's* 'conclusions' as to 'Two Act' entrenchment were only obiter, as the case was decided on the diminution point.

Legislature to alter the Constitution so as to confer the powers sought. That step, however, must be "preliminary" or antecedent to" and independent of the further step of carrying out that purpose. As we understand *Cooper's Case*, the Legislature must clothe itself, under its extraordinary and special powers to alter the Constitution, with the necessary authority to carry out legislation not authorised by the Constitution as it stands at the given moment, and unless that preliminary or antecedent step is taken, the subsequent effort is vain and useless.[64]

Although Lukin apparently picked up on Ryan's two 'steps' (rather than two 'Acts') terminology in this passage, he clearly used that term to mean wholly separate Acts. Since no such preliminary legislation had been enacted to modify the Constitution in a fashion which would permit the Legislature in a subsequent Act to abolish the Council, the Council could not be abolished.[65]

Lukin then reinforced this conclusion – drawing on Griffith's judgment in *Cooper* – by holding that while the Legislature was competent to delegate its lawmaking capacity on matters of *ordinary law* – and the Assembly plus referendum was an appropriate delegate for such matters – it could not delegate its power to modify *organic law*. On Lukin's view, the various Privy Council judgments upholding the power of colonial legislatures to delegate lawmaking power had all dealt only with matters relating to 'ordinary' law.[66] The judgments could not be considered authoritative in respect of organic law of the kind in issue in *Taylor*.[67] If the Council was to be abolished, the two Acts required would each have to be passed by the Assembly and Council and assented to by the Crown.

The hearing on 1 May ended in some levity. Ryan could not attend, and it fell to Blair to seek permission to appeal. 1 May was Tuesday and the referendum was scheduled for the Saturday, so some urgency obviously arose. According to *The Queenslander*,[68] Blair made two unsuccessful requests:

Mr Blair: And the leave to appeal?

The Chief Justice: We make no order.

Mr Blair asked for a stay of proceedings.

Real J: A stay of judgment?

Mr Blair: Yes, until the High Court intimates whether our leave to appeal is refused.

Real J: You are quite right to ask for it: you certainly do not expect to get it. (Laughter)

Mr Blair: The unexpected happens sometimes. I make the application. (Laughter)

The Court then adjourned.

The High Court scheduled an expedited appeal, and declined to grant Taylor interim relief to prevent the referendum being conducted. That decision was made on the Friday

---

[64] [1917] St R Qd 208, 241.

[65] Lukin did not indicate how this preliminary Act should be framed. Presumably what would be required would be along the lines of a Constitution Act Amendment Act which modified cl.22 to read: "shall have full power and authority ... to make laws altering or repealing all or any of the provisions of this Order-in-Council in the same manner as any other laws, *and such full power shall include the power to abolish the Legislative Council and reconstitute the Legislature as comprising only the Legislative Assembly acting with the assent of the Governor ...*".

[66] [1917] St R Qd 208, 241–42. Lukin referred to *Burah*, *Hodge* and *Apollo Candle*; pp 150–153 above.

[67] Given that these cases pre-dated *Cooper* and were not concerned with 'organic' law issues, their relevance to the *Taylor* issue is tenuous at best.

[68] 5 May 1917, http://trove.nla.gov.au/newspaper/article/22338401.

before the Saturday-scheduled referendum, leaving Ryan and other lesser Labour luminaries making frantic press and radio efforts to inform electors that the referendum was lawfully going ahead. The result rendered the appeal moot in an immediate sense; on 5 May 1917 Queenslanders rejected abolition by a clear majority (179,000 to 116,000).[69]

The State Supreme Court's Judgment in *Duncan v Theodore*

The *Taylor* litigation substantially compromised Ryan's capacity to campaign in the referendum. But it was not the only significant matter then before the state courts. On the day when the Supreme Court judgment in *Taylor* had been handed down, the appeal began in *Duncan Theodore*.[70] Ryan, assisted again by Macrossan, argued the appeal before the Supreme Court over nine days in early May. Feez appeared for the plaintiff/respondent. Judgment was handed down on 26 June.

The result was a qualified success for Ryan's government. Cooper – having been the trial judge – did not sit. The other *Taylor* judges did sit and were joined by William Shand, appointed in November 1908 by Kidston's (Kidston party) government. English born and educated (Harrow and Balliol), Shand qualified at the English Bar before emigrating to Queensland in 1886. He established a successful practice in Brisbane, and steered clear of any obvious party political affiliations. His appointment was not controversial.[71]

Shand followed Cooper in concluding that s.10 did not authorise acquisition of parts of a commodity, and so the June proclamation was unlawful.[72] However, unlike Cooper, Shand also considered s.7. On this point he found in the government's favour, although his reasoning, given the jury's finding as to bad faith, was ostensibly rather peculiar:

> It is not suggested that the persons guilty of the trespass were attempting, under the colour of law, to do an act which they knew to be unauthorised. I agree ... that s. 7 is a bar to the plaintiffs' action. I need hardly say I regret extremely that this case should be decided on such a point.

The peculiarity is explained by the fact that Feez apparently did not raise the bad faith point in his submissions.[73] Shand was, it seems, content to ignore Cooper's improper raising of the point rather than to confront and disapprove it directly.

Chubb took the same view of s.7 and saw no need to address the conclusions reached in Cooper's judgment. The protective clause would be effective if the defendants had acted in the honest belief that they had the power to do so. Like Shand, Chubb chose not to address the jury's bad faith finding.

---

[69] There are detailed results in *BC* 8 May 1917 p7, https://trove.nla.gov.au/newspaper/article/20153788; *Daily Mail (Brisbane)* 8 May 1917 p6, https://trove.nla.gov.au/newspaper/article/213496228.
[70] [1917] St R Qd 250.
[71] *BC* 4 November 1908 p5, https://trove.nla.gov.au/newspaper/article/19547833: "As soon as it was known that he had been offered and had accepted the Judgeship the feeling was freely expressed in the profession that the appointment had devolved upon a thoroughly sound lawyer and a cultured and courteous gentleman."
[72] [1917] St R Qd 250, 287 et seq.
[73] ibid 268–70.

Real produced a lengthy, rambling judgment.[74] Like Shand, Real also held that Cooper's view that s.10 required acquisition of a whole commodity was correct, and so the June proclamation was invalid. In finding that the defendants were protected by s.7, Real was also distinctly equivocal on the issue of bad faith. He had noted earlier in his judgment: "assuming (as I think we ought to assume) the State Government to be bona fide desirous of assisting the Imperial Government to the greatest possible extent in obtaining supplies of meat for the Imperial forces …",[75] and prefaced his conclusion as to s.7 by stating: "I feel compelled to hold that the defendants are protected from action by the plaintiffs …".[76] Like Shand and Chubb, Real was unwilling to make the point that no evidence was led at trial to sustain finding bad faith.

Lukin also avoided that issue. He dissented from his colleagues and resolved the appeal in Duncan's favour on two grounds, neither of which featured in Cooper's judgment. The first stemmed from Ryan's unwillingness to assert that the Sugar Act had in any sense repealed the Meat Act. That being so, and given the various differences between the acquisition regimes in the two Acts, it could not be correct that the general powers granted over all commodities in S.10 of the Sugar Act could take precedence over the specific power to deal with livestock and meat provided for in the Meat Act. If the government wanted to acquire livestock, it would have to do so under the Meat Act.[77]

Lukin decided the s.7 point against Theodore without raising any imputation of bad faith, which he thought unnecessary on the facts. His reasoning on this issue was linked to his first conclusion. S.7 could only be effective if the actions in issue had been taken under the auspices of the Sugar Act. But if the Sugar Act could not be used to acquire livestock and meat, neither it nor, consequentially, any proclamation issued under it was relevant to the seizure of Mrs Duncan's stock. Lukin did not explain why this line of reasoning was not overcome by the legislature's use of the word 'purporting' in the text of s.7.

The High Court's Judgment in Duncan v Theodore

The matter came promptly before the High Court, where it was argued on 6–10 August 1917. Feez again led for Mrs Duncan. Ryan, assisted by Macrossan and, perhaps surprisingly, Stumm, led the government's case. The bench comprised Barton, Isaacs and three judges appointed by Fisher's Labour government (effectively by Hughes qua Attorney-General) in 1913.[78]

The Judges

Called to the Bar in 1887, George Rich had combined a successful practice in commercial law and equity with an academic position at the University of Sydney. His career

---

[74] ibid 270 et seq. There is a bizarre passage at 281 in which Real invokes the Ten Commandments as an authority.

[75] ibid 278.

[76] ibid 284.

[77] Having reached this conclusion, Lukin saw no need to consider whether the Sugar Act authorised taking parts of rather than an entire commodity.

[78] Griffith suffered a stroke in March 1917, and did not return to the Court until February 1918.

accelerated rapidly after 1910. He became a KC in 1911, was appointed to the State Supreme Court in 1912 and just a year later to the Australian High Court, where he sat until 1950. Rich had no overt party political leanings, and soon developed a reputation as a conservative judge, especially in public law matters.

Rich shared that latter characteristic with Frank Gavan Duffy. Duffy was the son of Sir Charles Gavan Duffy, who had been variously a member of the House of Commons and, after emigrating to Australia, Premier of Victoria. Duffy began a hugely successful career at the Victoria Bar in 1874, which he combined with developing a substantial reputation as an academic author. Notwithstanding his father's influence, Duffy had no obviously partisan political affiliations.

The same could not be said of Sir Charles Powers, whose appointment generated considerable political controversy.[79] Powers qualified as a solicitor in Queensland in 1871. He sat as an independent in the Assembly between 1888 and 1896, and for some of that period led an informal Labour/Independent opposition coalition (to Griffith's administration). Powers left party politics to become Crown Solicitor in Queensland in 1899 and then Commonwealth Crown Solicitor in 1903. His High Court appointment was condemned as 'political' in the press; the New South Wales Bar described him as unqualified and boycotted his swearing-in ceremony.[80] He remained on the court until retiring in 1929.[81]

While Powers faced down that criticism, a fourth nominee, Albert Piddington, stepped aside on facing such attacks. Piddington, born in 1862 in New South Wales, was a clergyman's son. After attending Sydney University, he was called to the Bar in 1890 and elected to the Assembly in 1895 as a free trader. Piddington's political leanings were towards radical reformism. Although he lost his seat in 1898, Piddington's practice flourished, and he was deeply involved in promoting various reformist legislation in New South Wales over the next 10 years. He was apparently to his own surprise nominated to the High Court by Hughes, but was so perturbed by criticism from the legal profession that he was both insufficiently experienced as a lawyer (he was not then a silk) and overly partisan politically that he stood aside.[82]

The Judgments

The High Court divided three to two in Mrs Duncan's favour: Barton, Rich and Gavan Duffy formed the majority, with Isaacs and Powers dissenting.[83]

---

[79] http://adb.anu.edu.au/biography/powers-sir-charles-8092.
[80] *SMH* 4 April 1913 p7, http://trove.nla.gov.au/ndp/del/article/15410124.
[81] It has been suggested that national Labour governments were loath to make politically partisan judicial appointments to the High Court. Commenting on the 1913 appointees, Sawer labelled Powers a 'mediocrity', Gavan Duffy 'a States righter' and Rich 'non-political and constitutionally colourless': Sawer (1967) *Australian federalism in the courts* p65; cited in Tennant (1970) *Evatt: politics and justice* p72. In his earlier (1956) *Australian federal politics and law* pp 106–07, Sawer did not make such disparaging comments, but did make the curious observation (curious given Powers' career) that none of the appointees had been involved in party politics.
[82] http://adb.anu.edu.au/biography/piddington-albert-bathurst-8043. cf Sawer (1967) op cit p65; Piddington "was terrified into immediate resignation by the screams of rage which his appointment elicited from the reactionary Melbourne and Sydney bars".
[83] *Duncan v Theodore* [1917] HCA 38, (1917) 23 CLR 510.

The dissenting judgments decided every point in Theodore's favour. On the largest 'constitutional issue' – whether the Meat Act created rights for the Crown which could be altered only by subsequent legislation framed in express terms – Isaacs and Rich concluded that the underlying premise of the assertion was misconceived. Such rights as the Crown acquired under the Meat Act were not part of the Crown's prerogative, but statutory entitlements which the Legislature could remove or abrogate in the ordinary way.[84]

The primary issue was therefore the meaning of s.10 of the Sugar Acquisition Act, which was to be found in the words of s.10 itself, in s.10's immediate context of the Act as a whole and in the broader context of the obvious purpose which the Act was intended to serve. In Isaacs and Powers's view, s.10's meaning was to enable the government to issue a proclamation in respect of a particular commodity which, in turn, empowered the government to deal with that commodity in toto or in part, as it thought fit, by issuing subsequent proclamations. To assume that a first proclamation identifying a commodity precluded subsequent proclamations enabling only parts of that commodity to be acquired would be to adopt a strained reading of s.10 which would produce nonsensical results:[85] "nothing but the most intractable words ought to compel the Court to conclude that the second Proclamation must cover the whole area of the first".[86] Noting that other sections of the Act clearly referred to parts of a commodity,[87] Powers and Isaacs concluded that the only sensible reading of the Act was that: "discretion is entrusted to the Crown to acquire a given commodity in proportion to what it conceives to be the needs of the community".[88]

Isaacs and Powers also considered that the plain meaning of s.7's protective clause indicated that it had a similarly broad scope. It would be ineffective only if the plaintiff could show that the defendants acted in bad faith. On this point – although Isaacs and Powers did not refer to Cooper or Lukin expressly – the judgment was withering on the conclusions those two judges had reached: "We were not referred to any evidence fit to be submitted to a jury to support that finding ... The point ought never to have been submitted to the jury."[89]

Isaacs and Powers' analysis did not convince their colleagues, however, although the majority were not united in their reasoning. Rich and Gavan Duffy offered a joint opinion covering barely half a page.[90] Their conclusion was that the first proclamation had only authorised the Crown to take ownership of cattle as a class, and had not extended the reach of the Sugar Act to permit subsequent proclamations to identify only specific cattle within that general class. The judgment made no allusion to Cooper and Lukin's

---

[84] Rich and Isaacs did not question the correctness of the general principle, but held it inapplicable on the facts.

[85] Most obviously because within seconds of the first proclamation being issued for a given commodity (be it cows, coal or butter) the 'whole amount' of the commodity within the state would have changed; cows die or are born, coal is burnt, butter is eaten and so the second proclamation would be dealing with a different 'whole': "... If both Proclamations must refer to the same 'commodity' in the sense that identically the same articles – neither more nor less – must be covered by both, then every second Proclamation may be, and probably would be, invalid ...": (1917) 23 CLR 510, 532.

[86] ibid.
[87] ibid 534.
[88] ibid.
[89] ibid 544.
[90] ibid 544–45.

conclusions as to Theodore's (and, by extension, Ryan's) bad faith, an omission which left the accusation hanging. Nor did Rich and Gavan Duffy address at all the significance of the s.7 protective clause. All in all, their opinion is notable both for its intellectual laziness and for its transparently shabby political bias.

Barton's judgment could certainly not be classified as lazy. Barton offered a lengthy opinion, albeit one which was not especially cogent in its reasoning. Its core conclusion was that the first proclamation issued under s.10 had fixed the lawful scope of any subsequent proclamation relating to the identified commodity: "When the second paragraph of sec.10 allows the acquisition of 'any such commodity', it means the very commodity to which the Act has been extended by the first Proclamation, neither more nor less."[91] Barton did not address, still less rebut, the practical problems highlighted by Powers and Isaacs that such a construction of s.10 would entail.

Barton felt that he did not need to resolve the bad faith point, although he indicated that he did not think any such claim could be made out. That omission might be thought curious, given that he then concluded that Theodore could not rely on s.7. Rather than identify bad faith as negating the defence's reliance on s.7, Barton essentially followed Lukin's conclusion in the State Supreme Court. S.7 could only be effective if a valid proclamation was in force, but since Barton declared: "I gravely doubt whether the existence of the facts found affects a valid Proclamation",[92] s.7 was not in issue. Much like Lukin, Barton ignored the 'purporting' element of s.7's text.

There was little time for Ryan to digest the *Duncan* judgment, handed down as it was while argument in *Taylor* was still ongoing.

III. *Taylor* in the High Court

The scale of the government's defeat in the abolition referendum indicates that the Labour Party had misjudged the public mood on abolition. Nevertheless, the High Court proceedings in *Taylor* continued, given that they raised an issue of general significance. The Court heard argument on 10 and 13–15 August 1917.[93] The bench was the same as in *Duncan v Theodore*.

Counsel and Submissions

Ryan himself again led for Queensland. Feez and Stumm continued as counsel for Taylor. Neither side pressed the technical points unsuccessfully raised before the State Supreme Court. The record of submissions in the official law report is rather cursory, although there is extensive coverage in the *BC*.[94] Ryan began by reducing the

---

[91] ibid 523.
[92] ibid 525–26.
[93] So argument began on the same day that argument in *Duncan* ended.
[94] The account below is drawn from reports on 11 August 1917 p12, https://trove.nla.gov.au/newspaper/article/20164374; 14 August 1917 p13, https://trove.nla.gov.au/newspaper/article/20175326; 15 August 1917 p3, https://trove.nla.gov.au/newspaper/article/20178613; 16 August 1917 p3, https://trove.nla.gov.au/newspaper/article/20143719.

question before the Court to its substantive essentials: could Queensland's Legislature be abolished through the PBRA 1908's lawmaking process?

Ryan's starting point was to reject Lukin and Cooper's conclusion in the State Supreme Court that only the Imperial Parliament could abolish the Council. As in the court below, Ryan claimed that power was found in cl.22 (he suggested before the High Court that such a power also lay in s.2 of the 1867 Act).[95] Perhaps surprisingly – and not altogether accurately, since he ignored its 'Two Act' entrenchment element – Ryan invoked Griffith's judgment in *Cooper* to claim that the powers bestowed on the Legislature by cl.22 (and s.2 of the 1867 Act) included – and still included – the power to change the way in which it exercised its powers:[96] "My contention is that the continuation of government does not rest upon the *continuation of characteristics*, but on *succession of powers*."[97] In the alternative, Ryan asserted – as below – that the CLVA 1865 s.5 bestowed such a power.

Ryan readily accepted that this could lead to significant changes in the Legislature's identity:

> Duffy: You say you could abolish both Houses and substitute a dictator?
>
> Ryan: Yes. And if you did, you would not abolish the Legislature ... The dictator would exercise the powers of the Legislature.
>
> Duffy: ... [Y]ou mean you are at liberty to dispose of any part of the existing Legislature provided you form another in its place?

Barton continued this line of questioning:

> Barton: Then you could abolish the Legislative Assembly and continue to carry on the Government with a nominee Council and the Governor?
>
> Ryan: Yes.
>
> Barton: You could abolish the Legislative Council afterwards, and have everything in the hands of the Governor.
>
> Ryan: I contend there is power to do that.[98]

In essence, Ryan submitted that the lawmaker created by the PBRA 1908 was in a legal sense every bit as much 'the Legislature' of Queensland as the bicameral plus royal assent Legislature created by cl.22.

---

[95] (1917) 23 CLR 457, 466. On this point, Ryan did invoke Jenkyns (1902) *British rule* ... p75, but, as in the Supreme Court, did not expressly allude to the s.5 analysis at p73.

[96] Barton questioned this reading of *Cooper*, observing (accurately): "I thought the real result of Cooper's case was that you could not amend your Constitution by mere ordinary enactment, but in order to do so you have to make an enactment amending the Constitution in that part and then acting under the extended powers pass another Act to carry out your legislative purpose." Ryan's reply that this meant only that the Constitution could not be altered by implication drew the (again accurate per *Cooper*) rejoinder from Stumm that: "You could not repeal the Constitution by one Act."

[97] Emphasis added.

[98] Ryan was not pressed to explain – either by the bench or by Feez and Stumm – how his 'Council plus Governor Legislature' or 'Dictator/Governor Legislature' would satisfy the requirements of CLVA 1865 s.1 that it be 'representative', ie that 'half' of its members be elected. In closing the government's case, Blair (surprisingly) disagreed with that submission, albeit he endorsed the view that either cl 22 or s.5 provided a legal source for the PBRA: "Duffy: Do you go as far as your leader as to say that a Dictator could be set up? Blair: I would not like to assent to that ..." Later in the hearing, during Feez's submissions, Isaacs indicated that he doubted that CLVA 1865 s.5 could be used to remove a Legislature's representative character.

Blair took responsibility for rebutting any suggestion that the CAAA 1908 was invalid as it had not been passed with a (s.9) two-thirds majority. His submissions rehearsed the points Ryan made during the bill's passage, and placed particular emphasis on Berriedale Keith's analysis of the position.

Feez and Stumm offered little authority for their primary contention that only the Imperial Parliament could abolish the Council. They invoked only the Privy Council's (1896) judgment in *Attorney-General for New South Wales v Rennie*.[99] The submission was – at best – hugely optimistic. *Rennie* concerned the meaning of the legislation which had introduced payment for Assembly members. In rejecting the argument that the relevant Act applied only to the parliamentary session when the legislation was enacted, the Privy Council judgment referred to the New South Wales Legislature as a 'permanent' body.[100] 'Permanent' was manifestly used there only to mean that Assembly members would continue to be paid until the Act was repealed.

Feez's more elaborate argument on this point was that enactment of the Constitution Act 1867 – passed after the CLVA 1865 – had in some fashion 'exhausted' the Legislature's powers under cl.22 and s.5, and those powers could not be used again to alter the Legislature's fundamental, bicameral nature: "When that Constitution Act was passed Queensland had adopted an absolutely rigid form of Constitution so far as Parliament was concerned."

Feez doggedly insisted when faced with many questions from the bench that the Legislature could not – through either cl.22 or s.5 – remove its bicameral character. The details of that bicameral character might be altered in such matters as the numbers of members, their qualifications or their methods of selection, but bicameralism itself could not be abandoned. The bench showed some scepticism on this point.

> Powers: Do you say that the Legislature could reduce the number of the members of the Legislative Council?
>
> Feez: Yes, that is where the power is given.
>
> Powers: Then they could reduce to half, and if to half, to one?

Beyond suggesting the possibility of a one-person Council was 'absurd', Feez had no answer to that question.

Feez's secondary argument continued to be that if such a power did indeed exist, it could not be exercised through the PBRA process. His argument again had two strands. Firstly, s.5 used the term 'abolition' only in respect of courts, not legislatures: "If the Imperial authorities had intended to give power to abolish, they would have said so in clear words." Secondly, Feez pressed the argument that the PBRA lawmaker was not a 'Legislature', because it was inherent in that concept that the lawmaker's component parts were able to deliberate and consult with each other on the merits of a proposed law. The electors qua referendum could not perform that function. That submission ended with an apparently tetchy exchange:

> Feez: The Legislature is a well-known term and the Legislature is not the popular vote.
>
> Duffy: The Legislature as I understand it is the body capable of passing a law.[101]

---

[99] (1896) AC 376.
[100] ibid 379.
[101] Duffy was presumably alluding here to CLVA 1865 s.1; p 107 above.

The High Court indicated that it would not delay issuing its judgment for long. The decision was handed down on 6 September 1917.[102]

The Judgments in *Taylor*

Given the political significance of the abolition issue in Queensland, the judgment in *Taylor* is surprisingly brief. More noteworthy perhaps is that none of the five judges appeared to see any great difficulty in the question before them. Save for a (very) passing reference to the issue in Isaacs' opinion,[103] no member of the Court saw any need to engage with the legitimacy or political context of either the 1908 Acts or the Ryan government's plans to have the Council abolished.

Barton delivered the first opinion. He considered that the issue turned entirely on the meaning of CLVA 1865 s.5. Barton did not doubt – the matter seems not to have been in issue – that Queensland's Legislature was 'representative' per s.1 and s.5. Barton took a broad view of the meaning of 'constitution' within s.5: this would embrace the 'composition, form or nature' of the legislature. He also suggested – although he did not develop the point – that the s.5 power did not allow a representative legislature to divest itself of its representative character.

Having defined s.5's notion of 'constitution', Barton then concluded that the issue arising as to the validity of the PBRA 1908 concerned the Legislature's 'powers' rather than its 'constitution'. His rationale was that the 1908 Act provided a mechanism through which the referendum could be a 'substitute' for the Council. (On this analysis, of course – again, the point was not developed – the Legislature would remain bicameral, with one of its two components parts elected, and so would still likely be 'representative' for s.1 and s.5 purposes.[104])

Barton then returned to the question of the 'constitution', a concept which he held included the 'composition' of the legislature. Since the 1908 Act did not preclude the 'substitute' Legislature from changing the composition of the Legislature (whether in its substitute or original form), there was no basis to assume that the Council could not be abolished through the new procedure.

Barton referred briefly to *Cooper*. He held that s.5 overrode any 'Two Act' entrenchment requirement in relation to matters within the scope of s.5 itself. That conclusion seemingly accepts Ryan's submission that a 'colonial law' in the s.5 sense had to have an explicit statutory or Order in Council basis, rather than being rooted in a judicial implication into such measures. However, he did not cast on doubt on *Cooper*'s correctness in respect of Queensland's 'organic law' other than that brought within s.5.[105]

Isaacs also rejected Feez's submission that s.5's reference to the 'constitution' of a legislature precluded abolition of the legislature's component parts:

> I read the words "constitution of such legislature" as including the change from a unicameral to a bicameral system, or the reverse. Probably the "representative" character of the legislature

---

[102] [1917] HCA 45, (1917) 23 CLR 457.
[103] (1917) 23 CLR 457, 471.
[104] Barton did not explicitly quote from s.5 to say that the PBRA process was a new 'manner and form' of legislating.
[105] (1917) 23 CLR 457, 469.

is a basic condition of the power relied on, and is preserved by the word "such," but, that being maintained, I can see no reason for cutting down the plain natural meaning of the words in question so as to exclude the power of a self-governing community to say that for state purposes one House is sufficient as its organ of legislation.[106]

Nor could Isaacs find any reason in the circumstances surrounding s.5's enactment to justify lending 'constitution' a more narrow meaning. The Legislature had therefore been competent to enact the referendum legislation in 1908, and so long as the requirements of that Act were followed, the 'Legislature' might subsequently abolish the Council. S.5, Isaacs concluded, was: "a general standing power of all representative legislatures outside and irrespective of their own separate constitutions".[107]

Isaacs differed from Barton, however, in identifying just what the redefined Legislature comprised. In his view, the Legislature was now composed only of the Assembly (he did not consider the Crown to be part of the Legislature for s.5 purposes). The referendum itself was not a part of the Legislature, but rather an external mechanism which had to approve a bill passed by the Assembly before the measure could be presented for the royal assent:

> The effect, summed up briefly, is that the Legislature of Queensland – apart from the Crown, which must in all cases assent – henceforth consists of the two Houses concurring, except in the case of an irreconcilable difference, and in that case it is constituted by the Legislative Assembly alone, on condition that the electors approve of the Assembly's proposal.[108]

Isaacs also considered that the PBRA 1908 could have been enacted through the Legislature's powers under cl.22, which powers he suggested were "possibly even broader"[109] than those granted by s.5. He also made brief reference to *Cooper*, describing Griffith's judgment as 'correct'.[110] That observation must presumably be read as approving the 'Two Act' entrenchment thesis. Unlike Barton, Isaacs did not expressly suggest that s.5 overrode that thesis, and his opinion certainly implies that the *Cooper* principle was properly regarded as a 'colonial law' in the s.5 sense.

Gavan Duffy and Rich JJ delivered a joint opinion focused, like Barton's, solely on s.5. They lent s.5 a broad ambit:

> In our opinion the word "constitution" in this collocation means "nature," "composition," or "make up," and the enactment enables a representative legislature to alter its constitution as it chooses, to allot to the legislature such powers as it thinks fit, and to prescribe the method in which it shall conduct its proceedings.[111]

Their opinion acknowledged Feez's submissions as to the distinction drawn in s.5 between the explicit mention of 'abolition' of courts and the absence of that term in

---

[106] ibid 474.
[107] ibid.
[108] ibid 472.
[109] ibid 476; albeit that Isaacs doubted that s.5 or cl.22 could be used to remove the Legislature's representative character.
[110] ibid.
[111] ibid 477.

respect of legislatures, but did not accept that the distinction had the consequences which Feez suggested:

> It is said that the word "abolish" is used here where it is intended to give power to put an end to a Court, and that a similar word would have been used had it been intended to give power to destroy the Legislative Council, which is an integral part of the existing legislature. Had it been intended to give to a representative legislature power to enact that there should thereafter be no legislature, the word "abolish" might well have been used, but the vice of the argument lies in a confusion between two distinct notions – the abolition of a legislature, and the abolition of a constituent part of such legislature. Mere alteration of the constitution of a legislature negatives the notion of the abolition of such legislature, but may entail the abolition of an integral part of it.[112]

Queensland had to have a 'Legislature' (and, like Isaacs, Duffy and Rich suggested, that Legislature had to be 'representative'), but the form, powers and procedure of the Legislature were for the Legislature itself (acting in the correct manner and form) to determine.

Rich and Gavan Duffy offered a third perspective on the nature of the Legislature created by the 1908 Act. In their view, the 'true effect' of that Act was: "merely to limit the power of the Legislative Council by rendering its concurrence unnecessary in the making of laws in certain circumstances".[113] They appeared to reject the suggestion that the 1908 Act Legislature was a bicameral institution comprised of the Assembly and the referendum voters.

Powers produced a brief opinion, apparently concurring with all four other judges. He explicitly endorsed Isaacs's construction of the term 'constitution' in s.5 ("as including the change from a unicameral to a bicameral system, or the reverse")[114] and with the suggestion that the word 'such' in s.5 required any reconstituted Legislature to retain its representative character.

Ryan, Hughes and Conscription – Round 2

Taylor was a great success for Ryan both as a politician and as lawyer. The High Court refused Taylor permission to appeal to the Privy Council, and he subsequently decided to seek permission from the Privy Council itself. In the interim, ironically perhaps, the High Court judgment opened a legal route to Council abolition that seemed – for the present – politically impassable. At this juncture, Ryan sought to augment Labour numbers in the Council. Thirteen new members were appointed in October 1917. All the appointees made a pledge to support Council abolition.[115] The augmentation of Labour members was enough to afford the government the prospect of a majority on

---

[112] ibid 477–78.
[113] ibid 478.
[114] ibid 481.
[115] For biographical details of the 13 and an account of the selection process, see *Daily Standard* 10 October 1917 p1, https://trove.nla.gov.au/newspaper/article/179425490; *BC* 11 October 1817 p6, https://trove.nla.gov.au/newspaper/article/20192072.

most matters – but not abolition – given the generally poor attendance rates of opposition members.[116]

However, Ryan soon had a more personally pressing political matter to address. The referendum defeat on 5 May 1917 was accompanied by a sweeping win for Hughes's Nationalists in the 1917 Commonwealth election. The Nationalists took 53 of the House's 75 seats; Labour, the only opposition party, took just 22. The Nationalists held 24 of the 36 Senate seats. Hughes construed that electoral success as a justification to put the conscription issue to the electorate again.[117] A vote was set for December 1917.

Both in Queensland and on the national stage, Ryan steadfastly opposed conscription in the second referendum campaign. That opposition was initially rooted in ideological concerns, albeit that he consistently supported the war effort. However, as the referendum vote approached, Ryan had become convinced that Hughes's case was factually flawed. Hughes was so antagonised by Ryan's activities that Hughes initiated a prosecution of Ryan and Theodore for allegedly breaching regulations passed under the War Precautions Act 1914.[118]

The prosecution was triggered by Ryan's own investigations of the Hughes government's case that conscription was necessary. On Ryan's reading of the evidence, voluntary enlistment satisfied any foreseeable need for Australian troops to be deployed overseas. Ryan subsequently publicised his views to the press; and in a speech at a major anti-conscription rally in Brisbane on 19 November, Ryan argued that, on the basis of the government's own statistics, Australia had already recruited more than enough volunteers to provide the reinforcements that the British government requested. The Hughes government promptly censored press reports of the speech to excise the figures Ryan presented. Ryan then repeated the figures in a speech in the Assembly on 22 November, and arranged for 10,000 copies of the debate to be published as an official parliamentary report. Having been alerted to this, Hughes personally led a military raid on the Parliament's printers and seized all of the copies of the record of the debate. Ryan thereupon repeated his speech to a public meeting in Brisbane on 26 November.

Ryan and Theodore were charged under reg.42 of the War Precautions (Military Service Referendum) Regulations 1917 (No 290) (as amended):

> 42. – (1) Any person who, on or before the polling day for the Referendum, makes or authorizes to be made, verbally or in writing, any false statement of fact of a kind likely to affect the

---

[116] And as such prompted press reports of illegitimate swamping; see *Queensland Times* 12 October 1917 p4, https://trove.nla.gov.au/newspaper/article/121979235. *The (Brisbane) Courier* directed criticism at the Governor as much as at Ryan: "The Governor has consented to at least such a measure of swamping as is calculated to destroy the character of the chamber as one of independent mature second thought": BC 11 October 1917 p6, https://trove.nla.gov.au/newspaper/article/20192079. See further Murphy (1975) op cit pp 298–99 and fn 70 therein.

[117] Hughes sought to reload the electoral dice in his favour. Taking the view that Australians of German descent had mostly voted against conscription in the first referendum, Hughes promulgated regulations which prohibited Australians who had previously been, or whose father had been, of German descent; War Precautions Act (Military Service Referendum) Regulations 1917 reg.22. Bizarrely, both Feez and Stumm were caught by this proviso.

[118] The episode is recounted in detail in Murphy op cit ch 13. See also McPhee (2017) 'The deadliest enemies of Australia: the politics of intelligence during the Australian conscription controversies of 1916–1917' *Journal of Intelligence History* 1. There is substantial coverage of the trial, including Ryan's testimony, in *Queensland Times* 6 December 1917, https://trove.nla.gov.au/newspaper/article/121979458/10314361; *Daily Standard* 6 December 1917 p7, http://trove.nla.gov.au/newspaper/article/179432907.

judgment of electors in relation to their votes, or who prints, publishes, or distributes any advertisement, notice, hand-bill, pamphlet, or card containing any such statement, shall be guilty of an offence ...

Those regulations, purportedly promulgated by Hughes under powers granted by the War Precautions Act (although the regulations do not identify which section of the Act provides their legal source), were issued on 10 November 1917.[119] However, reg.42 was not in the original regulations (the last of which was reg.41). It was inserted by an amending regulation (No 304 reg.11) issued on 19 November 1917. The obvious inference is that reg.42 was specifically targeted at Ryan's critique of the government's statistics.[120]

If so, the initiative proved futile. The government ministers who produced the figures on which Ryan relied declined to give evidence; the one government witness who did appear confirmed that Ryan's estimates were accurate; and Ryan himself – as defendant and witness rather than counsel – proved as forensically persuasive in the former roles as in the latter. He urged the court to accept either that his estimates were not 'facts' per reg.42 but rather statements of opinion; or, if they were 'facts', they were not 'false'.

The *BC* of 7 December 1917 recounted proceedings at length. Ryan's counsel – Hugh Macrossan – had not stinted in attacking the prosecution's moral bona fides. Expressing amazement that the magistrate had not already dismissed the case, Macrossan concluded bluntly:

> If Mr Ryan was not the Premier of Queensland and made this speech, do you think for one minute you would have had the duty of adjudicating on this matter. You cannot get away from it. It is a political prosecution.[121]

The magistrate was apparently persuaded. Shortly afterwards he dismissed the case, stating that there were no 'facts' in Ryan's speech.

The extraordinary intensity of Ryan's workload as Premier and Attorney-General is perhaps best illustrated by the fact that the day after testifying in his criminal trial, he stood as counsel in the first stage of one of the most celebrated cases in British colonial constitutional history. Ryan's 'client' was Thomas McCawley.

---

[119] The regulations could conceivably also have been rooted in the Military Service Referendum Act 1916 s.12: "(1) The Governor-General may make regulations, not inconsistent with this Act, prescribing all matters which are necessary or convenient to be prescribed for carrying out or giving effect to this Act": www.legislation.gov.au/Details/C1916A00027.
[120] Murphy (1975) op cit pp 311–12.
[121] P8, http://nla.gov.au/nla.news-article20201521.

9

Constitutional Controversy in Queensland: Ryan, Theodore and *McCawley* in the Queensland Courts

> Neither jurymen, nor police officers, nor public defenders are likely to be intimidated by the comments of the Chief Justice, but he is no more justified in his adverse criticism of them than they would be if they attributed some of his erroneous decisions against the Government in such important cases as the insurance case or the Legislative Council case, to want of integrity rather than to an imperfect knowledge of the law.
>
> Tom Ryan, in a speech in the Legislative Assembly at *QLAD* 2 October 1917 p1515.

Thomas McCawley initially came to a position of minor political and legal prominence in Queensland during Kidston's first government. McCawley was born in Queensland in 1881, of Irish and German immigrant parents.[1] He began working life aged 14 as a solicitor's clerk, and subsequently entered the state's public service in the Justice Department when Blair was Attorney-General in Kidston's Labour administration. McCawley qualified as a barrister in 1907, but never practised in the courts. McCawley's career as a civil servant was not hampered by Kidston's abandonment of the Labour Party; in 1910, McCawley was appointed Crown Solicitor under Kidston's fused government.

McCawley's political instincts were strongly social democratic; he played a prominent role during Kidston's administrations in promoting and drafting reformist labour relations legislation. Although the political pendulum swung against that perspective during Denham's ministry, McCawley developed a close personal and political relationship with Ryan.[2] Ryan appointed McCawley in 1917 as the first President of Queensland's Arbitration Court under the terms of the Industrial Arbitration Act 1916.

The Act was one of the few measures that Ryan could push through the Legislative Council, a feat achieved only by acceding to Council demands that the original bill

---

[1] http://adb.anu.edu.au/biography/mccawley-thomas-william-7310. See further Scott, Kariyawsam and Hocking (2007) 'The philosophical ideals and political orientation of Thomas McCawley: a social democrat or a pragmatist?' *Bond LR* 57; Cope (1976) 'Political appointment of T.W. McCawley as President of the Court of Arbitration, Justice of the Supreme Court and Chief Justice of Queensland' *University of Queensland LJ* 224; Aroney (2006) 'Politics, law and the constitution in McCawley's case' *Melbourne ULR* 605.

[2] Ryan's biographer records: "It was to be McCawley on whose legal advice Ryan was to lean during the first two years of his government and on whom the cabinet was to rely in drafting its more contentious arbitration legislation": Murphy (1975) op cit p 110.

be significantly amended by reducing the number of occupations it affected.[3] The Act established in s.6 a 'Court of Industrial Arbitration' (hereafter 'Arbitration Court'), appointments to which were controlled by s.6(2)–(3):

> (2) The Governor in Council shall, by commission in His Majesty's name, appoint a Judge or Judges of the Court not exceeding three in number. One of such Judges shall be designated the President of the Court.
>
> (3) The Governor in Council may, if he deems it necessary, in like manner, appoint an additional Judge or additional Judges of the Court …
>
> (6) … The President and each Judge of the Court of Industrial Arbitration shall hold office as President and Judge of the said Court for seven years from the date of their respective appointments, and shall be eligible to be reappointed by the Governor in Council as such President or Judge for a further period of seven years.

Per s.7(i)(iv), the Arbitration Court would exercise a broad jurisdiction over industrial relations matters[4] to impose legally binding awards on employers and employees which would:

> … define and declare the relative rights and mutual duties of employers and employees according to what in the opinion of the Court should be the standard of fair dealing between an average good employer and a competent and honest employee.[5]

The political sentiments informing the 1916 Act were hardly new in the Australian context, either in the state or national sphere. The previous year, Higgins – by then deeply embedded both on the High Court and the Commonwealth Court of Conciliation and Arbitration – had used a *Harvard Law Review* article[6] to explain the policy underlying such legislation. Higgins presented the issue in class-laden terms:

> The war between the profit-maker and the wage-earner is always with us; and, although not so dramatic or catastrophic as the present war in Europe, it probably produces in the long run as much loss and suffering, not only to the actual combatants, but also to the public. Is there no remedy?[7]

The article was largely devoted to summarising the Court of Conciliation and Arbitration's judgments, and suggested that the 'war' metaphor was an exaggeration. Higgins indicated that the Court's jurisdiction was frequently invoked by employers' associations as well as by trade unions, with both 'sides' seeing the Court as a means to create a more consensual approach to industrial relations issues which fell within the Commonwealth Parliament's jurisdiction. Higgins also intimated that the judiciary's role in this 'new province' was necessarily rather different from its traditional responsibility. Higgins's political sentiments on such issues might credibly be thought to be

---

[3] For details, see Matthews (1949) 'A history of industrial law in Queensland' *Journal of the Historical Society of Queensland* 150, esp pp 155–62; Murphy (1975) op cit p212.

[4] A term very broadly defined to include all aspects of the employment relationship and the roles therein of trade unions.

[5] The Arbitration Court's jurisdiction could be triggered by a request from employees, employers, a trade union or at its own volition; s.7(1)(i)(ii).

[6] (1915) 'A new province for law and order' *Harvard LR* 13. The article acquired something approaching a seminal status in subsequent years.

[7] Ibid p13.

in reasonably close alignment with Ryan's.[8] But the legitimacy of the 'new province' per se – and especially of the appropriateness of selecting a new type of judge performing a new type of judicial role to govern that new province – was a fiercely contested issue in Queensland political and legal circles. Most pointedly, McCawley's appointment as President of the Arbitration Court provoked criticism on the ostensible basis that McCawley's lack of experience in practice left him unqualified to be a judge.[9] The criticism intensified in October 1917, when Ryan invoked a power apparently granted under s.6(6) of the 1916 Act to appoint McCawley qua judge of the Arbitration Court as a judge of the Supreme Court as well:

> S.6(6) … Notwithstanding the provisions of any Act limiting the number of Judges of the Supreme Court, the Governor in Council may appoint the President or any Judge of the Court to be a Judge of the Supreme Court … [and such appointee] shall hold office as a Judge of the said Supreme Court during good behaviour, and be paid such salary and allowances as the Governor in Council may direct … which shall not be diminished or increased during his term of office as a Judge of the Supreme Court or be less than the salary and allowances of a Puisne Judge of the Supreme Court.

I. In the Queensland Courts

Questions as to the constitutionality of McCawley's Supreme Court appointment circulated in the state press as soon it was announced.[10] Matters came to a (legal) head when Feez and Stumm, who led the criticism, intervened.

'Counsel' and 'Submissions'

While there are no records of submissions in the official law report,[11] there is an extensive (although not full)[12] account of the 'proceedings' before the Supreme Court on 6 December – proceedings which seem to have been attended by remarkable informality and tetchiness – in the *BC* of 7 December.

---

[8] Higgins and McCawley were on friendly terms by this time, and were in regular correspondence about the 1916 Act and McCawley's role on the Arbitration Court; Aroney (2006) op cit.

[9] That 'legal' criticism was likely underpinned by concern that McCawley qua judge would exercise the Court's jurisdiction in ways many employers would find politically unpalatable. See the leader titled 'Political Jobbery' in the *Bundeburg Mail* 8 January 1917 p2, https://trove.nla.gov.au/news-article216895072. See also the *Daily Examiner* 9 January 1917 p4 https://trove.nla.gov.au/news-article195769248. A contrasting view is offered in the radically inclined scandal sheet paper *Truth* 7 January 1917, https://trove.nla.gov.au/news-/article201556399.

[10] cf *Northern Herald (Cairns)* 19 October 1917 p10, https://trove.nla.gov.au/newspaper/article/150913606; *Gympie Times* 20 October 1917 p 6, https://trove.nla.gov.au/newspaper/article/188171179.

[11] *In re McCawley* [1917] St R Qd 62. The report oddly lists (at 62) the matter as having been heard for two days on 3–4 December. Press reports indicate that the 'hearing' was on 6 December, lasted just a few hours and was presumably conducted without either side having prepared formal skeleton arguments, which is unsurprising as no action had been issued. McCawley submitted further written arguments before judgment was given. See, however, n 18 below.

[12] The 'judgment' alludes to submissions not recorded in *The (Brisbane) Courier*.

Ryan's relationship with Cooper and Lukin was then extremely uncomfortable. Cooper's decision at trial in *Duncan v Theodore* to ask the jury to form a view as to Ryan and Theodore's good faith, and Lukin's refusal in the appeal to overturn the jury's conclusion on the point, lent a personal dimension to an obvious ideological tension.[13] On appearing before the Court on 5 December, Ryan was publicly upbraided by Lukin for not replying to a letter from Cooper disputing a government statement made in the Assembly some weeks earlier purportedly detailing (inaccurately in Cooper and Lukin's view) how often their judgments had been reversed on appeal.[14]

That spat followed a contretemps triggered in October when Cooper made a speech from the bench in which he attacked the moral propriety of a legal aid scheme introduced by Ryan's government[15] and went on to suggest that the government and some policemen were colluding to ensure that juries in some cases comprised persons who would secure the acquittal of the accused irrespective of the merits of the case.[16] Ryan responded promptly with an Assembly statement which criticised Cooper for overstepping his judicial role and undermining public confidence in the legal system, and which then, with undisguised sarcasm, cast obvious doubt on both Cooper's integrity and competence:

> Neither jurymen, nor police officers, nor public defenders are likely to be intimidated by the comments of the Chief Justice, but he is no more justified in his adverse criticism of them than they would be if they attributed some of his erroneous decisions against the Government in such important cases as the insurance case or the Legislative Council case, to want of integrity rather than to an imperfect knowledge of the law.[17]

No action of any sort relating to McCawley's appointment had been formally issued before 6 December, when McCawley presented himself to the Court to take his oath of office. It seemed, however, that a dispute was widely expected. The *BC* recorded that: "The knowledge that Mr Justice McCawley was to take his seat on the Full Court Bench yesterday for the first time had the effect of filling the spacious courtroom. The attendance of ladies was more than ordinarily large."[18]

---

[13] Pp 249 and 256 above.

[14] *BC* 6 December 1917 p6, https://trove.nla.gov.au/newspaper/article/20201386.

[15] The scheme was rooted in the Public Curator Act 1915 (a Ryan government measure assented to on 13 December 1915). The Act was concerned primarily with the administration of estates, but tucked away in s.114(1)(k) was a provision which empowered the Governor-General in Council to make regulations for "the provision of legal aid in any legal proceedings by or against poor persons, accused persons, and others". Cooper's 'critique' took the form of a series of assertions made to Blair (who had the misfortune to be the publicly funded defence counsel in the case), all of which Blair politely refuted; *BC* 2 October 1917 p5, https://trove.nla.gov.au/newspaper/article/20190535.

[16] ibid.

[17] *QLAD* 2 October 1917 p1515. Ryan's comment seems to have been made in the early hours of 3 October, but is found in the 2 October record of the Assembly's proceedings. The allusion to "the insurance case" is likely a reference to *Australian Alliance Insurance Co v A-G (Qld)* [1916] ST R Qld 135, in which the Supreme Court had invalidated many parts of legislation (and Cooper and Lukin in dissent had invalidated many more) which Ryan had promoted to establish a state-run insurance company designed primarily to deal with industrial injuries compensation. The matter bypassed the High Court and went directly to the Privy Council ([1917] AC 537), which – in very cursory terms – upheld the legislation in its entirety.

[18] 7 December 1917 p6, https://trove.nla.gov.au/newspaper/article/20201486. The account below comes largely from that source. In subsequent High Court proceedings, the following exchange occurred during Ryan's submissions relating to events on 6 December 1917 (reported in *BC* 11 September 1918 p7, http://nla.gov.au/nla.news-article20276165): "Mr Justice Barton: I suppose all the parties knew that the argument was to take place? Mr Ryan: Yes: everybody was quite prepared …".

McCawley entered the court with the other judges, evidently expecting to complete the formalities required for him to sit on the bench. Feez – supported by Stumm – thereupon stood and addressed the court, announcing with regret that he could not extend the customary congratulations and good wishes due from the legal profession to a new Court appointee, and stating that he spoke for all lawyers in the state, both barristers and solicitors. Ryan, ostensibly attending to witness McCawley taking his seat, promptly intervened:

> The Attorney-General Mr Ryan: "That is not so!"
>
> Mr Justice McCawley: "Does the court propose to permit a personal attack on me?"
>
> The Attorney General (Mr Ryan): "Mr Feez is not speaking on behalf of the Bar of Queensland – not on my behalf – and I am leader of the Bar".
>
> Mr Justice Real said he thought this must be very disagreeable to Justice McCawley to sit there and listen to.

Feez disclaimed any personal animosity against McCawley, but made it clear that he was attacking Ryan qua politician and, by extension, McCawley as an accomplice in Ryan's political project – that project being, by the expedient of the 1916 Act, to place judges on the Supreme Court whose limited seven-year tenure would make them vulnerable to deciding cases in accordance with the government's wishes to avoid the prospect of their appointments not being renewed:

> Such a method of appointment transgressed all traditions and propriety. It opened out a vista of corruption which it was appalling to contemplate … All judicial appointments should be free from any taint or suspicion of political fitness otherwise public confidence in the judiciary – one of the bulwarks of their freedom – must be shattered.

The crux of Feez and Stumm's argument lay again in the *Cooper* 'Two Act entrenchment' thesis. S.6 of Ryan's 1916 Act appointed judges of the arbitration court to seven-year terms of office, and simultaneously empowered the Governor to appoint by proclamation such judges as judges of the Supreme Court. Feez and Stumm argued that this amounted to an amendment of an 'organic law', in that the Constitution Act 1867 ss.15–16 only permitted Supreme Court judges to hold office during good behaviour: "An appointment to the Supreme Court Bench permanently … by this indirect and questionable method transformed the judge with this temporary office into one for life – it impliedly repealed the Supreme Court Act pro tanto …".

For the Legislature to permit a Supreme Court judge to hold office for a fixed term, ss. 15–16 would first have to be repealed by an explicit Constitution Amendment Act, which would then be followed by a statute authorising a fixed-term appointment. Since the first such measure had never been enacted, the appointment provided for in the 1916 Act was not valid (as were any and all other provisions of the 1916 Act inconsistent with the Constitution Act).

Feez and Stumm's secondary, narrower, argument was that even if s.6 was a valid law, the commission purportedly appointing McCawley was ultra vires s.6, insofar as the commission purported to appoint him to the Supreme Court for life even though s.6 itself provided that an appointment to the Supreme Court was consequential on the appointee holding a place on the Industrial Court, a position which could only be granted for a seven-year term.

Their third point, which, if correct, would have precluded McCawley from sitting on either court, was that McCawley did not satisfy the requirement in s.6(7) that an appointee to the Arbitration Court be a barrister or solicitor of at least five years' 'standing'. While McCawley had been called to the Bar in 1907, he had never practised, and it was that concept of practice that was meant by 'standing' in s.6(7).

The Judges

The bench, presided over by Cooper, was little changed from the one that sat in *Taylor*. Cooper was joined by Real, Chubb, Lukin and Shand.

The 'Judgment'

Quite what the judges thought they were doing in issuing a 'judgment' is a puzzle. There were no formal proceedings before the court; no application had been made; no writ had been issued. The Court nonetheless produced a 'judgment' which – at least de facto – pronounced on both s.6's validity and the lawfulness of McCawley's commission.

McCawley 'succeeded' on one point before the Supreme Court, which accepted that s.6(7)'s 'five years' standing' proviso required only a call to the Bar, not actual practice (albeit that Cooper felt compelled to add that such experience would be: "very desirable").[19] On every other point in issue – and one that had not – McCawley and (qua both counsel and Premier) Ryan were defeated.

Cooper gave the sole decision. In the first part, Cooper focused on establishing that the office of Supreme Court judge had two essential characteristics, each expressly provided for in the Constitution Act 1867. The first of these (ss.15–16) was that judges would hold office during good behaviour, and were dismissible by the Governor only on an address from both houses of the Legislature. The second (s.17) was that appointment to the Court carried a legislative entitlement to payment of a specified salary. Cooper traced the lineage of these provisions back through the 1859 Order into the New South Wales Constitution Act 1855, noted that they had never been repealed or amended, and concluded (somewhat grandiloquently) that in those measures Queensland had:

> … secured, and thereafter jealously preserved, those safeguards for ensuring the independence of the Judges of the Supreme Court, which found their first expression in the Act of Settlement more than two hundred years ago and have since come to be regarded as the cherished characteristics of the system under which justice is administered throughout the Empire.[20]

---

[19] [1918] St R Qd 62, 99.
[20] ibid 68.

Rather overlooking or ignoring the historical point that the Act of Settlement protected judicial independence against the Crown and not against Parliament,[21] Cooper then observed that the 1916 Act did not expressly address either of those issues:

> There is certainly nothing in these titles which suggests that the Act was intended to affect the constitution of the Supreme Court, nor does the Act itself demonstrate any intention to deal with matters other than those indicated by these titles, except so far as an intention is to be gathered from s.6.[22]

The opinion then devoted several pages to determining the meaning of s.6. Cooper identified two 'constitutional' objections to the route provided by s.6 for appointments to the Supreme Court. The first – an eminently plausible interpretation of s.6 – was that a s.6 appointment to the Supreme Court depended upon the appointee being a judge of the Arbitration Court. Since judges on that court held office only for a seven-year (albeit renewable) term, it necessarily followed that their tenure as Supreme Court judges was for that term rather than on the basis of good behaviour, which was inconsistent with the Constitution Act ss.14–15. The second – this, too, a perfectly credible reading of s.6(6)[23] – was that any salary that such judges received was paid because they were Arbitration Court judges. They received no salary qua Supreme Court judges, a position which was inconsistent with the Constitution Act s.16.

On Cooper's telling – although one imagines him rather putting words into Ryan's mouth – Ryan was candid as to the Act's proposed effect:

> The Attorney-General argued boldly that by this Act ... the Legislature has surrendered to the Executive Government power to pack the Supreme Court Bench with any number of Judges which the Executive Government may think fit to appoint, provided that each of them is at the time of his appointment a member of the Arbitration Court ...[24]

Having decided that s.6 was inconsistent with the Constitution Act 1867 ss.14–16, Cooper then moved to the next question: "... Can legislation inconsistent with the provisions of the Constitution Act 1867 be passed by the Queensland Parliament until after the enactment of a measure expressly intended to repeal or alter those provisions?"[25]

Unsurprisingly, Cooper returned to the High Court's judgment in *Cooper*, quoted extensively[26] from Griffith and Barton's opinions, noted Isaacs's agreement with Griffith and concluded: "They seem to us to have dealt most clearly and most exhaustively with the question which arises for our consideration."[27] And on Cooper's reading of that

---

[21] And strictly speaking – which point Cooper also overlooked – the Act of Settlement permitted removal of a judge without statutory intervention, requiring only Commons and Lords resolutions and not a new Act. With that proviso in mind, it is perfectly credible to see ss.15–16 as doing in Queensland precisely (and no more) what the Act of Settlement did in Britain: namely, safeguarding judicial independence against the *Executive*.
[22] [1918] St R Qd 62, 72.
[23] P 269 above.
[24] ibid 82. There is no record in press reports of Ryan using the term 'pack', and it seems most unlikely, given his skill as both counsel and politician, that he would have done so.
[25] ibid 84.
[26] Most of pp 86–90 is quotation from *Cooper*.
[27] ibid 90.

judgment, the High Court in *Cooper* had made it entirely clear that 'Two Act' amendment was required to alter any provision of Queensland's Constitution Act.

Cooper's next consideration was whether *Taylor* had affected the authority of *Cooper*, noting that some passages in *Taylor*: "are not easy to reconcile with … *Cooper*'s case".[28] The Chief Justice suggested at the outset that *Taylor*'s pronouncements on the constitutional issues were obiter, since when the matter was decided this issue was: "of no immediate practical significance",[29] given the result of the referendum.

Cooper then reasoned that Barton's judgment in *Taylor*, which had concluded that CLVA 1865 s.5 impliedly overrode the *Cooper* rationale, was misconceived, in that Barton had failed to appreciate that 'Two Act' entrenchment was a 'colonial law' for s.5 purposes and as such imposed a 'manner and form' requirement in the shape of 'Two Act' entrenchment for matters of organic law which fell within CLVA 1865 s.5[1] and/or 5[2].[30] That there was no explicit textual basis for that 'law' in the 1859 Order, the Constitution Act 1867 or any other Imperial or Queensland statute was apparently not a barrier to this conclusion.[31]

In respect of Isaacs's evident conclusion in *Taylor* that cl.22 and s.5 empowered the Legislature to amend or repeal any law in the 'ordinary way', *Cooper* noted – quite understandably – that this conclusion was 'hard to reconcile' with Isaacs's approval of Griffith's judgment in *Cooper* and his apparent endorsement of that judgment a year later in *Ah Way*.[32] *Cooper*'s solution to this evident conundrum was to conclude that: "It is possible then that the words we have quoted from the judgment of Isaacs J in *Taylor's Case* do not bear the meaning which they seem to suggest."[33] The 'possibility' on which *Cooper* alighted was that Isaacs had actually meant that the constitution was not entirely unamendable, and that the PBRA was a valid amendment.

Cooper also held in respect of Gavan Duffy, Rich and Powers's judgments in *Taylor* that: "there is nothing to suggest that they regarded the Parliamentary Bills Referendum Act as anything but a valid amendment of the Constitution Act of 1867".[34] As such, they could not in any sense be taken as disapproving of, still less overruling, the judgment in *Cooper*.

Cooper's reasoning here is not persuasive. *Cooper* leaves unsaid that 'validity' in the *Cooper* sense would require a 'Two Act' amendment process. The (very) best one can say is that Gavan Duffy, Rich, Powers and Isaacs impliedly accepted in *Taylor* (and the implication is a large one) that the CAAA 1908 was Act One and the PBRA 1908 was Act Two for the purposes of enacting the 'Assembly plus referendum plus royal assent' method of legislating. They certainly did not say so explicitly. The implication is very hard to sustain, given that all that the CAAA 1908 did was remove the two-thirds clause;

---

[28] ibid 91.
[29] ibid 92.
[30] This was not a point that had been determined, nor even raised, in either the Supreme Court or the High Court in *Cooper*, which had been decided without any reference being made to the CLVA 1865.
[31] *Cooper* did not seem alert to the irony that the conclusion that the Constitution required amendment in the most *explicit* of ways was produced by the Court as a matter of *implication* from the texts of the 1859 Order and the 1855 Act.
[32] P 225 n 79 above.
[33] Isaacs judgment in *Taylor* is summarised at pp 262–63 above.
[34] ibid 96.

there was nothing in it to suggest it was an enabling Act to permit subsequent alteration to the Legislature's composition. The PBRA 1908 was a free-standing measure in that respect. S.1 had expressly stated that the Act was amending the Constitution Act 1867, but that statement and the amendment itself appeared in just the one Act. If the PBRA was indeed a 'valid' amendment to the Constitution, it was achieved without any need for a preceding Act authorising the particular amendment that it enacted.

Cooper's reading of legislative history was also very selective. At 71–72, Cooper ran in some detail through several Supreme Court Acts enacted between 1889 and 1903 which had variously altered the numbers of judges and their salaries, both of which matters were specified in the Constitution Act. None of these measures had been preceded by an authorising Act One in the *Cooper* sense, yet Cooper expressed no doubt as to their validity. Nor did he identify any constitutional objection to statutes enacted in that fashion allowing for the appointment of temporary acting judges of the Supreme Court, even though such judges would obviously not hold office during good behaviour.

Despite Cooper's unconvincing analysis both of *Taylor* and Queensland's legislative history, for the majority of the *McCawley* Court the conclusion was clear. S.6 effected a constitutional amendment which would require Two Acts to be effective; s.6 itself would have to be preceded by an explicit Constitution Amendment Act permitting the Legislature to alter the tenure of Supreme Court judges or otherwise change their process of appointment. Absent such an Act, s.6 could not be a valid law.

Real evidently dissented on this broad constitutional issue. There is no reasoned dissenting judgment in the law reports, only a summary of it in the headnote and in Cooper's opinion, which states Real's conclusion as being that s.6's provisions: "though inconsistent with the constitution are valid and binding; or rather that, so far as inconsistent, they must be regarded as a modification of the provisions of the Constitution Act 1867".[35] This was precisely the position Real had taken in *Cooper*; which, given that his view on 'Two Act' entrenchment in *Cooper* had been reversed in the High Court, suggests he was unwilling to accept that judgment as binding on state courts or had concluded – contra Cooper's analysis – that the High Court in *Taylor* had *sub silentio* overruled its holding in *Cooper*.

Cooper had ended the 'judgment' by – rather unusually – addressing an issue not raised by counsel. Cooper noted that s.6 of the 1916 Act required that a judge appointed to the Arbitration Court be granted a salary when appointed. Since no mention was made of a salary in the commission, the commission itself was ultra vires the Act. Consequently, McCawley was not simply not a judge of the Supreme Court; he was not a judge of the Arbitration Court either! The Court did not accept a submission from Ryan – not backed with any documentary evidence – that McCawley's salary had been fixed, if not recorded, when the appointment was made.[36]

---

[35] [1917] St R Qld 19.
[36] Cooper did not engage with the obvious question flowing from that conclusion, which was whether any function McCawley had performed as such a judge was consequently invalid as well. Nor did he consider if the same flaw attached to other appointments to the Arbitration Court, in which event all of that Court's activities were prima facie unlawful.

II. Regularising the Proceedings

Hugh Macrossan had promptly petitioned the High Court for permission to appeal, only to be told that the Court had no jurisdiction, because the Supreme Court decision was not a 'judgment' but merely 'an expression of judicial opinion', since there had not been any extant legal proceedings. On 2 March 1918, Ryan commented that a formal action of some sort would have to be taken to bring the matter before the High Court.[37]

A peculiar sequence of events then unfolded. McCawley continued to sit on the Arbitration Court notwithstanding the Supreme Court's decision. If that decision was indeed not a 'judgment' but only an 'opinion', then he was in strict legal terms entitled to do so. That he had done so – one must assume with Ryan's blessing – before the High Court had expressed its view on the Supreme Court proceedings does rather suggest that Ryan's government had been willing to defy the Supreme Court on the issue.

Then on 6 March 1918 McCawley purported to take the oath required of a Supreme Court judge, administered to him not by the Chief Justice, but by a District Court judge, Allan Macnaughton. Macnaughton had been a District Court judge for many years, and had sat with McCawley on the Arbitration Court.

McCawley subsequently made a public statement from the bench at the start of Arbitration Court proceedings on 7 March.[38] He explained that he had taken the oath so that a *quo warranto* action[39] could be filed against him. That action was apparently to be filed by a senior state official – a Mr Carter, the Under-Secretary of Justice – albeit (curiously) in his 'private' capacity. The obvious implication is that Carter must have known that McCawley was about to take the oath, although McCawley refuted any suggestion that any Government *minister* was aware of this. McCawley's expectation was evidently that he would then file a defence to the action, the Supreme Court would find in Carter's favour by adopting its earlier 'opinion' as its judgment and the matter would then go on appeal to the High Court, where Feez and Stumm could seek to be joined as interveners.[40] It seems unlikely – despite McCawley's protestations – that Ryan was not involved in formulating this strategy.

Cooper was not impressed by this turn of events. Carter's application came before him in chambers on 7 March. Carter was represented by Neil Macrossan, Hugh Macrossan's brother. Hugh Macrossan appeared for McCawley.[41] Cooper initially refused to accept Macnaughton's capacity to administer the oath, and had to be taken by Neil Macrossan to the relevant statutory provision.[42] Cooper then told Hugh Macrossan that he was: "not disposed to help a litigant who had set at defiance the authority of the Supreme Court".[43] Cooper was either unaware of or unwilling to acknowledge the High Court's view of the Supreme Court's decision. On being informed of that view by Hugh Macrossan, Cooper set the matter down for the Supreme Court to hear on 12 March.

---

[37] Reported in the *Northern Herald (Cairns)* 7 March 1918 p10, http://nla.gov.au/nla.news-article147510404.
[38] *BC* 8 March 1918 p8, http://nla.gov.au/nla.news-article20215442.
[39] The substance of such an action being to challenge the lawfulness of an appointment to office.
[40] *Daily Mail (Brisbane)* 8 March 1918 p4, http://nla.gov.au/nla-news-article220504893.
[41] State Assembly elections were scheduled for 16 March and Ryan was busy campaigning. Neil Macrossan's first legal employment had been in McCawley's Crown Solicitor department.
[42] Presumably the Oaths Act 1867 s.2.
[43] *Daily Standard (Brisbane)* 8 March 1918 p5, https://trove.nla.gov.au/newspaper/article/178830655.

At that hearing, the judges were concerned to know if anything had been done to fix McCawley's salary qua judge of the Arbitration Court and were told to their evident irritation by Neil Macrossan (for Mr Carter) that he was not aware that any steps had been taken.[44] The matter was held over until 15 March, when Ryan could appear.

On 15 March, Ryan began submissions with some surprising information:

> He said that an executive minute had been discovered which was passed on January 5 of last year, and which was gazetted on the following day appointing Mr Justice McCawley to be president of the Arbitration Court and fixing the salary at £2000 per year.
>
> Mr Justice Lukin: And was that unknown to the Under Secretary for Justice [Mr Carter]?
>
> The Attorney-General: That is so.
>
> Mr Justice Lukin: Well that is a most astonishing thing.
>
> Mr Justice Real: If it had been known it would have saved me a good deal of work.[45]

The consequence of the revelation was that the lawfulness of McCawley's appointment to the Arbitration Court was no longer in issue on the salary point. And since the Supreme Court had determined the 'five years' standing' issue in McCawley's favour, his position as President of the Arbitration Court could not be seen as unlawful. Despite Cooper's aforementioned disposition not to be helpful, the Court accepted the parties' proposed course of action, and held on the basis of its previous opinion that McCawley was not a judge of the Supreme Court.

The 1918 Assembly Election

The Ryan government's defeat in the abolition referendum vote and in *McCawley* did not obviously impact upon its electoral popularity. Nor, it seemed, had Hughes's move to the Nationalists and his prosecution of Ryan and Theodore induced many former Ryan supporters to change their allegiance. Indeed, in the March 1918 Assembly election, held the day after Ryan had again been before the Supreme Court in *McCawley*, Ryan and Theodore led the Labour Party to an increased Assembly majority and an increased share of the vote.

Table 9.1 Queensland Legislative Assembly election, 1918 (16 March 1918)

Party	% vote	Seats	Change
Nationalist[a]	44.6	22	−3
Labour	53.6	48	+3
Queensland Farmers Union	–	–	−5
Independent Nationalist	1.0	2	+2

[a] The rebranded Liberals.

---

[44] *BC* 14 March 1918 p11, http://nla.gov.au/nla.news-article20216359.
[45] *Darling Downs Gazette* 16 March 1918 p6, http://nla.gov.au/nla.news-article171763772. The matter had not escaped everyone's attention. The *Daily Examiner* had reported McCawley's appointment and salary on 9 January 1917 p4, http://nla.gov.au/nla.news-article195769248.

III. *Taylor* before the Privy Council

The March election removed any possibility that Ryan might appear for Queensland in opposing Dr Taylor's application to the Privy Council for leave to appeal against the High Court's judgment. The application was heard on 18 March.[46] Ryan entrusted the brief to Sir Ernest Pollock, a scion of an especially distinguished legal family, who by 1918 was well established both as a King's Counsel and as a Conservative MP.[47] Dr Taylor's case was argued by Paul Lawrence, then Chairman of the General Council of the Bar, whose prominence at the Chancery Bar had latterly led him as counsel into several cause célèbre constitutional law cases in which he had appeared for companies seeking to resist government appropriation of their assets under war powers legislation.[48]

The Privy Council panel comprised three Law Lords: Haldane, Dunedin and Sumner.

Haldane[49] had no judicial experience when appointed as Lord Chancellor by the Liberal Prime Minister Asquith in 1912. His first government post was as Secretary of State for War in Asquith's 1905 Liberal administration, a role in which Haldane showed himself an energetic reformer. Haldane continued as Lord Chancellor until 1915, when the Conservative party made his removal a condition – to which Asquith acquiesced – of its entering a wartime coalition government. Haldane continued to sit as a judge in the Lords and on the Privy Council, and had been on the bench in the *Insurance Case* appeal.[50]

The panel's second member, Andrew Murray, Lord Dunedin, did have significant judicial (but also political) experience prior to entering the Lords. The son of one of Scotland's most eminent and politically well-connected (in Conservative circles) solicitors, Murray studied at both Cambridge and Edinburgh, before entering the Scots Bar. He took silk in 1891, was elected as a Conservative MP and appointed as Solicitor-General for Scotland. He became Secretary of State for Scotland in Balfour's 1903 Conservative government. Murray took judicial office as President of Scotland's Court of Session in 1905, and was appointed to the Lords by Asquith in 1913. By 1918, Dunedin was considered a very able appellate judge.[51]

Sumner (born John Hamilton)[52] – who had written the Privy Council judgment in the *Insurance Case*[53] – was born into a prosperous commercial family. After attending Manchester Grammar School and Balliol, he was called to the Bar and developed a successful commercial law practice. He was appointed to the High Court in 1909, and quickly became something of a favourite of Haldane, who as Lord Chancellor secured Sumner's promotion to the Court of Appeal in 1912 and then to the House of Lords

---

[46] [1918] St R Qd 194.

[47] Pollock subsequently served as Solicitor-General and Attorney-General in the post-war coalition administrations, and was later appointed Master of the Rolls; Samuels (2004) 'Pollock, Ernest Murray, first Viscount Hanworth' *ODNB*.

[48] Most notably *Re Petition of Right* [1915] 3 KB 649; *Attorney-General v De Keyser's Royal Hotel* 1917 D 582 (in the High Court), [1919] 2 Ch 197 (after *Taylor* in the Court of Appeal); see Loveland (1918) op cit pp 84–87. Lawrence was appointed to the High Court before *De Keyser* went to the House of Lords; [1920] AC 508. See Rubin (2004) 'Lawrence, Sir Paul Ogden' *ODNB*.

[49] Pp 177–179 above.

[50] P 270 n 17 above.

[51] Millar (2004) 'Murray, Andrew Graham, first Viscount Dunedin' *ODNB*.

[52] Lentin (2004) 'Hamilton, John Andrew, Viscount Sumner' *ODNB*.

[53] P 279 n 17 above.

just a year later. Originally of quite Liberal inclinations, Sumner's politics had moved substantially and visibly rightwards by 1918, and he did not regard his position on the bench as a reason to maintain a diplomatic silence on such issues.

The proceedings were brief, even cursory, in nature. Lawrence's primary submission was that the PBRA 1908 device could not be used to abolish the Legislative Council, and indeed that there was no mechanism available in Queensland law to achieve that objective. Imperial legislation that either abolished the Council per se or distinctly empowered the Queensland Legislature to do so would be required.

Haldane took the lead in posing questions to Lawrence, and focused repeatedly on two reasons for not granting permission, neither of which had any bearing on the legal merits of Dr Taylor's case.[54] The first, and apparently less significant, basis for the refusal was that the abolition proposal had been defeated in the 1917 referendum, so the issue was in political terms currently moot. The more pressing consideration was that the meaning of CLVA 1865 s.5, on which the High Court had founded its judgment, was an important matter for many parts of the Empire:

> That Act was passed, a very remarkable thing, I think, without much discussion, but it is a tremendous Charter, and the tribunals have refrained from expressing an opinion upon the extent to which that section has given Legislatures abstract powers to alter their own Constitution by virtue of the section. If that section applies to that case, all I can say is … that it is a "sleeping dog" which I am very reluctant to awaken …
>
> You know, if this question really were to be argued, it should not be argued in a litigation affecting only one litigant, the Legislature, and only a state Legislature. There is a procedure which is open to the Crown, which is under the Act, 3 and 4 Wm. IV., to refer to the Judicial Committee of the Privy Council a general question of this kind, and, when that is done, the advantage that the Judicial Committee possesses is that it can advise the Crown to mould the procedure. If that question was raised in an abstract form, we should probably direct that we should be attended by the Attorney-General of England as representing the Empire, and we should take care to secure that there should be a representation of the other parts of the Empire, so that this tremendous question which affects everyone should not be determined behind their backs; and we are most reluctant, speaking for myself, at any rate, to interfere now.[55]

Having been refused permission, Lawrence took some care to have the Privy Council confirm that the refusal should not in any sense be seen as offering any view on the merits of the appeal. Pollock's exertions were limited to asking for costs, which request was refused on the basis that the matter raised was genuinely one of substantial public interest.

Ryan – as Premier, if not counsel – was no doubt heartened by the Privy Council's conclusion. However, he had little time to dwell on it for, shortly afterwards, Ryan was appearing in the High Court on McCawley's behalf.

---

[54] The transcript of proceedings suggests that Haldane had not read the High Court judgment.
[55] [1918] Q St R 194, 196–97. Haldane's 'without much discussion' comment is an exaggeration: there was no parliamentary discussion of the Act at all; p 106 above. While the absence of discussion might have been remarkable in the sense that one might have expected the Commons and Lords carefully to discuss so important a measure, it was quite unremarkable in the sense that – as we have seen in earlier chapters – most 19th century colonial legislation passed through both houses with minimal or no examination. The procedure to which Haldane refers is found in s.4 of the Judicial Committee Act 1833: "It shall be lawful for His Majesty to refer to the said Judicial Committee for hearing or consideration any such other matters whatsoever as His Majesty shall think fit; and such Committee shall thereupon hear or consider the same, and shall advise His Majesty thereon in manner aforesaid."

10

Constitutional Controversy in Queensland: Ryan, Theodore and *McCawley* – In the High Court

The difficulty is that the Constitution of Queensland can be altered with the same machinery as you can amend the Dog Act.

Higgins J, during submissions in *McCawley v R* in the High Court on 10 September 1918.

All seven judges[1] sat in McCawley's appeal. The case was argued on 10–12 September 1918, and judgment was given on 27 September.[2] Ryan again led for McCawley, assisted by Sir Edward Mitchell KC[3] and Macrossan. Hayden Starke, a prominent member of the Victoria Bar, appeared for Feez and Stumm. Mr Carter was represented – in form if to no great substance – by a Brisbane barrister, JM Mahoney.

I. The Hearing

Ryan's opening submission was that CLVA s.5 controlled the issue; its grant in s.5[1] of 'full power' to the Legislature to abolish courts or alter their constitution meant the Legislature could legislate in the 'ordinary way' (ie by bicameral bare majority plus royal assent with express or implied effect). The precise basis of his submission is difficult to identify. Ryan seemingly accepted in *Taylor* that s.5 permitted enactment by the state legislature 'in the ordinary way' of legally enforceable 'manner and form' provisions which could prevent s.5[2] matters from subsequently being altered in the 'ordinary way'. It is not entirely clear if his position before the High Court in *McCawley* rested on

---

[1] Griffith (appointed 1903), Barton (1903), Isaacs (1906), Higgins (1906), Gavan Duffy (1913), Powers (1913) and Rich (1913); (1918) 26 CLR 9. There is no indication that Higgins thought he should recuse himself because of his friendly relationship with McCawley. The summary of submissions is from the official report and accounts in *BC*, respectively 11 September 1918 p7, https://trove.nla.gov.au/newspaper/article/20276165; 12 September 1918 p7, https://trove.nla.gov.au/newspaper/article/20241523; 13 September 1918 p7, https://trove.nla.gov.au/newspaper/article/20240131.

[2] (1918) 26 CLR 9.

[3] Mitchell was then an eminent member of the Victoria Bar (he took silk in 1904), with an extensive constitutional law practice. He was party politically a Nationalist; when briefed in *McCawley*, he was seeking (unsuccessfully) adoption as a Nationalist House candidate; http://adb.anu.edu.au/biography/mitchell-sir-edward-fancourt-7603.

the premise that s.5[3] applied only to s.5[2] and not s.5[1], or if s.5[3] applied to both but was not relevant on the facts as no such manner and form restraint existed, since the *Cooper* 'Two Act' entrenchment was not a 'colonial law' per s.5[3]. The *BC* records an exchange between Ryan and Isaacs which suggests that Isaacs felt Ryan pressed the former position, but the frequency with which Ryan (and Mitchell) invoked *Taylor* suggests they asserted the latter view, ie that the Legislature 'in the ordinary way' *could have* protected the tenure of Supreme Court judges from being altered in the 'ordinary way', but *had not* done so.

Griffith's interventions came as statements, not questions, and suggested that Ryan faced an uphill struggle:

> You cannot make law irrespective of the Constitution …
>
> If the Constitution says a thing shall not be done, and you say that you will do it, passing a law to do that thing will not alter the Constitution …
>
> In Cooper's case this court has decided the exact point that Mr Ryan is taking now …

Ryan was not cowed by Griffith's evident hostility. He responded with the submission that: "the Privy Council judgment in *Webb v Outtrim* was an answer to the High Court decision in *Cooper's* case". As discussed above, *Webb v Outtrim* had witheringly denounced Griffith's fondness for American constitutional law ideas in developing the implied immunities doctrine;[4] Ryan was likely intimating that Griffith's 'support for Pope Cooper's Two Act' entrenchment idea would receive equally dismissive treatment in London.

Higgins, in contrast, suggested that Ryan was on firm ground legally, even if that ground's political composition was not particularly palatable: "The difficulty is that the Constitution of Queensland can be altered with the same machinery as you can amend the Dog Act."[5] The 'difficulty' Higgins identified was one facing Feez and Stumm rather than Ryan and McCawley.

Ryan's second day submissions focused on s.6's meaning rather than its validity, his purpose being to establish – assuming s.6 was valid – that the commission was not ultra vires s.6. Mitchell closed submissions by returning to the larger constitutional point, ending in an exchange with Griffith which indicated that nothing he and Ryan had said had persuaded the Chief Justice that *Cooper* should be revisited:

> Sir Edward Mitchell: said that he thought the power of the Queensland Legislature included power to alter the tenure of the judges.
>
> The Chief Justice: But the safeguard is that it must be done openly as an amendment of the Constitution by both Houses. That is quite different from doing it by a sidewind.
>
> Sir Edward Mitchell: The Constitution could be altered like any other law.
>
> The Chief Justice: If you evade a law you do not alter that law. If you are restricted by law from doing a thing you do not get over the difficulty by doing the prohibited thing. You must amend the prohibiting law first.

---

[4] Pp 193–95 above.
[5] *BC* 12 September 1918 p7, https://trove.nla.gov.au/newspaper/article/20241523. Whether this was an allusion to events in Van Diemen's Land in 1847–48 is not clear; pp 24–27 above.

Starke began submissions on 12 September.[6] He reiterated the subsidiary points made by Feez and Stumm in the Supreme Court: namely, that even if s.6 was valid, the commission was ultra vires s.6; and even if the commission was good, McCawley could not be granted it because the 'five years' standing' proviso required practice and not merely call. The bulk of Starke's time was spent, however, challenging s.6's validity.

Starke relied squarely on *Cooper*, and adopted Cooper's reasoning below to the effect that *Taylor* had not undermined its correctness. Starke emphasised that *Cooper* did not prevent 'the Legislature' from amending any provision of the Constitution: it merely required the Legislature expressly to empower itself to do so (in Act One) before expressly doing so (in Act Two):

> [T]hey [by which he meant a bare bicameral majority in express terms] could not obtain the power and exercise it at one and the same moment. It was impossible, as a matter of law, that there could be want of shown and at the same time be an exercise of that power. This Act purported to obtain the power and to exercise it at the same time.

Isaacs responded with obvious scepticism to that submission. Griffith's support for it had already been made clear, and other judges appeared to approve it as well:

> Mr Justice Rich: The power must be given before it can be used.
>
> Mr Justice Duffy: I agree with that.

Starke also made submissions based on English company law. The proposition advanced – which he asserted was sustained by the cases he cited (*Imperial Hydropathic Hotel Co, Blackpool v Hampson* and *In re Patent Invert Sugar*[7]) – was that the statutory regime which controlled the operation of limited companies provided that if a limited company wished to exercise powers not identified in its articles of association, it must first formally amend those articles to acquire the new power sought. Neither the provenance nor the relevance of the submission is readily apparent. Starke did not explain why principles of company law were pertinent to matters of colonial constitutional law. Such ideas had not featured in *Cooper* (including most obviously in Griffith's judgment) or *Taylor*, nor in Feez and Stumm's Supreme Court submissions or Cooper's 'judgment' in *McCawley*. Neither were they invoked by the Privy Council in such leading colonial constitutional law cases as *Burah* and *Apollo Candle*.

The final comment came from Barton, and did not bode well for McCawley's argument: "The position is that you have broken the constitution because you have not altered it."[8]

II. The Majority Judgments

The Court deliberated for a fortnight before delivering judgment. Griffith, Barton and Powers concluded that s.6 was indeed invalid. Isaacs, Rich and Higgins dissented

---

[6] Mahony's submissions were perfunctory, indicating that 'Carter's' suit was a mere flag of convenience for Ryan's government.

[7] *Imperial Hydropathic Hotel Co, Blackpool v Hampson* (1882) 23 Ch D 1; *In re Patent Invert Sugar Co* (1885) 31 Ch D 166.

[8] 13 September 1918 p7, https://trove.nla.gov.au/newspaper/article/20240131.

on that point. The seventh judge, Gavan Duffy, decided against McCawley without addressing s.6's validity.

Griffith

If Ryan had hoped that invoking *Webb v Outtrim* might persuade Griffith to depart from or distinguish *Cooper* rather than risk another embarrassing dismissal of his constitutional theories by the Privy Council, he was to be disappointed. Griffith considered *Cooper* to be both correctly decided and dispositive of the *McCawley* issue. Griffith's conclusion was clear and straightforward. His reasoning was not. The judgment was a chaotic cavalcade of logical non sequiturs, historical misrepresentations and inappropriate analogy.[9]

Griffith began with the uncontentious proposition[10] that the 1859 Order gave Queensland a Legislature on which the Imperial government, in exercising its s.7 powers, had bestowed a general lawmaking authority, exercisable in the 'ordinary way' save for certain: "conditions and limitations".[11] Some of those 'conditions and limitations' had a clear textual basis in the Order. 'Two Act' entrenchment, the *Cooper* 'condition and limitation', had no such source. Griffith was no more successful than he had been in *Cooper* in finding a textual root – be it in an Imperial statute, an Order in Council or a Queensland Act – for the 'Two Act' entrenchment principle. The 'conditions and limitations' to which Griffith referred at the outset of his judgment would thus seem to be of two distinct types: firstly, those expressly created by a Legislature (Imperial or colonial) or by the Imperial government through an Order in Council and defined clearly in the relevant statutory/prerogative text; and secondly, those implied into such texts by the courts.

Griffith characterised ss.15–16 as giving effect to the: "great constitutional principle introduced by the Act of Settlement that the tenure of offices of Judges of the Superior Courts should be for life during good behaviour".[12] Griffith can surely not have been unaware – but must have deliberately omitted to acknowledge – that the life tenure provided for by the Act of Settlement was a protection against dismissal by the Crown, and was legally contingent both on Parliament not, at some future point, acting in the ordinary way, amending or repealing the 1701 Act by a later statute, and – should the 1701 Act not be amended – on the Commons and Lords not passing resolutions which would authorise the Crown to dismiss a judge. The Act of Settlement did not – and could not – safeguard judicial tenure against Parliament.[13]

But having decided that this 'great constitutional principle' could properly be implied into the 1867 Act as a matter attracting 'Two Act' entrenchment, Griffith

---

[9] It is possible that the stroke Griffith, then in his mid-70s, had suffered in 1917 had adversely affected his intellectual capacities. He sat in only 18 cases in 1918.
[10] Although it had apparently perplexed him in *Cooper*; p 222 above.
[11] (1918) 26 CLR 9, 21.
[12] ibid 22.
[13] Griffith could have suggested that the Imperial Parliament might have done so if it had the requisite power, and had passed on to Britain's colonies a benefit which Britain itself could not enjoy, but that reasoning is not evident in his judgment.

then reasoned[14] that the effect of s.106 of the Commonwealth Constitution Act was to endow the states' constitutions with the normative status of an Imperial Act.[15] Any 'Act' of a State Legislature inconsistent with the state's Constitution was therefore void by virtue of the CLVA 1865 s.2.

That is certainly a curious proposition.[16] But even were it correct, its pertinence in *McCawley* would obviously rest on there being a credible source for the 'Two Act' entrenchment idea. To reach that conclusion, the Chief Justice then launched into a lengthy passage in which he adopted the company law-based submissions made by Starke to sustain his constitutional analysis. Griffith cited at length from *Hampson* and *Invert Sugar*,[17] which he considered as raising: "An exactly similar point"[18] to the one before him. Like Starke in his submissions, Griffith did not explain why the company law case law was pertinent to constitutional law analysis. Griffith had not invoked such ideas in *Cooper*, and did not cite any Privy Council authority suggesting why such cases were relevant. Instead, very disingenuously,[19] Griffith ended this part of his judgment by asserting that *Attorney-General for the Commonwealth v Colonial Sugar Refining Co*: "strongly supports this view".[20] *Colonial Sugar* was certainly a constitutional law case in the broadest sense, and one recognised by the Privy Council as being of considerable significance. But its simple ratio was that if the Commonwealth Parliament wished to exercise powers that it was not granted under the Constitution, it would have to await an amendment of the Constitution through the s.128 process giving it such power. The Privy Council had not drawn any analogy with company law principles to sustain this conclusion, rooting the judgment instead in the twin sources of the text of the Constitution and the well-known political history that had led to the Constitution's creation. Nor could it credibly be said that *Colonial Sugar* supported the proposition – which underpinned Griffith's reasoning – that the *Commonwealth Parliament* could gain the power it lacked by giving itself the power it lacked. The s.128 lawmaker which would have to give the power was a *wholly separate entity* from the Parliament itself.

The CLVA 1865 s.5 merited just a few lines of Griffith's opinion. He saw it as a provision that: "does not carry the matter any further". It apparently did not occur to Griffith that 'Two Act' entrenchment might be categorised as a 'colonial law' which imposed a manner and form restraint on the way that legislation dealing with s.5[1] and s.5[2] issues could be passed. Griffith seemed to read s.5 as removing rather than imposing restrictions on a Legislature's power to make law in the 'ordinary way', but held that if such was s.5's effect it could not override the: "express provisions of a colonial constitution".[21] The analytical sleight of hand is not subtle; whatever status 'Two Act' entrenchment might have in normative terms, it was certainly not (linguistically) *express*; unless, of course, one finds that express quality in *Cooper*.

---

[14] (1918) 26 CLR 9, 22.

[15] In *Cooper*, Griffith had quoted s.106 without explaining its significance ((1907) 4 CLR 1304, 1313), and had accorded the 1867 Act the same normative status as Imperial legislation because of its roots in cl.22; pp 222–23 above.

[16] S.106's more obvious purpose and effect is to underline that the Commonwealth Parliament had no power to alter State Constitutions.

[17] N 7 above.

[18] (1918) 26 CLR 9, 22.

[19] Mendaciously might be a more apt descriptor.

[20] (1918) 26 CLR 9, 24.

[21] ibid.

In the final part of the judgment, Griffith turned to the meaning of s.6. Noting that the 1916 Act did not refer to or purport to amend the constitution, he observed that if s.6 sought to empower the Governor to appoint a Supreme Court judge for a seven-year term it was necessarily invalid. Griffith's reading of s.6 was that any appointment to the Supreme Court was consequential upon the appointee holding an Arbitration Court office; since that office could be only for a limited period, so too must any appointment to the High Court. In that event, McCawley's appointment to the Supreme Court had no legal base.

Griffith concluded, somewhat gratuitously it seems, by turning to the 'five years' standing' point. He did not decide the question (and so *sensu stricto* approved the Supreme Court's conclusion), but felt the need to describe McCawley as: "a mere clerk and not as a barrister".[22]

Although – or perhaps because – Griffith's reasoning to find a credible legal root for the principle that amendments to the Constitution Act 1867 required a 'Two Act' process was far from convincing, he evidently took care in his analysis – as he had in *Cooper*[23] – always to refer to 'the Constitution' or 'the Constitution of Queensland' rather than to 'the Constitution Act 1867'. That linguistic choice was again presumably made to try to underscore the assertion that there was something normatively superior to the political measures enacted in the 1867 legislation relative to any other Queensland statute.

Barton

Griffith's decision – whether conscious or unconscious – to deploy that particular presentational tail to wag the substantive legal dog also commended itself to Barton, who, especially in the latter parts of his opinion, consistently referred to 'the Constitution' rather than to the 'Constitution Act 1867'.[24] His lengthy judgment concurred with Griffith both as to result and – in large part – to reasons. Barton began by reaffirming the distinction between organic and ordinary law within Queensland's constitution and asserting that s.6 was inconsistent with that organic law in that it allowed appointment of Supreme Court judges for a limited term.

Barton certainly characterised Ryan's submission correctly:

> But it is said that the *Constitution Act of 1867* is not a Constitution, in the sense of the fundamental or organic law of Queensland, but is merely an ordinary legislative Act in no wise distinguishable from any other part of the common body of legislation.[25]

Barton accepted that the 1867 Act had been passed in the same way as an 'ordinary' statute – that is, by a bare majority[26] in the Assembly and Council with the royal assent.[27]

---

[22] ibid 28.
[23] P 224 above.
[24] He too had used the same labelling in *Cooper*; p 226 above.
[25] (1918) 26 CLR 9 at 31.
[26] ibid 32; emphasis added. He did not note that it had been passed as one element of a package deal of 30 bills, and had passed though both houses with no serious discussion; pp 124–127 above. Such facts might be thought to undermine claims that the Act had a fundamental character in the sense of its moral or political importance.
[27] Barton did not acknowledge that the Act would have impliedly repealed any inconsistent Queensland Act.

But that did not mean it was an 'ordinary' Act and could not have 'fundamental' status, since: "That is the only form in which the Parliament of Queensland is able to pass any Act, of, however, high authority ...".[28]

However, Barton rejected Ryan's assertions as to the effect of 'in the same manner as any other laws' proviso in cl.22. He did so on the basis that Ryan's argument could only be correct if: "Queensland no longer had a constitution in the sense of a fundamental law".[29] That premise was evidently misconceived, as in Barton's view the Legislature in 1867:

> amply throughout the Act manifested its intention that the thing it has framed is a *Constitution*, and, if it is so, amendments to cover excesses of the authority it grants must precede, so as to render valid, legislation which would otherwise be in excess.[30]

Despite his 'amply throughout the Act' reference, Barton – like Griffith before him – did not (presumably because he could not) offer a single express textual basis in the Act or the 1859 Order, or in any subsequent Imperial or Queensland statute which supported the 'Two Act' entrenchment principle. The rationale for his conclusion – again echoing Griffith – was that because the Constitution Act was 'the Constitution', it must per se have a normatively superior status to ordinary law. Cl.22 therefore could not be taken at face value:

> The words "in the same manner as any other laws for the good government of the Colony" do not in any way impair the necessity, if the necessity exists, of making by law an amendment of the Constitution authorizing any new legislation which but for such prior amendment would be a violation of the Constitution.[31]

Barton endorsed, at some length,[32] the relevance of the company law cases which Griffith had discussed, and added a few further such authorities of his own. He also approved of Griffith's characterisation of the effect of s.106 and quoted briefly from *Cooper*, characterising the case as providing a clear authority to support his reasoning.[33]

The 'Constitution's' superior status was rooted in Barton's peculiar assertion that the Constitution Act 1867, because it was enacted under the powers given by the 1859 Order, which, in turn, derived from s.7 of the 1855 Act, was itself normatively equivalent to an Imperial rather than to a Queensland statute. Thus, any Queensland law inconsistent with 'the Constitution' was per CLVA 1865 s.2 necessarily void for repugnancy.[34] That s.7 made no allusion to any such superior status did not seem to affect Barton's view of the correctness of that proposition, nor did the absence from s.7, the 1859 Order or the 1867 Act of any mention that such superiority was to be effected by 'Two Act' entrenchment.

---

[28] That is an extraordinary statement, given the High Court's decision in *Taylor*.
[29] (1918) 26 CLR 9, 32.
[30] ibid; emphasis added.
[31] ibid 31.
[32] ibid 35–37. Like Griffith, he had not used the idea in *Cooper*.
[33] Barton accepted that the relevant passages in *Cooper* on which he relied were merely obiter, but characterised the judgment as providing: "a reasoned opinion for future guidance"; ibid 35.
[34] Albeit Griffith had rooted this argument more in s.106 than in s.7 of the 1855 Act; p 284 above. Barton referred to s.106 at 33 as supporting the proposition that the Imperial Parliament must have then considered that Queensland had a 'fundamental law'.

Again like Griffith, Barton devoted barely any attention to CLVA s.5. Displaying a perhaps surprising readiness to accept the criticism that Cooper had made of his judgment in *Taylor*, Barton noted that he had perhaps exaggerated the effect of s.5, and that while he saw no need to doubt the correctness of his analysis in *Taylor* itself,[35] that analysis was not relevant to the matter raised in *McCawley*. It is not evident from his judgment if Barton misunderstood Ryan's s.5 submission, ie that s.5[3] permitted a representative legislature to enact all sorts of legally enforceable 'manner and form' exceptions to the ordinary way of legislating on s.5[1] and s.5[2] issues, but no such exception had yet been enacted in Queensland. Barton certainly did not address it explicitly, and simply seemed not to appreciate – or perhaps to acknowledge – that 'Two Act' entrenchment could be a 'manner and form' device in the s.5 sense which had not yet been given legislative effect by either the Imperial Parliament or Queensland's Legislature.

In Barton's view, the proper construction of s.6 of the 1916 Act was that appointment to the Supreme Court was contingent upon the appointee being a judge of the Arbitration Court. Since the Arbitration Court appointment was for a fixed term, so too was the appointment to the Supreme Court. And as such, that appointment contravened s.15 of 'the Constitution', and so could be enacted only through the 'Two Act' process:

> Now, this piece of attempted legislation can in no sense be truly said to be an amendment of the Constitution. It does not even profess to be one, and as the legislative power is restricted by the enactments numbered in the Constitution 15 and 16, it can only be regarded as a transgression of the limits of the legislative power.[36]

Gavan Duffy

Perhaps following Higgins's lead in *Cooper*,[37] Gavan Duffy restricted his opinion to considering the lawfulness of the commission vis-à-vis s.6. Gavan Duffy's reading of s.6 was that it permitted appointment to the Supreme Court only during the period of the appointee's tenure on the Arbitration Court (ie for seven years). Since, in his view, the commission purported to appoint McCawley to the Supreme Court during good behaviour, it was simply ultra vires s.6. Gavan Duffy did not express any view on the 'five years' standing' issue.

Powers

Powers accepted that the commission was not ultra vires s.6 of the 1916 Act, and also agreed that the 'five years' standing' test required only call and not practice.

---

[35] Since he considered that the PBRA 1908: "clearly described itself as amendment of the Constitution, and then took certain powers which did not previously exist"; ibid 38. That analysis is not impressive, as the purpose and effect of the PBRA was not to create *powers* that did not exist, but to create a new legislature which might exercise the powers previously exercisable only by the original legislature; or, if one prefers, to create a new method of legislating within Queensland.

[36] Barton concluded by noting that he saw no need to address the five years' standing issue, so presumably did not doubt that McCawley had been lawfully appointed to the Arbitration Court.

[37] P 226 above. Gavan Duffy's opinion is at (1918) 26 CLR 9, 76–80.

On the larger question of the Act's validity, however, Powers agreed with Feez and Stumm's contentions that *Cooper* controlled the issue:

> The question now raised came before this Court and was decided in 1907, in opinions expressed by four of the five Judges of this Court who then comprised the Full Court, in what is usually termed *Cooper's Case*. It is clear that the contentions raised in this case on this point were expressly raised in *Cooper's Case*.[38]

Powers then devoted two pages[39] to quoting extracts from the judgments of Griffith, Barton and O'Connor in *Cooper*, noted Isaacs's concurrence and then quoted Isaacs's apparent endorsement of *Cooper* in *Ah Way*. While acknowledging the *Cooper* opinions were *sensu stricto* obiter, Powers considered them to be correct as to the law and adopted them to dispose of the issue in *McCawley*.[40] Powers did not make any reference to the company law cases which Griffith and Barton had invoked.

III. The Dissenting Judgments

The unanimity (at least as to result) which the High Court had mustered in both *Cooper* and *Taylor* eluded its members in *McCawley*. Three of the seven judges concluded that s.6 was a valid provision and that – more broadly – the notion that 'Two Act' entrenchment was then a feature of state law was itself misconceived. Higgins produced a (quantitatively and qualitatively) slim judgment to that effect. Isaacs and Rich's presented a more substantial joint opinion.

Isaacs and Rich

While Isaacs and Rich did not record at the outset that they were dissenting, the timbre of their opening paragraph made their intention crystal clear:

> The principal question that emerges with great distinctiveness from the circumstances of this somewhat complicated case is ... whether the Parliaments of Queensland and the other States of this Commonwealth have powers of the noble character broadly framed by the Parliament of the Empire in 1865, or whether, in disregard of the plainly expressed will of the Imperial Parliament, the powers of the local Parliaments are still open to the embarrassing doubts and technical impediments that according to some opinions fettered the legislative action of a colony over half a century ago.[41]

The Isaacs/Rich opinion is not a model of lucidity in terms of either its structure or its detailed reasoning. The judgment broadly divides (albeit with various overlaps) into two parts. The first addressed the CLVA 1865; the second, the 1859 Order and

---

[38] ibid 83.
[39] ibid 84–86.
[40] Powers also accepted Cooper's reading of *Taylor* in the Supreme Court as decided on the basis that the PBRA 1908 had validly amended the constitution and so was consistent with the judgment in *Cooper*.
[41] ibid 44.

the 1867 Act. In short terms, their conclusion was that neither the Imperial Parliament nor the Order in Council had protected the tenure of Supreme Court judges through 'Two Act' entrenchment, and while the Queensland Legislature had the power to fashion such protection, that power had not yet been used. This was not, they suggested, a difficult conclusion to reach:

> [N]otwithstanding the wealth of argument that has been showered upon the case, we regard the law as affecting the present case to be simple and unattended with any real difficulty. The words of both the Imperial Act of 1865 and the Queensland Constitution of 1867, so far as they affect the present case, are so plain, in our opinion, that but for the respect we feel for the opinions from which we have the misfortune to differ, and but for the enormous importance of the question, our duty could be very briefly performed.[42]

On the CLVA 1865 s.5

Isaacs and Rich broadly endorsed Ryan's submissions as to s.5's meaning and effect. Isaacs and Rich were not suggesting that the powers of 'noble character' bestowed by the CLVA 1865 meant that all colonial legislatures had somehow had their lawmaking processes reset to a default position in which statutes were enacted only through bare majority plus royal assent with express or implied effect. Rather, they accepted that s.5 confirmed that representative legislatures could be placed in legally enforceable positions which departed from the default British lawmaking process by introducing 'manner and form' constraints against which the validity of statutes addressing s.5[1] and [2] issues could be measured. Their methodology, however, was structured more on demonstrating that Feez and Stumm were wrong rather than that Ryan and McCawley were right.

A central tenet of their argument – presumably targeted implicitly at the reasoning offered up by Griffith and Barton – was to refute the proposition that the terms of the Constitution Act enjoyed some normatively superior status to ordinary law simply because they appeared under the 'Constitution' label:

> The precise point taken is that secs. 15, 16 and 17 of the *Constitution Act* impliedly prohibit any legislation by the Queensland Parliament contrary to their provisions; and, therefore, in order to acquire the power to pass such legislation either under the *Imperial Act* or the local Constitution, those sections must first be expressly repealed. Implied repeal by antagonistic legislation of an affirmative character is said to be legally impossible. No doubt is raised as to the competency of the Queensland Parliament to pass the selfsame Act in the same terms, in the same way, by the same royal assent. But it is said to be dependent upon the condition that it previously passed an Act expressly labelled as an amendment of the *Constitution Act*, and expressly repealing or altering the sections referred to. All this, it is said, arises because the *Constitution Act of 1867* is labelled "Constitution". If such efficacy is given to that Act because of its label, it is self-evident that any other Act passed in the ordinary way, *provided no specific manner or form is prescribed for such an Act*, will be of equal validity if only it be similarly labelled.[43]

---

[42] ibid 48. Rich and Isaacs did not see any need even to mention the company law authorities which Griffith and Barton had invoked beyond dismissing them as 'foreign' to the issue before the Court; ibid 53.
[43] ibid 47 (emphasis added).

A little later in the same passage, Rich and Isaacs indicated that they took Feez and Stumm's argument to mean that 'Two Act' entrenchment was to be superadded to any explicit manner and form provision that attached to the law in question:

> It is manifest that, if this [argument] is sound, many Acts will be of doubtful validity. It will always be open to argument whether some provision of the *Constitution Act* is or is not as it stands at variance with a later Act; and, if that is so, then unless there be a label or announcement required – and even though the necessary majorities are obtained and the necessary reservation takes place – the Act will be void ...[44]

Without referring explicitly to Barton or Griffith, Isaacs and Rich indicated that their colleagues had failed to draw the necessary legal distinction between the two distinct ways in which the word 'Constitution' might be invoked. One such meaning, applicable, for example, to the Constitution of the United States or Australia, did indeed denote a body of 'fundamental' law, the alteration of which lay beyond the reach of the ordinary lawmaking process.[45] The second meaning was simply to denote the body of legal rules which regulated the way that governmental institutions – be they legislative, executive or judicial – were composed and could lawfully act. In that second sense – which was the sense in issue here – the state's various Supreme Court Acts were as much a part of the 'Constitution' as the 'Constitution Act' itself:

> There is no law of Queensland which draws a distinction between the comparative authority of the two classes of enactments.
>
> Consequently, there is nothing sacrosanct or magical in the word "Constitution"; the expression itself not indicating how far, or when, or by whom, or in what manner the rules composing it may be altered. All those things must depend upon the rules themselves.[46]

Isaacs and Rich were equally blunt in dismissing the notion that the Legislature did not already have the power to modify judicial tenure. That power was expressly given by CLVA 1865 s.5[1]; and even if the 1867 Act had sought to override s.5 on that point – which it had not – any such provision would be invalid per CLVA 1865 s.2.[47]

The passage is perhaps too bluntly stated. That s.5[1] gave the power is uncontentious. What was really in issue – and what Griffith and Barton had been unable or unwilling to clarify – was whether a valid s.5[3] constraint existed to prevent the s.5[1] power being used in the 'ordinary way'. On this point, Isaacs and Rich referred back to Collier and Palmer's report as an authority[48] for the proposition that there was no general principle

---

[44] ibid.

[45] In the Australian context, that would, of course, be the 'ordinary' Commonwealth Parliament lawmaking process; the Imperial Parliament could alter that fundamental law in the 'ordinary way'.

[46] (1918) 26 CLR 9, 52. Isaacs and Rich brusquely – disdainfully perhaps – dismissed Griffith's suggestion that the 1867 Act had the normative status of an Imperial Act, and so any Queensland statute inconsistent with it was invalid per CLVA 1865 s.2: "the Queensland Constitution Act of 1867 … is not an Imperial Act, order or regulation; and that ends the matter"; ibid 51.

[47] ibid 53.

[48] Isaacs and Rich emphasised that the report was of only persuasive (but very persuasive) authority: "The report cannot, of course, determine the construction of the Act, but the opinions of the eminent jurists who made it, and which will be stated later, are valuable on some propositions of law disputed in the course of these proceedings, and of extreme importance on the other branch of the case"; ibid 49. The relevant passage of the Report is discussed at pp 104–105 above.

in British colonial law that a colonial Act amending a colonial constitution had to be enacted with the (textually explicit) 'object' of so doing. This indicated that the reference in CLVA 1865 s.5 to a legislature's 'full power' created a *presumption* that s.5[1] and s.5[2] matters could be passed in the 'ordinary way'. But that was – because of s.5[3] – a rebuttable presumption:

> The 'full power' is to be exercised subject to any legal requirements as to 'manner and form' ...
>
> If no special provision as to the manner and form of passing a particular class of law exists, then the ordinary method may be followed; but if as to any given class of law a specific method is prescribed, it must be followed. For instance, if a certain majority is required, or if reservation for the King's assent is prescribed, such a condition is essential to a valid exercise of the power. An earlier instance is the invalidity of Act No 10 of 1855–1856 of South Australia, for non-reservation.[49]

Since the tenure of Supreme Court judges was manifestly a matter falling within s.5[1]:

> it only remains to be ascertained if any special "manner and form" of dealing with the subject matter is prescribed by Queensland law, so as to require *a special heading or descriptive introduction*. There is nothing of that nature to be found.[50]

'Found' seems to be the essential concept here; or – more precisely perhaps – where such a 'special' provision could properly be found. Isaacs and Rich appear to hold that any such 'manner and form' requirement would itself have to be express in providing that such linguistic precision[51] would in future be required, and such an express quality could be only a legislative and not a judicial creation.

'Two Act' entrenchment was a principle that could not be 'found' in any legislative text. Its cogency as a constitutional doctrine rested on a false, judicially constructed premise that the Constitution Act 1867 contained provisions that were normatively superior to other Queensland law simply because the Act had been entitled the *Constitution* Act:

> [T]the argument to support the suggestion that prior repeal is necessary rests, as we have said, on a doctrine of implied prohibition arising from the use of the word "Constitution." The suggestion in effect amounts to saying that a colonial legislature, by merely using the word "Constitution" in the title of an Act, may deprive itself of power to enact a different

---

[49] ibid 22, 54. The South Australia 'Act' mentioned is discussed at pp 93–94 above. On the logic of Isaacs and Rich's argument, immediately after the 1867 Act was passed, the Queensland *'Legislature' had no substantive competence* to enact in the ordinary way laws amending the provisions of in s.9 and s.10 (the respective special majority clauses). However, the 'Legislature' did have such competence if the requisite special majorities were achieved. Further, because the 1867 Act did not *expressly* require special majorities for 'the Legislature' to repeal or alter s.9 and s.10, the 'Legislature' *had substantive competence* to enact in the ordinary way (this being in essence Lilley's 'singular omission' point; p 128 above) statutory provisions repealing or amending s.9 and s.10 and thereby give 'itself' (the itself being 'the Legislature legislating in the ordinary way') powers that – acting in the ordinary way – 'it' did not previously possess.

[50] ibid 55; emphasis added. The passage indicates that Isaacs and Griffith recognised *linguistic entrenchment* through the mechanism of requiring express repeal as a valid manner and form restraint. Isaacs and Rich's question obviously misrepresents the nature of *Cooper* entrenchment, which required express provisions in two separate Acts.

[51] Or any other departure from the 'ordinary way', be it a special majority at one or more stages of a bill's passage in one or both chambers, reservation or laying before the Commons and/or Lords for a specified period.

rule of conduct, while the Act so labelled stands. No such condition is found in sec. 5 of the Act of 1865, *and no Court has any authority to insert it*. We think that no legislature can, by merely using such a word, abdicate the power created for the benefit of the community by the Act of 1865.[52]

On this reasoning, 'Two Act' entrenchment was a 'judicial insertion', and so could not be a 'colonial law' per s.5.

Taken in isolation, the final sentence of that passage might suggest that Isaacs and Rich considered that s.5[3] *precluded* the possibility of representative legislatures preventing themselves (whether by already enacted or future provisions) from legislating in any manner and form other than the 'ordinary way' on s.5[1] and s.5[2] matters.[53] It seems more likely, however, that the sentence is poorly drafted, as Isaacs and Rich clearly countenanced the prospect that s.5[3] provided representative legislatures with the means to create legally enforceable departures from the 'ordinary way':

> If in any Act it [the legislature] lawfully passes, and whether it be called a Constitution or not, it creates a law that requires in future some particular manner or form of legislation, that manner or form must be followed until the law requiring it is altered.

On this reasoning, if one found in the 1867 Act a proviso which stated, for example, that:

> 1(1). The Legislature may alter the tenure of Judges of the Supreme Court only by complying with the manner and form of legislating detailed below:
>
> (2) The Legislature must enact in the ordinary way a measure entitled the Constitutional Amendment (Judicial Tenure) Act, which Act shall contain only one section which shall state that:
>
>> "This Act amends the Constitution Act 1867 insofar as it empowers the Legislature if it so wishes to enact in the ordinary way a statute which alters the tenure of Judges of the Supreme Court".
>
> (3) At a date no sooner than one month after the Constitutional Amendment (Judicial Tenure) Act has come into force, the Legislature may if it so wishes enact in the ordinary way a statute which shall be titled the Supreme Court (Judicial Tenure) Act in which the tenure of Judges of the Supreme Court may be altered in such fashion as the Legislature may provide.

then one would be facing a legally enforceable 'manner and form proviso' which would in substance equate to *Cooper's* 'Two Act' express repeal entrenchment proviso. This reasoning seems to accept Ryan's submission that the effect of s.5 was that Queensland's Legislature could have enacted in the Constitution Act 1867, or at any point thereafter, enforceable manner and form restraints relating to judicial tenure, but simply had not done so.

There is, however, a peculiar passage, at 50, as to the effect of s.5 (emphasis below added):

> That section according to all recognized rules of construction works an implied repeal of *every prior enactment* with which it is inconsistent. The repugnancy to a former Act of a later Act competently passed is fatal to the earlier one.

---

[52] (1918) 32 CLR 9, 57 (emphasis added).
[53] A conclusion arguably reinforced by the 'noble character' comment at the start of their opinion.

At the moment, therefore, of the passing of the *Colonial Laws Validity Act 1865*, sec. 5 was, so far as its language extends, an absolute Charter, no matter what the British Legislature had previously said. It is as if the Imperial Parliament had said: "Notwithstanding anything contained in or omitted from the Constitutional law of any colony, be it enacted" &c.

This passage does suggest that Isaacs and Rich felt that s.5[3] had only prospective effect, ie that it allowed for new 'manner and form' restrictions to be created but did not preserve old ones. If that view were correct, then previously enacted restrictions. such as special majorities, requiring reservation to the Monarch or laying before the Commons and Lords. would all have disappeared with respect to s.5[1] and s.5[2] issues. That conclusion is not reconcilable with the text of either s.5[1] or s.5[2], both of which encompass future and existing law, nor with the sentiments expressed by Palmer and Collier as to the propriety of pre-1865 'special provisions'.[54] It may be that the better reading of Isaacs and Rich's position – a reading reinforced by other parts of their judgment – is that the issue raised in s.5 was not one of *date*, but one of *source*. What s.5 impliedly 'repealed' ('overrode' and 'invalidated' might be better terms) was any 'manner and form' restraint that was not expressly articulated in an Imperial statute, an Order in Council or a colonial statute,[55] ie a restraint created – as was the *Cooper* 'Two Act' entrenchment – by 'judicial insertion'. If taken at face value, the 'every prior enactment' phrase makes no sense at all.

What is somewhat clearer is that Isaacs and Rich accepted that 'manner and form' provisions per s.5 could have (many) quite different characters. They might be purely linguistic, in essence requiring express amendment or repeal; they might require special majorities; they might require reservation of assent to the Monarch in person; or they might, it seems, embrace any device that made enactment more difficult to achieve than the 'ordinary way' of legislating.

On the 1855 Act, the 1859 Order and the 1867 Act

The previous critique of the opinion's 'every prior enactment' passage is reinforced by the fact that Isaacs and Rich (one assumes by design rather than accident) also described the various pre-1865 provisions in the 1859 Order which prima facie prevented the Queensland Legislature from legislating on some matters in the 'ordinary way'

---

[54] P 103 above.

[55] One might alternatively suggest that what Isaacs and Rich meant here was that: "S.5[1] and [2] retrospectively validated any 'Act' previously passed by a colonial legislature on S.5[1] and s.5[2] matters which would otherwise have been invalid because its process of enactment failed to comply with pertinent manner and form requirements; and 5[3] underlines the point that the validity of any future Act produced by a representative legislature would be dependent upon compliance with any manner and form restraint", ie that CLVA 1865 s.5[1]–[2] was a generally applicable (to all colonies) version of CLVA 1865 s.7 (which applied only to South Australia; pp 68, 118–19 above). The obvious weaknesses of that supposition are that s.5[1]–[2] and s.7 are framed in completely different language, and it would have been a very simple matter for 'Parliament' to have enacted s.7 in terms that lent it general application had 'Parliament' wished to do so. 'Parliament' is used archly here because, as noted in ch 4, there was no discussion at all of the bill that became the CLVA 1865 in either the Common or the Lords. 'Parliaments's' role was one entirely of form, devoid of any substance (pp 105–06 above). Point (i) above in this footnote is, of course, the reading of s.5 rejected – on perfectly plausible grounds – by Boothby and Gwynne in *Walsh v Goodall* (pp 118–20 above).

as 'manner and form' restrictions. The 'full power … in the same manner' proviso in cl.22 should be taken as creating a presumption that legislation could be enacted in the 'ordinary way': "with certain exemptions mentioned as to manner and form".[56]

Such 'exemptions', however, had to be 'express', by which, it seems, was meant having an explicit textual basis in the Order:

> It is difficult now for us to see how any doubt could ever have existed that the Order in Council, so far from requiring a label marked "Constitutional amendment," studiously expressed the very opposite, apart from express exceptions, the mention of which strengthens the affirmative words – because, since a specific manner of passing the excepted classes of laws is stated, it is clear no other condition is to be implied.[57]

The 1867 Act replicated this methodology. The proviso in s.2 providing that the Queen Council and Assembly could make laws "in all cases whatsoever" created a presumption of lawmaking in the 'ordinary way'. That presumption could be rebutted, but only by textually express exceptions. In the 1867 Act, such express exceptions could be found in s.9, s.10 and s.13. But there were no such express exceptions in relation to the tenure of Supreme Court judges which was provided for in s.15 and s.16.

Drawing on Lord Selborne's (Roundell Palmer's) judgment in *Burah*,[58] Rich and Isaacs maintained that: "it is contrary to the settled rules of construing Constitutional Acts to introduce implied prohibitions on the legislature to cut down a clear affirmative grant".[59] Isaacs and Rich then repeated their earlier invocation of Selborne's view (qua Roundell Palmer as Attorney-General in authoring the 1864 Report) that there was no basis to assume that a requirement of express repeal could be implied into any colonial statute. Isaacs and Rich quoted the passage of the report cited at p 104 above, before concluding:

> In our opinion therefore – quite apart from the paramount effect of the *Colonial Laws Validity Act* – there was ample power also under sec.2 of the *Constitution Act of 1867* to do what has been done.[60]

On Empirical Inconveniences and Logical Inconsistencies

In analysing the legal effects of s.5, the 1859 Order and the 1867 Act, Rich and Isaacs repeatedly drew attention to some of the logical and practical difficulties that necessarily arose if the 'Two Act' entrenchment thesis was correct.

---

[56] (1918) 26 CLR 9, 61. Tracing the 1859 Order back to its roots in s.7 of the 1855 Act, Rich and Isaacs observed that: "That section does not use the word 'Constitution' at all"; ibid.
[57] ibid 62.
[58] Specifically on the passage quoted at pp 152–53 above.
[59] (1918) 26 CLR 9, 65.
[60] ibid 65–66. One point of potentially great significance seems to have escaped Rich and Isaacs's attention. If cl.22 of the Order and subsequently s.2 of the 1867 Act did indeed empower the Legislature in the 'ordinary way' to enact manner and form restrictions on the 'ordinary way', it arguably did so in a substantively much more expansive fashion than CLVA 1865 s.5. While CLVA s.5[3] was limited to matters within the scope of s.5[1] and s.5[2] (ie to 'identity' rather than 'competence' issues; pp 111–12 above), s.2 of the 1867 Act was applicable "in all cases whatsoever". So, for example, a statute could be passed in the 'ordinary way' which introduced a manner and form proviso (a two-thirds majority on both houses at third reading condition perhaps) relating to inter alia the rate of income tax, the nationalisation of private industrial undertakings (or denationalisation of state-owned undertakings), the qualifications required for employment in the state civil service and so on.

Echoing Ryan's submissions, Isaacs and Rich observed that the various Queensland Acts permitting the appointment of additional permanent judges or temporary judges to the Supreme Court and modifying the permanent judges' salaries had all been enacted without the preceding benefit of an Act expressly allowing for such changes to the relevant provisions of the Constitution Act 1867 having been previously passed. Such Acts would be: "if the argument of the Respondents is sound ... an open and flagrant breach of the Constitution".[61] (Although Rich and Isaacs did not labour the point, if the judges' appointment were unconstitutional, all of the judgments they had rendered were arguably invalid.) But that was merely one manifestation of a potentially much broader problem:

> ... How many more enactments there are open to the same criticism, we know not. But beyond that, how many such supposed violations of constitutional law – and consequently invalid enactments – have been and are acted on in other Australian States, and in parts of His Majesty's Dominions?[62]

Similarly, if Feez and Stumm's argument as to judicial tenure was correct because – and solely because – the judicial tenure provisions were found in the Constitution Act – then every other provision of the Constitution Act was similarly protected by 'Two Act' entrenchment, 'however trivial' in political terms that provision might be.[63] But since Feez and Stumm had offered no basis for distinguishing trivial and non-trivial matters within the Constitution Act, their argument necessarily entailed accepting the proposition that issues of great and minimal political significance enjoyed the same 'constitutional' status.

Rich and Isaacs also observed ("with the greatest respect") that Feez and Stumm's arguments as to the purposes of s.15 and s.16 rested on a "basic error".[64] That purpose, deriving from the English Act of Settlement 1701, was to safeguard judicial independence against the Crown, not against the Legislature – which could, of course, 'in the ordinary way' repeal or amend the 1701 Act. Further, the 1701 Act (and its Queensland echo in s.16 of the 1867 Constitution Act) provided for the dismissal of judges (without need for any legislation at all) by the mechanism of Crown action consequent on: "the request of the two Houses each acting on an ordinary majority by the comparatively informal method of an address, founded on a single resolution in each House".[65] To accept that dismissal could be effected in this way, but not by: "the more solemn and deliberate and authoritative way of legislation, which requires three readings and consideration in Committees", would not just be 'strange'; it would be 'absurd'.[66]

---

[61] (1918) 26 CLR 9, 56.
[62] ibid 57.
[63] ibid 56. Isaacs and Rich alighted on s.56, which contained a rule of evidence in relation to any legal proceedings in which their unauthorised publication of parliamentary proceedings was in issue. There are similarly 'trivial' issues in s.54 and s.55.
[64] ibid 58.
[65] ibid 60.
[66] ibid. Isaacs and Rich did not, however, acknowledge that a dismissal address would have to be very explicit as to its purpose, nor that the 'deliberate and authoritative way of legislation' of three readings and committees could be – and often had been – dispensed with by a simple majority vote in each house to suspend or alter their respective standing orders.

On Cooper

Feez and Stumm had made much in their submissions in both the Supreme Court and the High Court that Isaacs had approved Griffith's judgment in *Cooper*, and had seemed to underline that approval in *Ah Way*. The strategy underpinning those submissions is obvious: for Isaacs to find in McCawley's favour he would have to reverse his former position and acknowledge that it was misconceived. Feez and Stumm's hope was presumably that Isaacs would not take either step, whether for reasons of personal embarrassment or through a more principled adherence to notions of legal certainty.

If such was the hope, it was to be disappointed. Although Isaacs and Rich made no reference to *Ah Way*, they briefly explained why *Cooper* was not a controlling authority in this case. In the Supreme Court, Cooper had referred to Isaacs's judgment in *Taylor* – on its face hard to reconcile with *Cooper* – by suggesting that Isaacs's words in *Taylor* did not really mean what they seemed to mean. Isaacs deployed similar language in suggesting that Feez and Stumm's (and, by obvious implication, Cooper's) reading of *Cooper* was similarly misinformed. In part, this was because the 'Two Act' entrenchment point affirmed in *Cooper* was at best obiter; in part, it was because *Cooper* dealt with an issue (susceptibility to income tax) that did not fall with the scope of CLVA 1865 s.5; but primarily it was because to understand *Cooper* as enunciating a principle of general application was simply wrong:

> But, further, having considered the subject with all the care and responsibility that a direct decision requires, and sitting with the whole strength of this Court, and recognizing that our duty to ascertain the law with accuracy is higher than the convenience of following *dicta*, however, important, we have no hesitation in saying that if the words there used are to be understood in the unlimited sense in which they are now urged, they go beyond the law.[67]

On the Validity of the Commission and the Meaning of 'Five Years' Standing'

Having – at some length – decided that s.6 was valid and that the Legislature could in the 'ordinary way' enact a statute varying the tenure of a Supreme Court judge, Isaacs and Rich dealt quickly with the question of whether the commission was intra vires s.6. Their view, simply put, was since the commission was drafted in terms taken from s.6 itself, the only proper construction of the commission was that it meant whatever s.6 permitted it to mean: "If in that Act the tenure is a life tenure, the commission so operates; if by that Act the tenure is coterminous with the presidency, the commission should be so read."[68]

Isaacs and Rich also decided the 'five years' standing point' in McCawley's favour, and did so with such brevity that it seems they could see no merit at all in Feez and Stumm's submission.[69]

---

[67] ibid 66.

[68] ibid 67. Isaacs and Rich asserted that this was both a common law principle and a requirement of Queensland's Acts Shortening Act 1867 s.21A, which gave the common law principle a statutory basis.

[69] ibid 45.

Higgins

Higgins had not been willing formally to reach the constitutional question in *Cooper*, deciding that case on the narrow basis that liability to income tax was not a diminution in a judge's salary; he had, however, indicated that he agreed with the majority position on 'Two Act' entrenchment.[70] In *McCawley*, Higgins concluded that s.6 was not inconsistent with s.15 or s.16 of the Constitution Act 1867. On this occasion, however, he also went on squarely to address the larger question.

In *Cooper*, Higgins's comments on that larger question had consistently referred to 'the Constitution' rather than the 'Constitution Act'. In *McCawley*, however, he altered his labelling: he referred throughout to 'the Constitution Act'. Higgins did not explain why he changed his nomenclature. More significantly, perhaps, he did not acknowledge that he was changing the assumptions he made in *Cooper*. Rather, he prefaced his analysis of *Cooper* with this comment:

> These considerations lead me to the consideration of *Cooper's Case*, and of the *dicta* in that case *of my learned colleagues* (the *dicta* were admittedly unnecessary for the decision) to the effect that so long as a Constitution remains unaltered any enactment inconsistent with its provisions is invalid.[71]

Higgins's conclusion, reasoning and occasionally language echoed parts of the Isaacs/Rich dissent, albeit that Higgins's focus was primarily on the 1867 Constitution Act itself rather than the CLVA 1865, and it quite notably omitted any discussion of the implications of CLVA 1865 s.5. The thrust of his judgment is perhaps illustrated by quoting several brief excerpts:[72]

> Now, sec. 15 does not purport *on its face* to be a limitation of the powers of the Parliament, or a restraint on the action of the Parliament. It prescribes that the commissions of the present Judges and of all future Judges "shall … continue and remain in full force during their good behaviour." … But, under sec.2 of the *Constitution Act*, the Parliament has power, within the Colony of Queensland, to make laws for the peace, order and good government of the Colony "in all cases whatsoever"; there is *no exception from this power as to sec. 15, or as to any section of the Constitution Act except as to the constitution of the Legislative Council (sec. 9)*; and it would seem, therefore, that sec. 15 can be altered or excluded from operation by an ordinary Act of the Parliament. There is *no such provision* in this *Constitution Act*, as there is in most Constitutions, *excepting from the ordinary powers of legislation any of the provisions of the Constitution* (unless sec.9 makes an exception) …

> There is no magic in the words "Constitution Act"; what the Parliament can do is a matter of construction of the relevant Acts in each case. Indeed, the *Constitution Act* appears to be not an organic law in the strict sense, but the creature of the only organic law – the Order in Council made under 18 & 19 Vict. c. 54. The Order in Council is, as it were, the electric wire which carried the British power to make laws; and the *Constitution Act* is merely one of the laws made under that power …

---

[70] P 226 above.
[71] (1918) 26 CLR 9, 74; emphasis added. Higgins then suggested that if the majority view in *Cooper* was correct, it could at most apply to cl.22 of the Order, on the basis that cl.22 forbade the Legislature created by the Order from repealing or amending cl.22 itself. This reasoning is surely misconceived, given the wording of cl.22 and its (presumably unintended by the British government) obvious divergence from the provisions of the 1855 Act as to the competence of the New South Wales Legislature; pp 63–65 above.
[72] (1918) 26 CLR 9, ibid 72, 73 and 74 respectively (emphases added).

> *If Parliament*, in passing the Constitution *Act, had desired to except sec. 15 from the general power* to make laws contained in sec. 2, *it could easily have said so.*

Higgins devoted barely half a page to s.5, and his characterisation of its effect is difficult to discern. The argument is thin both quantitatively and qualitatively. Higgins did not explicitly confirm that s.5 empowered the Legislature to enact laws which removed s.5 issues from the (as he variously put it) 'ordinary' or 'general' power of legislating, but he did appear to accept that there could be exceptions to the 'ordinary' power and that such exceptions could be created by the Queensland Legislature through its 'ordinary power'.[73]

Conclusion

None of the High Court judges appeared to have grasped the point – or, if any of them did grasp it, they did not make their awareness explicit in their respective opinions – that their sharp (and also subtle) differences of view as to the correctness of the *Cooper* principle might lie in a lack of linguistic imagination which had to that point pervaded the relevant law, be it statutory or judicial, Imperial or colonial in origin.

Perhaps the one common point in the six positions taken in *McCawley* was the constant characterisation of '*the* Legislature', as though, for lawmaking purposes, 'the Legislature' was a homogeneous entity, to be identified solely as an institutional rather than a functional phenomenon. What was singularly lacking – in s.7, in the 1859 Order, in the 1867 Act and in all judicial interpretations thereof (in *Cooper, Taylor* or *McCawley*) – was any acknowledgement that 'the Legislature' was better seen as an umbrella term, which could quite properly encompass a (likely small, but possibly large) number of differently composed lawmakers, that difference being rooted in a (likely small, but possibly large) number of different lawmaking processes, with such differences being dependent upon the subject matter of the law that was being passed.

The criticism is perhaps more appropriately targeted at the politicians who proposed and enacted 'constitutional' legislation rather than the judges tasked with interpreting such Acts. The default style of legislative drafting of Imperial and Australian statutes in the mid-to late nineteenth century had been to create 'a' legislature and then locate somewhere in the relevant legal provision a statutory presumption of lawmaking in the 'ordinary way', with the presumption rebutted by one or more particularistic exceptions scattered here and there in other parts of the Act. Legislators did not provide courts with an easily comprehensible path to follow.

IV. Abolition of the Legislative Council and the 1919 National Election

Since Gavan Duffy had found against McCawley on the basis that the commission was ultra vires s.6 – and had not addressed the issue of s.6's validity – the outcome of the

---

[73] ibid 75. That 'ordinary' power was what had been used to create the 1867 Act. If the power derived from s.5[3], it was applicable only to s.5[1] and s.5[2] issues. If it derived from cl.22, it would apply to all matters.

judgment was that the High Court was evenly split (Griffith, Barton and Powers versus Isaacs, Rich and Higgins) on the correctness of the 'Two Act' entrenchment thesis. And within the majority judgments, there was obviously what one might kindly call a marked divergence of opinion as to the reasoning that underlay that conclusion. In such circumstances there was little doubt that Ryan (and McCawley) would promptly seek and be granted permission to appeal to the Privy Council. Some 18 months were to pass before the appeal was heard, in which time the war ended and significant developments occurred both in national and Queensland politics.

Abolishing Queensland's Legislative Council?

Despite the Labour Party's resounding victory in the March 1918 election,[74] the Council had maintained an intransigently obstructive stance towards much of the Government's legislative programme. There were some 49 members of the Council at the opening of the 1918 parliamentary session yet, despite the 1917 appointments, fewer than 20 of those 49 took the Labour whip. The obstructionism was not on minor issues; among the government bills rejected were measures on income tax and land tax reform. Ryan and Theodore had anticipated that action. The Labour Party had made Council abolition a prominent part of its 1918 election platform, and Ryan had indicated that a clear Labour victory would provide a proper basis for reopening that question notwithstanding the referendum result a year earlier. To Goold-Adams's evident discomfort, the opening speech with which he initiated the new legislative session in May 1918 ended with the following passage:

> Much of the useful legislation passed by the Legislative Assembly in the last Parliament was rejected, or seriously mutilated, by the Legislative Council. My advisers consider it their duty to take such steps as will in the future prevent such flouting of the expressed will of the people.[75]

Among the proposed measures included in the speech was a Constitution Act Amendment Bill, the sole purpose of which would be abolition of the Council.

Despite the election result, Goold-Adams initially indicated that he was not amenable to approving the appointment of any significant number of Labour members to the Council, for fear, it seems, that such swamping would promptly be used to abolish the Council. The Governor's position appeared to embolden opposition members in the Council, who by July 1919 had again rejected Theodore's Income Tax and Land Tax Bills, along with several other government measures.[76]

Ryan continued unsuccessfully to press Goold-Adams for further Council appointments, but Ryan's persistence seemed to be sufficient for the Nationalists to accept that the Governor might soon give way. In early August, the Council approved the Income

---

[74] P 277 above.
[75] *QLCD* 29 May 1918 p7. There was obvious irony in the fact that conventional practice was that the opening speech be delivered by the Governor in the Council and not the Assembly.
[76] Murphy (1975) op cit pp 384–86.

Tax and Land Tax Bills. The Nationalist's rationale for this strategic retreat was laid out in the Council on 20 August:

> We are now faced with the position, presumably, either to give in and not insist on our amendments and allow the Bills to go through as they are, or insist on our amendments and get them thrown out, thereby running the risk which we have been threatened with of reinforcements being introduced into this House ...
>
> We have had three threats during the last few months from ·Government supporters ... reinforcements would be brought in, and we have to face the possibility – and, to my mind, the probability – of that ... We know that last year eight new members would have brought the strength of the House up to forty-five, which was originally its highest number, but, instead of that, thirteen were brought here bringing the number up to fifty. As we know, if further reinforcements are brought in the future effectiveness of this side of the House will be absolutely gone.[77]

Ryan's determination to secure the Council's abolition was not assuaged by the passage of Theodore's bills. His attention was temporarily diverted by his appearance as counsel in *McCawley* before the High Court; but on 26 September 1918, the day before the High Court handed down judgment in *McCawley*, Ryan introduced another bill – the Constitution Act Amendment Bill 1918 – to abolish the Council. The content was slightly different from the 1917 measure. A minor amendment was added to make it clear that the King would continue to be part of the Legislature when the Council was abolished. More significantly, the bill made provision for a 'revisory committee' to be established within the Assembly to give additional consideration to contentious measures.[78] Ryan said little at first reading beyond invoking *Taylor* to confirm that there was no legal obstacle to the Council being abolished either through the PBRA device or by 'ordinary' legislation.

Second reading was held the next day.[79] Ryan's speech suggested that he envisaged abolition occurring through the PBRA mechanism rather than ordinary legislation consequent upon a swamped Council being created. He seemingly had little expectation that the bill would be passed by the current Council.[80] Invoking Canada as his primary example, Ryan observed that single chamber legislatures were a commonplace feature of British colonial constitutions and that there was thus no sound political reason to fear the creation of a unicameral legislature in Queensland.

But while the Council was willing – eventually – to acquiesce to the Income Tax and Land Tax Bills, it would not support its own abolition. Having passed through the Assembly, the abolition bill was defeated by 25–16 at Council second reading on 17 October 1918.[81]

---

[77] *QLCD* 20 August 1918 p1528. The speaker was Arthur Hawthorn. In his earlier political life, Hawthorn – a Brisbane-based solicitor – had been a political progressive. He was elected to the Assembly in 1902 as an 'Independent Ministerialist', but joined the Morganite faction a year later and subsequently served in Kidston's Kidston Party and Fusion governments (pp 211–214 above). His politics moved rightwards after his appointment to the Council by Denham in 1911; http://adb.anu.edu.au/biography/hawthorn-arthur-george-clarence-6608.
[78] *QLAD* 26 September 1918 pp 2585–86.
[79] *QLAD* 27 September 1918 p2626 et seq.
[80] ibid p2627.
[81] *QLCD* 17 October 1918. The debate begins at p3221; the vote is at p3233.

Ryan subsequently spent much of 1919 in England, in part because he was appearing in several matters before the Privy Council and in part in an effort to raise government loans on the London money market. The most significant litigation was *Theodore v Duncan*,[82] heard in March and April 1919.[83] The Privy Council, in a brief judgment delivered on 2 May, resolved the case in Theodore's favour without feeling the need to assess the effect of s.7 of the Sugar Acquisition Act 1915. The brief judgment, delivered by Haldane,[84] broadly endorsed Isaacs and Powers's dissenting opinion in the High Court as to the Act's meaning and the consequent validity of the proclamations, describing it as based on: "powerful reasoning".[85] Somewhat optimistically, or naively perhaps, Ryan greeted the judgment with the comment that he hoped it would encourage his government's political enemies to wage future battles through the electoral process rather than in the courts.[86]

In Ryan's absence, Theodore served as Acting Premier. Theodore succeeded where Ryan had not in persuading Goold-Adams to appoint some additional Labour members to the Council in August 1919. Theodore's success was modest: the Governor consented only to three appointees.[87] While all three could credibly be regarded as Labour loyalists, the party still stood some distance short of a Council majority. Two Nationalist members had died earlier in the year. The new appointees took the total membership of the Council to 50. The prima facie balance of power was Labour 21 and the opposition 29.[88]

Rumors were already circulating by this point that Ryan was considering entering the national arena. After some prevarication, Ryan announced the move in October 1919, having secured the national party's nomination for the safe Labour House seat of West Sydney.[89]

In Queensland, the immediate consequence of Ryan's 1919 move to the national sphere was Theodore's elevation to leadership of the Labour Party (on 14 October) and the premiership (on 22 October).[90] Theodore had reintroduced the 1918 Council abolition bill into the Assembly in August 1919.[91] Its passage though the Assembly was again straightforward,[92] but the bill met wrecking amendment in the Council on 4 November 1919, which carried by 27–17.[93] The bill having been 'lost' twice for PBRA

---

[82] [1919] AC 696.
[83] Twenty months had passed since the High Court's decision (in August 1917); p 257 above.
[84] See further pp 278–79 above.
[85] [1919] AC 696, 707.
[86] Murphy (1975) op cit p422. Ryan had also succeeded in *Lennon v Gibson* [1919] AC 709. The case turned on the meaning of various provisions of the Sugar Cane Prices Act 1915. The Act levied a tax on sugar refiners, payable when they received sugar for processing. The point taken by Gibson, a sugar producer and refiner, (Lennon was Agriculture Minister in Ryan's government) was that the Act was drafted in a manner that excluded the refiner from liability if the refiner was also the producer of the sugar. Perhaps to his surprise, Ryan had won the point before the State Supreme Court, Cooper, Lukin and Real all finding in the government's favour ([1918] St R Qd 1). On appeal, a three-man bench (Barton, Isaacs and Rich) in the High Court had reversed ((1918) 24 CLR 140) that judgment.
[87] *Daily Mercury* 19 August 1919 p3, https://trove.nla.gov.au/newspaper/article/178639808; *BC* 20 August 1919 p9, https://trove.nla.gov.au/newspaper/article/20379006.
[88] *Warwick Daily News* 30 June 1919 p4, https://trove.nla.gov.au/newspaper/article/177220616.
[89] Murphy (1975) ch 17.
[90] Fitzgerald op cit pp 106–07.
[91] QLAD 27 August 1919 p418 (first reading).
[92] Third reading was carried by 37–18; QLAD 22 October 1918 p1493.
[93] QLCD 4 November 1919 p1778 et seq (commencement of debate), pp 1793–94 (votes).

purposes, the government now had the possibility of invoking the PBRA process to secure abolition.

Although Theodore was widely regarded as intellectually brilliant, especially on financial matters, his personality was distinctly less convivial than Ryan's, and he lacked Ryan's almost innate capacity to generate both respect and affection within his own party, even among members who did not agree with him on ideological matters. Theodore was much more firmly identifiable with a particular faction in the party, given his long history of trade union activism, especially with the AWU, but he enjoyed the good fortune of presiding over a generally cohesive Assembly caucus, even though in the wider labour movement in the state a more militant industrial union faction linked with the American-based IWW (Industrial Workers of the World) was becoming more vocal. But within the national political arena, a different voice was making itself heard.

The 1919 National Election

Hughes's evident popularity as a war leader began to wane immediately the war was won. At the 1919 election, the Nationalists saw the 53 seats they had won in the House in 1917 slip to just 37. A single 'Independent Nationalist' member gave Hughes the slimmest of overall majorities,[94] but he governed in effect dependent upon support from the Country Party, which, with 11 seats, seized the opportunity to become an extremely effective power broker.[95]

Table 10.1 The 1919 Commonwealth election (13 December 1919)

House	% vote	Seats	Change
Nationalists	45.0	37	−16
Country	9.7	11	+11
Labour	42.5	26	+4
Independent Nationalist	1.2	1	
Senate[a]			
Nationalist	46.4	35	+11
Labour	42.8	1	−11
Country[b]	8.8	0	−

[a] 19 seats contested.
[b] See further n 96 below.

[94] The member concerned, Fred Francis, could not be relied upon to be a Hughes loyalist. He had stood in a Victoria seat against the official Nationalist candidate.

[95] In contrast to its precarious position in the House, the Nationalist party won 18 of the 19 Senate seats contested, leaving it with 35 of the 36 members. Hughes had, however, been defeated in a referendum proposal to amend the national Constitution to enhance the Commonwealth Parliament's powers over economic policy matters; see Coyne (1959) 'WM Hughes and the "powers" referendum of 1919: a master politician at work' *Australian Journal of Politics and History* 15.

The decentralised nature of the Australian polity both before and after confederation, coupled with the constant instability of party political alignments in the late nineteenth and early twentieth centuries, make it difficult to offer a clear linear narrative explaining the Country Party's emergence as a significant national force in 1919. Ward roots the party largely in former Free Traders who had not embraced Deakin's fusion, taking party political shape initially in the Farmers Party in Western Australia in 1912 and then spreading into Queensland (initially as the Farmers Party), Victoria and New South Wales by the end of the war.[96] Given its heterogeneous roots, the Country Party proved remarkably well-disciplined as an electoral and parliamentary force. Its ideology and electoral appeal lay partly in wistful nostalgia for an imagined vision of Australia as a land of sturdily independent small farmers, but many of its members also had a keen economic interest in seeing a reduction in the protective tariffs sheltering domestic manufacturers from overseas competition which meant they as agriculturalists and pastoralists paid more than open market rates for such item as farm machinery, fertilisers and – apparently an important commodity for pastoralists and farmers with thousands of acres to secure – barbed wire.

By 1919, the Country Party's leading and unifying light was Earle Page, a New South Wales born and bred medical doctor first elected to the Commonwealth Parliament in 1919 after having volunteered for military service in the war.[97] Page was born into economically modest but politically active family circumstances. He proved something of an academic prodigy, winning a scholarship to Sydney University at only 15 years old. He rapidly developed a successful medical practice and spent much of his earnings on buying land. Page entered politics through his involvement with a group called the Northern New South Wales Separation League, echoing arguments made to justify the state's pre-federation fragmentation to accommodate the creation of Victoria and Queensland, advocating the creation of a new state on the basis that Sydney was too remote – geographically and ideologically – properly to serve the interests of New South Wales's northern region and population.

Page was elected mayor of his hometown of Grafton in 1918, and ran successfully for the House seat of Cowper[98] on the northern coast in the December 1919 national election. He had initially stood as an 'Independent', but during the campaign accepted the endorsement of a pressure group called the Australia Farmer's Federal Organisation (AFFO), running on a platform which deprecated high taxes, governmental price fixing and state-run industries, and called for a fundamental review of Commonwealth-state financial relations.[99] The national 'Country Party' coalesced into a coherent group shortly after the election: "fortified", as Page put it, "by our political innocence and

---

[96] Ward (1978) op cit pp 133–36. See also Davy (2006) *The Nationals: the Progressive, Country and National parties in New South Wales 1919–2006* ch 1; Ellis (1958) *The Country Party: a political and social history of the party in New South Wales* chs 1–2.
[97] http://adb.anu.edu.au/biography/page-sir-earle-christmas-7941. Page has authored an engaging (if self-congratulatory) autobiography: (1963) *Truant surgeon*.
[98] The seat being named to honour Sir Charles Cowper (pp 56–58 above).
[99] Page op cit p49.

backed by an indestructible optimism which had not yet known the bitterness of defeat".[100]

By March 1920, as Theodore bedded into the role of State Premier and Page began to pull his disparate Country Party members into an ideologically coherent and tactically consistent bloc within the House,[101] *McCawley* arrived for hearing before the Privy Council.

---

[100] ibid p 61. At the election, seven seats were won by AFFO candidates and eight by 'Farmer Nationalists'. Four of the latter subsequently joined the Nationalists, leaving the newly named Country Party with 11 seats; ibid p53.

[101] Page was formally elected party leader in 1921, having received the support of all of his parliamentary colleagues; ibid p66.

11

Constitutional Controversies in Queensland: Ryan, Theodore and *McCawley* – Before the Privy Council

… embarrassing and even ridiculous …

Lord Birkenhead, on the argument advanced for Feez and Stumm, in the Privy Council's judgment in *McCawley v The King* [1920] AC 691, 705.

… I will allow no man in this House to insult me by interjections. If he does, he will get it in the teeth every time.

John Mullan, Attorney-General in the Queensland Labour Government, at second reading of the Judges' Retirement Bill 1921; QLAD 29 September 1921 p1008.

I. The Hearing

McCawley was argued before the Privy Council on 2 March 1920, and judgment delivered a week later. The bench was conspicuously strong: headed by Lord Birkenhead LC, joined by Viscount Haldane and Lords Buckmaster, Dunedin and Atkinson.

The Judges – A Court of Statesmen, Not Jurists?

Haldane and Dunedin had both sat in *Taylor*,[1] when they had refused permission to appeal. In the ensuing two years, they had both further consolidated their reputations as appellate judges. After *McCawley* was decided, Haldane greatly enhanced his standing as a colonial constitutional judge, proving particularly influential in relation to Canada's constitutional law.[2]

Lord Birkenhead LC was born Frederick (FE) Smith in 1872 in Liverpool.[3] His father was a barrister and prominent local Conservative politician. Smith excelled at Oxford

---

[1] Pp 278–79 above. Dunedin was also on the bench in *Theodore* and *Lennon*; p 301 above.
[2] The thrust of his jurisprudence being to restrict the national Parliament's powers in favour of enhancing the political autonomy of Canada's provinces. See especially *Reference re Board of Commerce Act* [1922] 1 AC 191; *Fort Frances Pulp v Man Free Press* [1923] AC 695; *Toronto Electric Commissioners v Snider* [1925] AC 396.
[3] Heuston (1964) op cit p353 et seq; Campbell (2004) 'Smith, Frederick Edwin, first Earl of Birkenhead' *ODNB*.

and at the Bar, and combined practice with politics when elected as Conservative MP for the Liverpool seat of Walton in 1906. Widely regarded (including very obviously by himself) as a brilliant barrister and orator, Smith was by turns a political reactionary and a pragmatist (he bitterly opposed House of Lords reform and women's enfranchisement, but eventually accommodated himself to both). Smith, appointed as Solicitor-General and then Attorney-General in Asquith's wartime coalition administration, was subsequently appointed Lord Chancellor by Lloyd George in 1919. When he sat in *McCawley*, he had no judicial experience of note.

Lord Buckmaster replaced Haldane as Lord Chancellor in 1915. He, like Birkenhead and Haldane, was appointed to the House of Lords without ever having sat in the High Court or Court of Appeal. Born in humble but upwardly mobile family circumstances in 1861,[4] Buckmaster made his way to Oxford and thence to the Bar. He built a successful chancery practice, taking silk in 1902, and also pursued a political career, being elected as Liberal MP for Cambridge in 1906. He was appointed Solicitor-General in 1913. He served as Lord Chancellor for barely a year, being dismissed when Asquith resigned as Prime Minister in favour of Lloyd George and being replaced by a Conservative, Sir Robert Finlay.

Lord Atkinson was also appointed to the Lords without previous judicial experience. Born (in 1844) and educated in Ireland, Atkinson built a formidable reputation at the Irish Bar and took silk aged only 36. He moved in Conservative political circles, and was appointed successively as Solicitor-General and Attorney-General for Ireland in the early 1890s in Lord Salisbury's administration. Atkinson was elected as a Conservative MP in 1895, and held office again as Attorney-General for Ireland until being appointed to the Lords by Balfour's Conservative government in 1905.[5]

Counsel and Submissions

Ryan's entry into national politics was sufficiently successful that by 1920 he was widely seen as the Labour Party's next leader. His increasingly high national profile precluded him from taking the *McCawley* brief before the Privy Council. Theodore's government instructed Sir John Simon as leading counsel in *McCawley*. Simon, the son of a Manchester clergyman, won scholarships to public school and then Oxford, where, after securing a first-class degree and being President of the Union, he had taken a fellowship at All Souls.[6] His career at the Bar flourished, and he was also elected as a Liberal MP in 1906. Asquith appointed him Solicitor-General in 1910 and Attorney-General in 1913. Appointed as Home Secretary in the 1916 coalition administration, Simon subsequently resigned from the government in opposition to the introduction of conscription and subsequently lost his Commons seat in the 1918 election. The resignation perhaps endeared Simon politically to Theodore, but the brief likely owed more to Simon's reputation as an advocate: he had appeared frequently in high-profile

---

[4] Goodhart (2004) 'Buckmaster, Stanley Owen' *ODNB*; Heuston (1964) op cit p243 et seq.
[5] Tobias (2006) 'Atkinson, John, Baron Atkinson' *ODNB*.
[6] Dutton (2011) 'Simon, John Allsebrook, first Viscount Simon' *ODNB*.

matters while Solicitor-General and Attorney-General, and Ryan had instructed him as co-counsel in the Privy Council in both *Theodore v Duncan* and *Lennon v Gibson*.

Feez and Stumm entrusted their case to Frederick Maugham. Maugham, who became Lord Chancellor in 1938 after being appointed to the High Court (in 1928), the Court of Appeal (1934) and the House of Lords (1935), was then an eminent silk at both the Chancery and the commercial law Bar. He had no obvious expertise as a constitutional lawyer, nor any particular track record in political terms. (He subsequently flirted with the prospect of contesting a Commons seat for the Conservatives, but was viewed very much as an apolitical appointment as Lord Chancellor in 1938.) He was ostensibly a strange choice for Feez and Stumm to have made.

The record of Maugham's submissions in the Appeal Cases covers barely half a page.[7] His argument was based squarely on *Cooper*; as he rather oddly put it: "that decision has never been questioned and is embodied in the textbooks".[8] The process of appointing Supreme Court judges and their tenure on the Court were matters of organic law, and so could be altered only by the 'Two Act' process. That three of the seven High Court judges who sat in *McCawley* had very obviously 'questioned' *Cooper* was a matter Maugham either overlooked or ignored.

Simon's submissions received more extensive coverage.[9] The submissions were succinct, rooted more in what one might term a received constitutional wisdom rather than the esoterica of colonial legislation and case law:

> The Constitution of Queensland is a "flexible," as distinguished from a "rigid," constitution. The distinction between those two classes of constitutions is pointed out and discussed in *Dicey's Law of the Constitution*, 8th ed., pp. 122, 123, 141. All the laws applying to Queensland which it is competent to the Queensland Legislature to alter can be altered in the same manner by ordinary enactment. In Queensland as in the UK there is no law within the competence of the Legislature which can be regarded as fundamental or supreme, or which tests the validity of laws subsequently enacted. The use of the word "constitution" in the title of the Constitution Act of 1867 does not restrict the power of the Queensland Legislature to pass subsequent laws which either expressly or impliedly vary the constitutional arrangements of the state.[10]

The Appeal Cases report does not record Simon invoking even one judicial authority to support his arguments (a wise strategy perhaps if one expected the Privy Council members to approach the task before them as statesmen rather than jurists). Instead, in addition to Dicey's treatise, Simon quoted from Anson's *Law and custom of the constitution*, Maitland's *Constitutional history of England* and Todd's *Parliamentary government*. Simon also referred (oddly, because clearly irrelevantly) to various British statutes which had affected the judiciary to demonstrate that such changes were made without any kind of special lawmaking procedure being undertaken.

---

[7] [1920] AC 691, 694–95. There was no significant coverage in the Queensland press; newspaper articles simply noted that the hearing was being held and identified the participants. There is no record of submissions in the CLR report.

[8] ibid 695. Although Maugham referred to textbooks, the only source recorded in the report is Berriedale Keith's *Responsible government in the Dominions*.

[9] [1920] AC 691, 693–94.

[10] ibid 693. The submission overstates the case, as obviously some bills had to be reserved for the royal assent and so were not passed in the 'same manner' as ordinary law. The prospect of legislation being enacted through the PBRA 1908 process does not contradict the submission, as such bills could have been passed in the ordinary way if a Council bare majority had been achieved.

II. The Judgment

Birkenhead's judgment – at least in form – paid tribute to the: "research and learning"[11] of all the High Court judges in *McCawley*. Substantively, however, Birkenhead caustically dismissed both the conclusions reached by the High Court majority and the Respondent's submissions before the Privy Council: "Their Lordships are clearly of opinion that no warrant whatever exists for the views insisted upon by the respondents, and affirmed by a majority of the judges in the Courts below."[12]

The strong bench convened was perhaps attributable less to the difficulty of the legal question raised than to its perceived political importance:

> Isaacs and Rich JJ. delivered one of two judgments dissenting from the majority of the Court, and with it their Lordships find themselves in almost complete agreement; indeed, if it were not for the general constitutional importance throughout the Empire of the matters under discussion, they would have been content to leave the matter where these learned judges left it. The circumstances, however, make it proper that they should attempt some examination of the matters which have been argued before them.[13]

Answered Questions

Most of Lord Birkenhead's judgment addressed the Respondent's first contention: namely, that the Queensland Court and the High Court majority had been correct to distinguish between 'ordinary law' and 'fundamental' or 'organic' law, and to conclude that 'fundamental' or 'organic' law could not be repealed or amended other than by the 'Two Act' process. Echoing the methodology (if varying the terminology of Simon's submissions), Birkenhead noted in fairly abstract terms that nations had adopted divergent views on the question of whether and, if so, how their governmental systems should differentiate between 'ordinary' and 'fundamental' laws:

> Some communities, and notably Great Britain, have not in the framing of constitutions felt it necessary, or thought it useful, to shackle the complete independence of their successors. They have shrunk from the assumption that a degree of wisdom and foresight has been conceded to their generation which will be, or may be, wanting to their successors, in spite of the fact that those successors will possess more experience of the circumstances and necessities amid which their lives are lived. Those constitution framers who have adopted the other view must be supposed to have believed that certainty and stability were in such a matter the supreme desiderata. Giving effect to this belief, they have created obstacles of varying difficulty in the path of those who would lay rash hands upon the ark of the constitution. It is not necessary, and indeed the inquiry would be a long one, to analyse the different methods which have been adopted in different countries by those who have framed constitutions under these safeguards. But it is important to realize with clearness the nature of the distinction.[14]

---

[11] [1920] AC 691, 700.
[12] ibid 706.
[13] ibid 701. Similarly at 704: "The inquiry ought not to be, and in fact is not, a very difficult one"; and at 711: "… their Lordships do not think it useful to expend time on a more detailed examination of the materials which were so much discussed in the courts below …". Haldane, Atkinson and Dunedin had been similarly impressed by Isaacs's reasoning in *Theodore v Duncan*; p 301 above.
[14] ibid 703.

Birkenhead's characterisation of the distinction as one between 'controlled' and 'uncontrolled' constitutions is not particularly well chosen. Birkenhead was certainly not thinking in terms of a simplistic dichotomy. He appeared to use 'uncontrolled' as equating with the British position (asserted by Simon) that any law could be made by a bare majority in each house plus the royal assent, and that such law would either expressly repeal or impliedly repeal or amend any previously enacted statutory provision. 'Controlled' was equated with any legally enforceable device – which devices were many and varied – that made lawmaking more difficult than that.[15]

The issue raised in *McCawley* is better described not as whether a *constitution* is controlled or uncontrolled, but how a given political society allocates the powers of the *lawmaking institutions which exist within it*. Birkenhead subsequently framed the question more precisely – albeit completely misunderstanding Higgins's comment in the High Court – as being whether the Queensland Constitution recognised a distinction between 'organic' and 'ordinary' law which required different lawmaking processes to be used depending upon what type of legal provision was in issue:

> Thus when one of the learned judges in the Court below said that, according to the appellant, the constitution could be ignored as if it were a Dog Act, he was in effect merely expressing his opinion that the constitution was, in fact, controlled. If it were uncontrolled, it would be an elementary commonplace that in the eye of the law the legislative document or documents which defined it occupied precisely the same position as a Dog Act or any other Act, however, humble its subject-matter.[16]

That many societies' constitutions did recognise such a distinction was a trite proposition. The question Birkenhead posed was why it should be assumed that the distinction was a feature of Queensland's Constitution in the specific (ie 'Two Act' entrenchment) sense for which Feez and Stumm argued?

The Privy Council proceeded on the basis that the British Parliament's lawmaking process had presumptively been exported to Britain's Australian colonies, ie that all matters within the colonies' substantive legal competence would be made by the bicameral bare majority plus royal assent process, with either express or implied effect on previously enacted colonial legislation. But that presumption was rebuttable. What Birkenhead variously referred to as 'shackles' or 'restrictions' could properly be placed on the default lawmaking process. And it seemed that in Queensland such 'shackles' could be imposed either by – obviously – the Imperial Parliament and/or by the Queensland 'Legislature' itself. Thus, Imperial legislation which required the Governor to reserve bills on certain matters for the Monarch's personal assent were a 'shackle', as were provisions requiring certain bills to be laid before the Commons and Lords for specified periods before assent was given. (Birkenhead did not refer explicitly to Isaacs

---

[15] Birkenhead did not note that the default British position could become *more* uncontrolled if, for example, as was arguably the consequence of the Parliament Act 1911, legislation equal in normative status to Acts enacted by the Common Lords and King could be passed without the consent of the House of Lords; ie an 'obstacle' had been removed.

[16] ibid 704, referring to Higgins's comment, which clearly accepted that the Constitution Act was no more normatively significant than a Dog Act exactly because the Constitution was 'uncontrolled' in Birkenhead's sense. Birkenhead was presumably not alert – Higgins likely was – to the significance of a 'Dog Act' in Australian constitutional law and history; pp 24–27 above.

and Rich's identification of various other types of 'shackles' which might exist,[17] but his judgment does not limit the forms such 'shackles' might take.[18])

For Birkenhead, the obvious difficulty that Maugham faced – and could not overcome – was that there was no legislative textual basis anywhere – whether in an Imperial statute, the 1859 Order or a Queensland Act which supported the existence of the particular 'shackle' which *Cooper* had identified – the 'Two Act' entrenchment hypothesis.[19] Addressing this issue, Birkenhead adopted language which – given prevailing niceties of professional courtesy from judge to counsel – was remarkably disparaging:

> [I]t is important at the outset to notice that the respondents do not find themselves in the position which they would occupy under any genuinely controlled constitution with which their Lordships are familiar. In such a case, confronted with the objections by which they are met in this appeal, they would have no difficulty in pointing to specific articles in the legislative instrument or instruments which created the constitution, prescribing with meticulous precision the methods by which, and by which alone, it could be altered. The respondents to this appeal are wholly unable to reinforce their argument by any such demonstration. And their inability has involved them in dialectical difficulties which are embarrassing and even ridiculous.[20]

Birkenhead seemed astonished, given the absence of 'specific articles', that Maugham: "was driven to contend – or at least ... did in fact contend"[21] that the two-stage entrenchment process could not even be achieved in separate provisions within a single statute, but would indeed require two wholly separate Acts.

The Privy Council readily accepted that Queensland's constitution had previously contained one such 'specific article' created by the Queensland Legislature itself, and Birkenhead cast no doubt on that 'specific article's' legal validity:

> The next section which requires examination is s.9, which required a two-thirds majority of the Legislative Council, and of the Legislative Assembly, as a condition precedent of the validity of legislation altering the constitution of the Legislative Council. We observe, therefore, *the Legislature in this isolated section carefully selecting one special and individual case* in which limitations are imposed upon the power of the Parliament of Queensland to express and carry out its purpose in the ordinary way, by a bare majority.[22]

The suggestion that there was anything 'careful' about the Queensland Legislature's 'selection' of s.9 in 1867 is fanciful. The 1867 Act – the product almost entirely of

---

[17] Pp 288–296 above.

[18] That is entirely consistent with the sequence of events that unfolded in Queensland and South Australia in the early 1860s, when the colonial legislatures failed to comply with various 'shackles', which failure led repeatedly to the retrospective validation of Imperial legislation being enacted.

[19] This was essentially the submission Ryan had made in the High Court and had aired previously in *Taylor*, although Birkenhead did not acknowledge the point.

[20] ibid 705. And then – with disdain accompanied by sarcasm – at 713: "The contention of the respondents upon [ss.15–16] ... is that they embody a judicial charter affording security of judicial tenure; that they cannot be modified except in some manner of which their Lordships take leave to observe that it is neither clearly conceived, nor intelligibly described; that the Act of 1916 is in conflict with these sections; that the Act does not comply with the formalities (whatever they may be) required for the effective modification of the sections; and, therefore, that the Act of 1916 is ultra vires and inoperative." Birkenhead had acquired a reputation, as both counsel and political orator, of being bitingly impolite to opponents, colleagues and judges, a trait which perhaps he was indulging here; Campbell (2004) op cit.

[21] ibid 705.

[22] ibid 712; emphasis added.

backroom work by Lilley and Cockle – sailed through both houses alongside a raft of consolidatory and revisory bills without any substantial debate.[23] The best that can credibly be said of s.9 and s.10 is that they were an echo of Wentworth's initiative in the 1853 New South Wales Bill (which initiative in that context was certainly 'carefully selected'). Nor is there any indication that Cockle, Lilley or any members of the Legislature considered that in enacting ss.9–10 they were exercising a power granted by CLVA 1865 s.5.

The passage's significance, however, is that Birkenhead clearly concludes that the Queensland Legislature had the power to depart from the 'ordinary way' of legislating. He had made the same point on the previous page:

> [U]nless the Act to consolidate the laws relating to the constitution of the colony of Queensland which was *passed in 1867 contributed some new and special quality* to, or imposed some new and special restriction upon, the constitution of that colony the argument for the respondents upon the matters heretofore discussed wholly fails.[24]

Affirming – if not expressly citing – the conclusion reached by Isaacs and Rich, Birkenhead stressed that such shackles or restrictions on the ordinary method of lawmaking had to come in very precise terms (with 'meticulous precision') from the Legislature; they could not be implied by a court.

Having dismissed the notion that 'Two Act' entrenchment was a feature of Queensland's constitutional landscape, Birkenhead, in an act of evident benevolence, reformulated Maugham's submissions in more moderate terms: namely, that the Queensland constitution required that any legislation which altered a provision of the Constitution Act do so in express terms, in "plain and unmistakeable language";[25] and which was 'plain and unmistakeable' both in announcing that a particular constitutional provision was to be changed and in then actually changing it; such an alteration to the constitution could not be achieved merely by the subsequent enactment of an inconsistent statutory provision. That reformulation in essence asserted that some aspects of Queensland's constitution were not subject to implied repeal in the orthodox British sense.

Birkenhead initially canvassed this issue early in his judgment when discussing the background to the CLVA 1865's enactment. Birkenhead's account was certainly accurate when recording that Palmer and Collier had thought that the doctrine of implied repeal could properly apply in the colonial constitutional context[26] (as in broader terms is his unspoken equation of his 'shackles' with Palmer and Collier's acceptance of the legitimacy and legality of 'special' restrictions on the ordinary way of lawmaking).[27] But Birkenhead's recharacterisation of Maugham's submission as being that provisions of the Constitution Act could not be altered by implied repeal led him into a curiously undisciplined passage:

> It must at once be observed that such a constitution as the respondents conceive of would be, so far as the Board is aware, unique in constitutional history. It is neither controlled nor

---

[23] Pp 124–26 above.
[24] [1920] AC 691, 711; emphases added.
[25] ibid 705.
[26] Pp 104–05 above.
[27] Pp 103–104 above.

is it uncontrolled. It is not controlled because posterity can by a merely formal Act correct it at pleasure. It is not uncontrolled because the framers have prescribed to their successors a particular mode by which, and by which alone, they are allowed to effect constitutional changes.[28]

Birkenhead's likely intention here was to heap further scorn on Feez and Stumm's case. But his analysis does not sit comfortably with the 'uncontrolled' versus 'controlled' dichotomy. If the British Parliament's mode of lawmaking is the 'uncontrolled' default mechanism, then the *Cooper* principle – as modified by Birkenhead – obviously contained a 'control', in that it required the consequential statute to identify its effect in explicit terms. (Isaacs and Rich had considered such 'linguistic entrenchment' as one means to depart from the 'ordinary way'.[29]) That the 'control' would not pose any significant obstacle to a government commanding even a tiny bicameral majority is beside the point; it is nonetheless an obstacle to inadvertent or mendacious legislative reform of existing law.

For Feez and Stumm to see the arguments on which they relied, which had been upheld in both the Queensland Supreme Court and by the majority in the High Court of Australia, dismissed as 'embarrassing and even ridiculous' was likely a chastening experience.[30] But they might equally have felt themselves legitimately aggrieved by Birkenhead's opinion, which – as yet another example of the Privy Council judges being 'statesmen' rather than 'jurists' – did not engage at all with the details of those (or any other) judicial authorities, and resolved the matter before it as essentially one of political theory. And the 'embarrassing and even ridiculous' label was presumably as applicable to the Australian judges who had approved the submissions in the courts below as to the counsel who made them before the Privy Council.

Notwithstanding the evident flaws in the details of Birkenhead's reasoning and its exposition, and its undiplomatically acerbic treatment of the Supreme Court and High Court majorities, the ratio and the broader implications of the judgment were clear, and are (respectively) neatly captured in passages towards the end of the decision:[31]

> [T]heir Lordships are wholly unable to discern in the language of ss. 15 and 16, or of any other sections in the Act of 1867, the slightest indication of an intention on the part of the Legislature to deal in any exceptional manner with legislation affecting judicial tenure in Queensland ...
>
> The Legislature of Queensland is the master of its own household, except in so far as its powers have in special cases been restricted. No such restriction has been established, and none in fact exists, in such a case as is raised in the issues now under appeal.

Putting the matter more starkly, Feez and Stumm did not fail because the Queensland legislature *could not* be subject to the 'shackle' of a 'Two Act' lawmaking process; they failed because the Legislature *had not* been so shackled.[32]

---

[28] [1920] AC 691, 705–06.
[29] Pp 288–92 above.
[30] Birkenhead evidently saw no need even to refer to, still less to engage with and refute, the reinforcement to their argument that Griffith and Barton had derived from company law principles. Those propositions, too, were perhaps 'embarrassing and even ridiculous'.
[31] [1920] AC 691, 713 and 714 respectively.
[32] Birkenhead's conclusion was essentially on all fours with Selborne's judgment 40 years earlier in *Burah*, although he made no mention of that authority; [1878] AC 889, 914, quoted at pp 152–53 above.

An Unanswered Question?

While the Imperial Parliament's power to impose shackles on colonial legislatures does not need explanation, the Privy Council also omitted to deal unambiguously with the distinctly less obvious issue of from where the Queensland Legislature derived the power to do so. In the High Court, Rich and Isaacs had suggested that CLVA 1865 s.5, cl.22 of the 1859 Order and s.2 of the 1867 Act all provided a legal root for such competence.

Birkenhead's statement that the Privy Council was "in almost complete agreement" with Isaacs and Rich might credibly be taken as an implicit endorsement of that dual source analysis (although, given Birkenhead's insistence on textual precision to sustain any 'restriction', there is something obviously unsatisfactory about leaving unanswered questions to be resolved by implication). That caveat aside, Birkenhead's focus on Constitution Act-created restrictions perhaps suggests that he had only s.5 in mind, given that the Constitution Act post-dated the CLVA. Birkenhead also noted that: "The important provision, however, of this Act [the CLVA] in relation to the present litigation is contained in s.5 ..."[33] The obvious rejoinder to that assertion is that cl.22 would seem to have been the Queensland equivalent of s.4 [BAA] and s.1 of sch.1 of the 1855 New South Wales Act, and the various shackles placed on the New South Wales Legislature's presumptively 'ordinary' lawmaking process pre-dated the CLVA.

Birkenhead's judgment might be taken to suggest that the Legislature's power to enact exceptions to the ordinary way of legislating was a 'once-in-a-lifetime' power exercisable only when the Legislature first deployed – in 1867 – the power granted in cl.22. The inference is not especially strong, and as an inference lacks the 'meticulous precision' which Birkenhead required of 'restrictions'. Further, Birkenhead's conclusion that the Queensland Legislature 'is', not 'was', master in its own household, which indicates a 'continuing' rather than 'exhausted' capacity.

Given that the Privy Council had alluded to the: "general constitutional importance throughout the Empire of the matters under discussion",[34] it was perhaps unfortunate that this issue was not expressly addressed. If the power to impose 'restrictions' derived from cl.22, the power could presumably be used on any and all political matters. If it lay in s.5[3], the power would be restricted to those issues identified in s.5[1] and s.5[2]. In both Queensland itself and in other colonies whose governmental systems derived from measures analogous to cl.22, that might be thought an obviously important question.

The 1867 Act had passed through Queensland's Legislature without division in either house. Members of the Assembly and those of the Council had not had any occasion to address the question of the legal and/or moral propriety of introducing the two-thirds restrictions (in ss.9–10) by a simple majority process. The Assembly had divided over the repeal of s.10 in 1871; a repeal that was carried on the basis that only a bicameral bare majority was required.[35] That point had been fiercely argued in 1908 over the repeal of s.9, but was resolved in favour of a bare majority repeal in *Taylor*. The Privy Council in *McCawley* made no reference to the 1871 or 1908 Acts, or to *Taylor*, but there

---

[33] [1920] AC 691, 710.
[34] ibid 701.
[35] Pp 128–29 above. That position was not challenged in the Queensland courts.

is nothing in Birkenhead's judgment to rule out the possibility that it was within the Legislature's power to re-enact (in the ordinary way) s.9 and s.10 in their original form; or, indeed, to enact other future 'restrictions' on the Legislature's capacity to make laws in that ordinary way.

The Meaning (and Vires) of the Commission

Birkenhead's evident impatience with Feez and Stumm's suit was further underlined by his comment on the suggestion that McCawley lacked seven years' 'standing' as a barrister: "this contention was not persisted in before their Lordships, was plainly insupportable, and may be treated as abandoned".[36] The claim that McCawley's commission was ultra vires s.6 was persisted in, but not in Birkenhead's view with much credibility. As he put it: "Common sense must be applied to the elucidation of these matters."[37] If that was done, the conclusion was "irresistible" that the s.6 permitted appointment for seven years, terminable within that period if the appointee was not of good behaviour, and the commission could not and should not be read as authorising anything else:

> The draftsman of the commission was in terms availing himself of the powers contained in that Act ... The Act was the only soil in which the commission had any root. When the commission therefore makes an appointment under the terms of the Act, and during good behaviour, it means, and can only mean, what the Act means – namely, for seven years (or an extended period) and during good behaviour.[38]

Reaction(s) in Queensland

The *BC* greeted the judgment with two cursory notes a few days apart,[39] and eschewed any editorialising. A lengthy editorial in *The Mail* – rather misleadingly titled 'WHAT IT MEANS' – offered a thorough account of the controversy, but seemed unwilling to express any view on the desirability of the Privy Council's conclusion.[40]

Among the Labour-leaning press, the reaction was distinctly more partisan and enthusiastic. For *The Standard*, *McCawley* confirmed the presumed inadequacy of the State Supreme Court:

> Having been repeatedly turned down by the Privy Council over their anti-Labor law decisions it seems about time the present Supreme Court Bench took a good look at itself and considered whether its legal outlook is in keeping with the spirit of the times.[41]

The pro-Labour scandal sheet *Truth* also greeted the judgment with delight, and placed credit where it might sensibly thought to be due: "It must be a bitter pill for opponents of Labour to swallow, as Ryan has beaten them constitutionally right along the line."[42]

---

[36] [1920] AC 691, 702.
[37] ibid 716.
[38] ibid 715 and 717.
[39] 10 March 1920 p7, https://trove.nla.gov.au/newspaper/article/20430695; 12 March 1920 p5, https://trove.nla.gov.au/newspaper/article/20414192.
[40] 10 March 1920 p5, https://trove.nla.gov.au/newspaper/article/215422275; original emphasis.
[41] 9 March 1920 p5, https://trove.nla.gov.au/newspaper/article/180953573.
[42] 14 March 1920 p4, https://trove.nla.gov.au/newspaper/article/204030291.

Ryan himself chipped in with a personal reminiscence relating to his professional (qua counsel) competence:

> It is a somewhat interesting fact that before the Governor of Queensland, Sir H. Goold-Adams approved the Executive minute appointing Mr. McCawley, and in consequence of the views of certain Judges, the Governor specifically required my legal opinion as Attorney-General as to the validity of the appointment before he would approve thereof. That opinion accordingly was given, and is now upheld by the Privy Council's decision.[43]

McCawley subsequently took his seat on the Supreme Court on 5 May 1920. Theodore was in London seeking to raise loans for the government on the capital markets, but Ryan made time to attend, as did: "apparently every member of the legal profession in Brisbane".[44] Ryan took the opportunity to make a short speech, welcoming McCawley to the bench and caustically suggesting that the Privy Council's conclusion was so obviously correct that Feez and Stumm's suit had been a wholly unmeritorious exercise.[45]

While there is no record of either Cooper or Lukin reacting to Ryan's comment,[46] Real interjected with a response intended, one assumes, to differentiate his own position from that adopted by the rest of the Court:

> You are hardly stating the case accurately. The attack was made by the Crown for the purpose of testing the matter, and one member of the court, at all events held exactly the same view as that held by the Privy Council.[47]

McCawley, too, spoke briefly, thanking Ryan and Macrossan for arguing on his behalf in the Australian courts. Theodore, on returning from London, turned the government's attention to other constitutional matters.

III. The Eventual Abolition of the Queensland Legislative Council

Theodore's distaste for the Council on grounds of what he regarded as democratic principle had always been profound, and that abstract hostility was coupled with a practical concern prompted by the Council's blocking of bills promoted during the first years of his premiership. Unlike Ryan, Theodore saw little prospect of achieving abolition through the referendum process. His preferred route was to promote an ordinary bill consequent on also having taken steps to alter the Council's composition. Those steps were initiated in January 1920. The then Governor Sir Hamilton Goold-Adams returned to England on leave prior to his expected retirement date before a successor

---

[43] *Daily Standard* 11 March 1920 p5, https://trove.nla.gov.au/newspaper/article/180953893.
[44] *Warwick Daily News* 6 May 1920 p2, https://trove.nla.gov.au/newspaper/article/175760132.
[45] ibid. Which analysis was presumably inferentially aimed at Cooper and Lukin.
[46] And it seems that neither *The (Brisbane) Courier*, *The Telegraph* nor *The Mail* covered McCawley's installation. The Brisbane-based *Worker*, an AWU-backed (and thus very pro-Theodore) paper, indulged dramatic licence and political partisanship by recording that there was: "an unusually cold and dejected aspect about the Judges and the older members of the Bar when the young, virile McCawley stepped determinedly forward on Wednesday and took his place amongst them …"; 6 May p6, https://trove.nla.gov.au/newspaper/article/71048616.
[47] *Queensland Times* 6 May 1920 p5, https://trove.nla.gov.au/newspaper/article/120738440.

was appointed. The usual practice in such circumstances (albeit a practice that had no express legal base) was that the State Chief Justice would serve as Lieutenant-Governor, exercising the Governor's powers.

Like Kidston a decade earlier,[48] Theodore had no desire to place Cooper in the Governor's chair, even temporarily. Goold-Adams's tenure was to end on 3 February 1920. On 5 January, Theodore announced that Goold-Adams had accepted Theodore's advice that until a new appointment was made, one William Lennon would serve as Lieutenant-Governor, exercising all of the Governor's powers.[49] Lennon, then 70 years old, was a long-term Labour Assembly member who had been a minister under Ryan[50] and had become Speaker in 1919.[51] Theodore sought to rebut accusations of political impropriety by informing the Assembly that both Philp and Griffith were offered the post but declined it; it was apparently (unsurprisingly) not offered to Cooper.[52]

In a startling manipulation of formal legal powers, one of Lennon's first actions as Lieutenant-Governor was to appoint himself to the Council and then elevate himself to President of the Council. There was a widespread expectation, which Theodore did nothing to dispel, that Lennon's appointment would be promptly followed – before any new Governor arrived in post – by Lennon being 'advised' by Theodore to swamp the Council with new members supportive of Theodore's administration in general and of Council abolition in particular.

As Fitzgerald notes, the Nationalist majority appeared oblivious to that possibility:[53]

> On 11 February 1920 the Council amended four clauses of the Income Tax Bill, rejected the Land Act Amendment Bill and amended the Profiteering Prevention Bill. The Council could hardly have picked items of legislation more important to the new Premier.

The Labour-leaning *Daily Standard* was one of the few newspapers to greet the prospect of swamping with enthusiasm:

> From Knibbs's Official Yearbook of the Parliament of Queensland: 'There is no limit to the number of members of the Legislative Council of Queensland'. Wherefore full steam ahead, Driver Theodore; crush out those obstructionists who have held up the chariot of progress for so long.[54]

Lennon subsequently appointed 14 new Council members on 19 February 1920. The Labour Party's own rules meant that the appointments were not directly in Theodore's gift; councillors would be 'elected' by the Assembly caucus from a shortlist of 50 nominees drawn up by the state party executive. Theodore's effective influence seemed strong: of the 14 appointees, six held office in AWU-friendly unions and three

---

[48] Pp 214–15 above.
[49] *Daily Standard* 6 January 1920 p5, https://trove.nla.gov.au/newspaper/article/180966835.
[50] In which capacity he was the titular plaintiff in *Lennon v Gibson*; n – at pp – above.
[51] http://adb.anu.edu.au/biography/lennon-william-7172. Lennon resigned as Speaker (and from his Assembly seat) that day; QLAD 9 January 1920 p2111.
[52] ibid pp 2118–19. Neither Philp nor Griffith contradicted this, and one might note that the generally very anti-Theodore *Daily Mail* (16 January 1920 p4) regarded those offers as having been made as an indication that there was nothing constitutionally improper about Theodore's behaviour; quoted in Fitzgerald op cit pp 119–20; https://trove.nla.gov.au/newspaper/article/215423937.
[53] Op cit p121. The episode is recounted in detail at ibid pp 119–29.
[54] 18 February 1920 p4, https://trove.nla.gov.au/newspaper/article/180951436.

were journalists on pro-Theodore newspapers. For *The Queenslander* newspaper, what it (one assumes sarcastically) called the 'Noble Fourteen' were a mix of anti-war pacifists lacking both political and economic experience, whose sole purpose was to turn the Council into a rubber stamp for government policy.[55] *The Worker* – unsurprisingly, given that its editor and managing director were among the nominees – greeted the news with the headline 'House of Privilege captured' and presented a much more positive characterisation of the new appointees.[56]

In an Assembly speech on 19 February, Theodore announced that the Government would deploy its new Council majority to secure the passage of various financial bills which had previously been blocked, but also confirmed that there were no immediate plans to seek the Council's abolition. That step would not be pursued until the Government received a popular mandate to do so, either through a PBRA referendum or by making abolition a prominent issue at a subsequent Assembly election.[57] Since an election was due later that year, Theodore's undertaking did not offer the Council any long-term guarantee of survival.

Lennon's tenure as Lieutenant-Governor ended in June 1920, when a new Governor, Sir Matthew Nathan, finally took office. Nathan was the child of middle-class Jewish parents. He initially had a successful military career, reaching the rank of major before being appointed to a series of governorships (Sierra Leone, the Gold Coast, Hong Kong and Natal) from 1899 onwards. He subsequently held posts in the British civil service before becoming Queensland's Governor in June 1920.[58]

Fitzgerald has suggested that Nathan was appointed by the then British government[59] – over Theodore's requests for an Australian Governor – in the expectation that he would be a conservative counterweight to Theodore's presumed radicalism. The two men nonetheless established congenial personal and political relations. At this point, Theodore's prime concern was what came to be known as 'the loan blockade'.[60] Philp had been prominent among a group of Queensland lobbyists who had with some success – and with Hughes's approval, if not active support – persuaded British lenders to decline to do business with Theodore's government until it adopted more conservative economic policies.[61] For Theodore, this was: "a sordid conspiracy that has been hatched against us in the dark recess of the Tory mind".[62] Among his prompt and various responses was

---

[55] 28 February 1920 p14, https://trove.nla.gov.au/newspaper/article/25316676.

[56] 26 February 1920 p11, https://trove.nla.gov.au/newspaper/article/71049931. A *Daily Mail* leader offered nuanced criticism, classing the appointments as poor political judgment rather than constitutional outrage; 23 February 1919 p4, https://trove.nla.gov.au/newspaper/article/215420178.

[57] *BC* 19 February 1920 p7, https://trove.nla.gov.au/newspaper/article/20401742.

[58] http://adb.anu.edu.au/biography/nathan-sir-matthew-7728.

[59] Op cit pp 129–32. Sir Alfred Milner then being Secretary of State for the Colonies in Lloyd George's coalition administration.

[60] For a detailed treatment, see Cochrane (1989) *Blockade: the Queensland loans affair 1920–1924*. For more succinct critiques, see Fitzgerald op cit pp 126–35; Attard (nd) 'How to organise a "capital strike": The British Australasian Society and the Queensland government, 1899–1924', www.ehs.org.uk/dotAsset/ba8ef532-867e-4c66-bc4e-36d67235d5ed.doc. Philp's role in the episode does make it seem extraordinary that Theodore had invited him to serve as Lieutenant-Governor, unless Theodore had reasoned that the appointment might remove a politically dangerous opponent from the stage.

[61] Their especial concern had been with bills – thus far blocked in the Council – dealing with reforms to land law, and especially to proposals to break up large pastoralist estates.

[62] Quoted in Fitzgerald op cit p131.

successfully to raise such loans on the New York market, and to promote legislation establishing a (very profitable) state lottery.[63]

Theodore fought his first election as party leader in October 1920. From one perspective, that election was not a success for him. Labour's representation in the Assembly fell from 48 to 38 seats; the party's overall majority dropped from 24 to just four. However, the electoral arithmetic was more complex than those bald figures suggest. Labour lost 10 seats, but the Nationalists lost 11. The Country Party, now with 21 seats to the Nationalists' 13, would be the official opposition.[64]

Labour had made clear in the election campaign that – notwithstanding the referendum result three years earlier– it was still committed to Council abolition. Theodore differed from Ryan on questions of method, however. Rather than hold a second PBRA referendum, Theodore's preference was to pursue abolition in the 'ordinary way'. That would, of course, require a majority in both the Assembly and the Council. The peculiar situation which now arose, consequent on the October election and the February appointments, was that Labour's Council majority was now perhaps more secure than its majority in the Assembly.

Table 11.1 Queensland Legislative Assembly election, 1920 (8 October 1920)

Party	% vote	Seats	Change
Nationalist	26.7	13	–9
Labour	47.8	38	–10
Country Party	24.7	21	+21
Independent Nationalist	–	–	–2

Theodore's effective position in the Assembly was more powerful than the bare figures would suggest; in part because the Labour caucus was (relatively) cohesive, but primarily because the Country and Nationalist parties, even though they fought the election without opposing each other in many seats, seemed as concerned on some matters to disagree with each other as to attack Theodore's government. And that Nationalist versus Country party tension was nowhere more evident than over Theodore's abolition plans. But before pressing that issue towards a conclusion, Theodore's government turned its attention to the Supreme Court.

That initiative was taken without benefit of any further input from Ryan. Ryan's achievements as both lawyer and politician in Queensland, and his growing reputation on the political stage, had been made against the background of constantly fragile

---

[63] On the latter, see Selby (2005) 'Social evil or social good: lotteries and state regulation in Australia and the United States' in McMillen (ed) *Gambling cultures: studies in history and interpretation*.

[64] The leader of the opposition was William Vowles, a Queensland-born solicitor from the small town of Dalby. Vowles, having been Mayor of Dalby, was elected to the Assembly as a Nationalist in 1911. He did not hold office under Denham, but subsequently became the party's Deputy Leader in opposition in May 1918; *Dalby Herald* 29 May 1918 p3, https://trove.nla.gov.au/newspaper/article/213753832. Vowles left the Nationalists for the Country Party shortly before the 1920 election; *BC* 29 July 1920, https://trove.nla.gov.au/newspaper/article/20401758. He remained leader until 1926, when he lost his seat and returned to legal practice and local politics; *Dalby Herald* 24 August 1943 p3, https://trove.nla.gov.au/newspaper/article/217497670/23449261.

health, often exacerbated by overwork. He had frequently been confined to bed during his premiership. Ryan was taken ill again during July 1921, falling victim to a fatal bout of pneumonia on 1 August. He was only 45. His death left a cavernous hole in the national Labour Party's ranks.

The Judges' Retirement Act 1921

Theodore's Judges' Retirement Bill had its first reading in the Assembly on 21 September 1921. Virtually all 72 members were present, and the public galleries were packed. The bill was presented as one element of a proposed three-Act scheme introducing wide-ranging changes to the state's court structure and processes. Notwithstanding the Privy Council's conclusion in *McCawley* that Queensland's Constitution could be amended (expressly or impliedly) by ordinary legislation, the text of the bill stated explicitly in its preamble and cl.1 that it was amending the Constitution of Queensland and, inter alia, the Supreme Court Acts 1861–1903. Cl.3 provided simply that every judge already 70 years old would retire immediately, and all current and future judges would retire automatically on reaching 70.[65] Per cl.4, existing judges would retain their pension rights (accrued after 15 years' service), but any subsequently appointed judge would not have any pension entitlements. Of the Supreme Court *McCawley* bench, all had long outlived Ryan. Cooper, Chubb and Real were in their mid-70s; Shand was 67; Lukin only 54.

In the Assembly

By September 1921, Labour's precarious four-seat Assembly majority had declined to two, raising the possibility that coordinated and well-disciplined action by the opposition parties could certainly obstruct, if not defeat, the passage of government bills. The Retirement Bill provided that opportunity. As the *Daily Mail* recorded on 22 September:

> For the first time that Labour came into power in Queensland in 1915, the Government was beaten on a division last night. The figures were 34–33 ... The result was received with acclamation by a number of ladies in the gallery.[66]

The defeat arose when – unusually at first reading – the Nationalists moved an amendment with Country Party support to limit the bill's effect to *future* Supreme Court appointees. The amendment was something of an ambush. One Labour member missed the vote because he was making a telephone call, another could not be found and accusations were raised from the Labour benches that a Nationalist member deliberately broke a pair with a Labour member called home because of a family illness. Theodore then immediately moved another amendment to overturn the previous amendment.

---

[65] Judges would complete any part-heard case.
[66] 22 September 1921 p7, http://nla.gov.au/nla.news-article213173199; *BC* 22 September 1921 p6, http://nla.gov.au/nla.news-article20499094. The acclamation being presumably the result of conscious political evaluation rather than bribery with 'delicious pies'; p 237 above.

The Labour whips retrieved their two missing members and, bolstered by the departure of a Country Party MP, the government won the second vote 35–33.[67] By then it was past midnight, and the bill was set down for second reading on 29 September.

In the interim, in a vein reminiscent of Lutwyche's 'political' activities 60 years earlier,[68] Lukin aired his views of government policy in comments from the bench on 27 September while sitting in Rockhampton.[69] Much of his lengthy address – delivered before he heard a list of matrimonial proceedings – was an accusation that the bill, if enacted, would violate the constitutional principles underlying the Act of Settlement and create a politicised judiciary:

> I feel that the political representatives have broken the pledged word of a previous government, supposedly secured by the express term of a statute, which statute aimed at securing the independence of the judges, so that the judges might be free from political or other undesirable influences.

Lukin also explained that he had given up – feeling duty bound to accept judicial office when Kidston had offered it – an income of £4000 per year, likely to rise further as his eminence at the Bar increased, for the much lesser judicial salary of £2000 per year. Had he known that he would have had to retire at 70, Lukin suggested, he would not have accepted the appointment.

Cooper eschewed public comment, even though he personally lobbied the Governor to express his opposition to the bill, which he characterised as a partisan retaliation against the Supreme Court for deciding various cases against the government.[70]

The third 'retiring' judge, Patrick Real, took a different approach. Immediately prior to second reading, the Assembly hosted an unusual guest. Real had sought – and been granted – the Assembly's permission to address the house on the bill. His speech[71] was seemingly not well-received on the Labour benches. Real, speaking without notes, had rambled across an eclectically landmarked constitutional terrain.

He began by pointing out, repeating the observation he had made when McCawley took his seat on the Court,[72] that he (alone of the Supreme Court) had found in the government's favour in *McCawley*, and expressed admiration for the Arbitration Court and its judges. Then, turning to the history of the House of Commons, Real invoked the political battles of Daniel O'Connell, Charles Bradlaugh and John Wilkes, and – going further afield – alighted to no evident purpose on America's: "second Washington, the martyr Abraham Lincoln". The references to O'Connell, Bradlaugh and Wilkes seemed to be intended to identify episodes in British constitutional history when worthy individuals had overcome unjust barriers, and as such were testament to an underlying fairness that informed British (and, by extension, Australian) political life. Real also told

---

[67] Having by the same majority approved Theodore's motion that there not be any debate on the 'new' amendment.

[68] Pp 77–80 above.

[69] *Morning Bulletin* (Rockhampton) 28 September 1921 p8, https://trove.nla.gov.au/newspaper/article/53985844. For a distinctly (and atypically) unsympathetic newspaper critique of Lukin's comments, see *Daily Standard* 28 September 1921 p5, https://trove.nla.gov.au/newspaper/article/184950028.

[70] Fitzgerald op cit pp 144–45.

[71] *QLAD* 29 September 1921 p1002.

[72] P 315 above.

the Assembly how able and hardworking he had been as a barrister in his early years, commanding the favour of both Cockle and Griffith.

More prosaically, Real pleaded that the bill, if enacted, would work a significant financial detriment on him. He claimed that he had sacrificed £100,000 of income to sit on the bench, and suggested that for financial reasons he would at his advanced age have to return to practise at the Bar. It seemed not to occur to Real that few Labour members would regard retirement on £1000 per year as a hardship, given that the minimum wage set by the Commonwealth Arbitration and Conciliation Court was then (for a man, wife and three children) £4 15s per week and that for many people the only source of retirement income would be the old age pension derived from Deakin's Invalid and Old-Age Pensions Act 1908,[73] then less than £1 weekly. Real concluded by touching briefly on the merits of judges holding office during good behaviour, noting that he, Cooper and Chubb were physically and mentally competent to continue their judicial careers.

Theodore's Attorney-General, John Mullan, opened the second reading debate. Mullan operated under the unusual handicap of being an Attorney-General who was not a lawyer,[74] a characteristic which perhaps in part explains his combative tone: "… I will allow no man in this House to insult me by interjections. If he does, he will get it in the teeth every time."[75]

Mullan began by invoking the Privy Council's judgment in *McCawley* to explain that the bill, if enacted, would not be invalid. The explanation seemed redundant: no opposition members raised any issue as to the proposed Act's legality; their concern was with its morality.

Mullan offered two policy justifications for the proposed Act. The first, far from convincing, ground was that the government's intended reforms to the court system would require judges to undertake more sittings in more (and more geographically remote) locations; men aged over 70 could not cope with the physical demands of travelling. The second – credible at least in principle – was that advanced age might dull a person's mental acuity, and 70 was a perfectly sensible upper age limit:

> It is far better for a judge to retire before he has outlived his usefulness than to have a feeble judge remaining unnecessarily long on the bench, piling up bad judgments and bad precedents probably to the disaster of the state. I am not suggesting that the judges are incapable, but I have sufficient experience of human nature to know that the last man in the world to admit that he is mentally defective or that he is declining mentally is the individual concerned. In my opinion, it is far better that we should have a definite age of retirement for our judges …[76]

---

[73] P 170 n 43 above. Labour members were not impressed by Real's address; for example, Mr Hartley considered it "pathetic and sad … His address was that of an old man who was inclined to ramble into reminiscences of the past"; QLAD 30 September 1921 pp 1077–78; Mr Ferricks "The appearance of Judge Real at the Bar of the House and the address he delivered was one of the strongest arguments they could have for the speedy passage of that Bill"; ibid 1084. Perhaps surprisingly, no one referred to Real's peculiar use of the Ten Commandments as an authority in *Duncan* (p 256 n 77 above) as a reason for doubting his continued judicial competence.

[74] Mullan, Irish by birth, emigrated to Australia as a 17-year-old in 1888. He worked variously as a postman and railway employee before involving himself in miners' union activism and being elected to the Assembly in 1908. Theodore appointed him Attorney-General after the 1920 election; http://adb.anu.edu.au/biography/mullan-john-7677.

[75] QLAD 29 September 1921 p1008.
[76] ibid p1010.

Mullan also noted that similar reforms to the court system, including a retirement age of 70 years for Supreme Court judges,[77] had been introduced in New South Wales some years earlier by a Nationalist government. This, he argued, made it clear that the government was not motivated by partisan antipathy towards the three judges immediately affected by the legislation. That, Mullan declaimed: "is an infamous suggestion".[78]

Within the Assembly, opposition to the bill rested on three grounds.[79] The first was a 'constitutional' objection relating to the independence of the judiciary – the argument Feez and Stumm had pressed in *McCawley* – expressed in quite abstract terms. The second focused on judicial independence in a narrower sense: the complaint being that Theodore expected Labour to lose the next election and would use new Supreme Court appointments to embed political sympathisers among the judiciary. A Mr Fletcher put the point most bluntly: "I say it is because the Government want a more weak and pusillanimous judiciary which they can control."[80] The third was the more prosaic criticism that the measure amounted to a 'repudiation' of the state's contractual arrangements with the current judges. The frequently voiced suggestion was that judges had given up lucrative practices, sacrificing their financial interests to the public service, and they should not be disappointed in their expectation of being guaranteed their salary until such time as they might choose to retire (notwithstanding that they would receive a pension of half of their final salary). This appeared to be the main concern. Many opposition members who spoke indicated that they would not oppose the bill if the present judges were excused from its effect. The point repeatedly also made was that if Cooper, Chubb or Real was no longer fit to serve and refused to retire, he could be removed through the s.16 process.[81]

Theodore took the floor midway through the first day's debate. His contributions were directed mainly to rebutting opposition claims of political vindictiveness and opportunism:

> I want to assure honourable members that the Bill is not intended as a measure of vindictiveness or anything of that kind. It arises from a desire to bring about a reform in the judiciary system ...
>
> There is no desire to humiliate the judges, nor is the legislation inspired or actuated by any political or other prejudice against the present occupants of the bench ...
>
> There has been no evidence of anything that the present Government have done in regard to the judiciary that justifies the suggestion we want to prostitute for political purposes and hon. Members opposite ought to be generous enough to acknowledge that.[82]

Theodore was, however, unable to complete his remarks without casting aspersions on the Supreme Court's current incumbents. Arguing that the provision made for pensions in the original 1867 Supreme Court legislation was an obvious indication that the

---

[77] Judges' Retirement Act 1918 s.3.
[78] *QLAD* 29 September 1921 p1008.
[79] Vowles was much the most prominent opposition speaker.
[80] *QLAD* 30 September 1921 p1075.
[81] Opposition MPs alighted on Lennon's appointment as Lieutenant-Governor when aged 70 as indicating the government's lack of good faith in selecting 70 as the retirement age. (Lennon eventually died at 88, having lived until then in fairly robust health.)
[82] *QLAD* 30 September 1921 pp 1020–21.

Legislature had anticipated that judges would retire of their own volition on the basis that advancing age would compromise their abilities, Theodore in effect accused Cooper, Chubb and Real of undermining that legislative intent: "Great delicacy is needed in touching upon these matters, because no one wants to reflect on the individual judges who come under the Bill, but it is somewhat unfortunate that some of them have not seen fit to retire."[83]

The only concession Theodore made was to undertake that if the bill were passed it would not come into force until March 1922.[84] Theodore was followed by a parade of opposition members, most of them exercised by the repudiation point, before the house adjourned at 10.40 pm.

Second reading resumed on 30 September (a Friday) at 10.30 pm. The Nationalists and Country Party cooperated with admirable determination to force the government and Labour backbenchers through an all-night sitting. This entailed occasionally innovative use of the chamber's facilities:

> After midnight some members began to get sleepy. Mr Costello was the first to seek the arms of Morpheus, finding a soft bed on the well-padded bench reserved for Legislative Councillors at the back of the Assembly. There he was joined by Mr Fletcher, and they calmly slept head to head for some time ... The benches presented a "literary" appearance – strewn with parliamentary papers ... and bulky volumes of Hansard that made handy pillows.[85]

Neither Theodore nor Mullan spoke again. Some 70 members attended for votes on opposition amendments – all narrowly won by the government – at the end of proceedings, and the government eventually won the second reading vote by 35–30 at 6.30 am on Saturday morning. Labour members remained sufficiently energised despite the late (early) hour to push the bill straight into committee. That stage, devoted solely to consideration of several (unsuccessful) opposition motions to limit the measure to future appointees, lasted until 9.15 am.

At third reading, on 4 October, opposition members again attacked the government's bona fides, and unsuccessfully (losing by 36–34) moved a motion to delay implementation of the measure should it pass.[86] Third reading was not pressed to division.

In the Council

The bill reached the Council on 11 October 1921.[87] The government's case was led by Alfred Jones,[88] the Secretary for Mines, who began proceedings by indicating that he proposed to press the bill though all its remaining stages with some haste. Given that Labour had a nominal majority in the Council rather larger than in the Assembly, and that the Labour Council caucus displayed great discipline in attending and voting, the bill's swift progress and approval were not in doubt.

---

[83] ibid p1020.
[84] ibid p1019.
[85] *Queensland Times* 3 October 1921 p5, http://nla.gov.au/nla.news-article109994383.
[86] *QLAD* 4 October 1921 p1118.
[87] *QLCD* 11 October 1921 p1263.
[88] Jones, variously employed in his youth as a teacher, shopkeeper and gold miner, was a long-time trade union and Labour Party activist first elected to the Assembly in 1904. Ryan appointed him Labour leader in the Council and Secretary for Mines in 1917; http://adb.anu.edu.au/biography/jones-alfred-james-6867.

At second reading,[89] opposition members repeated the repudiation arguments made in the Assembly, unsuccessfully tried to provoke Jones into identifying which judges the government presumed to be incompetent and again accused Theodore of seeking to create a party politically compliant judiciary. Few opposition members attended, however, and late on the evening of 14 October the bill completed its second reading, committee and report stages without divisions. Third reading was set for 18 October, when, despite some further rhetorical flourishes from opposition members, the bill passed without division.[90]

Having taken the necessary legal steps significantly to change the composition of the state's Supreme Court, Theodore's government turned its attention once again to the Council. The Legislative Council Abolition Bill was introduced to the Assembly on 24 October 1921. But before dealing with that matter of state constitutional law, Theodore found himself embroiled in a contentious policy dispute within the national Labour Party.

The Labour Party's (1921) 'Socialisation Objective'

Despite Hughes's fervent nationalism and general illiberalism on civil liberties issues, he had not wholly abandoned his Labour roots on matters of economic and social policy. This caused friction both within his own party and with the government's informal supporters in the Country Party. But such friction was at least in the short term eased by the national Labour Party's apparent embrace of a distinctly 'socialist' programme.

At the national Labour Party's 1921 annual conference in Brisbane, held in October, a youngish member of the House of Representatives from Victoria, James Scullin, moved a motion committing the party to the so-called 'socialisation objective',[91] a policy agenda proposing gradual nationalisation of all key industries, with control of each being ceded to their respective workers and Parliament's competence over economic policy matters being transferred to a 'Supreme Economic Council'.

Theodore had no enthusiasm for the socialisation policy either in principle or as a tool to gain electoral support. He had lobbied effectively at conference to have an explicit commitment added to the motion that Labour's economic policies would be pursued through 'constitutional' means. Theodore also took pains in subsequent speeches to present the socialisation objective as a (very) long-term ideal rather than an element of practical policy.

In Queensland, 'constitutional' methods placed few restraints on a Labour government's power. *McCawley* had confirmed that even the most radical of constitutional reforms could be effected through a bare majoritarian legislative process, and Lennon's fleeting tenure as Lieutenant-Governor had shown that the upper house existed essentially at the government's sufferance. Such direct legal routes to effecting political

---

[89] QLCD 13 October 1921 p1365; 14 October p1408.
[90] QLAD 18 October 1921 p1464. Royal assent was given on 3 November.
[91] Ward (1978) op cit pp 144–45; Lang (1956) op cit chs 27–28. Robertson (1974) *JH Scullin: a political biography* pp 63–67 explores Scullin's motivations.

change were obviously not available to a Commonwealth government, whatever its political hue. Formal constitutional change to equip the Commonwealth Parliament – and thence the government – with powers it did not yet possess required either successful navigation of the s.128 process or reinterpretation of the national constitution by the High Court and Privy Council; and a government with a House majority had no means to control the composition of the Senate to ensure it could invoke the powers that the Parliament already had. Theodore was surely well aware of this: socialisation on the national stage through constitutional means was at best a very distant prospect. In Queensland, however, radical constitutional change through 'ordinary' legislation was in the government's grasp.

The Legislative Council Abolition Legislation

Theodore introduced the abolition bill on 24 October. The bill was essentially identical to those the Council rejected in 1916 and 1917. Its key terms were short and to the point:

> 2. (1) The Legislative Council of Queensland is abolished.
>
> (2) The office of member of the said Legislative Council is abolished.
>
> (3) All offices constituted or created in or in connection with the said Legislative Council are abolished.
>
> (4) The Parliament of Queensland (or as sometimes called the Legislature of Queensland) shall be constituted.
>
> by His Majesty the King and the Legislative Assembly of Queensland in Parliament assembled.

Tongue presumably firmly in cheek, the Premier informed the house that the bill's passage would not be rushed:

> The Bill is a very important one, and we do not intend to take all its stages today. It is intended to take the first reading stage and make the second reading an Order of the day for tomorrow. That will furnish hon. Members with a full opportunity of preparing their remarks.[92]

In the Assembly

First reading again became more than a formality, as Vowles moved an amendment. The Country Party's position was to link abolition with the prompt subsequent creation of an elective second chamber, chosen on an unspecified but restricted franchise,[93] with three members returned – again on an unspecified basis – from each of the state's 10 national electoral districts. The Nationalists also proposed an amendment. They too favoured an elected Council, albeit achieved by modifying the existing house rather

---

[92] *QLAD* 24 October 1921 p1729. For further description of the abolition, see Fitzgerald op cit pp 118–45; Harding op cit; Twomey (2006) *The chameleon Crown* pp 33–35.
[93] Vowles intimated that a property or educational threshold would be used. One of his colleagues, a Mr Morgan, drew Labour laughter with the observation that: "I am not altogether in favour of adult suffrage"; *QLAD* 24 October 1921 p1730.

than by abolishing it and starting anew. Both amendments were defeated, and the government carried the first reading vote by 51 (with Country Party support) to 14.[94]

Theodore opened the second reading debate at 11.00 am on 25 October.[95] After explaining the origins of Australian second chambers as: "a check on the growing democracy of the people"[96] and dismissing the PBRA mechanism as cumbersome, entailing both considerable delay and substantial expense, Theodore explained that his government's understanding of 'democracy' was that a ministry should be able to give immediate legal effect to whatever political values currently commanded bare majority Assembly support. In times past, when the Council's conservative majority obstructed Labour governments, the Council thwarted the wishes of 'the people'; and now, with a Labour majority, it was a pointless 'echo' of the Assembly. The Council was: "now an anachronism upon our legislative system, and should not be tolerated any longer".[97]

Theodore devoted much of his speech to discussing *Taylor* and *McCawley*, underlining – as the government had done during the passage of the Retirement Bill – that abolition would be legally valid.[98] Noting also that the bill would have to be reserved for the King's assent per the Australian States Constitution Act 1907, Theodore took pains to describe the bill as "purely an internal question … I do sincerely hope that politicians within or without this Parliament will not attempt to influence the King in the free exercise of his discretion in connection with the assent to this Bill".[99]

Vowles in reply began by attacking the Nationalists for not supporting the Country Party's position of abolition followed by the immediate recreation of an elective Council. In his view, the current Council, as a mere echo of the Assembly: "is an excrescence on our parliamentary life, and the sooner it is got rid of the better".[100] Vowles also assured Theodore that he would not support any lobbying of the King to withhold assent.[101]

The Nationalist contribution was led by Charles Taylor,[102] who was to become party leader in 1925. Taylor's primary concern was to paint Theodore's justification of abolition by invoking the wishes of the people as essentially hypocritical, given the view expressed by the electorate in the 1917 referendum.[103]

Opposition members continued to dominate proceedings until mid-afternoon, when Theodore moved to curtail debate and hold the second reading vote. That vote was carried by 39–30. After a brief interlude – and to opposition cries of "Russia! Russia!" – the bill went into and through committee unamended. The third reading

---

[94] ibid p1744. First reading votes set a pattern for opposition behaviour. Country and Nationalist members consistently voted together in opposing curtailment of debate, but invariably divided on the substantive question of whether the appropriate route to 'reform' was modifying the existing Council (Nationalist) or abolishing it and creating a new body (Country).
[95] ibid p1773.
[96] ibid.
[97] ibid.
[98] ibid pp 1775–77.
[99] ibid p1779.
[100] ibid p1781.
[101] ibid p1782.
[102] www.parliament.qld.gov.au/members/former/bio?id=3045878422.
[103] *QLAD* 25 October 1920 pp 1783–85. Theodore offered some distinctly unconvincing suggestions as to why the referendum result should not be regarded as an accurate indicator of 'the people's' wishes; ibid pp 1774–75.

vote, held at 8.00 pm, saw the Country Party support the government to produce a 46 to 17 majority.[104]

The conservative-leaning press was distinctly unimpressed with the opposition parties' performances in the Assembly. For the *BC*, the parties were: "temporarily bewildered … engaged in a useless internecine squabble about something which, so far as the business before the House was concerned, was in the clouds".[105] *The Mail* expressed a similar view:

> The result was hopeless confusion which will be calculated to bring dismay to the large body of electors … The Bill, when passed by a characterless second chamber. will be presented for the Royal Assent, and, Instead of the Imperial authorities contemplating a measure agreed to by a majority of one in popular assembly, they will have the knowledge that a preponderating majority of the Legislative Assembly desire a change to the unicameral system of government. No thin sophistry can disguise the fact that, in this respect, the Country party has made a tragic mistake.[106]

In the Council

The bill began its Council passage at 8.40 pm on the day it left the Assembly.[107] Jones led for the government. First reading was moved without division, and the Council progressed immediately to second reading. Jones spent much of his speech refuting opposition allegations that the government was running scared of a referendum. He was, however, willing to agree to debate carrying over until the next day.

On that occasion, one Labour member, Gerald Page-Hanify,[108] broke ranks – and at some length – to oppose the bill, on the basis that it was unacceptably hypocritical for the government to invoke the wishes of the people to justify abolition without putting the matter to a referendum vote. William Taylor, now in his thirty-seventh year as a Council member, was among the most vocal of the opposition members to speak; his contributions, as of other Country Party and Nationalist members, re-trod the ground visited by their Assembly colleagues. However, with the exception of Page-Hanify, the Labour caucus held firm,[109] and the low division numbers suggest that the opposition

---

[104] ibid p1813.
[105] *BC* 25 October 1921 p6, https://trove.nla.gov.au/newspaper/article/20496079.
[106] 26 October 1921 p6, https://trove.nla.gov.au/newspaper/article/213100818.
[107] *QLCD* 25 October 1921 p1768.
[108] *QLCD* 26 October 1921 pp 1830–34. Page-Hanify was a 1917 Ryan appointee. He had worked for many years for Philp's firm before setting up his own small business, and had drifted into Labour politics because of his enthusiasm for temperance reform; *Daily Telegraph* 13 February 1922 p7, https://trove.nla.gov.au/newspaper/article/168431598. It is not immediately obvious why he was chosen. His position in the abolition debate was entirely consistent with his long-held beliefs as to the desirability of lawmaking by referenda; see his letter ('People or party') to the *Daily Standard* 15 September 1917 p10, https://trove.nla.gov.au/newspaper/article/179421464.
[109] Ryan's, and more particularly Theodore's (Lennon), appointees subsequently found themselves known as the 'Suicide Club'. Jones, in a stump speech made in March 1922, embraced the label proudly: "We Labour men of the Upper House called ourselves the Suicide Club. We were pledged to destroy the edifice of which were part … Could there be a better instance of unselfish legislation – of duty …"; *BC* 13 March 1922 p6, https://trove.nla.gov.au/newspaper/article/20554594. The label seems to derive from an article in the *Daily Standard* 10 October 1917 p1, https://trove.nla.gov.au/newspaper/article/179425490. The metaphor was also applied (pejoratively) by opposition politicians. See eg the hysterical (in both senses) letter to *The Telegraph*,

parties did not harbour any hopes of precipitating a more substantial Labour rebellion. Second reading passed by 28 votes to 10.

The committee stage passed at speed, with no amendments reported. Third reading began immediately. A wrecking amendment was defeated 28–8, and third reading subsequently passed without division. The last word in the bill's passage went to an opposition member, a Mr Leahy, who ended the debate with the prophecy that: "the day was not far distant when, Phoenix-like, the Council would rise from its ashes and be restored".[110] The house then, rather prosaically, moved without adjournment to the committee stage of the Miners Homestead Perpetual Leases Act Amendment Bill.

The Council's final session was held the very next day – 27 October 1921. A secure government majority attended, and the Council began by taking half a dozen bills through all of their stages. Thereafter, following some barbed opposition comments on the 'repudiatory' nature of the Theodore government's policy agenda, members coalesced in offering thanks to the Council's officials for the services they had rendered. Proceedings culminated – more, it seems, with a whimper than a bang – at 8.37 pm.[111]

Assent was reserved to the King under the Australian States Constitution Act 1907. Theodore had drawn assurances from the Country Party, but not the Nationalists, during the Assembly debate on the abolition bill that they would not lobby British ministers for refusal of assent. Some suggestions were made in the Queensland press that Nathan should advise the British government (the Secretary of State for the Colonies was then Winston Churchill, holding office in Lloyd George's second coalition ministry) to veto the bill. Several members of the Council also made written representations to the King, asking that he withhold assent until a referendum had been held.[112]

Theodore had laid the ground carefully to pre-empt that possibility, both by lobbying ministers in London and cultivating a mutually respectful relationship with Nathan. Despite the precarious nature of Theodore's Assembly majority, and the obviously contentious fashion in which the government had secured its Council majority, Nathan was not persuaded that there was any internal justification for Churchill to refuse assent. Nathan sent the bill to London with a despatch, in which he concluded: "Generally I am unable to say that there is evidence of any very strong or widespread feeling in the country against the assent being given."[113] Churchill saw no reason to controvert that opinion, writing in reply:[114]

> After careful consideration of all the circumstances, I cannot but regard the matter with which the Bill deals as essentially one for local determination. The policy of the Bill being one of purely local concern it would not be in accordance with established constitutional principles that His Majesty's advisers should intervene to prevent the Bill from becoming operative.

---

signed only by AN EXPELLED VICTIM, which decried the "suicidal band of reformers" who had deprived the EXPELLED VICTIM of his legislative seat and the people of Queensland of his political wisdom; 20 April 1922 p6, https://trove.nla.gov.au/newspaper/article/180064500; (original emphases).

[110] *QLCD* 26 October 1921 p1863.
[111] *QLCD* 27 October 1921 p1929.
[112] The episode is discussed in *BC* 31 March 1922 p8, https://trove.nla.gov.au/newspaper/article/20549714.
[113] Quoted in Harding op cit p175.
[114] Churchill's despatch is most easily found in *BC* 31 March 1922 p8, https://trove.nla.gov.au/newspaper/article/20549714.

Assent was given on 23 March 1922. Confirmation took some days to reach Australia. Theodore greeted the news with a blunt press statement:

> The Council, like Upper Houses in other countries where such existed, was the home of reactionary interests for many years, thwarting the will of the people and becoming a brake on democracy. Few would mourn its loss, and fewer still would hope for its resurrection.[115]

The 'New' Supreme Court

Council abolition was not the only event of constitutional significance to occur in March 1922. The Judges' Retirement Act received royal assent on 7 November 1921,[116] but, true to his undertaking at second reading, Theodore did not immediately have the Act brought into force. The necessary proclamation identified 30 March 1922 as the effective date.

Cooper, Chubb and Real's retirement was attended with great ceremony, much of it orchestrated by Feez and Stumm. An event initially set for 15 March, the Full Court's last scheduled sitting before the Act came into force, was delayed for a fortnight.[117] In what was presumably a calculated snub to Theodore, the judges announced a new 'final' sitting on 31 March. With many barristers and solicitors in attendance, Feez began proceedings with a speech that commenced with barely concealed criticism of the constitutional morality of the enforced retirement: "Not only is this a sad occasion, but it is certainly a very unique one. I suppose never in the course of judicial life in a British-speaking community has such an episode as has happened here to-day taken place."[118]

That comment aside, and with a brief reference to how physically and mentally vigorous the retiring judges still were, Feez limited his remarks to praising Cooper, Chubb and Real's achievements in office rather than attacking the government. Shand and Lukin expressed their thanks to and admiration of their retiring colleagues, whose own brief speeches eschewed any criticism of the policy underling the 1921 Act and focused instead on recording their pleasure at having passed so many years in public service and their gratitude for the comments offered by their colleagues and by Feez.

Lukin had likely once harboured hopes to become Chief Justice on Cooper's retirement. Given that the appointment lay in Theodore's gift, such hopes were hardly realistic. Theodore's choice was the 42-year-old Thomas McCawley.[119] Theodore resisted any temptation to replace Chubb and Real with obviously partisan appointments. Thomas O'Sullivan (then 66) was already sitting as a district judge (appointed by Ryan in 1915), and had previously served as a minister both in Kidston's Labour and Fusion governments and under Denham, in whose administration he had been Ryan's predecessor

---

[115] *Daily Standard* 11 March 1922 p7, https://trove.nla.gov.au/newspaper/article/184939605.
[116] *The Telegraph* 8 November 1921 p2, https://trove.nla.gov.au/newspaper/article/176886513.
[117] *The Telegraph* 16 March 1922 p2, https://trove.nla.gov.au/newspaper/article/181944116.
[118] *BC* 1 April 1922 p 7, https://trove.nla.gov.au/newspaper/article/20535197.
[119] McCawley's appointment was denounced as "executive favouritism" in *BC* 3 April 1922 p4, https://trove.nla.gov.au/newspaper/article/20548077. McCawley had little opportunity to make his mark as Chief Justice: he died very prematurely of a heart attack in 1925.

as Attorney-General.[120] Charles Jameson had been a district judge since 1910, having previously been a civil servant and Crown prosecutor, and had never pursued a party political career.[121] Allan Macnaughton – who had administered McCawley's Supreme Court oath in March 1918 – had a similarly apolitical background. Theodore chose as the final appointee one William Blair.[122]

IV. National Developments

As McCawley took his seat on Queensland's Supreme Court in May 1920, the Australian High Court was preparing to hear argument in a case which would signal a major departure in that Court's understanding of the national constitution and of the High Court's role with it.

A Judicial Rebalancing of Commonwealth–State Constitutional Relations? The *Engineers* Case and the Implied Immunity of Instrumentalities Doctrine

Griffith had retired from the Court in 1919, and so had no opportunity to respond in a judicial capacity to the Privy Council's ignominious dismissal of his reasoning and conclusions in *Cooper* and *McCawley*. 1920 was not a good year for Griffith's doctrinal legacy. As the Privy Council demolished one pillar of Griffith's constitutional jurisprudence, the Australian High Court set about undermining another.

Griffith's successor, Adrian Knox, was appointed directly as Chief Justice by Hughes in October 1919.[123] Born to wealthy parents in Sydney in 1863, and educated at Harrow and Cambridge, Knox returned to Sydney to practise at the Bar in 1883. He was elected to the Assembly as a Free Trader in 1894, but had no appetite for the formalities of party political life and did not contest his seat again. Knox nonetheless remained involved in conservative political circles. His legal practice blossomed, especially after 1901, when he frequently appeared in the High Court in constitutional matters. He took silk in 1906 and avoided involvement in overtly governmental activities; during the First World War, he was active in the Red Cross rather than a formal government role. Despite Knox's lack of judicial experience, his appointment was not widely contentious.[124]

---

[120] http://adb.anu.edu.au/biography/osullivan-thomas-7932; www.sclqld.org.au/judicial-papers/judicial-profiles/profiles/tosullivan.
[121] https://trove.nla.gov.au/newspaper/article/38467735; www.sclqld.org.au/judicial-papers/judicial-profiles/profiles/cjameson.
[122] Pp 219, 229–32 and 241 n 10 above. Blair subsequently succeeded McCawley as Chief Justice in 1925.
[123] http://adb.anu.edu.au/biography/knox-sir-adrian-6989.
[124] Theodore nonetheless regarded him as a partisan appointment, albeit accepting that quality per se did not preclude him proving an able judge: "The gentleman who has recently been selected for the high honour of the position of Chief Justice of the High Court, Sir Adrian Knox, was a bitter political partisan; one of the mainstays of the Conservatives in New South Wales"; *QLAD* 9 January 1920 p2120.

Barton's death in January 1920 enabled Hughes to make another Court appointment. His choice was Hayden Starke.[125] Like Knox, Starke had not previously been a judge. Born in Melbourne, Starke was raised by his mother in modest financial circumstances, and studied part time to qualify for the Victoria Bar while working as an articled clerk. He rapidly built a successful practice in Victoria and, although personally close to Deakin, never sought political office. In the constitutional law context, his most notable brief had been as Feez and Stumm's counsel before the High Court in *McCawley*.

Albert Piddington's withdrawal from his nomination to the Court in 1913 was prompted in part because of publication of correspondence between him and Hughes in which Piddington had indicated in response to a question from Hughes that he took – as did Hughes – a view of the Constitution which afforded greater powers to the Commonwealth Parliament than that favoured by Griffith, Barton and O'Connor. Piddington in retrospect considered the correspondence ill-judged, as it would raise suspicions that he owed his appointment to politically partisan considerations.[126] The same concern likely infused Hughes's choice of Powers in 1913, although there is no obvious basis to think that Rich or Gavan Duffy were of that view when appointed. By 1920, Isaacs, Higgins and Powers were widely regarded as favouring a reading of the Constitution less indulgent of state interests.[127] In 1919, Hughes had proposed constitutional amendments to extend the Commonwealth's economic powers, but both were defeated.[128] Since neither Knox nor Starke had previously held judicial office, their views on the extent of Commonwealth authority issue were something of an unknown. They were, however, soon offered the opportunity to make them clear. The so-called 'Engineers' case[129] was argued before the High Court in May and July 1920. The judgment, delivered in August, broke markedly in both substantive and methodological terms from the court's previous understandings of Australian federalism.

The prosaic question arising in *Engineers* was whether state bodies qua employers fell within the Commonwealth's jurisdiction for the purposes of awards being made by the Commonwealth Court of Conciliation and Arbitration under the Commonwealth Conciliation and Arbitration Act 1904.[130] The point would seem to have fallen squarely within *Railway Servants*, subject to the question of fact as to whether the state enterprise concerned was classified as a governmental or trading entity.[131] However, the Court's majority[132] judgment, authored by Isaacs, took a far more radical approach.

---

[125] http://adb.anu.edu.au/biography/starke-sir-hayden-erskine-8629.
[126] http://adb.anu.edu.au/biography/piddington-albert-bathurst-8043.
[127] Palmer op cit ch 23, especially pp 248–49. See also Cowen's invocation (op cit pp 17–119) of the intemperately expressed disagreement between Griffith and Isaacs on the point in *Federated Sawmill Employees of Australia v Jones Moore and Sons Pty Ltd* (1909) 8 CLR 465.
[128] Ward (1978) op cit pp 144–45; Joyner (1959) op cit.
[129] *Amalgamated Society of Engineers v Adelaide Steamship Co Ltd* (1920) 28 CLR 129. *Engineers* is likely the most commented upon of all Australian High Court judgments. I have drawn in this brief passage on a few of those many sources, notably Cowen op cit pp 149–64; Booker and Glass (2003) 'The Engineers case' in Winterton (ed) *State constitutional landmarks*; Garran (1924) 'The development of the Australian Constitution' *LQR* 221; Gaegler (1987) 'Foundations of Australian federalism and the role of judicial review' *Federal LR* 162; Meale (1992) 'The history of the federal idea in Australian constitutional jurisprudence' *Australian Journal of Law and Society* 25.
[130] Pp 169–170 above.
[131] Pp 195–196 above.
[132] Only Gavan Duffy dissented.

Just as he had (in dissent) in *McCawley*, Isaacs deprecated the fondness of some (former)[133] members of the Court to resolve constitutional questions by implying ('inserting', as he put it in *McCawley*) essentially political considerations into constitutional texts. The line of cases dealing with the principle of intergovernmental immunity was based on an unsound doctrinal principle, since the decisions:

> [I]ndividually rested on reasons not founded on the words of the Constitution or on any recognized principle of the common law underlying the expressed terms of the Constitution, but on implication drawn from what is called the principle of "necessity," that being itself referable to no more definite standard than the personal opinion of the Judge who declares it.[134]

Rather than countenance such implication, Isaacs held that the role of the Court was simply: "faithfully to expound and give effect to it according to its own terms, finding the intention from the words of the compact, and upholding it throughout precisely as framed".[135]

Construed in that fashion, s.51(xxxv) clearly afforded the Commonwealth Parliament jurisdiction over all industrial disputes with an interstate dimension. If an exception were to be made for state government bodies, such exception would have to be expressly found in the Constitution.[136] The only source offered to sustain that exception was s.107, which Isaacs construed as offering no support for the asserted principle:

> But it is a fundamental and fatal error to read sec.107 as reserving any power from the Commonwealth that falls fairly within the explicit terms of an express grant in sec.51, as that grant is reasonably construed, unless that reservation is as explicitly stated. The effect of state legislation, though fully within the powers preserved by sec.107, may in a given case depend on sec.109. However, valid and binding on the people of the state where no relevant Commonwealth legislation exists, the moment it encounters repugnant Commonwealth legislation operating on the same field the state legislation must give way.[137]

Isaacs also rejected the relevance of US constitutional principle – of which Griffith had been so fond – primarily on the distinctly less than obvious basis that because Britain and its colonies had adopted systems of responsible government rather than the rigid separation of powers prevalent in the United States, the Court should be disinclined to conclude that Commonwealth Parliament had overstepped its proper role since the

---

[133] Griffith, Barton and to a lesser extent O'Connor being the unnamed targets.

[134] (1920) 28 CLR 129, 142. See also Griffith and Barton's idea of reciprocal intergovernmental immunity: "It is an interpretation of the Constitution depending on an implication which is formed on a vague, individual conception of the spirit of the compact, which is not the result of interpreting any specific language to be quoted, nor referable to any recognized principle of the common law of the Constitution, or acknowledged common law constitutional principle, but arrived at by the Court on the opinions of Judges as to hopes and expectations respecting vague external conditions This method of interpretation cannot, we think, provide any secure foundation for Commonwealth or State action"; ibid 145.

[135] ibid.

[136] ibid 144.

[137] ibid 154. Isaacs spoke (ibid) of the need to find a 'special provision' in the text of the Constitution to justify such an exception. He perhaps missed an obvious trick in not borrowing Birkenhead's 'meticulous precision' phraseology to buttress this idea. On s.107 and s.109, see pp 161–163 above.

more appropriate remedy for any such abuse was political control through the electoral system.[138] Isaacs found a more pertinent authority in Selborne's (Palmer's) judgment in *Burah*. He quoted the same passage in *Burah* that he had quoted in *McCawley*[139] to refute the propriety of courts making 'judicial insertions' into legislative texts, and then continued:

> [T]he doctrine of "implied prohibition" against the exercise of a power once ascertained in accordance with ordinary rules of construction, was definitely rejected by the Privy Council in *Webb v. Outtrim*. Though subsequently reaffirmed by three members of this Court, it has as often been rejected by two other members of the Court, and has never been unreservedly accepted and applied. From its nature, it is incapable of consistent application, because "necessity" in the sense employed – a political sense – must vary in relation to various powers and various States, and, indeed, various periods and circumstances.[140]

The eventual consequence of the Court adopting this reasoning was that both *D'Emden* and *Railway Servants* were formally overruled.[141]

Subsequent commentators have been notably uncomplimentary about the clarity and coherence of Isaacs's opinion,[142] although on both counts it perhaps fares better than his judgment in *McCawley*. Whatever its presentational shortcomings however, the *Engineers*' decision's obvious implication was that the High Court would be more deferential than hitherto towards Commonwealth legislative attempts to intrude into areas of social and economic policy which had previously been assumed to be matters of state competence.[143]

Deposing Hughes

By this point, Hughes's position as leader of the Nationalist party was appearing increasingly anomalous. While bitterly at odds with most of his former Labour colleagues on the conscription issue, his personal political ideology on economic and social matters remained in broad terms more congruent with the more centrist element of his former party than his new one. Those ideological cracks had been papered over by the scale of the 1919 election victory, but they were starkly revealed in 1922. Hughes could not lead the Nationalists to outright victory in the December 1922 general election, even with the benefit of having been handed the opportunity by Labour's 1921 adoption of

---

[138] ibid 146. Electoral accountability as a justification for indulgent judicial approaches to the limits of legislative power seems prima facie no less applicable to laws enacted by Congress or state legislatures in the United States than to laws enacted by the Commonwealth Parliament or state legislatures in Australia. Where responsible government would provide an obvious basis for differential judicial approaches in each system would be in relation to control of the Executive branch, since in Australia but not in the United States the executive branch is accountable to majorities in the relevant legislative chamber and a government is vulnerable to dismissal on a vote of confidence in the lower house.

[139] ibid 149.
[140] ibid 151–52.
[141] ibid 156–57.
[142] See Booker and Glass op cit p36 and the sources cited therein.
[143] Ward (1978) op cit p145 has suggested that *Engineers* was an ironic counterweight to Hughes's failure to carry his 1919 referendum proposals, but it might be thought unlikely that as accomplished a politician as Hughes (himself an experienced barrister) had appointed Knox and Starke without having some informed sense of how they would decide such issues.

the socialisation objective to portray that party as in thrall to 'communist' influences. Labour was returned as the largest party, with 29 seats. The Nationalists won only 26. Their continued grip on power would depend on creating a formal or informal coalition with Earl Page's Country Party, now with 14 seats.[144]

Table 11.2 The 1922 Commonwealth election (16 December 1922)

House	% vote	Seats	Change
Nationalists	35.2	26	−11
Country	12.5	14	+3
Labour	42.3	29	+3
Liberal[a]	4.7	5	+5
Independent	4.5	1	–
Senate[b]			
Nationalists	36.2	24	−11
Labour	45.7	12	+11
Country	13.0	0	–

[a] 'Liberal' candidates were returned only in Victoria and South Australia.
[b] 19 seats contested.

Page held neither personal affection nor political admiration for Hughes. His price for bringing his party into formal coalition with the Nationalists was his own appointment as Treasurer and Hughes' removal as Nationalist leader and hence as Prime Minister. The Nationalist politician who emerged to replace Hughes was Stanley Bruce, who Hughes had appointed as Treasurer in 1921. Bruce was among the most Anglophile of Australian politicians. Born into a wealthy Melbourne family, Bruce was schooled in Australia but had attended Cambridge, qualified for the Bar in London and fought as a British officer in the war. Elected to the House as a Nationalist in 1917, Bruce rose rapidly through party ranks thanks to Hughes's patronage. However, he and his more long-standing Nationalist party colleagues had few qualms about ditching Hughes to form a viable coalition;[145] a coalition within which Page as Treasurer was to make a considerable mark.

A Political Rebalancing of Commonwealth–State Financial Relations? Control of the Note Issue and the Creation of the Loan Council

Prior to confederation, and for some years thereafter, private banks were permitted to issue currency in Australia. Fisher's government promoted a bill enacted as the

---

[144] Labour won 11 of 19 contested Senate seats, but given the chamber's 35–1 Nationalist-Labour composition before the election, the Nationalists retained a large majority.
[145] Ward (1978) op cit pp 145–54; http://adb.anu.edu.au/biography/bruce-stanley-melbourne-5400; Edwards (1965) *Bruce of Melbourne* chs 8–9.

Australian Note Act 1911 which removed private banks' currency powers and vested that authority solely in the Commonwealth Treasury. Fisher's administration also carried a bill to create a Commonwealth Bank in 1911. The bank's legal powers, entrusted to a Governor and Deputy (appointed per s.12 by the Governor-General), were initially very limited, akin more to those of a commercial bank rather than a central bank like the Bank of England.[146] Under its founding Governor, however, the Commonwealth Bank embarked on a very substantial lending programme – to individuals, companies and other government bodies – which financed a modest portion of Australia's economic growth and of its war effort.

The Treasury retained control over the note issue until 1920, when the Commonwealth Bank Act 1920 promoted by the Hughes government transferred that power to a new statutory body – a 'Note Issue Department'[147] – within the Commonwealth Bank, formally independent of the Treasury. However, in 1924, the Bruce government – largely at Page's instigation (prompted by his general distaste for even the prospect of large-scale government interference in financial affairs) – promoted an amendment to the 1920 Act which gave the Bank sole power to control the note issue.[148] Page described his intention as being to create a central bank: "free from political pressure and conducted solely on the lines of prudent finance".[149]

The Commonwealth Bank Act 1924 s.7 also replaced the Governor with a board of directors, each appointed by the Governor-General for seven-year terms, which chose its own chairman.[150] In 1926, Robert Gibson took on that role.[151] Gibson was born in 1863 in Scotland, the son a small businessman. He emigrated to Melbourne in 1890, where he established a successful iron foundry business, and became prominent in Victoria commercial circles. Gibson served on many arbitration and government bodies and was knighted in 1920 before becoming Chairman of the Bank Board. A biographer has suggested:

> Gibson brought to the position … a firm conviction that his prime legal and moral responsibility was to serve as senior trustee of the nation's currency. Money was interpreted as currency and bullion in its tangible form and excluded those balances which were the result of credit creation. "Real" money was seen as the outcome of thriftiness and the steady accumulation of savings. Gibson believed, with many of his contemporaries, in the strict separation of

---

[146] Sawer op cit p91.

[147] Per s.6 inserting an amended s.60C into the Note Issue Act 1910. The Department was to have a four-person Board of Directors, appointed by the Governor-General. The Board would be chaired by the Governor of the Bank; the three additional directors, one of whom was to be a Treasury Official, were appointed by the Governor-General (amended s.60D). Per amended s.60P, the Treasury retained the power to issue currency in emergency situations.

[148] Page describes his motivation and the processes of formulating and enacting the legislation in (1963) op cit ch XIII.

[149] Page op cit p115. Page would not have accepted that 'prudent finance' was itself a 'political pressure'.

[150] Per s.7, the directors were to be "(a) the Secretary to the Treasury; and (b) six other persons who are or have been actively engaged in agriculture, commerce, finance or industry". The Bruce government's initial appointees, mostly of a distinctly conservative political hue (one, MB Duffy, had Labour affiliations), are profiled in the *SMH* 4 October 1924 p16, https://trove.nla.gov.au/newspaper/article/16169893; Schedvin (1970) *Australia and the great depression* pp 83–84. Bruce announced their appointment to the House without explaining why they had been chosen; *HRD* 3 October 1924 p5141. None feature in Page's autobiography. Schedvin characterised their collective view on economic policy as: "intransigent conservatism"; (1970) op cit p83.

[151] http://adb.au.edu.au/biography/gibson-sir-robert-6310.

monetary management and government policy ... [G]overnments could not be trusted with other people's money.[152]

Page was also the chief mover in creating an (initially informal) 'Loan Council' to coordinate Commonwealth and state activities in the domestic and international loan markets.[153] In Page's view, the six states and the Commonwealth were competing against each other for loan funds in both domestic and overseas markets, thereby increasing demand for such loans and increasing their cost. This was particularly problematic given the national and state governments' continuing needs to refinance their still very substantial war loans. Under the Loan Council arrangement, the total size of loan funds sought, terms to be accepted from lenders and the allocation of total funds between the states and the Commonwealth would be determined by vote. States would have one vote each; the Commonwealth would have two and a casting vote in the event of a tie.

The proposal was not initially contentious within the states. Five of the six governments were then controlled by Nationalists or Nationalist/Country coalitions; only Queensland had a Labour administration. Theodore was coming increasingly to the view – particularly in light of the loan blockade – that the mild form of socialism he embraced could only be pursued effectively through the national governmental system: the prospect of a Loan Council controlled by a Labour Commonwealth government was an enticing one.[154]

V. An Opportunity Not Taken – Or Not Realised?

As his government moved to abolish Queensland's Legislative Council, Theodore did not seem alert to the possibility opened up by *McCawley* of invoking CLVA 1865 s.5 and/or cl.22 and s.2 to introduce a 'meticulously precise' legislative 'manner and form' provision to prevent a future government instigating the recreation of the Council by legislation enacted in the 'ordinary way' (which would post-abolition be simply a bare majority in a quorate Assembly plus the royal assent).[155] There would have been an ironic symmetry (or full circle perhaps) for Theodore to have reached back to the pre-CAAA 1908 position and promoted a provision which required a two-thirds majority in the Assembly for any bill that sought to reinstate the Council as a component part of the Legislature.

To the contrary, at second reading Theodore, as well as apparently not appreciating the legal possibility ("nothing we *can* do") of so doing, seemed also to reject the political legitimacy ("nothing we *intend* to do") of any such initiative:

> It is quite clear that if the people of Queensland do not endorse this policy and they want a Legislative Council, they can turn out of office the party that abolished it and they can

---

[152] ibid. Curiously, Gibson does not feature at all in Page's account of the Bank in this era.
[153] Page op cit ch 14.
[154] Fitzgerald op cit pp 170–80.
[155] To borrow Birkenhead's (imprecise) terminology, Queensland's Legislature was now even more 'uncontrolled' than when *McCawley* was decided.

restore it again if they wish. There is nothing to prevent them doing that. Nothing we can do – nothing we intend to do – can hamper the people in restoring the Legislative Council if they want it.[156]

There is no suggestion in Fitzgerald's Theodore biography that Theodore ever considered the entrenchment issue, nor in Murphy's Ryan biography that it ever occurred to Ryan. Contemporaneous press coverage (both of Birkenhead's judgment and the Council's subsequent abolition) also appeared not to take the point. Such an initiative would certainly have engendered controversy in terms of its politically legitimacy, both in the narrow party-based sense of being a mechanism to safeguard Labour policy objectives against future electoral disapproval and more broadly in the sense of its moral asymmetry, insofar as it would have sought a degree of entrenchment requiring that future reform command substantially more political support than required to enact the entrenching measure itself.

McCawley – An Unanswered (and Unasked) Question

Theodore's assertion that there "is nothing we can do" to prevent restoration of the Council may have been (albeit inadvertently) far- rather than short-sighted. While *McCawley* obviously opened the door to the new unicameral Legislature imposing 'shackles' on its presumptive 'ordinary way' power to recreate the Council, Birkenhead's judgment offered no obvious answer to the question of whether such a legislative innovation would in any event turn out to be legally futile.

Taylor stood as authority, albeit only High Court rather than Privy Council authority, for the proposition that even a formidable 'shackle' – the two-thirds majority requirement in s.9 – could be repealed in the 'ordinary way'. But when the Queensland Legislature had enacted s.9, it had not also provided that the repeal of s.9 itself should be subject to a similar 'shackle'. What Birkenhead had not done in *McCawley* (understandably, as the point did not arise on the facts) was confirm whether – and, if so, explain how – any prima facie legislative control *enacted by the Queensland Legislature* (or any representative legislature) which prevented legislation on particular matters[157] being passed in the 'ordinary way' could itself be protected against repeal or amendment passed in the 'ordinary way'. In other words, was Charles Lilley 'right' back in 1871[158] in suggesting that the Legislature had 'omitted' (presumably by inadvertence rather than design) from the 1867 Act what would have been a legally effective provision requiring that ss.9–10 could themselves only be repealed by legislation requiring (precisely identified) special majorities?

That question may not have been a live one in Queensland in 1923 as Theodore led the Labour Party to a convincing victory in the first post-abolition election. Despite being persistently decried by opposition politicians and much of the state's press as

---

[156] *QLAD* 25 October 1921 p1780.
[157] The 'particular matters' being those in s.5[1] and s.5[2] if the power came from s.5. Many more 'matters' would be in issue if the power came from cl.22.
[158] A view echoed by Berriedale Keith in 1908 in relation to the CAAA and PBRA; p 227–28 and 231 n 111 above.

socialistic and communistic, Theodore's Labour Party took 43 of the 72 Assembly seats, increasing its formal majority from just two to 14. The frequently expressed assertion by both Nationalist and Country Party members during the passage of the retirement and abolition bills that their respective parties would form a government after the next election proved distinctly ill-founded.

Table 11.3 Queensland Legislative Assembly election, 1923 (12 May 1923)

Party	% vote	Seats	Change
Nationalist	36.1	16	+3
Labour	48.1	43	+5
Country Party	10.8	13	−8

Theodore's case was much assisted, however, by some clumsy opposition machinations in August 1922. Frank Brennan,[159] a reputedly disaffected Labour backbencher (disaffected primarily because of his assumption that as the caucus's only barrister he should have been in the Cabinet as Attorney-General), was offered by two Country Party emissaries the (then huge) sum of £3500, with a judgeship to follow, to cross the floor and support a no-confidence motion. Unhappily for the putative bribers, Brennan shared the news with Theodore, and on the occasion of the next stage of negotiation Brennan invited a police officer to hide underneath his desk and take notes of the proposal. Criminal convictions followed.[160] As did an account to the Assembly by Theodore of an approach to him (scrupulously evidenced by verbatim reports made by hidden shorthand writers) by the Nationalists that he – like Kidston before him – abandon Labour to lead a new centrist but Nationalist-dominated party.[161]

The clandestine nature of the Country Party and Nationalists' manoeuvres evidently did not play well with potential Labour defectors among the electorate. More broadly, it seemed, Queensland's voters were sufficiently unconcerned by the 'constitutional' implications of the two Acts to decide that a Theodore-led government was no longer a palatable proposition. But in New South Wales, those constitutional questions raised on the one hand by *McCawley* and on the other by abolition of Queensland's Council were exercising the imaginations of a growing number of politicians and lawyers.

---

[159] http://adb.anu.edu.au/biography/brennan-frank-tenison-5348.

[160] What followed for Brennan was a Cabinet post and then (from a Labour government) a Supreme Court judgeship.

[161] *QLAD* 15 August 1922 p667 et seq. The speech was made in the context of a no-confidence motion moved by Vowles, which the government (with Brennan's support) won 36–35; ibid p682. The episodes are recounted in detail in Fitzgerald op cit pp 152–57. For contemporaneous coverage from divergent perspectives, see *BC* 15 August 1922 p7, https://trove.nla.gov.au/newspaper/article/20565380; *Daily Standard* 16 August 1922 p5, https://trove.nla.gov.au/newspaper/article/179024105.

BIBLIOGRAPHY

Aroney N (2006) 'Politics, law and the constitution in McCawley's case' *Melbourne ULR* 605
Atkinson A (1990) 'The first plans for governing New South Wales, 1786–87' *Australian Historical Studies* 22
Attard B (nd) 'How to organise a "capital strike": The British Australasian Society and the Queensland government, 1899–1924' Working Papers 13009, Economic History Society; https://ideas.repec.org/p/ehs/wpaper/13009.html
Bailyn B (1967) *The ideological origins of the American revolution*
Bell K and Morrell W (1928) *Select documents on British colonial policy 1830–1860*
Bennet J (2003) *Sir James Cockle; First Chief Justice of Queensland*
Bennet J (2003) *Sir John Pedder: First Chief Justice of Tasmania, 1824–1854*
Berriedale Keith A (1908) 'Judicial appeals in the Commonwealth' *Journal of the Society of Comparative Legislation* 269
Berriedale Keith A (1909) *Responsible government in the Dominions*
Berriedale Keith A (1916) *Imperial unity and the Dominions*
Berriedale Keith A (1933) *The constitutional law of the British Dominions*
Blackmore E (1894) *Law of the constitution of South Australia*
Bolton G (2006) 'Henry (later Sir Henry) Parkes' in Clune and Turner (eds) *infra*
Booker K and Glass A (2003) 'The Engineers case' in Winterton G (ed) *State constitutional landmarks*
Bothwell R (2006) *Penguin history of Canada*
Bridge C (1993) *Earle Page: the politician and the man*
Campbell E (1965) 'Colonial legislation and the laws of England' *University of Tasmania LR* 148
Campbell E (1966) 'Conditional land grants by the Crown' *Sydney LR* 267
Campbell J (2004) 'Smith, Frederick Edwin, first earl of Birkenhead' *ODNB*
Campbell T (2006) 'George (later Sir George) Richard Dibbs' in Clune and Turner (eds) *infra*
Castles A (1975) 'The judiciary and political questions: the first Australian experience 1824–25' *Adelaide LR* 294
Chalmers G (1814) *Opinions of eminent lawyers on various points of English jurisprudence*
Chilcott P (2004) 'Pakington [*formerly* Russell], John Somerset, first Baron Hampton' *ODNB*
Clark M (1993) *History of Australia*
Clune D and Griffith G (2006) *Decision and deliberation: the Parliament of New South Wales 1856–2003*
Clune D and Turner K (eds) *The Premiers of New South Wales 1856–2005*
Cochrane T (1989) *Blockade: the Queensland loans affair 1920–1924*
Cope M (1976) 'Political appointment of T.W. McCawley as President of the Court of Industrial Arbitration, Justice of the Supreme Court and Chief Justice of Queensland' *University of Queensland LJ* 224
Cowen Z (1967) *Isaac Isaacs*
Coyne J (1959) 'WM Hughes and the "powers" referendum of 1919: a master politician at work' *Australian Journal of Politics and History* 15
Creighton D (1970) *Canada's first century*
Currey C (1929) 'The first proposed swamping of the Legislative Council of New South Wales' *JRAHS* 282
Currey C (1943) 'The Legislative Council of New South Wales 1843–1943: constitutional changes attempted and achieved' *JRAHS* 337
Davy P (2006) *The Nationals: the Progressive, Country and National parties in New South Wales 1919–2006*
Dickey B (1969) *Politics in New South Wales 1856–1900*
Dickey B (1974) 'Responsible government in New South Wales: the transfer of power in a colony if settlement' *JRAHS* 217
Evans J and Lovelock L (2008) *Legislative Council practice*

Evans R (2007) *A history of Queensland*
Evatt H (1947) *Rum rebellion*
Fitzgerald R (1995) *"Red Ted": the life of E.G. Theodore*
Fitzmaurice A (2007) 'The genealogy of terra nullius' *Australian Historical Studies* 1
Friedmann W (1950) 'Trethowan's case, parliamentary sovereignty and the limits of legal change' 24 *Australian LJ* 103
Frost A (1981) 'New South Wales as terra nullius: the British denial of aboriginal land rights' *Australian Historical Studies* 513.
Gaegler S (1987) 'Foundations of Australian federalism and the role of judicial review' *Federal LR* 162
Garran R (1924) 'The development of the Australian Constitution' *LQR* 221
Gibbs H (1987) 'A nineteenth century cause Celebre: Queensland Investment and Land Mortgage Company v Grimley' 13 *Royal Historical Society of Queensland Journal* 73
Gibson P (2004) 'Russell, Francis Xavier Joseph [Frank] Baron Russel of Killlowen' *ODNB*
Glasson T (2010) '"Baptism doth not bestow freedom": missionary anglicanism, slavery, and the Yorke–Talbot opinion, 1701–30' *The William and Mary Quarterly* 279
Goldsworthy J (2006) '"Australia" – devotion to legalism' in Goldsworthy J (ed) *Interpreting constitutions: a comparative study*
Goodhart W (2004) 'Buckmaster, Stanley Owen' *ODNB*
Goodman D (2013) 'The gold rushes of the 1850s' in Bashford and McIntyre op cit
Graber M and Gilman H (2015) *The complete American constitutionalism vol 1: introduction and the colonial era*
Haldane R (1899) 'Lord Watson' *Juridical Review* 278
Harding J (2000) 'Ideology or expediency? The abolition of the Queensland Legislative Council 1915–1922' *Labour History* 162
Hawker G (1971) *The parliament of New South Wales 1856–1965*
Heuston R (1963) *The lives of the Lord Chancellors*
Higgins H (1905) 'McCulloch v Maryland in Australia' *Harvard LR* 559
Higgins H (1919) 'A new province for law and order' *Harvard LR* 13
Hogan M (2006) 'George (later Sir George) Houston Reid' in Clune and Turner *supra*
Hughes R (1987) *The fatal shore*
Irving H (2013) 'Making the federal Commonwealth 1890–1901' in Bashford A and MacIntyre S (eds) *The Cambridge history of Australia*
Jenkyns H (1902) *British rule and jurisdiction beyond the seas*
Joyce R (1974) 'SW Griffith: towards the biography of a lawyer' *Historical Studies* 235
Joyce R (1978) 'George Ferguson Bowen and Robert George Wyndham Herbert: the imported openers' in Murphy and Joyce *infra*
Joyce R (1978) 'Samuel Walker Griffith: a liberal lawyer' in Murphy and Joyce *infra*
Joyner C (1959) 'W M Hughes and the "Powers" referendum of 1919: a master politician at work' *Australian Journal of Politics and History* 15
Karskens G (2012) 'Naked possession: building and the politics of legitimate occupancy in early New South Wales Australia' in Shammas (ed) *Investing in the early modern built environments*
Karskens G (2013) 'The early colonial presence, 1788–1822' in Bashford A and MacIntyre S (eds) *The Cambridge History of Australia*
Keneally T (2007) *The commonwealth of thieves*
Kerr J (1961) 'The Macarthur family and the pastoral industry' *JRAHS* 131
Knox B (1976) '"Care is more important than haste": Imperial policy and the creation of Queensland, 1856–9' *Historical Studies* 64
La Croix S (1992) 'Sheep, squatters and the evolution of land rights in Australia' *3rd Annual Conference of the International Association for the Study of Common Property*
Lauchs M (2010) 'The return of manhood suffrage to Queensland, 1863–1872' *Journal of Australian Colonial History* 119
Leiboff M (2016) 'Theatricalising law in three, 1929–1939 (Brisbane)' *Law Text Culture* 93
Lentin A (2004) 'Hamilton, John Andrew, Viscount Sumner' *ODNB*
Loveday P and Martin A (1966) *Parliament, factions and parties: the first thirty years of responsible government in New South Wales, 1856–1889*

Loveday P (1956) '"Democracy" in NSW: the Constitution Committee of 1853' *JRAHS* 188
Loveland I (2015 7th edn; 2018 8th edn) *Constitutional law, administrative law and human rights*
Marginson G (1970) 'Andrew Fisher – the views of the practical reformer' in Murphy, Joyce and Hughes *infra*
Markey R (1987) 'Populism and the formation of a Labor party in New South Wales, 1890–1900' *Journal of Australian Studies* 39
Matthew H (2004) 'Haldane, Richard Burdon, Viscount Haldane' *ODNB*
Matthews B (1949) 'A history of industrial law in Queensland' *Journal of the Historical Society of Queensland* 150
Macnair M (2008) 'Talbot, Charles, first Baron Talbot of Hensol' *ODNB*
McMinn W (1979) *A constitutional history of Australia*
McPhee J (2017) 'The deadliest enemies of Australia: the politics of intelligence during the Australian conscription controversies of 1916–1917' *Journal of Intelligence History* 1
Meale D (1992) 'The history of the federal idea in Australian constitutional jurisiprudence' *Australian Journal of Law and Society* 25
Megarrity L (2006) '"White Queensland": the Queensland government's ideological position on the use of Pacific Island labourers in the sugar sector 1880–1901' *Australian Journal of Politics and History* 1
Melbourne and Joyce R (1963) *Early constitutional development in Australia*
Millar G (2004) 'Murray, Andrew Graham, first Viscount Dunedin' *ODNB*
Moore P (2103) 'The corruption of Benjamin Boothby' *ANZLH E-Journal Referred Paper No 2*
Morgan R (2004) 'The life and career of Sir Arthur Morgan' *JRHSQ* 555
Morrison A (1962) 'The town "liberal" and the squatter' *RHSQJ* 599
Morrison A (1970) 'The Brisbane general strike of 1912' in Murphy, Joyce and Hughes (eds) *infra*
Morton D (2006) *A short history of Canada*
Munsell D (2009) 'Clinton, Henry Pelham Fiennes Pelham-, fifth duke of Newcastle under Lyme' *ODNB*
Murphy D (1975) *T.J. Ryan: a political biography*
Murphy D (1978) 'William Kidston: a tenacious reformer' in Murphy and Joyce *infra*
Murphy D (1980) 'Abolition of the Legislative Council' in Murphy, Joyce and Hughes *infra*
Murphy D and Joyce R (eds) (1978) *Queensland political portraits 1859–1952*
Murphy D, Joyce R and Hughes C (eds) (1970) *Prelude to power: the rise of the Laour party in Queensland 1885–1915*
Murphy D, Joyce R and Hughes C (eds) (1980) *Labor in power: the Labor party and governments in Queensland 1915–1957*
Neal D (1991) *The rule of law in a penal colony*
O'Farrell P (1958) 'The Australian Socialist League and the labor movement 1887–1891' *Historical Studies* 152
Page E (1963) *Truant surgeon*
Palmer N (1931) *Henry Bourne Higgins*
Palmer R and Collier R (1864) 'Report of the Imperial Law Officers' in Blackmore E (1894) *Law of the constitution of South Australia*
Prest J (2004) 'Russell, John [*formerly* Lord John Russell], first Earl Russell' *ODNB*
Pugsley D (2004) 'Collier, Robert Porrett, first Baron Monkswell' *ODNB*
Robertson J (1974) *J H Scullin: a political biography*
Robinson J (1970) 'Lord Haldane and the BNA' *University of Toronto LJ* 55
Ross L (1947) 'The philosophy of the Australian Labor Party' *The Antioch Review* 109
Rubin G (2004) 'Lawrence, Sir Paul Ogden' *ODNB*
Sackville R (1969) 'The doctrine of immunity of instrumentalities in the United States and Australia: a comparative analysis' *Melbourne ULR* 15
Samuels A (2004) Pollock, Ernest Murray, first Viscount Hanworth' *ODNB*
Sawer G (1944) 'Injunction, parliamentary process, and the restriction of parliamentary competence' *LQR* 83
Sawer G (1956) *Australian federal politics and law 1901–1929*
Sawer G (1967) *Australian federalism in the courts*
Selby W (2005) 'Social evil or social good: lotteries and state regulation in Australia and the United States' in McMillen J (ed) *Gambling cultures: studies in history and interpretation*
Sharman C (2002) 'A web-based database on Australian government and politics' *Australian Journal of Political Science* 347

Shaw G (1980) '"Filched from us"; the loss of universal manhood suffrage in Queensland 1859–1863' *Australian Journal of Politics and History* 372
Shell D (1992) *The House of Lords*
Shinn R (2008) 'Keith, Arthur Berriedale' *ODNB*
Smith R (2006) *Against the machines: minor parties and independents in New South Wales*
Steele D (2004) 'Palmer, Roundell, first Earl of Selborne' *ODNB*
Stevens R (2004) 'Sankey, John, Viscount Sankey' *ODNB*
Stevens R (2004) 'Younger, Robert, Baron Blanesburgh' *ODNB*
Spencer H (2004) 'Atherton, Sir William' *ODNB*
Taylor G (2013) 'The early life of Mr Justice Boothby' *Adelaide LR* 167
Thomas P (2007) 'Yorke, Philip, first earl of Hardwicke' *ODNB*
Tobias T (2006) 'Atkinson, John, Baron Atkinson' *ODNB*
Todd A (1894) *Parliamentary government in the British colonies*
Turbeville A (1927) *The House of Lords in the eighteenth century*
Twomie A (2004) *The constitution of New South Wales*
Twomie A (2006) *The chameleon Crown*
Tyler P (2006) *Humble and obedient servants: the administration of New South Wales 1901–1960* vol 2
Wade HRW (1955) 'The basis of legal sovereignty' *Cambridge LJ* 172
Wanka K (1970) 'William Kidston – the dilemma of a powerful leader' in Murphy, Joyce and Hughes (eds) *infra*
Ward R (1978) *The history of Australia: the twentieth century 1901–1975*
Ward R (1992) *Concise history of Australia*
Weaver J (1996) Beyond the fatal shore: pastoral squatting and the occupation of Australia' *American Historical Review* 981
Wexler S (1983–84) 'The urge to idealise: Viscount Haldane and the constitution of Canada' *McGill LJ* 608
White M and Wessels P (1998) 'The Australian Feez family: its contribution to the law' *JRHSQ* 76
Williams G (2003) 'The emergence of the Commonwealth Constitution' in Winterton (ed) *infra*
Williams J (1998) 'The Tenterfield oration of Henry Parkes' *The New Federalist* 71
Winterton G (ed) (2003) *State constitutional landmarks*

INDEX

à Beckett, Thomas   179, 181n95, 189
Atherton, Sir William   78–9, 93
Atherton and Palmer's Report (1862)   93–4, 103
Atkinson, John (Baron Atkinson)   306
Australia, Commonwealth of *see also* **New South Wales; Queensland; South Australia; Tasmania; Van Diemen's Land; Victoria**
  Baxter v Commissioners of Taxation   196–9
  Braddon blot   163, 171
  Commonwealth Bank reforms   334–6
  Commonwealth Salaries Act 1907   199–200
  Conciliation and Arbitration Bill 1904   169–70
  conscription   245, 265–6
  Constitution Bill   154, 156
  constitutional amendment process   164–5
  constitutional change   325
  Conventions   153–4, 156
  Cooper litigation   222–8
  Country Party   302–4
  currency issue   334–5
  customs duties   162–3, 167, 171
  elections
    1901   167–8
    1903   169
    1906   170–1
    1910   171
    1913   243–4
    1917   265
    1919   302–4
    1922   333–4
  Engineers' case   331–3
  Excise Tariff Act 1906   201
  federation   149–56
  Financial Agreement of 1909   171
  Free Trade Party   147–8, 155n159, 167, 171
  governmental system   154
  Harvester case   200–1
  High Court   163–4, 168, 172
  judges   168
  Judiciary Act 1908   199–200
  Labour Party   166–7, 169–71, 333–4
  Liberal Party   171, 243
  Loan Council   336
  McCawley v The King   280–304
  military conscription   243–5, 265–6
  Military Conscription Referendum Act 1916   245
  National Party   245
  New Protection programme   170, 200–1
  old age pensions   170n43
  origins of   153–6
  Parliament   158–60
    composition   158
    deadlock provisos   159–60
    disallowance   160
    National Government   160–1
    powers   158–9
    reservation   160
    state autonomy   161–3
  political alignments   166–71
  Protectionist Party   147–8, 155n159, 167, 169–72
  Railway Servants case   195–6
  referendums   245, 265–6
  states, implicit limits on the powers of   172–3
  taxation   172–3
  terms of federation   157–65
  voting rights   168
  War Precautions Act 1914   244, 265–6
  'White Australia' policy   167
Australian Patriotic Association   18
Australian Workers Unions (AWU)   246

Bank of Toronto v Lambe (Quebec)   175–7, 178
Barton, Sir Edmund
  Baxter v Commissioners of Taxation   197, 199
  biography   155
  Cooper v Commissioner of Income Tax   226
  Deakin v Webb   190
  Duncan v Theodore   256–9
  election of 1901   166–7
  federation process   157
  McCawley case   282, 285–7
  as Prime Minister   168
  Taylor v Attorney-General   260, 262, 274
Bathurst, Henry   8
Berriedale Keith, Arthur   227–8, 231n111
Bigge, John   8
Birkenhead (Frederick Edwin Smith, 1st Earl of)   305–6, 308–14

Blair, Sir James William   219, 229–31, 233–5, 250, 254, 261, 330
Blake, Sir Henry   139n79
Bligh, Sir William   4–5
Boothby, Benjamin   80–3, 84, 86, 87–93, 98, 99–100, 116–22
Bourke, Sir Richard   18
Bowen, Sir George   65–6, 72–4, 78, 80, 124
Bowman, David   213, 235
Braddon, Edward   163
Braddon blot   163, 171
Bradlaugh, Charles   320
Brennan, Frank   338
Brentnall, Frederick   139n82, 140
Brisbane, Sir Thomas   12
Browne, Billy   212
Bruce, Stanley   334
R v *Burah* (India)   151–3, 175, 178, 227
Burke's Act   27, 43, 120–1
Byrnes, Thomas Joseph   143

Canada   35, 41, 102, 103, 149
  Hodge v *The Queen* (Ontario)   151–2
Cardwell, Edward (1st Viscount Cardwell)   67n1, 101, 106–7, 120, 122
Chelmsford (Frederic Thesiger, 1st Viscount)   214–15, 228
Chubb, Charles   221, 250, 253, 255, 272, 320, 322–3, 329
Churchill, Winston   209, 328
Citizens Insurance Co v Parsons (PC)   177
civil list payments   37
Clark, Andrew Inglis   154, 157, 183, 184
CLVA 1865 *see* Colonial Laws Validity Act 1865
Cockle, James   80, 123–4, 125–6, 217, 311
Collier, Sir Robert   67, 151–2, 311
Colonial Act Confirmation Act 1863   98–9, 119
colonial government   2n4, 29–32
Colonial laws validity report (Palmer and Collier) *see* **Palmer and Collier's Report (1864)**
colonial legislatures   110–12, 121–2, 150–3
Commissioners of Crown Lands   17–18
Commonwealth Bank   335
Connecticut   10
conscription   243–5, 265–6
convicts
  labour   3, 18, 29, 134
  transportation   7, 8, 17, 18–19, 29, 48, 63
Cook, Joseph   243–4
Cooper, Sir Charles   82, 84, 87, 92
Cooper, Sir Pope   214, 246–50, 270, 272–5, 276, 316, 320, 322–3, 329
Corn Laws   23

Country Party   302–4, 338
Cowper, Charles   58–9, 62, 144–5
customs duties   37, 145, 150–3, 162–3, 167, 171

Daly, Sir Dominick   93, 96, 98
Darling, Ralph   12–14, 15–16
Dawson, Anderson   210
Deakin, Alfred   155, 157, 166, 167, 168–71, 173n54, 188–91
Deas Thomson, Edward   45, 57–9
Denham, Digby   238, 239–40, 241
Denison, Sir William   24, 26–8, 48, 59–60, 61, 70–2
Dibbs, George   147, 154
Dickson, James   143
disentrenchment   56–63 *see also* **entrenchment**
Dodds CJ   183, 184–5
Donaldson, Stuart   57
Drake, James   185–6
Duffy, Frank Gavan   257, 258, 259, 263–4, 274, 287, 331
Dunedin (Andrew Murray, 1st Viscount)   278, 305

Elgin (Victor Bruce, 9th Earl of)   209
emancipists   3, 6–7, 9, 14, 19
entrenchment   50, 50n63, 97–9, 164, 336–7
  'Two Act' principle   220, 252, 271, 274, 281, 283–4, 286–7, 291–2, 296
exclusives   2, 3, 6, 7, 14

Farmers Party   303
Feez, Arthur
  biography   251
  Duncan v Theodore   248–9, 255, 256
  on enforced retirement of judges   329
  McCawley case   271, 312
  Taylor v Attorney-General   251–3, 261
Finlay, Sir Robert   192
Fisher, Andrew   170–1, 244
Fisher, James   96, 97
Fitzroy, Sir Charles   22, 32
Forbes, Francis   15–16
Free Trade Party   147–8, 155n159, 167, 171

Garran, Robert   155, 172
Gathorne-Hardy, Gathorne   138n70
Gavan Duffy, Frank   257, 258, 259, 263–4, 274, 287, 331
generalia specialibus non derogant   86n88
Gibson, Robert   335–6
Gipps, Sir George   18
Gladstone, William   35, 65
Glassey, Thomas   141, 144
Goderich (Frederick Robinson, 1st Viscount)   17n70

Index

gold rush of 1851 31
Goold-Adams, Sir Hamilton 242, 299, 301, 315–16
Gregory, Francis 139n76
Grey, Henry (3rd Earl Grey) 17n70, 22, 28, 29, 31–2
Griffith, Sir Samuel
   Baxter v Commissioners of Taxation 197–9
   biography 133
   Commonwealth constitution 154
   Cooper v Commissioner of Income Tax 222–5
   Deakin v Webb 190–1
   D'Emden v Pedder 186–8, 193, 194
   doctrinal legacy 330
   Excise Tariff Act 1906 201
   federation process 149, 156
   as High Court Judge 168
   Legislative Assembly of Queensland 133–4
   McCawley case 281, 283–5
   Premier of Queensland 134–44
   Railway Servants' case 195–6
Gwynne, Edward
   Auld v *Murray* 99
   biography 82–3
   Court of Appeals Act 1861 91
   denunciation of Boothby 120
   Driffield v *Torrens* 98
   McEllister v Fenn 92–3
   Payne v *Dench* 85–6
   The Queen v Neville 116–19
   Walsh v *Goodall* 122

Haldane, Richard (1st Viscount Haldane) 177–8, 195, 278, 279, 305
Halsbury (Hardinge Giffard, 1st Earl of) 191–2, 193–5
Hamilton, William 241–2
Hanson, Richard 91, 92, 98n127, 116, 119, 120
Hashemy (convict ship) 29
Herbert, Robert 65–6, 73, 78, 79, 124, 131
Herschell, Farrer 138n70
Higgins, Henry
   Baxter v Commissioners of Taxation 196, 199
   biography 179–80
   Cooper v Commissioner of Income Tax 222, 226
   Deakin v Webb 189–90
   Harvester case 200–1
   McCawley case 280n1, 281, 297–8
   Outtrim's Case 192
   Powell v Apollo Candle 180
Hobhouse, Arthur (1st Baron Hobhouse) 176, 178
Hodge v *The Queen* (Ontario) 151–2
Hodges, Henry 189
Hopetoun (John Hope, 7th Earl) 161n15
Hughes, Billy 244–5, 265–6, 302, 317, 324, 331, 333–4

implied intergovernmental immunities doctrine 173, 175, 180, 183–4, 187, 196, 197, 198, 201, 223, 224, 281, 332–3
implied repeal, doctrine of 49–50, 104, 216
income tax 214–28
indigenous peoples of Australia 1n1, 3–4, 132
Innes, Joseph Long 146n122
Isaacs, Sir Isaac Alfred
   Baxter v Commissioners of Taxation 196, 199
   biography 179
   Cooper v Commissioner of Income Tax 222, 225, 274
   Deakin v Webb 189–90
   Duncan v Theodore 256, 257–8
   Engineers' case 331–3
   Excise Tariff Act 1906 201
   McCawley case 281, 282, 288–96, 313
   Railway Servants' case 195
   Taylor v Attorney-General 262–3, 274
   Wollaston's Case 180

Jameson, Charles 330
Jenkyns, Sir Henry 251
Jones, Alfred 323–4, 327
judges 11–12, 17, 27–8, 73, 81–3, 89–93, 168, 319–24, 329–30
judicial review 15–16, 24–9
jury eligibility 11
jury trials 5–6

Keith, Arthur Berriedale 227–8, 231n111
Kidston, William 211–14, 228–30, 233–5, 237, 238
Knox, Adrian 330

Labour Party 144, 147–8, 166–7, 169–71, 210, 211–12, 213, 324–5, 333–4
land
   disposition policy 13–14, 17–18, 21–3
   grants 3–4, 6, 12, 13–14
   leases 23, 31
   licences 22
   naked possession 3–4, 7
   reforms 21–3, 60–3
   registration 81–3
   rights 7
Law Officers' (Palmer and Collier's) 1864 Report *see* Palmer and Collier's Report (1864)
Lawrence, Paul 278, 279
leases 23, 31
legal incapacity 6–7
Lennon, William 316, 324
Lesina, Joe 235
Lewis, Sir Elliot 183

Liberal Party   171, 202, 243
Lilley, Charles   123–9, 131, 132, 133, 217–18, 220, 231, 311, 337
Lilley, Edwyn   220, 222
Lincoln, Abraham   320
liquor licensing   239
Loan Council   336
Lowe, Robert   35–6, 47–8
Lukin, Lionel   220, 250, 253–4, 256, 270, 272, 320, 329
Lutwyche, Sir Alfred   72–80, 123, 133n53
Lyne, Sir William   161n15, 203

Macalister, Arthur   79, 124–5, 127, 129, 130, 131, 132, 133
Mcansh, John   139n82, 140
Macarthur, John   5, 6
McCawley, Thomas   267, 269–72, 275, 276–7, 282, 314–15, 329
McCulloch v Maryland (USA)   173–6
MacDonnell, Richard   81, 89, 91, 92, 93
Macgregor, Sir William   240
McIlwraith, Thomas   133–5, 136n32, 139, 141, 142–3
McIntyre JJ   183
Mackenzie, Robert   124–5, 127
Macnaghten, Edward   191, 192
Macnaughton, Allan   276, 330
Macquarie, Lachlan   5–6, 7–8
Macrossan, Hugh   248, 256, 266, 276, 280
Macrossan, Neil   276–7
Madden, Sir John   179, 181–2, 189
'manner (and form)' of lawmaking   49–50, 52, 58, 112–14, 121–2, 126, 208, 209, 217, 274, 287, 291, 293–4
Marbury v Madison (USA)   157
Marshall CJ   173–4, 178, 180, 181–2
Martin, James   144–5, 146, 150–1
Maugham, Frederick   307, 310, 311
military conscription   243–5, 265–6
Miller, Granville   219, 220
Ministerialists   143, 210–14
Mitchell, Sir Edward   280
Moffat, Thomas De Lacy   79
Montagu, Alfred   25n105, 27–8, 121
Moore, Harrison   180
Morehead, Boyd   141–2
Morgan, John   24–5
Morgan, Sir Arthur   212–13, 215
Mullan, John   321–2
Musgrave, Sir Anthony   137, 139n79

naked possession of land   3–4, 7
Nathan, Sir Matthew   317, 328
Nelson, Hugh Muir   142–3, 213
New South Wales

Commissioners of Crown Lands   17–18
Constitution Act 1857   56–8
Constitution Act 1902   202–8
Constitution Bill 1853   33–43, 44–5
convict transportation   7, 17, 18, 29
Court of Requests   17
courts   4, 5–6, 11–12, 26
  Court of Appeals   11n47
  Court of Requests   12
customs duties   37, 145, 150–3
elected representation   19–21
Electoral Act 1858   58–60, 71
Executive Council   12, 43, 54–5
geographical spread   14
gold rush of 1851   31
government of   1–2, 4, 7–8, 30–1, 34–42, 53–8
Governors   2–8, 12–14, 15–16, 22, 54–5
  see also Bligh, Sir William; Bourke, Sir Richard; Brisbane, Sir Thomas; Darling, Ralph; Denison, Sir William; Fitzroy, Sir Charles; Gipps, Sir George; Macquarie, Lachlan; Phillip, Arthur; Young, Sir John
Governor's Commission and Instructions   2–4, 13–14, 53–6
judiciary   11–12, 17, 42–3
jury eligibility   11
Labour Party   147–8
land disposition policy   13–14, 17–18, 21–3
land reforms   21–3, 60–3
legal incapacity   6–7
Legislative Assembly   34, 36–42, 148
Legislative Council   8–11, 16–21, 26, 34–6, 38–9, 41–2, 44, 58–62, 145–8
legislative powers   37–42
Liberal Party   202
'limits of location'   13–14
motives in founding   1n2
newspaper licences   15–16
Order in Council 1847   22–3
partitioning of   30
political divisions   7–8
political parties   147–8
Powell v Apollo Candle   150–3
Progressive Party   202
Quarter Sessions   12, 17
Reduction of Members Referendum Act 1903   206–8
repugnancy doctrine   8–11, 15–16, 16–17, 20
Supreme Court   5, 11, 26, 42–3
as *terra nullius*   4
two-thirds majority provisos   40–2, 48, 56–8
New Zealand   149–50
Newcastle (Henry Clinton, 5th Duke of)   32, 35, 62, 74–5, 78, 92, 93–4, 98

Index 347

newspaper licences 15–16
Nicholls, Sir Herbert 183–4, 186
Norman, Sir Henry Wylie 139n79
Norton, Albert 138n73

O'Connell, Daniel 320
O'Connor, Richard 168, 172, 190, 195, 197, 199, 222, 225
old age pensions 170n43
O'Sullivan, Thomas 329–30

Page, Earle 303, 334, 335–6
Page-Hanify, Gerald 327
Pakington, Sir John 32, 35
Palmer, Arthur 127, 131, 132
Palmer, Roundell (1st Earl of Selborne) 67, 78–9, 93, 151, 178, 227, 311
Palmer and Collier's Report (1864) 67–8, 101–5, 112–13, 119
pardons 3, 6–7, 8
Parker, Sir Henry 57
Parkes, Sir Henry 44n43, 144–8, 149, 153, 158
pastoralism 4–5, 14, 23, 44n42, 61, 63, 134
Pedder, John 24, 25–8, 121
Peel, Sir Robert 23
pensions 43, 170n43
Phillip, Arthur 3–4
Philp, Robert 143, 210, 212, 228, 232, 317
Piddington, Albert 257, 331
political parties 144, 147–8, 166–71 *see also* Country Party; Farmers Party; Free Trade Party; Labour Party; Liberal Party; Progressive Party; Protectionist Party
Pollock, Sir Ernest 278
Power, Francis Isidore 232, 236–7
Power, G. W. 221
Power, Virgil 221
Powers, Sir Charles 257–8, 264, 274, 287–8, 331
Pring, Ratcliffe 66, 73, 75, 76, 129
Privy Council *see* United Kingdom, Privy Council
Progressive Party 202
prohibition of alcohol sales 239
Protectionist Party 147–8, 155n159, 167, 169–72
Pugh, Theophilus 75–7, 131

Queensland
    appropriations bills 135–9
    Arbitration Court 271–2
    Brisbane general strike of 1912 239–40
    Constitution Act 1867 123–31, 215–19, 223–6, 271–5
    Constitution Act Amendment Act 1871 127–31
    Constitution Act Amendment Act 1908 229–32

Constitution Act Amendment Bill 1918 300–2
Cooper litigation 214–28
Country Party 338
creation of 63–6
Duncan v Theodore 246–50, 255–9
elections 211–12
    1860 73
    1899 210
    1902 212
    1904 212
    1908 228
    1912 240
    1915 241–2
    1918 277, 299
    1920 318
    1923 337–8
Electoral Act 1872 131–2
electoral law 70–80
electoral reform 58–60, 213
expenses for Assembly members 135–6, 138
government of 65–6
immigration 134, 142
Industrial Arbitration Act 1916 267–9, 271
judges 73–4
Judges' Retirement Act 1921 319–24, 329–30
juries 270
Labour Party 144, 210, 211–12, 213, 324–5
Legislative Assembly 123–32, 133, 135–6, 138
Legislative Council 74, 135–41, 213–14
    abolition 240–55, 264–5, 298–302, 315–19, 325–9
    restoration 336–7
liquor licensing 239
McCawley case 269–77, 337–8
military conscription 243–5
Ministerialists 143, 210–14
Mooraberrie case 246–50
Parliamentary Bills Referendum Act 1908 228–9, 233–7
population growth 134
prohibition of alcohol sales 239
referendums 245–6, 250–5, 259–64
seditious libel proceedings 75–7
shearers' strike of 1891 142, 143–4
sugar industry 134
Supreme Court 73–4, 269–72
taxation 214–28
Taylor v Attorney-General 250–5, 259–64
trade unions 239–40, 246
two-thirds majority provisos 68–70, 123–32, 337
Quick, John 155, 172

Ramsay, Robert 129, 131
Real, Patrick 221, 250, 253, 256, 272, 275, 315, 320–1, 322–3, 329

referendums   206–8, 228–9, 233–7, 243–6, 250–5, 259–64, 265–6
Reid, George   154, 155–6, 166, 169–70
'representative legislatures'   110–14
repugnancy doctrine   8–11, 15–17, 20, 24, 83–6, 95, 102, 115–16, 149–50
'responsible government'   39, 43, 53–5
Responsible government in the Dominions (Keith)   227–8, 231n111
Rich, George   256–9, 263–4, 274, 288–96, 312, 313, 331
Robertson, John   58–9, 60–2, 144–5, 146
Robinson, Sir Hercules   146n121
royal assent, matters reserved for   20, 21, 30, 34, 41, 55–6, 87, 96, 103
Russell, John (1st Earl Russell)   22n90, 23, 45, 48–9, 51–2, 53–4, 106
Ryan, Thomas Joseph
  anti-conscription policy   245, 265–6
  biography   240–1
  death   318–19
  Duncan v Theodore   249, 255, 256
  elections
    1915   241–2
    1918   277
  entrenchment   337
  Legislative Council Abolition Bill   242–3
  Legislative Council Abolition Referendum   245–6
  McCawley case   270–1, 273, 276–7, 280–1, 299–301, 314–15
  Taylor v Attorney-General   250–1, 259–60

Samuel, Saul   146n122
Scullin, James   324
seditious libel proceedings   75–7
See, Sir John   202–3, 206–7
Selborne (Roundell Palmer, 1st Earl of)   67, 78–9, 93, 151, 178, 227, 311
settlers *see* exclusives
Shand, William   255, 272, 329
Simon, Sir John   306–7
socialisation objective   324–5, 333–4
South Australia
  Auld v Murray   99–100
  Boothby dismissal proceedings   89–91, 93–5, 120–1
  constitutional crisis   67–8, 80–100
  Court of Appeals   85–7, 91, 92–3, 119
  Dawes v Quarrell   116–18
  Driffield v Torrens   97–9
  entrenchment   97–9
  establishment of   19n81
  Executive Council   85–6
  government of   30, 36
  Governors   81, 96
  Governor's *Instructions*   87–9
  Hutchinson v Leeworthy   83–5
  judges   81–3, 89–93
  land registration   81–3
  Local Courts   115–18
  McEllister v Fenn   87–9, 91, 92–3
  Payne v Dench   85–7, 92
  The Queen v Neville   115–16
  Real Property Act 1858   82–5, 87–9
  Real Property Act 1861   99–100
  Registration of Deeds Act 1862   118–19
  repugnancy doctrine   83–5, 86, 95, 115–16
  validity petitions   100
  Walsh v Goodall   118–19, 122
squatters   7, 14, 17–18, 21, 22, 23, 44n42, 59, 60–1, 79n54, 124n8, 127, 127n20, 140
Stanley, Frederick   137
Starke, Hayden   280, 282, 331
Stephen, Sir Alfred   71–2, 81n60
Stow, Randolph   97, 115, 118
Stumm, Charles   251–2, 256, 259, 261, 269, 271, 307, 312, 329
Sudds, Joseph   15
Sumner (John Hamilton, 1st Viscount)   278

Talbot, Charles   10
Tasmania *see also* Van Diemen's Land
  D'Emden v Pedder   182–8
taxation   172–3, 214–28
Taylor, Charles   326
Taylor, William   139n82, 245, 250–5, 264, 327
terra nullius   4
Theodore, Edward (Ted)
  anti-conscription policy   265
  biography   246–7
  Duncan v Theodore   247, 249
  entrenchment   336–7
  Judges' Retirement Act 1921   322–3, 324, 329
  Legislative Assembly of Queensland, election of 1923   338
  Legislative Council of Queensland
    abolition   299, 315–18, 325–6, 328
    appointments to   301
  as Premier of Queensland   301–2
Thompson, John Malbon   129, 131
Torrens system of land registration   81–3
trade unions   134, 142, 143–4, 239–40, 246
'Two Act' entrenchment principle   220, 252, 271, 274, 281, 283–4, 286–7, 291–2, 296
two-thirds majority provisos   40–2, 48, 56–8, 68–70, 123–32, 337

Index   349

United Kingdom
  Australian Colonies Act 1861   77–8
  Australian Colonies Constitution
      Act 1850   29–32
  Australian Constitutions Act 1842
      18–29
  Australian Constitutions Act 1862   94
  Australian Courts Act 1828   16–18
  Australian Land Sales Act 1842   21–2
  Australian States Constitution Act 1907
      208–9
  Colonial Laws Validity Act 1865   67–100,
      101–22, 165
  Colonial Leave of Absence Act 1782   27, 43,
      120–1
  Commonwealth of Australia Constitution
      Act 1900   157–65, 172–3, 180
  Crown exemption from legislation   50n61
  Federal Council of Australasia Act 1885   149
  Great Reform Act 1832   39
  New South Wales Act 1823   8–16
  New South Wales Constitution Act 1855   33–4,
      44–56
  Parliament of   37, 38, 39, 41, 49–50, 52
  Privy Council   10, 137–8, 172–8, 191–5,
      199–200, 278–9, 280–304
  Treaty of Utrecht   39
  Waste Land Occupation Act 1846 22–3

Van Diemen's Land *see also* **Tasmania**
  autonomy of   11n46
  Dog Act 1845   24–9
  government of   30–1
  judges   12, 27–8
  judicial review   24–9
  Legislative Council   26
  repugnancy doctrine   24
  Supreme Court   26

Victoria
  Deakin v Webb   188–91
  gold rush of 1851   31
  government of   30, 36
  Wollaston's Case   172–3, 175, 179–82
Vowles, William   318n64, 325, 326

Walsh, William   127n20
Watson, John   167n30, 169–71
Watson, William   177, 178, 195
Wauchope **principle**   52, 79, 104
Wentworth, D'Arcy   6
Wentworth, William
  biography   6
  Commons petition of 1828   16
  death   63n111
  emancipist interests   7, 18
  journalism   15
  Legislative Council of New South Wales   62
  New South Wales Constitution Bill 1853   33–41
  New South Wales Constitution Bill 1855   44–8
  pastoralist interests   23
  Petition on the general grievances of the colony
      (1851)   31
'White Australia' policy   167
Wilkes, John   320
Williams, Hartley   179, 181n95
Wills, Sir Alfred   191, 192
Wilson, Sir Arthur   191, 192
Wollaston, Sir Harry   173n54
Wood, Henry   139n82
Woolcock, John   248
World War I   243–4

Yaldwyn, William   219
Yaldwyn, William Henry   140
Yorke, Phillip   10
Young, Sir John   61–2

CPSIA information can be obtained
at www.ICGtesting.com
Printed in the USA
LVHW082047011021
699214LV00002B/162